AGAINST
ALL
ENEMIES

George Washington at Princeton, 1779, by Charles Willson Peale
Courtesy of the Pennsylvania Academy of the Fine Arts

The Army during the Eighteenth,

General of the Army George C. Marshall, chief of staff, seated before a portrait of an earlier chief of staff, General of the Armies John J. Pershing, 1 November 1943
Library of Congress (LC-USZ62-34070)

Nineteenth, and Twentieth Centuries

**Recent Titles in
Contributions in Military Studies**

The Stars and Stripes: Doughboy Journalism in World War I
Alfred E. Cornebise

Image and Reality: The Making of the German Officer, 1921–1933
David N. Spires

History of the Art of War: Within the Framework of Political History,
The Modern Era
Hans Delbrück, translated by Walter J. Renfroe, Jr.

In Peace and War: Interpretations of American Naval History, 1775–1984.
A Second Edition
Edited by Kenneth J. Hagan

America's Forgotten Wars: The Counterrevolutionary Past and Lessons for the Future
Sam C. Sarkesian

The Heights of Courage: A Tank Leader's War on the Golan
Avigdor Kahalani

The Tainted War: Culture and Identity in Vietnam War Narratives
Lloyd B. Lewis

Shaping a Maritime Empire: The Commercial and Diplomatic Role of the American
Navy, 1829–1861
John H. Schroeder

The American Occupation of Austria: Planning and Early Years
Donald R. Whitnah and Edgar L. Erickson

Crusade in Nuremberg: Military Occupation, 1945–1949
Boyd L. Dastrup

The Dogma of the Battle of Annihilation: The Theories of Clausewitz and Schlieffen
and Their Impact on the German Conduct of Two World Wars
Jehuda L. Wallach

Jailed for Peace: The History of American Draft Law Violators, 1658–1985
Stephen M. Kohn

AGAINST ALL ENEMIES

Interpretations of American Military History from Colonial Times to the Present

Edited by **Kenneth J. Hagan** *and* **William R. Roberts**

Foreword by Honorable Martin R. Hoffmann and General Fred C. Weyand, U.S.A. (Ret.)

Contributions in Military Studies, Number 51

GREENWOOD PRESS
New York • Westport, Connecticut • London

Library of Congress Cataloging-in-Publication Data
Main entry under title:

Against all enemies.

(Contributions in military studies, ISSN 0883–6884 ;
no. 51)
Bibliography: p.
Includes index.
1. United States—History, Military—Addresses,
essays, lectures. I. Hagan, Kenneth J. II. Roberts,
William R. III. Series.
E181.A3 1986   355'.00973   85–17660
ISBN 0-313-21197-3 (lib. bdg. : alk. paper)
ISBN 0-313-25280-7 (pbk.)

Library of Congress Catalog Card Number: 85–17660
ISBN: 0-313-21197-3
ISBN: 0-313-25280-7 (paperback)
ISSN: 0883–6884

First published in 1986

Greenwood Press, Inc.
88 Post Road West
Westport, Connecticut 06881

Printed in the United States of America

The paper used in this book complies with the
Permanent Paper Standard issued by the National
Information Standards Organization (Z39.48–1984).

10 9 8 7 6 5 4 3 2 1

For MARGARET CONNOLLY SHOWERS,
who loved a little boy long ago,

And for VIOLET ROBERTS,
with a grandson's love

Contents

Illustrations   xi

Foreword   xiii

Acknowledgments   xv

Introduction   xvii

1   Armed Force in Colonial North America: New Spain, New France, and Anglo-America   3
 JOHN SHY

2   The Anglo-American Military Tradition and the War for American Independence   21
 IRA D. GRUBER

3   Reassessing American Military Requirements, 1783–1807   49
 LAWRENCE DELBERT CRESS

4   From Peaceable Coercion to Balanced Forces, 1807–1815   71
 HARRY L. COLES

5   The Army in the Age of the Common Man, 1815–1845   91
 WILLIAM B. SKELTON

6   Military Education and Strategic Thought, 1846–1861   113
 JAMES L. MORRISON, JR.

7   The Old Army and the Confederacy, 1861–1865   133
 JUNE I. GOW

8   An Improvised Army at War, 1861–1865   155
 CRAIG L. SYMONDS

9   The Army's Search for a Mission, 1865–1890   173
    JERRY M. COOPER

10 Reform and Revitalization, 1890–1903   197
    WILLIAM R. ROBERTS

11 The Army Enters the Twentieth Century, 1904–1917   219
    TIMOTHY K. NENNINGER

12 Over Where? The AEF and the American Strategy for
    Victory, 1917–1918   235
    ALLAN R. MILLETT

13 The Interwar Army, 1919–1941   257
    RUSSELL F. WEIGLEY

14 The U.S. Army and Coalition Warfare, 1941–1945   279
    JAMES L. STOKESBURY

15 The Armed Services and American Strategy, 1945–1953   305
    STEPHEN E. AMBROSE

16 From the New Look to Flexible Response, 1953–1964   321
    DAUN VAN EE

17 The Vietnam War, 1962–1973   341
    B. FRANKLIN COOLING

18 The Army after Vietnam   361
    COLONEL HARRY G. SUMMERS, JR.

Index   375
About the Contributors   391

Illustrations

PLATES

George Washington at Princeton, 1779, by Charles
Willson Peale   frontispiece

General of the Army George C. Marshall, chief of staff,
seated before a portrait of an earlier chief of staff,
General of the Armies John J. Pershing, 1 November
1943   frontispiece

Nathanael Greene by Charles Willson Peale   24

The United States Military Academy in 1828   96

Brevet Lieutenant General Winfield ("Old Fuss and
Feathers") Scott   126

General Robert E. Lee, photograph by Matthew Brady,
April 1865   138

Major General Henry Wager ("Old Brains") Halleck   165

General Ulysses S. Grant, shown here as a lieutenant
general   166

General William Tecumseh Sherman, shown here as a
lieutenant general   180

Colonel Emory Upton, shown here as a major general   187

Soldiers of the Fifth Army Corps embarking for Cuba,
June 1898   206

Secretary of War Elihu Root, seated in his office before a
portrait of Winfield Scott   209

General of the Armies John J. ("Black Jack") Pershing
and his staff (Captain George C. Marshall, rear row,
second from right), 23 September 1919   250

GIs marching double file through barbed wire and tank
    traps of the Siegfried Line in World War II   299

GIs passing through a German village in World War II   299

American commanders in the European Theater of
    Operations   300

Heavy bombers high over Europe in World War II   300

General of the Army Douglas MacArthur near Suwon,
    Korea; Lieutenant General Matthew Ridgway, Eighth
    Army   315

The Pentagon   315

An army medic tending an injured lieutenant felled by a
    VC white phosphorus grenade booby trap   347

Helicopters of the First Air Cavalry Division returning to
    a landing field near An Khe after seeing action early in
    the Vietnam War   347

M A P S

The Revolutionary War in the North   31

The Revolutionary War in the South   41

The Mexican War   115

The Civil War   145

World War I: The Western Front   240

World War II in Europe   287

World War II in the Pacific   291

Korean War   312

Vietnam War   348

Foreword _____

This book of essays on the history of the United States Army will appeal to a wide range of interests. Serious students of military history will find it a valuable reference source. Policymakers who have a need to grasp and feel the evolution of the U.S. military establishment will find detail and perspective on the forces in the society which have given rise to and molded that establishment over the years and continue to shape it today. The book will be of particular appeal and make a particular contribution to members of the modern military profession of arms.

The book presents eighteen historical stepping stones across the history of the United States Army and, indeed, the nation. The great American experiment in democracy and freedom has included, importantly, continuing experimentation with the role and substance of the military establishment and its proper role in the larger fabric of a dynamic free society. Thus, the book collects up the beginnings of the American army in prerevolutionary times and traces it through its development in the seminal Revolutionary War and early nineteenth century periods. There initially was framed the national response to the tension between aspirations to be free from the complexities of and about standing military establishments on the one hand, and the certainties of the need for the availability of military power to underscore national will both at home and abroad on the other.

The clarity of the evolution of the concepts and patterns underlying the modern army are a chief utility of the work. The citizen-soldier concept; civilian control of the military; the combining of standing forces and militia-type reserves; the repeated rise and fall of national priorities and national capabilities as hopes for peace give way to the exigencies of conflict; the development and mutation of strategic and tactical doctrine; and the evolution of the current mission of credible deterrence through strength and readiness upon which the first sustained attempt to maintain a standing force in our nation's history is based—these are signal among the subjects to which the authors repeatedly return over the course of the eighteen essays. Acknowledging that perspective is improved with the passage of time, the essays produce a blend of history and interpretation that should prove accessible and digestible to all who serve in the military and all who wish better to support them.

The army through the years has been the element of the military establishment that has continued closest in its reflection of the society it has served. In addition to instructing on and memorializing that theme, this book serves as a reminder of the need for constancy of purpose and policy on the part of national leadership to maintain the essential capabilities of military forces of a free society, and to do so in a posture consistent with the hopes, aspirations and values to which that society is dedicated. The evident qualities that historically have provided the strength of the army in the past—resiliency, adaptability, flexibility and adherence to mission—will continue to be required in the years ahead.

Fred C. Weyand
General, U.S.A. (Retired)
Chief of Staff, U.S. Army, 1974-1976

Honorable Martin R. Hoffmann
Secretary, U.S. Army, 1975-1977

Acknowledgments _____

This book was first conceived as a companion-piece to *In Peace and War: Interpretations of American Naval History, 1775–1978* (Westport, Conn.: Greenwood Press, 1978, 1st ed.). In the intervening years the authors have shown remarkable patience with our editorial plodding, and to all of them we are most grateful. We also wish to thank Jimmy Haritos for his unparalleled "word processing," Bill Clipson for making maps with great rapidity and common sense, and Cookie Gold for taking time from her busy schedule to read the galleys. Three authors in particular—Ira Gruber, William B. Skelton, and James L. Morrison, Jr.—provided additional assistance in helping to locate paintings and photographs used to illustrate this volume. John W. Huston of the Naval Academy history department helped prepare captions for the World War II photographs, while Margaret Whitlock (Mort's wife) gathered photographs from the Library of Congress, and John Cummings gave us free rein in Nimitz Library.

In "Works-in-Progress" sessions dreamed up by our colleague Richard Abels, several members of the history department of the Naval Academy offered trenchant criticism of two of the chapters, and the book as a whole is better for their candor. Our thanks go also to Frederick C. Harrod, chairman of the history department, and LCDR Don Thomas Sine, USN, executive assistant to the chairman, for finding us a room at the top of Sampson Hall where we could arrange the historical affairs of the army without interruptions.

Fifteen years ago the U.S. Army Command and General Staff College at Fort Leavenworth invited Ken to teach an elective course on the history of American foreign policy and elected him to membership on its consulting faculty. From this experience he gained a high regard for the intellectualism of the officers of the U.S. Army. One of his best students went on to become aide-de-camp to the army chief of staff, General William C. Westmoreland. Now retired, Colonel Joe Felter inspired these pages in a subtle but profound way.

We thank finally our families—Vera, Doug, Muy, and Mugsy; Cookie and Jay—for their bemused love and understanding during the many late nights and weekends when we sat preoccupied, if not transfixed, before the glowing green screens of our computers. For their sake we pray that this book may in some small way help make the war that ended forty years ago the last total war of mankind.

KENNETH J. HAGAN
WILLIAM R. ROBERTS

Annapolis, Maryland
August 1985

Introduction _____

The eighteen chapters in this book are meant to be both interpretive and comprehensive. Each examines a particular period in the past and has been written by an author with a specialized knowledge of the military affairs of the era under scrutiny. These essays develop a number of salient themes about the American military and how it has changed over time. Three seem especially noteworthy to us: the increasing importance both on and off the battlefield the American military has come to have to the nation and indeed to the world in general; the changing geographical locale—from the North American continent before 1898 to every continent in the world since then—in which it has carried out its mission of defending the country; and the continuing tension between two different strategies—originally between a war of posts and a war of decisive battle, and more recently between a war of posts and a war of unrelenting actions—which has affected the way in which the American army has carried out its mission.

In one way or another, all of these essays testify to the growing importance of the military. Even as early as the eighteenth century, as John Shy points out in his comparative study of "Armed Force in Colonial North America," military institutions had the wherewithal to play a more vital role in the social, political, and economic development of the major European colonial systems of North America than has generally been recognized. For the most part, however, the army remained a small, relatively unimportant institution for more than a century after the War for American Independence. Harry L. Coles, for example, describes the cumbersome collection of short-term volunteers, militiamen, and "regulars" that could not prevent a smaller British force from occupying and burning the nation's capital during the War of 1812.

After the War of 1812, a number of changes took place within the regular army which made it a more cohesive, homogeneous organization. William B. Skelton shows how the officer corps developed common goals and a belief in the value of a formal military education once its members began to view the service as a way of life or profession rather than as a temporary civic obligation. James L. Morrison, Jr., describes the type of education officers received at West

Point before the Civil War, while Jerry M. Cooper and Timothy K. Nenninger demonstrate how the army transformed the professional development of its officers into a lifelong enterprise and produced the leaders competent to deal with overseas allies and adversaries in the twentieth century.

By the First World War, as Allan R. Millett details, those leaders had acquired the knowledge and the skills they needed to take an army, its equipment, and its men to Europe, where they contributed to the defeat of the Central Powers while largely maintaining the autonomy of the small expeditionary force they commanded. Afterwards army logisticians sought to ensure that in the event of another such conflict their country's industrial contribution—the one area in which the United States had clearly failed to pull its own weight during the war—would not be as disappointing as it had been in 1917 and 1918. Russell F. Weigley points out how these interwar leaders' plans for industrial mobilization eventually made it possible to tap the vast productive potential of American industry and forge the quantitative superiority of resources that enabled the service to fight a sustained war in Europe and the Pacific at the same time. Thus, in the opinion of both Weigley and James L. Stokesbury, by the Second World War the army emerged as one of the leading military organizations in the world and an institution touching the daily lives of the American people, not only on but off the battlefield. Stephen E. Ambrose, in his discussion of events during the Truman administration, adds that by the late 1940s and early 1950s the army had begun to reshape the political, social, and economic fabric of the very country it was created to serve.

Today, more than thirty years after the Korean War, at least 1.5 million men and women serve on active duty in the army or hold a paid position in the National Guard or army reserves, and the Department of the Army's budget for fiscal year 1986 is estimated at $80 billion. We see nothing to indicate that these changes have run their course or are likely to be reversed in the near future, but believe that the growing influence of the United States military makes the study of its history imperative for all Americans who want to understand the world in which they now live.

The following essays also bring out an important theme regarding the geographic locale in which army officers have upheld the oath they take on being commissioned to "defend the Constitution of the United States against all enemies, foreign and domestic." For more than a century after the War for American Independence, the army's efforts to accomplish its mission were restricted to the North American continent. Ira D. Gruber, Harry L. Coles, and James L. Morrison, Jr., show how American military leaders invaded Canada during the War for American Independence, burned the capital of Upper Canada during the War of 1812, and seized a large section of Mexico during the 1846–1848 Mexican War. Ironically, however, the foreign enemies that most occupied the army's attention were the European powers that were thought to be best equipped to launch an invasion of the United States from across the Atlantic. That possibility became unlikely once sailing ships gave way to coal-powered steamships, but William B. Skelton and William R. Roberts recount how army engineers nevertheless sought to defend America's coasts from attack well into the twentieth century. By building a series of fortifications and gun emplacements, the engineers hoped at least to slow down an invading force until regular army and local militia units could move into position to fend off the European foe.

In addition to defending the Republic from its foreign enemies, the regular army and militia were also responsible for defending it from domestic enemies. In the late eighteenth century these included, as Lawrence Delbert Cress relates, the followers of Daniel Shays in Massachusetts and the Pennsylvania farmers who participated in the Whiskey Insurrection, while in the nineteenth century they included for a time the South (see the chapters on the Confederate and Union armies by June I. Gow and Craig L. Symonds) as well as occasional groups of striking workers once Reconstruction ended (see Jerry M. Cooper's essay on the post-Civil War army).

Dissident farmers and workers, of course, were not the only domestic enemies with which the American military had to contend during the eighteenth and nineteenth centuries. William B. Skelton and Jerry M. Cooper point out that during most of this time the regular army amounted to little more than a constabulary force whose immediate mission was to keep the peace on the western frontier—sometimes by stopping white men from trespassing on Indian territory or taking advantage of the Indians, but more often by hunting down and relocating or killing the Indians—so that later generations of Anglo-Americans might fulfill their "manifest destiny" to rule the continent.

After Reconstruction the army at last subdued the Indians, and military leaders, as Jerry M. Cooper and William R. Roberts reveal, worried what would happen to the service and their careers when for the first time in its history the regular army did not have an enemy to fight. The future of the military establishment did not remain in doubt for long, however, as the nation's leaders soon extended the geographical area of American military operations to include the Caribbean and Pacific islands acquired during the 1898 Spanish-American War. The war had begun for reasons unrelated to the army's existential fears, but military officers, as Roberts notes, were quick to point out the army's need for more men and money in order to defend America's new island empire.

The army's defensive horizons have continued to expand during the present century. Membership in a world economy and a new-found belief in balance-of-power politics persuaded American leaders in the first half of the twentieth century that any enemy of Great Britain and western Europe was their enemy, too. But as Stephen E. Ambrose and Daun van Ee emphasize, by the middle of the century two new weapons—the long-distance bomber and the atomic bomb—momentarily renewed the anxiety that many officers had felt in the late nineteenth century when they had feared that the army might no longer have a mission. Nevertheless, the Cold War and an unprecedented peacetime alliance network combined to revive the fortunes of the country's ground forces. In the early 1950s the Korean War established the army's primacy in defending non-Communist allies from conventional attack or internal insurrection. The defeat of the army in another Asian country, Vietnam, almost a quarter of a century later caused military leaders and other Americans to urge greater selectivity in choosing when and where to defend non-Communist countries overseas, but the Vietnam War does not seem to have precipitated the same sort of identity crisis the army faced at the end of the nineteenth century and again after World War II.

A third theme worth noting in reading these essays has to do with strategy, that is, the way in which America's military leaders have chosen to apply the force at their disposal in order to accomplish their mission and the objectives of national policy. Ira D. Gruber's chapter on ''The Anglo-American Military Tradition and the War for American Independence'' seems particularly suggestive in this regard. Gruber believes that American military leaders such as George Washington and Nathanael Greene shared an ambiguous military tradition that taught them the value of ''two decidedly different ways of making war: a prudent, Continental war of posts and a much more hazardous, classical, and English war of decisive engagements.'' Gruber argues that Washington and Greene triumphed in the War for American Independence in part because of their persistence in fighting a war of siegecraft and maneuver (a war of posts) rather than a war of decisive battle. Nevertheless, his essay shows that the desire to fight a war of decisive battle existed long before Napoleon Bonaparte fired the imaginations of Dennis Hart Mahan and his students at West Point. Gruber's essay is important also because it implies the existence of a tension in American strategic thought which readers of this volume can trace from the eighteenth century to the present.

The attractiveness of a war of posts for American military leaders can be seen not only in the Revolution but also in such nineteenth-century conflicts as the War of 1812 when, as Harry L. Coles argues, President James Madison and General Jacob Brown clearly grasped the strategic desirability of fighting a war of siegecraft and maneuver with Montreal as the primary objective, or in the Civil War when, as Craig L. Symonds indicates, northern leaders at least initially followed a strategy similar to that used by Winfield Scott to outmaneuver and defeat General Santa Anna during the Mexican War. It can also be seen in twentieth-century conflicts such as the southwest Pacific campaign of Douglas MacArthur in World War II as well as MacArthur's conduct of operations, especially his amphibious landing at Inchon, during the Korean War.

While generally fighting a war of posts, early American military leaders tried to wage a war of decisive battle whenever possible. Andrew Jackson won a decisive victory over the British at New Orleans in 1815, while General Zachary Taylor later decisively conquered Mexican armies at the Battles of Palo Alto, Resaca de la Palma, Monterrey, and Buena Vista. During the Civil War, however, neither of these strategies proved capable of bringing matters to a successful conclusion—in part because of Robert E. Lee's tactical brilliance; in part because of the advantage new, long-range, rifled weapons gave a commander who did not wish to be drawn into a decisive battle; and in part also because of the nascent nationalism that drove Confederate armies on despite casualties far greater than American armies had endured before. Then in the final months of the war, the North capitalized on its sheer quantitative superiority of resources—enabling Ulysses S. Grant to maintain constant contact with Lee's army and fight a series of actions that in effect constituted one long battle, which raged more or less sharply, until the South surrendered. Grant's strategy of constant, unrelenting engagement was similar to that which American forces would later employ in Europe in World War II.

The United States has fought at least three wars that did not lend themselves all that well to a war of posts, a war of decisive battle, or a war of quantitative superiority and constant, unrelenting engagement: the nineteenth-century Indian wars, the Philippine Insurrection in the late nineteenth and early twentieth centuries, and the Vietnam War. In each the army faced a less sophisticated, but highly mobile and determined foe that was sometimes skilled in the use of guerrilla warfare. To overcome these enemies American military men were forced to develop greater mobility than the enemy—operating in the winter against the Indians, as Jerry M. Cooper explains, and nearly a century later in Vietnam relying on the helicopter as a form of flying artillery and transportation, as B. Franklin Cooling makes clear. Nevertheless, each of these wars tried the patience of American soldiers and civilians alike. They seemed to drag on forever and were sometimes attended by the angry, indiscriminate shooting of noncombatants (as at Wounded Knee in 1890 and at My Lai in 1968) by American soldiers who felt frightened and frustrated by an enemy who did not fight according to American rules. The only solution military leaders could find was to continue hunting, isolating, and killing the enemy until he could fight no more. In the case of Vietnam, however, the American people ultimately grew exasperated with a war in which both the quantitative and qualitative superiority of American military resources seemed impotent to break the enemy's ability and will to fight.

When regarding the essays which follow, the discerning reader will notice other themes worth considering. The regular army's relations with state and local forces as well as its relations with other services, for example, sometimes seem to have had as great an effect on the actions and thinking of military officers as have the larger needs of national defense and policy making. Several of the essays also offer insights into the kind of men—the Winfield Scotts, the Ulysses S. Grants, the Emory Uptons, the Douglas MacArthurs, the George Marshalls, the Dwight Eisenhowers, and the Creighton Abramses—who chose to make the army their career and who transformed it from the small Indian-fighting force which emerged soon after the War for American Independence into the global military establishment it is today.

Despite the many changes that have accompanied this transformation, we would caution the reader that no matter how much it changes, the army is an institution that in many respects always stays the same. James L. Morrison, Jr.'s description of the antebellum Military Academy, for instance, reveals a number of striking similarities between the education of officers then and now. Also striking is the analogous reasoning which led military leaders to recommend two of the more significant organizational reforms that have been enacted in the military in the last century: the General Staff and the Joint Chiefs of Staff. Indeed, many of the arguments that can be heard in favor of reforming the JCS today sound hauntingly like those the army first used in the late 1940s when it supported service unification as a means, at least in part, of improving its fortunes in dealing with Congress and the other services. Even the arguments of the military reform movement to which Colonel Harry G. Summers, Jr., refers in the concluding chapter are strongly reminiscent of the arguments used by Douglas MacArthur and other proponents of mobility between the two world wars. This lingering intellectual legacy is a final reason why the editors believe that serious students of military history—whether civilians or soldiers—will benefit from reading these eighteen essays.

W.R.R.
K.J.H.

AGAINST
ALL
ENEMIES

CHAPTER 1

Armed Force in Colonial North America: New Spain, New France, and Anglo-America

JOHN SHY

Military history continues to struggle to make its way within the historical discipline. Professional historians find it impossible to ignore war, but they are quite able to ignore other facets of the military experience that do not impinge on matters of immediate concern to them. Even when historians deal with questions of armed force, they give much less attention to the specialized nature of the subject than they would, say, to the technical aspects of economic growth, theological disputes, or democratic elections. War is an unpleasant subject, and military affairs do not seem very attractive to those who make history their profession. Yet these same scholars have devoted themselves to the close study of rebellion and revolution and are now scrutinizing the history of crime and punishment—subjects with perhaps as little intrinsic appeal as armies, navies, and war. The problem obviously goes deep and is difficult to understand fully.

One part of the problem seems clear enough, however, and easily remedied by the military specialist within whose domain it lies. Most published military history simply does not "connect" with general history. Too often military historians confine their research to military records and their search for explanations to military factors, as if the outcome of a battle or the life of an army was wholly self-contained and unrelated to its environment. The fallacy is too apparent to deserve argument. But the continuing reluctance of so many military historians to bring their work into effective touch with the modern ideal—shared by Marxists and non-Marxists alike—of a holistic history is surprising. What we get instead from too many military historians, aware of the lack of respect they receive from other historians, are programmatic pleas for the importance of their subject. Cries for new approaches and syntheses that will incorporate the military dimension are frequently voiced, but very little substantive work actually meets this high standard. The studies that effectively integrate military and nonmilitary sectors of life are usually done by scholars who would reject the label "military historian." What our apathetic and skeptical colleagues need is not programs and preaching, but performance; and this need establishes the task of this essay: to examine the projection of armed force by European states across the North Atlantic before the technological revolution of the nineteenth century transformed the very nature of both armed force and its projection over long distances.[1]

Superficially, the historical projection of military power by England, France, and Spain into North America appears similar. At first, very small increments of armed force, operating beyond effective control of these European governments, proved somehow sufficient to establish footholds on the North American continent. By the late seventeenth century, when the long series of European wars which shaped inter-American relations from 1689 to 1815 began, the military structure of English, French, and Spanish North America appears to have conformed roughly to a common pattern. This pattern included small garrisons of regular troops stationed at key points, a much larger but less professional militia recruited from among the European colonists themselves, friendly Native Americans (Indians) serving as auxiliaries, and more or less regular visitation and protection by warships based in European ports. An additional part of the pattern was chronic discontent with the pattern itself, a discontent expressed both by settlers in America and officials in Europe. These complaints themselves conformed to a pattern: regulars grew lazy and corrupt and cost too much to maintain; the militia was unarmed, untrained, and often cowardly; the Indians were treacherous and irresponsible; and the warships were seldom present when and where they were needed.

By the early eighteenth century, complaints about the military system of colonial North America had become so frequent, and proposals for reform so numerous, that a historian can only be reminded of the enormous physical difficulties of projecting military power and governmental control over thousands of miles in an age before steam transportation, electrical communication, and rapid-fire weapons had brought distance and population into a new relationship with armed force and state authority. During the long century of imperial conflict from 1689 to 1815, mutual inefficiency and weakness did as much to secure the European colonies of North America from external attack as did the skill and courage of their defenders, the strength of their fortresses, or the plans and expenditures of their respective governments.

Closer examination, however, reveals profound differences among the three colonial military systems; only a narrow focus on military organization and policy creates the superficial appearance of basic similarity. The main forces that set the American colonial empires on radically divergent military courses were geography, demography, and timing.

Spanish entry of the continent in 1519 found a very large, highly developed native population. Recent estimates based on new, careful research indicate that about 25 million people lived in the vast area that would become New Spain, most of them on the great Mexican-Guatemalan plateau.[2] This population, probably because of the "cold-screening" effect of migration from Asia through the Arctic zone and complete isolation for thousands of years, was virtually free of endemic disease.[3] The dominant force in the region was the Aztec Empire, a militarized state still in the process of expanding and consolidating its hold on peripheral areas when the Spanish arrived. The Aztec Empire, unlike earlier Mexican regimes, depended heavily on armed force, and resistance to its terrorist methods of control generated counterforce among subjected and threatened tribes.[4] Into this state of actual and incipient civil war, the first Spaniards moved. Their tiny armed band was no more than the increment needed to turn Indian rebellion against Aztec rule into civil war and revolution. Although Spanish arms are traditionally credited with the conquest of Mexico and the Aztec Empire, it is clear that Indians defeated Indians, although the Spaniards were the principal beneficiaries of this internecine strife.[5]

Spaniards could gather the fruits of civil war and military victory in part because of European technology, which was more frightening than it was lethal, and Native American theology, which foretold the conquest of Mexico by strangers from the east.[6] Nevertheless, the chief factor that led to Spanish rule was not weaponry but disease. Typhoid, smallpox, measles, and other diseases endemic among Europeans destroyed the native population in less than a century, leaving only a million disorganized, demoralized survivors by 1600, when France and England began to establish permanent footholds on the North American continent. Without natural resistance to disease, the Native American succumbed not to muskets and armored cavalry, but to conversation and kisses.[7]

Geography completed the imperial system of New Spain, in which organized armed force would play a surprisingly limited role. The incredible silver deposits at Potosí, Zacatecas, and Guanajuato were dug out by a dying native population, incapable of resistance, and soon by Africans as well.[8] This great Mexican treasure house and charnel house was secured by vast deserts to the north, by the inaccessibility of its western flank, and by the deadly diseases of the Caribbean coast and the constricted eastern routes to the interior. Veracruz, guarded by San Juan de Ulloa and a small regular garrison, thus blocked access to thousands of square miles of Mexico. Nature proved less cooperative, however, when it came to securing the line of supply and communication to Old Spain. Prevailing winds pushed silver-laden convoys through the Florida channel, and long before France or England could colonize the continent, the fortresses of Havana and St. Augustine guarded the one point where New Spain was truly vulnerable. On the mainland, along the frontier looking northward from St. Augustine, the courage and dedication of Franciscan monks did more than soldiers to bring the Indian tribes of the area under effective Spanish control.[9]

On the eve of permanent French and English colonization of North America, military organization as such played so little a part in New Spain that standard histories barely mention the military aspect of Spanish rule.[10] Militia existed, but more in name than in fact; the people were not armed. As long as Veracruz, Acapulco on the west coast, Havana, and St. Augustine could be held (or quickly retaken), and as long as a huge annual convoy could be assembled, New Spain could not be seriously threatened. Violence, or the threat thereof, readily controlled the native and African labor force. Institutionalized armed force was simply not important in New Spain before the eighteenth century.[11]

The early military history of New France stands in stark contrast to that of New Spain. Established Spanish bases thwarted early French efforts to colonize the more attractive southern part of the continent; and the magnificent fisheries off the Gulf of St. Lawrence, already well-known to seamen of the western ports, drew the French northward. But establishing a continental base at the natural strong point of Quebec in the early seventeenth century meant securing the constricted St. Lawrence valley above Quebec, and this strategic valley proved to be the "dark and bloody ground" of Canadian history. If fish drew the French to the St. Lawrence valley, fur kept them there; but the same fur trade, pouring down from the Great Lakes and Hudson Bay, was also a major factor in stunting and militarizing New France.[12]

When the French and English arrived in the early seventeenth century, the native population of eastern North America, more primitive and far less numerous than the native peoples of Mexico, had already felt the devastating effects of epidemic disease sweeping up from the south. Decimated, they tried, but could not effectively resist European invasion. Their weakness at the time of French and English colonization also made them susceptible to domination by the strongest Indian tribal grouping in the region, the Iroquois Confederation stretching from the Hudson valley to Niagara. In a primitive version of Aztec imperialism, the Iroquois used warfare and terror to assert hegemony over a vast tract of eastern North America, far into the best northern fur-bearing area and into the St. Lawrence valley itself. By establishing themselves when they did in the St. Lawrence valley, the French became—as had the Spanish a century earlier—the natural allies of those Indians who resisted a ruthless, aggressive Native American power. But unlike the Spanish, the French found themselves on the losing side. They could not protect their chief allies, the Hurons, from destruction by the Iroquois, and they could barely save themselves.

The military history of New France is grim but impressive. Not until the 1660s, when settlers, money, and troops began to pour into the St. Lawrence, was it clear that New France would survive. Survival depended on a large force of professional soldiers, who by 1665 made up more than a quarter, and later as much as a tenth, of the population.[13] The rest of the citizenry was organized into militia companies, and the militia captains were the chief officers of local administration.[14] After heavily subsidized immigration brought the population up to the level needed for survival, it was left to grow naturally; the Spartan conditions of New France described by priests and travelers and often embellished with tales of Indian atrocities did not attract settlers from Europe. The colony remained essentially a huge garrison, with all the strange mixture of rowdiness and order, authority and equality, that is part of a well-run regiment. Both economics and weakness gave New France an exceptional sensitivity to relations with Native Americans, and close ties with the western Indian tribes—all of them fearful of the Iroquois—brought Frenchmen and French outposts into the heart of the continent. Nonetheless, the military structure of New France set a fatal limit on its value to Old France.

The militarization of New France inhibited immigration and economic development, but it added a new weapon to the global strategy of eighteenth-century France. French ministers at Versailles saw Canada and its tough, combative people as a relatively cheap way of blocking the spectacular expansion of the Anglo-American colonies and making the British enemy divert military and naval resources from Europe, the West Indies, and India. Although some of the western posts and settlements of New France were economic liabilities, they had become military necessities. By mid-century French soldiers, militiamen, and Indian auxiliaries were pressing into the Ohio valley, not to expand the fur trade, but to keep Anglo-Americans penned behind the Appalachians. Despite the growing economic value of Canada within the French Empire during the eighteenth century, its strategic value overrode other considerations.[15] Whereas peaceful coexistence with the more numerous Anglo-Americans was what New France needed in order to develop socially and economically, its essentially military function forced it to be aggressive, in the end suicidally so.

When New France fell in 1760, after fighting heroically against great odds and after British naval victories had cut its lifeline to Europe, it was clear to all, including the Canadians themselves, that the government of Louis XV had simply abandoned the colony like a broken or worn-out weapon. A century of military history and more than half a century of French policy had shaped the fate of New France. In 1763 it became part of the British Empire, and 65,000 militarized Canadians accepted their fate because armed resistance seemed hopeless.

Military developments in the continental Anglo-American colonies fit neither the Spanish nor the French patterns. Tardy and feeble in the race for an American empire, England seemed remarkably unclear about its relationship to the settlements that by the 1680s dotted the coast between Florida and the St. Lawrence. While certain groups of English merchants and officials pressed for a legally defined, tightly controlled empire, the English crown gave away huge tracts of land and extensive powers of government in what would become New York, New Jersey, the Carolinas, and Pennsylvania.[16] The problem was that Anglo-America proved to be neither a vast treasure house like New Spain, which supplied wealth to the mother country, nor a tough military base like New France, which made an important contribution to French global strategy. As in New France, the Anglo-American was armed and lived (except in Pennsylvania) under a universal obligation to perform military service. But, as in New Spain, the issue of governmental control of armed force never clearly arose; for a moment in 1685–1688, when the English crown attempted drastic centralization of its colonies, the issue was almost confronted. Revolution in England resolved the crisis, however, and this key question of European political development remained largely muted in the British colonies until 1774–1775. Anglo-Americans instead were left to govern and defend themselves.[17]

The military history of the Anglo-American colonies offers at best a mixed and in general unhappy picture. Again and again Indians—often encouraged and supplied by New France or New Spain—would attack the Anglo-American frontier, driving settlement backward, spreading panic far beyond the point of actual attack, creating political crisis in provincial governments, and provoking efforts to retaliate massively and ruthlessly. Indian wars dragged Anglo-American provinces to the point of civil chaos more than once—in Virginia in 1675–1676, in Massachusetts and New York in 1688–1690, in South Carolina in 1719–1720, and in Pennsylvania in 1755 and in 1763–1764.[18] Hundreds of miles of ever-shifting frontier were not readily defensible; the only available strategy was retaliation so brutal that it would deter Indian attacks in the future along with the complete elimination of French and Spanish power from the North American continent. When the Anglo-Americans could persuade the government in London to help them in dealing with France and Spain, the help sent—munitions, ships, commanders, sometimes even soldiers—was usually inadequate or too late. Even along the southern frontier, where the outer defenses of New Spain seemed ever on the brink of collapse, Indians continued to seek shelter in the Spanish missions from the rapacity and cruelty of Anglo-American traders and frontiersmen.[19] The policy of relying on the numerous Anglo-Americans to defend themselves never worked satisfactorily; effective defense invariably seemed to demand offensive operations, which in turn were both very expensive and very difficult to mount. Seldom could Indians be caught and punished, and expeditions against Quebec and St. Augustine foundered more than once. Only in 1745, when New Englanders surprised the French defenders of Louisbourg, did Anglo-American military performance approximate the expectations of London policymakers.

The continuing failure of British military policy for the North American colonies reflected the nature of the British Empire. Haphazard and decentralized in its origins, it remained dependent on local elites who could command popular support and thus govern effectively. But decentralized, popular government in the Anglo-American provinces made military coordination almost impossible. At the same time an expanding agricultural society made wars inevitable. Recurrent wars and repeated military failure with all its attendant, unpleasant consequences posed a dilemma that colonial officials and theorists could never resolve.[20]

The murky, even contradictory quality of Anglo-American military policy and experience simply reflects the confusion within the British government itself about the value of the continental colonies. Fish, flour, lumber, and livestock were not valuable enough to justify the cost of a colonial military establishment. Tobacco saved Virginia but was hardly vital to the British economy; Carolina rice was highly profitable to the colonial planter but otherwise unimportant. Nothing produced on the continent could approach the value of West Indian sugar. The chief economic asset of the continental colonies lay in their land; but private persons—not the government—profited from land sales, while the sheer attraction of cheap land created serious military problems. Settlers dispersed uncontrollably over the land, pushing the Indians into small, bloody wars that the settlers could not win without expensive help from the seaboard, in some cases from England itself. Neither a treasure house nor a strategic base, Anglo-America was a gigantic real estate company from which London got little except trouble.

Persuasive arguments existed, on the other hand, for the adoption of a new military policy. The American fisheries bred seamen essential to British naval power. American farmers and fishermen fed West Indian slaves, and aggressive American merchants drained hard money out of the French and Spanish empires by selling products Great Britain did not need herself. But the strongest arguments centered on population. The spectacular growth of the Anglo-American population had by the mid–eighteenth century created a major new market within the British Empire. The rapidly rising volume of transatlantic shipping made the continental colonies a vital part of British sea power; about a third of the British merchant marine was American. Indeed, contemporary statistics indicate that the colonies had become the single truly dynamic sector of the British economy by the eve of the Industrial Revolution.[21]

When New France around 1750 attempted to contain the powerful but militarily inefficient giant to the south, a major policy change took place in London. The value of the continental colonies simply had become too great to continue the system of military laissez faire. After an intense debate, London decided to send regular troops to America, at first in numbers not so large as to be unprecedented, but later in great quantity. By 1760, when New France fell, the brunt of combat fell on more than twenty regiments of British regulars. The American colonial soldiers were, in the words of one British officer, recruited mainly "to work our boats, drive our waggons, to fell trees, and do the works that in inhabited countrys are performed by peasants."[22] In the aftermath of the decisive victories won by these British regulars and by the Royal Navy in the Seven Years' War (or French and Indian War, as it became known in the colonies), colonial Anglo-Americans felt that they had been relegated to second-class status within the British Empire. Anglo-America had become too valuable economically to leave its military affairs in the hands of the unruly, inept colonists.

The British decision in the treaty of 1763 to keep Canada, the trans-Appalachian West, and Florida as territorial buffers that would secure forever these dynamic continental colonies was of world-historical importance. Militarily, London had no choice except to garrison these great new territories with an expensive regular army. The expense of this new colonial military establishment led directly to the taxation of the colonies by Parliament and in turn to the fierce constitutional debate and the Anglo-American resistance movement that in time produced imperial civil war. But an armed population of more than two million people who lived three thousand miles away could not be defeated, not even by a British army and navy larger than the force that had defeated New France and New Spain in the Seven Years' War.[23]

While the American Revolution dominates the military history of North America in the latter part of the eighteenth century, the treaty ending the Seven Years' War in 1763 had important consequences not only for Anglo-America but for the colonial regimes of France and Spain as well. New France completely disappeared; even Louisiana was given to Spain as compensation for its wartime losses. The French population of the St. Lawrence valley, however, did not disappear. British occupation and rule were fairly benign. But the old system of local government through the militia captains did not continue. Catholics could not exercise judicial powers under the British constitution, and the militia captains retained the prestige but not the power of their office.[24] Moreover, the Old Regime of New France had effectively kept the seigneurial class from exercising political power by channeling seigneurial ambitions into the officer corps of the regular army regiments stationed in Canada; those regiments disappeared with the conquest in 1760.[25] As the British governors of Canada groped for political support in an occupied country and tried to curb the powers of the tiny Protestant minority that had entered Canada in the train of the British army, they moved toward ideas eventually incorporated in the Quebec Act of 1774. Often advertised as an outstanding example of British wisdom and toleration, the Quebec Act in fact gave the Catholic hierarchy and the seigneurial class stronger positions than either had ever achieved under the French regime.[26] Power shifted after the British conquest and especially under the Quebec Act from the rural mass of the population and its natural leaders to the educated, influential minority in Montreal and Quebec.

A clear sign of what British military conquest and its consequences did to the internal structure of French Canadian society was seen just a year after the Quebec Act, when Anglo-American rebel armies invaded the St. Lawrence valley. Seigneurs, priests, and French merchants rallied to the call to arms of the British governor, but the rural masses, when they were not apathetic, helped and even joined the rebels. Without active support from the *habitants*, Richard Montgomery's column would never have taken Montreal and Benedict Arnold's column, staggering down the Chaudiere toward Quebec, could not have survived. Despite a long history of bloody conflict between French and Anglo-American settlers, men from both sides acted together in late 1775 to seize the whole valley, except for the town of Quebec itself. The ultimate failure of the Anglo-American invasion is well known; in the debacle of 1776, *habitants* turned against the sick, retreating rebel army, but not before the desperate Anglo-Americans—unsupported from the south—had themselves begun to pillage the Canadian peasantry. The main point, however, is that British rule, by leaning so heavily on an urbanized elite, had effectively alienated the rural mass of the population.[27] The disarming of that population, the political emasculation of the militia captains, and the late, tentative steps taken to let French Canadians again play some limited military role did nothing to alter that alienation. And we are not yet done with its consequences.

New Spain after 1763 has some suggestive points of similarity with the demise of New France. The growth of population and trade since 1700 had taken place as rapidly in New Spain as it had in New France. Like the French after Quebec and Montreal had fallen, the Spanish were shocked when Havana and Manila fell to British attack during the Seven Years' War. Military defeat precipitated radical changes of colonial policy in both Madrid and Versailles. But while the French government abandoned Canada, deciding that its economic and military value could not justify the cost of retaining it, the Spanish government moved in the opposite direction.[28]

The Spanish colonies were seen as the key to the revival and modernization of Spain itself. Accordingly a plan of imperial reform—similar to that initiated in the British Empire after 1763, but far more comprehensive—was set in motion. A major element of Spanish colonial reform was the revival of a virtually defunct colonial military establishment. Defense of the Spanish Empire, in particular New Spain, against British attack or encroachment became the chief aim of military reform after 1763; Havana should be made impregnable, especially since Florida had been lost in the peace settlement, and Veracruz, Acapulco, and Campeche—the keys to Mexican trade and defense—needed to be equally strong. The questions, as always, were how to pay for defense, where to find the manpower, and how best to organize it.[29]

Spanish reformers recognized that an army large enough to defend the colony would have to draw on the colonial population; regular regiments from Europe were simply too costly. Moreover, experience had shown that European regulars deteriorated quickly in the American environment. They soon lost their discipline and tactical skills, they married locally and took up nonmilitary occupations, they sickened and died of unaccustomed diseases, and they grew old, lazy, and corrupt. Although a small force of European regulars would provide garrisons and a cadre, the bulk of the new army had to be found in America. But in drawing on the colonial population to create a new military structure, the Spanish confronted a major difficulty. Ever since the sixteenth century, the minority known as creoles—whites born in the colonies—had constituted the main obstacle to effective Spanish control of New Spain. Viceroy after viceroy had succumbed to opposition and seduction by creoles entrenched in commerce, agriculture, mining, and the church. To reform New Spain demanded that somehow the powerful network of vested creole interests, including the parochial mentality that characterized this network, be broken through. Creole interests and ways of thinking were so strong that the government saw creoles as the only serious internal threat; Indians, Negroes, and other nonwhites—together a vast majority of the population—were potentially dangerous but effectively controlled by the creoles themselves.[30] Obviously, a new military structure required creole participation, and yet the arming and military training of creoles seemed a prescription for imperial suicide.

Two schools of thought on the military reform of New Spain soon emerged. One stressed the creation of an indigenous professional army, with creole sons given at least junior commissions and trained and inspired by the cadre of European professionals. Creating a new class of creole military professionals would create a new mentality; obedient to orders from their supreme commander, thinking in terms of imperial security and welfare, the members of this class would outgrow the bad habits that had made New Spain so vulnerable. The other school of thought doubted the wisdom and feasibility of superimposing a European military institution onto the complex, delicately balanced social structure of New Spain. It called for the organization of an effective colonial militia which would be cheaper and larger and would fit more readily into colonial society than a professional army.

For more than forty years after 1763, the military establishment of New Spain grew steadily, but continual oscillation between the professional and the militia concepts of military organization occurred.[31] The professional concept was confronted by the disinclination of the population to become professional soldiers. Europeans dominated the regular officer corps of the new army, and creoles did not want to serve under the hated *peninsulares*. The regular regiments thus recruited heavily from the nonwhite dregs of society, in effect creating a small army dangerously alienated from the elite of the society it was supposed to defend. Only the militia concept could attract creoles. As militia officers they acquired a new status and enjoyed the privilege of being exempt from civil legal jurisdiction. It thus proved easy to induce young creoles to accept commissions in the provincial militia regiments. Whether those regiments were effective military units, however, was another matter. Regular officers sent to inspect the militia reported that militia officers were ignorant and inattentive, that the men were poorly trained and armed, and that in some cases the organization existed only on paper. Creole eagerness to become militia officers seemed to have little connection with the defense of New Spain. The new army effectively "militarized" a key segment of Mexican society. Despite its impressive growth, however, it never satisfied anyone.[32]

The Napoleonic invasion of Spain in 1808 and the destruction of central authority within the Spanish Empire shaped the consequences of these earlier military changes in New Spain. There had been no colonial tradition of military intervention in politics, but the inevitable contest between Spaniards and creoles for control of New Spain from 1808 onward inevitably dragged the new military establishment into the political arena. In 1810, an unexpected social revolution of Indian masses led by the enlightened creole priest Miguel Hidalgo y Costilla threw Spaniards and creoles back together. The post–1763 reforms had given the white minority the organized armed force needed to smash the Hidalgo revolt and subsequently to win a protracted, bloody, counterrevolutionary war against the oppressed nonwhite majority. But full mobilization in that war of the creole-dominated militia gave a preponderance of power to the creoles in their continuing struggle with Spaniards and Spanish authority—a struggle that the post–1763 changes had recast in a military form, with creole militia confronting Spanish professionals. And counterrevolutionary war turned creole Mexico in a conservative, militaristic direction. When Spain tried to abolish the legally privileged position of colonial militia officers in 1820, the creoles took the last step toward independence. But independence meant rejection of social reform, an emergent nation devastated by war that had begun in 1810, Spanish talent and capital driven out, and rule by armed force. By 1821, when Mexico declared its independence, the army had become as powerful as the church and the landowning elite and far less responsive to anything discernible as national interest.[33]

Perhaps the unhappy history of Mexico would have been much the same even without the unintended, unexpected effects of post–1763 military reform. Perhaps the great majority of French Canadians would have been alienated by British rule even if conquest had not unintentionally destroyed the militarized structure of political and social organization. But the links in the chain of causation joining narrow military factors to broader political and social consequences seem very clear in each case. Less clear is the relationship between military factors and broader consequences for Anglo-America.

The American Revolutionary War (itself a product of imperial military reform and the British government's decision to resolve constitutional deadlock by armed force) drove tens of thousands of Anglo-Americans to Nova Scotia, New Brunswick, and Ontario, giving British rule in Canada the popular basis on which it would thereafter depend. This splitting of the Anglo-American population probably weakened conservative political forces in the new United States; unlike the Mexican Revolution, in which independence was won by a counterrevolutionary army, the military mobilization of Anglo-America in the fight for independence favored democratization. Raising any army meant begging or bribing common men to fight, and many colonists became loyalists not because they approved of British policies but because they were disgusted and frightened by the corrosive effect of revolutionary war on social hierarchy and deference. The critical difference, of course, was that the United States did not have the submerged, nonwhite majority that turned revolution into counterrevolution in Mexico. Although the British tardily and half-heartedly tried to mobilize oppressed groups— Negro slaves, Indians, religious and ethnic minorities—against the Anglo-American rebels, they never succeeded in transforming a colonial war into a genuine civil war between Anglo-Americans.[34] If they had done so, even if Britain still had lost the war, the emergent United States would have been a very different sort of political and social entity.

Democratization—no part of the program of even the most radical leaders of Anglo-American resistance before 1775—was only one result of protracted war. National consciousness, equally invisible before 1775, was another. Armed struggle and ultimate military victory, coupled with the rhetorical explanation of the war, gave Anglo-American independence its peculiar meaning; the aims and results of a war that could not have been won without a unified military effort were equated with the word "American," meaning the United States. But the duration and character of the war also divorced American nationalism from the specific institutions of central government. Central government had conspicuously failed by 1778 to sustain and control the armed struggle for independence; the latter years of the war saw a devolution of effective government back to the provincial or state level, and respect for the Continental Congress steadily sank.[35] Even the Continental army lost prestige when it failed to defend the southern colonies against British invasion in 1779–1780, and only local guerrilla bands kept resistance alive. Had the United States split into two or three smaller republics—an outcome frequently predicted—the Revolution would have been reckoned a failure; in that sense, it was an ''American'' Revolution. But the actual experience of the Revolutionary War fostered skepticism toward higher levels of government, and from this wartime experience emerged that strange bundle of compromises and contradictions known as American federalism.

For a moment in 1782–1783, it looked as if the American Revolution might end as do so many revolutionary wars—in a military coup. The Continental army had gradually become less an army of citizen-soldiers and more a feeble imitation of an army of European regulars—arrogant young officers clamoring for lifetime pensions and damning the elected officials who resisted their demands, soldiers drawn by high enlistment bounties from the poorest, most obscure corners of Anglo-American society. Starved by the timidity and inefficiency of Congress and by the parochialism of the states, the Continental army had learned to take what it needed. But George Washington was no Caesar or Cromwell, and he refused to play the part assigned to him; instead, he used his own prestige to quash whatever plot existed to seize political power, and the British decision to end the war made it possible simply to dissolve the mutinous Continentals.[36]

The military problems British North America and the new United States faced in 1783 were not unlike those of the British Empire in 1763: vast spaces, a thinly settled but growing and moving white population, and on the frontier Indians often caught between rival groups of Europeans. The chief military threat, however, recalling the century before 1763, came from the proximity of Canada and the United States to one another. British policy, like French policy before it, emphasized the strategic value of Canada in curbing the growth of power to the south, and British expenditures kept a regular force in Canada that matched the small United States Army. The eventual clash in 1812–1814 was indecisive; both sides learned that they were too large and populous to be conquered by the other. Military stalemate, European powers preoccupied after 1815 with European affairs, and British naval forces in the North Atlantic left Canada and the United States to drift militarily until internal rebellions and new technology began to change the situation later in the century.[37]

Mexico, like Canada and the United States, a territorial giant with similar problems of control and security, points to the contrast with which this comparative survey will end. After independence the military in Mexico took on a life of its own, absorbing 80 percent of a swollen national budget imposed on a crippled, stagnant economy. The Mexican military gave little in return, except endless political chaos to which the army periodically pretended to bring some measure of order. So absorbed in the politics of central Mexico was this army that the government could secure the frontier province of Texas only by inviting Anglo-Americans to settle there and defend it. And so corrupted by its political absorption was this army that it could not protect Mexico against invasion by smaller forces from the United States in 1846–1847.[38]

To dwell exclusively on the very different ways in which military structures and events played themselves out in these three areas of North America would be to violate the admonition with which this essay began. But in seeking some satisfactory explanation for postcolonial histories that diverged so dramatically, we gain an important degree of understanding by tracing and comparing their military histories. The remarkable unimportance of organized armed forces in the political and social life of New Spain between the brief age of conquest and 1763 was the basic condition underlying what happened after 1763. By arming and organizing the creole population to defend New Spain, while keeping the creoles out of the most prestigious military positions in the regular regiments, the Spanish government planted the seeds of colonial insurrection and Mexican militarism. In contrast, the remarkable extent to which New France was militarized almost from its beginning, with military organization providing the French regime both its most effective instrument of local government and its chief means of controlling the aristocracy of the colony, remained a critical factor in the history of Canada after 1760. Projecting a false, anglicized picture of elite rule onto the strange society of the St. Lawrence valley, the new British regime abruptly shifted the balance of power within the French population, leaving the *habitants* alienated and apathetic. To the south, a constantly expanding, aggressive population of colonial Anglo-American farmers was both heavily armed and terribly vulnerable. When the British government eventually found the cost of colonial warfare intolerable and the value of colonial production and consumption indispensable, London ordered British regulars to take over the task of policing the Anglo-American colonies. The fiscal and constitutional ramifications of that change led to civil war, a war which the presence of regulars in North America encouraged London to begin, but a war that Britain, confronted by a numerous, armed people, simply could not win. Although the collapse of British imperial greatness was the predicted result, the actual result was the anglicization of the Canadian population.

The clear lesson of these three stories is that military arrangements represent vital allocations of power and interest, however invisible or unimportant such arrangements may seem in the day-to-day life of a society. The politicians and reformers who altered these arrangements in the eighteenth century seem to have shared an assumption fashionable in our own age, that armed force is best seen as an instrument of political action, a manageable means to a rational end. But the results of imperial military change in the eighteenth century went so far beyond the terms of this assumption, so far beyond anything foreseen or desired by those who initiated the changes, that the assumption itself comes into question. Whether this question still arises, or whether the revolutions that separate the early modern world from the late twentieth century have resolved it, is a matter beyond the scope of this essay.

NOTES

1. What follows is based primarily on my own research for colonial Anglo-America and the United States but draws heavily from the published work of William J. Eccles for New France, Christon I. Archer, Lyle N. McAlister, and Charles Gibson for New Spain, C. P. Stacey for Canada, and John Lynch and Charles C. Cumberland for Mexico.

2. Charles Gibson, *Spain in America* (New York: Harper and Row, 1966), p. 63.

3. T. D. Stewart, *The People of America* (New York: Charles Scribner's Sons, 1973), pp. 1–70, offers an up-to-date synthesis of knowledge about the pre-Columbian population of America.

4. Eric Wolf, *Sons of the Shaking Earth* (Chicago: University of Chicago Press, 1959), is a brilliant recreation of Indian history before and after the Spanish invasion.

5. Gibson, *Spain in America*, p. 26, et passim.

6. Ibid., p. 35.

7. Stewart, *People of America*, pp. 35–38; Gibson, *Spain in America*, pp. 3–65.

8. Gibson, *Spain in America*, pp. 143–47.

9. Christon I. Archer, *The Army in Bourbon Mexico, 1760–1810* (Albuquerque: University of New Mexico Press, 1977), pp. 1–3. A fuller, more systematic account is in María del Carmen Velázquez Chavez, *El Estado de Guerra en Nueva España, 1760–1808* (Mexico City: Colegio de México, 1950), pp. 9–29. On the northern frontier, see Gibson, *Spain in America*, pp. 182–92, and the fuller treatments in Philip Wayne Powell, *Soldiers, Indians, and Silver: The Northward Advance of New Spain, 1550–1600* (Berkeley: University of California Press, 1952), and John Jay TePaske, *The Governorship of Spanish Florida, 1700–1763* (Durham, N.C.: Duke University Press, 1964), pp. 3–7, 193–226.

10. E.g., Gibson, *Spain in America*.

11. Jonathan I. Israel, *Race, Class, and Politics in Colonial Mexico, 1610–1670* (London: Oxford University Press, 1975), especially his remark on p. 269 about the "almost total lack of arms" in the ruling white population.

12. What follows derives mainly from William J. Eccles, *The Canadian Frontier, 1534–1760* (New York: Holt, Rinehart and Winston, 1969), and *France in America* (New York: Harper and Row, 1972).

13. Eccles, *Canadian Frontier*, p. 101.

14. William J. Eccles, "The Social, Economic, and Political Significance of the Military Establishment in New France," *Canadian Historical Review* 52 (1971): 1–22.

15. On the impressive growth of the economy of New France, see Maurice Filion, *La pensée et l'action coloniales de Maurepas vis-à-vis du Canada, 1723–1749: l'âge d'or de la colonie* (Montreal: Leméac, 1972).

16. Wesley Frank Craven, *The Colonies in Transition, 1660–1713* (New York: Harper and Row, 1968), pp. 1–103.

17. John Shy, *Toward Lexington: The Role of the British Army in the Coming of the American Revolution* (Princeton, N.J.: Princeton University Press, 1965), pp. 3–44.

18. Wilcomb E. Washburn, *The Governor and the Rebel: A History of Bacon's Rebellion in Virginia* (Chapel Hill: University of North Carolina Press, 1957); Michael G. Hall, Lawrence H. Leder, and Michael G. Kammen, eds., *The Glorious Revolution in America: Documents on the Colonial Crisis of 1689* (Chapel Hill: University of North Carolina Press, 1964); and James H. Hutson, *Pennsylvania Politics, 1746–1770: The Movement for Royal Government and Its Consequences* (Princeton, N.J.: Princeton University Press, 1972).

19. TePaske, *Governorship of Spanish Florida*, pp. 108–58, 193–226.

20. The early volumes of Lawrence H. Gipson, *The British Empire Before the American Revolution*, 15 vols. (Caldwell, Idaho, and New York: Alfred A. Knopf, 1936–1970), provide the fullest account of these problems in the mid–eighteenth century.

21. Phyllis Deane and W. A. Cole, *British Economic Growth, 1688–1959: Trends and Structure* (Cambridge, Eng.: University Press, 1962), pp. 40–97; and James F. Shepherd and Gary M. Walton, *Shipping, Maritime Trade, and the Economic Development of Colonial North America* (Cambridge, Eng.: University Press, 1972).

22. Col. James Robertson to John Calcraft, 22 June 1760 (extract), Loudoun Papers, LO 6251, Henry E. Huntington Library, San Marino, California.

23. Shy, *Toward Lexington*; and Shy, *A People Numerous and Armed: Reflections on the Military Struggle for American Independence* (New York: Oxford University Press, 1976).

24. Alfred Le Roy Burt, *The Old Province of Quebec* (Minneapolis: University of Minnesota Press, 1933), pp. 28–35, 92. Frederick B. Wiener, *Civilians Under Military Justice: The British Practice Since 1689, Especially in North America* (Chicago: University of Chicago Press, 1967), pp. 37–63, contains useful details of civilians tried in Canada by "court martial" between 1759 and 1764 when military government ended, but because the author is preoccupied with *British* practice, the vital distinction between British military courts and French militia captains is obscured; see especially pp. 39–40.

25. Eccles, "Military Establishment," 17.

26. Burt, *Old Province*, passim.

27. John E. Hare, "Le comportement de la paysannerie rurale et urbaine de la région de Québec pendant l'occupation americaine 1775–1776," *University of Ottawa Review* 47 (1977): 145–50. This succinct article is based heavily on the investigation of the Quebec district parishes, published in the *Rapport de l'archiviste de la province de Québec pour 1927–1928* (Québec: L.-Amable Proulx, 1928), pp. 431–99, which is amply confirmed by evidence from the rebel side.

28. Stanley J. and Barbara H. Stein, *The Colonial Heritage of Latin America: Essays on Economic Dependence in Perspective* (New York: Oxford University Press, 1970), pp. 86–106.

29. This account is based on Archer, *Army in Bourbon Mexico*; Lyle N. McAlister, "The Reorganization of the Army of New Spain, 1763–1766," *Hispanic American Historical Review* 33 (1953): 1–32; and McAlister, *The "Fuero Militar" in New Spain, 1764–1800* (Gainesville: University of Florida Press, 1957).

30. Israel, *Race, Class, and Politics*, pp. 136–269, tells the story for the seventeenth century.

31. Archer, *Army in Bourbon Mexico*, tells this story in detail.

32. McAlister, "*Fuero Militar*," pp. 1–15. John J. Johnson, *The Military and Society in Latin America* (Stanford: Stanford University Press, 1964), pp. 13–23, stresses the importance of the wars of independence in creating "militarism."

33. This version of Mexican history from 1810 follows John Lynch, *The Spanish-American Revolutions, 1808–1826* (New York: Norton, 1973), pp. 294–330.

34. William Nelson, *The American Tory* (Oxford: Clarendon Press, 1961); Shy, *People Numerous and Armed*, pp. 183–224; and Shy, "British Strategy for Pacifying the Southern Colonies, 1778–1781," in Jeffrey J. Crow and Larry E. Tise, eds., *The Southern Experience in the American Revolution* (Chapel Hill: University of North Carolina Press, 1978), pp. 155–73.

35. Elmer James Ferguson, *The Power of the Purse: A History of American Public Finance, 1776–1790* (Chapel Hill: University of North Carolina Press, 1961), pp. 3–69, traces the revolutionary process for the critical issue of public finance.

36. Richard H. Kohn, *Eagle and Sword: The Federalists and the Creation of the Military Establishment in America, 1783–1802* (New York: Free Press, 1975), deals most fully with the military establishment that emerged from the Revolution.

37. Charles Perry Stacey, *Canada and the British Army, 1846–1871: A Study in the Practice of Responsible Government*, rev. ed. (Toronto: University of Toronto Press, 1963), pp. 1–45; Francis Paul Prucha, *The Sword of the Republic: The United States Army on the Frontier, 1783–1846*, The Wars of the United States (New York: Macmillan Co., 1968); Gerald S. Graham, *Empire of the North Atlantic: The Maritime Struggle for North America*, 2d ed. (Toronto: University of Toronto Press, 1958); and J. Mackay Hitsman, *Safeguarding Canada, 1763–1871* (Toronto: University of Toronto Press, 1968). Also containing useful information and documents is *A History of the . . . Military and Naval Forces of Canada from the Peace of Paris in 1763 to the Present Time* (Ottawa: Department of National Defence, 1919–20), especially vols. I–II.

38. Charles C. Cumberland, *Mexico: The Struggle for Modernity* (New York: Oxford University Press, 1968), pp. 141–89.

FURTHER READING

Aside from Alfred Thayer Mahan's early studies of sea power, the most important comparative study of armed force in the colonial history of North America is Gerald S. Graham, *Empire of the North Atlantic: The Maritime Struggle for North America*, 2d ed. (Toronto: University of Toronto Press, 1958). Unfortunately, there is no comparable, comparative study of the land forces with which this essay is primarily concerned.

Research on the native population both before and during European contact has been an active and exciting field in recent years, and the results have begun to change our understanding of the earliest military encounters. An introduction to this new research is James Axtell, "The Ethnohistory of Early America: A Review Essay," *William and Mary Quarterly*, 3d ser. 35 (January 1978): 110–44, while William C. Sturtevant, ed., *Handbook of the North American Indians*, 20 vols. (Washington: Smithsonian Institution, 1978–) will provide detailed accounts for each region.

For early Anglo-American military history, the standard account is Douglas E. Leach, *Arms for Empire: A Military History of the British Colonies in North America, 1607–1763* (New York: Macmillan Co., 1973). There are a number of studies of the colonial American militia in peace and war, but it was an elusive institution. More books of the quality of Fred Anderson, *A People's Army: Massachusetts Soldiers and Society in the Seven Years' War* (Chapel Hill: University of North Carolina Press, 1984) are needed. British policies and forces to 1757 are well treated in Stanley M. Pargellis, *Lord Loudoun in North America, 1756–1758* (New Haven, Conn.: Yale University Press, 1933); my own *Toward Lexington: The Role of the British Army in the Coming of the American Revolution* (Princeton, N.J.: Princeton University Press, 1965) continues the story to 1775. Of the many good books on the American Revolution, Piers G. Mackesy, *The War for America, 1775–1783* (Cambridge: Harvard University Press, 1964), on the British side, and Charles Royster, *A Revolutionary People at War: The Continental Army and American Character, 1775–1783* (Chapel Hill: University of North Carolina Press, 1979), on the American side, deserve special mention. Richard H. Kohn, *Eagle and Sword: The Federalists and the Creation of the Military Establishment in America, 1783–1802* (New York: Free Press, 1975) carries the story beyond the Revolution, while Russell H. Weigley, *The American Way of War: A History of United States Military Strategy and Policy*, The Wars of the United States (New York: Macmillan Co., 1973), is a stimulating interpretation of the whole American military experience.

For New France, the work of William J. Eccles is indispensable, especially *The Canadian Frontier, 1534–1760*, rev. ed. (Albuquerque: University of New Mexico Press, 1983), which is far broader than its title, and "The French Forces in North America during the Seven Years' War," an introductory essay in vol. III of the *Dictionary of Canadian Biography*. The sketches in the latter work of native, Canadian, and French military leaders are valuable. Eccles's view of the role of armed force in the government and society of New France is not universally accepted by Canadian historians, as I learned when this essay was originally presented in Ottawa at the international colloquium on military history in 1978, but his work is basic to all further study.

Study of the colonial wars begins with Francis Parkman's *France and England in North America: A Series of Historical Narratives*, 7 vols. (Boston: Little, Brown & Co., 1865–1892), particularly Pt. 5, *Count Frontenac and New France under Louis XIV* (1877); Pt. 6, *A Half-Century of Conflict*, 2 vols. (1892); and Pt. 7, *Montcalm and Wolfe*, 2 vols. (1884), all reprinted in various editions. Ian K. Steele, *Guerillas and Grenadiers: The Struggles for Canada, 1689–1760* (Toronto: Ryerson Press, 1969), takes issue with Parkman's emphasis on the baneful effects of Catholicism and authoritarian government on New France. Howard H. Peckham, *The Colonial Wars, 1689–1762* (Chicago: University of Chicago Press, 1964) is a usefully brief, modern account, while Lawrence H. Gipson, *The British Empire Before the American Revolution*, 15 vols. (Caldwell, Idaho, and New York: Alfred A. Knopf, 1936–1970) is exhaustive on the climactic campaigns of midcentury. Of special value are Christopher Moore, *Louisbourg Portraits* (Toronto: University of Toronto Press, 1982), and Charles P. Stacey, *Quebec, 1759: The Siege and the Battle* (Toronto: Macmillan Co., 1959).

Canada after the British conquest in 1760 is dealt with thoroughly in the older work of Alfred L. Burt, *The Old Province of Quebec* (Minneapolis: University of Minnesota Press, 1933) and *The United States, Great Britain and British North America From the Revolution to the Establishment of Peace After the War of 1812* (New Haven, Conn.: Yale University Press, 1940), but the important military dimension is buried in the general history, and the impact of a new military system on French-Canadian society is debated. Gustave Lanctot, *Canada and the American Revolution, 1774–1783*, trans. Margaret M. Cameron (Cambridge: Harvard University Press, 1967), offers a different view, and Fernand Ouellet, "Quebec, 1760–1867," in D. A. Muise, ed., *A Reader's Guide to Canadian History: Beginnings to Confederation* (Toronto: University of Toronto Press, 1982), pp. 45–77, sketches the general historiographical context of the debate. Charles P. Stacey, *Canada and the British Army, 1846–1871: A Study in the Practice of Re-*

sponsible Government (London: Longmans, Green and Co., 1936) carries the colonial story to its end.

The conquest of New Spain is best known through the classic work of William H. Prescott, *History of the Conquest of Mexico*, 3 vols. (New York: Harper and Brothers, 1843), but the subsequent military history of New Spain is not well studied. Professor Charles Gibson, whose *Spain in America* (New York: Harper and Row, 1966) is vital to my own understanding, remarked that Hispanic-American historians have been little interested in the subject between the conquest and the nineteenth century. John H. Elliott, *Imperial Spain, 1469–1716* (London: E. Arnold, 1963) is excellent, but brief and general for the Spanish side. Philip Wayne Powell, *Soldiers, Indians, and Silver: The Northward Advance of New Spain* (Berkeley: University of California Press, 1952), and John TePaske, *The Governorship of Spanish Florida, 1700–1763* (Durham, N.C.: Duke University Press, 1964) treat the northern frontier. Christon I. Archer, *The Army in Bourbon Mexico, 1760–1810* (Albuquerque: University of New Mexico Press, 1977), describes the military revival after the Seven Years' War and its results. The emergence of Mexican "militarism" can be traced in John Lynch, *The Spanish-American Revolutions, 1808–1826* (New York: Norton, 1963), and Charles C. Cumberland, *Mexico: The Struggle for Modernity* (New York: Oxford University Press, 1968).

CHAPTER 2

The Anglo-American Military Tradition and the War for American Independence

IRA D. GRUBER

In the late spring of 1755, Major General Edward Braddock led a small army of British regulars and colonial militiamen from Virginia into the mountains of western Pennsylvania. Braddock had been ordered to evict a force of French nd Indians from the Ohio River Valley, from lands that were claimed by both rrance and Britain. He had chosen to divide his small army so that an advanced party of about 1,200 men might reach the French outpost at Fort Duquesne before reinforcements arrived there from Canada. On 9 July, when within about eight miles of Fort Duquesne, the British suddenly encountered a party of 850 French and Indians. For once the British had failed to take routine precautions against surprise, and they found themselves engulfed in a destructive crossfire from brush-filled ravines along the line of march. When Braddock's van fell back and his main body rushed forward to join in the fighting, the whole of his army was compressed into a milling, disorganized, and terrified mass. In vain did he try to restore order—to lead his men from the narrow roadway and to drive the French and Indians from the adjacent ravines. The small British army was soon shattered; 977 of its officers and men were killed or wounded and the rest fled for Virginia.

Among the survivors were five men who, twenty years later, would lead opposing forces in the War for American Independence. Although three of them were regular British officers in 1755, only one would serve the king during the Revolution. Thomas Gage, a lieutenant colonel commanding the van of Braddock's army, would be commander in chief of British forces at Boston in 1775. But Horatio Gates, a captain in an independent company of foot, and Charles Lee, a lieutenant in the Forty-fourth Regiment, would resign their regular commissions, migrate to America, and become major generals in the Continental army at the beginning of the Revolution. They would find themselves serving under or with two other veterans of Braddock's expedition: George Washington and Daniel Morgan. Washington, an aide-de-camp on 9 July 1755, survived to command the Continental army; Morgan, a teamster with Braddock, would lead various light corps during the Revolution.

It was, of course, coincidental that five survivors of one small engagement in 1755 should become prominent commanders two decades later. But it was not unusual that Americans and Englishmen who had served together in the French and Indian War should rise to command opposing forces in the War for American Independence. At least seven veterans of the French and Indian War were among the most important generals in the Continental army. Four of them—Gates, Lee, Washington, and Morgan—had been with Braddock. But each of those four had gained further experience against the French and Indians: Gates as a regular during three campaigns in New York and one in western Pennsylvania; Lee as a British officer in five campaigns in New England; Washington as commander of Virginia militia and a volunteer with John Forbes's expedition to Fort Duquesne; and Morgan as a militiaman on the frontiers of Virginia. By 1775 each had the military experience and reputation as well as the republican zeal to win important commands in the rebel forces. So did three other veterans of the French and Indian War—Philip Schuyler, Benedict Arnold, and Benjamin Lincoln. Although Schuyler had not held a regular commission, he had had the social standing and military competence to manage the supply service for James Abercromby and Jeffery Amherst in their campaigns along Lake Champlain. No wonder that he would be appointed a major general in 1775 and charged with organizing patriot forces on the Hudson-Champlain line. Even Arnold and Lincoln, who had done no more during the French and Indian War than serve fitfully and inconspicuously in the militia—building roads and garrisoning remote outposts—were able to translate prior service into subordinate commands at the outset of the Revolution. Arnold took command of a detachment and went overland to attack Quebec; Lincoln became a major general of Massachusetts militia and commander of the state troops at Boston.[1]

Just as the colonists turned to veterans of the French and Indian War for leadership in the Revolution, so too did the British. Both Thomas Gage and Guy Carleton, who commanded British forces at the beginning of the Revolutionary War, had taken part in the conquest of Canada. After Braddock's defeat, Gage remained in America to serve without distinction at Louisbourg, Ticonderoga, and Montreal; but he had the seniority and the influence as well as the inclination to become governor of Montreal in 1760 and commander in chief in North America in 1763. Carleton, a much more accomplished soldier and a skillful administrator, had served with James Wolfe at the capture of Quebec in 1759 and returned in 1766 to become deputy governor. Although Carleton seemed quite competent to preserve Canada for the crown, there were serious doubts that Gage could do the same for the colonies to the south; and in early 1775 King George III began looking for someone who had the talent and determination to put down a rebellion. The king turned first to the most distinguished veteran of the French and Indian War—the man who had captured Louisbourg in 1758 and organized the final destruction of New France—Sir Jeffery Amherst. When Amherst refused to return to America, the king chose William Howe to assist and then supersede Gage. Howe, like Amherst, had made his reputation in the

French and Indian War—as a regimental commander at Louisbourg and Quebec. He would be commander in chief in North America from 1775 to 1778; and Amherst, commander in chief in Britain from 1778 to 1782.[2]

Of course, there were principal commanders on both sides of the War for American Independence who had not served in the French and Indian War, who had not known the peculiarities of warfare in the forests and on the lakes and rivers of North America. But even those who had not fought together at Louisbourg or Ticonderoga were heirs to a common military tradition. Nathanael Greene, Henry Knox, Anthony Wayne, and John Sullivan had been students during the French and Indian War. Yet after the war, each joined the militia and, through the militia and independent reading, imbibed military practices and ideas current in the British Empire. In their militia companies they learned how to march and fire according to Edward Harvey, *The Manual Exercise As Ordered by His Majesty in 1764* (New York, 1766, 1769, 1773), William Windham, *A Plan of Exercise for the Militia of Massachusetts Bay . . . From the Plan of Discipline of the Norfolk Militia* (Boston, 1768, 1771, 1772; New Haven, 1772; New London, 1772), or the dictates of a regular British soldier. In 1766 Henry Knox and other members of a Boston militia artillery company received instruction from British officers en route to Fort Ticonderoga; and eight years later Nathanael Greene hired a British deserter to train his Rhode Island Kentish Guards. Even more important, all were avid readers; and Greene, Knox, and Wayne were particularly interested in military history and theory. In the early 1770s Greene began to visit Knox's bookstore in Boston and to discuss the very books that were then being bought, read, and discussed by British officers. Greene especially admired Marshal Hermann-Maurice Saxe and Frederick II of Prussia, "the greatest General of the age."[3] Knox agreed that Saxe was the best guide to the principles of war, but Knox was also much interested in Vauban, Coehorn, and Muller—the standard authorities on fortification and gunnery. So it was that men like Greene, Knox, Wayne, and Sullivan, men who had not served in the French and Indian War, became soldiers in an Anglo-American tradition and rapidly won commands at the beginning of the Revolution: Greene as a division commander and adviser to Washington, Knox as chief of artillery, Wayne as commander of the Pennsylvania line, and Sullivan as a brigade and division commander in the Continental army.[4]

Although King George had turned first to veterans of the French and Indian War to lead his armies in the War for American Independence, he was soon forced to employ generals who had little or no experience in North America. Besides Amherst and Howe, there were no generals in 1775 who had served in America and who also had the talent and the desire to command against the rebels. But the men the king did choose and that did agree to serve were accomplished soldiers; they were thoroughly familiar with the theory and practice of war in mid-eighteenth-century Britain. Henry Clinton had begun his career skirmishing with the French and Indians on Prince Edward Island; spent the Seven Years' War in England and Germany as an aide-de-camp to two of the

Nathanael Greene by Charles Willson Peale
Courtesy of the Independence National Historical Park Collection

most celebrated generals of the day; and gained a reputation as a brave and studious officer. He used the ensuing years of peace not merely to study military history and theory—to analyze the tactics of Epaminondas, Scipio, Marlborough, Saxe, and Frederick—but also to visit the battlefields and armies of Europe. Much the same was true of John Burgoyne. Burgoyne had made his reputation in the Seven Years' War while serving as a volunteer in raids on the coast of France and as a cavalry commander in an allied force in Portugal. After the war he returned to the Continent to study the art of war—particularly the French authorities—and to write an essay analyzing the French, Austrian, and Prussian armies. Charles Earl Cornwallis, one of the few British officers of that generation to attend a military academy (Turin), had, like Clinton, served in Germany and emerged from the Seven Years' War as an officer of courage and competence. Clinton, Burgoyne, and Cornwallis were not then veterans of the French and Indian War. They were experienced and learned British officers, the kind of officers sent to America in 1775 and given, eventually, independent commands: Clinton of all British forces in America in 1778; Burgoyne of an expedition from Canada in 1777; and Cornwallis of the British army in the southern colonies in 1780.[5]

Not merely were the principal commanders of the Revolutionary War heirs to a common military tradition, but so were their lieutenants. The division, brigade, and regimental commanders and the most important aides-de-camp on both sides of the Revolution were remarkably like their superiors in training and experience. To be sure, half of those who rose to colonel or brigadier in the Continental army had had no military experience before 1775: youth or occupation had kept men like Alexander Hamilton, John Laurens, and Henry Lee out of the colonial wars. But the other half were either veterans of the French and Indian War or members of the colonial militia before the Revolution. At least fifty-seven officers of the second rank—William Alexander (Lord Stirling), John Glover, and John Stark among them—had served as militiamen with the British against the French and Indians, typically with James Abercromby or Jeffery Amherst along Lake Champlain or with John Bradstreet on Lake Ontario. Another five, including Richard Montgomery and Arthur St. Clair who took part in the conquest of Canada, had held commissions in the British army; and forty-four, including William Heath, Isaac Shelby, and Seth Warner, had trained and sometimes fought in the colonial militia in the years between the French and Indian War and the Revolution. Moreover, there were among those colonels and brigadiers of the Continental army serious students of war, men like Timothy Pickering who collected books about military history and tactics and who wrote an *Easy Plan of Discipline for a Militia* (1775) for the benefit of his fellow patriots.

British officers of the second rank were no more likely than their colonial counterparts to be veterans of the French and Indian War. But they were, on the whole, older and more experienced in British military practice. Only about one-fourth of British colonels and brigadiers of the Revolution—among them

Sir Robert Abercromby, Simon Fraser (killed at Bemis Heights), and Frederick Haldiman—had served in North America during the colonial wars. However, another 48 percent, which included Charles Grey, Charles O'Hara, and William Phillips, had seen action in France, Germany, Portugal, or the West Indies during the wars of midcentury; and six had served in America between the French and Indian War and the American Revolution. Thus, although only 24 percent had served in the French and Indian War, more than 70 percent were combat veterans and 30 percent had been in America. Even those who had never seen combat or America were regular officers with an average of four years' service before the Revolution began; and most of these relatively inexperienced young gentlemen became aides-de-camp rather than regimental commanders. Wealth and family could bring rapid promotion in the eighteenth-century British army, but they rarely brought independent commands to the very young. It was exceptional for a man like Banastre Tarleton to go to America a cornet in 1775 and to become by 1780 commandant of Cornwallis's light horse. Most of General Howe's regimental and brigade commanders were officers of long service in war and peace, officers thoroughly familiar with the art of war as practiced in mid-eighteenth-century Britain.[6]

If then commanders on both sides of the Revolution were heirs to a common military tradition and if some of those commanders were also veterans of the French and Indian War, it is important to know about the tradition they shared and the war they had fought together—to know about their common military origins. What was the traditional British way of making war and what were the peculiar requirements of fighting the French and Indians in North America? Did the British make war according to prevailing European ideas? Did they, too, prefer the fashionable war of posts—a war that was conducted mainly by siege-craft and maneuver and that was thought to be compatible with the small professional armies of that era, with the limited resources of absolute monarchy, and with the restrained reasonableness of the Enlightenment? In such a war commanders sought victory without the risks and costs of general engagements. They tried to use sieges and maneuvers to deprive the enemy of the means for making war—to deprive him of his cities, magazines, and lines of communication and to force him to accept defeat and make reasonable concessions. But did the British subscribe to these ideas—to the war of posts? Was such a war compatible with the topography, the climate, and the opposition to be faced in North America? Did the British have reasonable, limited objectives in going to war with the French and Indians? Moreover, did prolonged fighting in the American wilderness force changes in Anglo-American ideas about war? In short, what were the origins of British and American strategy in the Revolutionary War?

Although it is impossible to be sure, it seems likely that British officers entered the French and Indian War with a very ambiguous understanding of how wars should be fought. As those officers received no uniform training and as there were no general instructions governing tactics and strategy in the British army, it is impossible to be sure what officers thought about war. Yet to judge by the books that they read and wrote, by the commanders they most admired, and by the choices they made when in command, it does seem likely that they were attracted to two decidedly different ways of making war: a prudent, Continental war of posts and a much more hazardous, classical, and English war of decisive engagements. Consider the books that British officers of midcentury liked best: Feuquières's *Memoirs*, Saxe's *Reveries*, Vegetius's *Military Institutions*, and Caesar's *Commentaries*. Feuquières, Saxe, and Vegetius all suggested ways of achieving victory without a general engagement—Feuquières by destroying the enemy's baggage and artillery; Saxe by exhausting the enemy with frequent, limited attacks on his men and supplies; and Vegetius by starving the enemy into submission. Although each appreciated the value of destroying the enemy's principal force, each would have done so with the least possible risk to his own army. By contrast, Caesar had ever been willing to risk battle to destroy his enemy. Having had an abundant supply of men for his legions and unlimited political and military authority, Caesar had done whatever was necessary to find, engage, and destroy opposing forces. Here then were two distinctly different ways of making war, and the most popular British authors did nothing to reconcile the differences. The Earl of Orrery in his *Treatise of the Art of War* not only recommended "wearying" out the enemy with skirmishes, sieges, and maneuvers, but also celebrated Caesar's ability to engage and destroy an enemy and conceded that British soldiers probably lacked the patience for a war of posts. Similarly, Samuel Bever's *Cadet* advised both that war should be waged with moderation and that Caesar was the greatest of generals.[7]

It is scarcely astonishing that officers who went to war admiring Vegetius and Caesar as well as Marlborough and Saxe should have pursued ambiguous strategies in the French and Indian War. At the beginning of the war, the British government had limited objectives and sought to achieve them with a conventional war of posts. To secure the lands and trade of its subjects in the Ohio River valley, the government sent Braddock to besiege and capture Fort Duquesne; and to protect its settlers in Nova Scotia, it ordered Lieutenant Colonel Robert Monckton to reduce Fort Beauséjour and drive the French from Acadia. A few leading British colonists wanted to do more than secure lands, trade, and settlements; but it was not until 1756 that the British government and people as well as a substantial number of colonists began to dream of conquering Canada—of adding vast French territories to the British Empire. When they did, the Earl of Loudoun, commander in chief of British forces in America, recommended a strategy that was wholly consistent with these imperial dreams. He proposed going directly by sea to Quebec in order to precipitate the decisive battle that he thought necessary to destroy French forces and win Canada. In December 1756 the British government approved Loudoun's proposal.

Thus far the British had distinguished clearly and consistently between a war of posts and a war of decisive engagements. Thenceforth they would mix the two while pursuing the conquest of Canada. In December 1756 William Pitt, the new secretary of state, urged Loudoun to capture the French fortress of

Louisbourg on Cape Breton Island and destroy the French fleet in American waters before going to Quebec in pursuit of a decisive battle. Loudoun and his successors, James Abercromby and Jeffery Amherst, followed Pitt's instructions and put their trust in siegecraft. Although Loudoun failed because he was too cautious and Abercromby because he was too impatient, Amherst combined determination with prudence to reduce one French fortress after another, gain control of the principal waterways leading to Canada, and, without risking a general engagement and without suffering a single reverse, force the French to surrender all of Canada. Here it seemed was the quintessential war of posts. Yet the most spectacular victory of the war—a victory that was essential in bringing Amherst's plans to fruition—was won in the style of Caesar rather than of Saxe. In capturing Quebec in September 1759, James Wolfe deliberately precipitated a decisive engagement, defeated the French, and became one of the most celebrated generals in British history. Thus, the final campaigns of the French and Indian War did little to reconcile ambiguities in the British art of war.

Nor did the ensuing years of peace. In the fifteen years from the fall of Canada to the beginning of the War for American Independence, officers on both sides of the Atlantic continued to embrace indiscriminately a war of posts and a war of decisive battle. At least, to judge once more by the books that men bought, read, wrote, and discussed and by the commanders they admired, British officers and the future leaders of the Continental army continued to tolerate ambiguities in their military thinking. In Britain Amherst and Wolfe were equally famous for their roles in the French and Indian War; Saxe's *Reveries* and Caesar's *Commentaries* remained among the most popular books on war; and Vegetius and Saxe were considered as authoritative in sustaining or embellishing an argument as Scipio, Marlborough, or Frederick.[8]

Much the same was true in America. When George Washington ordered busts to grace the hall of Mount Vernon, he chose likenesses of Alexander the Great, Julius Caesar, Charles XII of Sweden, and Frederick the Great of Prussia. Although Alexander, Caesar, and Charles XII sometimes used siegecraft to defeat an enemy and although Frederick did not have enough reliable troops to sustain an offensive or exploit a victory, all of Washington's heroes were commanders of aggressive spirit who did not hesitate to rely on a general engagement to decide a campaign or a war. But Washington also bought books by a number of eighteenth-century soldiers—including Saxe and the leading authorities on siegecraft and fortification—who were considerably less aggressive than Charles XII or Frederick. Similarly, Nathanael Greene thought Frederick "the greatest General of the age" and admired other exponents of decisive, general actions such as Epaminondas and Turenne. Yet Greene also turned repeatedly to Saxe's *Reveries* as a source of military wisdom.[9]

There was one further encumbrance inherent in the Anglo-American military tradition. For those British or American officers who rose to command, making plans was not just a matter of resolving contradictions in their ideas about waging war—of deciding clearly between a war of posts and a war of decisive engagements. It was also a matter of adjusting their ideas to suit the wishes of kings and ministers and elected officials—of working within a political system that made generals subordinate to civil authority. An eighteenth-century British or American general might admire a Caesar or a Frederick. But he knew that he would never have the kind of political and military power that such men possessed. He knew that he could not alone decide how to wage war—that his government would determine not only when to go to war but also what kind of war the people could and would support. An Anglo-American general would have to receive instructions from or at least discuss his plans with his government before embarking on any campaign.

Occasionally, as at the beginning of the War for American Independence, a general found that he was narrowly bound by his instructions. In early 1775 General Thomas Gage, the commander in chief at Boston, learned that he was to use force to sustain British authority in America and that he was to do so in specific, limited ways. The British government assumed that most colonists were loyal to the crown and that protests against taxation and tyranny were the work of a few desperate, designing men. It also assumed that the colonists collectively had not the will—to say nothing of the discipline or military skill—to stand against regular troops. Thus, the government concluded that with modest reinforcements British troops stationed in America would be able to disperse any rebels in arms, destroy all congresses and committees, and restore royal government. By March 1775 the government had given Gage specific instructions: to secure Boston and Salem, to arrest leading rebels that they might be tried for treason, and to impose martial law, if necessary, throughout Massachusetts. He was also to occupy or destroy colonial fortifications and to confiscate all military stores. Here was no grand design for a campaign in New England—nothing to set generals debating the relative merits of siegecraft and decisive battle. But here was, the ministry hoped, a relatively inexpensive and prudent way of using regular troops to end opposition to British authority, to end an opposition that had disrupted the empire for more than a decade. Instead, this modest plan, which impelled Gage to send troops to Concord to confiscate stores and to Bunker Hill to secure Boston, brought on a long and difficult war.[10]

The colonists proved at the outset an inspired and dangerous enemy. Contrary to British expectations, the rebellion was more than the creation of a few designing men: the colonists may not as yet have favored independence; but they were united in defense of American self-government and liberty, and they were determined to resist what many thought to be a corrupt and tyrannical royal administration. The colonists were also, contrary to expectations, willing and able to fight against regular soldiers. The minutemen who gathered spontaneously to oppose the British on their march to Concord were filled with patriotic and religious zeal. They believed that service was a duty to country and to God, that faith and a few simple military skills would prevail over the corruption and sophistication of the British army, and that death would bring liberty and salvation. On the road from Concord, this simple faith seemed fully justified: the minutemen inflicted more than three times the casualties that they suffered.[11] Thereafter the colonists would find their zeal sorely tried by the killing and drudgery of war.

In the year after fighting began, the colonists did create an army and wage a successful war of posts, evicting the British from Boston and overrunning much of Canada. They began immediately after Lexington and Concord by surrounding Boston and sending men to capture the British outposts at Ticonderoga and Crown Point on Lake Champlain. Then in mid-June they pushed their lines closer to Boston, provoked Gage into an ill-conceived frontal assault, and killed or wounded more than 1,000 British troops before yielding Bunker Hill. George Washington, who took command of the rebel forces at Boston on 2 July, would have preferred to take the offensive, to attack the British in the town. Instead he decided to concentrate on making an army out of a mob of dirty, undisciplined men who had neither uniforms nor adequate ammunition. Gradually he improved and preserved his army, and with cannon taken from the forts on Lake Champlain, he forced the British to leave Boston for Halifax in March 1776. By then Richard Montgomery and Benedict Arnold had led other rebel forces into Canada, taking St. Johns by siege in early November 1775, capturing Montreal and laying siege to Quebec two weeks later, and failing only in their desperate effort to storm Quebec on New Year's Eve. Excepting this attack on Quebec, which was precipitated by expiring enlistments, the rebels had pursued a remarkably successful war of posts for more than a year after Lexington and Concord.[12]

At the same time, the British were gathering their forces and planning a far different type of war. News of Lexington and Concord and of Bunker Hill persuaded the British government that its efforts to intimidate the colonists had failed—that larger forces, a more vigorous commander in chief, and a completely different strategy would be required to end the rebellion. By early August 1775 the ministry had decided to increase its regular forces from about 6,000 men to more than 20,000 by the summer of 1776 and to order those forces from Boston to New York to strike "a decisive blow." Although the ministry also planned to impose a blockade on New England and to employ local colonists in recovering the Carolinas, it put its trust primarily in a war of decisive battle. General William Howe, who replaced Thomas Gage as commander in chief in November 1775, shared the ministry's priorities. During the winter of 1775–1776, he and the secretary of state for America, Lord George Germain, agreed that he should take his army to New York in order to engage and destroy the Continental army. Overconfidence might lead Washington to risk battle; if not, Howe would try to force an engagement by taking Manhattan and Rhode Island, by advancing up the Hudson to join forces with an army from Canada in isolating New England, and by sending ships and men to blockade and raid the Atlantic ports from New York to Maine. Capturing territory and waging a war of attrition against New England were clearly a means to an end—a means of provoking "a decisive Action, than which nothing is more to be desired or sought for by us, as the most effectual Means to terminate this expensive War." Sending regulars and

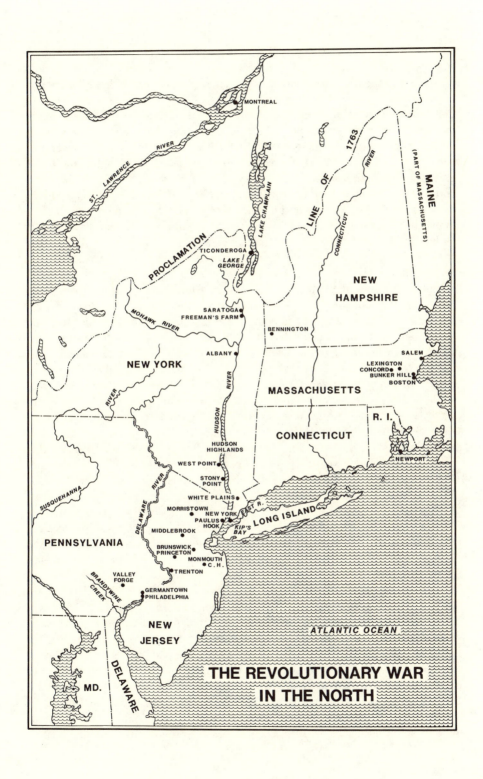

THE REVOLUTIONARY WAR
IN THE NORTH

arms to enlist loyalists in the Carolinas was never more than peripheral to British strategy in 1776.[13]

While the ministry and General Howe altered their strategy in hopes of ending the rebellion quickly, Washington and Congress persisted in a war of posts. They did so because siegecraft and skirmishing had been successful in 1775 and seemed essential for the campaign of 1776. Assuming that the British would go to New York in order to occupy the Hudson River Valley and cut communications between New England and the other rebellious colonies, Washington and Congress decided to shift their forces to New York, fortify Manhattan and adjacent portions of New Jersey and Long Island, and oppose British efforts to take New York City and ascend the Hudson. Such a strategy would require Washington to divide his army in the face of a superior fleet and army—to put detachments on both banks of the Hudson and East rivers. Yet in spite of the risks, such a strategy seemed politically and militarily essential. Congress was persuaded that abandoning a major city like New York without a fight would discourage the patriots and inspire the British and their loyal American colonists; Washington believed that maintaining communications across the Hudson was indispensable to "the Safety of America"; and both agreed that inexperienced patriot soldiers would fare better fighting regulars from prepared defensive positions than attacking them in open terrain. Indeed, so committed were Congress and Washington to the defense of New York and the Hudson River Valley that they would cling to their strategy through a succession of defeats and narrow escapes. Even at the end of the campaign—when forced to retire to Pennsylvania and when made desperate by expiring enlistments—Washington risked no more than counterattacks on detachments at Trenton and Princeton.[14]

But if Washington had been determined to defend New York City and the Hudson River Valley, and if Howe had been equally determined to engage and destroy the Continental army, why was there no decisive battle at New York in 1776? Primarily, because Howe changed his strategy after reaching New York. As late as 7 July he was "still of Opinion that Peace will not be restored in America until the Rebel Army is defeated."[15] Yet he changed his mind once he had had a chance to examine rebel defenses at New York and to confer with his brother, Admiral Richard Lord Howe, who arrived on 12 July to take command of the North American Squadron and serve as a peace commissioner to the colonies. It seems likely that General Howe found the rebel works too strong to invite a frontal assault and that his brother opposed any attempt at a decisive action until negotiations had been tried. By mid-August General Howe was clearly planning a war of posts—a series of turning maneuvers calculated to give him Long Island, Manhattan, and eastern New Jersey and to leave him free to send detachments up the Hudson and to Rhode Island. Moreover, his execution deviated little from this design. He employed prudent flanking movements to force Washington from Long Island, New York City, Manhattan, and much of New Jersey; he never engaged more than a portion of the Continental army; and he and his brother sought to use each success to promote a negotiated peace.

Only once—only at White Plains—was he even tempted to resort to a general action; and on that occasion rains promptly removed the temptation.

This war of posts proved by the end of 1776 not merely disappointing for the Howes, who favored a negotiated settlement, but disastrous for those British officials who wanted to destroy the Continental army and break the rebellion. While pursuing his war of posts, Howe had twice lost opportunities to capture substantial numbers of rebel troops: after the Battle of Long Island, when he let 10,000 demoralized rebels escape across the East River; and after his landing at Kip's Bay, when he failed to keep 5,000 rebels from fleeing New York City. More important, between August and mid-October he repeatedly rejected proposals to trap the whole of the Continental army at New York by sending troops to Westchester and by using Lord Howe's warships to block the Hudson and East rivers. But if Howe failed to exploit Washington's determination to defend New York—if he squandered Britain's best opportunity to destroy the Continental army and, perhaps, the rebellion—his prudent strategy nearly succeeded. By December 1776 he had driven the rebels from New York and New Jersey, captured Rhode Island, and sapped the morale of the Continental army and of the state militia. Had he not also grown overconfident and given Washington a chance to surprise his outposts at Trenton and Princeton, the rebellion might have collapsed early in 1777. But Washington's victories saved the Continental army, restored confidence in the Revolution, and ruined Howe's strategy—a strategy that had already cost the British their best prospects for a decisive victory.[16]

Notwithstanding the failure of Howe's strategy in 1776, he and General John Burgoyne proposed similar strategies for 1777. After Trenton and Princeton, Howe conceded that he saw no "prospect of terminating the war but by general action." Yet, doubting that he had the mobility to bring on such an action, he persisted in planning a war of posts for 1777. He would leave garrisons on Manhattan and Rhode Island, take an army by sea to capture Philadelphia, and win the help of loyalists, secure portions of Pennsylvania, New Jersey, and New York by the end of the campaign. He rejected the ministry's suggestion that he raid the coasts of New England and offered to do no more to assist British troops pushing south from Canada than clear a way for shipping through the Highlands of the Hudson. Seeking a decisive battle with the Continental army was not part of his plan. Nor was it part of John Burgoyne's reason for leading an army south from Canada to Albany. Burgoyne proposed taking 10,000 men south across Lake Champlain to join, or at least to cooperate with, another British army advancing up the Hudson from New York. The two forces would act together in controlling the Hudson-Champlain corridor, interrupting American communications and bringing steady pressure upon the hinterlands of New England. They would, with the support of ships and men based in Rhode Island, isolate and gradually subdue New England. They would not seek a single, climactic battle to end the rebellion.[17]

Although Howe's and Burgoyne's plans were clearly incompatible and although neither promised the prompt, decisive end to the war that the ministry desired, Lord George Germain, the secretary of state for America, approved both plans. Germain knew that Howe was going by sea to Pennsylvania and that he intended to do no more to assist Burgoyne than open the Hudson for British shipping; he also knew that Burgoyne expected Howe to do much more—to provide an army that would join or cooperate with the Canadian army in subduing New England. But Germain was so preoccupied with finding strategies that would not require larger regular forces and with discouraging Howe's interest in conciliation that he failed to order Howe to cooperate with Burgoyne. He intended and expected cooperation; he did not require it unequivocally. Nor did Germain object to Howe's or Burgoyne's choice of a war of posts. Germain thought that destroying the Continental army in a single, decisive engagement was the best way to end the rebellion and restore royal government. Yet when Howe maneuvered Washington out of New York without decisive results and when he proposed a war of posts for 1777, Germain said merely that Howe had "shewn great knowledge in his profession": "It is very clear that the Rebels will never face the King's troops, but as they understand the taking of strong posts and entrenching themselves so expeditiously it requires more than common abilities to carry on an offensive operation without considerable loss, and Sir Wm Howe has infinite merit in that particular." Having been reared a soldier, Germain understood that maneuver and siegecraft were as much a part of the British military tradition as decisive battle and that both methods of waging war might bring victory, as Amherst and Wolfe had shown. Thus, in spite of his preference for a decisive battle, he approved Howe's and Burgoyne's plans for a war of posts in 1777, plans that were patently incompatible.[18]

But poor planning did not alone account for Howe's and Burgoyne's failures in the campaign of 1777. Not only did Howe refuse to join or cooperate with Burgoyne along the Hudson, but he and Burgoyne each managed to mutilate his own strategy. Howe, who had proposed a war of posts to capture Pennsylvania and secure New Jersey, was so shaken by his defeats at Trenton and Princeton that he was unable to persist in any one strategy in 1777. He oscillated regularly and unproductively between the poles of British military theory—between a war of posts and a war of decisive battle. Notwithstanding his plans, he began the campaign in New Jersey in futile and time-consuming efforts to lure Washington into a general action. Then after refusing once again to cooperate with Burgoyne and sailing for the Delaware, he reverted to a war of posts: he would go to Pennsylvania by way of the Chesapeake to avoid an opposed landing in the Delaware and to force Washington to abandon Philadelphia by cutting off his supplies from York and Carlisle. But once he landed at Head of Elk and found the population hostile and Washington prepared to fight, Howe forgot about lines of supply and sought a decisive battle. At Brandywine he defeated but did not destroy the Continental army; and when rains prevented a second engagement, he occupied Philadelphia and devoted most of the autumn of 1777 to securing the city. Only briefly in December did he try again to bring Washington to action.[19]

While Howe went his separate way, failing to pursue any strategy long enough to achieve decisive results, Burgoyne was all too persistent in carrying out the plans he had made. An unusually ambitious man who had gained his command by criticizing his immediate superior—by telling the ministry that poor leadership alone had kept the Canadian army from reaching the Hudson in 1776—Burgoyne was determined to make his way to Albany in 1777 and to play a major role in ending the rebellion. He was also, after years of studying the art of war in France, unusually partial to a war of posts, to making war as carefully as possible. Ambition, then, would combine with strategic prudence to shape his performance in 1777 and contribute powerfully to his failure. Although he expected to meet strong opposition at the beginning of the campaign, he was able to capture Fort Ticonderoga without a siege on 6 July and to disperse the remnants of the garrison by 9 July. Had he been ready to continue south, he might have advanced virtually unopposed to Albany. But as he insisted on having an inordinate supply and siege train and as he had not wagons and carts enough to carry his train overland from the lakes to the Hudson, it took him a month to reach the Hudson and another month to prepare to cross and proceed to Albany. During that time the rebels were able to recover from the loss of Ticonderoga, reassemble their forces, defeat one of Burgoyne's detachments that had gone foraging to Bennington, and begin formidable defenses on the west bank of the Hudson, twenty miles above Albany. Knowing that Howe had gone to Pennsylvania and that he could not expect strong support from New York, Burgoyne might well have decided against going farther had he not been so deeply committed to reaching Albany. On 13 September he crossed the Hudson and proceeded south. Once he did, he could no longer wage a careful war of posts: he had to fight his way through to Albany, attacking the rebels in difficult terrain. Twice he tried and failed; and then, finding he could no longer retreat, he surrendered what was left of his battered army.[20]

In opposing the British offensives of 1777, both Washington and the commanders of American forces in northern New York relied primarily on wars of posts; but, under pressure from Congress, Washington also accepted and initiated general actions. For nearly six months after his victories at Trenton and Princeton, Washington remained in the hills near Morristown, watching the British in eastern New Jersey and harassing their foraging parties. Although members of Congress suggested and he considered attacking the enemy at Brunswick, Washington chose to avoid a general action. In late May he did move his army south to Middlebrook so as to be able to attack the British in flank or rear if they went overland to Pennsylvania; but he refused to allow his army to be lured into battle by mere feints. Indeed, it was not until August when Howe appeared in the Chesapeake to pose an immediate threat to Philadelphia that Washington agreed to risk a general engagement. Congress, popular feeling, and revolutionary ideology all required that he fight for Philadelphia, that he put aside what Samuel Adams called his Fabian tactics and engage the British army. Thus he fought— at Brandywine, in a nearly disastrous effort to keep the British from reaching Philadelphia, and at Germantown, in an ill-coordinated attempt to surprise the British after they had taken the city. These defeats persuaded Washington to concentrate on a defense of the Delaware—on holding fortresses that kept the British from navigating the river from the sea to Philadelphia. Yet so great was the pressure from Congress for "a short and violent War"—for a decisive battle—that Washington was forced repeatedly to reject proposals for attacking Philadelphia. Only in December did Congress acquiesce temporarily in a return to a war of posts.[21]

Unlike Washington, American generals serving against Burgoyne in the Champlain-Hudson corridor were free from the immediate interference of Congress, from importunate demands for a decisive battle. They were, therefore, able to pursue a war of posts that suited their means and that brought in time the decisive results that Congress sought. At the beginning of the campaign, Arthur St. Clair had not the men or provisions to defend Ticonderoga; and as soon as the British occupied commanding positions, St. Clair fled to save his army. While Philip Schuyler gathered some of the survivors from Ticonderoga to obstruct Burgoyne's advance to the Hudson, irregular forces like that led by John Stark of New Hampshire appeared to keep the British from foraging successfully and to attack their communications. By early September Horatio Gates had replaced Schuyler as commander of the northern army and had assembled a substantial army on the west bank of the Hudson above Albany. Gates intended to engage should Burgoyne try to force his way to Albany or to pursue him should he turn back toward Canada; he did not intend to attack Burgoyne, to initiate a general action. Choosing his ground to offset superior British discipline and musketry, he withstood Burgoyne's attack at Freeman's Farm on 19 September. Then he waited for reinforcements to strengthen his own forces and for shortages to force Burgoyne to act. When on 7 October Burgoyne advanced, Gates struck decisively, defeating the British and forcing them to withdraw. Ten days later Burgoyne succumbed to Gates's steady pressure, agreeing to a convention that would keep his soldiers prisoners for the remainder of the war. So much had American generals, who knew the advantages of the terrain and the limitations of their men, been able to accomplish with persistence in a war of posts.[22]

Burgoyne's surrender at Saratoga together with Howe's failure to achieve results in Pennsylvania and his subsequent resignation impelled the ministry to change its strategy as well as its commander in chief. The loss of Burgoyne's army not only substantially reduced the number of regular troops available for service in America, but also increased opposition to the war in England and the likelihood of overt French intervention on the side of the rebels. To forestall French intervention and hasten the end of the rebellion, the ministry organized a new peace mission to the colonies; and to carry on the war without asking Parliament for large, additional forces—without raising further opposition at home—the ministry developed a complex and largely unconventional new strategy. There were still lingering hopes that another, more aggressive commander might destroy the Continental army in a single battle and win the war. Thus, the ministry selected Sir Henry Clinton to replace Sir William Howe and ordered him to begin by trying to bring Washington to action. But should Clinton fail, he was to abandon offensive operations in the middle colonies, withdraw from Philadelphia if necessary, and cooperate with the Royal Navy and loyal colonists in ending the rebellion. During the summer he was to send expeditions to ravage the coasts of New England, and in the autumn, detachments to recover Georgia, the Carolinas, and Virginia. Once loyalists had been restored to power in the South, he was to let the rebellion in the North wither under a tight blockade. Here was a strategy designed to win the war with limited means: it reflected lingering hopes for a decisive battle, but it relied mainly on the unconventional idea of arming civilians to help recover and hold territory. If this strategy succeeded, it would save Britain lives and money, and it would demonstrate that the colonists were, as the ministry said, loyal to the crown and worthy of continued support.

But before the government could embark on its new strategy—before it could do more than recall Howe and organize another peace mission—France declared openly for the rebels and drove the ministry to adopt, temporarily, far different plans. On 13 March 1778 the French government announced it had concluded a Treaty of Amity and Commerce with the rebellious colonies. As this recognition of American independence was tantamount to a declaration of war, King George III and his advisers decided that combatting France was, for the time being, more important than putting down the American rebellion. On 21 March the king ordered his commanders in chief in North America to send 5,000 men with eleven warships to capture the French island of St. Lucia in the West Indies; to add 3,000 men to the British garrisons at St. Augustine and Pensacola; to make sure that Rhode Island, Canada, Nova Scotia, and Newfoundland were secure against attack; and to send home fourteen frigates and six sloops to strengthen the Channel Fleet. To do all of this, the commanders in chief would have to abandon Philadelphia and, perhaps, New York and postpone any attacks on the rebels.

These instructions, which reached Philadelphia on 8 May, and a French squadron, which arrived unexpectedly off New York on 11 July, would shape British strategy in America for more than six months. During that time Sir Henry Clinton and Admiral Lord Howe would be forced to concentrate on the war with France and to minimize operations against the rebels. In May Clinton did decide that he would try to use the evacuation of Philadelphia to lure Washington into a general action. As there was not shipping enough at Philadelphia to carry the army, its baggage, and loyal colonists to New York, Clinton decided to send only baggage and loyalists by sea and to take the army overland through New Jersey. By proceeding very deliberately, he made it possible for Washington to overtake and attack the rear of the British army near Monmouth Court House on 28 June. Clinton, who anticipated and welcomed the attack, soon precipitated a general action; but the day was hot and the result, far less favorable than he had hoped. During the remainder of the summer, Clinton and Howe were fully occupied defending themselves against Admiral d'Estaing, who reached New York on 11 July with eleven ships of the line, six frigates, and 4,000 troops to assist the rebels. D'Estaing first threatened New York and then sailed to join in an attack on the British garrison at Newport. Howe followed d'Estaing to Rhode Island, drew him to sea, and after a severe storm had damaged both fleets, followed him to Boston. Once the French put into Boston for repairs, New York and Newport were relatively secure; but not until additional ships arrived from England was Clinton able to send expeditions to St. Lucia and the Floridas or to consider resuming offensive operations against the rebels.[23]

Although Washington tried to take advantage of the British withdrawal from Philadelphia and the subsequent arrival of the French at New York—although he did risk one general action and considered several others—he never really abandoned a war of posts during the campaign of 1778. He was under considerable pressure to do more than watch and skirmish with the British. Congress continued to favor a short, violent war, a war decided by a general action; and the Continental army emerged from its winter at Valley Forge with better discipline and a more uniform grasp of infantry tactics than it had had in 1776 or 1777. Washington knew that Nathanael Greene was right when in recommending an attack he said, "People expects something from us and our strength demands it." Yet for all his pride in the Continental army and his admiration for aggressive commanders like Caesar and Frederick the Great, Washington was unwilling to seek and reluctant to risk a general action; and a majority of his generals were more cautious than he. Losing the Continental army in a single, climactic battle might destroy the rebellion. Thus Washington refused to attack the British at Philadelphia, agreed to do no more than detach 5,000 men to attack the rear of Clinton's army in New Jersey, and considered the Battle of Monmouth larger and less successful than he had intended. He would subsequently have joined the French in an attack on New York or Rhode Island and was bitterly disappointed when d'Estaing refused to continue the siege of Newport. But Washington would not alone attack either British port, and when the French declined further cooperative ventures and withdrew from Boston to the West Indies, Washington put his troops into winter quarters.[24]

By that time Sir Henry Clinton was considering the ministry's plans for resuming the war against the rebels, plans set forth in instructions of 5 August that reached New York on 10 October 1778. Clinton was not to delay the departure of the 5,000 men previously ordered to attack St. Lucia or the 3,000 destined to reinforce the Floridas. But once these detachments had sailed, he was to revert to the strategy, developed immediately after Burgoyne's surrender, that was designed to use the British navy and loyal colonists to supplement the diminished regular forces available for the American war. If unable to bring the Continental army to action at the beginning of a campaign, Clinton was to concentrate on raiding rebel ports in the North and on enlisting loyalists in the South to end the rebellion. The ministry still hoped that a conventional general action might prove decisive, but it relied primarily on an unconventional combination of regulars, sailors, and loyalists to carry on the war. This strategy of August 1778 would be restated repeatedly in 1779 and early 1780 and would remain, only slightly modified, the ministry's strategy until the spring of 1781.

But Clinton never carried out this strategy as the ministry intended, never consistently made raiding and recovering the South more important than waging a conventional war in the middle colonies. Thoroughly skeptical of relying on loyalists and uncomfortable with the admirals who succeeded Lord Howe, he clearly preferred to employ his army along the Hudson, defending New York, looking for a decisive battle with Washington, and disrupting rebel lines of supply and communication. Thus, in October 1778 when ordered to recover Georgia and the Carolinas, he complied most perfunctorily—adding 1,000 men to the 2,000 that were already being sent to reinforce East Florida and ordering the whole to attack Georgia. This attack was so much more successful than he expected that he was tempted in April 1779 to send additional troops to capture Charleston and help secure the interior of Georgia. But not at the expense of conventional operations in the North: he refused to spare any troops for the Carolinas until he had sent detachments to raid the Chesapeake and New England and had tried without success to force Washington into a general action by capturing rebel posts on the Hudson. Only when discouraged by his failures at New York and apprehensive for his forces in Georgia did he decide to go to South Carolina in force. He left New York in December 1779 (having been delayed by Admiral d'Estaing's unexpected return to North America), reached South Carolina in February, and took Charleston by siege in May 1780. Even after capturing the garrison and winning the greatest British victory of the war, he refused to remain in the South or to leave more than 27 percent of his total force to exploit his victory. Instead, he returned promptly to New York to expend another summer seeking a decisive battle with Washington, considering an attack on the French forces that occupied Rhode Island in July, and trying to secure West Point through the treachery of Benedict Arnold. So it was that for two years Clinton remained preoccupied with a conventional war in the middle colonies and gave only fitful and inadequate support to the ministry's plans for recovering the South. By the time that he began to do more, by the winter and spring of 1781, the best opportunities for British success in the South had been lost.[25]

While Clinton dissipated opportunities, Washington could do no more than wage a defensive war of posts from the autumn of 1778 until the spring of 1781. Because Congress was unable to tax to support its currency, and because worthless currency could not feed, pay, or clothe an army, Washington had to shape his plans for 1779 to suit dwindling resources. He kept the Continental army along the Hudson to oppose the main British army at New York. But he avoided a general engagement, used fortifications to protect his communications, and sent detachments to harass the enemy—punishing the Iroquois who had devastated the frontiers of Pennsylvania and New York and surprising British outposts at Stony Point and Paulus Hook. When in December Clinton sailed south, Washington remained at New York to watch the British garrison and to try to preserve his army through the winter. But Congress being unable and the states unwilling to support the army, the troops deserted, plundered, and mutinied; and by the summer of 1780, Washington had not men enough either to resist British forays from New York or to collaborate in offensive operations with the 5,500 French troops that reached Rhode Island in July. He did feel obligated to propose a combined attack on New York; but the French commander, the Comte de Rochambeau, was unwilling to risk an attack without a superior fleet to offset the weaknesses of the Continental army. Washington would have to endure another winter of shortages, mutinies, and shrinking numbers before he could again propose a Franco-American attack on the British.[26]

While Clinton and Washington waged a conventional war in the middle colonies—a war that occupied more than two-thirds of the British and Continental armies until early in 1781—Charles Earl Cornwallis employed the remainder of British troops and a combination of strategies in trying to recover the southern colonies. Cornwallis, who assumed command after Clinton captured Charleston in May 1780, hoped at first to use a cautious and unconventional strategy to restore royal government throughout the South: he would send small detachments of regulars to disperse the rebels, protect and organize the loyalists, and secure one region after another from Georgia and South Carolina to North Carolina and Virginia. This strategy seemed well suited to restoring order in a vast, sparsely populated, and primitive country where the only opposing army had been destroyed at the beginning of the campaign. Yet Cornwallis never managed to pursue this strategy consistently. He was repeatedly interrupted by the appearance of fresh rebel forces—repeatedly forced or tempted to abandon his prudent, unconventional strategy and seek a restoration of royal government through a conventional war of decisive engagements.

Thus Cornwallis made his way from South Carolina to Virginia, pursuing now one, now another strategy. In August 1780 he found his first efforts at gradual pacification jeopardized by the approach of Horatio Gates with more than 3,000 rebel troops. Cornwallis had to engage Gates or abandon the interior of South Carolina; but having defeated and dispersed the rebel army near Camden, he did not have to deviate from his strategy of gradually restoring loyalists to power in South Carolina: he did not have to advance into North Carolina in order to exploit his victory. In choosing to advance, and in calling on loyalists to rise against Gates, Cornwallis was attempting both to complete the destruction of the rebel forces and—somewhat prematurely and impatiently—to draw support from the people of North Carolina. When his militia was defeated at King's Mountain, he promptly returned to Winnsboro and reverted to his initial strategy of securing South Carolina for the crown. But a static defense was neither satisfactory for restoring loyalists to power nor satisfying for Cornwallis; and in

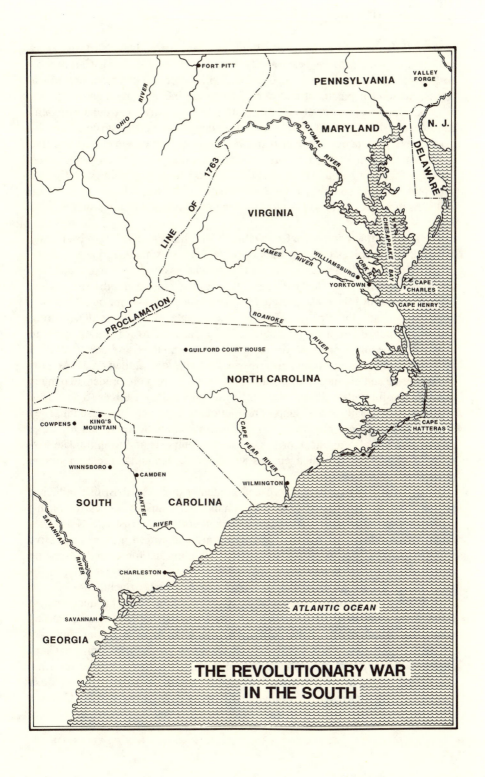

THE REVOLUTIONARY WAR
IN THE SOUTH

January 1781, as soon as he received reinforcements from New York, he again pushed north—to provide permanently for the security of South Carolina by destroying rebel forces in North Carolina. Only after weeks of chasing rebels across the sodden piedmont and after fighting an inconclusive battle with the principal American army at Guilford Court House, only then did Cornwallis concede that he could not gain a decisive victory in North Carolina, that he would have to conquer Virginia if he were to restore royal government in the Carolinas. Once in Virginia he forgot the strategy that brought him there, talked vaguely of making Virginia the seat of the war, and, after quarrelling with Clinton over plans for the summer, received instructions to establish a naval base on Williamsburg Neck. In early August he began fortifying Yorktown on the York River.[27]

The strategy that had driven Cornwallis to Virginia and that would eventually drive all British forces from the interior of the Carolinas and Georgia was a war of posts, offensively applied. Horatio Gates, who assumed command after the fall of Charleston, was the first to use this strategy in the South. He reached North Carolina in July 1780, gathered his forces, and set out for South Carolina, hoping to engage the British before they were able to assemble under Cornwallis—to induce battle on favorable terms, or at least to force the British to abandon some of their posts on the frontiers of South Carolina. But Gates advanced incautiously and lost his army in the Battle of Camden on 15 August. Thereafter he and his successor, Nathanael Greene, were more prudent and much more successful with their war of posts. They scattered their forces so as to feed their men more easily and to support revolutionaries throughout the South. They sent cavalry units not merely to disrupt British communications and to gather intelligence but also to attack or besiege enemy outposts and to intimidate loyalists. And they avoided engagements with large British units except on ground of their own choosing.

Thus Gates and Greene checked and gradually diminished British influence in the Carolinas and Georgia. In the months after Camden, Gates rebuilt his army, suppressed loyalists, and parried Cornwallis's first thrust into North Carolina. Greene then took over the southern army and waged a more aggressive and most skillful war of posts. He began by dividing his forces and advancing into South Carolina, where at Cowpens in January 1781 the right wing of his army under Daniel Morgan met and destroyed a British detachment of 1,150 men. When Cornwallis sought to retaliate, Greene reunited his army and retreated through the piedmont of North Carolina into Virginia, hoping to gather militia enough to be able to offer battle. In March, after receiving substantial reinforcements, he returned to North Carolina, took up strong ground near Guilford Court House, and invited attack. Cornwallis won the field but lost a third of his army and retired subsequently to Virginia. As North Carolina was then free of British troops, save for a garrison at Wilmington, Greene took his army to South Carolina where in the ensuing year he employed siegecraft, maneuver, partisan warfare, and limited engagements to drive the British into the lowlands about Charleston—to win a war without winning a single battle.[28]

Well before Greene saw the end of fighting in South Carolina, Washington had joined with the French to gain a decisive victory in the Chesapeake—a victory gained primarily with French forces and plans. It is true that as early as February 1781 Washington had persuaded Rochambeau to try to capture a British detachment in the Chesapeake. But once that attempt had failed, Washington consistently argued for an attack on Manhattan, and Rochambeau just as consistently for another attempt on the British in the Chesapeake. Rochambeau became particularly insistent once he learned that Cornwallis had gone to Virginia and that a powerful French fleet would come to North America during the summer of 1781. Washington resisted until he found that he was unable to raise enough men for an attack on the main British army at New York (in July he had only 6,425 men under his immediate command) and that Admiral de Grasse had decided to take his fleet to the Chesapeake. Indeed, as soon as Washington learned where de Grasse was bound, he joined Rochambeau on the road to Virginia. By mid-September, when the allied commanders reached Williamsburg, de Grasse had driven a British fleet from the Virginia Capes, escorted Rochambeau's siege train safely into the York River, and established a formidable blockade of the Chesapeake. With such support Washington and Rochambeau had merely to employ conventional siegecraft to capture Cornwallis and nearly a fourth of all British forces in America.[29] Cornwallis's surrender led in turn to a change of government in Britain, to peace, and to the confirmation of American independence. Although Washington might have preferred a decisive battle with Clinton at New York, he and his fellow revolutionaries were glad to celebrate their roles in a campaign won largely with French help and with a most conventional application of a war of posts.

Commanders on both sides of the War for American Independence were heirs to a common strategic tradition—a tradition that was ambiguous and restrictive and that troubled British generals far more than their American counterparts. Howe, Clinton, and Cornwallis all failed to achieve strategic consistency: Howe, because his preoccupation with conciliation made it impossible for him to persist in either a war of posts or a war of general actions; Clinton, because he could not satisfy both the ministry's preference for cooperating with loyalists to recover the South and his own desire for a conventional war in the middle colonies; and Cornwallis, because he was too easily tempted to abandon the ministry's plans for embodying loyalists—the tedious work of pacification—and to pursue the illusion of a decisive battle. Burgoyne alone among British commanders achieved consistency, and he did so in defiance of common sense and at the cost of an army. American generals, by comparison, were not so often distracted by strategic alternatives. From the beginning, nearly all were anxious enough about the quality of their troops to think a war of posts much more promising than a war of decisive battle. Washington, under pressure from Congress, did risk general actions at Philadelphia and in New Jersey, but thereafter he considered attacking Clinton only with the support of French ships and men. Similarly, Gates and Greene deviated little from a war of posts in their campaigns, and the French were even more cautious than their American allies.

What then were the consequences of British inconsistency and American consistency? In a war where the issue was long in doubt, where the difference between victory and defeat was often slight, inconsistency may well have kept the British from breaking the rebellion. Had Howe persisted in seeking a decisive battle at New York or Philadelphia while Washington was all too willing to fight, he might have destroyed the Continental army and ended the rebellion. Or, had Clinton pursued the ministry's southern strategy with more determination after capturing Charleston in 1780, had he been willing to devote most of his forces to a gradual restoration of loyalists to power in the South, he might even then have finished a rebellion that was suffering from inflation and crumbling morale. Conversely, consistency in a strategy that was well suited to unreliable troops and scarce resources, to carrying on a protracted defensive war, was of extraordinary importance to the survival of the rebellion. Had Washington more often responded to the demands of Congress and committed his army to decisive battles, it seems likely that he would eventually have lost his army; and had the Continental army been destroyed—had it been captured at New York or Philadelphia while making a desperate stand—the rebellion might have collapsed as well. Consistency in a war of posts was then as important to American victory as was strategic inconsistency to British defeat. Washington and Gates and Greene clearly made better use of their Anglo-American military heritage than did any British commander.

NOTES

1. See George Athan Billias, ed., *George Washington's Generals* (New York: William Morrow and Company, 1964), for interpretive essays and guides to the standard biographies for all except Gates. For Gates, see Paul David Nelson, *General Horatio Gates: A Biography* (Baton Rouge: Louisiana State University Press, 1976), pp. 8–30.

2. George Athan Billias, ed., *George Washington's Opponents: British Generals and Admirals in the American Revolution* (New York: William Morrow and Company, 1969), provides sketches and bibliographies for Carleton, Gage, and Howe. For Amherst see J. C. Long, *Lord Jeffery Amherst: A Soldier of the King* (New York: Macmillan Co., 1933).

3. Greene to George Washington, 3 December 1777, in Richard K. Showman, ed., *The Papers of General Nathanael Greene*, 3 vols. (Chapel Hill: University of North Carolina Press, 1976–), II, 235.

4. All are in Billias, ed., *George Washington's Generals*. For Knox's and Greene's tastes, see North Callahan, *Henry Knox: General Washington's General* (New York: Rinehart & Company, Inc., 1958), pp. 18–20, 29–30, 35–36; and Theodore Thayer, *Nathanael Greene: Strategist of the American Revolution* (New York: Twayne Publishers, 1960), pp. 20–21, 24, 44, 47–48.

5. Ira D. Gruber, "George III Chooses a Commander in Chief," in Ronald Hoffman and Peter J. Albert, eds., *Arms and Independence: The Military Character of the American Revolution* (Charlottesville: University Press of Virginia, 1984), pp. 166–90; Billias, ed., *George Washington's Opponents*; and Franklin and Mary Wickwire, *Cornwallis: The American Adventure* (Boston: Houghton Mifflin Co., 1970). Clinton's tactical reflections are undated in boxes marked "Memoranda" and "Military Notebooks" and in an unmarked box, Clinton Papers, William L. Clements Library, Ann Arbor, Michigan.

6. Mark Mayo Boatner III, *Encyclopedia of the American Revolution* (New York: David McKay Company, Inc., 1966), provides sketches of these officers.

7. Ira D. Gruber, "British Strategy: The Theory and Practice of Eighteenth-Century Warfare," in Don Higginbotham, ed., *Reconsiderations on the Revolutionary War* (Westport, Conn.: Greenwood Press, 1978), pp. 14–22.

8. Guy Frégault, *Canada: The War of the Conquest* (Toronto: Oxford University Press, 1969); Stanley McCrory Pargellis, *Lord Loudoun in North America* (New Haven: Yale University Press, 1933); J. Clarence Webster, ed., *The Journal of Jeffery Amherst . . . 1758 to 1763* (Toronto: Ryerson Press, [1931]); Beckles Willson, *The Life and Letters of James Wolfe* (London: William Heinemann, 1909).

9. Douglas Southall Freeman, *George Washington: A Biography*, 7 vols. (New York: Charles Scribner's Sons, 1948–1957), III, 27–28; John C. Fitzpatrick, ed., *The Writings of George Washington from the Original Manuscript Sources, 1745–1799*, 39 vols. (Washington: Government Printing Office, 1931–1944), I, 254; Showman, ed., *Papers of Nathanael Greene*, I, 1190; II, 28, 37.

10. Ira D. Gruber, *The Howe Brothers and the American Revolution* (Chapel Hill: University of North Carolina Press, 1972), pp. 3–23, 38–41.

11. Charles Royster, *A Revolutionary People at War: The Continental Army and American Character, 1775–1783* (Chapel Hill: University of North Carolina Press, 1979), pp. 3–53.

12. James Thomas Flexner, *George Washington*, 4 vols. (Boston: Little, Brown & Company, 1965–1972), II, 9–83; Robert McConnell Hatch, *Thrust for Canada: The American Attempt on Quebec in 1775–1776* (Boston: Houghton Mifflin Co., 1979).

13. Gruber, *Howe Brothers*, pp. 20, 24, 29–37, 77–79, 82–85; Germain to William Eden, 27 July 1775, and Howe to Germain, 25 April 1776, quoted in Gruber, *Howe Brothers*, pp. 27, 83.

14. Washington quoted in Christopher Ward, *The War of the Revolution*, ed. John Richard Alden, 2 vols. (New York: Macmillan Co., 1952), I, 205; Gruber, *Howe Brothers*, pp. 107–32. Nathanael Greene to John Adams, 3 March 1777, in Showman, ed., *Papers of Nathanael Greene*, II, 28–29, explains Washington's strategy in 1776. As Washington said, his strategy "has even been called a War of Posts"; quoted in Russell F. Weigley, "American Strategy: A Call for a Critical Strategic History," in Higginbotham, ed., *Reconsiderations on the Revolutionary War*, p. 50.

15. Howe to Germain, 7 July 1776, quoted in Gruber, *Howe Brothers*, p. 104.

16. Ibid., pp. 89–157.

17. Howe to Germain, 20 January 1777, quoted in ibid., p. 157; see as well pp. 174–83, 199–201; Hoffman Nickerson, *The Turning Point of the Revolution, Or Burgoyne in America* (Boston: Houghton Mifflin Co., 1928), pp. 83–89.

18. Germain to William Eden, 1 January 1777, Additions to the Manuscripts, 34,413, British Museum; Gruber, *Howe Brothers*, pp. 174–75, 180–81, 187–88, 212.

19. Gruber, *Howe Brothers*, pp. 227–66.

20. Nickerson, *Turning Point of the Revolution*, pp. 99–403; R. Arthur Bowler, *Logistics and the Failure of the British Army in America, 1775–1783* (Princeton: Princeton University Press, 1975), pp. 225–30.

21. John Adams to Abigail Adams, 2 September 1777, quoted in Royster, *Revolutionary People at War*, p. 148; Flexner, *George Washington*, II, 91–252; Showman, ed., *Papers of Nathanael Greene*, II, 24–238.

22. Nickerson, *Turning Point of the Revolution*, pp. 129–333; Nelson, *General Horatio Gates*, pp. 89–156.

23. Gruber, *Howe Brothers*, pp. 273–81, 297–321; William B. Willcox, *Portrait of a General: Sir Henry Clinton in the War of Independence* (New York: Alfred A. Knopf, 1964), pp. 211–54.

24. Greene to Washington, 24 June 1778, in Showman, ed., *Papers of Nathanael Greene*, II, 447; see as well ibid., II, 225–551; Royster, *Revolutionary People at War*, pp. 190–254; Flexner, *George Washington*, pp. 281–334.

25. Ira D. Gruber, "Britain's Southern Strategy," in W. Robert Higgins, ed., *The Revolutionary War in the South: Power, Conflict, and Leadership* (Durham, N.C.: Duke University Press, 1979), pp. 220–33; Willcox, *Portrait of A General*, pp. 260–346.

26. Freeman, *George Washington*, V, 132–250; Flexner, *George Washington*, II, 335–409; Royster, *Revolutionary People at War*, pp. 295–308; Charles H. Lesser, ed., *The Sinews of Independence: Monthly Strength Reports of the Continental Army* (Chicago: University of Chicago Press, 1976), pp. 136–99.

27. Gruber, "Britain's Southern Strategy," pp. 227–37; Wickwire and Wickwire, *Cornwallis*, pp. 133–353.

28. Nelson, *General Horatio Gates*, pp. 218–52; Thayer, *Nathanael Greene*, pp. 279–395.

29. Flexner, *George Washington*, II, 410–62; Freeman, *George Washington*, V, 251–393; Lesser, ed., *Sinews of Independence*, pp. 194–211.

FURTHER READING

Although this is the first essay to explore the origins of British and American strategy in the War for American Independence—the first to argue that there was a common and distinctive Anglo-American strategic tradition—other historians have studied British and American strategy extensively and intensively. Among those books that deal with the war as a whole, there are several that provide accurate and careful analyses of plans made by both sides—especially Don Higginbotham, *The War of American Independence*, The Wars of the United States (New York: Macmillan Co., 1971), and Willard M. Wallace, *Appeal to Arms* (New York: Harper and Brothers, 1951). Among the many books of essays dealing with the war, two contain sound studies of both British and American strategy: Don Higginbotham, ed., *Reconsiderations on the Revolutionary War* (Westport, Conn.: Greenwood Press, 1978), and Eric Robson, *The American Revolution in Its Political and Military Aspects, 1763–1783* (Hamden, Conn.: Archon Books, 1965).

For a more detailed analysis of strategy, it is necessary to see specialized studies of the men who made it. Piers Mackesy, *The War for America, 1775–1783* (Cambridge: Harvard University Press, 1964), provides a thorough, sympathetic account of the North ministry's efforts to manage the war. To complement Mackesy's work there are full-length studies of each of the men who held independent commands in America, including

Ira D. Gruber, *The Howe Brothers and the American Revolution* (Chapel Hill: University of North Carolina Press, 1974); Hoffman Nickerson, *The Turning Point of the Revolution, Or Burgoyne in America* (Boston: Houghton Mifflin Co., 1928); William B. Willcox, *Portrait of A General: Sir Henry Clinton in the War of Independence* (New York: Alfred A. Knopf, 1964); and Franklin and Mary Wickwire, *Cornwallis: The American Adventure* (Boston: Houghton Mifflin Co., 1970).

There is no book comparable to Mackesy's for the American side of the war—no book that is at once so comprehensive and so analytical. Yet there are studies of Washington as a strategist, including Thomas C. Frothingham, *Washington: Commander in Chief* (Boston: Houghton Mifflin Co., 1930), and Dave Palmer, *The Way of the Fox: American Strategy in the War for America* (Westport, Conn.: Greenwood Press, 1975). There are exhaustive biographies of Washington: Douglas Southall Freeman, *George Washington: A Biography*, 7 vols. (New York: Charles Scribner's Sons, 1948–1957), and James Thomas Flexner, *George Washington*, 4 vols. (Boston: Little, Brown & Co., 1965–1972). There are also two fine biographies of Washington's principal lieutenants, Gates and Greene: Paul David Nelson, *General Horatio Gates: A Biography* (Baton Rouge: Louisiana State University Press, 1976) and Theodore Thayer, *Nathanael Greene: Strategist of the American Revolution* (New York: Twayne Publishers, 1960). Taken together, these six studies do provide a remarkably full and coherent—if not consistent—description of American plans and planning in the Revolutionary War.

CHAPTER 3

Reassessing American Military Requirements, 1783–1807

LAWRENCE DELBERT CRESS

The Revolutionary War ended with the Treaty of Paris, signed by British and American representatives on 3 September 1783. In December a grateful nation accepted General George Washington's resignation as commander in chief and by the next summer virtually the entire Continental army had disbanded. Although a small constabulary force under the command of Lieutenant Colonel Josiah Harmar was soon organized to protect the frontier, the republican principles on which the nation was founded included the assumption that "a sufficient number of brave, loyal and determined citizens would always appear ready to support their government; [and] that a majority of the people would be too wise and too well informed to permit the basis of their rights and privileges to be overturned by a needy, desperate banditti."[1] It therefore seemed unlikely that many Americans would support a strong enough peacetime army to answer all of the new Republic's military needs.

A growing number of people found cause nevertheless to question traditional republican beliefs about national defense. The unpredictable battlefield performance of the citizen in arms during the Revolution convinced many nationalist-minded Americans that the decentralized and often haphazardly organized state militia system which existed after the war was incapable of preserving the external and internal security of the Republic.

News from Massachusetts in September 1786 that armed insurgents had closed the Courts of Common Pleas in Hampshire, Worcester, and Middlesex counties strengthened this conviction and provided solid evidence of the nation's internal vulnerability. Instead of rallying to defend the civil order, the local militia sided with the rebels led by Daniel Shays. Only a day after Governor James Bowdoin had called upon the citizenry to quell the rebellion, word arrived from Worcester that "there did appear universally that reluctance in the People to turn out for the support of Government as amounted in many instances to a flat denial: in others to an evasion or delay which amounted to the same thing."[2] From September through January reports of the militia's unreliability poured into the governor's office. Even the successful defense by the militia of the Continental arsenal at Springfield was marred when supposedly loyal militiamen joined the ranks of the insurgents during the skirmish.[3] Resistance to constitutional authority was by no means limited to the militia's rank and file. Surviving court records indicate that militia officers discouraged their companies from taking the field, prevented the distribution of powder and supplies, and actively recruited their subordinates for service with the insurgents.[4]

A joint resolution by the Massachusetts legislature described a systematic effort in the troubled western counties to raise and organize "regular military companies properly officered" for the "express purpose of opposing in arms, the Constitutional government of the state." The conduct of the militia thus raised serious questions about the state's ability to protect the liberties and property of its citizens. Bowdoin complained to the house and senate that the constitutional order depended on the fulfillment of "reciprocal duties" vested in the people and their leaders. He could only declare a state of emergency; the people had the responsibility to put it down. If the militia "refused to appear; or appearing join the insurgents, the laws cannot be executed," and the citizenry would soon find itself exposed to "all the evils, that may arise from the suspension, or prostration of law and justice." The governor believed that the crisis engulfing Massachusetts was in large part the result of the failure of its citizens to fulfill their constitutional military obligation. The rebellion was finally put down in early 1787 with the help of loyal local militia and a substantial body of soldiers raised in the eastern reaches of the state. But Bowdoin remained convinced that the militia would have to be made more responsive to the needs of the state if constitutional authority and civil order were to prevail.[5]

Three years later when the new Constitution granted federal authorities the power to preserve order and guarantee republican government in the states, George Washington probably recalled his own and Congress's sense of helplessness during Shays's Rebellion. He had been well informed of developments in Massachusetts and of Congress's surreptitious approach to the crisis. Short of men and fearful that direct intervention would only provoke more internal discord, Congress had requested just over 1,000 New Englanders for service on the frontier, planning covertly to use those troops to preserve order if Massachusetts failed to quell the rebellion. The same factors had led Congress to leave the defense of the Continental arsenal at Springfield in the hands of state officials. Washington had been exasperated by Congress's weakness. "What stronger evidence can be given of the want of energy in our government than these disorders?" he wrote James Madison at the time. "If there exists not a power to check them, what security has a man for life, liberty, or property?" The new constitutional arrangement gave the national government the ultimate responsibility for the preservation of liberty and property in the Republic. Washington recognized that to fulfill that responsibility, the militia would have to be made responsive to national policy.[6]

The Constitution divided control over the militia between the states and the national government, reserving for the former control over training and the power to appoint officers while granting to the latter the right to organize, arm, and discipline the militia. Congress had the authority to call out the militia "to execute the laws of the Union, suppress Insurrection and repel Invasion." The Constitution did not, however, prescribe either the organizational structure or the training apparatus necesary to prevent the confusion and uncertainty that had occurred during Shays's Rebellion. In January 1790 the Washington administration submitted to Congress a plan intended to transform the militia into an institution compatible with the tenets of republican theory, but more responsive to the needs and policies of the national government. To ensure the militia's dependability, the administration urged holding regular military encampments to inculcate discipline, discourage idleness and dissipation, and impart to the nation's young men a clear understanding of "the eminent advantages of free Government." Carefully organized and rigorously conducted, these summer training camps stood at the heart of a plan designed to provide the American people with a force able to silence domestic insurgency, discourage foreign invasions, and "effectively oppose the introduction of [domestic] tyranny."[7]

The plan provided by the administration also tried to deal more effectively with the growing economic complexity of American society. The principal burden of military service was to rest with the nation's youth. "The head of a family, anxious for its general welfare, and perhaps its immediate subsistence, will reluctantly quit his domestic duties for any length of time." According to the plan's author, Secretary of War Henry Knox, periodic militia service posed few economic hardships for young men under twenty-one, since they usually had no dependents and were still in the process of acquiring the skills they would use later to earn a living. Besides, regular attendance at summer encampments promised to lay the groundwork for a virtuous, productive, and industrious citizenry. In short, Knox's national militia plan promised for America the political and moral stability that had always eluded republics in the past; it envisioned "an institution, under whose auspices the youth and vigor of the constitution would be revived with each successive generation, secur[ing] the great principles of freedom and happiness against the injuries of time and events."[8]

At the same time, the Washington administration recommended numerous structural and organizational features designed to ensure that the national system would not degenerate into a confederation of state militias. The secretary of war's plan called for the national government to be given the power to mobilize the militia on its own authority as well as to conscript any militia member during wartime. Each state would appoint a general staff consisting of an inspector general, an adjutant general, and a quartermaster general. But the general staff would report to and be paid by the national government. Making the militia dependent on the national government for weapons and materiel would guarantee greater "uniformity, economy, and efficacy" throughout the system. Arming the militia from federal arsenals and supplying it from national stockpiles also would help to keep the militia from becoming a source of disorder within the Republic.[9]

Knox suggested other ways of making the militia more responsive to the policies of the national government. Federal remuneration of officers serving in the annual training camps would provide a degree of national influence through the state-appointed officer corps. Similar reasoning lay behind the administration's offer to pay and supply all officers and men mobilized for national service. The states were urged to select Continental army veterans for key militia commands. Experienced officers would provide much needed expertise. Veterans also had previous ties to the national government, and their appointment would help to assure that the militia did not become the special province of state political patronage—no small consideration at a time when many states were resisting the new government's attempt to establish a truly national structure. The secretary's proposal that all eighteen, nineteen, and twenty-year-olds make up an "Advance Corps" available for service anywhere in the Republic was designed with the same purpose in mind: surmounting local attachments which might prove detrimental to national security and domestic tranquillity.[10]

Congress rejected the administration's plan, passing instead, after a two-year delay, legislation that reflected a marked unwillingness to transform the historically state-oriented militia into a national institution. The Uniform Militia Act of 1792 included no provision to class the militia by age. It indiscriminately required every "free able bodied male citizen" aged eighteen through forty-five to enroll in a local militia unit. The act did not provide the fines and administrative organization needed to ensure compliance with federal training standards, and its authors rejected all recommendations to arm the militia from federal arsenals. The national government was given no power to enforce the generally vague organizational and training provisions of the act, nor was a system established to keep the president or Congress informed of the militia's readiness. An attempt to give the president authority to call out the militia to execute laws, suppress insurrections, and repel invasions failed to gain the approval of the Senate, leaving the chief executive dependent upon the cooperation of the state governments if he wished to call the militia to arms. Even then, the president could ask the states to call out their militia during domestic emergencies only after a Supreme Court justice certified the inability of local civil authorities to maintain order.[11] Congress had fulfilled its constitutional obligation to organize the militia, but it had done so without giving the national government a military force with which to meet its broader responsibility to "insure domestic Tranquility, [and] provide for the common defence."

The shortcomings of the Uniform Militia Act became apparent when resistance to federal excise taxes in western Pennsylvania boiled over into armed rebellion during the late summer and early fall of 1794. As had Shays's Rebellion, the Whiskey Insurrection pointed out the potential dangers of a local militia system over which the higher authorities had little or no control. The evidence is somewhat sketchy, but it appears that militia units provided the organizational base for the insurrection. Documents from Washington County, Pennsylvania, and nearby Ohio County, Virginia, indicate that militia officers, or individuals elected by the militia specifically for the purpose, planned and coordinated public demonstrations against the excise laws.[12] If the resistance was not actually coordinated by the militia leadership, few in positions of authority at the state and national levels doubted that the militia in Washington, Lafayette, Westmoreland, and Allegheny counties stood with the rebels. Pennsylvania Governor Thomas Mifflin, though anxious to avoid the use of military force, quickly conceded that the local militia had been rendered useless by popular support for the insurgents. President Washington's cabinet concurred, citing numerous reports that magistrates and militia officers had joined the insurrection and were threatening open warfare.[13] The situation was critical. Internal discord, supported by local allegiances which long predated the formation of the federal government, threatened to destroy the newly constituted Republic.

Having received word from Supreme Court Justice James Wilson that order could not be maintained by the civil authorities, Washington, on the advice of Secretary of War Henry Knox and Secretary of the Treasury Alexander Hamilton, ordered 13,000 militiamen readied for service in the western counties.[14] Half of the force was to be raised in Pennsylvania and the remainder in Virginia, Maryland, and New Jersey. The president's call to arms caught the state militias entirely unprepared. The militia had been allowed to deteriorate in most states after the Revolution. The Militia Act of 1792 had done little to improve its condition; and in the four states involved, inadequacies in existing militia laws hindered mobilization.[15] But there was another, potentially more serious problem that threatened the national government's first attempt to suppress domestic insurrection. If the western Pennsylvania militia had proven unreliable, might not the militia in the neighboring counties and states also prove undependable? Secretary of State Edmund Randolph suggested this possibility to Washington, fearing that a call to arms might prove even more embarrassing to the government than its inability to enforce national law with civil authority.[16] As Randolph predicted, mobilizing the militia raised additional questions concerning the government's ability to guarantee order.

Popular support for the Whiskey insurgents had to be overcome before New Jersey and Virginia could fill their quotas. The situation proved so serious in western Virginia that David Morgan, commander of the Virginia contingent of soldiers, requested arms from the state arsenal not only to train his men, but also to prevent civil and militia leaders in the Winchester area from disrupting preparations for the march into western Pennsylvania.[17] Efforts to mobilize the militia in Maryland produced massive resistance in the western counties, forcing Governor Thomas Lee to mobilize 700 additional men to protect the state arsenal in Frederick and to restore order in the mountainous region of the state. Maryland met its quota, but only by relying on the draft and looking to units raised outside western Maryland.[18] Pennsylvania did not try to call out the militia in the troubled western counties. Even the militia in the eastern counties proved unwilling to answer the governor's call to arms. Reflecting over reports that recruiting was going poorly, Governor Mifflin reminded the adjutant of the state's militia that "a free republic can only be established by the will of the people." If the citizens chose not to serve, they faced the prospect of living in anarchy or having to entrust their liberties to the "protection and support of a standing army."[19] Maryland's Governor Lee agreed, fearing that the states' inability to call the militia out would "ultimately render all dependence upon our militia in the moment of danger equivocal and precarious."[20]

Indeed, it had. Washington and Hamilton led a national force of impressive size into western Pennsylvania, and the president claimed that in ending the insurgency the militia had done "nothing less than to consolidate and to preserve the blessings of the Revolution."[21] But beyond the hyperbole, the Washington administration understood that the existing militia structure only reinforced the institutional localism that had the potential to destroy the fragile new nation. The militia system had to be made responsive to national authority. If it was not, cautioned Theodore Sedgwick in debate prompted by the militia's performance during the Whiskey Insurrection, "resort must then, in every instance, be made to a standing army. There was no other alternative."[22]

The fear in Federalist circles that the existing militia structure left the national government without a reliable emergency force—one congressman claimed that fewer than one in five militiamen had proven willing to serve during the Whiskey Rebellion—contributed directly to the Provisional Army Act of 1798. This legislation authorized the president not only to recruit officers and men for a 10,000-man reserve army for use in a national emergency but also to commission officers and accept into immediate service volunteer companies organized in support of the national government.[23] Although President John Adams did not elect to mobilize the provisional army, the 1798 act represented the culmination of Federalist efforts to place the militia on a national footing in order to overcome the political and military shortcomings of the state-controlled militia system. "If only the militia was wholly under the authority of the United States, and under the command of officers appointed by them," lamented a Federalist spokesman, "they might be more relied upon." Indeed, the decentralized structure of the nation's militia made the country particularly susceptible, many Federalists feared, to the rumored French effort to destroy the Republic from within.[24]

The provisional army and the volunteer corps therefore promised to give the nation forces of unquestionable loyalty at a time of rising domestic and international tensions. Had it ever actually been organized, the provisional army would have provided the government with a politically and militarily dependable infrastructure of men and equipment similar to that envisioned by Federalist proponents of militia reform since 1790.[25] The volunteer corps units, which were placed into service by the Adams administration in 1798 and 1799, were also intended to provide a force uninhibited by the restrictions and inadequacies of the state-controlled militia system. While the militia had proven weak and undependable, the volunteer corps would offer a formidable deterrent "to the invaders of our country—to the turbulent and seditious—to insurgents—to the daring infractors of the laws." In short, the addition of the volunteer corps to the military establishment represented for Federalists the "admission of a body of patriotic, respectable, generous youth, into the public service, who will form a firm phalanx against any internal or external enemy."[26] The provisional army and the volunteer corps thus reflected not only the Federalists' disillusionment with the existing militia structure, but also their continuing adherence to the principle that a republican government must base its coercive power on popular support. Not surprisingly, when Fries's Rebellion broke out in eastern Pennsylvania in March 1799, the Adams administration turned to the volunteer corps in conjunction with the regular army, although it lacked the authority to do so, and to loyal local militia to put down the insurrection.[27]

At the same time, the Federalist effort to create an alternative to the existing militia structure reflected more than a belief that the militia's ineffectiveness stemmed from its decentralized organizational structure. The sophistication of eighteenth-century warfare and the growing complexity of American society demanded a reassessment of the character and composition of the nation's military institutions. Mass mobilization disrupted many civilian activities that were essential for successful military operations. "You may occasionally call the militia," argued one Federalist, "but it would be immensely inconvenient to be constantly calling the husbandman from the field and the mechanic from his labors, and to have the whole country marching and countermarching." Just as important, militia soldiers were no match for the carefully trained and highly disciplined regulars that made up the armies of Europe. The success of a modern army depended on "something more than a disposition" to serve. Certainly the classical republican claim that the union of arms and property was the principal ingredient of a victorious army had proven erroneous in America. "Though composed of persons who had the greatest stake in the country," the militia during the Revolution too often had "wanted discipline, and was far from being prompt in obedience to orders." Modern soldiers had to have specialized skills; their effectiveness depended upon discipline and order far more than valor and patriotism.[28]

Hamilton and other Federalists hoped that the provisional army and the volunteer corps would constitute a select citizen reserve that would overcome the inadequacies of the state-controlled militia system. Nevertheless, the social and economic structure of the new Republic and the sophistication of eighteenth-century warfare led many of these same men to conclude that the regular army should provide the cornerstone for the nation's defenses. Associating the stability of American republicanism with the nation's ability to marshal an effective military force, Hamilton and his followers at various times during the 1790s had argued that a professional army was compatible with and necessary for the preservation of republican liberties. The 12,000-man new army created during the summer of 1798 was an important manifestation of that belief.[29] Secretary of War James McHenry expressly articulated the reasons for placing greater reliance on a standing army in a series of letters to the Speaker of the House early in 1800. The issue at hand was a plan for a military academy, but the overriding concern of the secretary of war was the need for a reassessment of the Republic's military requirements and capabilities.

Proponents of militia reform, argued McHenry, ignored the social, economic, and military realities of American society. "To qualify and keep our citizens . . . prepared to take the field against regular forces, would demand the most radical changes in our militia system, and such an uninterrupted series of training, discipline, and instruction, to be applied" that the nation would lose more "by the abstraction of labor or occupation" than it would cost to maintain a modest regular army. Making a citizen a "master of the several branches of the art of war" made no more sense than to employ every man in the community in the construction of houses while expelling "as useless, architects, masons, and carpenters." Neither, argued McHenry, did the militia's past record suggest that it should retain a central role in the nation's military establishment. The militia had performed poorly in the Revolutionary War and its conduct on the northwest frontier during the recent Indian campaigns of Josiah Harmar and Arthur St. Clair had been less than commendable. On the other hand, recent history abounded with evidence that "the perfect order, and exact discipline" of regular troops gave them "a decided advantage over more numerous forces composed of un-instructed militia, or undisciplined recruits." Military expertise had become the critical factor in any armed encounter. Strategic theory and tactical principles had to be learned and then applied with precision and care to quickly developing circumstances to secure victory on the battlefield. Part-time militia officers and soldiers could neither master nor apply these techniques with the precision re-quired in the heat of battle. The militia might occasionally serve brilliantly, but it was "universally felt, that regular and disciplined troops were indispensable, and that it was utterly unsafe for us to trust to militia alone the issue of war."[30]

McHenry's contention that the nature of American society necessitated a reap-praisal of the traditional republican suspicion of military professionalism reflected the influence of British attitudes toward military professionalism that, like the arguments marshaled by proponents of the citizen-soldier, dated back to the great late seventeenth-century debate over the English military establishment. Begin-ning with Daniel Defoe's defense of William III's request for a standing army and continuing through the eighteenth century, a host of prominent Englishmen had defended the compatibility of military professionalism with the institutions of a free people. Their ideas were summarized by Adam Smith in *An Inquiry into the Nature and Cause of the Wealth of Nations* published in 1776. An examination of Smith's ideas, thus, not only will help to clarify the assumptions that shaped McHenry's analysis of the nation's military requirements but also will help to explain why many Americans could support a professional military establishment with little concern that it would undermine the social and consti-tutional fabric of the young Republic.

Smith argued that the rise of military professionalism was an expression of social complexity; it was not, as republican theorists contended, a step toward political tyranny. The noncommercial, agricultural societies of ancient Greece and Rome had been, he maintained, the most sophisticated cultures in which the functions of citizen and soldier could be combined. The paramilitary activities of domestic life and an abundance of leisure had allowed the Greeks and Romans to train in the martial arts without sacrificing their economic standing in society. More sophisticated economic and social structures, however, did not lend themselves to universal military training. Commercial societies thrived on an efficient and effective division of labor. Military training only distracted the artisans from their crafts, reducing production for society and income for the craftsmen. The same applied to farmers. A universal military obligation reduced the farmers' ability to develop and apply the more sophisticated agricultural techniques required to meet the greater demands of an economically interdependent society. In short, the ability of the citizenry to defend society decreased in inverse proportion to the commercial sophistication of society itself. Paradoxically, as a society became more complex and more wealthy and, thus, had more reason to worry about being attacked, it became less able to defend itself. When the division of labor progressed to a point that the citizenry could no longer effectively shoulder military responsibilities, Smith argued, the state must assume the obligation for defense.[31]

Smith believed a commercial society could be defended adequately only by making soldiering ''a particular trade, separate and distinct from all others.'' Defense, like other aspects of a commercial society, depended upon an efficient division of labor. The militia, according to Smith, was inefficient because ''the character of the labourer, artificer, or tradesman, predominates over that of the soldier.'' A professional soldier, paid by the state and trained in the martial arts, would view his trade in the same manner as the craftsman. Thus, among the members of the military profession, the character ''of the soldier predominates over every other,'' leaving the defense of society to its most capable members. Admittedly, the coercive power of professional armies had been abused by civilian leaders in the past. But so long as the interests of civil society remained merged with those of the army, a professional military posed no threat to civil freedoms. To the contrary, it guaranteed national security and eliminated the threat of domestic disorder, while also freeing society from the disruptions associated with the mobilization of the militia.[32]

The Federalists succeeded neither in transforming the nation's regular army from a frontier constabulary to a skeletal professional force nor in replacing the militia with a national reserve such as the provisional army. Dissension in their own ranks and the rise of the Jeffersonian Republicans prevented the organization of the provisional army and contributed to the demobilization of the new army during the summer of 1800.[33] Nevertheless, the Federalists' assessment of the militia's unreliability as well as their analysis of the military requirements of a republican society in a modern world raised questions about the adequacy of the nation's military establishment that could not be ignored. Indeed, the decentralized organization of the militia and the need to come to terms with both the sophistication of modern warfare and the complexity of American society were very much on the minds of Jeffersonians concerned with the Republic's military requirements.

During the 1790s Republicans had resisted Federalist efforts to place the militia on a national footing, arguing that militia reform was only a thinly disguised plan to subvert the federal constitutional structure.[34] Once in power, the party's congressional leaders made clear their continued reluctance to alter the local character of the nation's militia. As a House committee explained in 1803, using language that would be repeated again and again while Thomas Jefferson was president, the Militia Act of 1792 "embraces all the objects of a militia institution, delegated to Congress; the principles of that law lay the foundation of a militia system on the broad basis prescribed in the Constitution, and are well calculated to insure a complete national defence." Jefferson himself, however, annually urged a reexamination of the nation's militia structure.[35] By the end of his second administration, he, like his Federalist predecessors, had become convinced that the existing decentralized militia system was incapable of preserving the nation's domestic tranquillity.

Aaron Burr's foray into the Southwest in 1806–1807 provided the Jeffersonians with strong evidence of the militia's ineffectiveness. Local militia units did not ally themselves with the insurgents as they had done during Shays's Rebellion and the Whiskey Insurrection. The sparsely populated Southwest simply lacked a militia organization capable of responding to the emergency.[36] The administration had tried to pass militia legislation that would have given it the ability to respond to such an emergency, sending to Congress in 1805 a classification plan similar to that recommended by Washington and Knox in 1790. Congress, though, had refused to act.[37] Following what it considered to be treasonous activity on the western frontier, the administration thereupon did what Federalists of the Hamiltonian persuasion had only dreamed of: it moved to add the regular army to the coercive force available to the national government during domestic emergencies. In 1807 Jefferson sought and received from Congress authority to use land or naval forces in any domestic crisis that would otherwise require militia service.[38]

Similar legislation provided the principal means by which the Jefferson administration maintained order in the Republic during the embargo year of 1808. Faced with widespread civil disobedience, Jefferson never considered a systematic mobilization of the coastal and frontier militia. Instead, the administration used the small standing army and the newly created fleet of gunboats to enforce compliance with federal laws along the New England coast and the Canadian frontier—areas in which the militia was reported to be sympathetic with or active in the violations of the embargo. The militia was occasionally called out to assist federal revenue officers, but usually only until regulars could be brought into an area or after special care had been taken to ensure that it would be mobilized under officers loyal to the administration.[39]

Ironically, the Jeffersonians, once the chief critics of Federalist efforts to increase the coercive power of the national government, were the first to use the regular army legally to ensure domestic tranquillity. Factionalism and internal dissent had destroyed republics in the past. It was with this lesson in mind that the Jefferson administration, unable to fashion the militia into a force responsive to national needs, turned elsewhere to ensure order. The decision to use the regular army for this purpose, moreover, reflected certain basic changes that had recently been made in that body. As Theodore Crackel has pointed out, the Republicans had used the provisions of the Military Peace Establishment Act of 1802 to do more than reduce military expenditures. Through changes in the army's organizational structure and removals from, promotions within, and appointments to the officer corps, they had "Republicanized" the country's small standing army.[40] The establishment of the United States Military Academy at West Point, New York, in the same year was expected to facilitate the entrance of young Republicans into the officer corps in the future and further persuaded the president and his chief aids that the army had come to represent a far more certain guarantor of the republican principles espoused by the administration than the state-controlled militia system.

Jefferson's use of the regular army to enforce the embargo, however, did not necessarily reflect the same commitment to military professionalism that had informed the Federalist defense of the new army during the Adams administration. Certainly there were some Jeffersonians, most notably Joseph Priestley, who used the insights of Adam Smith to argue that a professional peacetime army was compatible with the republican foundations of American society.[41] Nevertheless, Jefferson, who tripled the size of the regular army on paper to over 10,000 men in 1808 when faced with mounting international tension and the continued refusal of Congress to take up militia reform, perversely continued to believe that "a classified militia . . . specially trained" could best meet the nation's peacetime requirements.[42] Indeed, most critics of the American military establishment during the first decade of the nineteenth century exhibited a marked reluctance to endorse military professionalism. While recognizing that the structure of American society and the sophistication of contemporary tactics had altered the military needs of the Republic, they continued to look to the militia as the military institution most compatible with the ideological foundations of American republicanism.

Commentators concerned with the nation's external security repeatedly warned of the dangers inherent in a military system that separated the responsibility for national defense from the functions of citizenship. As one analyst noted, "With us, all should be soldiers as well as citizens." Nevertheless, the citizen militia recommended in the Republican press and elsewhere had little in common with the decentralized system extant in America. As had Federalist proponents of militia reform in the previous decade, most commentators chose to merge a sensitivity for the growing complexity of modern warfare and society and a recognition of the national government's need to have access to a dependable emergency force with an appreciation for the Republic's longstanding suspicion of standing armies. The result was an assortment of recommendations—some, not unlike the plan proposed by the Washington administration in 1790, urging classification of the nation's militia by age. In its simplest manifestation, classification entailed little more than the imposition of more frequent training sessions for the nation's young men, its aim being to develop only a force capable of withstanding the initial thrusts of a foreign invader while giving valuable time for raising a larger army. Other proposals were more ambitious; one even envisioned a comprehensive militia system capable of replacing the regular army on the frontier during peacetime. These plans often included proposals for the establishment of military training camps and academies designed to instill both military discipline and republican virtue. In their most extreme form, they urged that service in the national militia become a prerequisite for public office. Whatever the details of their prescriptions, the proponents of these militia reforms understood that the structure of modern society and the sophistication of contemporary warfare required a reassessment of the assumptions supporting the existing militia structure. At the same time, they were convinced that the militia, properly reformed, remained the best means to ensure the nation's security.[43]

William Duane—the editor of the *Philadelphia Aurora* and one of the most persistent critics of American military preparedness—articulated as well as anyone the assumptions behind the continuing American unwillingness to abandon the militia for the military expertise offered by a professional army. Duane conceded that militia service had "become a matter of institution and positive law, rather than a habit or opinion." In part that was the result of the growing complexity of war. But it was also the consequence of the infusion of luxury and wealth into European society that had followed the invention of the printing press, the discovery of America, and the rise of commerce. This understanding of the development of Western society, borrowed from the political tracts of the English radical Whigs who had provided the intellectual context for the Revolution, led Duane to link the rise of "new occupations, necessities, riches, and speculations" with the decline of "the practice of military exercise." In short, as money became the basis of exchange, the union of citizenship and military service that had ensured constitutional balance and political stability among free societies during the classical and feudal periods was destroyed, leading to the rise of professional armies and the proliferation of political tyranny. For Duane, the lessons of history were inescapable. The nation that failed to provide itself with an armed and disciplined citizenry as it grew in wealth and economic complexity—by institutionalizing the citizen's obligation to perform militia service—faced the inevitable loss of its political freedom.[44]

The American Republic was particularly vulnerable. Its growing wealth made it increasingly susceptible to external attack. At the same time, the Republic had failed to develop a system of national defense capable of performing well in a modern war. The navy was too small, fortifications were too widely scattered, and the militia was too poorly disciplined and too inexperienced to provide an effective deterrent against surprise attack. Indeed, wrote Duane, Americans seemed bent on discouraging the cultivation of militia skills. State governments had allowed their militias to deteriorate, and Congress had proven reluctant to leg-islate an effective national militia law. In his judgment the "current militia law seemed calculated to frustrate military discipline, to discourage patriotics, and to discredit [military] talents." With the renewal of hostilities by Britain and France in 1803 after the Peace of Amiens and the growing likelihood that the United States would become involved in the conflict between them, the Repub-lic's very survival, he argued, depended upon the enactment of "some general law for enforcing an effective system of defense."[45]

Duane rejected out of hand any suggestion that the Republic's interests might best be served by a professional military establishment. He reminded Americans that the standing armies that supported the tyrannical governments of Europe had been created "when the holders of the soil ceased to be the armed defenders of the country." Representative government required a citizenry prepared by "skill and will" to defend it. "Any other system but militia, would be as fatal to the liberties of this country as any invading enemy could possibly be." Modern military maneuvers depended upon rigid discipline and tactical expertise; "the tactics of our revolution would not answer at the present time." Nevertheless, the militia soldier could be expected to master the tactical skills required for success on the battlefield. Duane warned Americans to be wary of plans to lift the burden of military service from the citizenry—he himself believed all men eighteen to forty-five should be enrolled in the active militia—and to be suspicious of claims that "vast scientific acquirements were indispensable to be competent to study tactics." Intrigue and deception had robbed free people of their liberties in the past. Only as long as "the citizens were the only soldiers" could the Republic be secure from both external attack and internal intrigue. "It is for these solid reasons," concluded Duane, "that the whole wisdom and energy of the American nation should be directed to the perfection of that only system of safe and effective defense—a well disciplined militia."[46]

Duane's pleas fell on deaf ears, however, and by the end of Jefferson's second term national authorities had come to rely on the army and not the militia to guarantee domestic tranquillity. After the Whiskey Rebellion, no national admin-istration had dared to use the militia exclusively to ensure domestic peace. The ensuing demise of the militia had not been the consequence of a conspiracy to make the regular army the nation's police force. The militia—always more responsive to local issues and frustrations than to state and national policy—had become the victim of the localism that had once caused republican theorists to identify it with the preservation of constitutional balance and civil order. It lost its status as a symbol of American republicanism because it had proven to be more often the perpetrator of discord than the guarantor of domestic tranquillity. It was for that reason that the Republic's national leadership turned first to auxiliary military units drawn from civil society and then to the regular army itself to ensure domestic tranquillity. But there was more. Even if the militia had not been at least implicitly involved in challenges to the authority of the state and national governments, the nation's leading political and military commentators had grave doubts about the compatibility of the citizen-soldier ideal with the military requirements of the age and the structure of American society. For some, the discipline and expertise inherent in a force of professional soldiers offered the only realistic way to meet the nation's military needs. Others remained suspicious, favoring instead a major reform of the existing militia structure. Unfortunately for the immediate military requirements of the Republic, a national select militia system was as politically unacceptable in America as a professional army. That circumstance left the Republic woefully unprepared for the military challenges of its second war for independence.

NOTES

Portions of this essay were read at the 1979 meeting of the Organization of American Historians. The author would like to thank George A. Billias and Russell F. Weigley for their helpful comments. Grants from the National Endowment for the Humanities and the American Council of Learned Societies supported the research.

1. Theophilus Parsons, *Memoir of Theophilus Parsons. . . . By His Son Theophilus Parsons* (Boston: Ticknor and Fields, 1859), pp. 128–31.

2. Instructions to the Sheriff of Worcester from the Council Chamber, 2 September 1786, and Jonathan Warner to James Bowdoin, 3 September 1786, vol. 189, 7–8; vol. 190, 230, Massachusetts Archives, Massachusetts State Library. George R. Minot, *The History of the Insurrection in Massachusetts* (Worcester, Mass.: Printed by Isaiah Thomas, 1788), pp. 40–41, 74–75, 92–94.

3. Council Chamber Minutes, 7 and 9 September 1786; Narrative of a riot in the County of Worcester, by Artemas Ward, 5 September 1786; Joseph Henshaw to James Bowdoin, 7 September 1786; Sheriff Greenleaf to Bowdoin, 16 September 1786; Sheriff Caleb Hyde to Bowdoin, 13 September 1786; William Shepard to Bowdoin, 25 and 29 September 1786; An Account [of events in Springfield] by Nathan P. Sargent and David Sewall, 2 October 1786; Shepard to Bowdoin, 4 December 1786; Jonathan Warner to Bowdoin, 5 January 1787; and General Brooks to Bowdoin, 28 January 1787, Massachusetts Archives, vol. 189, 9–14; vol. 190, 131–33, 237–37a, 235–35a, 263–64, 266, 291–92, 294a–d; vol. 318, 202–3, 223, 299. See also Levi Lincoln to George Washington, 4 December 1786, George Washington Papers, ser. 4, Library of Congress, Washington, D.C.; and [commentary on the reluctance of the Third Division to support the government], undated and unsigned, Misc. Doc. Folder, Shays's Rebellion Collection, American Antiquarian Society.

4. Writ vs. Aaron Board, 4 February 1787; Testimony and Trial of Dr. Issac Chenery, 20 February 1787; Writ vs. Major Francis Willson, 28 February 1787; Writ vs. Samuel Richardson; and General Court Martial, 2 June 1787, Shays's Rebellion Collection.

5. Proclamation, 2 September 1786; House and Senate Resolution, 4 February 1787; Bowdoin's Speech to the Massachusetts House and Senate, 28 September 1786; Bowdoin to Massachusetts House and Senate, 3 February 1787, Massachusetts Archives, vol. 189, 1–2, 108–9; vol. 190, 267–76, 330.

6. Henry Lee to Washington, 3 September, 1 October, and 17 October 1786; Henry Knox to Washington, 28 October 1786; D. Humphreys to Washington, 1 November 1786, Washington Papers. Washington to Henry Lee, 31 October 1786; Washington to James

Madison, 5 November 1786; Washington to Levi Lincoln, 24 February 1787, in George Washington, *Writings of George Washington, 1745–1799*, ed. John C. Fitzpatrick (Washington: Government Printing Office, 1931–44), XXIX, 34–35, 51–52, 168. Knox to Washington, 14 January 1787, and Madison to Washington, 16 March 1787, in Jared Sparks, ed., *Correspondence of the American Revolution*, 4 vols. (Boston: Little, Brown & Co., 1853), IV, 161, 166–67. John C. Fitzpatrick et al., eds., *Journals of the Continental Congress, 1774–1789*, 34 vols. (Washington: Government Printing Office, 1904–1937), XXXI, 391–93, 895–96. C. Joseph Bernardo and Eugene H. Bacon, *American Military Policy: Its Development Since 1775* (Harrisburg, Pa.: Military Service Publishing Co., 1955), pp. 66–69.

7. Henry Knox to Speaker, House of Representatives, 18 January 1790, in U.S., Congress, House, *The Debates and Proceedings in the Congress of the United States, 1789–1824* [hereafter cited as *Annals of Congress*], 1st Cong., 2d sess., 1790, II, 2087–2107.

8. Ibid.

9. Ibid.

10. Ibid.

11. For the text of the Militia Act of 1792, see *Annals of Congress*, III, Appendix, 1370–72.

12. Circular of the Western Insurgents to the Militia Officers, 28 July 1794, and Resolves of Ohio County, Virginia, 9 September 1794, *Pennsylvania Archives*, 2d ser., 19 vols. (Harrisburg, Pa.: Printed by J. Severns & Co., 1887–1896), IV, 78–79, 269–71. Washington County, Hamilton District, Resolution, 11 and 28 February 1794, in Rawle Family Papers, I, 15, 18, Historical Society of Pennsylvania, Philadelphia, Pennsylvania.

13. William Bradford to Elias Boudinot, 1 August and 7 August 1794, in Wallace Papers, II, Historical Society of Pennsylvania. Bradford to Washington, 17 August 1794, Pennsylvania Whiskey Rebellion Collection, Library of Congress. Bradford to Washington, August 1794, Washington Papers. Alexander Hamilton to Washington, 5 August 1794; Governor Thomas Mifflin to Washington, 5 August 1794, *Pennsylvania Archives*, 2d ser., IV, 100–104, 104–9. Hamilton to Washington, 2 August 1794; Henry Knox to Washington, 4 August 1794, Washington Papers.

14. James Wilson to Washington, n.d., Pennsylvania Whiskey Rebellion Collection. Hamilton to Washington, 2 August 1794; Knox to Washington, 4 August 1794, Washington Papers.

15. Governor Thomas Lee to Henry Knox, 11 and 15 August 1794; Lee to Joseph Wilkinson, 4 September 1794; Lee to John Carlile, 4 September 1794; Lee to Hamilton, 4 September 1794; Lee to Henry Hollingsworth, 5 September 1794, Council Letter Books, 1793–1796, 39, 40, 49, 51–52, 52–53, Maryland Hall of Records, Annapolis, Md. Col. Alexander Russell to Gen. Harmar, 3 September 1794; Governor Mifflin to the Militia of Philadelphia, 10 September 1794, *Pennsylvania Archives*, 2d ser., IV, 263–64, 273–74. Arthur Campbell to Governor Henry Lee, 21 August 1794; Thomas Matthews to Lieutenant Governor Wood, 12 October 1794, Virginia Executive Papers, Henry Lee, Boxes 87, 88, Virginia State Library.

16. Edmund Randolph to Washington, 5 August 1794, Washington Papers.

17. Proclamation of the Governor of New Jersey, 16 September 1794, *Pennsylvania Archives*, 2d ser., IV, 306–7; David Morgan to Henry Lee, 7 September 1794, Virginia

Executive Papers, Box 83; Lee to Secretary of War Knox, 17 September 1794, Virginia Executive Letter Book, Virginia State Library.

18. Thomas Lee to Montjoy Bayley, 6 September 1794; Lee to James Lloyd, 8 September 1794; Lee to Philip Reed, 8 September 1794; Lee to Hamilton, 12 September 1794; Lee to Bayley, 13 September 1794; Lee to Samuel Smith, 13 September 1794; William Pickney to Hamilton, 18 September 1794; Lee to Thomas Sprigg, 21 September 1794; Lee to Hamilton, 23 September 1794; Lee to Smith, 30 September 1794; Lee to Luther Martin, 5 October 1794, Council Letter Books, pp. 53–54, 55–56, 57, 59–60, 60–61, 64–66, 74–75, 78–79, 80, 80–82, 92, Maryland Hall of Records. John Lynn to Governor Lee, 11 and 25 September 1794, Maryland State Papers, Ser. A, Box 76, nos. 35, 49, Maryland Hall of Records.

19. Mifflin to General Harmar, 8 September 1794; Secretary of State Dallas's Report to the Senate, 10 September 1794; Mifflin to Lancaster Militia, 26 September 1794; Mifflin to Pennsylvania House and Senate, 6 December 1794, *Pennsylvania Archives*, 2d ser., IV, 264–65, 280–82, 373–75, 488–94.

20. Lee to Philip Reed, 8 September 1794, Council Letter Books, 57, Maryland Hall of Records.

21. Washington to Edmund Randolph, 16 October 1794; Washington to Henry Lee, 20 October 1794; Washington's Address to Congress, 19 November 1794, in Fitzpatrick, ed., *Writings*, XXXIV, 3–4, 6, 34–35. Henry Knox to Governor Mifflin, 5 December 1794, *Pennsylvania Archives*, 2d ser., IV, 486–87.

22. *Annals of Congress*, IV, 3d Cong., 2d sess., 1067–79, 1217–18.

23. For the text of the Provisional Army Act, see *Annals of Congress*, IX, Appendix, 3729–33, 3743–44.

24. *Annals of Congress*, IV, 3d Cong., 1st sess., 500–504; VI, 4th Cong., 2d sess., 1690–91, 2099, 2223–24; VIII, 5th Cong., 2d sess., 1384–86, 1772–73. "Measures in the War Department Which It May Be Expedient to Adopt" [December 1794]; Hamilton to Timothy Pickering, 11 May 1797, in Alexander Hamilton, *Papers of Alexander Hamilton*, ed. Harold C. Syrett, 26 vols. (New York: Columbia University Press, 1961–1979), XVII, 582–84; XX, 83–84.

25. *Annals of Congress, VIII*, 5th Cong., 2d sess., 1729–31, 1734–39, 1747, 1758. [Hamilton], "The Stand, No. VI" (originally published in the *New York Commercial Advertiser*, 19 April 1798); Hamilton to Harrison Grey Otis, 27 December 1798; Hamilton to Theodore Sedgwick, 2 February 1799; Hamilton to Jonathan Drayton, [ca. October-November 1799], in Syrett, ed., *Hamilton Papers*, XXI, 438–49; XXII, 394, 453; XXIII, 599–602. Secretary of War James McHenry to John Adams, 24 December 1798, printed in the *Philadelphia Aurora*, 10 January 1799.

26. *Annals of Congress*, VIII, 5th Cong., 2d sess., 1703–7, 1725–72, 1934–54, passim. Robert Goodloe Harper to his Constituents, 23 July 1798 and 20 March 1799, in James A. Bayard, *Papers of James A. Bayard*, ed. Elizabeth Donnan (New York: Da Capo Press, 1971), pp. 55–59, 83–84. James Ross to James McHenry, 15 June 1798, in Bernard C. Steiner, *The Life and Correspondence of James McHenry* . . . (Cleveland: Burrows Brothers Co., 1907), pp. 437–38. Harper to Hamilton, 27 April 1797, in Syrett, ed., *Hamilton Papers*, XXI, 449.

27. Bennett M. Rich, *The Presidents and Civil Disorder* (Washington: The Brookings Institution, 1941), pp. 21–26.

28. *Annals of Congress*, VIII, 5th Cong., 2d sess., 1525–42, 1630–1703, passim.

29. *Annals of Congress*, II, 2d Cong., 1st sess., 343–48, and 2d sess., 750, 762–68,

773–802; IV, 3d Cong., 1st sess., 534–35, 735–38, 774–79, and 2d sess., 1163–72, 1220–23; V, 4th Cong., 1st sess., 905–13, 1418–23, passim. Also Timothy Pickering, "Objects of the Military Establishment of the United States," 3 February 1796, and James McHenry, "Report of the Peace Establishment," 14 March 1796, *American State Papers*, Class V: *Military Affairs*, 7 vols. (Washington: Gales and Seaton, 1832–1861), I, 112–13, 114. For a defense of the new army based explicitly on the need for professional soldiers, see *Annals of Congress*, X, 6th Cong., 1st sess., 304–6, 365.

30. James McHenry to Speaker, House of Representatives, 5 January 1800, with an endorsement by President John Adams; and McHenry to Speaker, House of Representatives, 31 January 1800, *American State Papers: Military Affairs*, I, 133–39, 142–44. George Washington, Noah Webster, and David Ramsay, among others, shared McHenry's understanding of the relationship between the structure of American society and the need to reassess the implications of military professionalism. See Lawrence Delbert Cress, "The Standing Army, the Militia, and the New Republic: Changing Attitudes Toward the Military in American Society, 1768 to 1820" (Ph.D. diss., University of Virginia, 1976), pp. 139–40, 173–74, 190–92, 200–203.

31. Adam Smith, *An Inquiry into the Nature and Causes of the Wealth of Nations*, ed. Edwin Cannan (New York: Modern Library, 1973), pp. 653–59.

32. Ibid., pp. 659–68.

33. Richard H. Kohn, *Eagle and Sword: The Federalists and the Creation of the Military Establishment in America, 1783–1802* (New York: Free Press, 1975), pp. 256–73.

34. See, for example, *Annals of Congress*, II, 1st Cong., 3d sess., 1851–75, passim; III, 2d Cong., 1st sess., 418–23, 552–55, 574–79; IV, 3d Cong., 2d sess., 1067–71, 1214–20, 1233–37; VI, 4th Cong., 2d sess., 1675–83. Also William Findley, *History of the Insurrection, in the Four Western Counties of Pennsylvania . . .* (Philadelphia: Printed by Samuel Harrison Smith, 1796), pp. 153–58.

35. Jefferson asked for militia reform during every year of his presidency except 1803. Congress, however, always refused. See, for example, the exchange between Jefferson and the House during the winter of 1802–1803. James D. Richardson, comp., *A Compilation of the Messages and Papers of the Presidents, 1789–1897*, 10 vols. (Washington: Government Printing Office, 1896–1899), I, 345. *Annals of Congress*, XII, 7th Cong., 2d sess., 521–22.

36. Leonard W. Levy, *Jefferson and Civil Liberties: The Darker Side* (Cambridge: Belknap Press of Harvard University Press, 1963), pp. 114–20.

37. Jefferson, "Fifth Annual Message to Congress," in Richardson, comp., *Messages*, I, 385–87. The bill passed the Senate, but never reached the House floor. See *Annals of Congress*, XV, 9th Cong., 1st sess., 327–29, 1069–75.

38. The legislation passed with no recorded debate. The text is printed in *Annals of Congress*, XVI, Appendix, 1286.

39. *Annals of Congress*, XIX, 10th Cong., 2d sess., 247–49, 254–55, 269–72, 286–97, 312–19, 931–38, 982–1025. Jefferson to Robert Smith, 14 February 1808; Gallatin to Jefferson, 9 August, 17 August, and 14 September 1808; Jefferson to James Wilkinson, 30 August 1808, Jefferson Papers, Library of Congress. Henry Dearborn to Governor Israel Smith, 1 June, 1 July, and 7 October 1808; Letters by the Secretary of War, vol. 3, Records of the Office of the Secretary of War, Record Group 107, National Archives, Washington, D.C. Note by Gallatin, 5 October 1808, in Daniel Parker Papers, Box 13, Historical Society of Pennsylvania. Dearborn to Alexander Walcott, 14 April 1808, Letters

by the Secretary of War, vol. 3, Record Group 107, National Archives. Dearborn to Governors of the States, 17 January 1809; Jefferson to Charles Simms, 22 January 1809; Jefferson, Proclamation, 22 January 1809, Jefferson Papers.

40. Theodore Joseph Crackel, "Jefferson, Politics and the Army: A New Look at the Military Peace Establishment Act of 1802" (Paper delivered at the 1979 meeting of The Society for Historians of the Early American Republic in Annapolis, Maryland).

41. Joseph Priestley, *The Theological and Miscellaneous Works, of Joseph Priestley,* 25 vols. (London: Printed by G. Smallfield, 1817–1832), vol. XXIV, *Lectures on History and General Policy* . . . (1826), pp. 381–90. See also Maximillian Godefroy, *Military Reflections, on Four Modes of Defence, for the United States* . . . , trans. Eliza Anderson (Baltimore: Printed by Joseph Robinson, 1807), pp. 5–38.

42. Jefferson to Samuel Dupont de Nemours, 2 May 1808; Jefferson to Charles Pinckney, 30 March 1808, Jefferson Papers. Jefferson to James Madison, 5 May 1807; Jefferson to Henry Dearborn, 28 August 1807; Jefferson to John Armstrong, 2 May 1808, in Thomas Jefferson, *The Writings of Thomas Jefferson*, ed. Paul Leicester Ford, 10 vols. (New York: G. P. Putnam's Sons, 1892–1899), IX, 49–50, 132, 193–94.

43. David Humphreys, *Considerations on the Means of Improving the Militia for the Public Defence* . . . (Hartford, Conn.: Printed by Hudson & Goodwin, 1803). William Henry Harrison, "Militia Discipline," nos. 1 and 2, *Washington National Intelligencer*, 21 September and 1 October 1810. See also the following articles in the *National Intelligencer*: unsigned essay, 4 November 1807; "On the Military Constitution of Nations," 18 November 1808; "JURISCOLA," 17 October 1810; and "AURORA," 14 December 1811. James Kendall, *Preparation for War the Best Security for Peace* . . . (Boston: Munroe & Francis, 1806), pp. 22–23.

44. William Duane, *The American Military Library; or, Compendium of the Modern Tactics* . . . , 2 vols. (Philadelphia: By the author, 1809), I, i, 5–8, 29–36.

45. *Philadelphia Aurora*, 30 and 31 October 1807.

46. Ibid., 2, 3, 4, 5, 10, 11, 12, 14 November 1807. Duane, *American Military Library*, I, i–iv.

FURTHER READING

General studies of American military history treat the early national period only lightly, assuming that the small size and incomplete organization of the military offer few insights into the nation's military development. Emory Upton, *The Military Policy of the United States From 1775* (Washington: Government Printing Office, 1904) and John McAuley Palmer, *Washington, Lincoln, Wilson: Three War Statesmen* (Garden City, N.Y.: Doubleday, Doran & Co., 1930) discuss developments between 1783 and 1808 only briefly. These early works also are marred by a conscious presentism that reflects a marginal interest in understanding the past. Russell F. Weigley's *History of the United States Army*, enlarged edition (Bloomington: Indiana University Press, 1984), Marcus Cunliffe's *Soldiers & Civilians: The Martial Spirit in America, 1775–1865* (New York: Free Press, 1973), and Samuel P. Huntington's *The Soldier and the State: The Theory and Politics of Civil-Military Relations* (Cambridge: Harvard University Press, 1957) are among the best modern surveys of the military in the early Republic, although they pass too quickly through the early national period. Of use, too, is C. Joseph Bernardo and Eugene H.

Bacon, *American Military Policy: Its Development Since 1775* (Harrisburg, Pa.: Military Service Publishing Co., 1955).

The best analyses of military policy between the Revolution and the War of 1812 are to be found in studies of the political affairs of that period. Richard H. Kohn's *Eagle and Sword: The Federalists and the Creation of the Military Establishment in America, 1783–1802* (New York: Free Press, 1975) is an excellent blend of intellectual, political, and institutional history centering on the place of the military in Federalist politics between 1783 and 1802. Lawrence Delbert Cress, *Citizens in Arms: The Army and the Militia in American Society to the War of 1812* (Chapel Hill: University of North Carolina Press, 1982) examines the impact of political ideology on military policy during the revolutionary and early national eras. Also of interest is Reginald C. Stuart, *War and American Thought: From the Revolution to the Monroe Doctrine* (Kent, Ohio: Kent State University Press, 1982). The final chapters of Don Higginbotham's *The War of American Independence: Military Attitudes, Policies, and Practice, 1763–1789*, The Wars of the United States (New York: Macmillan Co., 1971) and Robert Middlekauff's *The Glorious Cause: The American Revolution, 1763–1789* (New York: Oxford University Press, 1982) offer useful insights into military policy in the immediate postwar period. Howard White, *Executive Influence in Determining Military Policy in the United States* (Urbana: The University of Illinois, 1925), is dated but still valuable. The opening chapters of J. C. A. Stagg's *Mr. Madison's War: Politics, Diplomacy, and Warfare in the Early American Republic, 1783–1830* (Princeton: Princeton University Press, 1983) are also very useful. Richard Alton Erney, "The Public Life of Henry Dearborn" (Ph.D. diss., Columbia University, 1957), and Mary P. Adams, "Jefferson's Military Policy with Special Reference to the Frontier, 1805–1809" (Ph.D. diss., University of Virginia, 1958), provide sound discussions of military policy during the Jefferson administration. Dumas Malone, *Jefferson and His Time*, vol. V, *Jefferson the President: Second Term, 1805–1809* (Boston: Little, Brown & Co., 1974), also includes a good account of Jeffersonian policy. James Ripley Jacobs, *The Beginning of the U.S. Army, 1783–1812* (Princeton: Princeton University Press, 1947), and Francis Paul Prucha, *The Sword of the Republic: The United States Army on the Frontier, 1783–1846*, The Wars of the United States (New York: Macmillan Co., 1969), are two particularly strong studies of military operations in the West. Stephen Ambrose, *Duty, Honor, Country: A History of West Point* (Baltimore: Johns Hopkins Press, 1966), discusses officer training and military thought.

Articles concerning the origins and evolution of American military policy include Charles A. Lofgren, "War-Making under the Constitution: The Original Understanding," *Yale Law Journal* 81 (March 1972): 672–702; Lofgren, "Compulsory Military Service Under the Constitution," *William and Mary Quarterly*, 3d ser., 33 (January 1976): 61–88; Richard H. Kohn, "The Washington Administration's Decision to Crush the Whiskey Rebellion," *Journal of American History* 59 (December 1972): 567–84; William H. Gaines, Jr., "The Forgotten Army: Recruiting for a National Emergency (1799–1800)," *Virginia Magazine of History and Biography* 16 (1948): 267–279; and Reginald Horsman, "American Indian Policy in the Old Northwest, 1783–1812," *William and Mary Quarterly*, 3d ser., 18 (January 1961): 35–53. Of interest, too, is Lawrence Delbert Cress, "Republican Liberty and Military Policy: The Problem of the Military in American Ideology, 1783–1789," *William and Mary Quarterly*, 3d ser., 38 (January 1981): 73–96. Theodore J. Crackel's "Jefferson, Politics, and the Army: An Examination of the Military Peace Establishment Act of 1802," *Journal of the Early Republic* 2 (Spring

1982): 21–28, offers a major revision of the intent and effect of Jeffersonian policy regarding the army.

The institutional history of the army is covered in Leonard D. White's *The Federalists: A Study in Administrative History, 1789–1802* (New York: Macmillan Co., 1948) and *The Jeffersonians: A Study in Administrative History, 1801–1829* (New York: Macmillan Co., 1951). Well documented but weak in analysis is Harry M. Ward, *The Department of War, 1781–1795* (Pittsburgh: University of Pittsburgh Press, 1962). William H. Guthman, *March to Massacre: A History of the First Seven Years of the United States Army, 1784–1791* (New York: McGraw-Hill, 1975), is concerned with the operations and organization of the First Regiment.

Few published works exist analyzing the militia as an institution or as an instrument of policy. Frederick B. Weiner, "The Militia Clause of the Constitution," *Harvard Law Review* 54 (1940): 181–220, is a good starting point. Jim Dan Hill, *The Minute Man in Peace and War: A History of the National Guard* (Harrisburg, Pa.: Stackpole Co., 1964), is somewhat uneven. John K. Mahon, *The American Militia: Decade of Decision, 1789–1800* (Gainesville: University of Florida Press, 1960), is better.

Biographies treating the military leaders of the early national period are old and of mixed quality. St. Clair's career is covered in William Henry Smith's *The St. Clair Papers: The Life and Public Services of Arthur St. Clair . . .* (Cincinnati: R. Clarke & Co., 1882). Thomas A. Boyd, *Mad Anthony Wayne* (New York: Charles Scribner's Sons, 1929), provides a colorful but still competent account of Wayne's service in Ohio. James Wilkinson's controversial career is justified in heroic terms in his *Memoirs of My Own Times*, 3 vols. (Philadelphia: Printed by Abraham Small, 1816). Royal O. Shreve, *The Finished Scoundrel: General James Wilkinson . . .* (Indianapolis: Bobbs-Merrill, 1933), and James Ripley Jacobs, *Tarnished Warrior: Major-General James Wilkinson* (New York: Macmillan Co., 1938), draw more unflattering conclusions.

The intellectual context within which the young Republic's military institutions developed needs to be noted by any student of the nation's early military history. Lois G. Schwoerer, *"No Standing Armies!": The Antiarmy Ideology in Seventeenth-Century England* (Baltimore: Johns Hopkins University Press, 1974) provides important background. Also of use are Alfred Vagts, *A History of Militarism: Civilian and Military* (New York: Meridian Books, 1959), and J. F. C. Fuller, *The Conduct of War, 1789–1961: A Study of the Impact of the French, Industrial, and Russian Revolutions on War and Its Conduct* (New Brunswick, N.J.: Rutgers University Press, 1961). Reginald C. Stuart, *The Half-way Pacifist: Thomas Jefferson's View of War* (Toronto: University of Toronto Press, 1978), is of limited value. Relevant articles include Edward Mead Earle, "Adam Smith, Alexander Hamilton, Friedrich List: The Economic Foundations of Military Power," in Earle, ed., *Makers of Modern Strategy: Military Thought from Machiavelli to Hitler* (Princeton, N.J.: Princeton University Press, 1952), and Lawrence Delbert Cress, "Radical Whiggery on the Role of the Military: Ideological Roots of the American Revolutionary Militia," *Journal of the History of Ideas* 40 (1979): 43–60.

The best single bibliography addressing the period is Robin Higham, ed., *A Guide to the Sources of United States Military History* (Hamden, Conn.: Archon Books, 1975), with supplements. For readers interested in primary sources, two collections offer insights into the actions and motivations of the executive branch and Congress during the early national period: *American State Papers*, Class V: *Military Affairs*, 7 vols. (Washington: Gales and Seaton, 1832–1861) and *The Debates and Proceedings in the Congress of the United States, 1789–1824* [*Annals of Congress*], 42 vols. (Washington: Gales and Seaton,

1834–1856). The correspondence of the secretaries of war can be found scattered in Gayle Thornbrough, ed., *Outpost on the Wabash, 1787–1791* . . . (Indianapolis: Indiana Historical Society, 1957); William Henry Smith, ed., *The St. Clair Papers* . . . (Cincinnati: R. Clarke & Co., 1882); and Bernard C. Steiner, *The Life and Correspondence of James McHenry* . . . (Cleveland: Burrows Brothers Co., 1907). Henry Dearborn's papers are unpublished, but they served as the basis for the study of Dearborn by Richard Erney cited above. Of considerable value, too, are the volumes pertaining to the 1790s in Harold C. Syrett, ed., *The Papers of Alexander Hamilton*, 26 vols. (New York: Columbia University Press, 1961–1979).

CHAPTER 4

From Peaceable Coercion to Balanced Forces, 1807–1815

HARRY L. COLES

On 22 June 1807, just outside territorial waters, the U.S. frigate *Chesapeake* was fired on at practically point blank range by the British ship *Leopard*. After sustaining brutal punishment for about fifteen minutes, the American ship surrendered, and British officers came on board and took four seamen who were allegedly deserters from the Royal Navy. With three men killed and eight seriously wounded, *Chesapeake* hobbled back to Norfolk. There were of course many other instances of British impressment, but earlier episodes involved merchant vessels, not armed naval vessels. News of the outrage reached President Jefferson on 25 June and rapidly spread throughout the East Coast. The president said that nothing had so affected the country since the battle of Concord and he doubted even that encounter had produced such unity of feeling. Assurances of support poured in upon the president from all sections of the country, producing that great consensus he had always wanted. Congress and the people were now prepared to follow wherever he might lead. But instead of asking for a declaration of war or vigorous preparedness measures, Jefferson decided to deal with—and exploit—the crisis on three levels. His policy for the next several weeks was to preserve and enhance, while at the same time controlling and containing, public indignation against Great Britain; to launch a diplomatic offensive aimed at persuading Great Britain to disavow and to make reparations for the attack on the *Chesapeake*; and to deal with the immediate crisis arising from the presence of British ships in Norfolk and other American ports.

Good sense as well as international usage suggested that a government be allowed time and opportunity to disavow what might have been an unauthorized act by one of its agents. Hence it was decided in cabinet to send a small armed vessel, *Revenge*, to England with instructions for the American minister, James Monroe, to demand a disavowal of this particular act and the general practice of searching public armed vessels; restoration of the men taken; and a recall of Admiral Sir George Berkeley, who had ordered the search. Had Monroe's instructions ended here, he might have succeeded with reasonable promptitude. But apparently Jefferson felt that the *Chesapeake* affair gave him additional leverage in dealing with Great Britain. Hence the instructions, drawn up by Secretary of State James Madison, forbade Monroe to agree to any settlement that did not provide for the abolition of impressment from American merchant vessels on the high seas. "Reparation for the past, and security for the future," was the phrase repeated in Jefferson's private letters.[1] The cabinet also discussed whether Congress should be summoned before its regular December session. The decision was to call Congress in October, by which time it was hoped that *Revenge* would have returned with the answer of the British government.

Just as interesting as the substance of these measures is the manner in which they were carried out. Jefferson made no effort to publicize his measures and made no general announcement of his plans for the future. His biographer says: "He would not endanger diplomacy by publicizing its processes."[2] Probably this was part of his plan, but one suspects there was more to his method. Although Jefferson felt strongly that he should defer to Congress in legislative matters, he jealously guarded the president's prerogative in foreign affairs. At the moment he had no clear-cut policy and wanted none, unless the play for time can be regarded as a policy. Jefferson knew that the problems of the United States grew out of the general European war and the war might take a new turn or be ended at any time.

One of the president's immediate concerns was to retain control, and therefore he had to prevent further clashes. The Norfolk district presented a potentially explosive situation to which he turned his personal attention. On 2 July he issued a proclamation terminating the hospitality hitherto enjoyed by the Royal Navy in American ports and required all armed vessels to depart. Though he referred to "uncontrolled abuses," he did not denounce the *Chesapeake* affair as an act of war and he issued no ultimatum. Even before the president's proclamation, a citizens' committee of Norfolk had published a resolution calling for the suspension of any communication between the Americans and the British. It was to this local ordinance, rather than to the president's proclamation, that a local British commander reacted with anger. On 3 July a British squadron under Commodore J. E. Douglas sailed into Hampton Roads, sounded the passage to Norfolk, and began a blockade. Incensed at what he considered an insult to the British flag, Commodore Douglas pointed out that he had the power to obstruct all trade in the Chesapeake Bay. In a spirited reply the mayor of Norfolk, Richard E. Lee, informed the British officer that the people of Norfolk were prepared to receive the worst he could send. If His Majesty's officers were unwilling to await the settlement of the *Chesapeake* affair by the two governments, then they must accept the responsibility for commencing hostilities.

Genuinely alarmed at the situation, Jefferson instructed the governor of Virginia, William H. Cabell, to call out the militia. Only such portions as Cabell thought necessary for local defense were to be called immediately to duty; the remainder should be put in a state of readiness, but not called out until given further notice. These measures may have caused Commodore Douglas to have second thoughts and his ire may have been further tempered when David Erskine, the British minister to the United States, advised him to avoid all hostile measures until His Majesty's commands were made known. By 11 July Jefferson could report that the officers of the British ships had "solemnly protested they mean no further proceeding without further orders."[3] While encouraging a cooling off in every way he could, Jefferson assured the Virginia militia that in enforcing his proclamation of 2 July, "force is to be employed without reserve or hesitation." When no further incidents occurred and the crisis passed, Jefferson advised Governor Cabell to discharge about 2,000 militiamen who had been called in the emergency. "This is rendered expedient," he explained, "not only that we may husband from the beginning those resources which will probably be put to long trial, but from a regard to the health of those in service, which cannot fail to be greatly endangered during the sickly season now commencing and the discouragement, which would thence arise, to that ardor of public spirit now prevailing."[4] It was the end of July and Jefferson had in mind not only the welfare of the militia but his own concerns. Having dismissed the troops, he headed for Monticello where he could preserve his health during the sickly season, attend to private affairs, and plan his next moves.

During the summer Jefferson repeatedly said that he did not expect satisfaction from England, that the public mind was made up for war, and that he considered war inevitable.[5] Jefferson's statements, however, belie the fact that the president was stalling for time, rather than planning or preparing for war.

On 25 July Secretary of the Treasury Albert Gallatin sent Jefferson a long memorandum setting forth the measures that should be taken to prepare for war. Gallatin's memo is an impressive paper, comparable in its thoroughness and sophistication to some of the better planning papers produced by the Operations Plans Division of the War Department in World War II. Divided generally into defensive and offensive measures, it gave due consideration to enemy capabilities, American resources, and national strategy.

In view of what happened five years later, it is interesting to note what Gallatin recommended with regard to strategy. "Lower Canada," he said, "must be taken as far down as Montreal, to cut up the communication with Indians and Upper Canada. The taking of Quebec will better secure the object. At all events, it would be better to have the seat of war between Montreal and Quebec than predatory incursions at home." Moreover, Gallatin recommended extending the offensive beyond the line of the St. Lawrence, to include an attack on the maritime provinces aimed at threatening or perhaps taking Halifax, the main British naval base in North America.

Gallatin estimated manpower needs for both defensive and offensive operations at 30,000 regulars and militiamen. And where were the troops to come from? For Upper Canada: Ohio and Kentucky; for the Niagara area: upper Pennsylvania and the western parts of New York; for Lower Canada: from New York principally; for New Brunswick and Nova Scotia: principally from New Hampshire,

Massachusetts, and Rhode Island. From the states south of Pennsylvania, he would draw nothing for the North, because the men there were too distant and not used to the climate.[6]

Gallatin produced a useful plan, but it had defects. He mentioned the salt water navy only in a defensive role; he made little mention of the navy on the lakes; and he made no mention of privateering. Another glaring omission was the political factor, but it must be remembered that Gallatin wrote his memo at a time of near unanimous support for war. Finally, he assumed complete success all along the line in a single campaign.

Whatever its defects, Gallatin's plan provided a sound basis for putting the country on a war footing. Jefferson did not record his opinion of this document. He made no use of it except in its defensive phases, and even that only partially. Gallatin's approach to the question of national defense was direct and unambiguous; Jefferson's mind, however, ranged over a wide spectrum of possibilities. He was trying to see the world situation as a whole and to manipulate a complex equation to benefit his country. After the *Chesapeake* incident Jefferson wrote William Duane, editor of the *Philadelphia Aurora*, that Russia was the country most worthy to be cultivated since its interests, particularly with regard to neutral rights, coincided with those of the United States. Jefferson lauded the virtue but patronized the intelligence of Alexander I. "He is not of the very first order of understanding, but he is of a high one. . . . Our nation being like his, habitually neutral, our interests as to neutral rights and our sentiments agree."[7]

In addition to his project of persuading neutrals of the world to act together, Jefferson looked to science as a means of challenging England's tyranny on the seas. During the summer he encouraged Robert Fulton's experiments with torpedoes (in modern parlance, mines), but he was even more hopeful that the submarine would bring about a revolution in naval warfare.[8] These international and technological developments might alter power equations of the world for the better, but obviously they would take time; and time was quickly running out. While still at Monticello, Jefferson was informed of the Peace of Tilsit, 7 July 1807, by which Russia withdrew from the Third Coalition against Napoleon and joined the French emperor's Continental System. This reversal meant that Jefferson could no longer hope for aid from Russia and economic warfare between France and England would enter into high gear.

Returning to Washington early in October, Jefferson began work on a message to Congress. Since nothing had been heard from *Revenge*, he did not know the outcome of his negotiations. But it was clear that the intervening weeks had brought no improvement: lacking fresh provocation the war sentiment had subsided, the hope of manipulating the European situation through Russia had vanished, and the outlook for neutrals had darkened. With these developments in the background and probably in the hope of maintaining public indignation, the first draft of Jefferson's message to Congress was belligerent in tone. Asked for advice, Gallatin said that he would "wish its general color and expression to be softened."[9] Working through two more drafts, Jefferson presented a message that was mild and vague. The greatest amount of space was devoted to explaining and justifying the precautionary measures taken since the *Chesapeake* affair. The appropriations for seaport towns and harbors and the existing gunboats had been assigned principally to New York, Charleston, and New Orleans as the places most likely to suffer in case of attack. In gathering additional military stores for the magazines, the president had exceeded available appropriations, but he hoped Congress would understand and approve. As for expanding the regular army and navy, the president advised Congress to await information expected shortly from Europe.[10]

The information so long awaited arrived at the end of November. George Canning, the British foreign secretary, disavowed the actions of Admiral Berkeley but maintained that in issuing his proclamation of 2 July, Jefferson had taken reparations into his own hands. Turning the whole case around, Canning insisted Great Britain was the injured party and categorically refused to link the settlement of the *Chesapeake* incident with the general issue of impressment.

With every dispatch from Europe, the picture darkened. A proclamation signed by George III on 16 October 1807 reasserted the right, regardless of any naturalization papers they might possess, to remove British seamen from neutral merchant vessels and even claimed the right to take them from war vessels under prescribed procedures. This was followed by the British order in council of 11 November which blockaded all ports of Europe from which the British flag was excluded. About the same time Napoleon made it clear that his Berlin Decree, which closed the Continent to all British products, applied to the United States as well as to other nations. The rival systems of orders and decrees would go to further lengths, but by December 1807 it was evident that the United States was caught between the upper and nether millstones. As Jefferson explained to one of his friends: "The whole world is . . . laid under interdict by these two nations and our vessels, their cargoes, and crews are to be taken by one or the other, for whatever place they may be destined, out of our limits."[11]

Faced with such a situation, the president reconsidered his options. Since the end of June he had been stalling, but time had served merely to eliminate one option after another. By early December Jefferson concluded: "What is good in this case cannot be effected; we have therefore only to find out what will be *least* bad."[12] Madison apparently took the lead in advocating an embargo. Gallatin, who earlier had favored planning and preparing for war, said, "I also think an embargo for a limited time will at this moment be preferable in itself, and less objectionable in Congress." But he quickly added: "In every point of view, privations, sufferings, revenues, effect on the enemy, politics at home, etc. I prefer war to a permanent embargo." It is clear that while Gallatin wished to get American ships and sailors home, he regarded the embargo only as the lesser of evils for the time being. Prophetically he warned: "Governmental prohibitions do always more mischief than had been calculated."[13]

On the very day he received this warning, 18 December, Jefferson sent Congress a bundle of recent communications on the state of war in Europe with the casual remark that Congress would "doubtless perceive all the advantages which may be expected from an inhibition of the departure of our vessels from the ports of the United States." Equally casually, he added: "Their wisdom will also see the necessity of making every preparation for whatever events may grow out of the present crisis." No arguments for the embargo and no specific suggestions concerning the army or navy were presented.[14]

Meeting behind closed doors, the Senate passed the embargo bill after a single day of discussion and the House required only three days of deliberation. The bill prohibiting American vessels from sailing to foreign ports and foreign vessels from taking on cargoes in the United States received the president's signature on 22 December 1807. Since there is no record of what was said in Congress and since the president communicated no supporting arguments, the administration's reasons for introducing this measure remain unclear. One day after the bill became law, however, a series of anonymous articles began to appear in the administration organ, the *National Intelligencer*. These articles had to be written by an insider with advance information and in all likelihood the author was Secretary of State Madison. At any rate the author represented the embargo as both precautionary and coercive in its aims. The recent actions of the warring powers left no alternative but "a dignified retirement within ourselves; a watchful preservation of our resources." But much more could be expected: "It is singularly fortunate that an embargo, whilst it guards our essential resources, will have the collateral effect of making it to the interest of all nations to change the system which has driven our commerce from the ocean." While recognizing that the embargo would involve sacrifices on the part of Americans, the author maintained that the deprivations soon to be felt by the British and French, especially in supplying their colonies, would be greater and would induce those powers to alter their policies. "With other injured nations there may be no choice but between disgraceful submission or war. A benignant providence has given to this nation a happy resource for avoiding both." Tongue in cheek, one historian has noted: "As thus described, the God-given embargo was little short of a flawless weapon."[15]

It is unlikely that Gallatin, on whose shoulders the enforcement of the law would fall, shared all this optimism; from first to last he made it clear that he favored the embargo only as a temporary means of getting ready for war. As to what other Republicans thought, it is difficult to say. Jefferson's biographer, who has made a minute study of the question, concludes: "Nobody knew just what it would lead to—peace or war or a redress of grievances—and anybody was at liberty to see in the measure what he wanted to."[16]

People could find whatever they wanted in the measure, but few Americans then or later realized the magnitude of the undertaking. The embargo was not unprecedented: economic pressure had been used during the American Revolution and during the 1790s, but on former occasions it was used as one of several means of seeking redress. At the time of the earlier experiments, furthermore, the United States possessed a relatively simple and unintegrated economy in which dislocations were apt to be felt locally but have little national impact. By the time of the embargo, the northern states earned what cash they had by trade; the southern by export; and the middle by a combination of the two. Never before in the history of the Republic—and never since—was the economy seized root and branch and wielded as an instrument of foreign and military policy.

Until the actual enactment of the embargo and for several weeks afterward, Jefferson seems to have regarded it as a precautionary measure, a means of saving seamen and property. But as time went by the emphasis shifted from the precautionary to the coercive aspects. On 15 May 1808 Jefferson wrote Gallatin: "I place immense value in the experiment being fully made, how far an embargo may be an effectual weapon in future as well as on this occasion."[17] As the administration attempted to enforce the law, it met with smuggling, evasion, and outright defiance. Jefferson asked for stricter laws and heavier fines, and Congress responded. The laws were progressively strengthened and more and more power was given to the executive.

Congress in April 1808 passed a law that gave the president power to suspend the embargo if conditions warranted. The effect of this law was to transform the embargo from a measure to preserve neutrality to a means of seeking an alliance. When the American ministers in London and Paris attempted to use this provision to obtain an alteration in maritime practices, they met with no success whatever. Several reasons account for the failure of the embargo as a coercive measure. Although shortages existed in England, none were of crucial proportions. The most vulnerable spot in England's economy was export, not import, and the embargo touched export only slightly. Furthermore, the British found alternatives to the American market in the Spanish colonies, where restrictions on trade ended after the Iberian rising against Napoleon in the spring of 1808.[18]

As Jefferson neared the end of his term, he faced the necessity of calling for stronger measures of enforcement or abandoning the embargo. He chose the latter course—but very reluctantly. One of the criticisms of Jefferson made by political opponents at the time and repeated by historians is that he was doctrinaire. Viewing his political career as a whole, this charge is not supportable. And yet in the case of the embargo, it must be admitted that he lost some of his usual flexibility; he came close to being doctrinaire. Jefferson believed he had failed for reasons beyond his or anybody else's control. He wrote to Monroe: "There never has been a situation of the world before in which such endeavors as we have made would not have secured our peace. It is probable there never will be such another."[19]

Ironically, Jefferson was right in the short run, but wrong in the long. A combination of circumstances by 1812 did induce Great Britain to abandon the orders in council; but a hundred years later in World War I, the United States as a neutral confronted as baffling a situation as Jefferson faced in 1807–1809.

Did Jefferson realistically prepare for war while giving peaceable coercion a fair trial? It is not possible to give an unqualified answer to this question. Jefferson developed something close to an obsession about the embargo: he yearned during the last months of his presidency to teach Europe yet another useful lesson. Thus, it cannot be said that he gave wholehearted and constant attention to preparation for war. But he did make an effort, and he never ceased to try to create the kind of army he thought a republic ought to have.

Though refusing to make any fundamental change in the militia system, Congress did improve the method of providing arms. In the original militia law of 1792, the problem of providing arms had been solved by the simple expedient of requiring each man to furnish his own musket. In the spring of 1808, Congress authorized an annual appropriation of $200,000 to be apportioned among the states to provide arms and military equipment. Unable to persuade Congress to go beyond this limited improvement, Jefferson asked for an increase in the standing army. In fact, Secretary of War Henry Dearborn prepared a plan originally designed not only for passive defense, but for a military initiative against Canada as well. It will be recalled that the planning paper drawn up by Gallatin in the summer of 1807 called for 30,000 men to invade Canada. Jefferson knew that Congress would not enact a law calling for 30,000 regulars and even if the legislators did, he could not raise such a force. Hence Dearborn's plan called for an additional 6,000 regulars and a force of 24,000 volunteers. Congress ignored the plan for 24,000 volunteers, but on 12 April 1808 enacted a law calling for 6,000 additional regulars to bring the standing army to a total strength on paper of 10,000 men. Actual strength reached nearly 7,000 men in 1809, but thereafter declined until war was declared.[20]

Madison's concept of the presidency and the role of the executive was essentially the same as Jefferson's. Both men believed that the executive should faithfully carry out the laws but should not encroach on Congress's legislative prerogatives. Hence their formal communications with Congress were quite similar in tone. But if one looks to the actual conduct of the office during the two administrations, there were significant differences. Although he subscribed to a self-denying theory, Jefferson in fact was a strong president—at least for about six of his eight years in office. In the case of Madison, theory and practice tended to coincide; or to put it another way: personal limitations reinforced theoretical ones. In contrast to Jefferson, Madison never had firm control of his own cabinet, let alone extensive influence with his party or with Congress.

On matters of substance the two presidents had much in common: both retained a fondness for the embargo even after it was discarded, and both had little faith in a stronger military. Madison spent practically the whole of his first term trying to find some form of peaceable coercion that might work. His belief in moral and legal considerations was more doctrinaire than Jefferson's. On matters pertaining to the army and navy, Madison was less well informed, less flexible, and, if possible, less interested than Jefferson.

Until well into Madison's administration, the United States was in excellent financial condition and could afford to build up its armed strength. On 8 December 1809, however, Secretary of the Treasury Gallatin reported a deficit of $3,000,000; he proposed to make up part of this sum by cutting army and navy expenditures by 50 percent. By this time there was strong opposition to Gallatin not only in the Federalist party but also within a faction of the Republican party known as the Invisibles. Aware of this opposition, Madison did not wish to restrain Gallatin and possibly lose a man for whom he had the highest regard. The president therefore allowed the secretary to recommend his budget cuts to Congress. Only a few weeks afterwards, however, Madison himself recommended a substantial, though not extensive, program for strengthening national defenses. He suggested that Congress renew the act (due to expire on 30 March 1810) authorizing the federal government to call 100,000 men from the state militias in case of emergency and repeated Jefferson's often made but never adopted plan of classifying and organizing the militia in such manner "as will best insure prompt and successful aids from that source." In addition he asked Congress for a force of 20,000 volunteers. Thus, Congress had before it contradictory recommendations and could pick and choose what tune it wanted to hear.[21]

But even if the administration had presented a united front for improving the army, it is unlikely the Congress would have reacted favorably. By 1810 leaders in both parties had reason to suspect that money spent on the army was soapsuds down a rat hole. The leadership of the army, both military and civilian, was weak and vacillating. Secretary of War William Eustis was a veteran of the American Revolution, but his knowledge of military affairs was limited and he was even more of a penny pincher than his predecessor Henry Dearborn. The ranking brigadier was James Wilkinson, noted mainly for his appetite for money, women, and intrigue. Over the course of a long career, Wilkinson's name was linked with several disreputable episodes.[22]

It was against a background of mismanagement and neglect that Congress considered the conflicting recommendations on army policy. John Randolph, a simon-pure Jeffersonian Republican, led off the debate by introducing a resolution that the army and navy be reduced. In the course of the discussion, it became clear that it was not just the old Republicans who were disillusioned with the armed forces. Henry Adams later commented: "Three fourths of the Republican party and all the Federalists were of the same mind with Randolph— that any army led by Wilkinson and a navy of gunboats . . . were not worth maintaining."[23] But Congress was just as incapable of moving along a consistent course as the administration. Although it passed a motion to reduce both the army and the navy, the House proceeded to turn down bills for actually carrying out the resolutions.

It was obvious by the summer of 1811 that American diplomacy had reached a dead end and that the military capability of the country had fallen to its lowest point since the founding of the Republic. The demand for new departures and stronger measures came from the bottom up. The very sections of the country— the South and the West—that had borne the self-denying measures most patiently at length lost their patience. In the congressional elections of 1810–1811, nearly half of the incumbents lost their seats. Disgusted by what they considered the do-nothing policies of recent years, a new generation of legislators demanded and got action. Among the new congressmen were John C. Calhoun from the piedmont area of South Carolina; Felix Grundy, an Anglophobe from the frontier settlement of Nashville, Tennessee; Peter B. Porter from the Niagara frontier of New York; and John Adams Harper, a firebrand from New Hampshire. These and other so-called War Hawks elected Henry Clay of Kentucky as Speaker. Though only thirty-four years old at the time, Clay had already served in the Senate, but had switched to the House where he believed he could be more effective. Hitherto the Speaker had been little more than a presiding officer; Clay proceeded to give the office power and prestige. Packing the principal committees with War Hawks, Clay was determined to move ahead with preparations for war.

From the time it met in November 1811, the Twelfth Congress took on a new tone. Was the executive branch in step? Madison's biographer says that the president probably made up his mind for war in the summer of 1811.[24] If so, there is room for doubt that his mind was completely made up. When Madison delivered his third annual message on 5 November, he repeated the old litany of grievances that had been part of presidential messages since 1805 and added some fresh examples of British perfidy. His conclusion must have been something of a disappointment to the most ardent spirits: "With this evidence of hostile inflexibility in trampling on rights which no independent nation can relinquish, Congress will feel the duty of putting the United States into an armor and an attitude demanded by the crisis, and corresponding with the national spirit and expectations."[25]

Congress responded with reasonable promptness. The House Committee on Foreign Affairs, headed by Peter B. Porter, presented a report that recommended bringing the regular army up to authorized strength, adding 10,000 regulars and 50,000 volunteers, and outfitting existing warships. By 19 December all the resolutions offered by the committee were carried in the House by comfortable majorities. But the vote on the resolutions suggested a unanimity that did not exist. Some Federalists voted with the War Hawks, hoping to bring on a war that would discredit the Republicans and return the Federalists to power. Some Republicans called Scarecrows voted for preparations not with the idea of fighting a war, but with the object of deterring one. To frighten Great Britain, the naval vessel *Hornet* was sent to Europe laden with warlike resolutions, newspapers with patriotic editorials, and records of the debates in Congress.[26]

After the Christmas recess Congress took up the defense and tax measures to put the resolutions into effect. The Committee on Foreign Affairs recommended that the army be brought up to its authorized strength of 10,000 men and that an additional force of 10,000 be raised for three years. When this bill came before the House, it was opposed by some, including John Randolph, who repeated the ancient arguments about the dangers of standing armies. William Branch Giles, the Republican senator from Virginia, followed a different tack. An inveterate enemy of both Madison and Gallatin, Giles brought in a bill to raise a force of 25,000 regulars in addition to the existing 10,000. Knowing such an army could not be raised, Giles hoped to embarrass the administration. The War Hawks, however, called his bluff and passed the measure on 9 January 1812. Thus, at least on paper, the regular army was increased to 35,000.[27]

During the debate the possibility of invading Canada as a means of winning maritime concessions was raised. It was recognized that the regular army, scattered as it was among various posts, could not be enlarged and concentrated in time to invade Canada in 1812. Hence a bill authorizing the president to accept 50,000 volunteers was introduced. Though called "volunteers," these recruits would in effect be militia since they were to be officered by state authorities. Soon there arose the question of whether the president had the constitutional authority to send militia outside the territorial limits of the United States. Even some of the most ardent War Hawks maintained that the president had no such authority. In order to get the bill on the statute books, the constitutional question was simply ignored. Of these preparedness measures the president remarked: "With a view to enable the Executive to step at once into Canada they have provided after two months parlay for a regular force requiring twelve to raise it, and after three months for a volunteer force, on terms not likely to raise it at all for that purpose."[28] The legislation with regard to the army was weak enough, but for the navy Congress would provide no additional strength whatever. When a bill to build twelve ships of the line and twenty frigates was brought in, a combination of the Pennsylvania delegation, southerners, and westerners sent it down to defeat. One historian remarks: "With it died the chance of strengthening the war spirit in coastal areas."[29]

Obviously the War Hawks and other members of Congress were still of a divided mind. The preparedness measures were woefully inadequate either as deterrents of war or as genuine preparation for fighting. Nevertheless, by the spring of 1812, the country was on a new tack and, barring some dramatic development, retreat would be difficult. One of the last excuses for delay was removed when the *Hornet* returned on 22 May with news from Europe. The vessel brought supplementary instructions to Augustus John Foster, the British minister, but they merely repeated what had been said before: since the French had not in fact repealed their decrees, Britain could not repeal her orders in council. With no relief in sight and having exhausted every diplomatic avenue, President Madison notified Congress and war was declared on 18 June.

In most situations a declaration of war unites a people, releases energies, and subordinates selfish ambitions to general goals. Such was not the case in the War of 1812. At no time was there anything approaching general harmony and unity of effort; rather, for the most part it was business as usual and politics as usual. Next to the fighting in Vietnam, the War of 1812 was perhaps the most unpopular war in American history. Real enthusiasm was to be found only in the South and the West and even in those sections for only about a year. The war received support along party lines in the middle states and from a minority of the populace in New England. But it was opposed by Federalists generally and especially by New England Federalists who denounced the whole affair as "Mr. Madison's war." The opposition, and the location of the opposition, greatly affected the conduct of the war in all its phases, especially when it came to organization, manpower, and strategy.

A few weeks before war was declared, President Madison recommended that the secretary of war be given two assistant secretaries. In support of this modest proposal, one friend of the administration declared: "In the wretched, deplorably wretched organization of the War Department it is impossible either to begin a war or to conduct it. In its present organization, it is a mere counting house establishment." John Randolph saw the matter in a different light and helped to defeat the administration's attempt to improve the organization of the War Department. "This system, if pursued, will effectually create all our great departments of government into sinecures."[30] Other than a modest increase in the number of clerks, the secretary never, even after the beginning of hostilities, received any substantial increase in his civilian staff who were engaged in record keeping as well as dealing with accounts and claims of former soldiers and with Indian affairs.

Even in administering the vastly increased army, the secretary had only weak and uncertain assistance. During the American Revolution there had been a commander in chief; but in the War of 1812, there was no central military authority and only a weak headquarters staff. Early in the war Henry Dearborn, who had served as secretary of war under Jefferson, was made a major general; yet though he outranked all other generals, he never exercised command over the army as a whole. The country was divided into geographical divisions, and at the head of each of these divisions was a brigadier general who was responsible directly to the secretary.

After military defeats along the Canadian border in 1812–1813, a General Staff was created; but it differed in significant ways from the modern organization of the same name. The 1813 General Staff included the following departments: quartermaster, engineering, topographical engineering, adjutant and inspector general (both functions performed by the same officer), ordnance, hospital, purchasing, and pay. The principal officers of these departments did not act as a body and they were not concerned with broad policy and planning. Rather, they were more akin to what today is called a special staff.[31]

The establishment of the General Staff has often been hailed as a far-reaching step that relieved the overburdened secretary of some of his housekeeping duties. That it was a step in the right direction can scarcely be denied, but whether it produced any immediate benefits during the war seems doubtful, as can be shown by looking more closely at the situation with regard to supply. The act establishing the General Staff provided for the appointment of eight quartermasters general (one for each geographical division), eight deputy quartermasters general, and thirty-two assistant deputy quartermasters general. The quartermaster general attached to the principal army was to have the brevet rank and pay of a brigadier; all other quartermasters general were to have the rank of colonel.[32]

Soon after this legislation was passed, Robert Swartout succeeded Morgan Lewis as the quartermaster general of the principal army in the Ninth Military District with headquarters in Albany, New York. During the war Swartout never resided in Washington. Except for estimates that included all forces, he never exercised general jurisdiction over the Quartermaster's Department, and orders to other quartermasters general were issued not by his office but by the secretary of war.[33] The 1813 legislation clearly left considerable discretion to the secretary in defining the duties of the General Staff. In working out regulations Secretary John Armstrong and his successors tended to make the General Staff a permanent management staff of the War Department, but this was an accomplishment of several years, not a few months. In the area of military administration, the main contribution of the War of 1812 was to emphasize the need for reform; the war itself was fought with little improvement over the Revolution.

Organizational problems were matters of concern primarily to the executive branch and certain congressional committees. Manpower problems, on the other hand, touched the people directly and had to be handled with attention to public opinion. During the course of the conflict, Congress lurched from one crisis to another, passing a series of measures that were incoherent, overlapping, and self-defeating. Manpower policies were improvised without any fundamental guidelines other than injunctions to maintain the Republican principles of minimal government and states' rights.

A brief review of the wartime legislation will suffice to show how quickly the government exhausted the possibilities allowed by these self-imposed restrictions. When the war broke out, the administration sought to raise three types of forces: 35,000 regulars, 50,000 volunteers, and 100,000 militiamen allotted among the various states. Congress hoped to recruit a regular army for a period of five years by offering to pay privates five dollars per month as well as a sixteen dollar bounty at enlistment and three months' pay and 160 acres of land on discharge. The volunteer army was to be raised on the same basis, except that the volunteers had to serve only one year. Under these terms, however, fewer than 20,000 regulars enlisted during the first year, and the federal volunteer program fared even worse: only about 5,000 men served in it during the first year. The military defeats, the refusal of some state governors to answer the government's call for troops, and the unsteadiness of the militia soon convinced Congress to rely primarily on the regular force. In January 1813 Congress therefore approved legislation increasing the enlistment bounty to twenty-four dollars, raising the authorized strength of the regular army to above 60,000 men, repealing the earlier laws relating to volunteers, and reducing the term of service to one year. As a result of other similar enactments, the period of enlistment went up and down like a yoyo. By the middle of 1813, the regular army had some recruits serving for one year, some for eighteen months, others for five years, and still others for the duration.[34]

But neither shorter enlistments, higher pay, nor increased bonuses produced a regular army of the size needed. In 1813 the United States achieved naval control of Lake Erie, retook Detroit, and secured the Northwest from invasion, but was unable to carry out a major invasion of Canada. At the beginning of 1814, Secretary of War John Armstrong reported that the army stood at about half its authorized strength, but even these figures masked the gravity of the situation. An abstract furnished by the adjutant general gave the number of regular troops as 23,614—adding that "although the numerical force in January 1814 was 23,614 the actual strength was less than half that number. . . . "[35] In an effort to correct this situation, Congress passed no fewer than five laws in January and February 1814. Still unwilling to resort to a draft, the legislators attempted to fill the ranks by increasing the bounties in land and money.[36]

After the burning of Washington and the suspension of specie payment by most banks, Congress met in September 1814 in order to raise additional men and money to continue the war. In place of the discredited Armstrong, President Madison asked James Monroe to take over the War Department in addition to his duties as secretary of state. Since the Capitol was a smoke-stained hull, Congress met in the incommodious old Patent Office Building. In such circumstances the congressmen proved willing to consider desperate measures, and they asked Monroe for his recommendations. Pointing out that the Treasury Department had been unable to pay the bounties due the few recruits who had enlisted during the last three months, Monroe attributed the failure of recruiting to the higher bounties paid for substitutes in the militia. To invade Canada and to defend the coastal areas against incursions, a regular army of 100,000 men would be necessary. In an attempt to break completely with Republican dogma, Monroe recommended that the federal government deal directly with the individual without the states as intermediaries. Stoutly he affirmed both the need and the legality of a draft. Realizing that his party was probably unready for so drastic a change, he then outlined four possible plans for Congress to consider. The last of these—the one Monroe considered least desirable—was to continue the existing system with an increase in the land bounty. After much debate, Congress opted for continuing the old system.[37] News of the Peace of Ghent reached the United States a few weeks after this measure was enacted.

There were grave weaknesses in organization and manpower, but some historians feel that the greatest weakness was in strategy. According to this view, the Americans failed to formulate and carry out an effective strategy because they lacked an intellectual grasp of the geographical situation confronting them. With admirable perspicuity one historian writes: "From England came almost everything that made Canadian defense possible—the arms and munitions, the red coated regiments . . . and from Montreal they passed to Upper Canada by the great river or by primitive roads along its banks. There was no alternative means of communication, and the interruption of this line would necessarily cause the whole of Upper Canada west of the point of severance to fall into American hands." In failing to understand these simple facts of geography, the Americans exhibited "perverse stupidity" and lack of "common sense."[38]

Such a view vastly oversimplifies the strategic problem and ignores political and logistical considerations. Gallatin, in his comprehensive plan drawn up soon after the *Chesapeake* incident, clearly demonstrated a firm grasp of the importance of the Montreal-Quebec line. General Dearborn had grave defects as a field officer, but early in the war he recommended an advance against Montreal by way of Lake Champlain. President Madison's knowledge of things military was limited, but he too had no difficulty in recognizing the essentials of the strategic problem. Writing to Dearborn, he maintained that the United States should have concentrated a force that "could have seized Montreal, and thus at one stroke, have secured the upper province, and cut off the sap that nourished Indian hostilities."[39] Thus, the American leaders at the time saw the essentials of the strategic problem clearly; they simply lacked the physical means for implementation of a winning strategy.

Early in the war President Madison requested the governors of New England to order into service as many men as General Dearborn considered necessary "for the defense of the sea coast." Regular troops, the president explained, would be marching to the northern frontier. The Constitution provides that the militia can be called into federal service to suppress insurrection, to repel invasion, and to execute the laws of the United States. The Federalist governors of Massachusetts and Connecticut informed the president that the determination of when these exigencies existed would be made by themselves rather than by the federal government. This haughty response precluded convenient federal use of the best and most conveniently located militia and made it impossible to launch a strong invasion of Canada in 1812. "The seditious opposition in Massachusetts and Connecticut," wrote Madison, "with the intrigues elsewhere . . . have so clogged the wheels of the war that I fear the campaign will not accomplish the object of it." Poor enlistment, the president added, "leaves us dependent for every primary operation on militia, either as volunteers or draughts for six months."[40]

With the opposition in a position to withhold men, money, and moral support in such a way as to frustrate the main object, something less than an ideal strategy had to be found. The emphasis had to be shifted to the West, not because quick and decisive results could be achieved there, but because those were the areas where manpower and support could be assembled. Postponement of concentration was excusable in 1812; it was less so in later years of the war. At no time was there adequate coordination of effort and none of the commanders in the field knew what was expected of him in relation to other commanders. There was a strategy, but it was inadequately developed and inadequately communicated to those expected to carry it out. This generalization applies not only to 1812, but to all three unsuccessful campaigns against Canada.

It was not until the war was practically over that a sound strategic plan was developed. Soon after the burning of Washington, James Monroe wrote the president: "I have been twice brought into [the War Department] by circumstances. . . . I made arrangements for the campaign of 1813, and had I continued in the Department would have conducted it on different principles from those observed by General Armstrong. I must now lay the foundation for the next campaign.''[41] Over the next several weeks, Monroe matured his plan, and on 6 February 1815 General Jacob Brown arrived in Washington to discuss strategy. General Brown, along with Winfield Scott, was one of the few able generals to emerge from the war. Brown, too, had been laying plans for the next campaign and was gratified to learn that his ideas and those of the secretary of war corresponded very closely. The new plan was superior to those that had preceded it because it called for concentration on the crucial east end of the British line of communications and subordinated all other considerations to this. The general plan was Monroe's, but the execution would be left to Brown. Given the opportunity, there seems little doubt that this able and energetic man would have exerted every effort to make the plan work.

The United States now had a well-thought-out and coordinated strategy and an able general to carry it out, but formidable obstacles remained. Lower Canada was crawling with British troops, many of them experienced and well-equipped veterans of the Napoleonic wars; the Treasury was empty, Congress had as yet found no means of raising an army; and the Hartford Convention had met and concerted its plans for opposing the war and the federal government. Whether this last campaign against Canada would have succeeded in such circumstances, there is no means of knowing. Before he reached his headquarters near the Canadian frontier, General Brown learned that the peace treaty ending the war had been signed.

But the influence of the experience along the Canadian border and the slow maturing of plans did not end with the peace. As commander of the Northern Division (1815–1821) and as commanding general of the army (1821–1828), General Brown repeatedly indicated the importance he attached to the Lake Champlain route to Canada. One of his ideas—never realized—was to construct a fortress on the American bank of the St. Lawrence so that in case of another conflict, cutting the line of communications would be facilitated. Another idea resulting from the war experience was the beginning of two military roads to the St. Lawrence—one running west from Plattsburg, the other east from Sackett's Harbor. These projects were initiated as the result of a tour of inspection of the northern frontier made by President Monroe in 1817.

Thus in the field of strategy, as in the fields of organization and manpower, the most efficacious measures were adopted only after the war was over. Even the greatest military victory, the Battle of New Orleans, came after the peace treaty was signed. Historians have argued and in all probability will continue to argue about the military significance of the Battle of New Orleans. Nearly all agree, however, that this battle had tremendous psychological significance. Twice within a few years—once in the autumn of 1811 and again in the autumn of 1814—the country had faced crises in which it was unable to defend itself or to exercise true independence in a hostile world. The victory at New Orleans and the unrelated but welcome peace that followed tended to blot out the memory of earlier defeats and disasters. The people emerged from the conflict convinced they had won, and a wave of nationalism swept the country.

Influenced by the new nationalism, Congress made provisions after the war for a permanent army of 10,000 men and appropriated $1 million to build nine ships of the line and twelve 44s.[42] William H. Crawford succeeded Monroe as secretary of war in 1815 and set about immediately to remedy some of the defects made evident by the war. Concerning the General Staff, Crawford advised Congress, "The experience of the two first campaigns of the last war furnished volumes of evidence upon this subject. . . . The stationary staff of a military establishment should be substantially the same in peace as in war." Congress approved Crawford's recommendation to make the General Staff a permanent part of the military establishment on 24 April 1816. The new secretary also secured an appropriation of nearly $1 million to launch a major program of fortifications.[43] There had thus been a complete change since 1807 from confidence in peaceable coercion to reliance on balanced forces. In the future men might argue about the size and composition of America's standing army, but few seriously questioned the need for a permanent national force after the war ended in 1815.

NOTES

1. Henry Adams, *History of the United States in the Administrations of Jefferson and Madison, 1801–1817*, 9 vols. (New York: Antiquarian Press, 1962), IV, 1–26; Dumas Malone, *Jefferson and His Time* (Boston: Little, Brown & Co., 1948–1981), vol. V, *Jefferson the President: Second Term, 1805–1809* (1974), 415–38; Bradford Perkins, *Prologue to War: England and the United States, 1805–1812* (Berkeley and Los Angeles: University of California Press, 1961), pp. 140–45.

2. Malone, *Second Term*, p. 427.

3. Jefferson to Barnabus Bedwell, 11 July 1807, in A. A. Lipscomb and A. E. Bergh, eds., *The Writings of Thomas Jefferson*, 20 vols. (Washington: Thomas Jefferson Memorial Association of the United States, 1903–1904), XI, 271–72.

4. Jefferson to Cabell, 24 and 27 July 1807, in Lipscomb, *Writings*, XI, 294–97.

5. See, for example, his letters to William Duane, 20 July 1807, and to J. Crowninshield, 3 September 1807, in Lipscomb, *Writings*, XI, 290–91, 357.

6. Gallatin to Jefferson, 25 July 1807, in Henry Adams, ed., *The Writings of Albert Gallatin*, 3 vols. (Philadelphia: J. B. Lippincott, 1879), I, 340–53.

7. Jefferson to William Duane, 20 July 1807, in Lipscomb, *Writings*, XI, 290–91.

8. Malone, *Second Term*, pp. 503–6.

9. Gallatin to Jefferson, 21 October 1807, in Adams, *Writings*, I, 358–64.

10. James D. Richardson, ed., *A Compilation of the Messages and Papers of the Presidents, 1789–1902*, 11 vols. (Washington: Bureau of National Literature and Art, 1905–1906), I, 425–30.

11. Jefferson to John Mason, ca. December 1807, in Lipscomb, *Writings*, XI, 401–2.

12. In making this remark Jefferson was commenting on the Non-Importation Act, but his comment indicates his general frame of mind. Jefferson to Gallatin, 3 December 1807, in Adams, *Writings*, I, 367.

13. Gallatin to Jefferson, 18 December 1807, in Adams, *Writings*, I, 368.

14. Richardson, *Messages*, I, 433.

15. Malone, *Second Term*, pp. 485–89.

16. Ibid., p. 487.

17. Lipscomb, *Writings*, XII, 56.

18. Perkins, *Prologue*, pp. 168–78.

19. Quoted in Malone, *Second Term*, p. 644.

20. Ibid., 516–17; Russell F. Weigley, *History of the United States Army*, enlarged ed. (Bloomington: Indiana University Press, 1984), p. 597.

21. Irving Brant, *James Madison*, 6 vols. (Indianapolis: Bobbs-Merrill, 1941–1961), V, 124; Richardson, *Messages*, I, 478–79.

22. James R. Jacobs, *The Beginning of the U.S. Army, 1783–1812* (Princeton, N.J.: Princeton University Press, 1947), pp. 270–71, 352–56.

23. Adams, *History*, V, 200.

24. Brant, *Madison*, V, 362–64, 390–92.

25. Richardson, *Messages*, I, 494.

26. Perkins, *Prologue*, pp. 356–59, 375–76.

27. Ibid., pp. 360–61.

28. Quoted in Reginald Horsman, *The War of 1812* (New York: Alfred A. Knopf, 1969), p. 20.

29. Perkins, *Prologue*, p. 362.

30. Quoted in Leonard D. White, *The Jeffersonians: A Study in Administrative History, 1801–1829* (New York: Macmillan Co., 1959), pp. 235–36.

31. Ibid., pp. 236–40.

32. Raphael P. Thian, comp., *Legislative History of the General Staff of the Army of the United States . . . from 1775 to 1901* (Washington: Government Printing Office, 1901), pp. 200–1.

33. Erna Risch, *Quartermaster Support of the Army: A History of the Corps, 1775–1939* (Washington: Government Printing Office, 1962), pp. 152–54.

34. Emory Upton, *The Military Policy of the United States from 1775* (Washington: Government Printing Office, 1904), p. 108; C. Joseph Bernardo and Eugene H. Bacon, *American Military Policy: Its Development Since 1775* (Harrisburg, Pa.: Military Service Publishing Co., 1955), pp. 124–27.

35. Adams, *History*, VII, 380–81.

36. Bernardo and Bacon, *Military Policy*, p. 132.

37. Marvin A. Kreidberg and Merton G. Henry, *History of Military Mobilization in the United States Army, 1775–1945* (Washington: Department of the Army, 1955), pp. 53–56.

38. C. P. Stacey, "An American Plan for a Canadian Campaign," *American Historical Review* 46 (January 1941): 348–58.

39. Brant, *Madison*, VI, 45, 53.

40. Ibid., VI, 50.

41. Quoted in Stacey, "An American Plan," 349.

42. Since this essay deals with the army, it makes only occasional reference to the navy in order to indicate the general picture. For naval policy see Linda Maloney, "The

War of 1812: What Role for Sea Power?'' in Kenneth J. Hagan, ed., *In Peace and War: Interpretations of American Naval History, 1775–1984*, 2d ed. (Westport, Conn.: Greenwood Press, 1984), pp. 46–62.

43. Chase C. Mooney, *William H. Crawford, 1772–1834* (Lexington: University Press of Kentucky, 1974), pp. 78–92.

FURTHER READING

The best modern survey of military policy from the American Revolution through the Vietnam War is Russell F. Weigley, *The American Way of War: A History of United States Military Strategy and Policy*, The Wars of the United States (New York: Macmillan Co., 1973). This classic may be supplemented by the same author's *History of the United States Army*, enlarged ed. (Bloomington: Indiana University Press, 1984). Older surveys include C. Joseph Bernardo and Eugene H. Bacon, *American Military Policy: Its Development Since 1775* (Harrisburg, Pa.: Military Service Publishing Co., 1955), and Emory Upton, *The Military Policy of the United States from 1775* (Washington: Government Printing Office, 1904).

The best general history treating all aspects of the era covered in this essay is Henry Adams, *History of the United States in the Administrations of Jefferson and Madison, 1801–1817*, 9 vols. (New York: Antiquarian Press, 1962). In spite of Adams's prejudices against both Jefferson and Madison, his account remains indispensable because of its thoroughness and breadth of vision. Some of Adams's misjudgments have been corrected by Dumas Malone in his six-volume biography, *Jefferson and His Time* (Boston: Little, Brown & Co., 1948–1981). In vol. V, *Jefferson the President: Second Term, 1805–1809* (1974), Malone made a minute study of the embargo, naval policy, military policy, and diplomacy. Merrill Peterson, *Thomas Jefferson and the New Nation* (New York: Oxford University Press, 1970) is an excellent summary of modern scholarship. Both the Malone and Peterson biographies are generally sympathetic to Jefferson and his policies. Irving Brant seeks to understand and defend Jefferson's successor against all criticism. Nevertheless, Brant, *James Madison: Commander in Chief*, 6 vols. (Indianapolis: Bobbs-Merrill, 1941–1961) is extremely valuable.

Nearly all the general histories of the War of 1812 concentrate primarily on operations rather than policy. This is true of Harry L. Coles, *The War of 1812* (Chicago: University of Chicago Press, 1965), but one can also find brief summaries of the causes and consequences of the war in this volume. More extended treatments may be found in Reginald Horsman, *The War of 1812* (New York: Alfred A. Knopf, 1969), and John K. Mahon, *The War of 1812* (Gainesville: University of Florida Press, 1972). For the administrative aspects of the war, see Leonard D. White, *The Jeffersonians: A Study in Administrative History, 1801–1829* (New York: Macmillan Co., 1959), a pioneering work that may be supplemented by Noble E. Cunningham, *The Process of Government Under Jefferson* (Princeton, N.J.: Princeton University Press, 1978).

CHAPTER 5

The Army in the Age of the Common Man, 1815–1845

WILLIAM B. SKELTON

From its formation in the 1780s to the end of the War of 1812, the dominant features of the United States Army had been administrative decentralization, fluctuating size and organization, and a rapid turnover of commissioned personnel. The army had expanded and contracted in relation to specific crises and the party composition of Congress, and had lacked a consistent, well-defined conception of its role. In contrast, the thirty years of general peace following the Treaty of Ghent were marked by institutional reform and consolidation. During this period the "old army" assumed the basic character it would retain into the early twentieth century.

The chief source of reform was the generation of young officers who had risen during the war to the middle and upper ranks of the officer corps. Although relatively few of these men had received formal military training, they had experienced directly the mismanagement and the repeated humiliations of the early war years. They also recalled with exaggerated pride the campaigns on the northern frontier in 1814, in which the army appeared to have achieved a degree of professional competence. In their opinion the Republic could not afford to rely again on the spontaneous mobilization of its citizenry, either as militiamen or short-term volunteers. A more permanent and efficient regular army seemed necessary to supply experienced officers, to supervise logistical and support services, and generally to provide direction to a future war effort. Moreover, many of these men had grown attached to military life and hoped to continue their careers in peacetime. The preservation of a relatively large and well-organized military establishment thus appealed to both their personal ambitions and their professional judgment.

The drive for military reform coincided for a time with favorable conditions in the larger society. The effusive nationalism of the postwar years, especially the shift of the dominant Democratic-Republican party from its traditional states' rights philosophy toward neo-federalism, temporarily weakened popular opposition to a standing army. Important leaders in Congress and the executive branch shared officers' concerns about the condition of the nation's defenses. Foremost of these was John C. Calhoun, secretary of war under James Monroe. While he considered the War Department as a stepping stone to the presidency, Calhoun proved to be an exceptionally able and energetic administrator, perhaps the most influential secretary of war of the nineteenth century. Less an original thinker than a synthesizer of ideas, he drew heavily on the advice of military men and served as a conduit for the emerging professional consciousness of the officer corps.[1]

Governmental support for a strong military establishment was a brief phenomenon. The absence of a viable foreign threat, the temporary economic slump after 1819, and political infighting over the presidential succession revived congressional antimilitarism, leading in 1821 to the reduction of the army from its authorized postwar strength of 12,000 officers and men to 6,000. By that time, however, the outlines of the nineteenth-century military establishment were evident.

Central to the postwar reforms was a partial redefinition of the army's mission. Before the War of 1812, the regular army had served almost exclusively as a frontier constabulary, performing such essentially peacetime tasks as the extension of federal authority into the West, Indian control, and the suppression of domestic disorders. Individual officers, especially in the Corps of Engineers, had suggested a more important function: continual preparation for war with a major European power. Beyond the construction of seacoast fortifications, sporadically pursued through the 1790s and early 1800s, these ideas had not influenced policy. Memories of the wartime mobilization and the quest for career security led high-ranking officers to develop the preparedness theme further during the postwar years. When Congress debated the reduction of the army in 1820, regular army generals expressed their views in a series of reports to Calhoun. Unsettled conditions in Europe and the extended frontiers of the United States made any cutback undesirable. If one proved necessary, the commanders favored confining it mainly to the enlisted ranks. The retention of a disproportionately large number of officers would provide a pool of experienced leaders capable of directing a future mobilization, in effect a cadre system. During a major crisis, the government could expand the army quickly and efficiently by fleshing its understrength units with recruits.[2]

Calhoun incorporated these ideas in his report of 12 December 1820 to the House of Representatives, one of the most famous documents in United States military history. In his opinion war was "an art, to attain perfection in which, much time and experience, particularly for officers, are necessary." While the army must continue to perform its constabulary role, its principal task "ought to be to create and perpetuate military skill and experience; so that, at all times, the country may have at its command a body of officers, sufficiently numerous, and well instructed in every branch of duty, both of the line and staff." This goal could best be attained through a cadre arrangement which would give the army the staff apparatus and the basic organization of a much larger force. In effect, the army must become an educational institution, a reservoir of trained leadership, as well as a force-in-being.[3] Because of congressional suspicions of military influence, the act reducing the army in 1821 did not adopt Calhoun's proposals fully. Implicit in the bill, however, was a diluted version of the cadre plan, and that concept became a staple of executive and congressional discussions of military policy in the decades that followed.[4] Within the officer corps preparedness and the cadre plan served as a unifying ideology, a basis for justifying the army's existence before a skeptical public and an incentive for professional development.

A related theme of military reform was structural—a tightening and a rationalization of the army bureaucracy. As they emerged from the War of 1812, the army's support and logistical services amounted to an uncoordinated jumble of offices, overlapping in jurisdiction and lacking systematic procedures. While some departments had chiefs stationed in Washington, such key branches as the Quartermaster and Medical Departments had no central headquarters at all. Officers called for a more efficient general staff to reduce waste and to facilitate a future mobilization. During his early months in office, Calhoun began to concentrate all support operations at the capital, under his immediate supervision. An act of April 1818, sponsored by the War Department, established the offices of surgeon general and commissary general of subsistence, and replaced the two divisional quartermaster generals with a single quartermaster general of the army.[5] To these and other staff offices, Calhoun appointed young and energetic veterans of the War of 1812 and encouraged them to introduce standardized regulations for the conduct of their operations. As time passed most departments developed relatively permanent complements of officers who devoted their careers to administrative duties. There resulted the bureau system or nineteenth-century general staff: a collection of small, centralized bureaucracies—quartermaster, medical, engineering, pay, subsistence, and ordnance—in charge of the army's support functions, headquartered in Washington, and responsible directly to the secretary of war. Although the reduction of 1821 caused reorganization and cutbacks in certain departments, this arrangement continued without substantial change through the rest of the century.

Calhoun made no initial attempt to centralize control in the line, the combat arms of infantry and artillery. No individual had officially exercised overall command of the army since George Washington's nominal tenure as general in chief during the Quasi War with France, a situation consistent with both a Jeffersonian suspicion of concentrated power and the sprawling, amorphous nature of American society. After the War of 1812, the War Department divided the nation for purposes of military administration into two geographical divisions, each under a major general who reported separately to the secretary of war. As part of a compromise between Congress and the Monroe administration on the size of the army, however, the reduction act of 1821 retained a single major general. In an apparent quest for bureaucratic symmetry, Calhoun ordered the senior division commander, Jacob Jennings Brown, to Washington and gave him command of the line regiments, a move which brought "the military administration of the army, as well as the pecuniary, through the several subordinate branches, under the immediate inspection and control of the Government.''[6]

As with the general staff bureaus, the office of commanding general became a permanent fixture of nineteenth-century army administration, ultimately succeeded by the army chief of staff after the Spanish-American War. From the start, however, it occupied an uncertain place in the military hierarchy. Neither Congress nor the executive branch had anticipated the office and neither defined its functions clearly. The staff bureaus jealously guarded their independence and their direct relationship with the secretary of war. Officially subordinate to the commanding general, senior line officers stationed at remote frontier posts often enjoyed a similar autonomy, ordering troop movements on their own initiative and even calling out state militia. General Brown suffered a stroke soon after assuming office and thereafter lacked the energy to develop his command powers. His successors, Alexander Macomb (1828–1841) and Winfield Scott (1841–1861), strove more vigorously to make their office the administrative hub of the army, but slow communication between Washington and the frontier, the lack of disciplinary powers at their disposal, and the weight of tradition largely frustrated their efforts. While the commanding general served as a military adviser to the executive branch and occasionally took a field command, he remained through most of the antebellum period a rather superfluous figure, overshadowed in matters of policy by the president and secretary of war and in routine administration by the bureau chiefs and high line commanders.[7]

Less obvious than the changes in army structure was a quiet trend throughout the service toward systematic procedures. Administrators at the capital brought order to the chaotic military records inherited from the War of 1812 and compelled field commanders to submit regular returns for the troops and property under their control. Standardized forms and manuals proliferated. In 1821, for example, the War Department adopted the first really comprehensive set of general regulations in the army's history, compiled by Brigadier General Winfield Scott from European sources and the mass of regulations and standing orders issued since the 1790s.[8] Beginning in the postwar period, a series of military boards updated the army's infantry tactics and approved manuals for the artillery and for the mounted regiments added during the 1830s. The Ordnance Department embarked on a long-term project to standardize the design of ordnance and other types of military materiel.[9] While the erratic behavior patterns of the prewar army did not entirely disappear, military administration assumed an unprecedented regularity and system, coming to resemble in important ways modern bureaucratic organization.

A final aspect of postwar reform was a vitalization of military education. Founded as a school for engineers in 1802, the Military Academy at West Point had languished during its early years. It had lacked a set organization and curriculum, and bitter officers' quarrels had repeatedly disrupted its operations. Graduates had been few in number and had concentrated in the artillery and engineers. However, military education was an important component of the emerging professional ideology of the officer corps, which increasingly viewed the army as a reservoir of expertise to direct a future war effort. In 1817 an innovative administrator, Captain Sylvanus Thayer, became superintendent of West Point. With the support of the War Department, he reformed the academy, introducing uniform administrative regulations which included a merit system for ranking cadets and establishing a fixed four-year curriculum.[10] For more than a decade after 1821, virtually all military appointments other than those to the Pay and Medical departments went to West Point graduates; by 1830, they constituted 63.8 percent of the officer corps.[11] Not all regulars were enthusiastic about Thayer's system, especially the curricular emphasis on engineering and mathematics. Inspector General John E. Wool expressed a line of criticism which would persist to the present when he recommended greater attention to history, geography, and languages, especially in the training of infantry officers. The great victories of history "were not achieved by the 'rule and compass' or the 'measurement of angles.' They were the product of enlarged minds, highly cultivated and improved by a constant and accurate survey of human events."[12] Nevertheless, the reform of West Point and its designation as the principal entry point into the officer corps indicated the army's growing conception of military leadership as a science, to be acquired through prolonged study, rather than an intuitive art or a trade.

The emphasis on an educated officer corps was not limited to the reform of West Point. During the early 1820s officers recommended the founding of advanced "schools of practice" for the artillery and infantry, modeled on the French military school system. Not only would such institutions provide training in practical military subjects slighted by the West Point curriculum, they would permit officers to work with relatively large bodies of troops, offsetting the isolation inherent in the army's constabulary role. The War Department established the Artillery School of Practice at Fortress Monroe, Virginia, in 1824 and a similar school for the infantry at Jefferson Barracks, Missouri, two years later. This early experiment in advanced military education proved too ambitious for the antebellum army; lack of congressional funding and the conflicting demands of frontier service caused the schools to close during the early 1830s.[13] The War Department sponsored other projects, however, to encourage professional development within the officer corps. Of special importance was the practice of sending officers to Europe to study at military schools, observe military operations and installations, and procure equipment and manuals.[14]

The reforms of the post–War of 1812 years gave the army a consistent mission, a permanent structure, and a considerable degree of regularity in its internal operations. The cadre principle and the emergence of West Point encouraged a view of officership as a distinct profession, requiring specialized training to master. Moreover, the reduction of 1821 was the last significant cutback of the regular army in the nineteenth century. From that point forward, the trend was toward a gradual increase in the size of the peacetime establishment: from an actual strength of 5,746 officers and men in 1821 to 8,349 in 1845 and 16,367

The United States Military Academy in 1828
National Archives (111-SC-87212)

on the eve of the Civil War. Interacting with these changes in the army's official organization and functions were developments in the informal aspects of military society—the career patterns, attitudes, and life styles of military personnel.

Between 1821 and the Mexican War, the officer corps evolved into a relatively homogeneous group of long-term careerists. Before the War of 1812, the army's commissioned personnel had been a rather diverse lot. While it would be an obvious exaggeration to describe the early officer corps as a reflection of the larger society, officers had derived from a variety of backgrounds and levels of education and had entered the service by several routes; at least 29.7 percent of the officers on the 1785 army list and 14.5 percent of those on the 1797 army list had served in the ranks before acquiring their commissions. The virtual monopoly of military appointments enjoyed by West Point graduates after 1821 narrowed the social base of the officer corps. By 1830, for example, only 19 of 522 officers (3.6 percent) had begun their careers as enlisted men, and only 2 of these individuals had been commissioned after the War of 1812.[15] Military administrators righteously denied that West Point was an elitist institution and their claims were at least partially correct. The War Department sought geographical balance in cadet appointments, distributing most of them among the states on the basis of congressional representation. Frequent references to poverty and parental death in applications to West Point indicate that many prospective officers were attracted to military life by economic considerations: hopes of a free education and a secure, "respectable" career.[16] Nevertheless, the relatively demanding academic standards of the Military Academy and the tendency to favor applicants with distinguished forebears increasingly restricted access to the officer corps to established old-stock families with records of public service. While the American officer corps was not as narrowly based as the aristocratic military elites of most European nations, the vast majority of West Pointers were the sons of government officials, professional men, merchants, and landholding farmers and small planters, clearly middle or upper middle class in education and social status if less so in economic circumstances.[17]

West Point lost its monopoly of military appointments during the 1830s. The ideology of the dominant Democratic party rejected formal higher education as a prerequisite for public office, opposed monopolies of any sort, and stressed equality of opportunity for white male citizens, unrestricted by birth, wealth, or family influence. Moreover, the expansion of the army to meet the demands of Indian removal combined with an exceptionally high officers' resignation rate in 1836 and 1837 to create more openings than West Point graduates could fill. Thus, the Jackson and Van Buren administrations appointed a sizable number of citizens directly to the army and commissioned a handful of sergeants. Most of the citizen-appointees resembled West Pointers in background, however, and this gesture toward democracy therefore failed to broaden significantly the social base of the officer corps. In any case, the Military Academy continued to supply the great majority of officers—75.6 percent by 1860, excluding pay and medical officers.

A related trend was the lengthening of military careers. The reform of military administration and the gradual expansion of the army after the reduction of 1821 eased the career anxieties which had plagued the officer corps in the past. Egalitarian critics notwithstanding, the rising prestige of West Point gave the profession of arms a more reputable standing than it had previously enjoyed. While regulars complained about low pay, slow promotion rates, the isolation of garrison life, and frequent family separations, most of them found the army sufficiently attractive to make a long-term commitment. The overall increase in career lengths was dramatic. The median length of service of officers whose names appear on the 1797 army list was ten years; for those on the 1830 list, it was twenty-two years. During the same time span, the portion of the officer corps remaining in service twenty or more years rose from 14.5 percent to 58.3 percent, and those remaining thirty years increased from 3 percent to 37.8 percent.[18] For the first time in the history of the United States Army, the average officer would conform to Morris Janowitz's minimal definition of a professional soldier as "a person who has made the military establishment the locus of his career."[19]

A variety of informal ties interacted with social origins and career patterns to unify the officer corps. Whatever the academic merits of a West Point education, four years at the Military Academy had the effect of socializing young men into military life, providing a web of friendships and shared experiences which bound them to a unique milieu. Authoritarian values instilled at the academy—discipline, regularity, order—set them subtly apart from the expansive individualism which permeated contemporary civilian society. Service identities deepened after graduation, as young officers settled into tightly knit garrison communities along the seaboard and the western frontier. Many of them married the daughters or sisters of fellow officers; rare was the senior commander who raised a family and lacked at least one son or son-in-law in uniform. Regulars filled their private letters and journals with service news: assignments, promotions, troop movements, garrison events. Gradually there emerged a distinct military subculture, sharing many characteristics of the larger society but containing its own configuration of values and traditions and commanding loyalty as an institution. Captain Ethan Allen Hitchcock expressed an increasingly common sentiment in 1835 when he assured a friend that he did not intend to resign. "This insane attachment; as you may properly call it, is nevertheless real and I cannot bear the thought of separating myself from those with whom I have been associated all my life. Whatever may be the errors of soldiers I verily believe our little army contains a better body of men than can be found in any other profession."[20]

The rhetorical antimilitarism of the Age of Jackson reinforced the trend toward cohesion within the officer corps. Through the 1830s and early 1840s, the regular army and the Military Academy came under frequent attack by congressmen, state legislators, journalists, and militia leaders who denounced the alleged elitism and authoritarianism of these institutions and praised the citizen-soldier as the safest defender of a free people.[21] The military establishment was not alone in facing egalitarian criticism; institutions as divergent as the Bank of the United States, professional associations in law and medicine, and the Masonic Order were denounced as "aristocratic" barriers to the aspirations of the much venerated common man. For the officer corps, the actual impact was slight. Most critics of the army wished not to abolish it altogether but merely to democratize access to military commissions. The army's functions as a frontier constabulary and constructor of internal improvements won it at least the grudging support of important segments of the population. In fact, the military establishment grew significantly during the 1830s, as Congress added three new regiments and expanded several staff departments.

Military men often exaggerated the extent of public hostility. Their most common reaction was to draw inward and lament the fate of the military profession in an egalitarian era. Politicians, at least in the abstract, appeared as adversaries—"demagogues" who appealed to the "mob" by attacking the army and who placed party and sectional loyalties over the nation's welfare, defined of course as a strong military establishment. Compared to the spirit of duty and sacrifice which allegedly permeated the officer corps, civilian society as a whole seemed rather degenerate. Lieutenant Peter V. Hagner bridled at public criticism of the army's performance in the Second Seminole War:

Could some elevated being, see with one eye the poor fellows here tossing and rolling in a burning fever and trudging breast high through mud and mire, that the hardest shudder to look at, and at the same moment let the other rest upon the crowds collected in gay lively circles about our fashionable and elegant cities and hear their remarks, sneering and disrespectful as they always are, . . . where would he suppose the soldier was to find his reward? Not in the hearts of his countrymen most assuredly.[22]

Regulars reserved their most biting remarks for citizen-soldiers: militiamen and short-term volunteers. The public praise for such troops and the government's occasional reliance on them for border crises and Indian removal seemed an affront to the army, a challenge to its claims to special expertise. Almost unanimously, officers denounced citizen-soldiers as extravagantly expensive, undisciplined, politically motivated, and brutal in their conduct of warfare.[23] There was a legitimate basis for these charges, but the intensity of officers' expressions on this subject indicate that amateur soldiers served as a foil for the emerging professional consciousness of the officer corps. Gradually, regulars developed a conception of themselves as a devoted band of brothers, committed to politically neutral national service, but scorned and mistreated by petty politicians and an ungrateful public. However exaggerated this image might be, it grew stronger during the Mexican War and became a permanent feature of the army's perception of its relationship to the larger society.

The trend toward uniformity in the recruitment, career patterns, and attitudes of the army's commissioned personnel did not result in a monolithic officer corps. As before the War of 1812, officers' quarrels constantly disrupted the small service world. One source of friction was the perennial quest for individual advancement, aggravated by the seniority system which strictly governed most types of promotion and forced ambitious young officers to grow gray in the rank of captain. The practice of duelling, pervasive in the army before and during the war, gradually declined as a means of settling officers' personal differences. Military men jealously guarded their honor, however, and sought desperately to circumvent the ubiquitous promotion bottlenecks. They did not hesitate to publicize their grievances in the press or to appeal to political friends for redress.

Especially troublesome was the question of brevet rank. Introduced into the American service in 1812, brevet rank was a type of honorary rank higher than the holder's regular grade, granted for gallant or distinguished conduct or for ten years' service in one grade. The government did not clearly define the prerogatives of brevet rank or its relationship to regular rank, however, and the result was continual bickering. The exceptionally bitter controversy between Generals Winfield Scott and Edmund P. Gaines, which ran from the 1820s to Gaines's death in 1849 and at times threatened the stability of the entire army, had its roots in the brevet question.[24]

A second source of internal tension was more central to the institutional history of the army—branch and departmental rivalries. Branch distinctions had existed since the 1790s, but they intensified greatly in the post–War of 1812 period with the emergence of the bureau system and a permanent regimental structure. While the staff departments and the combat arms occasionally quarreled among themselves, the principal division ran between staff and line. Line officers resented the size, independence, and political influence of the bureaus and the alleged privileges in pay and stations enjoyed by their staff colleagues. In the opinion of many, the army as a whole had become ''a mere machine for the accommodation of the staff.'' Staff officers argued with some justification that the army's widely dispersed garrisons, its multiple functions, and its commitment to the cadre system and preparedness made a relatively large staff essential.[25] All branches pushed their cases in the press and made use of political channels. The staff departments had the advantage in this bureaucratic warfare, as their headquarters were concentrated in Washington in close contact with the War Department and Congress. Intraservice friction continued through the nineteenth century and shaped a distinctive pattern of political action in the army, focusing on branch goals rather than a unified ''army interest.'' One of its indirect effects was to diffuse the political influence of the officer corps and thereby reinforce civil control over the military.[26]

By far the deepest cleavage in the old army was the one which separated commissioned officers from enlisted men. Inherited from the standing armies of Europe, this distinction was reinforced by class and ethnicity and constituted a nearly unbridgeable social chasm. Until 1833 soldiers enlisted for a five-year term of service and received pay ranging from five dollars a month for privates to nine dollars for sergeants major. In order to spur recruiting and combat a high desertion rate, Congress raised the pay of the rank and file slightly in 1833 and lowered the enlistment term to three years, though the five-year stint was restored in 1838. If subsistence, medical care, clothing, and various bonuses are considered, the compensation of the enlisted men probably compared favorably with the wages of unskilled civilian laborers.[27] The prospect of conforming to rigid military discipline at isolated and often unhealthy frontier posts did not prove attractive in an expansive, egalitarian age, however; and few individuals with a stake in society could be induced to enlist. In contrast to the old-stock, middle-class backgrounds of most officers, the vast majority of enlisted men came from the working classes. In the depression year of 1837, when an exceptional variety of men might be expected to have enlisted, one batch of 200 recruits included 66 laborers, 96 artisans, and 19 others from such semiskilled manual occupations as machinist, porter, soldier, and sailor; only 11 were listed as farmers, 4 as clerks, and 1 each as engineer, teacher, peddler, and druggist.[28] Although the government officially barred aliens from the army before 1844 and for several years required special permission to enlist naturalized citizens, recruiting officers did not enforce these restrictions rigidly and immigrants made up a sizable portion of the rank and file, about 40 percent between 1834 and 1843. Indeed, many American soldiers did not know enough English to understand commands.[29]

In theory, the relationship between officers and enlisted men was a strict but compassionate paternalism. More commonly, however, officers treated soldiers with elitist contempt tinged with nativism. Few commanders questioned the eighteenth-century European conception of military leadership which rested on the threat of physical punishment to elicit unquestioning obedience. In 1818 the surgeon general complained that there was ''probably no service in which officers appear to pay so little respect to the character of the soldier as in ours, or in which so little attention is given to their comfort[,] convenience and health.''[30] While a high attrition rate among the rank and file made promotion to noncommissioned officer relatively easy, advancement to the commissioned grades was virtually impossible. Only seven soldiers received commissions during the quarter century before the Mexican War. In this respect, the officer corps of the world's leading republic in an age of egalitarian democracy was more closed than those of contemporary European monarchies; even tsarist Russia drew a higher percentage of its officers from the enlisted ranks than did the United States.[31] A former enlisted man recalled that there was ''just as almighty a distance preserved between a *Sergeant-Major*, who is the highest noncommissioned officer in the service, and a *Brevet Second Lieutenant*, who is the lowest commissioned officer, . . . as though it were sacrilege in the former to approach the latter in a familiar manner.''[32]

Needless to say, discipline was a continual problem. Drinking provided one of the few recreations at remote frontier garrisons for officers and enlisted men alike, and observers agreed that American soldiers were an intemperate lot. Through the Jacksonian era, desertion raged at epidemic levels; one historian has calculated that 27 percent of the soldiers enlisting in nineteen selected years between 1821 and 1845 deserted before completing their term of service, and many absconded more than once.[33] Military administrators blamed the problem on liquor and the allegedly depraved character of the rank and file. Perhaps a more basic cause was the discrepancy between the rigid, often arbitrary nature of military discipline and the egalitarian spirit pervading civilian society. Congress had abolished flogging in the army in 1812, and the president invariably commuted sentences of death for desertion in peacetime. Officers often disregarded these restrictions, however, or circumvented them by inflicting a variety of exotic corporal punishments, either unofficially or by sentence of court-martial. In 1821, for example, a private stationed at Green Bay complained to the secretary of war that he had been repeatedly flogged and "ducked almost to strangulation" with buckets of water poured over his head. "If, Sir, personal malice and revenge . . . are allowed to pervert the Laws of the constitution, then is the Army (I speak boldly, for I have always thought freely) instead of being the bulwark of the national defense, *a nursery of traitors and incendiaries.*"[34]

The officer corps closed ranks on the question of discipline, supporting the opinion of Brigadier General Edmund P. Gaines that *"Stripes and lashes* stand . . . next to *Ball Cartridges"* as an effective means to control the American soldier's unruly nature. In 1833 officers' reports led Congress to restore flogging as a punishment for desertion if ordered by a general court-martial.[35] Still, arbitrary punishments continued. When the War Department tried to prevent physical abuse of enlisted men in the early 1840s, a series of courts-martial either acquitted officers accused of such actions or awarded only token sentences. In one case a court found a senior commander guilty of beating, threatening, and otherwise mistreating soldiers, forcing one to fight his slave and confining another at hard labor for twenty-seven days without trial, but recommended that the sentence—a four-month suspension from rank and command—be remitted because of the officer's "long and gallant services."[36] Not all officers were insensitive to the lot of the enlisted men. Influenced by the humanitarian impulse abroad in the larger society, reform-minded officers sponsored temperance societies for the improvement of their men, convinced the government to appoint chaplains at the larger military posts, and lobbied for the establishment of "military asylums" for old soldiers. In general, though, the gap between officers and enlisted men widened during the "Age of the Common Man" and left a legacy of resentment and low morale among the rank and file.

While preparation for a major war dominated the officers' conception of their collective role, routine garrison duty and the demands of westward expansion continued to absorb much of their everyday attention. Between the War of 1812 and the Mexican War, the army was usually scattered along the seaboard and the western and southern frontiers in small posts containing no more than three or four companies. Much to the disgust of professionally oriented officers, the War Department required troops to perform physical labor at the expense of military training. They constructed posts, fortifications, and military roads, and cultivated crops for their own subsistence. As they had done since the 1780s, regulars served as a frontier constabulary, a complex and thoroughly unpopular duty. Particularly aggravating was enforcement of the trade and intercourse laws, the basic legislation regulating relations between whites and Indians. Military commanders strove diligently to suppress the illegal liquor trade, expel white intruders from Indian lands, and generally keep the peace along the extended Indian frontier. Their efforts, sometimes heavy-handed, embroiled them in almost continual controversies with state and territorial officials and local citizens; officers were frequently compelled to defend themselves against lawsuits in civilian courts.[37] Not surprisingly, these experiences reinforced the officer corps's antipathy toward the civilian world, its sense of isolation and martyrdom.

The most important task of the frontier army during the Age of Jackson was Indian removal. From the late 1820s to the early 1840s, the army served as the federal government's main instrument to force the remaining eastern tribes to settle on new lands west of the Mississippi River. The principal combat operations of this period—the Black Hawk War of 1832, the Creek War of 1836, and the Second Seminole (or Florida) War of 1835 to 1842—arose from this policy. The army had conducted sporadic Indian operations in the past, of course, but the particularly controversial, morally repugnant character of the removal process deeply affected military thinking on Indians and Indian warfare.

Generally, army officers were sympathetic to the plight of the eastern tribes. While they considered red men to be culturally inferior to whites and endowed with such traits of savage character as bloodthirstiness, vengefulness, and treachery, they accepted the prevailing environmentalist view of race, which assumed that Indians could be converted from their primitive ways through the civilization process. Officers saw themselves as neutral agents of the government, striking a balance between the demands of the whites and the rights of the Indians. They thoroughly disliked frontier civilians whom they considered unruly and troublesome; thus, the Indians, usually the victims of white aggression, appeared in a relatively favorable light. As "good soldiers," regulars carried out the removal policy, but many of them considered it unjust and attempted to shield Native Americans from white pressure. Brigadier General Gaines stated that he "would just as soon seek for fame by an attempt to remove the Shakers, or the Quakers, as to break up the Indians, take their lands and throw together twenty tribes speaking different languages where the most ferocious savage will cut the throat of the most civilized and orderly."[38]

Most Indian removals were relatively brief and bloodless affairs. The principal exception was the interminable Second Seminole War, the army's first prolonged encounter with guerrilla warfare. For seven years, from 1835 to 1842, the bulk of the regular army and thousands of militiamen and volunteers pursued elusive bands of Seminoles and blacks through the Florida wilderness; no fewer than eight commanders tried their luck without decisive success. Probably no conflict in American history other than the Vietnam War was so frustrating or so unpopular within the army. Oriented toward the cadre system and European-style warfare, the officer corps was unprepared to counter the mobile, hit-and-run tactics of the Indians. Because the war was controversial in the larger society,

Florida service offered little chance for glory or promotion, the chief rewards of the military profession. Moreover, many regulars admired the courage and tenacity of their adversaries and had sincere moral doubts about their own part in the conflict.[39]

Early in the war the army employed relatively conventional strategies, marching large columns through the interior of Florida in hopes of engaging the Indians in a decisive battle. As the years passed and the frustration mounted, however, commanders resorted to more irregular methods. On several occasions they violated flags of truce and promises of immunity in order to seize Seminoles and ship them west, a practice ironically justified by the alleged "treachery" of the Indians. The army systematically struck at the economic base of Indian society, destroying villages and food supplies.[40] By the closing years of the conflict, sympathy for the Seminoles was on the wane and officers openly proposed extermination. During 1841 and 1842 Colonel William J. Worth used small detachments of light troops to pursue the remaining bands relentlessly, offering a bounty for each dead or captured warrior. According to his aide-de-camp, he issued the "simple injunction 'Find the Enemy, capture, or exterminate,' " and removed all restraints on the conduct of operations. Worth's strategy did not succeed fully—a small number of Indians continued to elude the army in the swamps of southern Florida—but the government finally declared the long conflict at an end.[41]

Indian removal accentuated the ambivalence of the army's relationship with the Native American. Under peaceful conditions regulars saw Indians as innocent victims of the white man's greed. As an impartial agency of the government, the army had an obligation to protect the native tribes from white pressure and, if possible, guide them on their path to civilization. When fighting broke out, however, the officers' unfavorable estimation of Indian character and the frustration of guerrilla combat caused them to distinguish informally between "civilized" and Indian warfare and to employ exceptionally harsh, even brutal methods against their Indian adversaries. This ambivalence continued to characterize the army's handling of Indian affairs through the rest of the century.

A branch of the army which largely avoided frontier service was the Corps of Engineers. Organized in 1802, the engineers formed an elite within the officer corps; they drew the top graduates of West Point and their duties were defined as "the most elevated branch of military science."[42] The principal functions of the corps were the design and construction of seacoast fortifications. While the government had built forts at coastal towns as early as the 1790s, the program had received only sporadic attention before the disastrous experiences with the British navy during the War of 1812. As part of the postwar military reform movement, the War Department established a board of engineers in 1816 which examined the coastline and drew up systematic plans, emphasizing large masonry works at the major ports and bays. Indeed, the board's summary reports of 1821 and 1826, occasionally updated and extended, remained the basis for American defense planning until the late nineteenth century.[43] Although congressional skeptics criticized and sometimes delayed particular projects, appropriations continued at a relatively high level into the 1830s and work progressed steadily, hampered mainly by a shortage of engineer officers to supervise construction. Beginning in the mid–1830s, however, individual officers in both the army and the navy questioned the viability of the entire program, arguing that developments in military technology—steam-powered naval vessels, railroads which made possible the rapid concentration of forces at exposed points, rifled cannon, and explosive shells—had rendered large coastal works obsolete.[44] In response, the engineers pushed the fortification system in the press and in Congress and with difficulty retained governmental support until the Civil War.[45] Ironically, involvement in the fortification program made the Corps of Engineers at once the most professionally oriented and the most politically active branch of the military establishment.

Regulars engaged in another controversial activity during the Age of Jackson—civil works. Despite the opposition of strict constructionists in Congress, the army gradually entered this field after the War of 1812 through explorations, surveys for transportation routes, harbor and river improvements, and the military road program—all designed to serve both military and commercial ends. The key event was the General Survey Act of 1824, which authorized the president to employ military engineers on surveys for roads and canals deemed of national importance. By 1830 the War Department listed sixty civil projects under its supervision.[46] Although officers of all branches participated, this duty fell increasingly to the topographical engineers, a group of officers originally attached to the Corps of Engineers but organized as a separate staff bureau in 1831. Even more than the Corps of Engineers, the topographical engineers led an existence virtually independent of the rest of the army. Inevitably, they developed close ties with congressmen, local politicians, and entrepreneurs; until prohibited by law in 1838, they were granted extended leaves to work for private transportation firms. Line officers complained that internal improvements distracted the army from its legitimate functions and some favored divesting the topographical engineers of military rank. With the emergence of pork barrel politics, however, the construction of civil works became a permanent feature of the army's peacetime role.[47]

By the time of the Mexican War, the United States Army had assumed the basic form which it would retain through the rest of the century. It had developed a relatively permanent organizational structure: fourteen regiments of infantry, artillery, and dragoons under the commanding general and several semiautonomous general staff departments reporting directly to the secretary of war. In contrast to the chaotic administrative practices of the Jeffersonian era, the introduction of standardized regulations and tactical manuals had brought system and order to all phases of military bureaucracy. Increasingly, the officer corps consisted of long-term, West Point–trained careerists who identified strongly with the army, especially their particular branches, and who viewed the civilian world with suspicion. Class distinctions and ethnic prejudice combined to keep relations between officers and enlisted men in the rigid mold inherited from the aristocratic armies of eighteenth-century Europe. Soldiers had virtually no access to the commissioned grades and were subjected to an arbitrary, often brutal discipline. The more articulate officers shared a budding professional ideology which centered on the cadre system, preparedness, and the value of formal military education. The demands of a rapidly expanding nation, however, forced most regulars to devote their careers to the mundane, inglorious tasks of a frontier constabulary. As time passed the army would grow progressively more isolated, both physically and intellectually, from the mainstream of American life.

NOTES

1. The best sources for Calhoun's career as secretary of war are Charles M. Wiltse, *John C. Calhoun: Nationalist, 1782–1828* (Indianapolis and New York: Bobbs-Merrill, 1944), pp. 142–87, 198–264; and John C. Calhoun, *The Papers of John C. Calhoun*, ed. Robert L. Meriwether and W. Edwin Hemphill, 13 vols. (Columbia: University of South Carolina Press, 1959–1980), II–IX, passim.

2. Henry Atkinson to John C. Calhoun, 18 October 1820; Edmund P. Gaines to Calhoun, 27 July 1820; Winfield Scott to Calhoun, 20 August 1820; Andrew Jackson to Calhoun, 8 August 1820; Alexander Macomb to Calhoun, 30 September 1820, Letters Received by the Secretary of War, Registered Series, Records of the Office of the Secretary of War, Record Group 107, National Archives, Washington, D.C.; Jacob Brown to Calhoun, 6 October 1820, Jacob Brown Papers, Library of Congress, Washington, D.C.; Thomas S. Jesup to Calhoun, 31 March 1820, *Papers of Calhoun*, IV, 744–53.

3. John C. Calhoun to John W. Taylor, 12 December 1820, *American State Papers*, Class V: *Military Affairs*, 7 vols. (Washington: Gales and Seaton, 1832–1861), II, 188–93.

4. Abner R. Hetzel, comp., *Military Laws of the United States: Including Those Relating to the Army, Marine Corps, Volunteers, Militia, and to Bounty Lands and Pensions* (Washington: George Templeman, 1846), pp. 213–15. The bill did not mention the cadre principle specifically, but while it cut the enlisted strength of the army by over one-half, it reduced the officer corps by only one-fifth. The cadre principle was discussed recurrently in military correspondence and congressional debates; in 1838 and 1846, Congress expanded the army in part by filling its understrength regiments with recruits.

5. *Papers of Calhoun*, II, liii–lxix; Hetzel, *Military Laws*, pp. 200–202.

6. John C. Calhoun to James Monroe, 27 November 1822, *American State Papers: Military Affairs*, II, 450.

7. William B. Skelton, "The Commanding General and the Problem of Command in the United States Army, 1821–1841," *Military Affairs* 34 (December 1970): 117–122.

8. U.S., War Department, *General Regulations for the Army; Or, Military Institutes* (Philadelphia: n.p., 1821).

9. William B. Skelton, "The United States Army, 1821–1837: An Institutional History" (Ph.D. diss., Northwestern University, 1968), pp. 159–65, 259–71, 333–38; Stanley L. Falk, "Artillery for the Land Service: The Development of a System," *Military Affairs* 28 (Fall 1964): 97–110; William E. Birkhimer, *Historical Sketch of the Organization, Administration, Matériel and Tactics of the Artillery, United States Army* (Wash-

ington: J. J. Chapman, 1884), passim; Stephen W. Kearny, *Carbine Manual: Or Rules for the Exercise and Maneuvers for the U.S. Dragoons* (Washington: War Department, 1837). The general problem of bureaucratic reform is discussed in William B. Skelton, "Professionalism in the U.S. Army Officer Corps During the Age of Jackson," *Armed Forces and Society* 1 (Summer 1975): 450–55.

10. Stephen E. Ambrose, *Duty, Honor, Country: A History of West Point* (Baltimore: Johns Hopkins Press, 1966), pp. 62–105.

11. Of 522 officers in the officer corps (excluding the "semi-military" departments— medical, pay, and purchasing), 333 were West Point graduates. Based on the army register for 1830 and on Francis B. Heitman, comp., *Historical Register and Dictionary of the United States Army, From Its Organization, September 29, 1789, to March 2, 1903*, 2 vols. (Washington: Government Printing Office, 1903).

12. John E. Wool to John C. Calhoun, undated inspection report approved by Jacob Brown on 12 December 1819, John E. Wool Papers, New York State Library, Albany, New York.

13. Skelton, "U.S. Army, 1821–1837," pp. 165–83, 338–41.

14. For examples of officers' activities in Europe, see R. Ernest Dupuy, *Where They Have Trod: The West Point Tradition in American Life* (New York: Frederick A. Stokes, 1940), pp. 69–103; Charles W. Elliott, *Winfield Scott: The Soldier and the Man* (New York: Macmillan Co., 1937), pp. 194–207; Daniel Tyler, *Daniel Tyler: A Memorial Volume Containing His Autobiography and War Record*, ed. Donald G. Mitchell (New Haven: privately printed, 1883), pp. 8–28; Stanley L. Falk, "Soldier-Technologist: Major Alfred Mordecai and the Beginnings of Science in the United States Army" (Ph.D. diss., Georgetown University, 1959), pp. 172–81, 254–75; Thomas E. Griess, "Dennis Hart Mahan: West Point Professor and Advocate of Military Professionalism, 1830–1871" (Ph.D. diss., Duke University, 1968), pp. 120–33; Philip Kearny, "Service with the French Troops in Africa," *Magazine of History*, extra no. 22 (1913): 1–54.

15. Based on the army lists for 1785, 1797, and 1830, and on Heitman, *Historical Register*. For purposes of this analysis, medical officers have been omitted from the 1797 list and officers of the medical, pay, and purchasing departments have been omitted from the 1830 list.

16. U.S. Military Academy Cadet Application Papers, 1805–1866, passim, Records of the Adjutant General's Office, Record Group 94, National Archives, Washington, D.C.

17. This generalization is based on the author's research into the social origins of nineteenth-century army officers.

18. Based on the army lists for 1797 and 1830 and on Heitman, *Historical Register*.

19. Morris Janowitz, *The Professional Soldier: A Social and Political Portrait* (Glencoe, Ill.: Free Press, 1960), p. 54.

20. Ethan Allen Hitchcock to Richard Bache, 13 December 1835, Ethan Allen Hitchcock Papers, Missouri Historical Society, St. Louis, Missouri.

21. Marcus Cunliffe, *Soldiers and Civilians: The Martial Spirit in America, 1775– 1865* (Boston: Little, Brown & Co., 1968), pp. 101–11; Ambrose, *Duty, Honor, Country*, pp. 106–20; Arthur A. Ekirch, Jr., *The Civilian and the Military* (New York: Oxford University Press, 1956), pp. 60–89.

22. Peter V. Hagner to Peter Hagner, 7 June 1837, Peter Hagner Papers, Southern Historical Collection, University of North Carolina Library, Chapel Hill, North Carolina. Officers' political attitudes are discussed in William B. Skelton, "Officers and Politicians:

The Origins of Army Politics in the United States Before the Civil War,'' *Armed Forces and Society* 6 (Fall 1979): 22–48.

23. See, for example, *The Army and Navy Chronicle*, 2 (25 February 1836): 116–17, 6 (8 March 1838): 154–56, 9 (17 October 1839): 244–46; John T. Sprague, *The Origin, Progress, and Conclusion of the Florida War* (New York: D. Appleton, 1848), pp. 424–27; Jacob Rhett Motte, *Journey Into Wilderness: An Army Surgeon's Account of Life in Camp and Field During the Creek and Seminole Wars, 1836–1838*, ed. James F. Sunderman (Gainesville: University of Florida Press, 1953), pp. 3, 195–97; Philip St. George Cooke, *Scenes and Adventures in the Army; Or, the Romance of Military Life* (Philadelphia: Lindsay and Blakston, 1857), pp. 156, 158–59, 164, 167, 215–25.

24. Hetzel, *Military Laws*, p. 155. For the Scott-Gaines dispute, see Elliott, *Scott*, pp. 227–28, 238–39, 241–46, 294–303, 322–31, 385, 422; James W. Silver, *Edmund Pendleton Gaines: Frontier General* (Baton Rouge: Louisiana State University Press, 1949), pp. 130–36, 167–90, 161–62, 260–61.

25. Staff-line controversies are aired extensively in *The Military and Naval Magazine of the United States* and *The Army and Navy Chronicle*, the semiofficial service journals of the 1830s and early 1840s. See also [John L. Gardner], *Military Control, or Command and Government of the Army* (Washington: A. B. Claxton and Co., 1839), passim; [Braxton Bragg], "Notes on Our Army," *The Southern Literary Messenger* 9–10 (February 1844–February 1845), passim; Skelton, "U.S. Army, 1821–1837," pp. 92–101, 235–54. The quotation is from *Army and Navy Chronicle* 3 (18 August 1836): 104.

26. Skelton, "Officers and Politicians," passim.

27. Stanley S. Graham, "Life of the Enlisted Soldier on the Western Frontier, 1815–1845" (Ph.D. diss., North Texas State University, 1972), pp. 150–58.

28. *Army and Navy Chronicle* 4 (15 June 1837): 376.

29. Graham, "Enlisted Soldier," pp. 44–45; Francis Paul Prucha, *Broadax and Bayonet: The Role of the United States Army in the Development of the Northwest, 1815–1860* (Lincoln: University of Nebraska, 1953), pp. 41–45; George Croghan, *Army Life on the Western Frontier: Selections from the Official Reports Made Between 1826 and 1845 by Colonel George Croghan*, ed. Francis Paul Prucha (Norman: University of Oklahoma, 1958), pp. 142, 148; Cunliffe, *Soldiers and Civilians*, pp. 115–16.

30. Joseph Lovell to John C. Calhoun, 1 November 1818, *Papers of Calhoun*, III, 249.

31. The Russian army drew approximately 5 percent to 7 percent of its infantry and cavalry officers from the enlisted ranks. John S. Curtiss, *The Russian Army Under Nicholas I* (Durham, N.C.: Duke University Press, 1965), p. 177. In the Restoration period, over half the officers in the French army were former enlisted men. Douglas Porch, *Army and Revolution: France, 1815–1848* (London and Boston: Routledge and Kegan Paul, 1974), pp. 43–44.

32. *Recollections of the United States Army. A Series of Thrilling Tales and Sketches* (Boston: James Monroe, 1845), p. ix.

33. Graham, "Enlisted Soldier," p. 194.

34. Joseph Baxter to John C. Calhoun, 25 July 1821, Letters Received by the Office of the Adjutant General, Record Group 94, National Archives, Washington, D.C. See also, John Van Want to Calhoun, 1 October 1820, and James Simpson to Calhoun, 12 February 1821, ibid. A former dragoon private attributed the high desertion rate in his regiment to the contrast between the glowing promises of recruiting officers and the labor and harsh discipline actually encountered by the enlisted men. [James Hildreth], *Dragoon*

Campaigns to the Rocky Mountains; Being a History of the Enlistment, Organization, and First Campaigns of the Regiment of United States Dragoons (New York: Wiley and Long, 1836), pp. 44–46.

35. Edmund P. Gaines to the Adjutant General, 14 January 1824, Letters Received by the Office of the Adjutant General, Record Group 94, National Archives, Washington, D.C.; Hetzel, *Military Laws*, p. 232.

36. Decision in court-martial of Lt. Col. William S. Harney, General Order No. 39, 13 August 1845, Orders and Circulars, Record Group 94, National Archives, Washington, D.C. For other trials of officers for mistreating enlisted men, see the following general orders: No. 34, 9 June 1842; No. 63, 27 September 1842; No. 2, 6 January 1843; No. 4, 17 January 1843; No. 6, 21 January 1843; No. 13, 20 February 1843; No. 17, 3 March 1843; No. 68, 18 December 1843; No. 2, 13 January 1844, ibid. The commanding general denounced arbitrary punishments in General Order No. 53, 20 August 1842, ibid.

37. For the army's role as a frontier constabulary, see Prucha, *Broadax and Bayonet*, passim; Francis Paul Prucha, *The Sword of the Republic: The United States Army on the Frontier, 1783–1846*, The Wars of the United States (New York: Macmillan Co., 1969), pp. 118–248, 307–18, 365–95; Tommy R. Young II, "The United States Army in the South, 1789–1835" (Ph.D. diss., Louisiana State University, 1973), pp. 244–343, 487–522.

38. Edmund P. Gaines to Mr. Miller, 20 August 1830, quoted in Silver, *Gaines*, p. 137. For officers' opinions of Indians, see William B. Skelton, "Army Officers' Attitudes Toward Indians, 1830–1860," *Pacific Northwest Quarterly* 67 (July 1976): 113–24.

39. For examples of officers' sympathy for the Seminoles, see Reynold M. Wik, "Captain Nathaniel Wyche Hunter and the Florida Indian Campaigns, 1837–1841," *Florida Historical Quarterly* 39 (July 1960): 73–74; Motte, *Journey*, pp. 199–200; Ethan Allen Hitchcock, *Fifty Years in Camp and Field: The Diary of Major-General Ethan Allen Hitchcock, U.S.A.*, ed. W. A. Croffut (New York and London: G. P. Putnam's Sons, 1909), pp. 120, 122, 125; William T. Sherman to Ellen Ewing, 7 September 1841, William T. Sherman Papers, Ohio Historical Society, Columbus, Ohio; *Army and Navy Chronicle* 6 (25 January 1838): 55–56.

40. Sprague, *Florida War*, passim; John K. Mahon, *History of the Second Seminole War, 1835–1842* (Gainesville: University of Florida Press, 1967), passim.

41. Sprague, *Florida War*, pp. 274, 275, 278–80, 360–76, 450–51, and passim; Mahon, *Second Seminole War*, pp. 294–320. For officers' calls for extermination, see William G. Grandin to Samuel P. Heintzelman, 5 May 1839, Samuel P. Heintzelman Papers, Library of Congress, Washington, D.C.; Thomas S. Jesup to John Bell, 26 April 1841, Thomas S. Jesup Papers, Library of Congress, Washington, D.C.; *Army and Navy Chronicle* 9 (29 August 1839): 132, 138–39; 9 (31 October 1839): 284–85; 9 (7 November 1839): 289–91; 10 (23 April 1840): 267–68; 11 (1 October 1840): 220–21; 11 (3 December 1840): 361–62.

42. Hetzel, *Military Laws*, p. 116.

43. *American State Papers: Military Affairs*, II, 305–10, III, 283–98.

44. See, for example, Silver, *Gaines*, pp. 223–35; Lewis Cass to Andrew Jackson, 7 April 1836, *American State Papers: Military Affairs*, VI, 366–76; report of Lt. L. M. Powell, U.S.N., 1841, in U.S., Congress, House, 27th Cong., 2d sess., H. Exec. Doc. No. 220, pp. 2–34.

45. The Corps of Engineers' political activities can be followed in the unofficial

letterbooks of Chief Engineer Joseph G. Totten, Record Group 77, Records of the Office of the Chief of Engineers, Letters and Reports of Col. Joseph G. Totten, 1803–1864, National Archives, Washington, D.C. See also Henry W. Halleck in U.S., Congress, Senate, *Report on the Means of National Defence*, 28th Cong., 2d sess., S. Exec. Doc. No. 85, pp. 2–76; John G. Barnard, "Harbor Defence by Fortifications and Steam-Vessels," *Southern Library Messenger* 11 (January 1845): 25–30.

46. *American State Papers: Military Affairs*, IV, 597–600.

47. The army's role in civil works is covered in Forest G. Hill, *Roads, Rails and Waterways: The Army Engineers and Early Transportation* (Norman: University of Oklahoma Press, 1957); Harold L. Nelson, "Military Roads for War and Peace, 1791–1836," *Military Affairs* 19 (Spring 1955): 1–14; William H. Goetzmann, *Army Exploration in the American West, 1803–1863* (New Haven: Yale University Press, 1959); Richard G. Wood, *Stephen Harriman Long, 1784–1864: Army Engineer, Explorer, Inventor* (Glendale, Calif.: A. H. Clark, 1966).

FURTHER READING

The best general studies of the army and military policy, all of which include important sections on the post–1815 years, are Walter Millis, *Arms and Men: A Study in American Military History* (New York: G. P. Putnam's Sons, 1956), and three works by Russell F. Weigley: *Towards an American Army: Military Thought from Washington to Marshall* (New York: Columbia University Press, 1962); *History of the United States Army*, enlarged ed. (Bloomington: Indiana University Press, 1984); and *The American Way of War: A History of United States Military Strategy and Policy*, The Wars of the United States (New York: Macmillan Co., 1973). In *Soldiers and Civilians: The Martial Spirit in America, 1775–1865* (Boston: Little, Brown & Co., 1968), Marcus Cunliffe provides provocative insights on both civil-military relationships and the internal history of the old army. The problem of military professionalism is considered in chap. 8 of Samuel P. Huntington's classic, *The Soldier and the State: The Theory and Politics of Civil-Military Relations* (Cambridge: Harvard University Press, 1957), and in William B. Skelton, "Professionalization in the U.S. Army Officer Corps During the Age of Jackson," *Armed Forces and Society* 1 (Summer 1975): 443–71. Leonard D. White's admirable works on the federal bureaucracy, *The Jeffersonians: A Study in Administrative History, 1801–1829* (New York: Macmillan Co., 1951) and *The Jacksonians: A Study in Administrative History, 1829–1861* (New York: Macmillan Co., 1954), should be consulted for administrative issues, as should William B. Skelton, "The Commanding General and the Problem of Command in the United States Army, 1821–1841," *Military Affairs* 34 (December 1970): 117–22. Roger J. Spiller discusses the development of the cadre plan in "Calhoun's Expansible Army: The History of a Military Idea," *South Atlantic Quarterly* 80 (Spring 1980): 189–203, although he erroneously concludes that Congress rejected the plan in 1821.

The most satisfactory published histories of the U.S. Military Academy are Sidney Forman, *West Point: A History of the United States Military Academy* (New York: Columbia University Press, 1950), and Stephen E. Ambrose, *Duty, Honor, Country: A History of West Point* (Baltimore: Johns Hopkins Press, 1966). A number of unpublished dissertations also provide details on the antebellum period. See especially Thomas E. Griess, "Dennis Hart Mahan: West Point Professor and Advocate of Military Professionalism, 1830–1871'' (Duke University, 1968), and James L. Morrison, Jr., ''The United States Military Academy, 1833–1866: Years of Progress and Turmoil'' (Columbia University, 1970). The army's role in internal improvements and exploration is covered in Forest G. Hill, *Roads, Rails and Waterways: The Army Engineers and Early Transportation* (Norman: University of Oklahoma Press, 1957); William H. Goetzmann, *Army Exploration in the American West, 1803–1863* (New Haven: Yale University Press, 1959); and Harold L. Nelson, ''Military Roads for War and Peace, 1791–1836,'' *Military Affairs* 19 (Spring 1955): 1–14. Robert S. Browning examines seacoast fortification in *Two if by Sea: The Development of American Coastal Defense Policy* (Westport, Conn.: Greenwood Press, 1983).

The army's frontier experience is the subject of a large historical literature. General studies include Edgar B. Wesley, *Guarding the Frontier: A Study of Frontier Defense from 1815 to 1825* (Minneapolis: University of Minnesota Press, 1935); Grant Foreman, *Advancing the Frontier, 1830–1860* (Norman: University of Oklahoma Press, 1933); Francis Paul Prucha, *Broadax and Bayonet: The Role of the United States Army in the Development of the Northwest, 1815–1860* (Lincoln: University of Nebraska, 1953); and Prucha, *The Sword of the Republic: The United States Army on the Frontier, 1783–1846*, The Wars of the United States (New York: Macmillan Co., 1969). Garrison life is discussed generally in a dissertation by Richard D. Gamble, ''Garrison Life at Frontier Military Posts, 1830–1860'' (University of Oklahoma, 1956) and more specifically in such post histories as Bruce E. Mahan, *Old Fort Crawford and the Frontier* (Iowa City: State Historical Society of Iowa, 1926), and Edwin C. Bearss and Arrell M. Gibson, *Fort Smith: Little Gibraltar on the Arkansas* (Norman: University of Oklahoma Press, 1969). Stanley S. Graham's dissertation, ''Life of the Enlisted Soldier on the Western Frontier, 1815–1845'' (North Texas State, 1972), provides important information on a badly neglected subject. John K. Mahon, *History of the Second Seminole War, 1835–1842* (Gainesville: University of Florida Press, 1967) is by far the most reliable study of that conflict, though John T. Sprague, *The Origin, Progress, and Conclusion of the Florida War* (New York: D. Appleton, 1848) is still useful for the later stages of the war. William B. Skelton discusses army-Indian relations in ''Army Officers' Attitudes Towards Indians, 1830–1860,'' *Pacific Northwest Quarterly* 67 (July 1976): 113–24.

Among the many biographies of army officers whose careers touched the period 1815–1845, the following stand out: Charles W. Elliott, *Winfield Scott: The Soldier and the Man* (New York: Macmillan Co., 1937); James W. Silver, *Edmund Pendleton Gaines: Frontier General* (Baton Rouge: Louisiana State University Press, 1949); Brainerd Dyer, *Zachary Taylor* (Baton Rouge: Louisiana State University Press, 1946); and Volume I of Douglas Southall Freeman, *R. E. Lee: A Biography*, 4 vols. (New York: Charles Scribner's Sons, 1934–1935). The flavor of military life is captured in such personal accounts as [James Hildreth], *Dragoon Campaigns to the Rocky Mountains; Being a History of the Enlistment, Organization, and First Campaigns of the Regiment of United States Dragoons* (New York: Wiley and Long, 1936); Ethan Allen Hitchcock, *Fifty Years in Camp and Field: The Diary of Major-General Ethan Allen Hitchcock, U.S.A.*, ed. W. A. Croffut (New York: G. P. Putnam's Sons, 1909); and Philip St. George Cooke, *Scenes and Adventures in the Army: Or, the Romance of Military Life* (Philadelphia: Lindsay and Blackston, 1857). The principal military journals of the period, *The Military and Naval Magazine of the United States* and *The Army and Navy Chronicle*, are available on microfilm and contain a vast amount of information on military life in the 1830s and early 1840s. Finally, two multivolume documentary collections are essential for a serious study of the post–1815 army: *American State Papers*, Class V: *Military Affairs*, 7 vols. (Washington: Gales and Seaton, 1832–1861), and John C. Calhoun, *The Papers of John C. Calhoun*, ed. Robert L. Meriwether and W. Edwin Hemphill, 13 vols. (Columbia: University of South Carolina Press, 1959–1980). Hemphill's introductions to vols. II to IX of the later series constitute the best study of Calhoun as secretary of war.

CHAPTER 6

Military Education and Strategic Thought, 1846–1861

JAMES L. MORRISON, JR.

When the United States went to war with Mexico in 1846, the service was well on the way toward becoming a professional force. The next fifteen years saw graduates from the Military Academy master many of the skills they would use as general officers to command the army in the Civil War. Although only one officer who had gone to West Point became a general before 1861, academy graduates had long dominated the rest of the officer corps.[1] The lessons they learned at West Point and the experience they gained while fighting the Mexican army from 1846 to 1848 strongly influenced their behavior in the positions of greater responsibility they later occupied.

The Mexican War grew out of a long-standing disagreement over the location of the southern boundary of Texas. In early 1846, less than a year after the annexation of Texas, President James K. Polk sent Colonel Zachary Taylor with 4,000 soldiers to take possession of the disputed territory between the Nueces River and the Rio Grande. Polk wanted to draw Mexico into a war which would not ony decide its boundary with Texas, but also give the United States an opportunity to seize Upper California and the deep-water ports of San Diego, Monterey, and San Francisco.

To achieve these aims the military required a much larger force than the 7,400-man regular army which already existed in April 1846 when Mexican soldiers fired on a small party of dragoons north of the Rio Grande. Neither the Constitution nor the Mililtia Act of 1792 said anything about sending militiamen outside the United States, yet Taylor and his immediate superior, Brigadier General Edmund Gaines, convinced more than 11,000 men from militia units in the Southwest to volunteer for duty in Mexico. This unauthorized call to arms cost the overzealous Gaines his command and spurred national leaders to find other ways of strengthening the military. When Congress declared war against Mexico on 13 May, for example, it authorized the War Department to assign more enlisted men to each regular army regiment. A subsequent increase in the number of those regiments enabled the regular army to expand in size until it included more than 30,000 men before the war ended.

Many of these wartime "regulars" came from existing militia units. Indeed, volunteers from the organized militia made up a majority of the more than 100,000 men who served their country during the war. Often such men signed up for federal service on condition that they remain in the same state organizations to which they already belonged. By relying on state volunteer units of this sort in order to circumvent worrisome legal questions, the nation's leaders established a precedent which would be followed on a much larger scale in both the Civil War and the Spanish-American War.

Recruiting enough soldiers to fight proved less difficult, however, than did supplying and caring for those soldiers while on enemy soil. The navy controlled the waters around Mexico and provided the army with most of its supplies. Away from the coast, men either had to live off the countryside or take what they needed with them. Transportation overland proved particularly troublesome, as poor communications between the field and the Quartermaster's Department resulted in a severe shortage of wagons and mules at the beginning of the war. Inadequate sanitation posed an even more serious problem for the army; after securing the Rio Grande in early May 1846 at the Battles of Palo Alto and Resaca de la Palma, Taylor lost approximately 1,500 men to illness in a single month while preparing an assault on the northern Mexican stronghold of Monterrey. Dysentery, cholera, and yellow fever accounted for more than 85 percent of all American soldiers who died during the war.

America's success at the beginning of the war depended not only on the courage and persistence of commanders like Taylor but also on the weakness of Mexico's northern defenses. When Colonel Stephen W. Kearny led 1,800 regulars and volunteers from Fort Leavenworth to Santa Fe in June–August 1846, he encountered no opposition from the few Mexican regulars and the many untrained militiamen who were supposed to defend New Mexico. Taking 100 men with him, Kearny continued on to California, where Commodore Robert Stockton, the commander of the navy's Pacific Squadron, and Captain John C. Frémont, an army engineer in charge of an exploring expedition to the West Coast, had already arrived. By January the small forces these men commanded had joined together to wrest control of the province from Mexico. Despite brief uprisings by the citizens of both New Mexico and California, the absence of any serious oppposition by professional soldiers made the conquest of these two northern provinces a relatively easy matter.

Operations in the north bore little resemblance to those farther south, however, where American forces were often outnumbered and opposed by Mexican regulars. Armed for the most part with old-fashioned, muzzle-loading flintlocks and smoothbore artillery pieces, the Americans nevertheless enjoyed one very important advantage: their field artillery, despite its limitations, was vastly superior to that of the enemy. The more mobile, mounted batteries of "flying artillery" that had been introduced in the army during the previous decade proved their worth early in the war when they helped Taylor to defeat an enemy force almost

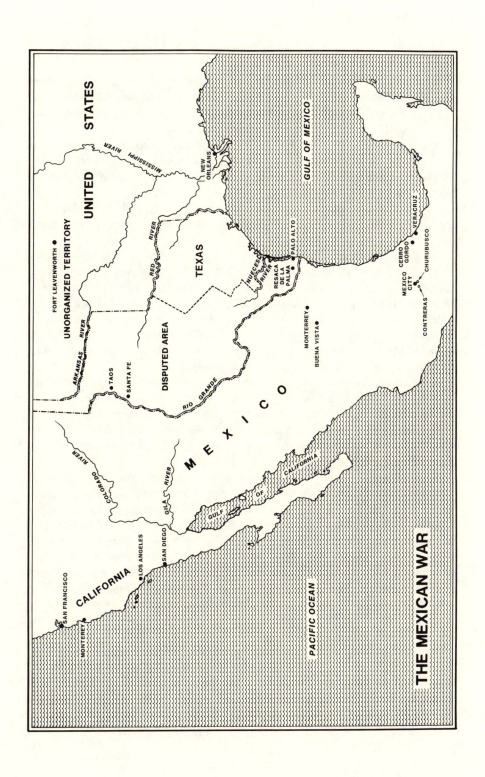

THE MEXICAN WAR

three times as large as the army he commanded at the Battle of Palo Alto in May 1846.

If the field artillery came into its own in Mexico, so too did the engineers who planned and coordinated marches, reconnoitered, and assisted in besieging enemy fortifications. Scott in particular made good use of the engineers who accompanied him when he set out from the central Mexican port of Veracruz in March 1847 for Mexico City. Following the first major amphibious landing ever attempted by American forces, "Old Fuss and Feathers" marched inland with 10,000 men (almost half of whom he had taken from Taylor's force to the north). Scott relied heavily on West Point–trained engineers such as Captain Robert E. Lee and First Lieutenant Pierre G. T. Beauregard to scout ahead in order that the army might avoid or overcome any opposing forces it encountered on the way.

Scott's initial progress was aided by the decision of General Antonio Lopez de Santa Anna to hurry north with 15,000 soldiers to attack Taylor's much smaller army near the hacienda of Buena Vista. When Santa Anna returned after failing to defeat Taylor, Scott fought a limited war of posts in which he consistently outmaneuvered and outflanked the Mexican commander in chief. After winning the bloody Battles of Contreras and Churubusco, American soldiers occupied Mexico City in September. Fighting between the two armies diminished thereafter until the war finally ended in February 1848.

All in all, the Mexican War had a remarkable impact on the nineteenth-century United States Army and on many of the officers who later became its most important leaders. Academy graduates such as Lee and Beauregard were greatly influenced by all they saw and did in this, their first brush with war. Serving under the pompous, albeit highly capable Scott, they learned invaluable lessons about leadership, tactics, and strategy.

In addition to Lee and Beauregard, a number of other West Point graduates distinguished themselves during the war. Colonel Jefferson Davis (class of 1828) resigned his seat in Congress to command a volunteer regiment known as the Mississippi Rifles, fought bravely under Taylor, and was wounded at the Battle of Buena Vista. Joseph E. Johnston (class of 1829) was wounded five times during the war; as quartermaster general he subsequently became the first academy graduate to achieve the rank of general. Second Lieutenant Ulysses S. Grant (class of 1843) served under both Zachary Taylor and Winfield Scott as an infantry officer and regimental quartermaster, while Second Lieutenant George B. McClellan (class of 1846) served as an engineer in both northern and central Mexico.

The accomplishments of these and other academy graduates prompted Scott in later years to write: "I give it as my fixed opinion, that but for our graduated cadets, the war between Mexico and the United States might, and probably would, have lasted some four or five years." Following the Battle of Contreras in 1847, Scott had paid even stronger tribute to engineers such as Robert E. Lee, without whose unstinting efforts Contreras would never have fallen to

Scott's forces; the general proclaimed, "If West Point had produced only the Corps of Engineers, the country ought to be proud of that institution."[2] A staunch supporter of the Military Academy, the commanding general's praise was calculated to draw attention to the performance of West Pointers in the conflict with Mexico and to help win their alma mater's acceptance as a permanent American institution. For some time to come, fusty Jacksonians, harking to the past, might rail spasmodically against the "bastion of aristocracy" on the banks of the Hudson River and demand its extirpation, but by the early 1850s these attacks had degenerated into pro forma sorties, staged mainly to impress the most gullible element of the electorate; no one else took them seriously any more.[3]

In his 1847 encomium to the Corps of Engineers, Scott inadvertently revealed another crucial feature of the educational experience of the men who would command the army during the Civil War. West Point, which trained and taught the majority of regular army officers, was more an engineering school than a military college. The chief of engineers in Washington exercised staff supervision over the academy; the superintendent at West Point was invariably an engineer; and, not surprisingly, the curriculum canted heavily toward engineering courses. Also, on graduation the top students in each class entered the Corps of Engineers almost as a matter of course.[4]

A candidate for admission to West Point in the years between 1846 and 1861 could scarcely have gained a hint of the academic rigors he was about to face from the lax entrance requirements. To gain admission a boy had to demonstrate only rudimentary proficiency in arithmetic, spelling, and writing. In answer to periodic criticisms of these slack standards, the responsible authorities usually defended themselves on the grounds that they kept open the doors to worthy sons of the poor—a sop to egalitarianism which had some validity. The statistics illustrate, however, that the greatest number of cadets came not from the indigent, but from the middle class; the intent, therefore, may well have been to ensure access to ill-prepared, but not necessarily impecunious, southerners and mid-westerners as much as to guarantee a leavening of economic democracy.

The entrance examinations were administered from mid-June to early September. This lengthy period of testing accommodated aspirants who had to travel from distant parts of the country and at the same time afforded those who failed on their first try a second chance before being sent home. After successfully negotiating this initial hurdle, the new cadet reported to camp, where he passed the remainder of the summer learning military fundamentals. At the beginning of September, the fourth class (freshmen), along with the older cadets, moved into barracks. For the novices this encounter marked the start of a four-year confrontation with an academic program that exacted a toll of some 25 percent of each class before graduation.

Survival at the academy depended to a large extent on mathematical aptitude. In fact, of all the cadets discharged for academic failure in the antebellum period, more than 85 percent had come to grief either in mathematics alone, mathematics together with some other subject, or a course closely allied with mathematics, such as natural and experimental philosophy or engineering. During these same years not a single cadet failed military tactics.[5] These figures leave no question as to the *sine qua non* for success at West Point in the years between 1846 and 1861.

Academic instruction was conducted in accordance with the "Thayer System"—so called because during his fourteen-year term as superintendent, Sylvanus Thayer, the putative "Father of the Military Academy," had instituted a series of reforms which have been associated with his name ever since. In conformity with these precepts, cadets attended classes in small, academically homogeneous groups. The dozen or so students who ranked highest in a given subject constituted the first section of that subject; the next dozen, the second, and so on down the line to the "Immortals" of the last section, cadets like Henry Heth, George Pickett, John B. Hood, and George A. Custer, who teetered on the brink of academic disaster. Regardless of section or subject, each student recited daily to an instructor who awarded him a numerical grade denoting the precision with which the cadet's answers to the teacher's questions matched the study assignment; thus, rote memory rather than analytical thought was encouraged.

Each semester ended with comprehensive oral examinations in every subject. At the end of the academic year in June, the cadet received his annual class standing which consisted of a weighted composite of his grades in all subjects for both terms. When he graduated, he was also assigned a general order of merit ranking derived from his performance in every subject for the entire four years. This final, overall standing was of critical importance, for it determined the branch of service a graduate could enter and his place on the promotion list of his corps or regiment. Nowhere was the institutional bias of the academy more evident than in the computation of general order of merit. Although several curriculum revisions necessitated changing the weights allotted to performance in different subjects in the years between 1846 and 1861, never did mathematics, science, and engineering encompass less than 54 percent of the total, whereas military tactics never counted more than 14 percent.[6]

Every cadet recited daily in mathematics during his first two years at West Point. The course began with algebra in the fall of the fourth-class year, progressed through plane and solid geometry, plane and spherical trigonometry, analytics, descriptive geometry, differential and integral calculus, and ended in the spring of the third-class (sophomore) year with surveying. In addition to mathematics, the third and fourth classes pursued a two-year program in French with sections meeting every other day. Since the purpose was to prepare students for translating scientific and military works, the focus of the course was more on grammar and literature than on the spoken language. During the third-class year, recitations in French alternated with English composition, rhetoric, and geography.

Third classmen also took drawing on alternate days throughout the academic year. The initial portion of the course dealt with studies of the human figure and topographical sketching. In the second-class (junior) year, drawing sections met daily, the final sequence of the program being devoted to landscape drawing and advanced topography. The aim of this instruction was practical, not aesthetic. It trained a cadet to make field sketches and terrain studies and simultaneously provided an underpinning for the extensive work he would do in engineering and fortification drawing as a first classman (senior).

In addition, second classmen recited in chemistry on alternate days for the entire academic year. Occasionally, the instructor would perform illustrative experiments to demonstrate principles and show their relevance to military technology, but cadets did not work in the laboratory. However, in the summer encampment following completion of the course, members of the new first class were able to apply some of the concepts they had learned in chemistry to the manufacture of pyrotechnics and other explosives in the ordnance workshop.

Natural and experimental philosophy, which included physics, mechanics, and astronomy, was the most demanding of the second-class courses; sections met daily in both terms. Like chemistry, natural and experimental philosophy was taught almost exclusively by the classroom-recitation method except for infrequent demonstrations put on by the professor. The departmental head, William H. C. Bartlett, resolutely refused to permit the slightest alteration in the purely mathematical style of teaching these courses, despite suggestions that he adopt a less abstruse approach.

The final year exposed students to a wider variety of subjects than the first three. On alternate days in both terms, first classmen took a course called "ethics," which included international and constitutional law, political science, and logic as well as moral philosophy. The course took its name from the ethics department, chaired by the chaplain, which was responsible for teaching this hodgepodge. In the spring semester, cadets recited in mineralogy and geology on the days they did not attend ethics classes. This course in natural science qualified the students to make technical observations on the western frontier and also acquainted them with the properties of construction materials indigenous to that area.

Their broader professional implications notwithstanding, neither ethics nor mineralogy and geology enjoyed the prestige and emphasis of the capstone course: civil and military engineering and the science of war. This series of studies, taught by the department which Dennis Hart Mahan headed, not only consumed the lion's share of the time allocated to first-class subjects, it also counted more than the others in determining general order of merit. In the fall cadets took civil engineering for an hour and a half and engineering drawing for three hours daily. By a similar arrangement the spring semester was given over to military engineering, fortification drawing, and a short subcourse in the science of war. The available evidence does not permit exact measurement of the time devoted to the science of war, a subject to which certain scholars have attached signal importance, but the best estimates are that only between nine and eleven hours were spent on it in the classroom. Furthermore, the topic embraced army organization as well as grand tactics and strategy.[7] It was therefore a rare genius indeed who obtained from the course anything more than the shallowest perception of strategic principles.

Seniors attended recitations in military tactics, too. Artillery and infantry tactics had been taught since the earliest days of the academy, but instruction in cavalry tactics was not introduced until 1849. In infantry and cavalry classes, cadets learned the formations and movements set forth in army manuals. They studied the same subjects in their artillery classes but in addition took up other aspects of ordnance: the manufacture and testing of guns, powder, and projectiles; the operation of siege, seacoast, and field batteries; and ballistics. In 1851 practical military engineering, another professional subject, was added to the first-class curriculum; as the name implies, however, students learned practical military engineering not in the classroom, but in the field, where they surveyed positions, made route reconnaissances, laid out fortifications, and erected bridges under the supervision of officers from the resident engineer company.

Only first classmen recited in tactics and took practical military engineering, but all cadets participated in artillery and infantry drills while at the academy. In addition, first and second classmen received instruction in equitation and fencing. All military training followed a natural sequence, beginning with the school of the soldier, cannoneer, or trooper and advancing through the duties of the commissioned officer. In the course of their military training, all students fired artillery and infantry weapons and practiced using the saber while mounted. In four years at the academy, a cadet devoted 540 hours to infantry drills, 268 to riding and mounted exercises, and 204 to artillery drills.[8]

Professional training did not end on the drill field or in the classroom. The environment was totally martial. Cadets lived in barracks from September until June and under canvas in the summer. They walked guard, ate in a mess hall, and marched almost everywhere they went. Moreover, the student body was organized as an infantry battalion under officers and noncommissioned officers selected from the three upper classes. Overarching the whole was a disciplinary system designed to regulate every human activity from bathing to conduct on furlough. Buttressed by a graduated scale of demerits and punishments, this pervasive code of conduct was enforced by practically every member of the garrison, including the cadets themselves. And while it is no doubt true that the humanitarian impulses of some officers, not to mention the ingenuity of the more daring members of the student body, may have softened the impact to a degree, the disciplinary system remained a highly effective tool for securing instantaneous, unquestioning obedience to a multitude of minutely detailed rules.[9]

Despite the thoroughness of professional military education at antebellum West Point, the quality of that education was at best uneven. From time to time after 1846, the Board of Visitors and, more significantly, ad hoc boards of army officers reported that the cadets were being trained with obsolete weapons and that tactics instructors were so dogmatic they discouraged initiative. In addition, commanders of mounted regiments observed that new graduates were deficient in horsemanship, and other officers voiced concern that excessive time was being spent on close order infantry drills to the detriment of skirmisher training and instruction in the other arms. Similarly, it was noted that cadets did not always receive sufficient opportunities to fire some of the artillery pieces or to use surveying instruments.[10]

Long-standing dissatisfaction with the quality of military instruction, together with equally old complaints of overemphasis on mathematics, science, and engineering, as well as the high rate of attrition, induced Secretary of War Jefferson Davis and Chief of Engineers Joseph Totten to initiate a five-year program of studies in 1854; except for a temporary interruption in 1858, this change remained in force until the eve of the Civil War. Consistent with the purpose of this reform, the courses in mathematics, science, and engineering were not expanded. Instead, more time was spent on English and professional military subjects and new courses were introduced in Spanish, history, and military law. The reformed curriculum led to other changes as well. The commandant of cadets, a line officer, assumed responsibility for all tactical training in addition to portions of the science of war; a Department of Ordnance and Gunnery was also established to teach the technical aspects of artillery. Still, much remained the same. The attrition rate did not decline under the five-year program, and mathematics continued to be the leading producer of academic casualties; furthermore, the relative weights of mathematics, science, and engineering, even though diluted by the introduction of new subjects, continued to prevail in determining general order of merit.[11]

Whether he pursued the four or the five-year program, every graduate passed from adolescence to manhood in a unique environment. Since not all people respond identically to the same stimuli, any attempt to assess the impact of that environment must remain tentative and general. Nevertheless, it is safe to conclude that each alumnus left the academy with strong preconceptions about the profession he was entering. Certainly, he had been made aware that the Corps of Engineers embodied an intellectual elite in the envious eyes of other officers. The academy graduate was also isolated from his civilian contemporaries by the curriculum he had followed as a cadet and the value system he had acquired at West Point. Considered in this light, the notorious contempt for the militia which West Pointers displayed and their bitter resentment of officers appointed to the regular army from civil life become more understandable, if no less reprehensible.

More difficult to detect and impossible to measure were the psychological effects of the authoritarian milieu. Obviously, any contention that the West Point environment reduced every graduate to an automaton would be absurd. The likes of Jeb Stuart, Fitz Lee, Phil Sheridan, John Buford, and Joe Wheeler immediately give the lie to such an assertion. On the other hand, many cadets of less robust psyche undoubtedly emerged from the experience convinced that the answers to all of life's problems lay in drill manuals, regulations, and textbooks. Other youngsters, though succumbing less completely to the mechanistic pressures, must have come away with a deep mistrust of innovation and creativity.

Subsequent experience at least afforded the graduate a chance to broaden his psychological outlook. But the same cannot be said for his intellectual horizons, particularly in the field of strategic theory. As long as an officer remained on active duty, he would find few opportunities and no material incentives to increase his store of professional knowledge by study. It is true that schools of application operated from time to time in the antebellum era, but only on a haphazard basis. Almost invariably other exigencies would disrupt or cancel the programs, and in any case the orientation of these schools was exclusively tactical and technical. Unit commanders were also supposed to conduct classes for junior officers, but the evidence suggests this requirement was mostly honored in the breach; when it was observed, the thrust of such instruction, like that of the schools of application, was not strategic. Even at Saumur, the one foreign military school which a few Americans attended in the antebellum era, the curriculum was devoted to advanced equitation, veterinary science, and cavalry tactics.[12]

Some officers turned to self-study in order to improve their professional knowledge, but the promotion system, founded on seniority without regard to merit, provided little motivation. Equally important, even when intellectual curiosity inspired an officer to study on his own, he found it exceedingly difficult to obtain the reading material he needed for this purpose. Post libraries on the frontier were either nonexistent or poorly stocked, and maintaining a private collection of books was rendered next to impossible by frequent, sudden moves and the need to travel light. Nor did the excellent professional journals characteristic of the 1830s and early 1840s flourish after 1846. Although civilian periodicals occasionally carried military pieces, these consisted mainly of uncritical biographies of war heroes, travelogues, and frontier adventure stories—material of scant value to the serious student.[13]

A notable exception to this general dearth of opportunity for advanced study in military theory was the academy itself. Of the four American officers who published works bearing on strategy in the antebellum period, three had served as instructors at West Point. Foremost among these was the fecund and indefatigable Dennis H. Mahan. The professor and his small band of disciples—Henry W. Halleck, George B. McClellan, and James St. Clair Morton—had all been commissioned in the Corps of Engineers on graduating from the Military Academy.[14] Despite their substantial pro-French bias, they deserve recognition for pioneering in the effort to create a discrete body of American strategic literature.

Scholars have charged these engineer-strategists, especially Mahan, with imparting a Jominian tinge to American military thought.[15] To be sure, this contention is more sophisticated than the naive claim that most officers on both sides in the Civil War were trying to implement the principles of Baron Antoine Henri de Jomini on the battlefield, but it is still too simplistic to stand alone. Undeniably, the four Americans were close students of Jomini's 1838 *Précis de l'art de guerre*, and clearly they cherished several of his tenets: a prejudice in favor of regular troops, a preference for limited war, a geometric view of strategy, a faith that the study of Napoleon's campaigns would reveal eternal truths, a reverence for French military institutions, an obsession with strategic localities, and a qualified emphasis on the offensive. Nevertheless, none of the four Americans subscribed to Jomini's interpretation of Napoleonic strategy without important qualifications.

Mahan, for instance, was less restrained in his admiration of Bonaparte than Jomini. In his voluminous writings the West Point professor stressed audacity, swiftness, maneuver, and the offensive as well as defensive use of fortifications with a verve not found in Jomini's works. In fact, Mahan outdid Napoleon himself in advocating masked movements and other strategems.[16]

In contrast, Henry W. Halleck was more the pure Jominian, counseling caution in maneuver and accentuating concentration as an overriding consideration in campaign planning. When it came to the efficacy of permanent and field fortifications, however, "Old Brains" stood as one with Mahan. Both Americans, unlike Jomini, considered such works necessary for an army which in wartime would be forced to rely on short-term, poorly trained citizen-soldiers. But Halleck was more than an intellectual cross between Jomini and the West Point professor; his *Elements of Military Art and Science*, first published in 1846, was both broader and more philosophical in scope than the books of the others. Halleck made an exhaustive and imaginative attempt to adapt European principles to the American scene. He did not go so far as to reflect meaningfully on the peculiar dictates of Indian warfare, but he did expound at length on the strategic implications of a hypothetical conflict involving European powers on the North American continent. He also developed a detailed, if somewhat convoluted rationale for war and military preparedness. Moreover, Halleck was the sole American strategist to evince an awareness of Carl von Clausewitz's *Vom Kriege*, but since "Old Brains" merely mentioned the title without comment in a list of recommended readings, it is impossible to ascertain what effect, if any, the Prussian's thought had on him.[17]

One-time engineer George B. McClellan was a cavalry officer when he wrote *The Armies of Europe*, a report of his experiences in the Crimean War, published commercially in 1861. Even though the author's primary interests were operational analysis, organizational structure, and military education, it is not difficult to deduce the canons of McClellan's strategic thought from his treatment of these other topics. Like Mahan, the cavalryman favored speed, boldness, maneuver, and stratagem, and, like both Mahan and Halleck, he took considerable pains to state the case for fortifications. Although typically enthralled by the French, McClellan nevertheless noted developments in other countries and their applicability to the United States in a much more thoroughgoing fashion than either of the other two authors. Noteworthy in this vein were his recommendations that friendly Indians be recruited to form irregular cavalry along Cossack lines and his suggestion that American mounted units employ different techniques in mountain combat from those then in vogue. In an appendix written to update the army's cavalry regulations, McClellan also manifested greater sensitivity to the changes which the advent of rifled weapons would necessitate than did his colleagues. Despite these insights, the future commander of the Army of the Potomac retained an outlook which was essentially European.[18]

A West Pointer of a younger generation also wrote on strategic problems, albeit in a narrower, more derivative vein than his predecessors. On the eve of the Civil War, Captain James St. Clair Morton published two treatises, each applying Mahan's concepts of fortifications to American defense issues.[19] Bright and articulate, Morton nevertheless did not make an original contribution to strategic thought; he is mainly significant as an exemplar of the strong continuity of older ideas.

Another occasional resident of West Point, Winfield Scott, the ablest strategic practitioner of the antebellum period, wrote extensively on tactical matters but never committed his guiding military principles to paper other than by inference.[20] Nonetheless, Scott, a master of limited warfare and maneuver, unquestionably influenced those who did write on strategy. Mahan and Halleck, in the revised editions of their works, and McClellan in *The Armies of Europe* all paid homage to Scott's classic campaign in central Mexico because it illuminated many of the rules they espoused.[21] In fact, their adulation seems to have blinded the engineer-strategists to a relevant point: Santa Anna, the loser, had followed orthodox Jominian methodology more faithfully than his opponent had.

Winfield Scott also influenced military thought in less direct ways. The fact that as commanding general and quondam field commander he had to cope with picayune logistical and administrative matters indicated one aspect of a fundamental problem; his episodic removals of army headquarters to New York from 1849 to 1850 and again from 1853 to 1860 as well as his unseemly feud with Secretary of War Jefferson Davis signified other aspects of the same issue. Undoubtedly, prickly egos, partisan politics, and bureaucratic bungling exacerbated this problem, but its roots lay deeper. As Halleck and McClellan intimated, and as the Civil War was soon to show, the ramshackle army hierarchy needed thorough structural overhauling.[22] Until that could be accomplished, the ambiguous nature of Scott's position, together with his penchant for creating animosities, would continue to obfuscate command relationships, impede staff functioning, and deprive the army of the full benefit of his wisdom and leadership.

Despite Scott's failure to articulate a set of strategic principles and his limited role in the conduct of military affairs after the Mexican War, there can be no doubt that he loomed large in the eyes of his contemporaries. The letters and reminiscences of antebellum officers rarely mention Jomini; references to Mahan, Halleck, and McClellan are almost as scarce and are invariably made in an offhanded fashion having little connection with their strategic works.[23] But Winfield Scott was different; he and Napoleon Bonaparte captivated the American military imagination to a unique degree. Some officers were repelled by the personalities of these two giants, but everyone recognized their singular professional status.[24] This is not to suggest that the operations of either commander were subjected to serious, analytical scrutiny outside the engineer-strategist school. Such was manifestly not the case. Instead, the typical officer saw Bonaparte and the portly Virginian as archetypes—Titans of the sword who, heedless of the odds, won glory by paralyzing the foe with daring maneuvers of large columns and devastating fire of massed artillery, all in one swift, decisive campaign.

The leaders of the American Revolution never achieved the status of Scott or Napoleon in the eyes of antebellum officers, perhaps because history received such short shrift at the Military Academy. George Washington, of course, was admired as a folk hero and as a champion of the permanent military establishment, but no professional officer appears to have given more than cursory attention to the means by which Washington and his lieutenants triumphed in the face of well-nigh insurmountable difficulties. Needless to say, the strategic exploits of Nathanael Greene and Daniel Morgan in the South attracted even less notice.[25] That the unreflective failed to see the pertinence of the Revolution is hardly surprising, but it is difficult to comprehend why the engineer-strategists fell into the same trap, especially since Mahan and Halleck perceived a connection between the American Revolution and the later conflagration which gave birth to Napoleon's exploits. Despite that tie, neither man ever probed deeply into the military history of his own country.

In a similar manner the larger implications of Indian warfare were virtually ignored, not only by the engineer-strategists, but also by the authors of the army's tactical manuals—some of whom were experienced Indian fighters.[26] Admittedly, McClellan did touch on the matter, but only in a superficial way. Some frontier commanders also attempted to delineate a coherent operational strategy in their official reports; otherwise, no one wrote about the subject from a strategic or tactical viewpoint.[27] This reticence seems all the more striking because it is clear that while European-style techniques occasionally proved successful against Indians, in most instances more ruthless methods had to be employed—a fact every frontier soldier quickly learned. A kindred paradox was the failure of American officers to perceive that if the techniques of civilized warfare sometimes proved effective in Indian fighting, the reverse might also obtain. This inability to visualize a broader application of the strategy of social and economic destruction which characterized so much of American frontier warfare could only have resulted from a rigid, compartmentalized way of thinking. For most officers, real war meant fighting in the traditional style of Scott and Napoleon, whereas attempting to starve out or exterminate savages remained a mere ancillary activity, something only incidentally related to the profession of arms.

If intellectual intransigence prevented the antebellum officers from appreciating the potential significance of the American Revolution and frontier experience, the origins of that intransigence can be traced to the banks of the Hudson where cadets were conditioned to think in an unimaginative, mechanistic way. The lessons they learned at the academy were reinforced by subsequent service, whether in the combat arms or the scientific corps, under seniors who had also graduated from West Point and who were just as unlikely to have an inquiring mind or a flexible outlook.[28] It is small wonder that the outbreak of war in 1861

Brevet Lieutenant General Winfield ("Old Fuss and Feathers") Scott
U.S. Army Military History Institute, Carlisle Barracks, Pennsylvania

found so many officers unprepared to make the sudden leap to large unit command or to deal with the other complex problems created by a conflict whose magnitude had no parallel in American history.[29] But whatever their weaknesses as strategists, the Mexican War had shown that West Pointers excelled as small unit tacticians, disciplinarians, trainers, and administrators. Throughout their battlefield careers they exhibited unflinching devotion to duty, iron integrity, and stubborn courage. For these skills and virtues, which soon would shape the armies of both North and South, the antebellum Military Academy and the regular army deserve due credit.

NOTES

1. Several West Point graduates received the rank of a brevet general officer, but only one (Joseph E. Johnston) received a substantive (nonbrevet) promotion to brigadier general. For the number of West Point graduates in the antebellum officer corps, see chap. 5 of this volume.

2. U.S., Congress, Senate, *Report of Commission*, 36th Cong., 2d sess., 1860, Misc. Doc. No. 3, p. 176; T. Harry Williams, *P. G. T. Beauregard: Napoleon in Gray* (Baton Rouge: Louisiana State University Press, 1955), p. 26.

3. James L. Morrison, Jr., "The United States Military Academy, 1833–1866: Years of Progress and Turmoil" (Ph.D. diss., Columbia University, 1970), pp. 23, 25, 196–97. In the early years of the Civil War, the academy came under attack as "a hotbed of secession." Ibid., pp. 247–49.

4. Morrison, "Military Academy," pp. 13, 22, 23, 55; U.S., Congress, House, *Army Staff Reorganization*, 42d Cong., 3d sess., 1873, Reports of Committees, No. 74, X, 277–88; *Register of Graduates and Former Cadets of the United States Military Academy, 1802–1963* (West Point, N.Y.: West Point Alumni Association, 1963), p. 16.

5. Of the cadets entering between 1842 and 1861, about 1.9 percent reported their families as "Indigent." Failures in mathematics, of course, were concentrated in the third and fourth classes; natural and experimental philosophy took the heaviest toll of second classmen and engineering of seniors. Morrison, "Military Academy," pp. 93–94, 174, apps. I and III; James L. Morrison, Jr., "Educating The Civil War Generals: West Point, 1833–1861," *Military Affairs* 38 (October 1974): 108–11.

6. Morrison, "Military Academy," pp. 147–48, 223.

7. Ibid., pp. 139–66.

8. Ibid., pp. 166–72.

9. Ibid., p. 114.

10. Ibid., pp. 172–73; Senate, *Report of Commission*, 36th Cong., 2d sess., 1860, pp. 89–109, 124–52.

11. Morrison, "Military Academy," pp. 200–35.

12. Senate, *Report of Commission*, 36th Cong., 2d sess., 1860, pp. 83–91, 107–9, 143, 190–92, 108; William A. Ganoe, *The History of the United States Army*, rev. ed. (1942; reprint, Ashton, Md.: Eric Lundberg, 1964), pp. 192, 239. Robert M. Utley, *Frontiersmen In Blue: The United States Army and the Indian, 1848–1865*, The Wars of the United States (New York: Macmillan Co., 1967), p. 41; Marcus Cunliffe, *Soldiers and Civilians: The Martial Spirit in America, 1775–1865* (Boston: Little, Brown & Co.,

1968), p. 174; Maurice Matloff, ed., *American Military History*, Army Historical Series (Washington: Government Printing Office, 1969), p. 182; Russell F. Weigley, *History of the United States Army*, enlarged ed. (Bloomington: Indiana University Press, 1984), p. 153. Attending Saumur were Henry S. Turner, 1839–1841; W. J. Hardee, 1840–1842; and James Morrison Hawes, 1850–1852, *Register of Graduates*, pp. 220, 224, 232. George B. McClellan, *The Armies of Europe* (Philadelphia: J. B. Lippincott, 1862), pp. 364–70. Dabney H. Maury, *Recollections Of A Virginian in the Mexican, Indian, and Civil Wars*, 3d ed. (New York: Charles Scribner's Sons, 1894), pp. 103–05; Dwight L. Clarke, ed., *The Original Journals of Henry Smith Turner* (Norman: University of Oklahoma Press, 1966), p. 11.

13. Cunliffe, *Soldiers and Civilians*, pp. 166–67; Weigley, *History*, pp. 151–53.

14. *Register of Graduates*, pp. 210, 223, 225, 238.

15. Charles P. Roland, *Albert Sidney Johnston, Soldier of Three Republics* (Austin: University of Texas Press, 1964), pp. 13–15; T. Harry Williams, *McClellan, Sherman, Grant*, 2d ed. (New Brunswick, N.J.: Rutgers University Press, 1962), p. 23; David Donald, *Lincoln Reconsidered*, 2d ed. (New York: Alfred A. Knopf, 1966), pp. 87–89, 86–102; J. D. Hittle, *Jomini and His Summary of the Art of War* (Harrisburg, Pa.: Military Service Publishing Co., 1947), p. 2.

16. Edward Hagerman, "From Jomini To Dennis Hart Mahan," in John T. Hubbell, ed., *Battles Lost and Won* (Westport, Conn.: Greenwood Press, 1975), pp. 35–40; Joseph L. Harsh, "On The McClellan Go-Round," *Civil War History* 19 (June 1973): 102–10; Edward Hagerman, "The Professionalization of George B. McClellan and Early Civil War Field Command," *Civil War History* 21 (June 1975): 113–15; Dennis H. Mahan, *An Elementary Treatise on Advance-Guard, Out-Post, and Detached Service of Troops*, new ed. (New York: John Wiley, 1862), pp. 8–9, 33; Dennis H. Mahan, *A Complete Treatise On Field Fortifications* (New York: John Wiley, 1836); Russell F. Weigley, *Towards an American Army: Military Thought From Washington to Marshall* (New York: Columbia University Press, 1962), pp. 46–51.

17. Henry W. Halleck, *Elements of Military Art and Science*, 3d ed. (New York: D. Appleton, 1862), pp. 7–32, 39, 42, 44–48, 51–54, 60–87, 125, 151–230, 327–74; Weigley, *Towards an American Army*, pp. 57–67; Weigley, *The American Way of War: A History of United States Military Strategy and Policy*, The Wars of the United States (New York: Macmillan Co., 1973), pp. 84–89.

18. McClellan, *Armies of Europe*, pp. 25–35, 208–10, 364, 386, 469–82; Hagerman, "The Professionalization of McClellan," 113–116; Weigley, *Towards an American Army*, pp. 68–72.

19. Hagerman, "The Professionalization of McClellan," 16; Hagerman, "From Jomini to Mahan," p. 43; *The Centennial of the United States Military Academy at West Point, 1802–1902*, 2 vols. (Washington: Government Printing Office, 1904), II, 322.

20. Weigley, *American Way of War*, pp. 66–67; Weigley, "To the Crossing of the Rhine," *Armed Forces and Society* 5 (Winter 1979): 304; Winfield Scott, *Infantry Tactics*, rev. ed., 3 vols. (New York: Harper, 1861); Charles W. Elliott, *Winfield Scott: The Soldier and the Man* (New York: Macmillan Co., 1937), pp. 228–29; Winfield Scott, *Memoirs of Lieutenant General Scott*, 2 vols. (Freeport, N.Y.: Books for Libraries, 1864), I, 118, 154, 207, 259.

21. Mahan, *Out-Post*, pp. 46–47; Halleck, *Elements*, pp. 143, 409–11, 415; McClellan, *Armies of Europe*, p. 10; Lynn Montross, *War Through the Ages*, rev. ed., (New York: Harper and Row, 1946), p. 579; Matloff, *American Military History*, pp. 176–78;

K. Jack Bauer, *The Mexican War: 1846–1848*, The Wars of the United States (New York: Macmillan Co., 1974), pp. 261–320.

22. Otis A. Singletary, *The Mexican War* (Chicago: University of Chicago Press, 1960), pp. 21, 77–98; Halleck, *Elements*, pp. 239–46; McClellan, *Armies of Europe*, pp. 33, 81, 312.

23. John C. Tidball, "Getting Through West Point," Tidball Papers, U.S. Military Academy, West Point, New York; Maury, *Recollections of a Virginian*, pp. 50–62; William T. Sherman, *Memoirs*, rev. ed., 2 vols. (New York: D. Appleton, 1896), I, 16–17, II, 396; Lloyd Lewis, *Sherman: Fighting Prophet* (New York: Harcourt, Brace & Co., 1932), p. 75; Grady McWhiney, "Jefferson Davis and the Art of War," *Civil War History* 21 (June 1975): 103–5; George D. Bayard Papers, U.S. Military Academy, West Point, New York; Henry A. DuPont Letters (Xerox of Longwood MSS), U.S. Military Academy, West Point, New York; James L. Morrison, Jr., ed., *The Memoirs of Henry Heth* (Westport, Conn.: Greenwood Press, 1974), pp. 18, 141, 152, 199–200.

24. Frank E. Vandiver, *Mighty Stonewall* (New York: McGraw Hill, 1957), p. 44; Maury, *Recollections of a Virginian*, pp. 29–31, 63; Douglas S. Freeman, *R. E. Lee*, 4 vols. (New York: Charles Scribner's Sons, 1934), I, 456–58; Warren W. Hassler, Jr., *General George B. McClellan: Shield of the Union* (Baton Rouge: Louisiana State University Press, 1957), p. 15; Ulysses S. Grant, *Personal Memoirs*, 2 vols. (New York: Charles L. Webster, 1885), I, 41–42, 139–66; Sherman, *Memoirs*, I, 82; Williams, *Beauregard*, p. 33; Morrison, *Heth*, pp. 24–25, 53–54, 75–76, 112–13, 135, 140; Weigley, *American Way of War*, p. 90; Thomas L. Connelly and Archer Jones, *The Politics of Command: Factions and Ideas in Confederate Strategy* (Baton Rouge: Louisiana State University Press, 1973), pp. 3, 29–30; Lenoir Chambers, *Stonewall Jackson*, 2 vols. (New York: William Morrow, 1959), I, 120–21, 265; Charles W. Elliott, *Winfield Scott: The Soldier and the Man* (New York: Macmillan Co., 1937), p. 734.

25. Weigley, *The American Way of War*, pp. 10–37; Weigley, "To The Crossing of the Rhine," 302–4.

26. John K. Mahon, *History of the Second Seminole War, 1835–1842* (Gainesville: University of Florida Press, 1967), pp. vii, 118, 320, 325; Utley, *Frontiersmen in Blue*, pp. 33, 48, 57; Randolph B. Marcy, *Thirty Years of Army Life on the Border* (New York: Harper, 1866), pp. 67–75.

27. Marcy, *Thirty Years*, pp. 48–56, 73–74, 85, 102, 110–18; Weigley, *History of the Army*, pp. 161–62.

28. The scientific corps included the Corps of Engineers, the Topographical Engineers, and the Ordnance Corps. The combat arms consisted of the artillery, dragoons, mounted rifles, cavalry, and infantry.

29. Weigley, *History of the Army*, pp. 242–46; Weigley, *Quartermaster General of the Union Army: A Biography of Montgomery C. Meigs* (New York: Columbia University Press, 1959), pp. 29, 165; Williams, *Beauregard*, pp. 7, 33–38, 95; Williams, *McClellan, Sherman, Grant*, pp. 16–39; Warren W. Hassler, Jr., *Commanders of the Army of the Potomac* (Baton Rouge: Lousiana State University Press, 1962), pp. 248–56.

FURTHER READING

Russell F. Weigley stands without peer as the foremost student of the evolution of American military thought. Especially useful for placing the intellectual facets of the antebellum United States Army into the broad context of American history are his *History of the United States Army*, enlarged ed. (Bloomington: Indiana University Press, 1984); *Towards an American Army: Military Thought From Washington to Marshall* (New York: Columbia University Press, 1962); and *The American Way of War: A History of United States Military Strategy and Policy*, The Wars of the United States (New York: Macmillan Co., 1973).

The introductory section of a trenchant little book on the Civil War era, Thomas L. Connelly and Archer Jones, *The Politics of Command: Factions and Ideas in Confederate Strategy* (Baton Rouge: Lousiana State University Press, 1973), contains a uniquely useful, thorough, and scholarly exegesis of the nuances of Jominian thought. Equally relevant to antebellum strategic thinking are the first four essays in John T. Hubbell, ed., *Battles Lost and Won: Essays From Civil War History* (Westport, Conn.: Greenwood Press, 1975).

Two volumes on strategic thought, Conrad H. Lanza, *Napoleon and Modern War*, rev. ed. (Harrisburg, Pa.: Military Service Publishing Co., 1949), and J. D. Hittle, *Jomini and His Summary of the Art of War* (Harrisburg, Pa.: Military Service Publishing Co., 1947), provide accurate translations of the great Swiss military thinker, but both books offer simplistic interpretations of Jomini's impact on the United States Army. Hittle's unproven assertion concerning the substantial influence of Jomini on Civil War strategy unfortunately has been accepted without question by so eminent a scholar as T. Harry Williams, whose recent book, *The History of American Wars from Colonial Times to World War I* (New York: Alfred A. Knopf, 1981), is less dogmatic about Jomini's influence on Civil War generalship than his earlier works, but in it Williams still refuses to abandon Hittle's thesis.

Carl von Clausewitz, *On War*, ed. and trans. Michael Howard and Peter Paret (Princeton, N.J.: Princeton University Press, 1976), on the other hand, has greatly facilitated the accurate appreciation of Jomini's Prussian rival, Clausewitz. Theirs is the first English translation to render Clausewitz comprehensible without taxing the reader's patience.

Horrendous titles notwithstanding, the following firsthand works provide irreplaceable insights into the military precepts, personalities, and prejudices of America's foremost antebellum strategic thinkers: Winfield Scott, *Memoirs of Lieutenant-General Scott*, 2 vols. (Freeport, N.Y.: Books for Libraries, 1864); Dennis H. Mahan, *An Elementary Treatise on Advanced-Guard, Out-Post, and Detached Service of Troops and the Manner of Posting and Handling Them in the Presence of an Enemy with a Historical Sketch of the Rise and Progress of Tactics* (New York: John Wiley, 1862); Henry W. Halleck, *Elements of Military Art and Science, or Course of Instruction in Strategy, Fortification, Tactics of Battles, Etc., Embracing the Duties of Staff, Infantry, Cavalry, Artillery and Engineers*, 3d ed. (New York: D. Appleton, 1862); George B. McClellan, *The Armies of Europe: Comprising Descriptions in Detail of the Military Systems of England, France, Russia, Prussia, Austria and Sardinia, Adapting Their Advantages to all Arms of the United States Service: and Embodying the Report of Observations in Europe During the Crimean War, As Military Commissioner From the United States Government in 1855–56* (Philadelphia: J. B. Lippincott, 1862).

The most penetrating analyses of the strategic aspects of the Mexican War can be found in Otis A. Singletary, *The Mexican War* (Chicago: University of Chicago Press, 1960) and K. Jack Bauer, *The Mexican War, 1846–1848*, The Wars of the United States (New York: Macmillan Co., 1974). Bauer's book in particular brings modern scholarship to bear on both the military and political issues of the conflict.

Serious treatments of army life on the frontier, a sadly neglected phase of antebellum military history, may be found in the memoirs of a contemporary soldier, Randolph B. Marcy, *Thirty Years of Army Life on the Border* (New York: Harper, 1866), and in two volumes by modern historians, Robert M. Utley, *Frontiersmen in Blue: The United States Army and the Indian, 1848–1865*, The Wars of the United States (New York: Macmillan Co., 1967), and John K. Mahon, *History of the Second Seminole War, 1835–1842* (Gainesville: University of Florida Press, 1967).

Amplification of the points made in this chapter may be found in James L. Morrison, Jr., *"The Best School in the World": West Point, The Pre-Civil War Years, 1833–1866* (Kent, Ohio: Kent State University Press, 1985).

CHAPTER 7

The Old Army and the Confederacy, 1861–1865 _____

JUNE I. GOW

The Civil War began on 12 April 1861, when General Pierre G. T. Beauregard's guns fired on Fort Sumter in Charleston Harbor, South Carolina. To President Abraham Lincoln the attack on the fort was an act of rebellion; to many Southerners it was the opening blow in a struggle which recalled the American Revolution and sought to preserve the true Constitution of the United States. But whether rebel or revolutionary, the new Confederate States of America was little prepared for the war which awaited.

The Confederacy was still only in the process of formation. Territorially it consisted of the seven states of the Deep South, with the eight other slave states remaining in the Union. The new government and its constitution were the creations of a Provisional Congress meeting in a temporary capital at Montgomery, Alabama, and had not yet been sanctioned by elections. President Jefferson Davis, chosen by the Provisional Congress, had been in office for only eight weeks, during which he and his fledgling cabinet had labored to set up the necessary machinery of government and to find the talented men who could staff the executive departments. All this work was in train only, the Confederacy essentially incomplete, when war for survival came in April.

The outbreak of war gave a new dimension to the secession issue. What the South saw as northern aggression stirred regional loyalties and accorded the Confederate government a new political legitimacy. Four states of the Upper South—Virginia, North Carolina, Tennessee, and Arkansas—refused to join in the use of military coercion against the seceded states, and themselves joined the Confederacy. In the meanwhile an embryonic War Department found itself with the crucial and immediate task of defending the new nation. The political crisis had become a military one.

In these circumstances the rapid recruitment, organization, and strategic disposition of southern military forces were essential. Enthusiastic volunteers had to be converted into an army by whatever professional experience the Confederacy could summon to its aid. Obviously and inevitably, that experience owed much to the antebellum United States Army and to the training its officers received at West Point. Whatever experiments might later be made under pressure of war, the Confederate army started out as an American army which drew on an American inheritance.

Despite the proud victories of the Mexican War, the inheritance was a troubled one. In the three decades before the Civil War, neither formal, written rules nor practical experience had succeeded in producing the "perfect yet simple machine" which, as idealized by a career officer such as Beauregard, would act in disciplined responses to the clear and unquestioned authority of its commander.[1] Rather, the army's record, while generally one of success against foreign foes, revealed structural flaws which were especially dangerous in any domestic crisis. Critical weaknesses existed in the areas of institutional order, cohesion, and discipline.

At the topmost levels of command, roles and relationships were not clearly defined.[2] Under the president as the constitutional commander in chief, authority was divided between the secretary of war and the general in chief of the army, according to the traditional American belief that military administration and military command were distinct functions. In practice, of course, these functions overlapped, but with no general staff there was no institutional means of coordinating them. Instead the civilian secretary and the military general wrangled over issues of authority and proper jurisdiction, with each trying to assert his own supremacy over the other. Entangled in these disputes was the adjutant general, the senior officer of the staff, whose department was responsible for issuing the orders of secretary and general alike. Personality conflicts further underlined the ambiguities of the divided command system. The authors of that system intended to provide an orderly division of functions which avoided any dangerous concentration of military power; the unintended result was controversy at the political-military intersection of command, confused lines of authority, and factionalism among the subordinate officers of line and staff.

The character of the American military hierarchy before 1861 only exacerbated these problems.[3] Rank was no simple reflection of past performance and present responsibility, stating unequivocally its holder's place in a vertical chain of command. A dual system of commission produced the phenomenon of double rank, whereby the same officer might hold one rank in the line and another on the staff. A dual system of promotion also made it possible for officers to have two ranks, one reflecting seniority in the regular military establishment and the other marking extraordinary achievement in the form of a special brevet. Henry Wager Halleck labeled this state of affairs "absurd and ridiculous," blaming it for the dangerously deficient staff work of the American army.[4] Certainly it lent itself to continuous controversy over which rank should apply, under what circumstances, and with what responsibilities. Attempts to clarify the situation through definition in the Articles of War or to eliminate it by thoroughgoing reform proved unsuccessful, and problems related to double rank continued to undermine the institutional structure of the antebellum army.

Thus, if the measures of an efficient military institution include coordination at the topmost levels of command, together with a clear definition of roles and relations within an ordered hierarchy, the old army met these requirements to a limited degree only.[5] In fact the army, by its intrinsic military character supposedly an authoritarian and highly disciplined organization, contained within itself considerable potential for resistance and challenge to its own authority structure. Officers were very familiar with a long history of arguments over orders, assignments, and issues of precedence.[6] Ulysses S. Grant later recollected that as a young lieutenant, Braxton Bragg had been so "naturally disputatious" that he had even quarreled in writing with himself over his own duties.[7] This contentious tradition had a double significance. On the one hand, concern over status, dignity, and responsibility was one indicator of an emerging professionalism. On the other hand, the frequency of idiosyncratic rather than disciplined responses among the military elite might, in a situation sufficiently critical, threaten both the institution and its ability to carry out its primary functions.

Institutional weaknesses had not, however, precluded a nascent professionalism in the old army. As William B. Skelton and James L. Morrison, Jr., have shown, the basis of this professionalism lay in the predominantly West Point officer class, with its increasing interest in military theory and military literature and its developing sense of identity, competence, and legitimate function.[8] These characteristics survived the strains of internal dissension, the counterattraction of civilian career opportunities, and the doubts of politicians and civilians in general about the military's role in a democratic society. But the old army's limited professionalism could not survive the double shocks of secession and civil war. These events caused officers to react less as a cohesive class facing a clear military duty than as individual citizens confronting a choice both personal and political. Their decisions made the military yet another institutional casualty of the political crisis.[9]

The army split. From 1802 to 1860 West Point had graduated a total of 1,887 officers, of whom 75 percent were from northern and eastern states, and 25 percent from southern states. The same regional ratio still prevailed in 1860 on the eve of the Civil War among the 752 officers who were then alive and in the service. Of those 752, 74 percent elected to fight for the Union and 24 percent for the Confederacy.[10] The consistency of this pattern suggests that the old army both reflected and retained a sense of civilian loyalty conceived in state and regional terms. That regional loyalty was not, as has commonly been maintained, predominantly southern, but was also characteristic of the North and West. Although it might function constructively when faced with an external enemy, it worked divisively when the conflict was domestic.[11] Private loyalties combined with institutional weaknesses to diminish the effectiveness of the United States Army as a professional, coercive agency of the federal government in the Civil War. Instead, the army drew upon a common American inheritance to provide military theory, military experience, and military leadership for both sides.

This source of military expertise proved crucial for the Confederacy. When the war began, five of the leading figures in the antebellum army chose to fight for the South: Samuel Cooper, the adjutant general; Albert Sidney Johnston, the commander of the Department of the Pacific; Robert E. Lee, the acting commander of the Department of Texas and a possible successor to Winfield Scott as general in chief; Joseph E. Johnston, the newly appointed quartermaster general; and P. G. T. Beauregard, then maneuvering for appointment as superintendent of the United States Military Academy at West Point.[12] These men, with the addition of Braxton Bragg, a former artillery officer and Mexican War hero, commanded the major armies of the Confederacy and worked to set up an effective command system at army headquarters in Richmond. Together with other old army officers of lesser rank, they converted the 340,250 men recruited during the first year of the war into a military force and led them in battle for four years.[13] Without the professional leadership of these six men, the South's struggle for independence would have been swiftly lost.

These officers had come to personal decisions which overrode their group loyalty to their profession. Neither their West Point training, nor their oaths of allegiance, nor the years they had spent in the military service of the United States swayed their response to the Civil War situation. To say that they replied in terms of regional loyalty is, especially for Southerners, undoubtedly true, but that very broad explanation leaves many questions unanswered. On what more specific grounds did individual men make their decisions and justify them? For what did the generals think they were fighting? Some answers at least can be suggested by looking at the six highest ranking Confederate leaders.

Samuel Cooper was not even a Southerner, but a New Yorker by birth and upbringing, the son of a Revolutionary War hero.[14] By 1861 he had been forty-six years in the United States Army, twenty-three of them in the Adjutant General's Department, with the last six as adjutant general. Yet he resigned in March 1861, while the crisis was still in its secession phase, offered his services to the Confederacy, and was appointed adjutant and inspector general of the Confederate States Army. Cooper was sixty-two when he thus transferred his allegiance as an officer and a citizen to the new southern nation. Why he did so he did not himself explain. But he had married into Virginia society and during his long years on duty in Washington, he had lived on the Virginia side of the Potomac. The resulting inference that family ties determined Cooper's choice was, however, denied by Jefferson Davis, who as secretary of war in the 1850s had known the adjutant general both socially and professionally. Writing after the war, Davis maintained that Cooper had not acted for private reasons but out of political conviction. The United States, Cooper had argued, was formed under a constitutional compact by member states. Although no member state was subject to military coercion by the federal government, by March 1861 it was already apparent that the federal government would exceed its powers by warring on the seceded states. Without waiting for the outbreak of war or for the secession of his adopted state of Virginia, Cooper anticipated events by resigning his commission and joining the Confederacy—thus, according to Davis, consciously aligning himself with the party of constitutional law and right.

Conviction that the southern cause was just may have made Cooper's decision easier, but Albert Sidney Johnston liked neither of the alternatives facing him.[15] On the one hand lay his duty and honor as an officer, sworn to uphold the federal government and the integrity of a Union in which he deeply believed; on the other lay the loyalty and gratitude due his adopted state of Texas. In normal times these two allegiances need not have conflicted, but the secession of Texas on 1 February 1861 set them at odds with one another. Forced to choose, Johnston placed his allegiance to his state first and resigned from the old army. He did not make this decision lightly. The southern states were, he believed, exercising their "right of revolution" in a nation marred by the hostility of the North toward the South, by the attacks of fanatical abolitionists, and by the Republican failure to respect legitimate southern interests. Johnston hoped that there would be peaceful settlement of the issues, but he feared that a final decision would come only "by the sword." He sought to reconcile his honor and his conscience by continuing to serve faithfully at his Pacific post until notified of the formal acceptance of his resignation; only then did he turn to what he perceived as his superior duty to his state. A West Point education and years of service in the old army had encouraged in Johnston a natural military conservatism, his son and biographer later affirmed, but never outweighed his lasting sense of responsibility as "the citizen of a republic."[16]

Robert E. Lee's distaste for the events forcing him toward a personal decision was even more marked than Johnston's, for while he conceded the aggressiveness of northern actions against the South, he could not justify the remedy of dissolving the Union.[17] In his view the patriots of the American Revolution had not set up merely a constitutional compact with all its encouragement to anarchy, but a perpetual union within which the rights of all states would be protected. At the time of the Hartford Convention in 1814–1815, Virginians had declared secession from that union to be treasonous. Lee believed that it was still an act of treason which could only bring on revolution and civil war. But although his convictions were firm and his condemnation of secession complete, Lee could find no attraction in a nation which must be maintained by force. He sadly chose to withdraw to Virginia, and in retirement there to mourn alike his country and the welfare and progress of mankind. In April 1861 the outbreak of war at Fort Sumter, together with the impending secession of Virginia and the possibility that he could be recalled to duty in order to take up arms against his own state, forced Lee to come to a new decision. Without changing his political views, he nevertheless resigned from the army, explaining his action in terms of loyalty to his relatives, his children, and his home.[18] These same loyalties took him not into private life, but into the service first of Virginia and then of the Confederacy. In the difficult struggle between loyalties, private responsibilities eventually overcame public responsibilities, as the Virginian overshadowed the American.

Joseph E. Johnston shared Lee's loyalty to the state where he had been born, raised, and educated.[19] But Johnston was able, where Lee was not, to justify the secession of Virginia by appealing to the revolutionary principles on which

General Robert E. Lee, photograph by Matthew Brady, April 1865
Library of Congress (USZ62-20244)

the new American nation had been founded in 1789. Implicit in Johnston's position was the doctrine of a constitutional compact, voluntarily entered into by the member states, and from which they could voluntarily withdraw. In 1861 the legitimate occasion for Virginia's withdrawal from the Union lay in her refusal to deny the right of secession to the states of the Confederacy. When she rejected the northern demand for troops to help subjugate the South, Johnston found no difficulty in deciding his allegiance. His natural and primary loyalty was to his state, whereas his obligations as an American army officer were purely contractual and could readily be dissolved by the formalities of resignation. Thus, his decision to resign implied neither treason nor professional failure, he argued, while asserting that his own action and that of Virginia would in the event be justified by the lasting success of the Confederacy.

Like Lee and the two Johnstons, Beauregard could for a time hold in suspension the conflict implicit in his private loyalty to his own state, Louisiana, and his public duty as an officer in the United States Army.[20] But the secession of Louisiana on 26 January 1861 forced him also to a decision about his primary allegiance. His choice followed the same pattern: the formal resignation of his military commission, relieving him of his duties to the Union, and assumption of the responsibilities of a state citizen. After twenty-two years in the old army, Beauregard did not make his decision without reluctance; but it was the easier, he wrote, in that he was "strongly imbued with the constitutional doctrine of States' Rights and State Sovereignty," and believed the South in danger from a northern tendency toward democracy and despotism, two interacting elements which threatened the rule of law. Family loyalties, state citizenship, and political views coincided for Beauregard, dictated his resignation from the American army, and rapidly brought him a new commission in the service of the South.

Curiously, among the Confederate generals-to-be it was the civilian Braxton Bragg, who—although he had resigned from the army five years earlier—was most conspicuously impressed by military values.[21] He advised that for efficiency and profit southern plantations should be run as small military establishments embodying discipline, system, regularity, and economy; inculcating due sub-ordination among blacks and children; rooting out laxity; and quashing any notions of revolt or rebellion. Bragg called his own Louisiana plantation Bivouac. He confided his views on the need for military discipline and order in civilian life to his friend William Tecumseh Sherman, then superintendent of the Lou-isiana state military academy, and regretted that in the coming political crisis similar convictions of duty would place the two men on opposite sides. They both despised the "few old political hacks and barroom bullies" who had brought on the crisis, but loyalty to self, family, and friends meant that each man would serve a different "country." By late January 1861 Bragg considered separation inevitable and his choice equally clear. In the three months before formal hos-tilities began at Sumter, he commanded both state troops in Louisiana and the Confederate forces at Pensacola, Florida. Any residual loyalty that Bragg might have felt toward the old army was apparently satisfied when he granted the federal garrison at the Baton Rouge arsenal full military honors in their surrender to the Louisiana authorities.

Thus, for all six Confederate generals-to-be, the problem of their duty as officers and members of an embryonic professional class could be met through a nice respect for the formalities of military honor and etiquette. Each could then reach his personal decision as a citizen rather than as an officer, defining for himself the issues in the domestic crisis and his own response to them. They did not find their answers easily. Albert Sidney Johnston faced division within his family; Lee was the proud descendant of a family closely associated with the founding of the Republic; Cooper had also inherited the revolutionary tradition and was, moreover, a Northerner. While all six framed their individual debates in political and constitutional terms, they disagreed in their perception of those terms. P. G. T. Beauregard and Joe Johnston believed secession a right, but for Robert E. Lee it was treason; Lee and Samuel Cooper thought in terms of the Constitution, although with totally divergent interpretations; Albert Sidney Johnston and Braxton Bragg showed a shrewder political awareness of the northern threat to legitimate southern interests. But for all of them—even for Lee, in whom professional and broad political allegiances most closely corresponded— the final decision was based on a combination of family and state loyalties. Personal and regional connections proved stronger than institutional and national ties, revealing the old army as yet another institution reflecting the divisions of mid-nineteenth-century America.

This emphasis upon personal loyalties and individual values was to have an important effect on the Confederacy. Just as it had undermined the institutional structure of the old army, so would it affect the cohesion and discipline of the Confederate forces. For along with the military skills they had learned in the antebellum years, West Point officers exhibited in their new organization the familiar tradition of challenge and resistance to military authority, as they quarreled over who should wield it and how. With notable exceptions, factionalism accompanied expertise; and if "died of democracy" is an appropriate epitaph for the Confederacy, it epitomizes not only southern civilian society but also its military professionals.[22]

The contribution of West Point to the southern war effort has always attracted attention.[23] During the Civil War Jefferson Davis—himself a West Pointer, Mexican War hero, past secretary of war, and the chairman of the 1860 Senate commission to examine the military education provided at West Point—considered training at the United States Military Academy an obvious criterion for the selection of Confederate officers. His critics, on the other hand, blamed the West Point influence for stifling talent and innovation. The resulting disputes over appointment and assignment, rank and command, spilled from the military arena into the political and added to the difficulties of managing and commanding the Confederate armies.

The contemporary debate over the West Point role has since been joined by military historians. In the centennial celebration held at the academy in 1902,

Colonel Charles W. Larned analyzed the contribution of West Point graduates to military leadership in the Civil War. He claimed that they had commanded the armies of both sides in fifty-five of the sixty major battles of the war and had led the winning side in the remaining five.[24] In following up this analysis, later writers have underlined additional elements common to the leaders of both armies during the war: education in the same military principles and techniques and broadly similar experience in Florida, on the frontier, and in Mexico. These writers have also made certain distinctions: Confederate leaders were on the whole older, more prone to sickness, less able to stand the stresses of active campaigning, and more conservative in their military thinking.[25]

Larned's investigative framework has been useful, but it has certain limitations. His leaders are defined by virtue of an experience they underwent when they were approximately twenty-one years old—graduation from West Point— and not in terms of what happened to them afterward. In addition, they are considered solely as individuals, the generals of victory, and are not seen as part of institutional structures which themselves need analysis and comparison. Even a cursory investigation of the career experience and institutional context of selected senior officers on either side raises interesting questions. Of the six Union generals closest to high command in the Civil War—Winfield Scott, George B. McClellan, Ethan Allen Hitchcock, Henry Wager Halleck, Ulysses S. Grant, and William Tecumseh Sherman—only Scott was still in service in 1861. The others had all resigned their military commissions in favor of civil occupations. For the six comparable Confederate generals, the situation was reversed. This contrast, usually neglected even though it might add to the old and dubious argument for a specifically southern military tradition in America, has important implications about the character and variety of experiences which contributed to successful generalship.[26]

Furthermore, in 1861 the Union army at least had institutions in place which, whatever their weaknesses, had provided direction and command over American forces for the past forty or more years. Confederate organizational arrangements, although skeletal at best, resembled those of the northern army, because in the initial crisis experienced officers were more concerned to reproduce the old system they already knew than to develop a new one. Both sides therefore drew on the institutional experience of the antebellum army, and both encountered the problem of expanding and adjusting a familiar system to meet the unfamiliar demands of a large-scale war. T. Harry Williams has argued that by the spring of 1864 the Union had succeeded in developing a new command system which contributed significantly to the final victory of the North one year later.[27] The Confederacy proved less adaptable.

Central to the Confederate command system, in the absence of any general staff, was the Adjutant General's Department headed by Samuel Cooper.[28] In a sea of unending paperwork, department headquarters at Richmond functioned as an office of orders and correspondence, as an office of military record, and as an office of inspection. Many of its tasks were narrowly bureaucratic, but

General Fitzhugh Lee, the nephew of both Robert E. Lee and Cooper, considered the department's work to be of the broadest significance.[29] On it depended the creation and maintenance of a flexible but precisely articulated fighting machine—one served by the coordinated efforts of the various staff departments and capable of executing the strategic and tactical plans of its leaders. Fitzhugh Lee and Jefferson Davis argued that the labors of Cooper and his department, while not bringing ultimate victory, contributed importantly to the Confederate war effort.

Cooper's own view of his role as adjutant and inspector general was rooted in his old army experience. He ran his department and, beyond it, the Confederate army as a whole according to United States Army Regulations, now taken over wholesale for use by the southern forces. He considered himself a *de facto* chief of staff, communicating the military decisions of the president and the secretary of war to senior commanders, and providing through the staff departments the means by which the generals might carry out their instructions. He was ready to offer professional military advice to his civilian superiors, if asked to do so, but would not himself make decisions or exercise command. These responsibilities were outside his province. In short, Cooper saw his functions as administrative only, in accordance with antebellum military theory. Following familiar antebellum practice, the adjutant general associated himself in matters of the highest importance with the War Department rather than with the generals of the line. Cooper's interpretation of his place in the Confederate command system thus reflected a mixture of the institutional and the personal, as he carried out the combined roles of adjutant and inspector general, chief of staff, and military adviser. His work in all of these areas, moreover, brought him into close touch with Jefferson Davis.

As president of the Confederacy, Davis was also its constitutional commander in chief. Sometimes he used his legal prerogative to intervene in the conduct of Confederate military operations, as did Lincoln in Union operations.[30] In the eyes of his critics, Davis usurped the offices of both secretary of war and general in chief. His assertion of the military powers of the presidency is usually explained in very simple terms: his antebellum military experience had given him such knowledge of, and taste for, military matters that in the Civil War he sought to direct the War Department and, through it, the Confederate armies. This explanation, however, does not reveal how Davis's antebellum experience affected the development of the Confederate command system.

That experience, as so often in the old army, combined elements both personal and institutional. Davis, for example, had long thought Cooper a gentleman of high character and cultivated taste. The two men had known each other since the late 1830s when, as a junior member of the Adjutant General's Department, Cooper had acted as military adviser to Secretary of War Joel R. Poinsett. When Davis became secretary of war in 1853, Cooper was the adjutant general, and the two men maintained a harmonious association through which the civilian secretary first received professional advice and then transmitted his orders to the army.[31]

In marked contrast to this successful relationship were Davis's dealings with Winfield Scott.[32] The two men were mutually antipathetic, exchanging vituperative insults in official, public correspondence. From insignificant beginnings the occasion for their hostility had become in the secretary's mind a challenge by the general in chief to duly constituted civilian authority over the army. This conflict was defused for Davis when Scott transferred his headquarters to New York and Cooper remained in Washington as the principal link between the secretary and the army. With this experience behind him, it is little wonder that Davis as president of the Confederacy should lean heavily on Cooper and his department in the management of the Confederate armies, while strenuously resisting the appointment of a general in chief to command them, preferring instead a system of regional commands.[33]

However understandable in the light of his earlier experience, Davis's command arrangements were subjected to much criticism.[34] Robert Garlick Hill Kean, chief of the Confederate Bureau of War, charged that Davis usurped the functions of the secretary of war and through his reliance on Cooper manifested a narrow West Point favoritism that was blind to the adjutant general's limited capacity, professional conservatism, and inability to make independent decisions even on minor matters. One of Cooper's own assistants, Major Samuel W. Melton, asserted that experience in the old army inhibited rather than promoted the efficient management of the unprecedentedly large Confederate forces. A congressional committee of inquiry recommended that the Adjutant General's Department be reorganized to permit more attention to its crucial but neglected inspection duties. Robert E. Lee called for a new staff system to provide discipline and direction in the largely inexperienced southern armies. Joseph E. Johnston complained that his 1863 assignment to regional command of the Western Department gave him a theater, but no army, and reduced him to military impotence. And the Senate Military Affairs Committee argued persistently, but vainly until 1865 for the appointment of a general in chief.

To some degree this criticism sprang from a growing political and military factionalism in the Confederacy.[35] Davis's own leadership was called in question. His removal of Beauregard from command in 1862, following the Shiloh and Corinth campaigns, and of Johnston in 1864 on the eve of the battle for Atlanta became highly sensitive and controversial issues, as did his long retention of Braxton Bragg as commander of the Army of Tennessee. Military decisions were complicated by family connections, political associations, and the old institutional quarrels over control of the army. To some extent this criticism was prejudiced and self-serving, but it also reflected genuine concern for the most effective use of the limited southern resources. Efforts at reform sought to adjust the command system originally evolved under Davis and Cooper to meet the growing pressures of the war.

The critical link in the system was that connecting the civilian political authorities and the generals in the field. What was needed was a coordinating agency to advise the political leaders on strategy, calculate the military means necessary to achieve strategic decisions, and give direction and cohesion to the work of independent-minded staff departments and equally independent-minded field commanders. Lincoln and the Union tried to meet these problems, and encountered numerous difficulties in doing so, through the old army practice of appointing a commanding general, also known as the general in chief. This Davis hoped to avoid by his use of the adjutant general and other extrainstitutional military advisers. When he finally did consent in January 1865 to appoint a Confederate general in chief, some interesting variations emerged in the contemporary theory of generalship.

The appointment, if it were to be made, had always been intended for Robert E. Lee, commander of the Army of Northern Virginia since June 1862, victor of Fredericksburg and Chancellorsville, and the most prestigious general in the Confederacy.[36] The president and Congress believed that Lee could combine active field command in Virginia with the general direction of all Confederate forces, thus concentrating in his own person the familiar heroic functions of military leadership and the newer managerial responsibilities of a large-scale, modern war.[37] A similar expectation, that the general in chief could and should combine these functions, was widespread in the North and contributed to the early dissatisfaction with McClellan and Halleck and the later approval of Grant. In the South, however, Lee had declared the combination impossible. In the summer of 1862, he forced Davis to choose between keeping him in Richmond and assigning him to the field with the Army of Northern Virginia. When Lee finally accepted the double responsibility in 1865, he did so reluctantly, under pressure, and with doubts about his ability to do more than "maintain a harmonious action" among the major armies while relying on the various field commanders for the actual conduct of military operations.[38]

Lee's reservations about his new appointment were shared by General Joseph E. Johnston.[39] A general's proper role and the only true basis of his usefulness, Johnston argued, was active command of an army. Without an army he became "a comparatively insignificant official"; but unless he gave up his army, he could not exercise "an impartial supervision of the whole service." Thus, the new office of Confederate general in chief, intended to combine the functions of command and direction, in fact contained irreconcilable elements which Lee was expected somehow to resolve, and Johnston warned of disappointment to come.

His warning proved apt. Lee's two-month tenure as general in chief coincided with the last struggles of the Confederacy, culminating in the fall of Richmond and the surrender on 9 April 1865 at Appomattox. In this final campaign Lee's attention had to be given to the immediate problems of countering Grant and saving the Army of Northern Virginia. Time and the enemy did not permit any real occasion to experiment with the wider implications of his appointment.

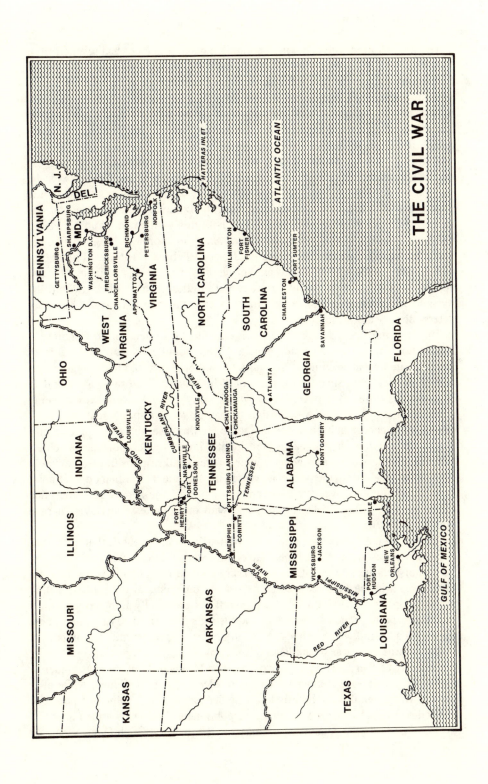

The long Confederate delay in appointing a general in chief had resulted from a combination of factors: the president's earlier experience as secretary of war; Lee's doubts about the feasibility of an assignment so wide-ranging in its duties; and the continuing Confederate dispute involving the president, successive secretaries of war, Congress, and generals sensitive about their military prerogatives and the proper relationship between the military and political aspects of command. But these difficulties over the appointment of a general in chief did not prevent Davis from experimenting with an alternative method of linking the central direction of the war with its military execution in the field. Twice he assigned a general officer "to duty at the seat of government, . . . under the direction of the President, . . . charged with the conduct of military operations in the armies of the Confederacy."[40] Lee held this assignment from 13 March 1862 until called to the command of the Army of Northern Virginia in June 1862. Braxton Bragg held the same job from 24 February 1864 until his return to field duty in October of that year. For neither man did this assignment mean appointment to a specific military office with duties clearly defined within the recognized structure of command. In each case the role was an ad hoc one, determined by the president.

The day after Lee's assignment, Davis explained his intentions to Congress.[41] He did not want a "commanding general" who would conduct operations from his headquarters at Richmond and also be authorized to assume command of armies in the field. Such an officer would be much too close to a general in chief for his taste. Moreover, Davis wrote, army generals would resent being superseded on the eve of a campaign or battle, so an appointment with such power was unacceptable in a military sense. It was also unacceptable constitutionally because it challenged the president's powers as commander in chief. What Davis did want was a general whose tenure and responsibilities he would determine. In addition, the president wanted the "conduct of military operations" defined as authority over "the movement of troops, the supply and discipline of the Army." It was in these terms and with these duties that Davis charged both Lee and Bragg.

For this he has been much criticized, primarily on the grounds that for selfish or legalistic reasons, wishing himself to command and jealous of his prerogatives, he diminished the powers of his new assignees and by refusing them the right to command in the field reduced them to mere bureaucrats, the echoes of their political superiors.[42] This line of argument reflects a generally derogatory estimate of Davis's performance as president and also implies a basic assumption about military leadership which echoes Johnston's, that the proper and most important place for a general was at the head of an army.

Certainly neither Lee nor Bragg expressed enthusiasm about their assignments. Lee could not foresee "either advantage or pleasure" in his duties, while after the war Bragg recollected bitterly his struggles against the "combined power of imbeciles, traitors, rogues and intriguing politicians."[43] Yet both men accepted the definition of "the conduct of military operations" by which Davis separated the organization and management of the Confederate forces from the active command of specific armies. Lee watched over the condition of military affairs at crucial points, checking Confederate needs and enemy threats, providing information and advice to the field commanders, and, where possible, arranging for supplies and reinforcements.[44] In trying to coordinate the functions of the various staff departments, he acted in effect as an unofficial chief of staff. Bragg's role was similar to that of Lee, although with a greater emphasis on inspection duties, and Bragg described it as "almost entirely ministerial . . . [requiring] an amount of labor, investigation and *pruning* both thankless and appalling."[45]

The duties of both Lee and Bragg were primarily those of military management. To these Davis added the role of "military adviser," consulting their professional opinion on important questions of strategy, command, and the allocation of Confederate resources.[46] The two generals were therefore in a position to exert considerable influence on military decisions, but only informally at the president's discretion and without any necessary expectation that their advice would be adopted.

Clearly, Davis was not using Lee and Bragg as either "commanding general" or "general in chief." Rather, he used them much as he had earlier used Adjutant and Inspector General Cooper, extending their functions as the pressures of the war increased. Whereas the tremendous burden of the adjutant general's work, as well as his advancing age, confined Cooper more and more closely to his bureau duties, Lee and Bragg could be sent on missions outside of Richmond. In 1862 Lee went to the Carolinas, and the summer of 1864 found Bragg in Georgia and Alabama. Even after Lee had taken over command of the Army of Northern Virginia, he continued to act as a military adviser; and Bragg was not only an adviser to the president but also worked specifically to develop the inspection department whose neglect under Cooper had weakened the discipline, control, and coordination of the Confederate forces.[47] Indeed, it had been suggested that Bragg be appointed inspector general and even that he replace Cooper as adjutant and inspector general.[48] This substitution, however, Davis never made, preferring to leave Cooper where he was and to call on Lee and Bragg when the conduct of military operations required.

Thus, the president changed neither the formal institutional structure of command nor his personal assignment of Cooper as chief officer of the Confederate staff. Instead, he sought through ad hoc arrangements to provide for the much expanded organizational needs of the army while at the same time maintaining both the separation of administration and command and his own control over the general direction of the war.

While these adjustments of the command system had the merit of recognizing the importance of military management, their weakness lay precisely in their lack of institutionalization. Too much depended on the personal factor, and the burdens were too heavy to be carried by individuals. Davis, whatever his experience or inclination, was not the Confederate secretary of war but the president, with extensive executive and political responsibilities. Cooper was a desk officer, imbued with the traditions and methods of the old army and, by the time of the Civil War, nearing the end of his career. Lee was persistently drawn, both by his talents and by events, to the concerns of command in the crucial Virginia theater. And Bragg, while an admittedly able administrator, had his usefulness seriously impaired by a "naturally disputatious" and authoritarian temper which by 1864 had been strained to the breaking point. For assistance these overburdened men could call variously on the civilian officials of the Bureau of War, on the chiefs of the separate staff departments, on the eight assistant adjutants already fully occupied with departmental routine, or on the five staff officers assigned to each general officer conducting military operations. Such help was simply inadequate. There was no central agency to collate information, construct plans, make recommendations, or help execute decisions once reached. The Confederate leaders worked, in short, without the assistance of a general staff.

That they did so did not indicate any lack of concern over the problem of ensuring an efficient staff at all levels and in all areas.[49] They worried, as had the leaders of the old army, over the recruitment, assignment, and promotion of staff officers, fearing that nepotism and personal prejudice too often outweighed merit. And they debated the highly significant alternatives defined by Davis as "a staff for generals, or a general staff," with Generals Johnston and Beauregard and powerful Senator Louis T. Wigfall arguing for the first, while Lee, Bragg, and the president supported the second.

"A staff for generals" implied a group of officers selected by an individual commander and by him assigned to specific staff duties; the president would confer the formal commission in accordance with congressional military legislation, but the staff would in practice be attached to the person of the general and would be responsible to him. The resulting close integration of field staff and line command would, so its proponents claimed, serve the army best by maintaining the discretionary authority of the general and preserving his relative independence from the Richmond bureaucracy. The basic argument was that the general was the best judge of his own needs: Beauregard, for example, was convinced that the great generals of history, Alexander and Caesar, Frederick and Napoleon, owed their success to their freedom from stultifying central control.

"A general staff," on the other hand, signified a reduction in the personal influence of field commanders through the creation of a staff corps on, as Lee said, "the French model." Officers would be selected for their aptitude for staff work, receive special training, and then be appointed and promoted according to merit within their own corps. They would be responsible to the heads of the various staff departments, who would assign them to field work as required in particular theaters or commands. This organizational pattern emphasized the need in Confederate staff work for experience, coordination, and centralization. What its advocates understood by "general staff," therefore, was not a superior branch of the staff to meet the complex demands of modern war (that did not come in the American army until 1903), but rather the existing system reformed to encourage professionalism in its officers and to tighten institutional control over the army.

In theory and on paper, the argument for a general staff was successful, and General Order No. 44 of 29 April 1864 and the Senate act of 14 June 1864 were designed to implement the desired changes. But substantial reorganization proved impossible. In the fourth year of the war, with mounting pressure from the great Union assaults in Virginia and Georgia, neither the Adjutant General's Department nor the generals in the field had the resources or the time to reconstruct the staff system. Thus, the field staff remained essentially the personal creation of the commander, and the staff departments at Richmond functioned as before, unable to develop even the modest general staff envisaged by Davis and his closest advisers.

Southerners had made a political revolution, but they failed to make a military one. They debated, as the leaders of the old army had done in the 1850s, the need to train highly professional officers and develop new institutions of command, and they were aware of European changes along these lines. But serious reform proposals stirred both political and military jealousies, and proved impossible to implement in a war situation. The Confederacy remained the captive of its American military inheritance, benefiting from its experience but struggling with its limitations throughout the Civil War.

Defeat ended the Confederate efforts to devise from the old army a modern command system. Victory had the same effect in the Union, and the workable system constructed by Grant to meet the command problems of 1864 was allowed to lapse once the Civil War was over. The familiar organizational patterns of the old army, with all their problems, had almost forty years of contentious life yet to run and another war to fight before substantial institutional reform was finally achieved in the 1903 General Staff Act.

NOTES

1. U.S., Department of War, *The War of the Rebellion: A Compilation of the Official Records of the Union and Confederate Armies*, 128 vols. (Washington: Government Printing Office, 1880–1901), ser. I, X, pt. 2, 443 (hereafter cited as *OR*).

2. Emory Upton, *The Military Policy of the United States* (Washington: Government Printing Office, 1917), pp. 155–59; William H. Carter, *The American Army* (Indianapolis: Bobbs-Merrill, 1915), pp. 184–204; Leonard D. White, *The Jacksonians: A Study in Administrative History, 1829–1861* (New York: Macmillan Co.,1954), pp. 190–96; Samuel P. Huntington, *The Soldier and the State: The Theory and Politics of Civil-Military Relations* (Cambridge: Harvard University Press, 1957), pp. 208–11.

3. H. L. Scott, *Military Dictionary* . . . (1861; reprint, Westport, Conn.: Greenwood Press, 1968), s.vv. "brevet," "command," and "rank."

4. Henry Wager Halleck, *Elements of Military Art and Science* (1846; reprint, Westport, Conn.: Greenwood Press, 1971), pp. 242, 245.

5. This chapter makes no attempt to apply any fixed institutional model to the antebellum American army, but sociological concepts relevant to the nineteenth-century

experience have been drawn from Morris Janowitz, *The Professional Soldier: A Social and Political Portrait* (New York: Free Press, 1960); Bengt Abrahamsson, *Military Professionalization and Political Power* (Beverly Hills: Sage Publications, 1972); Hans Gerth and C. Wright Mills, *Character and Social Structure: The Psychology of Social Institutions* (New York: Harcourt, Brace and World, 1953); and Huntington, *The Soldier and the State*.

6. For example, see Marcus Cunliffe, *Soldiers and Civilians: The Martial Spirit in America, 1775–1865* (Boston: Little, Brown & Co., 1968), pp. 140–42.

7. Grady McWhiney, *Braxton Bragg and Confederate Defeat*, vol. I, *Field Command* (New York: Columbia University Press, 1969), 33–34.

8. See Russell F. Weigley, *Towards an American Army: Military Thought from Washington to Marshall* (New York: Columbia University Press, 1962), p. 39; Huntington, *The Soldier and the State*, pp. 193–221. Contemporary evaluations of West Point training are found in U.S., Congress, Senate, *Report of the Commission . . . to examine into the organization, system of discipline, and course of instruction of the United States Military Academy at West Point*, 36th Cong., 2d sess., S. Misc. Doc. No. 3, 1860.

9. The argument here is derived from David Donald's thesis in "An Excess of Democracy: The American Civil War and the Social Process," in David Donald, ed., *Lincoln Reconsidered: Essays on the Civil War Era*, 2d ed., enlarged (New York: Vintage Books, 1956), pp. 209–35, especially pp. 234–35.

10. Analysis of West Point cadets and graduates rests on their records in George W. Cullum, *Biographical Register of the Officers and Graduates of the U.S. Military Academy . . . 1802, to 1890 . . .* , 6 vols., 3d ed., rev. and extended (Boston: Houghton Mifflin Co., 1891), I and II, passim. The regional definitions are essentially geographic: included with the northern and western states are those border states which remained in the Union in 1861; and included with the southern states are those of the Southwest and the Confederate border. Percentages have been rounded to the nearest whole number. The missing 2 percent in the 1861 figures consists of officers who died during the crisis or who declined to serve either side.

Those officers who transferred their regional loyalties in 1861 constituted 12 percent of the graduates serving at that time; forty-six from the North and West fought for the Confederacy, forty-seven from the South for the Union; 73 percent of this especially divided group were from border states. As the numbers of transfers are virtually even, the overall percentages are not affected.

11. The regional framework within which this analysis has been set was suggested by Frank L. Owsley, "The Fundamental Cause of the Civil War: Egocentric Sectionalism," *Journal of Southern History* 7 (1941): 3–18.

12. Biographical information on Confederate generals may be obtained from Ezra J. Warner, *Generals in Gray: Lives of the Confederate Commanders* (Baton Rouge: Louisiana State University Press, 1959). A companion volume is Warner, *Generals in Blue: Lives of the Union Commanders* (Baton Rouge: Louisiana State University Press, 1964).

13. *OR*, ser. IV, I, 962–64.

14. *Dictionary of American Biography*, s.v. "Samuel Cooper"; General Fitz Lee, "Sketch of the Late General S. Cooper," *Southern Historical Society Papers* 3 (1877): 270–76.

15. Albert Sidney Johnston to F. J. Porter, 25 February 1861, in William Preston Johnston, *The Life of General Albert Sidney Johnston . . .* (New York: D. Appleton and Company, 1879), p. 270; Johnston to W. P. Johnston, 9 April 1861, ibid., pp. 270–71;

Johnston to John J. Griffin, 14 April 1861, ibid., pp. 271–72; Johnston to Eliza Gilpin, 1 June 1861, ibid., pp. 273–74. A fuller discussion of Johnston's conduct during the secession crisis can be found in Charles P. Roland, *Albert Sidney Johnston: Soldier of Three Republics* (Austin: University of Texas Press, 1964), pp. 244–52.

16. Johnston, *The Life of General Albert Sidney Johnston*, pp. 256–60.

17. R. E. Lee to W. H. F. Lee, 29 January 1861, quoted in full in William M. E. Rachal, ed., " 'Secession is Nothing But Revolution'; A Letter of R. E. Lee to His Son 'Rooney,' " *The Virginia Magazine of History and Biography* 69 (1961): 4–6.

18. Lee to Winfield Scott, 20 April 1861, *The Wartime Papers of R. E. Lee*, ed. Clifford Dowdey and Louis H. Manarin (Boston: Little, Brown & Co., 1961), pp. 8–9; Lee to Anne Marshall, 20 April 1861, ibid., pp. 9–10; Lee to Sydney Smith Lee, 20 April 1861, ibid., p. 10.

19. For Johnston's views, see Joseph E. Johnston, *Narrative of Military Operations* . . . (New York: D. Appleton and Company, 1874), pp. 9–11.

20. For Beauregard's views, see Alfred Roman, *The Military Operations of General Beauregard in the War Between the States, 1861–1865*, 2 vols. (New York: Harper and Brothers, 1883), I, 14–27; and, T. Harry Williams, *P. G. T. Beauregard: Napoleon in Gray* (New York: Collier Books, 1962), pp. 66–68.

21. For Bragg's views, see Braxton Bragg to W. T. Sherman, 19 December 1859, *General W. T. Sherman as College President: A Collection of letters, documents, and other material . . . ; 1859–1861*, ed. Walter L. Fleming (Cleveland, Ohio: The Arthur H. Clark Company, 1912), pp. 80–83; Bragg to G. Mason Graham, 27 June 1860, ibid., pp. 236–38; Bragg to Sherman, 26 December 1860, ibid., pp. 319–21; Bragg to Sherman, 27 January 1861, ibid., p. 351; Bragg to Elise, 7 March [1861], quoted in McWhiney, *Braxton Bragg and Confederate Defeat*, p. 155. A more extensive discussion of Bragg's ideas and actions appears in McWhiney, *Braxton Bragg and Confederate Defeat*, pp. 141–56.

22. David Donald, "Died of Democracy," in David Donald, ed., *Why the North Won the Civil War* (New York: Collier Books, 1962), pp. 79–90.

23. Useful material may be found in Ellsworth Eliot, Jr., *West Point in the Confederacy* (New York: G. A. Baker and Co., Inc., 1941).

24. Colonel Charles W. Larned, "The Genius of West Point," *The Centennial of the United States Military Academy at West Point, New York, 1802–1902*, 2 vols. (Washington: Government Printing Office, 1904), I, 488–94.

25. David Donald, "Refighting the Civil War," in *Lincoln Reconsidered*, pp. 82–102; T. Harry Williams, "The Military Leadership of North and South," in *Why the North Won the Civil War*, pp. 33–54.

26. For a critical discussion of this argument, see Cunliffe, *Soldiers and Civilians*, pp. 335–84.

27. T. Harry Williams, *Americans at War: The Development of the American Military System*, new, enlarged ed. (New York: Collier Books, 1962), pp. 71–91.

28. For a more detailed examination, see June I. Gow, "Theory and Practice in Confederate Military Administration," *Military Affairs* 39 (October 1975): 119–23.

29. Lee, "Sketch of the Late General S. Cooper," 269–70.

30. For assessments of Davis, see Rembert W. Patrick, *Jefferson Davis and His Cabinet* (Baton Rouge: Louisiana State University Press, 1944), pp. 27–76, 103–54; Bell I. Wiley, *The Road to Appomattox* (New York: Atheneum, 1968), pp. 1–42; David Potter, "Jefferson Davis and the Political Factors in Confederate Defeat," in *Why the North Won*

the Civil War, pp. 91–112; Clement Eaton, *Jefferson Davis* (New York: Free Press, 1977).

31. Davis To Fitzhugh Lee, 5 April 1877, in Lee, "Sketch of the Late General S. Cooper," 274–76.

32. The subject matter and style of this dispute can be sampled in Dunbar Rowland, ed., *Jefferson Davis, Constitutionalist: His Letters, Papers and Speeches*, 10 vols. (Jackson, Miss.: Mississippi Department of Archives and History, 1923), III, 1–25.

33. For discussions of Davis's command system, see Frank E. Vandiver, *Rebel Brass: The Confederate Command System* (Baton Rouge: Louisiana State University Press, 1956); and Thomas Lawrence Connelly and Archer Jones, *The Politics of Command: Factions and Ideas in Confederate Strategy* (Baton Rouge: Louisiana State University Press, 1973), pp. 87–136.

34. R. G. H. Kean, *Inside the Confederate Government: The Diary of Robert Garlick Hill Kean*, ed. Edward Younger (New York: Oxford University Press, 1957), pp. 87–88, 90, 100–101; *OR*, ser. IV, II, 945; *OR*, ser. IV, I, 890–91; *OR*, ser. IV, II, 447–48.

35. See Potter, "Jefferson Davis and the Political Factors in Confederate Defeat," pp. 91–112; Wiley, *Road to Appomattox*, pp. 1–42; Connelly and Jones, *The Politics of Command*, pp. 49–86, 170–200.

36. The classic biography of Lee is Douglas Southall Freeman, *R. E. Lee: A Biography*, 4 vols. (New York: Charles Scribner's Sons, 1934–1935); a more recent study is Thomas L. Connelly, *The Marble Man: Robert E. Lee and His Image in American Society* (New York: Alfred A. Knopf, 1977).

37. "Heroic" and "managerial" are terms derived from Janowitz, *The Professional Soldier*, sec. II, pp. 21–22 and passim.

38. *OR*, ser. I, XLVI, pt. 2, 1091–92; *Wartime Papers of R. E. Lee*, pp. 884–85, 891, 892–93.

39. Joseph E. Johnston to Louis T. Wigfall, 12 February 1865, Wigfall Family Papers, Library of Congress, Washington, D.C.

40. *Wartime Papers of R. E. Lee*, p. 127; *OR*, ser. I, XXII, pt. 2, 799.

41. *OR*, ser. IV, I, 997–98.

42. Freeman, *R. E. Lee*, II, 4–7; Don C. Seitz, *Braxton Bragg: General of the Confederacy* (Columbia, S.C.: The State Company, 1924), p. 410.

43. *Wartime Papers of R. E. Lee*, pp. 127–28; Bragg to E. T. Sykes, 8 February 1873, in William E. Polk, *Leonidas Polk: Bishop and General*, 2 vols. (New York: Longmans, Green, and Co., 1893), II, 310.

44. Walter H. Taylor, *Four Years with General Lee* (New York: Appleton and Company, 1877), pp. 37–38.

45. Braxton Bragg, Notes of Movements from December 1863 to July 1864, MS in Braxton Bragg Papers, William P. Palmer Collection, Western Reserve Historical Society, Cleveland, Ohio; see also *OR*, ser. IV, III, 327.

46. Connelly, *The Marble Man*, pp. 202–3; Seitz, *Bragg*, p. 410; Kean, *Inside the Confederate Government*, p. 142.

47. Bragg, Notes of Movements from December 1863 to July 1864, Bragg Papers.

48. Leonidas Polk to Jefferson Davis, 30 March 1863, in Polk, *Leonidas Polk* II, 201–2; Kean, *Inside the Confederate Government*, p. 128; T. G. Richardson to Braxton Bragg, 5 January 1864, Bragg Papers.

49. For a discussion of the Confederate debate over the type of staff the army needed, see Gow, "Theory and Practice in Confederate Military Administration," 120–21.

FURTHER READING

An excellent introduction to the complex issues involved in the American Civil War is provided by James G. Randall and David Donald, *The Civil War and Reconstruction* (Lexington, Mass.: D. C. Heath, 1969). Included in this work is an extensive bibliography, classified according to subject matter and offering an important guide to the wide-ranging literature on the war. That literature began to appear even before the war was over, and it reached new heights during the Civil War centennial of the 1960s. A historiographical analysis and overview appear in Thomas J. Pressly, *Americans Interpret Their Civil War* (New York: Collier Books 1962).

Other helpful bibliographies include David Donald, *The Nation in Crisis, 1861–1877* (New York: Appleton-Century-Crofts, 1969), and Allan Nevins, James I. Robertson, Jr., and Bell I. Wiley, eds., *Civil War Books: A Critical Bibliography*, 2 vols. (Baton Rouge: Louisiana State University Press, 1967–1969). Regular bibiliographic updates are published annually in the journal *Civil War History*.

Just as the Civil War, to be properly understood, must be placed in the general context of American history, the military aspects of this upheaval must be seen in the context of the nineteenth-century United States Army. Critical studies include Emory Upton (himself an officer of the old army), *The Military Policy of the United States* (Washington: Government Printing Office, 1917); Russell F. Weigley, *History of the United States Army*, enlarged ed. (Bloomington: Indiana University Press, 1984); and Marcus Cunliffe, *Soldiers and Civilians: The Martial Spirit in America, 1775–1865* (Boston: Little, Brown & Co., 1968). All three works examine from different perspectives the problems of the emergence of a professional army in a society committed to civilian, democratic values.

Similarly, an American rather than a specifically Union or Confederate perspective is reflected in Bruce Catton's thoroughly researched and highly readable three-volume *Centennial History of the Civil War*: vol. I, *The Coming Fury* (Garden City, N.Y.: Doubleday, 1961); vol. II, *Terrible Swift Sword* (Garden City, N.Y.: Doubleday, 1963); and vol. III, *Never Call Retreat* (Garden City, N.Y.: Doubleday, 1965).

For the Confederate experiment in nation-building, the classic work remains E. Merton Coulter, *The Confederate States of America, 1861–1865* (Baton Rouge: Louisiana State University Press, 1950). Other studies include Charles P. Roland, *The Confederacy* (Chicago: University of Chicago Press, 1960), and Frank E. Vandiver, *Their Tattered Flags: The Epic of the Confederacy* (New York: Harper's Magazine Press, 1970).

The military history of the Civil War has been fashioned from the tremendous wealth of primary material which characterizes this research field. The greatest single source is the massive collection of battle reports, campaign records, military orders, and correspondence contained in U.S., Department of War, *The War of the Rebellion: A Compilation of the Official Records of the Union and Confederate Armies*, 128 vols. (Washington: Government Printing Office, 1880–1901). This massive collection is accompanied by a three-volume *Atlas* . . . (Washington: Government Printing Office, 1891–1895). More readily accessible are Vincent J. Esposito, ed., *The West Point Atlas of the Civil War* (New York: Praeger, 1962), and Craig L. Symonds, *A Battlefield Atlas of the Civil War* (Annapolis, Md.: Nautical & Aviation Press, 1983).

In addition to the official military records of the war, there exists a vast range of autobiographies, memoirs, diaries, sets of letters, and other personal accounts by participants and observers. Many of these have been published in Robert U. Johnson and Clarence C. Buel, eds., *Battles and Leaders of the Civil War*, 4 vols. (New York: The Century Co., 1887–1888) and the *Southern Historical Society Papers* (1876–1959). The major autobiographies of generals cited in the footnotes should be supplemented with those of John Bell Hood, *Advance and Retreat* . . . , new ed. (Bloomington: Indiana University Press, 1959), and James Longstreet, *From Manassas to Appomattox: Memoirs of the Civil War in America*, ed. James I. Robertson, Jr., new ed. (Bloomington: Indiana University Press, 1960). Perceptive memoirs by staff officers include those of Irving Ashby Buck, *Cleburne and His Command* (Jackson, Tenn.: McCowat-Mercer Press, 1959), and Walter H. Taylor, *Four Years with General Lee*, ed. James I. Robertson, new ed. (Bloomington: Indiana University Press, 1962). Inside information about the Confederate war effort may be found in John B. Jones, *A Rebel War Clerk's Diary at the Confederate States Capital*, 2 vols. (Philadelphia: Lippincott, 1866), and R. G. H. Kean, *Inside the Confederate Government: The Diary of Robert Garlick Hill Kean* . . . , ed. Edward Younger (New York: Oxford University Press, 1957).

This great wealth of primary material has fueled a series of controversies over the Confederate conduct of the war. For the traditional view which underscores the importance of the eastern theater, the Army of Northern Virginia, and Robert E. Lee, see in particular the classic works of Douglas S. Freeman, *R. E. Lee: A Biography*, 4 vols. (New York: Charles Scribner's Sons, 1934–1935), and *Lee's Lieutenants: A Study in Command*, 3 vols. (New York: Charles Scribner's Sons, 1942–1944). For the major challenge to this view, see principally the studies of the western theater, the Army of Tennessee, and its successive commanders by Thomas Lawrence Connelly, *Army of the Heartland: The Army of Tennessee, 1861–1862* (Baton Rouge: Louisiana State University Press, 1967), and *Autumn of Glory: The Army of Tennessee, 1862–1865* (Baton Rouge: Louisiana State University Press, 1971). For a critical reevaluation of the Lee historiography, see Connelly, *The Marble Man: Robert E. Lee and His Image in American Society* (New York: Alfred A. Knopf, 1977). Other significant works which address the issues of command and coordination are Frank E. Vandiver, *Rebel Brass: The Confederate Command System* (Baton Rouge: Louisiana State University Press, 1956); Archer Jones, *Confederate Strategy from Shiloh to Vicksburg* (Baton Rouge: Louisiana State University Press, 1961); and Thomas Lawrence Connelly and Archer Jones, *The Politics of Command: Factions and Ideas in Confederate Strategy* (Baton Rouge: Louisiana State University Press, 1973).

CHAPTER 8

An Improvised Army at War, 1861–1865

CRAIG L. SYMONDS

The American Civil War was the nation's first experience with total war. A good argument can be made that it remains the nation's *only* experience with total war. In no other conflict before or since did so large a percentage of American manpower experience combat; in no other conflict were so many American cities and farms devastated or so many American civilians rendered homeless. Until the Vietnam War, battle casualties from the Civil War exceeded the totals of all of America's foreign wars combined. Such a ubiquitous struggle confronted the United States Army with fundamental challenges to many of its basic institutional assumptions. The nature of the war necessitated a national effort, and as the war lengthened the federal government assumed more and more power and authority over state militia forces. In addition to this nationalization of the war effort, basic organizational changes were implemented whenever they seemed to be warranted by the crisis. But although many of these changes presaged future developments and reforms, they were ad hoc responses to an immediate crisis and almost without exception they were abandoned after the war. The creation of the "Grand Army of the Republic," therefore, was the result of improvisation in the midst of crisis and was not part of a conscious revolution in military organization and thought.

It is a perverse distinction of American society that its armed forces have never embarked on a war fully prepared. The American Civil War was no exception. At the war's outset the army consisted of some 15,000 men organized into 198 companies, 186 of which were scattered along the western frontier in strategically insignificant "forts."[1] But if lack of peacetime preparedness is a characteristic weakness of American armed forces, the ability to adjust to crisis is a particular strength. Almost from the beginning of the war, army and civilian leaders experimented with innovative approaches to recruiting, unit organization, command structure, logistics, and, of course, technology. It is tempting to view all these changes as a kind of conscious revolution, but in each case, when the crisis of war passed, the country discarded such innovations as part of the baggage of war.

The war began with the Confederate bombardment of Fort Sumter on 12 April 1861. This overt act prompted President Abraham Lincoln to issue a call to the individual states for 75,000 volunteers to serve for a period of three months in order to suppress "combinations too powerful to be suppressed by the ordinary course of judicial proceedings." It is significant that the authority which Lincoln cited to justify his call for troops was the Militia Act of 1792; he was, in effect, calling up the states' militias. His proclamation allowed the states to determine the structure and composition of individual units, and even left to the state governors the responsibility of naming all the officers up to and including five major generals (two each from New York and Pennsylvania, and one from Ohio).[2] Besides abjuring responsibility for the character of the units called up, Lincoln's proclamation underestimated by a considerable margin the vast numbers that would be required. Before the war ended four years later, no less than 2,673,567 men would serve in the Union armies. But in 1861 the very thought of an army numbering over a million was beyond the imagination of soldiers and civilians alike.[3]

Though Lincoln's request for 75,000 soldiers appears modest enough now, the machinery of the federal government, and in particular of the War Department, was totally unprepared to handle the administrative burden it created. The disorganized and unimaginative secretary of war, Simon Cameron, was part of the problem, but the fundamental source of difficulty was the simple fact that the structure of government was inadequate to meet the demands of total war; Cameron's personal staff, for example, consisted of only two clerks. In 1861 neither Cameron nor anyone else in the administration had any idea of the magnitude of the challenge that lay ahead. As a result, the War Department moved uncertainly and haphazardly in the early months of the war.

The lack of organization first became apparent in the government's attempt to deal with the new levies. The arrival of the first few regiments from northern states eased fears in Washington that the Rebels would seize the capital, but their arrival created a whole new set of problems. Troops were arriving faster than the government could provide them with campsites, rations, supplies, and arms. Cameron confessed to Lincoln that "the Government presents the striking anomaly of being embarrassed by the generous outpouring of volunteers" and expressed a desire to "keep down the proportions of the army."[4] But the troops continued to flow into the capital. Regiments arrived attired in uniforms of their own design: some in gaudy silken Zouave outfits, some in blue wool, and some in outfits of no recognizable uniformity at all. At least one regiment—the Eighth New York—arrived in civilian clothes. Many units were unarmed, and those that did have arms could not be supplied with ammunition. The lack of any central direction in all this led to confusion, delay, and shortages.

Cameron and the army commander, Brevet Lieutenant General Winfield Scott, could not agree on which governmental bodies were responsible for what. Scott believed that the states should provide a blanket and a rifle for each soldier, and the federal government the rest. But the federal government was virtually without resources and as hordes of variously uniformed and undisciplined soldiers made their way to Washington in the spring of 1861, citizens were treated to what under other circumstances might have seemed an opéra bouffe. Soldiers were quartered and fed wherever room could be found: in parks, hotels, restaurants, and even in the Capitol itself, often creating chaos in the process. To local citizens it must have seemed a stiff price to pay for such dubious security. Historians have generally held Cameron to be responsible for this state of administrative anarchy, but few men could have dealt effectively with the unprecedented situation that existed in the spring of 1861.

Clearly some new arrangement, some new organization, was needed to bring order out of this chaos. Since Secretary Cameron appeared unwilling or unable to come up with such a plan, Secretary of the Treasury Salmon P. Chase ordered Generals Irvin McDowell and William B. Franklin to work up a proposal. Immediately they faced a critical decision: whether to consider the new levies as state troops, identified as such and with officers appointed by the state governors, or to attempt to integrate them into a truly national army. They chose the latter alternative. According to their recommendations, units would be identified as, say, the Eighty-eighth U.S. Infantry rather than the Eighth New York. Governors would continue to nominate officers, but the president would grant the commissions. Recognizing the value to troop morale of retaining the familiar state identification, Secretary Chase rejected this advice. Thus, a recommendation that might have led to a genuine organizational revolution was stillborn.[5]

This was unfortunate for several reasons. First, these new regiments lacked effective professional leadership. In the early days of the war, many regular army officers requested permission to accept commissions—usually with a dramatic leap in rank—in state units. General Scott refused to grant permission. He preferred to think of the regulars as a hardened cadre that would serve as the core of an expanded army. The thought of disbursing this core of veterans into volunteer state units was repugnant to him. His decision was regrettable, for the greatest weakness in the volunteer regiments early in the war was a lack of experienced leadership at the regimental level. Though many of the amateur officers of 1861 eventually became excellent commanders, their lack of expertise at the outset of the war contributed to the confusion that was characteristic of early battles and perhaps prevented a quick Federal victory. A few years after the war, General Jacob D. Cox wrote what remains the prevailing view: "There can be no doubt that the true policy would have been to encourage the whole of this younger class [of officers] to enter at once the volunteer service. They would have been field officers in the new regiments, and would have impressed discipline and system upon the organization from the beginning."[6]

Second, state supervision of recruiting offered many opportunities for interstate competition, duplication of effort, and occasional fraud. Local governments offered bounties to new recruits in order to fill their quotas, and these bounties varied not only from state to state, but from town to town. These differences gave rise to the practice of ''bounty jumping,'' as daring entrepreneurs enlisted, collected their bounty, and then deserted to enlist elsewhere for another bounty.

Finally, as Confederate bullets and the ravages of disease exacted a toll on the troops, many state regiments were dramatically reduced in size, but state recruiting continued to be conducted in such a way as to encourage the creation of new units rather than to provide replacements for existing units. Service with a newly created regiment offered recruits the opportunity to enter the army with friends and neighbors and the prospect of creating a new unit tradition. Neither of these attractions was present for a prospective volunteer who enlisted as a replacement for a veteran unit already at the front, where the recruit would arrive as a green outsider among hardened and unfamiliar faces. Recruitment of replacements for older units was also discouraged by would-be colonels who often assumed the burden of recruiting their own regiments. They signed up followers by making hyperbolic public appeals and offering membership in what they invariably described as an elite unit. There was no such vocal advocate to attract replacements. The result, as the war lengthened, was an army composed of veteran regiments that were too small to be effective and new, full-size units that lacked experience.[7]

After his appointment to supreme command of the Union armies, Major General George B. McClellan tried to rectify this unsatisfactory situation by promulgating War Order No. 105 on 3 December 1861. His order took recruiting out of the hands of the state authorities and placed it under the aegis of the War Department. For each state, a federal supervisor of recruiting was appointed whose primary objective was to maintain existing regiments at something approximating full strength. After he became secretary of war on 15 January 1862, Edwin Stanton joined in this effort by combining several undersized regiments, despite howls of protest from state authorities.[8]

Unfortunately for the Union war effort, these initiatives did not lead to the creation of a permanent federal authority to oversee state recruiting. Stung by continued congressional sniping about extravagance and waste in the War Department, and perhaps slightly euphoric after McClellan's ''victories'' at Yorktown and Williamsburg during the Peninsular Campaign, Stanton closed down the recruiting offices on 3 April 1862.[9] He apparently believed that the soldiers already under arms, if managed properly, would be sufficient to end the war. But his decision was monumentally ill judged. There were fewer than half the federal troops then under arms that eventually would prove necessary to extinguish the rebellion. Stanton soon recognized his error, for on 19 May, after the success of Thomas J. (''Stonewall'') Jackson's Valley Campaign, he issued new calls for troops to the state governors. But by abolishing the federal recruiting offices established by McClellan, Stanton had forfeited control of recruiting to the states.

There were other experimental initiatives during the war that expanded the national government's responsibility for army organization. The unprecedented demands of the war created specialized needs which led to the formation of several army units that had no state affiliation and therefore became federal units by default. In each case, however, the initiative was an ad hoc response to the crisis and not part of a conscious attempt to nationalize the army.

The first of these was the product of Secretary Stanton's desire to establish a regiment composed exclusively of sharpshooters. Since such a body of men had to be drawn from several states, it came to be called the First U.S. Sharpshooters. When its commander, Colonel Hiram Berdan, expressed concern about the legality of his unit, President Lincoln's response was a pragmatic one: " . . . put the corps into the most effective form, regardless of existing regulations; and I will recommend to Congress to ratify it, giving Commissions, pay &c."[10] Lincoln's response was representative of his attitude about the whole question of authority in the creation of new fighting units. He was less concerned with the principle of state versus federal control than he was with practical results. For example, he compromised with the prerogative-conscious governor of Missouri, Hamilton R. Gamble, allowing him titular authority over the issuance of commissions; the president urged Governor Richard Yates of his own home state of Illinois not to stand on "punctilio," but to get on with recruiting under any authority; and to Governor Edwin D. Morgan of New York, Lincoln wrote, "We are in no condition to waste time on technicalities."[11]

This pragmatic view also helped forestall objections to another body of troops with a federal rather than a state genesis: the so-called Invalid Corps. This organization, whose unfortunate name was later changed to the Veteran Reserve Corps, was created to employ veteran soldiers who had been lightly wounded in earlier battles and who were unfit for field service but who were still able to perform garrison duty. Established on 28 April 1863, the Invalid Corps eventually included 60,000 men in twenty-four regiments. It provided its most important service defending Washington against Jubal Early's large-scale raid in 1864. Members of its regiments came from several states and, significantly, were known as "U.S. Veterans."

The federal government was also the supervisory organ for the men recruited from Confederate prisoner of war camps to fight against hostile Indians on the western plains. For these men as well, there was no state identification; they became U.S. Volunteers and wore the collar insignia "USV."[12]

The most far reaching of all national recruiting efforts was the organization of former slaves into fighting regiments. Initiated by Major General David Hunter on the occupied South Carolina coast in the spring of 1862, the first such regiment was designated as the First South Carolina Volunteers. Despite the designation, it was obvious that the federal government and not the state of South Carolina sponsored the unit. As northern states struggled to fill the quotas imposed upon them by Lincoln's repeated calls for troops, some state officials reluctantly adopted the idea of recruiting black soldiers. The Fifty-fourth and Fifty-fifth Massachusetts were among the first and most famous of the black units, but neighboring states complained that Massachusetts had recruited free blacks from outside its boundaries. To avoid squabbles between the states and to regularize the recruitment of black soldiers, the War Department took over all recruitment of "colored" troops on 22 May 1863. In November of that year, Secretary Stanton had to write the governor of Ohio that a recently created black regiment from that state could not be designated an Ohio regiment. Instead, under War Department aegis blacks enlisted as "United States Colored Volunteers"—a truly national force. It was a significant step not only because blacks were finally included in the Grand Army but because they had been recognized as *United States* troops. Once again, however, the revolution was incomplete. Though some 180,000 blacks served in the Union armies, black regiments had white officers and were confined largely to garrison duty or used as a labor force. Moreover, the designation as United States troops did not last beyond the end of the war.[13]

The legislation with the greatest immediate impact on recruiting resulted from Lincoln's decision to hold the states accountable for their quotas by implementing a draft to complete unfilled quotas. The Enrollment Act of 3 March 1863 imposed a military obligation on all male citizens aged twenty to forty-five. Married men over thirty-five were put in a special category to be called upon only after all others had been tapped. The act is significant not only because it established a draft, but because it was based on the constitutional power to raise armies rather than on the militia system. The abuses of the national draft have been well documented. The practice of hiring substitutes was so common that very little social stigma attached itself to those who chose to opt out in this way. Perhaps partly because of such abuses, the draft was never completely successful. Of the 500,000 men "called" in Lincoln's proclamation of 18 July 1864, only 240,000 ever came into federal service. The principal result of the Enrollment Act was that it encouraged volunteers to enlist before they were conscripted, a situation akin to that existing during most of America's subsequent wars.[14]

The war also witnessed great strides in the nationalization of the noncombatant arms of the service. The civilian-sponsored United States Sanitary Commission sprang from a widely recognized need for better hospital facilities for the troops. And perhaps the most monumental effort of the war years was that required of the United States Army's Quartermaster Corps which had to oversee the purchase and transportation of the mountains of material needed to support the Grand Army of the Republic. It required literally hundreds of wagonloads of food a day just to feed McClellan's army during the Peninsular campaign. To keep the soldiers marching and clothed, the armies in the field needed no less than 3,000,000 pairs of shoes and 1,500,000 uniforms a year. Clearly, supply had to be a national and not a state effort. Whatever the generative agency for individual units, it was the federal government that assumed responsibility for feeding and supplying the troops once they entered federal service.[15]

Nevertheless, these developments suggesting a general movement toward the establishment of federal authority over army organization fell short of a permanent revolution. Most veterans of the war felt that their unit loyalty was to their regiment rather than to their army. Though some brigade and division commanders were successful in building unit pride by authorizing special head-gear or issuing divisional shoulder patches, pride in state units remained dom-inant. The monuments at Gettysburg were erected by the states, in memory of state units and of the sons of the states who fell there, and paid tribute much less frequently to the brigade or division that claimed them. Thus, while cen-tralization and integration characterized many aspects of the war effort, the army remained a mosaic of state units rather than a truly national force.

With the exception of Lincoln himself, the men who bore the burden of guiding the Union war effort during the first year of the war made up a particularly unimpressive team. While Simon Cameron struggled ineffectually with the her-culean task of readying the Republic for total war, Brevet Lieutenant General Winfield Scott pondered how the tools of war might be employed. Scott was a gargantuan 300-pound man in his seventies who was plagued so badly with gout that he had difficulty walking and occasionally nodded off during staff meetings. He was the hero of two earlier wars and his heroism had been well earned. But neither the War of 1812 nor the Mexican War, where he had commanded an army of some 10,000 men, had prepared him for the total conflict that the Civil War would prove to be; Scott's organizational planning and strategic thinking were irrevocably linked to an earlier era. His personal staff consisted of only two aides, and he remained convinced even after his forced retirement that two were sufficient. His army table of organization did not include anything larger than a brigade. By contrast, Scott's successor, Major General George B. McClellan, relied upon a staff of no less than sixty-five, and by the spring of 1862 the Army of the Potomac had been organized into divisions and corps as well as brigades.

Scott's one great contribution to the Union war effort was the so-called An-aconda Plan which he proposed to Lincoln in the early days of the war: rely on the main army along the Potomac to hold the principal Confederate army in check; blockade the Confederate coastline; and employ joint operations to take and hold the Mississippi River Valley. Scott hoped that the Confederacy, thus weakened and sundered, would come to realize the extent of its dependence on the North and a reconciliation could be effected. His expectations were unfulfilled in that regard, but his recommendations nevertheless served as the framework for Union strategy.

While the overall strategic plan may have been sound, the improvised army of 1861 and 1862 was unable to fulfill even the most modest expectations. In the East the Union armies fought only one major battle in 1861, Bull Run or First Manassas, the results of which were enough to evoke concern in the most sanguine Union mind. The price which the Union field commander, Major General Irvin McDowell, had to pay for his defeat was the loss of the army's confidence. Despite Lincoln's initial assurances of support, the president soon came to the conclusion that in order to restore morale, McDowell would have to give way to a new commander.

The man Lincoln chose for the job was apparently ideally suited to it. George Brinton McClellan was one of the many officers who had possessed too much talent and ambition to be happy in the peacetime army of the 1850s and had left it to find success in business, in his case as a railroad executive. Within a very few years, he had become president of the Eastern Division of the Ohio and Mississippi Railroad. Executive administration was his particular talent, but he was also a superior propagandist. When small units under his command cleared Confederate troops from the spur of what is now part of West Virginia between Ohio and Pennsylvania, his after-action report described the modest campaign in hyperbolic terms that caught the attention of the press and the government at a time when reports of victories were sorely needed.

McClellan came to Washington at the beckoning of the president to assume command of the Federal armies. Around him he saw confusion and disorganization with no apparent order being imposed on the rabble that was the national army. He gradually became convinced that he was virtually the only man who could bring order out of this chaos. He may have been right. McClellan was a general who would have been successful in the twentieth century: he was a manager of men. He was also a man of great personal presence and he enjoyed life most when he cast himself in the role of leader as well as manager. When the army began to take shape, he conducted massive reviews where thousands of infantrymen and hundreds of cavalrymen would pass to salute him. At night and during other off-hours, he would ride through the camps and receive the cheers and hurrahs of the men. It was not long before McClellan began to lobby actively for Scott's job, and by November 1861 he had it.

Historian T. Harry Williams has called McClellan "the problem child of the Civil War." Ulysses S. Grant claimed that he was "one of the mysteries of the war." Few controversies have engendered as much historical editorializing as Lincoln's dismissal of McClellan in the late fall of 1862. Perhaps only Harry S. Truman's firing of Douglas MacArthur has evoked more argument about civil-military relations in the United States. McClellan's biographer and principal defender, Warren Hassler, claims that "political enmity toward him was largely his undoing." Williams counters with the simple explanation that "McClellan was not a fighting man."[16] But whatever McClellan's merits or limitations as a field commander, historians agree that he was a superb organizer. Even his enemies gave him credit for rebuilding the demoralized and disorganized remnants of the Bull Run disaster into an effective fighting force.

McClellan's first order after assuming overall command of the army called for the reorganization of the staff. "I at once designated an efficient Staff," he later wrote, and though some might argue that the staff's efficiency left something to be desired, it was most certainly large. It included a personal entourage of no fewer than twenty "aides" who accompanied McClellan wherever he went. Allan Nevins credits McClellan with "early recognition of the vital importance of apportioning precise duties among a large body of officers." Unfortunately, McClellan's personal insecurity led him to select "trusted" staff officers who could generally be relied upon to provide the answers the general wanted to hear. His chief of staff, Randolph B. Marcy, was his own father-in-law. Contrariwise, there were certain officers whom McClellan distrusted, and his initial reluctance to establish divisions and later corps within the army stemmed in part from the fact that the four most senior major generals who would presumably command such units were all on his "enemies list." In short, McClellan was jealous of his perquisites and authority, and he was reluctant to share either with division commaders whose political motives and loyalty he suspected.[17]

In the end it was Lincoln, not McClellan, who promulgated the order to establish corps in the Federal armies. The president's General War Order No. 2, issued on 18 March 1862, directed McClellan "forthwith" to divide the army into four corps and named as the four commanders the very men whom McClellan had been so reluctant to endow with increased authority. Thus, the two most important organizational reforms in the Union army—the creation of a military staff and the reorganization of the army itself—were less the result of prescience on McClellan's part than circumstance, a certain amount of Napoleonic imitation, and presidential directive. McClellan's successors retained the staff structure and improved upon it, and by 1863 the principal staff officers wore the stars of brigadier generals, but with the end of the war came the end of any apparent need to retain the innovation.[18]

The most important organizational novelty of 1862 resulted from Lincoln's decision to appoint a general in chief to exercise command authority over all the Union field generals. Lincoln wanted a competent military man at his elbow to help him make military decisions and take some of the burden off the presidency. From the beginning of the war, Lincoln had recognized that a coordinated national strategy was necessary if the North were to take advantage of its enormous superiority in resources, but so far coordination was the one element most conspicuously lacking in the Union war effort.

The man Lincoln appointed to this critical post on 11 July 1862 was Henry Wager Halleck, who up to that point had been Grant's senior in the western theater. Halleck had been accorded rave reviews by the eastern press, mostly because of Grant's capture of Forts Henry and Donelson early in 1862. But Halleck himself was not the answer to the Union's organizational problems. In fact, though he possessed a high service reputation as a tactician (largely because of his authorship of a book on the subject), he lacked the insight and decisiveness of an effective field commander. Furthermore, he was physically unattractive: flush faced and virtually popeyed, he always looked like he had been holding his breath for several minutes and was about to exhale violently. Lincoln soon discovered that while Halleck was perfectly willing to give advice to the administration and to pass on the president's decisions to generals in the field, he was unwilling to make those decisions himself. Halleck thus became not so much a general in chief as a chief of staff to the president. In this sense Halleck's appointment was fortuitous, for "Old Brains," as he was known in the army, was an excellent chief of staff.

Halleck got little credit, then or later, for his efforts. Contemporary news-papers, previously so kind, ridiculed both his peculiar looks and his apparent lack of activity. Halleck complained to his wife that "the great difficulty in the office of general in chief is that it is not understood by the country. The re-sponsibility and odium thrown upon it does not belong to it." Halleck knew that his position was as much political as military; it was, in fact, the kind of job that few military professionals would enjoy. "I am utterly sick of this political hell," he wrote his wife.[19] Halleck's discomfiture notwithstanding, his appoint-ment was significant because it acknowledged the need for a chief of staff to coordinate the armies of the Union. In the twelve months that followed Mc-Clellan's repulse before Richmond in June 1862, the administration experimented with several new field commanders in the eastern theater, trying John Pope, Ambrose Burnside, Joe Hooker, and finally George Gordon Meade. Halleck outlasted them all. When Grant subsequently was promoted to lieutenant general, superseding Halleck as general in chief, "Old Brains" remained in Washington and continued to serve as the communications link between the administration and the generals in the field, including Grant. This arrangement was the precursor of the modern command system; but like other such arrangements made during the war, it was not a permanent "reform." Rather, it came as a fortuitous and accidental result of Lincoln's unflagging efforts to find an effective general for the army.

The kind of organization established in the eastern theater came much later to the armies in the West. The Battle of Shiloh, fought on 6–7 April 1862, was essentially a confrontation between armed mobs. In the words of Bruce Catton, "These were not armies that fought" at Shiloh but "huge assemblies of citizens thrown into an enormous combat and left to fight their way out of it."[20] The staggering casualties—24,000 killed and wounded on both sides—testified to the personal valor of these amateur soldiers, but the carnage testified also to the absence of skilled leadership on either side. The Union commanders, none other than Ulysses S. Grant and William T. Sherman, were clearly caught by surprise and barely survived the first day's onslaught, then failed to follow up the suc-cessful counterattack made by their troops the next day.

Naturally there were recriminations, but they were not as numerous or noisome as they might have been if Shiloh had been fought in Virginia. Indeed, Mc-Clellan's performance at Antietam on 17 September 1862, disappointing as it was, was far better than Grant's at Shiloh. But because Grant and Sherman fought in the West, comfortably removed from the direct scrutiny of the eastern press and the highly political congressional Committee for the Conduct of the War, they were allowed the time to mature into the winning team they eventually became. Mistakes like Shiloh, which might have proven fatal to a commander in the eastern theater, were eventually overcome in the public mind by successes like Grant's triumph at Vicksburg the next year. Given the same opportunity to profit from errors, others might have been equally successful. McDowell in particular, never completely trusted after Bull Run, might have become a suc-

Major General Henry Wager ("Old Brains") Halleck
U.S. Army Military History Institute, Carlisle Barracks, Pennsylvania

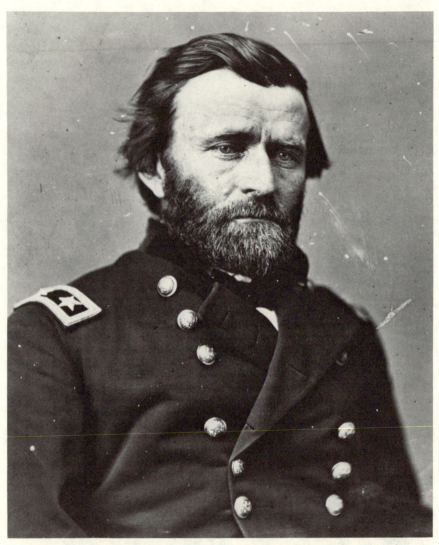

General Ulysses S. Grant, shown here as a lieutenant general
Library of Congress (USZ62-51046)

cessful commander had he been given two years to practice in the West before coming east.

The Union's supremacy in the West, which in the long run was the decisive factor in the war, was due largely to its ability to command the all-important river system. Because the North had the industrial capability to construct specialized riverine fighting vessels, it was able to seize control of the Tennessee and Mississippi rivers at an early date. The Union gunboats provided secure logistic lines for the western armies and could be called upon for the rapid transportation of troops or the provision of fire support. As a communications line, the rivers were even more important than the railroads. While the iron rails could be torn up by Rebel raiders, the flow of the Mississippi could not be stopped.

But the Union's superiority on the rivers could not have been decisive without the close cooperation of naval and military forces. Joint operations were the most difficult aspect of nineteenth-century warfare. On the Atlantic coast, for example, naval commanders on the blockade frequently refused to accept orders from army officers of any rank. The interservice cooperation evident at the capture of Hatteras Inlet in 1862 and the second assault on Fort Fisher in 1864 are remarkable precisely because they were exceptions to this rule. The key to Union victories in the Mississippi Valley, therefore, was the practically unprecedented situation that placed naval vessels under the strategic control of army officers. Though the gunboats themselves were commanded by naval officers, they were subject to the orders of the commander of the department, invariably an army officer. This command relationship was a fortuitous, but in the end temporary, response to an immediate problem and not a precedent for future command arrangements. The lessons that might have been learned about the benefits of unified command in joint operations had to be relearned in the twentieth century.[21]

Grant's arrival in the national capital in March 1864 marked the beginning of the last phase of the American Civil War. In retrospect it may appear that the outcome could not have been in much doubt even at that date, but contemporaries did not see it that way. Lee was waiting with his unvanquished host behind the line of the Rapidan-Rappahannock rivers, where so many Union armies—and Union generals—had come to grief. Despite their defeat at Gettysburg in July 1863, Lee and his army had been endowed in the public mind, North and South, with an almost mystical strength, and his veterans appeared as tough as ever. Moreover, 1864 was a presidential election year. If the war-weary North turned the Lincoln administration out of office, a negotiated peace was not unthinkable.

By the winter of 1864–1865, however, the handwriting on the wall was clear to all. Grant had pounded Lee almost daily from May to June, and by midsummer he had the Confederate army pinned inside its own fortifications around Richmond and Petersburg. In September Sherman had captured Atlanta, an event with profound importance for the November elections in the North, and from there he had driven to the sea, presenting Lincoln with Savannah as a "Christmas present." From that point on, the Confederacy's capitulation was only a matter of time.

The story of Union success in the American Civil War is one of adjustment to crisis. The Lincoln administration and the army leadership were both willing to experiment—to tinker with the system—in order to meet the unprecedented demands of total war. But in the end it was only tinkering after all. Though the Union army, initially a conglomeration of state militia units, gradually developed many of the characteristics of a national army with the organization, command structure, and logistic support of a truly national force, the adjustments were pragmatic, ad hoc responses to a temporary crisis, and they did not outlast the war. Administratively, the government never fully relinquished the concept of state regiments or surrendered its dearly held belief in militia troops and the citizen-soldier. Organizationally, the concept of a specialized group of staff officers, of a chief of staff, and of a regularized hierarchy of corps and divisions, had proven their worth but did not become regular parts of the postwar army. Strategically and tactically, though the Civil War provided unmistakable examples that the murderous accuracy of rifled muskets and artillery made massed infantry charges futile, Union generals never completely abandoned their faith in frontal assault. But Union generals were not alone in their inability to grasp this truth. The British and German commanders at the Somme and Verdun a half century later showed that they had not profited from a study of Fredericksburg, Cold Harbor, and Petersburg. Thus, the Civil War's strategic and tactical lessons, as well as its organizational and administrative lessons, had to be relearned at enormous human cost in the next century. The sins of the fathers would be repeated by the sons.

NOTES

1. U.S., Department of War, *Report of the Secretary of War*, 36th Congress, 2d sess., 1860, S. Exec. Doc. 1, pp. 216–17, 224–29.

2. Roy P. Basler, ed., *The Collected Works of Abraham Lincoln*, 9 vols. (New Brunswick, N.J.: Rutgers University Press, 1953–1955), IV, 332 (hereafter cited as *Lincoln Papers*). U.S., *Statutes at Large*, vol. I, 271. U.S., Department of War, *War of the Rebellion: A Compilation of the Official Records of the Union and Confederate Armies*, 128 vols. (Washington: Government Printing Office, 1880–1901), I, 68–69 (hereafter cited as *OR*; unless otherwise noted, all citations are from series III).

3. The figure cited is from Frederick H. Dyer, *A Compendium of the War of the Rebellion*, 3 vols. (1909; reprint, New York: Thomas Yoseloff, 1959), I, 11. Dyer is the most authoritative source for such figures. Other estimates range from a low of 1,556,678, which does not include the ninety-day volunteers, to a high of 2,778,304. These estimates are offered by Thomas L. Livermore, *Numbers and Losses in the Civil War in America, 1861–1865* (Bloomington: Indiana University Press, 1957), p. v; and Fred A. Shannon, *The Organization and Administration of the Union Army, 1861–1865*, 2 vols. (Cleveland: Arthur H. Clark, 1928), II, 278, respectively. Russell F. Weigley

places the figure at 2,666,999 in his *History of the U.S. Army*, enlarged ed. (Bloomington: Indiana University Press, 1984), p. 216.

4. Cameron to Lincoln, 1 July 1861, *OR*, I, 303.

5. Allan Nevins, *The War for the Union*, vol. I, *The Improvised War* (New York: Charles Scribner's Sons, 1959), 168–69.

6. Jacob D. Cox, "War Preparations in the North," in Clarence Buel and Robert Johnson, eds., *Battles and Leaders of the Civil War*, 4 vols. (New York: The Century Co., 1887–1888), I, 94.

7. Wisconsin regiments were an exception in this regard, and many Union generals late in the war came to regard a Wisconsin regiment as the equivalent of an entire brigade composed of depleted units.

8. The order is printed in *OR*, I, 722–23.

9. See Nevins, *The War for the Union*, vol. II, *War Becomes Revolution* (New York: Charles Scribner's Sons, 1960), p. 63; and Weigley, *History*, p. 206.

10. See Jim Dan Hill, *The Minute Man in Peace and War: A History of the National Guard* (Harrisburg, Pa: Stackpole, 1963), pp. 84–90; Weigley, *History*, p. 213; Lincoln to Stanton, 20 September 1862, *Lincoln Papers*, V, 431.

11. Lincoln to Gamble, 6 November 1861; Lincoln to Yates, 23 April 1862; Lincoln to Morgan, 20 May 1861, *Lincoln Papers*, V, 15–17; IV, 375.

12. Weigley, *History*, p. 214. See also *OR*, III, 170–72.

13. Weigley, *History*, pp. 211–13; John K. Mahon, *History of the Militia and the National Guard*, The Wars of the United States (New York: Macmillan Co., 1983), p. 103. See also Benjamin Quarles, *The Negro in the Civil War* (Boston: Little, Brown & Co., 1953).

14. Eugene C. Murdock, *One Million Men: The Civil War Draft in the North* (Madison: State Historical Society of Wisconsin, 1971).

15. William Q. Maxwell, *Lincoln's Fifth Wheel: The Political History of the United States Sanitary Commission* (New York: Longmans, Green and Co., 1956); and Charles J. Stille, *History of the United States Sanitary Commission* (Philadelphia: J. B. Lippincott & Co., 1866). For the Quartermaster Corps, see Russell F. Weigley, *Quartermaster General of the Union Army: A Biography of M. C. Meigs* (New York: Columbia University Press, 1959). The statistics are from Nevins, *The Improvised War*, p. 241.

16. T. Harry Williams, *Lincoln and His Generals* (New York: Alfred A. Knopf, 1952), pp. 25, 178; Warren Hassler, *General George B. McClellan: Shield of the Union* (Baton Rouge: Louisiana State University Press, 1957), p. xvi.

17. George B. McClellan, *McClellan's Own Story* (New York: William C. Prime, 1887), p. 113; Nevins, *The Improvised War*, p. 268.

18. President's General War Order No. 2, *Lincoln Papers*, V, 149–50. Weigley claims that despite the large number of staff officers, McClellan was "ill served" by them on the peninsula. Weigley, *History*, p. 241.

19. *OR*, ser. I, XXXII, 2, 402. See also Stephen Ambrose, *Halleck: Lincoln's Chief of Staff* (Baton Rouge: Louisiana State University Press, 1962), pp. 158, 143.

20. Bruce Catton, *U. S. Grant and the American Military Tradition* (Boston: Little, Brown & Co., 1954), p. 87.

21. Bern Anderson, *By Sea and By River* (New York: Alfred A. Knopf, 1962); Rowena Reed, *Combined Operations in the Civil War* (Annapolis, Md.: Naval Institute Press, 1980).

FURTHER READING

The literature on the American Civil War is voluminous and much of it is very good. The basic source for all studies of the Union army is the U.S., Department of War, *War of the Rebellion: A Compilation of the Official Records of the Union and Confederate Armies*, 128 vols. (Washington: Government Printing Office, 1880–1901), which is divided into four series. The first series is the longest and deals with military operations. The third series is especially relevant to the subject of this essay since it contains "the correspondence, orders, reports and returns of the Union authorities" (I, v). The best one-volume treatment of the war as a whole is the textbook by J. G. Randall and David Donald, *The Civil War and Reconstruction* (Lexington, Mass.: D. C. Heath, 1969), which also contains a superb annotated bibliography. For a more exhaustive treatment, Allan Nevins's eight-volume *Ordeal of the Union* (New York: Charles Scribner's Sons, 1959–1971) is a masterpiece of American history. The last four volumes treat the war itself: *The Improvised War, War Becomes Revolution, The Organized War*, and *The Organized War to Victory*. Nevins concentrates on the North and especially singles out Lincoln for extensive and sympathetic coverage. Herman Hattaway and Archer Jones focus on military operations in *How the North Won: A Military History of the Civil War* (Urbana: University of Illinois Press, 1983).

For somewhat lighter reading, the three-volume account by Shelby Foote, *The Civil War: A Narrative* (New York: Random House, 1958–1974) is great fun, though it is totally without notation and Foote succumbs to the temptation to root for the underdog. Bruce Catton's many offerings are well written and scholarly; they deserve the wide audience they have attracted over the years. The two best are trilogies: one on the Army of the Potomac—*Mr. Lincoln's Army, Glory Road*, and *A Stillness at Appomattox* (Garden City, N.Y.: Doubleday, 1951–1953)—and the other a centennial history of the war: *The Coming Fury, Terrible Swift Sword*, and *Never Call Retreat* (Garden City, N.Y.: Doubleday, 1961–1965).

On more specialized topics, Lincoln's relations with his generals have been the subject of several fine books. Kenneth P. Williams has treated the subject at length in *Lincoln Finds A General*, 5 vols. (New York: Macmillan Co., 1950–1959). But T. Harry Williams has written a fine one-volume work with a similar title: *Lincoln and His Generals* (New York: Alfred A. Knopf, 1952). Both are highly sympathetic to Lincoln, and Williams in particular treats McClellan roughly. For a contrasting viewpoint, see Warren W. Hassler, Jr., *General George B. McClellan: Shield of the Union* (Baton Rouge: Louisiana State University Press, 1957). Craig Symonds, *A Battlefield Atlas of the Civil War* (Annapolis, Md.: Nautical & Aviation Press, 1983) provides a cartographic overview of the war.

The biographies of other Union generals are an excellent source of information on the armies which they commanded. Those particularly worth noting include Bruce Catton's short paperback in the Library of American Biography series entitled *U. S. Grant and the American Military Tradition* (Boston: Little, Brown & Co., 1954). More detailed coverage of Grant's early career is provided by Lloyd Lewis, *Captain Sam Grant* (Boston: Little, Brown & Co., 1950), and continued by Bruce Catton in *Grant Moves South* (Boston: Little, Brown & Co., 1960) and *Grant Takes Command* (Boston: Little, Brown & Co., 1968). The best coverage of Grant, however, is found in his own *Personal Memoirs* (New York: Charles L. Webster and Co., 1885–1886), one of the few genuinely readable presidential memoirs. By contrast, Sherman's memoirs are unreliable. See instead Sir Basil Liddell-Hart, *Sherman: Soldier, Realist, American* (New York: Praeger, 1929), which is somewhat dated by the author's attempt to portray Sherman as a master of the indirect approach, and James M. Merrill, *William Tecumseh Sherman* (Chicago: Rand McNally, 1971).

Many of the relevant volumes on special aspects of the war are cited in the footnotes above. One source that deserves repeated mention is Clarence Buel and Robert Johnson, eds., *Battles and Leaders of the Civil War*, 4 vols. (New York: The Century Co., 1887–1888), a collection of essays by most of the generals who fought in the war. It is a virtual mine of firsthand information and should not be overlooked as a reference or for enjoyable reading. On army organization, Fred A. Shannon, *The Organization and Administration of the Union Army, 1861–1865*, 2 vols. (Cleveland: Arthur H. Clark, 1928), is still the only full-length work on the subject, though many of his conclusions have come under attack since its publication. The administration of the War Department is admirably covered by two volumes: A. H. Meneely, *The War Department, 1861* (New York: Columbia University Press, 1928), and Benjamin P. Thomas and Harold M. Hyman, *Stanton: The Life and Times of Lincoln's Secretary of War* (New York: Alfred A. Knopf, 1962). Two other important subjects are the U.S. Sanitary Commission and the Quartermaster General's Department, covered by William Q. Maxwell, *Lincoln's Fifth Wheel: The Political History of the United States Sanitary Commission* (New York: Longmans, Green and Co., 1956); Charles J. Stille, *History of the United States Sanitary Commission* (Philadelphia: J. B. Lippincott & Co., 1866); and Russell F. Weigley, *Quartermaster General of the Union Army: A Biography of M. C. Meigs* (New York: Columbia University Press, 1959).

CHAPTER 9

The Army's Search for a Mission, 1865–1890

JERRY M. COOPER

The grand review of the victorious Union army in Washington, D.C., on 23 and 24 May 1865 served as much as any single event to mark the end of the Civil War. The Confederacy did not surrender, it simply dissolved. Consequently, the nation, North and South, was left to its own private means to digest the meaning of the Civil War. The rancor and eventual failure of Reconstruction demonstrated that military victory did not provide ready answers to pressing constitutional, political, and social problems. The nation spent ten years after the war in a vitriolic political struggle attempting to redefine the South's relation to the rest of the nation and to resolve the question of the freedmen's place in American life. In the confusion the purpose of the war was never explained nor fully comprehended. The rapid dissolution of southern military resistance and the absence of a formal surrender document perpetuated the wartime belief among most Americans that there was no relationship between what occurred on the battlefield and the underlying social and political causes of the conflict. The purpose of war was to defeat the enemy, not to achieve specific social or political ends.[1]

Victory and peace left unanswered as well the effect of the war on American military policy. In the conduct of the Civil War, civilian and military leaders had adopted policies and practices unthinkable in 1861. The experience of a nearly total war, however, did not lead to dramatic alterations in the course of the nation's military affairs. Prewar attitudes toward a professional regular army persisted in rhetorical form after 1865. Congressional and editorial comments on the army repeated old fears of the potential threat of a standing army to democratic government—however unrealistic such a threat was in the late nineteenth century. A refurbished version of the antebellum state volunteer militia, the National Guard, ostensibly offered a reserve of amateur soldiers eager and willing to serve in wartime. The most important factor shaping civilian perceptions of the army and preventing the development of a well-defined military program, however, was a civilian realization that the nation was secure for the immediate future from any outside threat.

Throughout the nineteenth century Americans refused to consider any substantive connection between an army raised to wage war and a military force maintained in peace. The latter served to meet minimum peacetime needs and act as a repository of military knowledge. Career soldiers manned the peacetime service, but the war army belonged to all the people and should be open to all comers. John A. Logan's *The Volunteer Soldier of America* epitomized the deeply held belief that the volunteer citizen-soldier remained the most reliable defense for the nation. Volunteers, recruited by their states and officered by men they knew and often chose, fought with their hearts and not for pay. Even Ulysses S. Grant lauded a military system which relied on "men who knew what they were fighting for, and could not be induced to serve as soldiers, except in an emergency when the safety of the nation was involved."[2]

The war army concept mirrored prewar society in its decentralization, strong local ties, emphasis on volunteering, and overtones of individualistic entrepreneurship. Reliance on the states as the focal point of manpower recruitment offered ambitious military amateurs the opportunity for military command, depending on their ability to raise troops, as seen in the career of Nelson A. Miles. Many West Point graduates eschewed institutional loyalty in 1861 by turning their backs on the army and seeking commissions from their home states. Ulysses S. Grant, George B. McClellan, Oliver O. Howard, John M. Schofield, and Philip H. Sheridan, among others, entered the Union army through state volunteer service. Despite inefficiency, expense, and waste, Americans embraced the practice enthusiastically. A volunteer army raised only for war kept peacetime military expenditures low, obviated the need to maintain an always dangerous and generally useless peacetime army of any size, and retained the conduct of war in the hands of the people. Secure behind their ocean barriers, Americans believed they would always have time to raise an army for war and clung to these antebellum attitudes.

The Civil War demonstrated that freebooting individualism was an effective way to recruit an army in the early stages of mobilization but was a decidedly ineffective means of sustaining the conduct of mass war. By 1865 Washington dominated nearly all the aspects of manpower recruitment. The reality of war faded quickly, however. The recent conflict merely reinforced faith in the old way of doing things, for whatever its weaknesses, the war army practice had never failed. After the Grand Army of the Republic paraded down Pennsylvania Avenue in May 1865, it returned to the states, taking its battleflags with it for deposit in the state capitals.[3]

Congress revealed its sympathy for popular thinking by reducing federal military expenditures and army manpower levels. The acrimony surrounding Reconstruction added to the general desire to curtail the army's size. Congress made one serious attempt to consider military reform and long-range policy when it created a joint committee on army reorganization chaired by Senator Ambrose Burnside in 1878. The Burnside committee's limited recommendations for change barely passed in the House and met defeat in the Senate. After 1878, if the solons gave any thought to future military needs, the war army concept guided their thinking. It remained the basic constant affecting congressional thinking on military affairs in the twenty-five years following the Civil War. The superb Grand Army of the Republic, in which many congressmen had served, resided in their minds as the embodiment of the American military method and positive proof of the nation's ability to create a viable force for war.[4]

Inevitably, then, immediate demobilization of wartime volunteers and gradual reduction of the regular army followed the Confederate collapse. An army whose peak strength numbered at war's end over 1 million men quickly dwindled to just under 200,000 by late 1865. A year later only 11,000 volunteers remained in federal service and Congress authorized a regular force of just under 60,000 officers and men. In a final concession to the valor and contribution of citizen-soldier volunteers, the legislature provided that all lieutenancies and half of all other commissioned grades in the reorganized army would go to men from the volunteer service. Reduction of regular troops continued during the ensuing decade. Congress cut the postwar army organization in 1869, reducing the infantry regiments from forty-five to twenty-five but keeping the previously authorized ten cavalry and five artillery regiments. This reduction provided for an enlisted strength of 45,000 and cost 750 aspiring career officers their commissions. Finally, in 1876 Congress authorized a force of 27,442 officers and men, an authorization basically unchanged until war came again in 1898.[5]

The end of hostilities in 1865 did not eliminate the need for an army, and military cutbacks complicated substantially the service's immediate tasks. Army leaders could only speculate as to their institution's future place in American society, for the cuts were based on cost, not on some rational program aimed at long-range goals. Lacking civilian guidance on the functions of a regular army in peace, the army reflexively resumed the constabulary duties it had met since its founding.

Occupying the South and implementing congressional Reconstruction was the service's first postwar assignment. Reconstruction embroiled the army in the most contentious political issue of the late nineteenth century. Almost all the leading generals exhibited little desire to become involved in the acrimonious political struggle attending Reconstruction. Many, most notably Generals Sherman, Sheridan, Schofield, and Hancock, viewed with personal distaste the intent of congressional Reconstruction to empower former slaves with fundamental political and civil rights. But the army could not avoid involvement in Reconstruction for it was the only national force capable of restoring and maintaining order in the South. Abraham Lincoln's early death left the North with no guide for restoring the rebellious southern states to the Union. In the ensuing political struggles between President Andrew Johnson and Congress, both looked to the army as the means for implementing their opposing policies. The service was forced to make a choice, and following the lead of its general in chief, Ulysses S. Grant, it opted for Congress.[6]

Grant and the army went with Congress in order to protect occupation forces and to ensure a modicum of northern victory. Southern physical and legal harassment of Union occupation troops forced officers to accept the fact that leniency towards their erring southern brothers merely encouraged recalcitrant ex-Confederates to act as though rebellion had never occurred. Grant, Sherman, and Sheridan believed that slavery caused the war and that if nothing else, the war ended slavery. Nonetheless, with the apparent encouragement of Andrew Johnson, Southerners adopted black codes and relied on violence to drive free blacks back to plantation labor. Only with black political participation could Reconstruction state governments be maintained, and only Reconstruction governments would ensure ex-slaves minimal political, economic, and civil rights. Grant originally opposed an immediate vote for blacks but soon concluded that a guarantee of that vote by military occupation "became an absolute necessity . . . because of the foolhardiness of the President and the blindness of the Southern people to their own interests."[7] Sheridan, too, overcame his initial opposition to the use of force to reform the South. White harassment of freedmen in Texas and Louisiana was so virulent and violent that he saw it as a "plain duty" to use military means to ensure blacks their freedom and "screen them from the bitter political resentment that beset them."[8]

The essence of the military occupation of the South was to ensure victory by supporting freedmen, not to punish the South or plunder the prostrate region. Reconstruction duty placed military commanders in the uncomfortable position of administering otherwise civil functions. General officers in command of the five military districts established by the 1867 Reconstruction acts suppressed disorder, provided justice for loyal citizens, and supervised the operations of provisional state and local governments. District commanders bore the responsibility for registering Southerners eligible to vote in constitutional conventions required for readmission to the Union. They unofficially advised and cajoled convention delegates to accept the inevitable and speed up the readmission process. Military commanders provided as well military protection for the uniformed agents of the Freedmen's Bureau, commanded by Major General Oliver O. Howard, until the bureau ceased most of its activities in 1868. From late 1866, when 20,000 troops occupied the eleven states of the Confederacy, until 1870, when the last three states gained readmission, fully one-third of the army served in the South. This manpower use placed a severe physical strain on the undermanned army.[9]

Reconstruction also generated an enormous strain on the Constitution and traditional American civil-military relations. It not only put military commanders in uncomfortable and unwelcome positions as governors of civil populations, but forced the army to choose between its commander in chief, Andrew Johnson, and the United States Congress. The brunt of this unhappy choice fell upon Ulysses S. Grant. In retrospect it is clear he served his country as well in this crisis as he did in the last years of the war. Grant's tremendous public popularity and his unquestioned authority within the army made him the focal point of the presidential-congressional struggle. The three Reconstruction acts of 1867, Section 2 of the Army Appropriation Act of 1867 (which forbade transfer or dismissal of the general in chief without consent of the Senate), and the Tenure of Office Act of 1867 ostensibly gave Congress control of the army. Grant's active support, however, was absolutely necessary as well. Without his endorsement the army would not have accepted congressional direction. Grant acceded to Congress's intent in these acts and made crucial decisions, particularly when he returned the office of secretary of war to Edwin Stanton in early 1868, thereby giving Congress domination in southern policy.[10]

Not all of Grant's actions appear open and straightforward, but he was in a most awkward position. Deeply committed to civilian control of the army, he did not want openly to defy his commander in chief, but neither did he want to see the fruits of victory lost to unrepentant Southerners. Grant never directly disobeyed an order from President Johnson, though he resolutely rejected Johnson's clumsy attempt in 1866 to pack him off to Mexico as a special envoy. Fortunately for the future of civil-military relations, the president never pushed his power as commander in chief to the ultimate. He refrained from ordering Grant's removal, trying instead to eliminate the far less popular Stanton. Failing in this, Johnson gave up further attempts to outflank Congress.[11]

The army generally followed Grant's restrained but steady opposition to Johnson's efforts to thwart congressional Reconstruction. Grant, not the president, assumed the executive function of implementing the Reconstruction acts, a bold step for a commanding general. In unofficial letters as well as general orders, Grant advised the district commanders on the meaning and intent of legislation. The generals in turn referred their problems and queries directly to Grant, bypassing the secretary of war and normal army channels. Nonetheless, when relations between President Johnson and individual district commanders, most notably Philip Sheridan of the Fifth District, reached the breaking point, the generals reluctantly but obediently accepted presidentially ordered transfers. Conversely, Grant's influence restrained Johnson's most outspoken military supporter, Winfield S. Hancock, from materially altering Sheridan's general policies in the Fifth District when Hancock replaced him in September 1867. Grant and his brother generals did not directly disobey their president, but neither did they hide the fact that they intended to implement congressionally designed Reconstruction.[12]

The struggle over reforming the South posed difficult problems for army generals, men so recently committed to meeting battlefield problems head on with all available force. Political conflict called for different strategies and tactics. Generally the soldiers acquitted themselves well. Lacking a firm policy guide, facing constant alterations in army size, and coping with the unprecedented example of the executive and legislative branches vying for army support, the officer corps followed the guide of Grant and remained committed to civilian control of the military. The heart of Reconstruction politics was not whether a civilian or a military peace would be settled on the South but *which* civilian peace, that of the president or that of Congress, would prevail. The army did not step in to offer a third program of its own, but sought as best it could to support the policy it believed most likely to secure the victory of 1865. That the final peace was a lost peace was not the army's fault, though many officers were lukewarm at best about a drastic reformation of southern society; it was the nation's fault for failing to give freedmen their rightful place in American life.[13]

Formal military rule of the South came to an end in 1870 with the readmission of the last ex-Confederate states, and 1877 marked the removal of the majority of federal troops from the South. Reconstruction left a confused legacy. Most Americans, civilian and military, found the experience distasteful. Opponents of black civil rights attacked the army and argued against military reform or expansion. Military men considered Reconstruction service a temporary assignment and took exception to what they felt was a mission unworthy of a professional force. In addition, soldiers complained that occupation duty kept them from more legitimate tasks. Military resources were needed west of the Mississippi where since the end of the war the army had been struggling to establish order on the high plains and break the power of the Indians. Suppression of the Indians, like the occupation of the South during Reconstruction, challenged a severely undermanned army with assignments lacking general public support, sound conception, or firm civilian direction. This was the service's major problem throughout the late nineteenth century. The army needed policies defining its place and role in American life, indicating what civilians expected of the military. Neither Congress nor the executive branch provided a design for military policy.

Originally a creature of the frontier, the army returned to border duty even before Reconstruction took full form. There it remained for the next thirty years. The need for a military presence on the Mexican-American border in Texas prevented Major General Philip H. Sheridan from participating in the Grand Review. By early June 1865, Sheridan had assembled 52,000 men along the Rio Grande to contain the Mexican civil war and to suggest to the French that their presence in Mexico was not appreciated by the United States. In July Sheridan's compatriot, Lieutenant General William T. Sherman, established headquarters for his new assignment, command of the Division of the Mississippi, in St. Louis, where he oversaw the conduct of operations against Indians in territory west of the Mississippi River.[14]

Service in the West after the war highlighted the lack of a cogent Indian policy, let alone an overall military program. The post–Civil War thrust of settlement deep into the trans-Mississippi West, spurred by construction of the transcontinental railroads, meant that Indian-white relations could no longer be governed by a treaty system which presumed the Indians could be given large land tracts far removed from white settlement. The Bureau of Indian Affairs (BIA), with the strong support of President Grant after 1869, developed a policy which granted annuities to Indians willing to give up their nomadic way of life and settle on reservations. Underlying the reservation program was the presumption that the Indians would eventually adopt an agricultural way of life. Unfortunately, neither whites nor Indians accepted fully the agreements which established reservations. Whites continued to encroach upon Indian lands, while significant minorities of red men refused to confine themselves to reservations or give up the old ways.[15]

The army's task under the reservation system was to keep whites off Indian land and the red men on it. Either action stimulated severe criticism. Eastern humanitarian interests, on the one hand, roundly condemned the use of military force to chastise marauding Indians and force their return to reservations. Westerners, on the other hand, attacked the army whenever regulars moved to drive white intruders from Indian land or when military efforts to return marauding Indians to reservations fell short of annihilation.

General Sherman believed firmly that the army's difficulties with Indian affairs stemmed from divided control of Indian policy. In his eyes civilians in Congress, the Interior Department, and the BIA created conflicting policies bound to anger the Indians. Misguided civilian concerns and inconsistent policy led to pampering as well as confusing the red men. Sherman strongly advocated total military control of Indian policy. That policy, he argued, should be to confine Indians to the reservations, punish them severely whenever they left designated areas, and maintain a constant military presence throughout Indian territory as the visible hand of a powerful government ready to use force at the slightest sign of Indian misbehavior. Sherman saw the Indian question in terms of order and control. The Indians constantly disrupted settlement of the West and were not easily controlled by BIA policies. At his gloomiest, he viewed military subjugation as the only answer. "The more we can kill this year," he wrote to his brother in 1868, "the less will have to be killed in the next year, for the more I see of these Indians the more convinced I am that they will all have to be killed or maintained as a species of pauper. Their attempts at civilization are simply ridiculous."[16]

Sherman at his darkest did not advocate genocide, but he disliked the constraints a mixed policy imposed on him. For a time in the late 1860s, troops could not enter reservations, even in pursuit of off-reservation Indians, unless requested by BIA agents. The annuities and reservation program gave Indians weapons, a haven from military pursuit, and a convenient winter camp for recuperation from the campaign season. BIA administrators, however, too often cheated Indians on their rations, broke promises, and interfered in tribal politics. Angry Indians sometimes fled reservations simply to obtain adequate food and shelter. Many army officers admired aspects of the Indian way of life, especially the red man's affinity with his environment and his ability as an individual soldier. Professional soldiers in a decidedly civilian-dominated society could not totally disparage a culture which exalted the warrior above all others; however, the indiscipline of Indian life and the savagery of their warfare did not appeal to military men. Thus, many officers confronted the Indians with an underlying ambivalence which often led to white savagery in war and high praise for the enemy they had destroyed when they later wrote their memoirs.[17]

The conditions under which the army fought the Indian wars undoubtedly

General William Tecumseh Sherman, shown here as a lieutenant general
Library of Congress (BH82-1979)

provoked many of Sherman's bitterest condemnations of his enemies, for he was forced to fight them with a flawed instrument. The postwar army was simply too small and too poorly supported to patrol adequately all points where Indian-white conflicts might develop. With a force of approximately 30,000 combat effectives in the late 1860s, reduced to 20,000 by the mid–1870s, Sherman had to ensure peace in the vast territory stretching from Mexico to Canada and from the Mississippi River to the Pacific Ocean. Local political pressures and the felt need to display some force at as many places as possible led to the creation of innumerable two- and three-company posts throughout the West. When large-scale uprisings occurred in West Texas in 1868–1869, during the Red River War of 1874–1875, the great Sioux uprising of 1876, and the Nez Percé outbreak of 1877, undersized local garrisons met temporary defeat or at the least failed to prevent full-fledged hostilities. An inevitable delay ensued while higher commands concentrated sufficient troops, usually 2,000 to 3,000 men, to quell the uprising.[18]

Once the army created an offensive force large enough to deal with the hostilities, the mobility of the Indians and the tremendous logistical difficulties of operating in the West often led to only partial success, stalemate, or even defeat. The fact that two-thirds of the white military force was infantry and that the army's cavalry simply could not match Indian horsemen created further frustration. Institutional inertia and the legacy of the Civil War kept the army from adopting unconventional organizations or tactics. The heavy column with cavalry in the van and infantry as the main body guarding supply wagons was the standard formation in army operations against western Indians. General George Crook developed relatively mobile mounted offensives supplied by mule pack trains in Arizona, but his liberal use of Indian scouts and white irregulars brought on his transfer out of Arizona. General Philip Sheridan insisted that regular troops be used regardless of Crook's success with unconventional means. Colonel Nelson A. Miles proved that infantry could effectively pursue and fight Indians, but his methods placed enormous demands on the men of his Fifth Infantry, and few officers possessed the megalomania which drove Miles to his successes.[19]

The army relied on a strategy drawn from the Civil War to overcome its structural limitations. As first applied by Sheridan in the 1868–1869 Southern Plains War, this approach combined surprise, converging columns, and winter campaigns. Sheridan used similar methods in the 1874–1875 Red River War. The strategy failed temporarily in 1876 when poor coordination by Generals George Crook and Alfred H. Terry brought on the defeat in detail of Lieutenant Colonel George A. Custer's cavalry column. An ensuing campaign by Miles's Fifth Infantry during the bitter winter of 1876–1877 finally broke the power of the Sioux tribes. The essence of converging columns was to keep the Indians on the move and never allow them to come to rest for refitting. Constant military pressure prevented all-male warrior bands from leading pursuing troops away from Indian villages. Surprise attacks, especially in winter, allowed regulars to demolish villages, kill or disperse Indian horse herds, and destroy food supplies.

This was nothing less than total war, a method Russell Weigley labels a strategy of annihilation. Army officers consistently asserted that it was never their intent to kill noncombatants. The assertion was moot and of small comfort to those who died, for regardless of the army's intent, Indian women, children, and the aged died in the attacks, and many more succumbed to starvation or the weather after villages were obliterated.[20]

General Sherman declared in his final report as commanding general in 1883: "I now regard the Indians as substantially eliminated from the problems of the Army. There may be spasmodic and temporary alarms, but such Indian wars as have hitherto disturbed the public peace and tranquility are not probable."[21] Sustained military campaigns, supported by the expanding western railroad network, enforced the reservation system. The burgeoning white population hemmed in the Indians and destroyed the economic foundation of Indian society, the buffalo herd. Yet however inevitable the Indians' defeat now appears, it was not an easy task. Most whites wanted the Indians subdued, but the public and Congress were unwilling to approve the manpower levels needed to make the job easier. Nearly a thousand officers and men died in combat or from wounds, and another thousand suffered wounds. Policing the West absorbed the majority of effective combat manpower. Just prior to the end of Reconstruction in 1870, 50 percent of all regulars served in the West. From 1870 to 1890 a minimum of 70 percent remained in the region.[22]

Frontier service condemned regulars to a monotonous, insular, and often thoroughly uncomfortable life. However taxing, it was more likely to be boring than dangerous, with every day spent in pursuit of hostilities matched by fifteen or twenty given over to unvarying garrison duty. Political and military needs forced widespread distribution of troops. Regulars occupied 103 camps, posts, and forts in the West in 1870, a number which reached 129 in 1875 as the Indian wars peaked. Neither the army nor Congress intended to keep so many garrisons permanently, but ostensibly temporary facilities served as home for some troops for up to twenty years. Westerners lobbied successfully to keep many small posts for local protection and to benefit the local economy long after the military need for them had passed. By 1890 regulars occupied only 79 western posts, but far too many of these remained two- and three-company garrisons.[23]

Military duty in the West accentuated problems intrinsic to the army since its founding. Miserable living conditions compounded the service's perennial difficulties in recruiting and retaining an adequate enlisted force, a problem exacerbated by persistent civilian animosity toward the regulars. Native-born Americans composed 50 to 60 percent of the recruits, while immigrants provided the remainder. Four of the regiments, the Ninth and Tenth Cavalry, and the Twenty-fourth and Twenty-fifth Infantry, recruited black men exclusively. Economic necessity, society's prejudice and indifference to immigrants and blacks, as well as a desire to escape the law or an unhappy family life impelled men "in the main . . . to enlist from other than patriotic motives or love of the military profession."[24]

Except for the black regiments, desertion, drunkenness, and indiscipline plagued units stationed in the West. The army attempted throughout the late nineteenth century to discover remedies for desertion and intemperance and to devise methods of attracting better educated and more highly motivated men to the enlisted ranks. The attempts failed, however, principally because only Congress could alleviate the underlying causes of enlisted discontent by improving the nature of military service, which it refused to do. Enlisted life offered low pay, a meager and dull diet, poor living conditions, little opportunity for advancement, a severe and unbending disciplinary system, and few social and recreational facilities. When not in the field campaigning, enlisted men performed arduous, nonmilitary duties such as gathering wood, tending vegetable gardens, or constructing and maintaining garrison buildings. Otherwise, they were kept at the never-changing routine of post duties: reveille, guard mount, retreat, and tattoo daily; Sunday inspections weekly; reviews monthly. Military training outside of incessant company drill played little part in their lives. The mindlessness and boredom of garrison duty, overseen by far too many unimaginative and autocratic officers, contributed significantly to the service's inability to get and keep enlisted men of quality.[25]

Routine garrison life was enervating for most officers also. Daily post duties rarely occupied more than two hours a day for most officers and, lacking imagination or ambition, "cards, billiards and liquor attracted many."[26] Insular life in the West tested officers and their wives in maintaining the genteel life expected of people of their social class. An endless round of teas, dinners, hops, and theatricals all too often assumed the same thoughtless routine attending military duties, with the same guests and dance partners appearing regularly. Judging from the number of courts martial of both enlisted men and officers, preferring charges against one's inferiors, peers, and superiors must have been one of the few readily available methods of breaking up an otherwise tiresome existence.[27]

A serious institutional problem underlay the tedium and aimlessness of postwar military service. As with Reconstruction, Indian duty would not go on forever and this dawning realization caused introspective officers of the late nineteenth century to consider as never before the army's mission in American society. Superficially, there was little difference between antebellum and postwar peacetime military service, but the Civil War had affected the officer corps far more profoundly than had the Mexican War. The nature of the Civil War, with its enormous logistical demands and costly battlefield stalemate, altered the corporate consciousness of a significant element of officers. These men also possessed an acute awareness of the important changes in military command methods and weapons technology which were occurring in contemporary European armies and were convincingly demonstrated in the Franco-Prussian War of 1870–1871. American army officers came to see themselves as professional soldiers, not overseers of a frontier constabulary, and called for wide-ranging military reform. The flowering of a military renaissance in the 1870s and 1880s came from within the army, not from changes in civilian attitudes fostered by industrialization or alterations in fundamental military policy.[28]

An archaic, rigid personnel system stimulated many calls for reform. The prewar system of promotion by seniority, coupled with the rapid reductions in force following the Civil War, condemned a relatively young officer corps to excruciatingly slow advancement. Realizing that merit and performance played no role in promotion below the rank of brigadier general and that only death, resignation, or retirement opened up opportunities to advance, younger officers lobbied for reform. In 1882 Congress finally mandated compulsory retirement at age sixty-four but did not open up advancement beyond the individual officer's regiment until the early 1890s. The latter practice was a constant source of envy between staff and line officers since the staff tended to advance more rapidly than the line. The boy generals of 1865, men like John R. Brooke, George A. Custer, Ranald Mackenzie, Wesley Merritt, Nelson A. Miles, and Emory Upton, wartime general officers by their midtwenties, faced twenty years of service before again pinning stars on their shoulders. Eager young graduates of West Point could anticipate decades of duty before having an opportunity to acquire the field rank of major, and then many more years of service before making lieutenant colonel or colonel. Reformers not unnaturally called for promotion by examination to reward the intelligent and studious, and for expansion of the army to provide more openings.[29]

A developing sense of professionalism further spurred reform-minded officers. In the late nineteenth century, soldiers on both sides of the Atlantic argued that modern war was too complex and demanding for any but those who devoted a lifetime of study, practice, and application to it. War must be waged not simply by career soldiers but by professionals. The Prussian-imperial German military system exemplified the professional acme for most soldiers of the industrializing Western world. Professionalism demanded a fully developed postgraduate school system and constant historical analysis of past wars. William T. Sherman attempted to meet these requirements by encouraging intellectually curious officers like Emory Upton, supporting the numerous professional journals and associations which appeared in the 1870s, and instituting a nascent postgraduate school system with the establishment of such institutions as the School of Application for Cavalry and Infantry at Fort Leavenworth in 1881. Sherman recognized, too, the stultifying effect of garrison duty in the West and approved the detailing of bored officers to such off-post assignments as professors of military science and tactics at land grant colleges and as instructors to the state National Guards. The army's school system was slow to develop into a truly professional educational system, despite Sherman's efforts. West Point remained enamored with its antebellum methodology and curriculum, and the school at Fort Leavenworth failed to rise much above the level of a refresher course for company officers. Truly professional education lay in the future.[30]

By stressing constant study and postgraduate education, reformers redefined the meaning of officership. They implied that four years at West Point and twenty

years of service on the frontier with troops at the company level did not automatically qualify a man for high command in modern war. The changing nature
of war evidenced in the Civil War and the Franco-Prussian War placed increasing
demands on the managerial talents of general officers and less emphasis on their
possessing the qualities of a warrior. Modern war necessitated well-conceived
mobilization plans, elaborate logistical calculations, coordination of mass armies
over large geographical areas, and detailed staff work during battle. Purely
personal bravery was no substitute for the skills and knowledge needed to wage
modern war, and frontier constabulary service provided little experience in these
areas.[31]

Military reformers also advocated a Prussian-style general staff system to
replace the bifurcated American administrative and command system. Despite
the Civil War experience which had revealed the fallacy of a system of organization which did not let the commanding general command both the field
armies and the logistical elements of the service, postwar army organization had
returned to prewar arrangements. The separation of line and staff branches often
complicated and delayed operations in the West during the Indian wars, where
logistical needs were so great. Reform of the command system was needed to
give the army a centralized agency capable of coordinating all service branches
in peace and war. The prevailing system provided no means for planning for
war, hence preventing rapid and efficient mobilization when war came.

Neither law nor army regulations defined very clearly the precise powers and
duties of the commanding general, despite the informal arrangements worked
out between Lincoln, Stanton, and Grant during the war. Despite earlier promises, President Grant did not allow General Sherman to assert authority over the
administrative bureaus and thereby stand between the army and the secretary of
war as the sole uniformed spokesman for the service. Unable to command the
entire army and fed up with what he saw as the political machinations of Secretary
of War William W. Belknap, Sherman emulated Winfield Scott and left Washington, establishing his headquarters at St. Louis from October 1875 to April
1876. Philip Sheridan, Sherman's successor as commanding general, took on
Secretary of War Robert T. Lincoln in 1883 with the same vigor he had once
used to attack Rebel troops and asserted the commanding general's right to
command the bureau chiefs. Uncharacteristically, Sheridan retired in full retreat,
never to raise the issue again.[32]

The fundamental issue of the commanding general's powers went beyond the
question of his right to command and coordinate the logistical bureaus. His
relationship with the president and secretary of war, the crux of civil-military
relations, was also unclear. Winfield Scott had asserted that only the president
could give orders to the commanding general, an assertion both presidents and
secretaries of war had rejected in Scott's time and also after 1865. In the eyes
of many military men, the secretary should have restricted himself to the purely
fiscal and legal needs of the War Department because of his civilian background,
leaving all military matters to the expertise of the commanding general, who

would confer on policy and strategy directly with the president. Sherman enjoyed greatly his brief stint as both commanding general and acting secretary of war in late 1869, informing his brother, "United [authority] in one person settles all disputes. In the present attitude of things, it would be a good thing to dispense with a Secretary of War."[33]

Sherman's desire to do away with the secretary of war not only revealed a dangerous spirit in postwar military reform but also exposed its fundamental weakness and reason for ultimate failure. Reformers were so disenchanted with the truncated nature of military service and the lack of a meaningful mission that they advocated a total revolution in the institutional arrangements governing civil-military relations. Reformers offered suggestions for a number of badly needed changes in the army: regimental reorganization, improvement and expansion of the service's education system, rationalization of the personnel system, redefinition of the government's relationship with the state militias, and moderate expansion of the army. As epitomized in the writings of Emory Upton, however, the call for change went much farther than technical alterations. Upton argued forcefully and with copious historical documentation "that our military policy is weak and that it invites and inevitably produces long wars." He contended that such a policy had been for a hundred years "a crime against life, a crime against property and a crime against liberty." Only far-reaching changes in American military policy would eliminate the criminality of the past.[34]

Upton prescribed a total change in the American military system. He recommended a regular army that could quickly absorb large numbers of recruits in order to provide a field army ready to fight in wartime; a reserve system of national volunteers raised, equipped, officered, and trained in peace by the federal government; and a general staff system. The general staff, officered by products of a fully developed professional educational system, would prepare war plans, instruct the national volunteers in peace, and write the legislation necessary to ensure a sound military system. Upton's reformed military system would eliminate the wasteful and inefficient war army and give total control of military affairs to the highly trained, fully professional regular army. Based upon the German system, the scheme not only would replace the amateur citizen-soldiers of the Civil War, but would relegate the secretary of war to the position of the army's lawyer. The Civil War portions of Upton's *Military Policy of the United States*, highly critical of Lincoln's interference in the conduct of the war, implied that the president, too, should take a back seat to the soldiers. Asserting boldly that "a professional soldier should be the best judge of what constitutes a good military system," Upton gave Congress the right to say only yes or no on military legislative programs. Congress might "refuse to incur the expenses of reforms," but it should not "question the wisdom of the details."[35]

Upton and other reformers believed sincerely that their program for change ensured efficient mobilization, the immediate creation of a force ready for combat, and a leadership trained to avoid the costly blunders of the Civil War. Such a program also provided a mission worthy of a professional army: perpetual

Colonel Emory Upton, shown here as a major general
National Archives (111-BA-257)

training for war in defense of the nation. While technically correct, the reformers nonetheless failed to gain executive or legislative support. Political leaders did not share the sense of urgency evident in the writings of military officers because, like most civilians, they were satisfied with traditional military policy and retained their faith in the viability of the war army idea. Uptonian reformers, despite considerable intellectual effort, could not produce a convincing threat to American security which justified root and branch reform. They could not because there was none. General Sheridan admitted as much in his 1884 annual report, concluding, ''I do not think we should be much alarmed about the probability of wars with foreign powers.'' He estimated that it would take an army of 1.5 million men to wage a successful land war against the United States. All of the shipping of Europe would be needed to transport and support such an invading force. The realities of European power politics precluded the likelihood of any effort of this kind.[36]

Military reformers failed to recognize that the low profile the United States maintained in international relations negated drastic changes in the American military system. Until outside events or internal policy decisions by civilians altered the nation's position in relation to the rest of the world, politicians would ignore military affairs. Emory Upton and his peers either did not comprehend that fact or failed to reconcile their desire for theoretically correct military policy with political reality. The thinly veiled professional contempt for civilian control of military policy represented an early version of the myth that ''political'' interference in military affairs was the fundamental weakness in American civil-military relations. As the Civil War had shown, however, military affairs in a democracy could not be divorced from politics. Peacetime decisions governing the size, organization, and role of the army were of as great a public importance as basic social and economic decisions. Uptonian proposals to circumvent the civilian political process in military affairs were alien to the American system, as flawed as it was, and were doomed to rightful failure.

Professionally myopic and politically naive, Uptonian reformers ignored the political context within which military policy had to be made. Their desire to end the war army practice and eliminate dual state-federal control of the militia led them to reject out of hand the developing National Guard. Political reality demanded *some* professional accommodation with the amateur citizen-soldier tradition. However professionally pure a wholly federal reserve system might have been, it was doomed to failure as long as it ignored the National Guard. Furthermore, despite Upton's contentions in *The Military Policy of the United States*, the record of the citizen-soldier was not one of unmitigated failure. It deserved more consideration than Upton gave it. His insistence on eliminating state soldiers not only failed to bring a new manpower system; it delayed reform for decades, leaving the nation in the meanwhile with no rational manpower system whatever.[37]

Upton's program was flawed because it was divorced from all aspects of the American experience. Ignoring the past, he firmly believed that ''it is to the armies of Europe that we ought to look for best military models."[38] He then chose imperial Germany, a system which had long been the sole creature of monarchy, nearly devoid of parliamentary control, officered by aristocrats, and maintained by thoroughgoing conscription. No European army could have been less fit as a model for military reform in the United States. The choice revealed far more about Emory Upton and his instincts than it did about American military needs. As Stephen Ambrose concludes, the program "was progressive in almost every detail and reactionary in sum."[39] The United States Army in the late nineteenth century unquestionably needed rationalization and centralization, but reform had to be built on the existing political-military system and past national experience.[40]

In taking their cues from Europe, the reformers erred also in assessing the Civil War and, hence, the nature of modern war. Bedazzled by the stunning Prussian successes, Uptonians argued that the Civil War degenerated into bloody stalemate because the American system allowed amateurs to man and lead the armies and encouraged civilian political interference in the conduct of war. The wars of the future, they argued, would be short because modern weaponry and Prussian command methods would give victory to professionally led armies. Those nations which failed to adopt professional methods would be easy prey to the better organized countries. Upton was not alone in failing to assess the Civil War as a harbinger of modern war. Few professional soldiers realized that stalemate came in the Civil War because new technology favored defense over offense and because a people's war demanded destruction of the enemy army and the breaking of the enemy people's will. Highly trained professional armies were not the wave of the future; modern war would be conducted by mass citizen armies.[41]

Caught up in their fascination with the enviable position armies and professional soldiers held in Europe, American military reformers rejected their own past and ignored current needs. They offered few suggestions to lessen the difficulties frontier constabulary duty imposed on the army, nor did they posit workable programs for integrating the National Guard into a single national military system. Frustrated in their attempts to establish continual preparation for war as the singular mission of the army, some reformers turned to pure technicism by devoting themselves to refurbishing the nation's dilapidated coastal fortifications. Such work did not solve the army's underlying institutional problems but it gave the officers involved a means of utilizing their professional knowledge.[42]

Others, intellectually as well as physically isolated from their fellow citizens, proferred dubious nonmilitary justifications for reform. The failure of many state militias in the 1877 railroad strikes necessitated use of the army to restore order. Suppression of domestic disorder, despite its constabulary nature, seemed to offer a means of winning civilian support for military reform. Despite the occasional use of federal troops in labor disorders in the 1880s and 1890s, however, neither the army as a whole nor most civilians exhibited a genuine interest in making the service a national gendarmerie. Military reformers made the appeal out of desperation, and their arguments for domestic disorder duty rang hollow when they were written. They were blatant appeals for civilian support which could not be secured by purely professional arguments.[43]

In the twenty-five years following the Civil War, the American people and many of the men who officered their army lost touch with each other. The relationship between Americans and career soldiers had always been an uneasy one, but the war effort had overridden former hostilities and suspicions to bind soldiers to civilians. After the aura of victory faded, however, the army once again faced penury, physical isolation, stunted careers, and civilian indifference. A developing sense of professionalism fostered by the war and European example produced an intelligent inquiry into the nature of officership and a search for a mission for the army which would give it a purpose worthy of a high calling. Unfortunately, the quest took many ardent reformers too far afield. Their search led many to contend that civilians had to adapt their values to meet the needs of soldiers, an inversion and perversion of traditional American civil-military relations. By looking to Europe, young reformers ignored or forgot the examples of Grant, Sheridan, Schofield, Hancock, and even the morose Sherman. The majority of officers, however, did not succumb to Uptonian pessimism. They understood that the greater mission of the army was to subordinate itself to the society it existed to serve.

For all its faults, the army managed to carry out the assignments society gave to it. It subdued the Indians, instructed the National Guard when asked to do so, fostered an expanding interest in professional inquiry and education, and nurtured a generation of junior officers—Bliss, Bullard, Crowder, Liggett, March, Pershing—who would successfully lead a mass citizen-soldier army in twentieth-century warfare. Military professionalism did not create an officer corps imbued with a set of values distinct from civilian values. In their search for a mission, officers sometimes flirted with the notion that the singular nature of their calling justified reordering the institutional character of civil-military relations. Ultimately, however, the spirit of Ulysses S. Grant prevailed at the end of the period as it had at the beginning.[44]

NOTES

1. Thomas E. Leonard, *Above the Battle: War Making in America From Appomattox to Versailles* (New York: Oxford University Press, 1978), chap. 1. See also William L. Barney, *Flawed Victory: A New Perspective on the Civil War* (New York: Praeger Publishers, 1975), pp. 185–91.

2. Ulysses S. Grant, *Personal Memoirs of U. S. Grant*, 2 vols. (New York: Charles I. Webster and Co., 1886), II, 531. John A. Logan, *The Volunteer Soldier of America* (Chicago: R. S. Peale and Co., 1887) is worth reviewing, and Russell F. Weigley, *Towards an American Army: Military Thought from Washington to Marshall* (New York: Columbia University Press, 1962), chap. 7, has a useful discussion of Logan's ideas.

3. Most general treatments of American military policy and practice discuss the volunteer, ad hoc method of raising an army for war utilized by the United States throughout the nineteenth century. Emory Upton, *The Military Policy of the United States* (1904; reprint, Westport, Conn.: Greenwood Press, 1968); Marvin A. Kreidberg and Merton G. Henry, *History of Military Mobilization in the United States Army, 1775–1945* (Washington: Department of the Army, 1955); and C. Joseph Bernardo and Eugene H. Bacon, *American Military Policy: Its Development Since 1775*, 2d ed. (Harrisburg, Pa.: The Stackpole Co., 1961), have been valuable to this analysis, although all three are quite critical of the practice. Walter Millis, *Arms and Men: A Study of American Military History* (New York: G.P. Putnam's Sons, 1956); Russell F. Weigley, *History of the United States Army*, enlarged ed. (Bloomington: Indiana University Press, 1984); and Jim Dan Hill, *The Minute Man in Peace and War* (Harrisburg, Pa.: The Stackpole Co., 1964), provide useful and insightful antidotes to the Uptonian criticism of the citizen-soldier system.

4. For the thesis that "business pacifism" prevented military reform in late nineteenth-century America, see Samuel P. Huntington, *The Soldier and the State: The Theory and Practice of Civil-Military Relations* (Cambridge: Harvard University Press, 1957). See Allen Guttman, *The Conservative Tradition in America* (New York: Oxford University Press, 1967), chap. 4, for one critique of the Huntington thesis. Bernard L. Boylan, "The Forty-fifth Congress and Army Reform," *Mid-America* 41 (July 1959): 134–40, discusses the Burnside committee's work.

5. Weigley, *History of the U.S. Army*, pp. 266–67; William A. Ganoe, *The History of the United States Army*, rev. ed. (New York: D. Appleton-Century Co., 1942), pp. 302–9, 324–25, 334; Maurice Matloff, ed., *American Military History* (Washington: Office of the Chief of Military History, 1969), pp. 281–82.

6. James E. Sefton, *The United States Army and Reconstruction, 1865–1877* (Baton Rouge: Louisiana State University Press, 1967), is the standard work.

7. Grant, *Memoirs*, II, 512.

8. Philip H. Sheridan, *Personal Memoirs of P. H. Sheridan, General, United States Army*, 2 vols. (New York: Charles L. Webster and Co., 1888), II, 262. See also William T. Sherman, *Personal Memoirs of W. T. Sherman*, 2 vols. (New York: Charles L. Webster and Co., 1892), II, 381, and Grant, *Memoirs*, II, 542, on slavery as the cause of the Civil War. Weigley, *History of the U.S. Army*, pp. 257–64; Barney, *Flawed Victory*, pp. 185–90; and Martin E. Mantell, *Johnson, Grant, and the Politics of Reconstruction* (New York: Columbia University Press, 1973), passim, provide the chief ideas for interpreting the army's Reconstruction experience.

9. Sefton, *The U.S. Army and Reconstruction*, passim; William S. McFeely, *Yankee Stepfather: General O. O. Howard and the Freedmen* (New Haven: Yale University Press, 1968), passim.

10. James G. Randall and David Donald, *The Civil War and Reconstruction*, 2d rev. ed. (Lexington, Mass.: D. C. Heath and Co., 1969), pp. 576–77, 593–98, 603–4; Mantell, *Johnson, Grant, and the Politics of Reconstruction*, chaps. 1–3; Sefton, *The U.S. Army and Reconstruction*, passim.

11. Sefton, *The U.S. Army and Reconstruction*, pp. 105–6, 178–82; Mantell, *Johnson, Grant, and the Politics of Reconstruction*, chaps. 1, 2, 5, and 6; Randall and Donald, *The Civil War and Reconstruction*, pp. 603–4.

12. Sefton, *The U.S. Army and Reconstruction*, pp. 157–60; and Mantell, *Johnson, Grant, and the Politics of Reconstruction*, pp. 35–37.

13. Barney, *Flawed Victory*, pp. 185–91; Weigley, *History of the U.S. Army*, pp. 262–64; and Mantell, *Johnson, Grant, and the Politics of Reconstruction*, pp. 129–50.

14. Clarence C. Clendenen, *Blood on the Border: The United States Army and the Mexican Irregulars* (New York: Macmillan Co., 1969), pp. 50–59; Robert G. Athearn, *William Tecumseh Sherman and the Settlement of the West* (Norman: University of Oklahoma Press, 1956), chap. 1; Robert M. Utley, *Frontier Regulars: The United States Army and the Indian, 1866–1891*, The Wars of the United States (New York: Macmillan Co., 1973), chap. 1.

15. Utley, *Frontier Regulars*, chap. 9; Athearn, *Sherman and the Settlement of the West*, pp. 69–70; and Ray H. Mattison, "The Indian Reservation System on the Upper Missouri, 1865–1890," in Allen G. Bogue, Thomas D. Phillips, and James E. Wright, eds., *The West of The American People* (Itasca, Ill.: F. E. Peacock Publishers, Inc., 1970), pp. 102–7.

16. Sherman quoted in Athearn, *Sherman and the Settlement of the West*, p. 223. See also Athearn, "War Paint Against the Brass: The Army and the Plains Indians," in Bogue et al., *The West of the American People*, pp. 133–37.

17. Athearn, *Sherman and the Settlement of the West*, pp. 95–97; Leonard, *Above the Battle*, chap. 3; Utley, *Frontier Regulars*, pp. 7–8, 133–39.

18. Utley, *Frontier Regulars*, chap. 3 and passim.

19. Ibid., pp. 48–55, 286–90; Russell F. Weigley, *The American Way of War: A History of United States Military Strategy and Policy*, The Wars of the United States (New York: Macmillan Co., 1973), pp. 153–59.

20. Weigley, *The American Way of War*, pp. 160–63; Utley, *Frontier Regulars*, pp. 44–56.

21. U.S., Department of War, *Annual Report of the Secretary of War for 1883* (Washington: Government Printing Office, 1883), p. 45.

22. Utley, *Frontier Regulars*, pp. 410–11.

23. Statistics on the number of posts maintained by the army in the West were compiled from the annual reports of the secretary of war.

24. Brig. Gen. August V. Kautz, "Our National Military System: What the United States Army Should Be," *Century Magazine* 36 (October 1888): 934.

25. Jack D. Foner, *Blacks and the Military in American History: A New Perspective* (New York: Praeger Publishers, 1974), chap. 4; Jack D. Foner, *The United States Soldier Between Two Wars: Army Life and Reforms, 1865–1898* (New York: Humanities Press, 1970); Arlen L. Fowler, *The Black Infantry in the West, 1869–1891* (Westport, Conn.: Greenwood Press, 1971); William H. Leckie, *The Buffalo Soldiers: A Narrative of the Negro Cavalry in the West* (Norman: University of Oklahoma Press, 1963); William B. White, "The Military and the Melting Pot: The American Army and Minority Groups, 1865–1924" (Ph.D. diss., University of Wisconsin, 1968), chap. 5; Edward M. Coffman, "Army Life on the Frontier, 1865–1898," *Military Affairs* 20 (Winter 1956): 195–201; Utley, *Frontier Regulars*, pp. 22–28.

26. James Parker, *The Old Army: Some Memories, 1872–1918* (Philadelphia: Dorrance and Co., 1929), p. 23.

27. Oliver Knight, *Life and Manners in the Frontier Army* (Norman: University of Oklahoma Press, 1978), passim; Coffman, "Army Life on the Frontier, 1865–1898"; and Utley, *Frontier Regulars*, pp. 18–22.

28. Contemporary comment includes Kautz, "What the Army Should Be," 935–36; "The Army and the Future," *Army and Navy Journal* 28 (8 November 1890): 174.

Historical analyses include James Leonard Abrahamson, "The Military and American Society, 1881–1922" (Ph.D. diss., Stanford University, 1977), chaps. 1–3; Ganoe, *History of the U.S. Army*, p. 355; and Weigley, *History of the U.S. Army*, pp. 271–72.

29. Ganoe, *History of the U.S. Army*, pp. 355–56, 365; Matloff, *American Military History*, pp. 289–90; Weigley, *History of the U.S. Army*, p. 291.

30. Allan Millett provides a very useful discussion of military professionalism and its genesis in the United States Army in "Military Professionalism and Officership in America," *A Mershon Center Briefing Paper* (Columbus: The Mershon Center of the Ohio State University, May, 1977), pp. 2, 5–6, 17, 20–21. See also Timothy K. Nenninger, *The Leavenworth Schools and the Old Army: Education, Professionalism, and the Officer Corps of the United States Army, 1881–1918* (Westport, Conn.: Greenwood Press, 1978), pp. 5–10, 16–18; Weigley, *History of the U.S. Army*, pp. 271–81; Weigley, *Towards an American Army*, pp. 101–05; Matloff, *American Military History*, pp. 288–90; and Stephen Ambrose, *Duty, Honor, Country: A History of West Point* (Baltimore: The Johns Hopkins Press, 1966), chap. 10.

31. Stephen Ambrose, *Upton and the Army* (Baton Rouge: Louisiana State University Press, 1964), pp. 99–104; Abrahamson, "The Military and American Society, 1881–1922," pp. 49–57, 72–77; Millett, "Military Professionalism and Officership in America," pp. 13, 17; Nenninger, *The Leavenworth Schools and the Old Army*, pp. 9–18; Weigley, *History of the U.S. Army*, pp. 279–80, and *Towards an American Army*, pp. 104–5, 120–24.

32. Weigley, *History of the U.S. Army*, pp. 284–89, and *Towards an American Army*, pp. 109–17; Utley, *Frontier Regulars*, pp. 28–35; Robert F. Stohlman, *The Powerless Position: The Commanding General of the Army of the United States, 1864–1903* (Manhattan, Kans.: Military Affairs/Aerospace Historian Publishing, 1975), chaps. 1–3; Leonard D. White, *The Republican Era, 1869–1901: An Administrative Study* (New York: Macmillan Co., 1958) pp. 134–44.

33. William T. Sherman to John Sherman, 12 September 1869, quoted in Stohlman, *The Powerless Position*, p. 58. See also pp. 53–70.

34. *The Military Policy of the U.S.*, pp. ix, 4.

35. Ibid., pp. xi, 423; Ambrose, *Upton and the Army*, passim; Weigley, *Towards an American Army*, chap. 7.

36. Quoted in Weigley, *The American Way of War*, pp. 168–70. See also Ambrose, *Upton and the Army*, pp. 107–9 and 123–24.

37. Ambrose, *Upton and the Army*, pp. 90–96, 99, 107–9; Weigley, *Towards an American Army*, pp. 119–26; Martha Derthick, *The National Guard in Politics* (Cambridge: Harvard University Press, 1965), chap. 2; William H. Riker, *Soldiers of the States: The National Guard in American Democracy* (Washington: Public Affairs Press, 1957), chap. 4.

38. Peter S. Michie, *The Life and Letters of Emory Upton . . . U.S. Army* (New York: D. Appleton and Co., 1885), p. 406.

39. Ambrose, *Upton and the Army*, p. 135.

40. Weigley, *Towards an American Army*, pp. 119–26; Ambrose, *Upton and the Army*, pp. 90–96, 99, 107–9; Nenninger, *The Leavenworth Schools and the Old Army*, pp. 12–15; Richard C. Brown, "General Emory Upton—The Army's Mahan," *Military Affairs* 17 (Fall 1953): 125–31.

41. Weigley, *The American Way of War*, pp. 167–70; Ambrose, *Upton and the Army*, pp. 132–35; Leonard, *Above the Battle*, pp. 75–79, 83–94; Jay Luvaas, *The Military*

Legacy of the Civil War: The European Heritage (Chicago: The University of Chicago Press, 1959), chap. 6 and pp. 226–34.

42. Weigley, *History of the U.S. Army*, pp. 283–84; Millis, *Arms and Men*, pp. 134–36; Abrahamson, "The Military and American Society, 1881–1922," pp. 135–47.

43. See Jerry M. Cooper, "The Army As Strikebreaker—The Railroad Strikes of 1877 and 1894," *Labor History* 18 (Spring 1977): 179–96; Ambrose, *Upton and the Army*, pp. 105, 123–24.

44. Weigley, *History of the U.S. Army*, pp. 291–92.

FURTHER READING

The history of the United States Army in the twenty-five years after the Civil War can only be accurately understood if placed in the full context of the history of American military affairs. Robin Higham, ed., *A Guide to Sources of United States Military History* (Hamden, Conn.: Archon Books, 1975) remains a convenient bibliographic source. Walter Millis, *Arms and Men: A Study of American Military History* (New York: G. P. Putnam's Sons, 1956), currently available in paperback, and Russell F. Weigley, *History of the United States Army*, The Wars of the United States (New York: Macmillan Co., 1967), also now available in an enlarged, paperback edition from Indiana University Press, and Weigley's *Towards an American Army: Military Thought from Washington to Marshall* (New York: Columbia University Press, 1962) give the student the necessary background for any period of the army's history. A very different, but nonetheless stimulating book, is Thomas E. Leonard, *Above the Battle: War-Making in America From Appomattox to Versailles* (New York: Oxford University Press, 1978), which provocatively assesses the impact of the Civil War on three generations of Americans.

The memoirs of Grant, Sherman, and Sheridan are most useful for understanding Civil War and Reconstruction issues, but the postwar army is perhaps more fully revealed in John M. Schofield, *Forty-Six Years in the Army* (New York: The Century Co., 1897) and Nelson A. Miles, *Serving the Republic: Memoirs of the Civil and Military Life of Nelson A. Miles* (New York: Harper and Brothers, 1911). The many writings by Charles King, fictional and factual, tell us much about the late nineteenth-century army. See, for example, *Campaigning with Crook and Stories of Army Life* (New York: Harper and Brothers, 1890).

The army's role in Reconstruction can be traced in Martin E. Mantell, *Johnson, Grant, and the Politics of Reconstruction* (New York: Columbia University Press, 1973), and James E. Sefton, *The United States Army and Reconstruction, 1865–1877* (Baton Rouge: Louisiana State University Press, 1967).

The best single work on the army in the Indian wars is Robert M. Utley, *Frontier Regulars: The United States Army and the Indian, 1866–1891*, The Wars of the United States (New York: Macmillan Co., 1973), valuable for its bibliography, analysis, and narrative. An interesting, comparative cultural approach to the army and the Indian is Stephen E. Ambrose, *Crazy Horse and Custer: The Parallel Lives of Two American Warriors* (Garden City, N.Y.: Doubleday and Co., 1975). For very different aspects of military life and service on the plains, read Arlen L. Fowler, *The Black Infantry in the West, 1869–1891* (Westport, Conn.: Greenwood Press, 1971); Oliver Knight, *Life and Manners in the Frontier Army* (Norman: University of Oklahoma Press, 1978); and Don

Rickey, Jr., *Forty Miles a Day on Beans and Hay: The Enlisted Soldier Fighting the Indian Wars* (Norman: University of Oklahoma Press, 1963).

All students of post–Civil War army reform must begin with Emory Upton, *The Military Policy of the United States* (1904; reprint, Westport, Conn.: Greenwood Press, 1968). Stephen E. Ambrose, *Upton and the Army* (Baton Rouge: Louisiana State University Press, 1964), and Samuel P. Huntington, *The Soldier and the State: The Theory and Politics of Civil-Military Relations* (Cambridge: Harvard University Press, 1957), take contrasting views of the thrust of late nineteenth-century military reform. Timothy K. Nenninger, *The Leavenworth Schools and the Old Army: Education, Professionalism, and the Officer Corps of the United States Army, 1881–1918* (Westport, Conn.: Greenwood Press, 1978); Allan R. Millett, *The General: Robert L. Bullard and Officership in the United States Army, 1881–1925* (Westport, Conn.: Greenwood Press, 1975); and James L. Abrahamson, *America Arms for a New Century: The Making of a Great Military Power* (New York: Free Press, 1981), all see the Indian-fighting army as a source of professionalism and reform. On enlisted men, see Jack D. Foner, *The United States Soldier Between Two Wars: Army Life and Reforms, 1865–1898* (New York: Humanities Press, 1970). Jerry M. Cooper, *The Army and Civil Disorder: Federal Military Intervention in American Labor Disputes, 1877–1900* (Westport, Conn.: Greenwood Press, 1980), examines the army's role in policing industrial disorder.

Until recently scholars have slighted or ignored the development of the National Guard in the late nineteenth century. See the appropriate chapters in the following: John K. Mahon, *History of the Militia and National Guard*, The Wars of the United States (New York: Macmillan Co., 1983); Martha Derthick, *The National Guard in Politics* (Cambridge: Harvard University Press, 1965); Jim Dan Hill, *The Minute Man in Peace and War: A History of the National Guard* (Harrisburg, Pa.: The Stackpole Co., 1964); and William H. Riker, *Soldiers of the States: The Role of the National Guard in American Democracy* (Washington: Public Affairs Press, 1957). For one description of the guard in a labor dispute, see Jerry M. Cooper, "The Wisconsin National Guard and the Milwaukee Labor Riots," *Wisconsin Magazine of History* (Fall 1971): 31–48.

CHAPTER 10

Reform and Revitalization, 1890–1903

WILLIAM R. ROBERTS

The waning years of the nineteenth century and the early years of the twentieth century were a time of reform and revitalization for the army. Military leaders during this period sought to defuse the institutional crisis which elimination of the army's Indian-fighting mission and the nation's volatile economy had brought to a head. Reform-minded officers set out initially to impart a greater sense of unity and vitality to the service by improving the living and working conditions of both enlisted and commissioned personnel. Public alarm over wartime mistakes and public pride arising from wartime accomplishments combined after the Spanish-American War in 1898, however, to allow a small group of officials in the War Department to make important structural and procedural changes in the military establishment itself. By 1903 these men claimed to have laid the foundation for a "new army"—one which they believed would serve their needs and the needs of the country in the coming century better than the small constabulary force on which Americans had relied largely in the past.

The crisis threatening the army at the end of the nineteenth century did not occur abruptly or unexpectedly. Most officers, for example, knew well in advance that the Indian wars were drawing to a close. Not everyone had been as confident as William T. Sherman, when in 1883 the commanding general had announced that the army no longer faced a serious threat from the Indians.[1] But by the beginning of the next decade, Sherman's claim had become more credible. The last major confrontation between the army and the Indians took place near Wounded Knee Creek, South Dakota, in December 1890. Although fears of future uprisings persisted, this bloody tragedy brought organized hostilities in the West to an end.

Leaders such as Sherman were proud of the part the army had played in conquering the frontier. Yet they also felt uneasy in the absence of other enemies to whom they could call attention after they had defeated the Indians. The election of Grover Cleveland to the White House in 1892 and the seesaw battle between the Democratic and Republican parties for control of Congress during the depression of 1893–1897 made the officers all the more apprehensive. They feared that inactivity on their part would give Democratic politicians an opportunity to reassert that party's traditional opposition to a large standing army. Unless they moved quickly to demonstrate a need for their services, one junior officer admonished his colleagues in 1890, "we may wake up some day from our Rip Van Winkle sleep to find our occupation gone."[2]

The persistently high desertion rates of the post–Civil War period gave the officers further cause to worry. Desertion was an especially serious crime in the small, widely dispersed units of the old army. An annual desertion rate that averaged more than 16 percent of the army's aggregate strength during the 1870s and almost 13 percent in the early 1880s greatly alarmed the leaders responsible for those units. The number of deserters depended primarily on the job opportunities available to unskilled workers in the boom-and-bust economy of the day, but explanations of this sort offered little comfort to commanding officers. Given their choice, many would have tried to discourage would-be offenders by reviving the harsh forms of corporal punishment used earlier in the century. But as long as Congress refused to revive the use of capital punishment for deserters (or to pay enlisted men more than thirteen dollars a month), military leaders reluctantly concluded that they would have to find some more creative means of lowering the desertion rate.[3]

Taking the lead in addressing this problem, the adjutants general, the chief personnel officers of the army, sought to improve the living conditions of the troops. Beginning in the early 1880s, Adjutant General R. C. Drum proposed a series of reforms designed to make the soldier's lot more palatable. From 1889 to 1893 Drum's successor, Brigadier General John C. Kelton, waged an even more vigorous and successful campaign to reduce desertion rates. Kelton and other reformers like him shortened the required term of enlistment from five years to three and replaced the old bimonthly system of pay with monthly payments for all enlisted men. In 1889 military authorities even went so far as to abolish Sunday inspection, one of the army's oldest traditions. Despite formidable opposition from patriarchs such as Sherman, weekly inspections took place thereafter on Saturday morning, leaving Saturday afternoon and Sunday free for sports and other forms of recreation.

Another change that heralded the growing concern of military leaders for the general welfare of the soldier occurred in the same year when the army abolished the post and regimental funds which had used money obtained by selling a portion of each soldier's rations to finance educational, recreational, and similar activities. Post libraries, schools, bands, and other amenities of garrison life were treated thereafter as public responsibilities of the institution rather than private responsibilities of the individuals who stood to benefit from them.

The desire to strengthen the allegiance of the individual to the organization also led the War Department to phase out the controversial system under which secretaries of war licensed private businessmen to operate post stores. The traders or sutlers who held these licenses sold supplies, tobacco, and even whiskey to their customers for a profit. During the late 1880s and 1890s, however, cooperative canteens replaced many of the sutlers' stores. Later renamed the post exchange, the canteen offered reasonably priced commodities (to include for a time wine and beer, but not whiskey) to both officers and enlisted men and promised to reduce the dissatisfaction that had arisen in the past because of the questionable practices of some of the traders.

Although these and other reforms diminished the high rate of desertion in the army, they did not eliminate the problem. Neither the abolition of the post and regimental funds nor the introduction of the post exchange could make up for the failure to provide soldiers with reasonable monetary and social rewards. Innovations of this sort nonetheless promised to unify and revitalize the army by encouraging what would eventually become a far-reaching transformation in the attitudes of enlisted men toward the organization in which they served.

It proved more difficult to effect a similar change among the officers, possibly because they appear to have felt a stronger attachment to the subordinate units or functional groups to which they belonged than to the service as a whole. To make matters worse, fear that the military would soon fall on hard times exacerbated a number of long-standing rivalries and quarrels, as various groups of officers tried all the harder to defend their particular interests against those of their comrades.

One of the more divisive struggles to come to the fore during these years pitted army commanders (line officers) against administrators (staff officers). Worried about keeping their jobs in the near future and influenced by the conventional wisdom that the government should save, not spend, its way out of its economic difficulties, the staff officers systematically sought to improve the army's "fiscal arrangements."[4] They introduced new rules and regulations which they said would standardize military procurement and accounting procedures. They then checked to see that everyone complied with the new requirements and to measure how well those requirements kept expenses down. Through these and other means, they tried to persuade Congress that any significant decrease in administrative personnel would cost the government more than it would save.

The line officers resisted these changes. Commanders disliked having to rely on the staff bureaus for the many services and supplies their units needed. They suspected the administrators of paying more attention to the interests of their bureaus than to the needs of the combat units they were supposed to serve. The administrative reforms that were enacted during the late nineteenth century heightened these suspicions. If allowed to continue, the line officers warned, the proliferation of "red tape, . . . forms and papers" required to keep the bureau chiefs informed of what happened outside Washington would soon turn the "army into a mere *paper* machine" and destroy its ability to operate as a military organization.[5]

The line officers were naturally looking out for their own interests as well as those of the service when they objected to these administrative changes. They made light of their personal motives, but prestige, career advancement, and job security all played a much more important part in the struggle between line and staff than most men cared to admit. Afraid of future budget and personnel cuts, the commanders automatically opposed any move that might strengthen the position of the staff at their expense. Because they recognized a need to justify their actions in politically acceptable terms, the line officers claimed that the army had too large a staff. The number of administrators could be reduced, they said, by consolidating the different staff bureaus performing closely related tasks. What the commanders did not point out was that they hoped by this means to satisfy demands for a smaller officer corps without having to give up any of the billets they themselves held.

Army commanders were willing to go to great lengths to get what they wanted, as shown by the actions of Lieutenant General John M. Schofield upon succeeding General Philip H. Sheridan as commanding general in 1888. Ever since he had served as secretary of war in the late 1860s, Schofield had shown an interest in clarifying the ambiguous responsibilities of the secretary, the bureau chiefs, and the commanding general. As early as 1876 he had recommended uniting the bureaus into a single staff department under the supervision of a chief of staff, "second in rank and importance only to the General-in-Chief." Schofield had abandoned this suggestion when faced with the determined opposition of senior staff officers. But the more he thought about the problem, the more he began to wonder whether in an army as small as that of the United States, the duties of the commanding general and the chief of staff could not be combined and made the responsibility of one man. After his appointment as commanding general, he worked hard to accomplish that goal.[6]

Perhaps because he himself had once occupied the secretary's office, Schofield realized that he needed the assistance of the secretary of war if he hoped to control the staff. He promised not to challenge the secretary's authority to command the army as other commanding generals before him had. Schofield even offered to substitute the title of "chief of staff" for that of "commanding general" and "to lay before the Secretary for his approval . . . every order" issued by the army's new "Chief Staff Officer." All he asked in return was that the secretary observe more closely an 1876 War Department directive specifying that "all orders and instructions relative to military operations or affecting the military control and discipline of the Army" be routed through the commanding general (or chief of staff, as Schofield called himself) to the rest of the army. Schofield thought this informal arrangement would enable him to supervise the bureau chiefs in all but the most routine administrative matters. Because he alone would direct the flow of information between the army and the nation's political leaders, he also felt confident that he would occupy a much more important position in the civil-military chain of command than his new title indicated.[7]

Schofield sought to curtail the semiautonomous powers of the administrators in order to give the men who would command the army in time of war more control over its peacetime affairs. Staff officers had little personal contact with units in the field, and line officers such as Schofield were determined to revitalize the service by placing it in the hands of experienced leaders who understood those units and their needs. In addition, he believed that subordinating the staff to the line would end the struggle between commanders and administrators and thereby allow military leaders to pay more attention to the problems of the army as a whole.

The war between line and staff was not the only conflict within the officer corps. Junior and senior officers had not always seen eye to eye before, and fears of a reduction in the size of the army and its budget greatly aggravated their disagreements with one another. Junior officers resented the rules that governed their chances for preferment and prevented them from rising as far or as quickly as they desired. Despite the existence of a mandatory retirement law after 1882, the long-established practice of promoting officers only when a vacancy occurred in their own regiment continued to make advancement a slow and uncertain process. This was especially true for anyone near the bottom of the promotion ladder or unfortunate enough to find himself assigned to a regiment commanded by relatively young men.

The bottleneck blocking the rise of junior officers gave little sign of easing until 1890, when the adoption of new procedures ensured that an officer no longer had to wait for the promotion, death, or retirement of a senior colleague in his regiment to advance in rank. Promotions below the level of brigadier general instead took place in each staff department or combat arm of the service (infantry, cavalry, and artillery) whenever an opening appeared among the officers of that particular department or arm. This reform, together with the closely timed adoption of a system of efficiency reports and the requirement that all lieutenants and captains had to pass a written examination before being promoted, did not satisfy all of the army's "Young Turks." Nonetheless, the hope that promotions might one day depend more on individual merit cheered many low-ranking officers and made them feel a more vital part of the organization to which they belonged.

Evidence that the army had found a new mission (really an old mission in a new guise) to replace that of a frontier constabulary also helped to revive the spirits of military leaders. By the late 1880s those officers who espoused Emory Upton's idea that the peacetime army should act as a school to teach soldiers how to win future wars had succeeded in giving institutional expression to some of their goals. From 1885 to 1889 a small Military Intelligence Division took shape in the Adjutant General's Department; its members collected and disseminated information about the armed forces of other countries. Earlier efforts to consolidate the various units scattered throughout the West continued, and in 1889 the army held the first large-scale exercises in which different regiments came together to practice battlefield maneuvers.

The importance of preparing for war before it began was underscored during the 1890s as a result of the efforts of army and navy officers to call attention to America's deteriorating coastal defense system. Protecting the nation from sea-borne attack was a responsibility the army had long shared with the navy. Except for those occasions when war with an overseas power such as Great Britain or

France had seemed likely, however, army officers had usually attached less importance to the mission of coastal defense than they had to their constabulary duties. As the latter responsibilities grew less demanding, military leaders began to pay more attention to their ability to defend the coast against attacks from abroad.

As early as 1885 Congress had directed Secretary of War William C. Endicott to convene a Board on Fortifications or Other Defenses in order to determine how best to protect the nation from offshore bombardment and coastal raids. The Endicott board found that the United States had not kept up with defensive developments in other countries. Existing fortifications had fallen into bad repair and no longer afforded adequate protection for the harbors and navy yards on which American commerce depended. In order to correct these conditions, the board recommended installing an ambitious new system of fixed shore batteries, underwater mine fields, and shallow-draft vessels along the Atlantic, Gulf, and Pacific coasts, as well as on the Canadian border.

Construction of these defenses did not begin in earnest until the following decade, when the Ordnance Department overcame the problems that had delayed production of the heavy guns and carriages on which the new system depended. Additional funds to implement the Endicott board's recommendations became available after a number of officers took advantage of the Japanese invasion of China in 1894 to warn of the vulnerability of the United States to a similar attack. It was not until the Republican party gained control of both houses of Congress in 1895, however, that legislative appropriations for coastal defenses approached the levels requested by military leaders. The army spent $540,000, or approximately 1 percent of its expenditures for that year, on coastal defenses. It spent $2.5 million, 6 percent of military spending, the following year. Army engineers complained that even these sums were not enough to complete the vast defensive system envisioned by the Endicott board, but by 1900 (when annual military expenditures for coastal fortifications exceeded $22 million) engineer and ordnance officers had already installed 53 rapid-firing guns, 242 twelve-inch mortars, and 237 eight-inch, ten-inch, and twelve-inch guns mounted on both disappearing and barbette carriages.[8]

The growing interest shown by many officers in coastal fortifications, large-scale field maneuvers, and the characteristics and capabilities of other armies stemmed almost exclusively from a traditional concern for continental development and defense that gave no sign of changing until after the Spanish-American War began in 1898. Although they frequently sought to persuade their countrymen that the United States should have an army capable of holding its own in case of conflict with a major European power, military leaders revealed no plans to use such a force in offensive operations overseas. General Schofield, for example, recommended in 1894 that the size of the army be increased so that it might "bear a reasonable proportion to that maintained by other great nations." The commanding general said nothing about sending the larger force he requested abroad. Rather, he pointed to the Sino-Japanese War as an example of how easy it would be for another country to invade the United States if Congress failed to appropriate the funds for an army large enough to thwart such an attack.[9]

Thus, despite their misgivings over what would happen if the United States had to fight a European power in the 1890s, when war finally came in 1898, it was not the type of conflict military leaders had expected. Indeed, the army's emphasis on national defense continued to influence military thought and actions even after it became apparent that a war with Spain was imminent.

In March 1898 President McKinley rushed a special appropriation bill through Congress in order to intimidate the Spanish government as well as to strengthen the armed forces in case the talks then underway with Spain collapsed and war broke out. The new law authorized the expenditure of $50 million "for the National defense."[10] The navy used its share of the money to prepare for offensive operations at sea. Secretary of War Russell A. Alger interpreted the language of the law more narrowly, however, and had the War Department spend most of what it received on coastal fortifications. The shortsightedness of these and earlier defensive arrangements quickly became apparent once the war began and the army was called on to conduct offensive operations overseas.

Caught off guard by this requirement, military leaders hastily assembled the forces they would send to the Pacific and the Caribbean. From the time the United States declared war in April until Spain requested an armistice in August, the regular army more than doubled in size, adding approximately 30,000 officers and enlisted men to the 28,000 already in uniform. In addition to the regulars, the War Department recruited more than 200,000 volunteers, some 18,000 of whom came from throughout the country to serve in ten regiments of federal volunteers. The most famous of these units was the First United States Volunteer Cavalry Regiment, or Rough Riders, led by Colonel Leonard Wood and Lieutenant Colonel Theodore Roosevelt.

The eager response of the state National Guard units to the president's call to arms satisfied the remaining need for volunteers. Because the courts had never settled the question of whether the president could send militiamen out of the country, National Guardsmen volunteered for federal service individually. They then reconstituted their old units and served out the war alongside the neighbors with whom they had marched and drilled for most of their adult lives—making this the last major conflict in which a majority of American soldiers belonged to homogeneous, hometown units.

Relying on a mixed organization of this sort had a number of disadvantages. Most of the officers in the guard, for example, were community leaders whose neighbors had elected them to the positions they held. Regular army officers complained that this was no way to select officers for units that would soon see combat. According to the professionals, discipline in the guard suffered because its officers were too friendly with the men they commanded. There was something to be said for the guard's method of choosing leaders, however, for it avoided many of the problems encountered in designating officers for other units.

All general officers, all staff officers at the division and corps levels, and all officers in the federal volunteers were appointed by the president acting on the advice of the secretary of war. As many as 25,000 men applied for the approximately 1,000 commissions granted in this manner. Applicants for these commissions, an assistant adjutant general later recalled, "filled the rooms and corridors" of the War Department and left the secretary of war and adjutant general little time to "attend to the proper functions of their offices." Unable to handle the sudden onslaught of men trying to gain favor by day, these officials and their subordinates took to "secreting themselves for a few moments at a time, or during the night, when most of the real business of the department had to be conducted, to avoid the pressure from office seekers."[11]

Such problems were not new, but in previous wars staff officers had usually had more time to deal with them than they did in 1898, when the first soldiers went overseas one month after the war began and the fighting stopped two and a half months later. In addition, earlier bureau chiefs had often had more administrative experience than they had in 1898. Prior to the introduction of mandatory retirement in 1882, it had not been uncommon for bureau chiefs to head the same department for thirty or forty years. When Brigadier General Henry C. Corbin became adjutant general in 1898, however, he was the fifth officer in nine years to hold that post. Corbin was an especially capable administrator, but this was not true of all the officers who had become bureau chiefs in the 1890s. New to their jobs, the bureau chiefs felt overwhelmed by the many demands suddenly made of them in 1898. The confusion and mistakes that ensued contributed to the popular impression that military leaders were sometimes their own worst enemies during the war.[12]

Graham Cosmas has since tried to correct that impression, noting that "by working hard and in the main sensibly, officials in Washington and commanders in the field had solved their most serious problems" by the time the fighting stopped.[13] Sometimes operations went smoothly from the start, as in the case of the more than 10,000 men of the Eighth Army Corps who left San Francisco during May and June to serve under Major General Wesley Merritt in the Philippines. But more often the army's failure to prepare properly for the war, coupled with the absence of experienced bureau chiefs, caused it to make a number of early mistakes which overshadowed its later accomplishments. This was certainly true of the only other corps to serve overseas as an operational unit during the war, the Fifth Army Corps, which fought under the command of Major General William R. Shafter in Cuba.

Once the president decided to intervene in Cuba, the soldiers of what would later become known as the Fifth Corps gathered at a few large assembly areas in the southeastern United States where they could draw their equipment and train. Eager to leave as soon as possible, commanders paid little attention to the future needs of their men should they have to stay in these camps longer than expected. The crowded, unsanitary conditions which resulted accounted for most of the war's casualties. The many volunteer units that were left behind when the Fifth Corps departed for Cuba were especially hard hit. Moreover, some of the troops who went with Shafter contracted typhoid fever and dysentery prior to their departure; tropical diseases such as malaria and yellow fever added to the medical emergency that seriously depleted the force Shafter led into battle. Before the war ended local commanders and military doctors working together in the United States and Cuba eliminated many of the unsanitary conditions which were largely responsible for this crisis. But the army's wartime achievements in medicine and sanitation came too late to quiet the criticism caused by the knowledge that disease killed almost 93 percent of the servicemen who perished during the war.[14]

Military officials also found it difficult to live down the many mistakes they made in transporting and supplying the Fifth Corps overseas. Shafter received orders to embark at Tampa, Florida. The naval officers responsible for protecting the troop transports and supply ships bound for Cuba wanted to keep the voyage as short as possible, and Tampa was the closest port to the Caribbean. Tampa proved a poor choice, however, because it did not have adequate rail or port facilities. Only two railroads led into the town, and from there a single line extended to the harbor some ten miles distant. Trains backed up as far away as South Carolina, and miles of unopened boxcars sat on sidings outside Tampa waiting delivery. Matters came to a head on 6 June when Shafter began embarking the Fifth Corps on board too few transports to take everyone who had counted on going. Individual units literally fought to keep from being left behind in the free-for-all which followed.

The mistakes and lack of coordination that marked the army's departure from Tampa continued to bedevil the Fifth Corps after its arrival off the southern coast of Cuba on 20 June. There Shafter rendezvoused with the North Atlantic Squadron, which had blockaded the main Spanish squadron in the harbor at Santiago since the beginning of the month. The American naval commander, Rear Admiral William T. Sampson, hesitated to enter the narrow channel leading to the harbor where the Spanish ships were anchored for fear the passage was mined. Sampson wanted the army to attack the batteries and fortifications overlooking the channel so that minesweepers might then clear the way for his squadron to advance and engage the enemy naval force.

The admiral hoped Shafter would comply with his request; but he could only ask, not order the general to cooperate. The Fifth Corps commander soon made it clear that he had no intention of playing a subordinate role. Landing southeast of Santiago, Shafter's force of mostly regular army units followed the coast toward the harbor entrance for a short distance, then turned inland, and headed for Santiago. The Americans encountered little resistance and on 1 July seized the main line of defenses to the east of the city. There Shafter's advance stopped. Overcome by illness, exhaustion, and worry, the general did not think his men could continue the assault and warned that they might have to withdraw from the positions they held if the enemy launched a counterattack.

The tables had turned and Shafter now found it necessary to seek the navy's

Soldiers of the Fifth Army Corps embarking for Cuba, June 1898
National Archives (111-SC-100412)

assistance. He urged the admiral to advance and shell the city in order to "have the business over."[15] Sampson refused, reminding the general that until his soldiers silenced the Spanish artillery overlooking the passageway to the harbor, the navy could do nothing to help.

Fortunately for the American commanders, Santiago's defenders were in even worse straits. The Spaniards saw no way to avoid defeat and tried to cut their losses, only to play into their opponents' hands. On the morning of 3 July, the Spanish naval commander attempted to run the blockade. Sampson's ships gave pursuit and in less than four hours easily destroyed the enemy squadron. Encouraged by this victory, Shafter held his position until the garrison commander in Santiago surrendered two weeks later. Shortly thereafter the United States and Spain agreed to stop fighting and broke off all military and naval operations after American forces captured Manila on 13 August.

Despite its brevity the Spanish-American War had a number of important consequences for the United States and its army. In July, while American soldiers were still fighting in the Caribbean and preparing to attack Manila in the Philippines, Congress had satisfied the need for a naval base in the Pacific by annexing the Hawaiian Islands. Other American possessions acquired as a result of the war included the former Spanish colonies of Guam, the Philippines, and Puerto Rico. Although Cuba became a nominally independent country after the departure of the last American soldiers in May 1902, the United States reserved the right to intervene in the island's internal affairs in the future. These scattered possessions led to the development of new foreign policies and thrust political leaders more fully into the mainstream of international affairs than they had chosen to venture before. Such changes pleased military men, who saw in them an opportunity not only to complete the process of reform and revitalization, but also to create a new army capable of advancing American interests overseas even as it defended them at home.

The appointment of a new secretary of war in August 1899 gave army officers the leader they needed to accomplish these goals. When Secretary Alger resigned in July, President McKinley chose a well-known New York lawyer, Elihu Root, to replace him. McKinley thought Root's legal experience would prove useful in governing the island empire occupied by the army. Root did not disappoint the president. The new secretary helped establish the conditions under which American soldiers eventually withdrew from Cuba and was largely responsible for drafting the instructions to the civilian commission which took over the government of the Philippines by mid–1901. In addition, he played a key role in winning congressional approval for the 1902 Philippine Government Act, which declared the islands an unorganized territory and promised the Filipinos a greater degree of self-government in the future.

While he attended to his colonial responsibilities, Root also did all he could to settle the organizational crisis which had troubled the army since the late 1880s. Historians have often looked to Root's experience as a corporate lawyer and his ties to the Progressive movement to explain his enthusiasm for institutional reform. Certainly, his work with large industrial enterprises and the men who ran them had shown him the importance of what he once described as "effective and harmonious organization" and left him predisposed to improve institutional relations and procedures in the army.[16] Nevertheless, contrary to what his admirers have sometimes said, the innovations he sponsored were shaped less by the structure of the modern business firm than by ideas that had originated almost entirely within the army.

The Progressive movement, of which Root was a leader, also inclined the secretary to reform the army. While the changes he made exhibited little of the humanitarian concern often associated with Progressive measures, they did improve organizational efficiency, another important goal of the movement. Like a number of other Progressives, Root wanted to see the United States become a world power. He thus sought to strengthen the executive branch of government—especially the means by which it made its influence felt abroad. As a Progressive, moreover, the secretary showed a high regard for professional expertise and relied heavily on the advice of his military assistants. He did not follow their suggestions blindly, but instead immersed himself in the affairs of his office and acted as if the military men working under him were clients on whose behalf he had promised to intercede with Congress and the American public.

Root quickly became known as one of the more capable secretaries the service had ever had. His formidable skills as an advocate and political tactician stood him in good stead as he guided his reform program through Congress. His success was all the more remarkable, since he openly held Congress responsible for many of the army's ills. He did not deny that the military had been woefully unprepared for the war it had just won, but he blamed political leaders more than anyone else for the mistakes which had detracted from that victory.

Echoing the opinions of the officers about him, Root complained that short-sighted legislators had so pared down the size of the army after the Civil War that its overworked commanders had had all they could do just to keep up with their "police duty" on the frontier. Congress's emphasis on "pecuniary accountability and economy of expenditure" had further discouraged military leaders from paying attention to their "true purpose" of preparing for the next war. The secretary did not go so far as to say that these pressures excused the blunders and mismanagement of the army once that war began, but he clearly felt they explained many of the problems the military had encountered in 1898.[17]

Soon after taking office, Root announced that one of his principal goals as secretary would be to guard against a resurgence of the legislative apathy which he believed had crippled the army in the past. He fought to prevent any decrease in the size of the military and to give the nation the strong peacetime army military men had long demanded. At the end of the Spanish-American War, the authorized strength of the regular army had stood at 65,000 men. Secretary of War Alger had had little trouble getting an eighteen-month extension for this force or securing legislative approval to send an additional 35,000 volunteers

Secretary of War Elihu Root, seated in his office before a portrait of Winfield Scott *Library of Congress (262-37255)*

abroad once fighting broke out in early 1899 between the Filipino army of Emilio Aguinaldo and the 20,000 American troops still stationed in the Philippines. During the next two years, the demand for more soldiers to suppress the Philippine Insurrection and to relieve the Peking legations during the Boxer Rebellion greatly increased America's military commitment in the western Pacific. Although the latter expedition lasted but a short while, the army found it necessary to devote most of its resources and attention to the ruthless guerrilla conflict that persisted in the Philippines even after Aguinaldo's capture in 1901. As the number of units sent overseas grew and the deadline established by Congress for retaining many of those units neared, Root asked the legislators to create a permanent regular army as large as the existing regular and volunteer forces combined. Congress approved this and other changes requested by the secretary in the Reorganization Act of 2 February 1901.

The 1901 act was one of the most important pieces of military legislation adopted while Root was in office. It not only gave the secretary the size military establishment he sought, but also promised to restore the army to its "true purpose" of preparing for combat. The act called for the establishment of a staff detail system in order to counter what Root described as the "excessive bureaucratic tendency" of the military.[18] Line officers had long hoped to give new vitality to the staff by following the proposals of reformers such as Emory Upton, who had urged that all staff positions be filled by line officers temporarily detached from their regiments. A small circle of former line officers who had joined the Adjutant General's Department and the Inspector General's Department in the late 1880s and 1890s remained true to this goal even after they became staff officers. These men introduced Elihu Root to the idea of line-staff interchange and persuaded him to make it one of the cornerstones of his program to reform and revitalize the service.

The 1901 act ended the practice of making permanent staff appointments and thereby undermined the strong position of the bureau chiefs and their assistants in directing the internal affairs of the army. Officers already filling permanent positions on the staff and staff officers assigned to the more technical bureaus were not affected by the new law.[19] All other staff officers, however, including the bureau chiefs themselves, were to serve a four-year tour of duty with the staff and then rejoin the line. With the exception of adjutants and inspectors general, no one could be reassigned to the staff until he had served at least two years with the combat arm in which he held his commission.

At the same time Root realized that preparedness for future wars depended on more than simply maintaining the size or changing the prevailing distribution of power within the military. As early as November 1899, he had foreseen that the army would continue to have to rely on the support of a large number of citizen-soldiers in any major war it fought in the future. The secretary was therefore especially concerned by the lack of discipline and uniformity professional officers had observed in many National Guard units during the Spanish-American War. He wanted to repeal the 1792 law which governed the use of the militia and to reform the hybrid system of state and federal volunteers who had fought alongside the regulars in 1898.[20] He favored creating a permanent organization of federal volunteers under the command of regular army officers to serve as the primary backup force for the regular army in time of war. The National Guard would be used only as a last resort to provide individual replacements for soldiers who had fallen in battle.

The National Guard Association rejected this plan and drew up its own, parts of which the War Department incorporated in legislation it sent to Congress in January 1902 and which President Theodore Roosevelt signed into law twelve months later. Named for Charles Dick, president of the National Guard Association and chairman of the House Committee on the Militia, the Dick Act asserted the primacy of the National Guard over all other volunteer organizations. While it acknowledged the right of local authorities to control the guard, it also recognized the need for greater regulation and supervision of the guard by national authorities. In return for increased federal subsidies and equipment, guard units had to adopt certain uniform training standards and submit to annual inspections by regular army officers. Root was unable to free the reserve system from political control by state officials, but as was often the case, he decided it better to accept half a loaf than none at all.

In addition to making guardsmen better soldiers, Root sought to ensure that regular army officers mastered the professional skills they had sometimes neglected when commanding the small-unit operations of a constabulary force on the frontier. One of the first things the secretary did after taking office was look into the possibility of creating an institution modeled after the Naval War College in Newport, Rhode Island. He believed that the resident faculty of the Army War College ought to supervise the overall "instruction and intellectual exercise of the Army," but he expected many of the courses the new school offered to be taught by correspondence or by teachers at the different service schools. The resident faculty and the few students actually attending the War College would thus have an opportunity to apply the knowledge and practical skills they had already acquired to important problems other military leaders did not have the time or experience to solve. In addition, the secretary directed the members of the War College to study the war plans prepared by their counterparts in Newport and to cooperate with the older institution in the development of joint plans for both services under "all contingencies of possible [future] conflict."[21]

Root originally wanted the War College to perform another function as well. He thought that the officers teaching there could meet periodically with the commanding general and the bureau chiefs for the purpose of advising the secretary of war and the president. The idea of an advisory group of this sort was not new. As recently as May 1899, Root's predecessor Russell A. Alger had held weekly meetings of the bureau chiefs or "Secretary's Cabinet," as the chiefs who attended the meetings had become known. Root envisioned the Army War College acting in a somewhat similar fashion, while also serving as the center of higher education and strategic planning for the army.[22]

Some of Root's military advisers in the War Department cautioned against combining so many different responsibilities in one organization. Lieutenant Colonel William H. Carter, the assistant adjutant general who wrote the Reorganization Act of 1901, emerged as the most outspoken and influential exponent of this view. Carter objected to having the same men who oversaw the professional "instruction of the Army" perform "the duties of a general staff." He believed that a different group of officers should plan and supervise the overall operations of the army.[23]

The assistant adjutant general nonetheless had difficulty convincing Root to support this reform as aggressively as some of the other improvements the secretary made. Carter later remembered that when he first brought the matter to Root's attention, the secretary wanted to "spread information as to the need of a General Staff Corps" before committing himself further. Afterward, when Root suggested to President McKinley that authority to create the new organization be incorporated in the Reorganization Act of 1901, the president rejected the idea as too controversial. Root appears then to have dropped the issue until shortly after the president's assassination in September 1901, when the *Army and Navy Journal* reported that the secretary would soon ask Congress to approve the creation of a general staff.[24]

Historians have usually assumed that the contemporary German General Staff provided a model for this request. Although both Root and Carter tried to learn as much as they could about the German institution, neither man had a very good understanding of its organization and operating procedures or the relationship of its members to the rest of the German army. The staff reform bill Carter drafted and sent to Congress in February 1902 thus did little more than revive ideas that had long been discussed by military men in the United States and that had formed the basis of earlier reform proposals Carter found in the War Department archives. Supporters as well as opponents of the new institution did not hesitate to compare it to its German counterpart when it served their purposes. In part because of the argument that a general staff was better suited to a monarchical than a democratic form of government and in part because of other far-reaching changes Carter included in his proposal, the general staff bill encountered considerable resistance within the army and Congress. So strong was this resistance that Carter had to modify many of his initial suggestions for reform in the new bill the War Department submitted to Congress after the November 1902 elections.

The second bill encountered a more favorable reception than the first. This was no doubt due to the persistent, behind-the-scenes efforts of Root to drum up as much political support as he could for Carter's proposals. But passage of the December 1902 bill depended also on the more modest goals Root and Carter chose to pursue after they observed the storm of opposition the first bill provoked. The December bill, for example, no longer sought to eliminate the Inspector General's Department or to consolidate the Quartermaster's Department, the

Subsistence Department, and the Pay Department into a single Department of Supply, as the February bill had done.

Another important difference between the February and December bills involved the way each dealt with the commanding general. Lieutenant General Nelson Miles's repeated attempts to take advantage of the office he had held since 1895 in order to secure the Democratic nomination for the presidency left Root determined to see to it that no other officer ever followed suit. The February 1902 bill thus called for the replacement of the commanding general by a "Chief of General Staff" who would "supervise the employment and operations of the General Staff officers . . . and perform such other duties as may be assigned to him by the Secretary of War."[25]

Root thought that if the chief's authority were carefully circumscribed by army regulations, he would be less likely to oppose the secretary and cause trouble than Miles and his predecessors had been. Although Root did not openly discuss all of the limitations he had in mind until after Congress approved the General Staff Act, the secretary wanted the chief to serve at most a four-year tour of duty; anyone appointed to the new position would have to step down sooner if the president or secretary asked him to resign or if the presidency changed hands.[26] The February bill further implied that the chief would have no authority to command anyone other than the officers of the General Staff Corps itself. Many commanders objected to these changes. Even those who agreed on the importance of patching up the long-standing feud between the commanding general and the secretary complained sometimes that Root had gone too far when he tried to replace the ranking line officer in the army with what amounted to another bureau chief.

A slight change in the wording of the December bill overcame these objections. Acting on the advice of retired Lieutenant General John M. Schofield, Root had Carter substitute the less restrictive title of "chief of staff" for "chief of the general staff."[27] The chief of staff would supervise line officers and staff officers alike. Although he would not ordinarily command the army, he would occupy an intermediate position between it and the secretary—thus firmly establishing the secretary's authority over the chief while giving the army the same pyramidal structure that Schofield had recommended when he was commanding general.

Carter's enthusiasm for the legislation he revised in time for the Fifty-seventh Congress when it reconvened in December 1902 sprang from somewhat different reasons than those of the secretary. The assistant adjutant general felt confident that after people had had a chance to observe the General Staff at work, it would "establish itself in public esteem beyond cavil or assault." Once that happened, Carter predicted that the collective professional expertise of its members would help the army avoid what he and other military men thought of as political meddling in their affairs—a goal that the commanding generals had struggled unsuccessfully to achieve throughout much of the nineteenth century. He eagerly looked forward to the day when the General Staff would become the principal source of military policy, and "it will be discreditable in the eyes of the Nation for Congress to enact a military law which has not received the approval of the General Staff Corps."[28]

Within the army itself, Carter expected the General Staff to fulfill a second, no less important function. He insisted that anyone appointed to the new corps be chosen on the basis of "recognized merit," rather than "personal, social, or political influence," in order to make the General Staff "the mecca toward which the roads of professional endeavor lead." Like other reformers before him, the assistant adjutant general wanted to find new ways to reward "the capable and ambitious young and middle-aged officers of the Army." Although he had begun to move up rapidly in rank after joining the Adjutant General's Office as a major in 1897, Carter had never forgotten how discouraged he and other junior officers had grown over the absence of adequate rewards for their services after the Civil War. After graduating from West Point in 1873, he had served in the cavalry as a second lieutenant for six years, a first lieutenant for ten years, and a captain for seven years before coming to Washington. Because almost three-quarters of the positions on the General Staff were to be filled by lieutenants, captains, and majors, Carter proudly told Root that the new institution would ensure "that this class of officers be not disheartened or waived aside."[29]

The law Congress eventually passed called for General Staff officers to serve for four years. They would then return to the line and (except in time of war) remain ineligible for reassignment to the General Staff for the next two years. A majority of the forty-six officers serving on the General Staff, furthermore, would actually spend their four years on the staffs of major subordinate commanders stationed outside Washington. By assisting general officers with their military duties (much as staff officers from each of the bureaus helped the general officers with their administrative duties), Root and his advisers believed that the members of the new institution would better prepare the army for combat and thereby help in returning it to its "true purpose."[30]

After Congress approved the General Staff Act in February 1903, the period of reform and revitalization which had begun during the late 1880s rapidly came to a close. A final change took place in June when Root and Secretary of the Navy William H. Moody ordered the creation of a Joint Army and Navy Board. The eight members of the Joint Board included the chief of staff, the admiral of the navy, and three other officers from each service. The secretaries directed these men to deal with "all matters calling for the cooperation of the two services." Root predicted that "the common understanding and mutual assistance" which resulted would contribute to "much greater efficiency, at much lower cost . . . [than could] be obtained . . . by separate services working in entire independence of each other. If the two forces . . . [were] ever called upon to cooperate" in the future, the secretary of war believed that the Joint Board would enable any combined operations which might take place to proceed more smoothly than they had during the Spanish-American War.[31]

Military leaders in Washington insisted even as the reform impulse waned that their work kept them busier than ever, but they spent much of their time during the spring and summer of 1903 either implementing reforms already in place or planning how to implement changes due to occur in the near future. Earlier disputes over the nature and shape of the General Staff, for example, gave way to the need to decide who its first members would be in time for the official commencement of their duties on 15 August. By December Root openly admitted the army's need to rest after the "very great and radical changes" it had made. No "important legislation regarding the Army will be advisable," he cautiously explained, until military men had had "time to put the new laws into operation and work out the new methods under the direction of the General Staff without further disturbance. Experience will of course develop occasion for some improvements in the new statutes, but these should not be attempted until the full results of experience have been attained."[32]

When Root resigned from the cabinet at the end of January 1904, it was still too early to assess the overall impact of the various reforms that had taken place in the service since the late 1880s. At the very least those changes had revitalized the military and given its members renewed hope for the future by improving their working and living conditions and making them feel less isolated from the rest of society than before. In addition, many observers thought that by clarifying the regular army's relations with the National Guard and overhauling the nineteenth-century system of command and administration, Root had laid the foundation for a new army that would take shape in the future and represent national interests at home and abroad better than the old one had done. Whether that hope would prove well-founded or not—indeed, whether the many reforms that had occurred since the late 1880s had returned the army to its "true purpose" or not—were questions that only time and subsequent events could answer.

NOTES

1. For amplification of this point, see the preceding essay by Jerry M. Cooper.

2. Second Lt. Frank Eastman quoted in Peter Karsten, "Armed Progressives: The Military Reorganizes for the American Century," in Jerry Israel, ed., *Building the Organizational Society: Essays on Associational Activities in Modern America* (New York: The Free Press, 1972), p. 217.

3. Jack D. Foner examines the problem of desertion during this period along with the different measures that were used to correct the problem in *The United States Soldier Between Two Wars: Army Life and Reforms, 1865–1898* (New York: Humanities Press, 1970), especially pp. 6–10, 77–113, 222–24.

4. U.S., War Department, *Regulations of the Army of the United States and General Orders in Force on the 17th of February, 1881* (Washington: Government Printing Office, 1881), p. 20.

5. Maj. Charles P. Hatfield to Adj. Gen. Henry C. Corbin, 25 August 1900, 335338, Document File, 1890–1917, Records of the Adjutant General's Office, Record Group 94, National Archives, Washington, D.C.; Brig. Gen. John Gibbon, "Needed Reforms in the Army," *North American Review* 156 (February 1893): 216–18.

6. U.S., Congress, House, *Reduction of Army Officers' Pay, Report to Accompany H.R. 2817, 2935, and 2952*, 44th Cong., 1st sess., 1876, H. Rept. 354, p. 28; *Remarks of Major General John M. Schofield, United States Army, Upon the Reorganization of the Army* (Washington: Government Printing Office, 1876), pp. 8–9.

7. Schofield to Secretary of War Stephen B. Elkins, 27 February 1892, and Schofield to Elkins, 9 November 1892, John M. Schofield Papers, Library of Congress, Washington, D.C.; General Order No. 28, 6 April 1876, in *Army and Navy Journal* 13 (15 April 1876): 576; Schofield, *Forty-Six Years in the Army* (New York: The Century Company, 1897), pp. 6–7, 406–23, 467–83, 536–39.

8. Robert S. Browning III, *Two If By Sea: The Development of American Coastal Defense Policy* (Westport, Conn.: Greenwood Press, 1983), pp. 170, 172, 192 n. 11.

9. Quoted in James L. Abrahamson, *America Arms for a New Century: The Making of a Great Military Power* (New York: The Free Press, 1981), p. 40.

10. Quoted in David F. Trask, *The War with Spain in 1898*, The Wars of the United States (New York: Macmillan Co., 1981), p. 34.

11. U.S., Congress, Senate, *Creation of the American General Staff: Personal Narrative of the General Staff System of the American Army, by Major General William Harding Carter*, S. Doc. 119, *Senate Miscellaneous Documents*, 68th Cong., 1st sess., 1924, XXII, 17.

12. Arthur P. Wade, "Roads to the Top—An Analysis of General Officer Selection in the United States Army, 1789–1898," *Military Affairs* 40 (December 1976):162.

13. Graham Cosmas, *An Army for Empire: The United States Army in the Spanish-American War* (Columbia: University of Missouri Press, 1971), p. 4.

14. See Trask, *War with Spain*, pp. 158–62, 324–34.

15. Shafter quoted in ibid., p. 150.

16. "Speech of Honorable Elihu Root, . . . August 15, 1903," Henry C. Corbin Papers, Library of Congress, Washington, D.C. See also William H. Carter, "Elihu Root—His Services as Secretary of War," *North American Review* 178 (January 1904):120.

17. U.S., War Department, *Annual Report of the Secretary of War for the Year 1899*, 3 vols. (Washington: Government Printing Office, 1899), I, 46.

18. Root to William C. Church, 20 February 1900, Elihu Root Papers, Library of Congress, Washington, D.C.; and "Army Reorganization," *Army and Navy Journal* 37 (3 March 1900):621.

19. The law did not affect officers in the Corps of Engineers, the Medical Department, the Judge Advocate General's Department, and the Pay Department. The Reorganization Act of 2 February 1901 may be found in U.S., *Statutes at Large*, vol. XXXI, 751–57.

20. *Annual Report of the Secretary of War for the Year 1899*, I, 52–54.

21. Ibid., I, 46–7, 49.

22. A brief description of the events leading up to the establishment of the 1899 "Secretary's Cabinet" may be found in Cosmas, *Army for Empire*, p. 305.

23. William H. Carter, "Memorandum: Subject,-War College," 8 July 1900, and Carter, "Memorandum for Colonel Sanger, Acting Secretary of War," 27 August 1903, 31124, Document File, Record Group 94, National Archives, Washington, D.C.

24. *Creation of the American General Staff: Personal Narrative of . . . Major General William Harding Carter*, pp. 2–4; "A General Staff for the Army," *Army and Navy Journal*, 39 (14 September 1901): 36.

25. Quoted in *Creation of the American General Staff*, p. 23.

26. U.S., War Department, *Annual Report of the Secretary of War for 1903*, 8 vols. (Washington: Government Printing Office, 1903), I, 65–67.

27. See the statement of Lt. Gen. John M. Schofield in U.S., Congress, Senate, Committee on Military Affairs, *Efficiency of the Army, Hearings on S. 3917*, 57th Congress, 1st Sess., 1902, pp. 104–105; and M. O. Chance to William H. Carter, 20 November 1902, Elihu Root Papers, Library of Congress, Washington, D.C.

28. William H. Carter, "Memorandum for the Secretary of War," n.d., quoted in *Creation of the American General Staff*, p. 50.

29. Ibid.

30. U.S., *Statutes at Large*, vol. XXXII, pt. 1, 830–31.

31. *Annual Report of the Secretary of War for 1903*, I, 9–10.

32. Ibid., I, 36.

FURTHER READING

The crisis of the late nineteenth century and the efforts of military and naval reformers to deal with that crisis have been described by Peter Karsten, "Armed Progressives: The Military Reorganizes for the American Century," in Jerry Israel, ed., *Building the Organizational Society: Essays on Associational Activities in Modern America* (New York: Free Press, 1977), pp. 197–232; and at greater length by James L. Abrahamson, *America Arms for a New Century: The Making of a Great Military Power* (New York: Free Press, 1981). Each takes a very different view of the reformers' motives and the changes they introduced.

For a closer examination of the personnel reforms mentioned here as well as other improvements in the living and working conditions of enlisted men before the Spanish-American War, see Jack D. Foner, *The United States Soldier Between Two Wars: Army Life and Reforms, 1865–1898* (New York: Humanities Press, 1970). Graham Cosmas looks at some of the other changes that transformed the late nineteenth-century military into *An Army for Empire: The United States Army in the Spanish-American War* (Columbia: University of Missouri Press, 1971). The best overall treatment of the army's role in the war is that of David F. Trask, *The War with Spain in 1898*, The Wars of the United States (New York: Macmillan Co., 1981), although Walter Millis, *The Martial Spirit: A Study of Our War with Spain* (Boston: Houghton Mifflin Co., 1931), remains unsurpassed for pure reading pleasure. Another book worthy of mention is Gerald F. Linderman's *The Mirror of War: American Society and the Spanish-American War* (Ann Arbor: University of Michigan Press, 1974)—a collection of essays about the army and the Spanish-American War that provides a fascinating glimpse of the end of the small-town "social consensus that had shaped post–Civil War America" (p. 177).

The Elihu Root reforms have attracted much attention over the years, although a critical analysis of both the military and political origins of the Root reforms has yet to be written. Root's actions as secretary of war are detailed by Philip C. Jessup, *Elihu Root*, 2 vols. (New York: Dodd-Mead, 1938), I, chaps. 11–19, and in more succinct fashion by Richard W. Leopold, *Elihu Root and the Conservative Tradition* (Boston: Little, Brown & Co., 1954). Root's reforms are placed in broad historical perspective in James E. Hewes, Jr., *From Root to McNamara: Army Organization and Administration, 1900–1963* (Washington: U.S. Army Center of Military History, 1975), chap. 1. John K. Mahon examines the origins of the National Guard and the Dick Act in his *History of the Militia and the*

National Guard, The Wars of the United States (New York: Macmillan Co., 1983), pp. 108–41, while the best discussion of the creation of the General Staff remains that of Root's close adviser, William H. Carter, in U.S., Congress, Senate, *Creation of the American General Staff: Personal Narrative of the General Staff System of the American Army, by Major General William Harding Carter*, S. Doc. 119, *Senate Miscellaneous Documents*, 68th Congress, 1st sess., 1924, vol. XXII.

The military occupation of Cuba and the Philippines during this period is described in David F. Healy, *The United States in Cuba, 1898–1902: Generals, Politicians, and the Search for Policy* (Madison: University of Wisconsin Press, 1963), and John M. Gates, *Schoolbooks and Krags: The United States Army in the Philippines, 1898–1902* (Westport, Conn.: Greenwood Press, 1973). A much less flattering view of American involvement in the Philippines may be found in Stuart C. Miller, *"Benevolent Assimilation": The American Conquest of the Philippines, 1899–1903* (New Haven: Yale University Press, 1982).

CHAPTER 11

The Army Enters the Twentieth Century, 1904–1917

TIMOTHY K. NENNINGER

Between 1904 and 1917 the United States Army remained small compared to the armies of other major powers. It was scattered from Governor's Island in New York Bay to Zamboanga in the Philippines at posts which varied in size from a company to a brigade. Its tactical units were usually understrength, with enlistments often lagging, desertions high, and officers away on detail. It was also a period of heightened activity for the army, activity described by one historian as "cosmopolitan and diverse." An officer could be student, instructor, governor, judge, constructor, executive, peacemaker, and fighter, all in a single year.[1] America's recently acquired overseas possessions required the army to perform a variety of novel functions in the realms of civil engineering, administration, and government.

It remained a fighting force, however, and often undertook difficult if not necessarily bloody operations. Indeed, in the Philippines there were skirmishes, most small but a few involving several hundred casualties, between regular army troops and Moro bands in every year until the final pacification of the Moro Province in 1913–1914. In 1906 the army reoccupied Cuba; troops remained there for over two years. Although not engaged in combat operations during the occupation, the Cuban intervention represented a major planning, mobilization, and logistics effort for the army. Following the Mexican Revolution in 1910, there were border clashes between American soldiers and various Mexican factions, eventually culminating in the 1914 Veracruz Expedition and the 1916–1917 Mexican Punitive Expedition. Throughout these years there was seldom a time when some element of the army was not deployed on active operations somewhere in the world. But this was not only a period of intense military activity, it was a time of institutional change as well. In three important areas—relations with the militia, War Department administration, and military education—the army attempted to reconcile the reforms inaugurated by Elihu Root during his tenure as secretary of war (1899–1904) with past practice, current doctrine, and future need.

A major facet of Secretary Root's reform program was the increased subordination of the state militias to federal, essentially regular army, control. Although the 1903 Dick Act did not go as far in that direction as Root would have liked, it authorized the federal government to mobilize state National Guard units to repel invasion or maintain internal order. For duty outside the boundaries of the United States, however, the militia would have to volunteer. Essentially, the Dick Act recognized the National Guard or organized militia as the country's first-line military reserve, a recognition most regular officers were loath to grant. In return for this recognition, the militia of each state had to meet minimum federal standards of efficiency. The regular army became responsible for assuring that these standards were met and for providing weapons, equipment, and instruction to the state units.[2]

To foster cooperation between the National Guard and the regular army, to improve the tactical skills of individual militia units, and to broaden the military skills of National Guard officers, Secretary Root admitted guardsmen to army schools and inaugurated a series of joint maneuvers. The results were disappointing.

From 1904 through 1916 only three militia officers graduated from the School of the Line at Fort Leavenworth (all with the class of 1906), while another, Captain W. O. Selkirk of the Texas National Guard, graduated from the Line School and the Leavenworth Staff College. Another guardsman, Major General John F. O'Ryan of New York, was the only militia officer in this period to graduate from the Army War College. Both Selkirk and O'Ryan were unique citizen-soldiers. Selkirk was highly intelligent and particularly diligent in his studies at Leavenworth. O'Ryan was a lawyer by training but was in fact a full-time militiaman too busy to practice the law. During World War I he ably commanded the Twenty-seventh Division in France.

Although the War Department paid lip service to the attendance of militia officers at the service schools, with these few exceptions, the effort was futile. Most guard officers could not take a year away from their families and professions. Others failed to pass the admissions tests to the schools. After 1906 no guard officer even attended Leavenworth, much less graduated. A guardsman who graduated from the School of the Line in that year levelled such acrimonious charges against what he considered prejudiced regular army instructors that other guardsmen lost their enthusiasm for army schools. At the same time the Leavenworth commandant, J. Franklin Bell, expressed the misgivings of the regulars that only a "devilish few" militia officers could pass the admissions requirements and fewer still could successfully complete the course.[3] The experience at the service schools did little to engender cooperation between the regular army and the militia. It did much to reinforce skepticism among the regulars about the professional ability of the guardsmen while confirming the belief among guardsmen that the regulars were prejudiced against them.

Joint maneuvers were another means by which Secretary Root proposed improving militia efficiency and discipline while at the same time fostering good feeling and cooperation among the regulars and the National Guard. The first modest maneuvers took place in September 1902 on the New England coast.

More ambitious operations followed. With the exception of 1905 when Congress failed to appropriate funds, some form of joint maneuvers or summer instruction encampments was held every year until 1916 when conditions in Mexico required mobilization of the National Guard for duty on the border.

In 1904 over 25,000 guardsmen and 10,000 regulars participated in maneuvers at American Lake, Washington, at Altascadero, California, and at Manassas, Virginia. Two years later there were seven major joint maneuvers; in 1908 there were eight; and in 1912 over 125,000 troops took part in maneuvers. There were several drawbacks to those maneuvers: they were expensive; the tactical situations played out by the experienced regulars and the inexperienced militia were often unrealistic and thus inappropriate for training; on a number of occasions regular troops were not available in sufficient numbers to support large-scale exercises satisfactorily. On those occasions when joint maneuvers were infeasible, many state militias held local summer instruction camps with regular army officers and noncommissioned officers (NCOs) acting as instructors and observers. Sometimes these camps were for entire organized militia units, sometimes for training officers only. They had the advantage of providing instruction under more controlled conditions than maneuvers and made it possible to concentrate on improving the specific weaknesses of a militia unit.

For both regulars and militiamen, the joint maneuvers and instruction camps of the early twentieth century had mixed results. Regular officers assigned as instructors and observers had a splendid opportunity to control and witness large bodies of troops in active field operations. Many of these regulars were recent service school graduates; normally most of the graduating classes at the Leavenworth Staff College and the School of the Line went to the joint maneuvers and summer encampments as umpires, observers, instructors, or temporary staff officers assisting the maneuver directors. At the maneuvers they could observe on a large scale with live troops some of the lessons they had studied in the classroom. They had to feed, clothe, equip, transport, and maneuver forces composed of several thousand troops. Normally regular officers faced similar problems but on a smaller scale with only a few hundred men. The opportunity to handle live troops afforded the service school graduates a good antidote to their recent work in the classroom, where they solved military problems on a map with little regard for the morale, fatigue, and discomfort of the troops.[4] Similarly, the militia benefited from the up-to-date knowledge and professional expertise of the regulars. The militias of a number of states developed relationships with particular regular officers which lasted a number of years. For instance, John F. Morrison, an instructor at the Leavenworth schools and an authority on tactical training, became very friendly with Charles R. Boardman, the adjutant general of the Wisconsin National Guard. Morrison was the principal instructor at a number of Wisconsin militia summer encampments. It is difficult to assess accurately how much of an impact these regular officers had on state National Guard units. But in at least a few instances, such as Morrison in Wisconsin, there were benefits for militiamen and regulars alike.

Despite some successes in training, major difficulties remained. Most state militias consisted overwhelmingly of infantry with few support troops such as engineers, signalmen, and ordnance personnel. The guard was often ill equipped, with obsolete artillery, little or no motor and wagon transport, and inadequate quartermaster support. To compound these deficiencies, too many of the joint maneuvers emphasized only tactical exercises with no attention given to logistics, especially for extended operations. As a result, the National Guard of 1917 was nearly as unprepared for war as the state militias had been in 1898.

Between the time of the Root reforms and World War I, service with militia deepened the conviction of many regulars that the National Guard was still unsuitable as the nation's principal militiary reserve. Too many guard units had too many deficiencies in organization, equipment, and leadership. Beyond that, federal control over the National Guard remained limited. But the experience with the militia also had convinced many regulars that short-service citizen-soldiers, with proper leadership from the regular army professionals, could furnish the primary manpower pool necessary for any major war or mobilization. Service with the militia and the experience of European armies demonstrated that troops could be trained much more rapidly than the previous Uptonian doctrine proclaimed—in six months rather than two years. Regulars also learned from service with the militia that citizen-soldiers could provide the army with important technical and administrative skills in time of emergency, skills possessed by carpenters, plumbers, accountants, draftsmen, railroadmen, and a host of others not often found in abundance among the regulars.[5] The appreciation by the regulars that most short-service volunteers, conscripts, and militiamen could, with proper organization and leadership, provide a suitable basis for a mass wartime army was an important psychological barrier that had already been overcome when the United States mobilized for World War I.

Root's most important, most controversial, but in the short run least successful reform was his attempt to restructure the command relationship within the War Department. He wanted to centralize responsibility for planning future operations and supervising current operations in the newly created War Department General Staff. The chief of staff of the army headed that staff, served as the principal military adviser to the secretary of war, and issued orders to the rest of the army in the name of the secretary. The decade and a half between the creation of the General Staff and American entrance into the First World War saw administrative turmoil, several reorganizations, and some small successes as the army sought to blend Root's organizational innovations with the traditional ways of doing business in the War Department. That there were numerous problems in the implementation and functioning of the new system was clear, although the causes of many of the problems remain open to debate.

A number of historians have attributed the shortcomings of the early General Staff to ignorance among American officers about proper staff functions. There was a striking lack of preparation of early General Staff officers. Of the 202 officers who served between 1904 and 1916, 112 lacked the postgraduate military education common to staff officers in all the European armies. The remaining 90 War Department General Staff officers had attended the Army War College, the service schools at Leavenworth, or both.[6] But even those schools emphasized planning and executing field operations rather than strategic planning and administration.

Nevertheless, Americans were not totally ignorant of how a general staff should function. Many officers had studied the operations of the European staffs; read von Schellendorf's *The Duties of the General Staff* and Spenser Wilkinson's *The Brain of an Army*, two contemporary treatises on how the European staffs, especially that of the German army, worked; and also read the reports of American attachés and observers on foreign general staffs. Thus, while some officers were unprepared for and uninformed about general staff duty, others had a reasonable conception of what such a staff should do. The problem was not that Americans had no understanding of general staffs but that they had a variety of conflicting ideas. There was no unanimity largely because Americans had no experience operating a War Department–level general staff of the sort common to European powers. Because it was impossible constitutionally, politically, and practically to impose an exact replica of the German General Staff on the United States Army, the Americans had to experiment with a variety of organizational forms and lines of authority in a process disruptive to the smooth administration of any large organization.

Between 1903 and 1917 seven officers served as chief of staff, three within the first three years. Few who held that post had sufficient time in office in addition to the intellectual, administrative, and political ability to mold the General Staff into an effective agency. Leonard Wood is the only chief of staff during the period 1903 to 1918 generally mentioned by name in standard military histories of the era. S.B.M. Young and Adna Chaffee, the first two chiefs, were fine field soldiers whose appointments recognized past service, not administrative ability. John Bates briefly held the post while J. Franklin Bell completed unfinished business before beginning his tour as the fourth chief of staff. Neither Young, Chaffee, nor Bates had his heart in the job. Chaffee did not even insist that all of the bureau chiefs, theoretically his subordinates, submit their reports to him for transmission to the secretary of war. They continued to communicate directly with the secretary.[7] William W. Wotherspoon succeeded Wood in 1914 but held the office less than a year before Hugh L. Scott succeeded him. Scott, another good field soldier, was loyal, conscientious, and of strong character; but he was not an administrator, nor was he very imaginative. Former President William Howard Taft said of Scott as chief of staff, "He is wood to the middle of his head."[8] Of all the chiefs of staff of the pre–World War I era, only Wood (1910–1914) and Bell (1906–1910) tried to energize the War Department General Staff and make it an efficient operating agency.

When Bell became chief he found the General Staff bogged down in petty administration. It considered such individual cases as assignment of surgeons to particular posts, compensation for civilian employees injured at work, and allocation of specific supplies to units. Because previously the bureaus had made these decisions, the bureau chiefs regarded the General Staff as interfering in their affairs. Many line officers, especially those with a high regard for the German General Staff, criticized administrative work as irrelevant to the principal functions of a general staff: intelligence gathering and strategic planning. Bell recognized that although the criticisms were pertinent, there were other considerations.

When Bell was chief of staff, the bureaus had yet to acknowledge the supremacy of the General Staff. In order to impose its authority throughout the army, the General Staff had to confront the bureaus in the realm of administrative minutiae. When the positions of two or more bureaus overlapped or differed on a particular issue, the General Staff would sort out the competing positions, force the necessary compromises, and undertake a course of action. In addition to flexing its institutional authority, the General Staff had to be cognizant of the day-to-day administration of the bureaus in order to perform its long-range planning functions. Routine bureau procurement decisions made during Bell's tenure could have an important impact years later when the General Staff attempted to mobilize and supply an army for field duty.[9]

For these several reasons Bell recognized the need for the War Department General Staff to coordinate and administer as well as gather intelligence and plan strategy. But he agreed with those critics who saw too many staff officers engaged in routine administration. He wanted the General Staff to establish generalized precedents upon which to base future administrative decisions rather than to decide each issue on a case-by-case basis. To accomplish that and to assure that the planning and intelligence functions were not neglected, Bell established two separate General Staff sections in June 1908. The First Section, housed in the War Department building in downtown Washington and supervised closely by the chief of staff, was responsible for all administration and coordination of the bureaus. The Second Section, located across town along with the Army War College and supervised by the college president, was responsible for planning, intelligence, and the instruction of War College students. The physical separation of the two sections and the assignment of the War College president to supervise the Second Section meant that in effect the United States Army had two chiefs of staff: one advised the secretary of war and coordinated the bureaus; the other supervised planning, intelligence, and education.[10] When Wood succeeded Bell he did not change the essence of the 1908 reorganization, although he added a few administrative offices and adopted a functional nomenclature. Thus in 1910 the Second Section became the War College Division and the First Section divided into the Mobile Army, Coast Artillery, and Militia Affairs Divisions.

By freeing the planners from administration, Bell's reorganization assured that all the important functions of the War Department General Staff would be carried out. On the other hand, it failed to bring War College students into the active role of neophyte General Staff officers that Bell envisaged for them, largely because too many of the students lacked the experience Bell expected they would have. Most importantly, the physical separation of the two sections led to the gradual isolation of the chief of staff from the planning and intelligence functions. In one of the periodic Mexican crises, Wood and two assistants spent an entire night preparing mobilization tables even though tables for such a contingency were already on file at the War College.[11]

A second reorganization effort by Bell did not come to fruition. He wanted to increase the number of General Staff officers and expand the staff's range of authority by merging it with the Inspector General's Office (IGO) and the Adjutant General's Office (AGO). The 1903 legislation gave responsibility for monitoring the overall efficiency and effectiveness of the service to the General Staff, although that was also the principal duty of the IGO. Bell wanted the AGO to join the staff because as records keeper, records manager, and communications center that bureau occupied a strategic position in War Department administration. Also, officers assigned to the AGO were often among the most efficient, intelligent, and politically well connected in the army. That was especially so for the chief of the bureau, Adjutant General Fred C. Ainsworth. Although most of the officers involved, including Ainsworth, generally agreed to Bell's consolidation scheme, the timing was poor. Bell made the proposal too near the end of his tour as chief of staff for anything to come of it.[12] As a result, the problems that Bell tried to solve or at least avert by consolidation confronted his successor, Leonard Wood, with dire consequences for the General Staff.

Wood and Henry L. Stimson, the secretary of war from 1911 to 1913, united in a further effort to improve War Department administration and shift the locus of control permanently to the General Staff and the chief of staff. They believed that Ainsworth, the adjutant general and most powerful of the bureau chiefs, had to relinquish some of his responsibilities and power to the chief of staff. If Ainsworth and his office submitted to General Staff supervision, the other bureaus would likely acquiesce. Wood confronted Ainsworth directly and over a period of months challenged his authority in three areas. In December 1910 Wood informed Ainsworth that all orders, instructions, and other information issued by the War Department would come through the office of the chief of staff and would have to be signed by him, the chief, rather than flowing through the Adjutant General's Office as was previously the case. Shortly thereafter, Wood sent the adjutant general a restricted list of names from which to select recruiting officers. In the past Ainsworth had enjoyed unlimited authority to select whomever he wanted. Finally, Wood challenged the adjutant general's sole responsibility for supervising records keeping. He recommended abolishing the muster roll and consolidating other returns in an effort to reduce army paperwork. Wood intended to impress upon Ainsworth that the adjutant general was subordinate to the chief of staff and had to perform all of his responsibilities in accordance with "the policy and wishes of his superior." The succession of attacks on his prerogatives infuriated Ainsworth, as Wood expected. Ainsworth's response, particularly to the muster roll question, was intemperate and deemed insubordinate by Wood, Stimson, and eventually the judge advocate general. Rather than face a court-martial, Ainsworth retired. The question of the General Staff's supremacy over the bureaus apparently had been resolved.[13]

The Wood-Ainsworth imbroglio confirmed the civil-military alignment of the army, with the chief of staff and the General Staff representing the professional interests of the line officers and the secretary of war representing the civilian political leadership. Further, it confirmed the supremacy of the chief of staff over the technical and support bureaus which were responsible to him, not to the secretary. Thus, the immediate apparent result was a triumph for the General Staff and the supremacy of its chief.

The cost of this victory, however, was high. General Ainsworth harbored a grudge and, with the help of congressional allies, he retaliated. In 1912 Ainsworth collaborated with James Hay of the House Military Affairs Committee to pass legislation reducing the size of the General Staff by one-fifth, to thirty-six members. The so-called Manchu Law also limited the length of time line officers could serve away from their regiments. This law was particularly disruptive to the smooth functioning of the advanced professional schools like Leavenworth and the War College. Four years later the National Defense Act of 1916 increased to fifty-four the number of General Staff officers but strictly limited the number of those who could be assigned to Washington. Only nineteen officers were on the War Department General Staff in April 1917 when the United States entered World War I. Besides numerical limitation, the 1916 act restricted the General Staff to war planning only. Administration and supervision, seen by the bureaus as interference, were strictly forbidden. The act abolished the Mobile Army Division of the General Staff and assigned its functions to the Adjutant General's Office. War Department bureau chiefs could again report directly to the secretary of war, bypassing the chief of staff. The 1916 act became known as the "Magna Carta" of the bureau chiefs because it restored their independence.[14]

On the eve of America's entrance into World War I, the War Department General Staff was thus politically, numerically, and structurally weak. Despite the apparent victory of Wood and Stimson over the most powerful bureau chief, the chief of staff was unable consistently to dominate, coordinate, and supervise the bureaus. At the same time, however, the War College Division was undertaking important planning and intelligence activities. It prepared a series of contingency plans for intervention in Mexico and recommended force structures for the army in the event of national mobilization. The War College Division also supervised intelligence gathering in potential theaters of operation. The information collected from such sources as mobile radio intercept stations on the Mexican border and from attachés and observers in Europe eventually proved useful when the army took the field in both Mexico and France. Because of structural deficiencies, the War College Division's efforts sometimes occurred in a vacuum, while the lack of sufficient General Staff officers limited the scale of virtually all of its activities.

The turmoil in War Department administration during the period from 1904 to 1917 was probably a necessary prelude to the efficient operation of a general staff in an American setting. New ideas and administrative structures had to be tried and occasionally discarded. In 1918 a strong chief of staff, Peyton C. March, supported by a strong secretary of war, Newton D. Baker, finally forced the rest of the War Department to submit to centralized wartime control by the General Staff.

While Secretary Root's attempts to streamline War Department administration and improve relations between the regular army and the National Guard had mixed results at best, his efforts to reform the army school system met immediate and continuing success. A number of Root's associates in the War Department advocated the systematic education of all officers. They convinced the secretary that the "rapid advance of military science" had created a growing need for "thorough and broad education for military officers."[15]

The existing army schools had impressed Root. Their graduates performed well during the Spanish-American War. But too few army officers were graduates. Expansion during and after the 1898 war brought young, untrained officers into the army. Of 2,900 line officers serving in 1902, over 1,800 had received commissions since the beginning of the war with Spain. Only 276 were West Point graduates. Nearly half of all line officers and almost all lieutenants of the line had virtually no formal military education.[16] Besides providing a basic program of military instruction for this group, Root wanted a coherent plan of continuing education for officers at all levels of the army. There had been no system of postgraduate military education before, only individual schools with no relations to one another. Root assigned his closest adviser, Colonel William H. Carter, the task of planning a system of army schools. The result, General Order No. 155 of 27 November 1901, outlined the structure of postgraduate army education until World War I.

Carter and Root designed a school system to meet the changing educational requirements of an officer as he advanced through his career. Beginning with classes conducted at each post and progressing to the Army War College, the student officers at each level concentrated on one aspect of military studies—basic tactics, tactics of combined arms, staff functions, or national strategy. Only the best graduates went to the school at the next higher level.

The first step in the system was the garrison schools. In the 1890s many units held lyceums where officers studied, discussed, and presented papers on military problems. Many of the lyceums met high intellectual and military standards, but others did not because they depended on the interests and idiosyncrasies of individual unit commanders. Orders issued by the War Department in 1902 standardized the regulations and curriculum of all garrison schools. A one-year preliminary course included study of the drill and firing regulations of the student's branch (cavalry, infantry, artillery) as well as field engineering, hygiene, and company administration. The regular three-year course concentrated on the *Field Service Regulations* and the basic tactics of a single arm or branch of the service. Often the garrison commander himself would direct postgraduate work which consisted of practical problems such as map maneuvers, terrain exercises, and war games. All captains with less than ten years' service and all lieutenants had to attend garrison schools. More experienced officers on the post served as instructors. Examinations followed the annual period of instruction which normally lasted from 1 November to 30 March. Results of the examinations went to the War Department and became part of each officer's official record. Performance in the garrison school often determined fitness for promotion and was always considered when determining eligibility to attend other army schools.[17]

The garrison schools were a unique innovation. They were the army's first systematic effort to provide all junior officers with a formal, theoretical grounding in the basic functions of their profession. Initially many of those charged with supervision and instruction at the schools disparaged the attempt to teach officers what they needed to know from a book. These older "moss backs" had become soldiers by soldiering, not by reading. Not surprisingly, some of their efforts at instruction were disappointing. One young officer was especially candid in criticizing the garrison school he attended: "Our distinguished post commander is making a grand bluff at teaching us . . . by means of what he calls a map problem. It is about as much a map problem as I am a suffragette."[18] But as the number of graduates of the War College and the Leavenworth Schools increased and replaced the original instructors at the garrison schools, the quality of instruction improved. Most young officers undergoing instruction recognized and appreciated the difference.[19] They correctly believed that the garrison schools inaugurated by Secretary Root and Colonel Carter were a successful first step in improving professional knowledge throughout the officer corps.

The second level of the postgraduate school system expanded on the service schools existing before the Spanish-American War: the Artillery School at Fort Monroe, the School of Application for Cavalry and Light Artillery at Fort Riley, the Engineer School of Application at Washington Barracks, and the School of Submarine Defense at Fort Totten. By World War I the system had grown considerably. While the Artillery and Engineering schools remained, a separate Mounted Service School and a School of Fire for Field Artillery had evolved at Fort Riley and Fort Sill, respectively. Three additional institutions, the Signal School, the Army Field Engineer School, and the Field Service and Correspondence School for Medical Officers, opened at Fort Leavenworth and another, the School of Musketry, began at Fort Sill. The schools for engineering, signals, and field artillery reflected the growing complexity of twentieth-century warfare. Branch specialists, presumably the most promising garrison school graduates, attended these institutions. Because special service schools had existed during the nineteenth century, the branch schools represented no innovation, only an expansion and an improvement. Their curricula were more demanding than those of the garrison schools, but concentrated on the technical and tactical employment of a single branch only. For combined arms training an officer had to attend the Army Service Schools at Fort Leavenworth, Kansas.

Root and Carter believed that before 1898 the Infantry and Cavalry School at Leavenworth had provided sufficiently advanced instruction to warrant the title "war college." Although that designation may seem rather inflated, Leavenworth in the 1890s had been the site of the most advanced, sophisticated, and innovative instruction in the army. Arthur L. Wagner and Eben Swift, the two leading Leavenworth instructors, introduced practical problem solving as a means of learning tactics. Their methods and the reputation of Leavenworth began spreading throughout the service. Impressed with what had gone before, Root and Carter wanted to build on this solid foundation. They envisioned Leavenworth as only slightly less important than the Army War College itself.

Leavenworth reopened in 1902 (it had closed during the 1898 war and the Philippine Insurrection) as a one-year course with the title General Service and Staff College. Initially, Root used it to provide basic tactical instruction to some of the untrained, recently commissioned lieutenants, but in 1904 Brigadier General J. Franklin Bell, then commandant, reorganized the course to reflect Root's higher purposes. Leavenworth became two one-year schools, with only the best graduates from the first-year school advancing to the second. Students were mostly captains, although some junior majors as well as a few highly promising lieutenants also attended. The first-year curriculum at the Infantry and Cavalry School encompassed military engineering, foreign languages, and military law, but military art was the heart of the course. Students learned troop leading of mixed tactical units (artillery, cavalry, and infantry) up to a division. In the second-year curriculum at the Leavenworth Staff College, military art again predominated but with emphasis on General Staff duties, logistics, and the operational control of units as large as an army corps.

Military art at both schools was taught largely by means of practical problem solving: map exercises, terrain problems, and war games. The heavy work load required considerable study outside the classroom and consisted of solving "problem after problem." George C. Marshall, a Leavenworth student from 1906 to 1908, remembered: "It was the hardest work I ever did in my life."[20] The studies were difficult and the competition among first-year students to make the second-year Staff College class was fierce, but this arduousness only added to the growing prestige of Leavenworth. The leadership of Bell and of able instructors like Matthew F. Steele, Arthur L. Conger, and especially John F. Morrison further enhanced the institution's reputation. Leavenworth could emphasize quality in part because the number of graduates remained small. The twelve graduating classes of the first-year school (redesignated the School of the Line in 1908 to signify attendance of artillerymen as well as infantry and cavalry officers) between 1905 and 1916 averaged only thirty-six officers; Staff College classes averaged twenty-one graduates.

Despite the small number of graduates, Leavenworth contributed much to the army. It attracted the best young officers in the service. Marshall is perhaps the outstanding example, but he was not unique; his class at the School of the Line included eight future generals. Graduates filled most of the important General

Staff positions in the American Expeditionary Forces during World War I and also served as regimental and brigadier commanders. Only lack of age, time in service, and grade kept most from division and corps command. During the 1920s and 1930s, members of the Leavenworth generation of 1904–1916 became the leaders of the army as they came to dominate many positions on the General Staff. Besides this cadre of leaders, Leavenworth helped create an atmosphere in which the army came to appreciate the intellectual content of the military profession. Leavenworth instructors, students, and graduates filled the professional journals of the period with articles on a variety of technical, tactical, and historical topics. American officers wrote numerous books and translated significant foreign military works for use as textbooks at the schools. Finally, Leavenworth students and instructors were instrumental in producing the 1910 *Field Service Regulations*, a comprehensive guide to the organization, administration, and tactics governing the army in the field. With only minor revision, the *Regulations* were the basis of American field operations in France during World War I. As Secretary Root had hoped, Leavenworth became an intellectual center of the army. Its graduates had a sense of pride and of cooperativeness not found among graduates of other army schools. Leavenworth enjoyed a reputation far above that of the other service schools of the era, even the War College.[21]

The Army War College had been established in 1903 as the apex of Root's school system to instruct students in "the higher branches of professional study." Root did not want theory to displace practical application, but he had originally planned on making the college the army's highest academic institution. The first college president, Tasker H. Bliss, however, interpreted the term college in the Latin meaning of the word *collegium*: a body of men associated in a community of interest for the purpose of doing something rather than merely learning how to do it. Under Bliss students learned by doing as the college became an adjunct to the War Department General Staff. Students prepared war plans and mobilization tables in addition to participating in lectures, discussions, and map exercises. Initially the course had neither a specified length nor a required curriculum.[22] But gradually the War College changed, becoming more and more like the Leavenworth Staff College in its methods of instruction and course content. Most War College students were not Staff College graduates, as Root had wanted, and thus they had no preparation as General Staff officers. They were poorly qualified to prepare strategic plans or even an operations order. Of necessity, therefore, the faculty of the college had to provide instruction in many of the subjects covered at Leavenworth before turning to more advanced topics.[23]

Despite these shortcomings, the War College met with limited success in the years before World War I. In contrast to the other army schools, it made some effort to study military problems in the context of national policy. The college tried to connect military operations with strategic, diplomatic, economic, and political considerations. In addition, it provided advanced operations training to many officers who later became senior commanders in the American Expeditionary Forces in France.

The system of postgraduate military education inaugurated by Secretary of War Elihu Root was considerably more successful than his efforts to reform War Department administration and improve relations between the regular army and the National Guard. Between 1904 and 1917 the army literally went to school. The classroom experience produced a heightened awareness of the intellectual content of the military art and improved professional expertise within the officer corps, particularly in the realm of conducting combat operations with large units. The results became obvious by 1918 in France. By the end of the war, General John J. Pershing had concluded that without the preparation given in the army schools, "our successful handling of great masses of partially trained troops in operation while at the same time providing for their enormous needs of food and material could not have been possible."[24]

NOTES

1. William A. Ganoe, *The History of the United States Army*, rev. ed. (1942; reprint, Ashton, Md.: Eric Lundberg, 1964), p. 460.

2. Walter Millis, *Arms and Men: A Study in American Military History* (New York: G. P. Putnam's Sons, 1956), p. 161; Jim Dan Hill, *The Minute Man In Peace and War: A History of the National Guard* (Harrisburg, Pa.: Stackpole Co., 1964), pp. 175–89.

3. J. Franklin Bell to Adjutant General, 3 July 1906, AGO Document File 1146007, Records of the Adjutant General's Office, Record Group 94, National Archives, Washington, D.C.; Bell to W. W. Wotherspoon, 14 April 1905, Army Service Schools Miscellaneous File, Records of United States Army Continental Commands, 1821–1920, Record Group 393, National Archives, Washington, D.C.

4. Timothy K. Nenninger, *The Leavenworth Schools and the Old Army: Education, Professionalism, and the Officer Corps of the United States Army, 1881–1918* (Westport, Conn.: Greenwood Press, 1978), pp. 113–14.

5. Allan R. Millett, *The General: Robert C. Bullard and Officership in the United States Army, 1881–1925* (Westport, Conn.: Greenwood Press, 1975), pp. 209–12; Jack C. Lane, *Armed Progressive: General Leonard Wood* (San Rafael, Calif.: Presidio Press, 1978), pp. 174–83.

6. Nenninger, *Leavenworth Schools*, p. 159.

7. U.S., War Department, *Annual Report of the Chief of Staff, U.S. Army, 1906* (Washington: Government Printing Office, 1906), p. 26.

8. William Howard Taft quoted in John P. Finnegan, *Against the Specter of a Dragon: The Campaign for American Military Preparedness, 1914–17* (Westport, Conn.: Greenwood Press, 1974), p. 45.

9. Edgar Frank Raines, Jr., "Major General J. Franklin Bell and Military Reform: The Chief of Staff Years, 1906–1910" (Ph.D. dissertation, University of Wisconsin, 1976), pp. 255–57; James E. Hewes, Jr., *From Root to McNamara: Army Organization and Administration, 1900–1963* (Washington: U.S. Army Center of Military History, 1975), pp. 10–11.

10. Raines, "Bell and Military Reform," pp. 225–34.

11. Johnson Hagood, *The Services of Supply* (Boston: Houghton Mifflin Co., 1927), p. 24.

12. Raines, "Bell and Military Reform," pp. 249–52, 258–63.

13. Hewes, *Root to McNamara*, pp. 12–18; Lane, *Armed Progressive*, pp. 156–67.

14. Hewes, *Root to McNamara*, p. 21.

15. U.S., Congress, House, *Report of the Secretary of War, 1901*, 57th Cong., 1st sess., 1901, H. Exec. Documents, pp. 20–21.

16. U.S., Congress, House, *Report of the Secretary of War, 1902*, 57th Cong., 2d sess., 1902, H. Exec. Documents, p. 30.

17. Ira L. Reeves, *Military Education in the United States* (Burlington, Vt.: Free Press Publishing Co., 1914), pp. 298–314.

18. Capt. William D. Chitty to Secretary, 19 January 1911, Army Service Schools File 5001, Record Group 393, National Archives, Washington, D.C.

19. See, for instance, the testimonials of young officers as to the instruction and guidance they received from Leavenworth graduates during the years 1912 to 1917 in William Geffen, ed., *Command and Commanders in Modern Warfare: Proceedings of the Second Military History Symposium, U.S. Air Force Academy* (Washington: Government Printing Office, 1969), pp. 62–78.

20. Transcript of interview between Forrest C. Pogue and George C. Marshall, 4 April 1957.

21. Nenninger, *Leavenworth Schools*, pp. 112–30.

22. George S. Pappas, *Prudens Futuri: The U.S. Army War College, 1901–1967* (Carlisle Barracks, Pa.: Alumni Association of the U.S. Army War College, 1967), pp. 15–83.

23. Nenninger, *Leavenworth Schools*, pp. 122–24.

24. John J. Pershing quoted in Hanson E. Ely, *Address at Opening of General Service Schools* (Fort Leavenworth, Kans.: General Service Schools Press, 1922), pp. 11–12.

FURTHER READING

Army history for the period between the Spanish-American War and World War I is embodied in a particularly rich literature, much of it the result of recent scholarship. In part this is a reflection of the wealth of extant primary sources in the National Archives, numerous manuscript collections in federal and private depositories, and the voluminous published *Annual Reports of the War Department*.

The best overview of institutional developments in the army during this era may be found in Russell F. Weigley's *History of the United States Army*, enlarged ed. (Bloomington: Indiana University Press, 1984), chaps. 14–15. James L. Abrahamson provides sympathetic coverage of the movement for military reform and modernization from the 1880s through World War I in *America Arms for a New Century: The Making of a Great Military Power* (New York: The Free Press, 1981). Focusing on matters which long proved frustrating to reformers in the regular army, Jim Dan Hill ably argues the promilitia view in *The Minute Man in Peace and War: A History of the National Guard* (Harrisburg, Pa.: Stackpole, Co., 1964), chaps. 7–11. Although Hill includes much interesting detail not readily accessible elsewhere, his treatment of army–National Guard relations for this period has been superseded largely by John K. Mahon, *History of the Militia and the*

National Guard, The Wars of the United States (New York: Macmillan Co., 1983)—the best single-volume history of the guard.

The administrative evolution of the General Staff and War Department are well summarized in the first chapter of James E. Hewes, Jr., *From Root to McNamara: Army Organization and Administration, 1900–1963* (Washington: U.S. Army Center of Military History, 1975). Edgar F. Raines, Jr., "Major General J. Franklin Bell and Military Reform: The Chief of Staff Years, 1906–10" (Ph.D. dissertation, University of Wisconsin, 1976), ably describes and analyzes Bell's tenure as chief of staff. But Raines's focus is wider than his title indicates, and he provides an excellent administrative history of the army for the years 1906 to 1910. Jack C. Lane has described Leonard Wood as chief of staff, Wood's confrontation with Ainsworth, and Wood's subsequent role in the preparedness movement in *Armed Progressive: General Leonard Wood* (San Rafael, Calif.: Presidio Press, 1978). Ainsworth's case is presented by Mabel E. Deutrich, *Struggle for Supremacy: The Career of Fred C. Ainsworth* (Washington: Public Affairs Press, 1962). Three additional monographs analyze the role of the War Department General Staff in making strategy, shaping preparedness legislation, and planning the 1906 Cuban occupation: Richard D. Challenger, *Admirals, Generals, and American Foreign Policy, 1898–1914* (Princeton, N.J.: Princeton University Press, 1973); John Patrick Finnegan, *Against the Specter of a Dragon: The Campaign for American Military Preparedness, 1914–1917* (Westport, Conn.: Greenwood Press, 1974); and Allan R. Millett, *The Politics of Intervention: The Military Occupation of Cuba, 1906–1909* (Columbus: Ohio State University Press, 1968).

Only the very dated and prosaic Ira L. Reeves, *Military Education in the United States* (Burlington, Vt.: Free Press Publishing Co., 1914), offers an overview of the army school system in the post-Root reform years. Two individual institutions do have recent histories: Timothy K. Nenninger, *The Leavenworth Schools and the Old Army: Education, Professionalism, and the Officer Corps of the United States Army, 1881–1918* (Westport, Conn.: Greenwood Press, 1978); and George S. Pappas, *Prudens Futuri: The U.S. Army War College, 1901–1967* (Carlisle Barracks, Pa.: Alumni Association of the U.S. Army War College, 1967).

Biography has always been an important form of military history. There are a number of excellent recent biographies of officers which bear on army history in the immediate pre–World War I era. The role of junior officers in an army in transition is described in Martin Blumenson, *The Patton Papers, 1885–1941* (Boston: Houghton Mifflin Co., 1972); D. Clayton James, *The Years of MacArthur*, vol. I, *1880–1941* (Boston: Houghton Mifflin Co., 1970); Forrest C. Pogue, *George C. Marshall: The Education of a General, 1880–1939* (New York: Viking Press, 1963); and Barbara Tuchman, *Stilwell and the American Experience in China* (New York: Macmillan Co., 1970). The premier American soldier of the era has two recent biographies: Donald Smythe, *Guerrilla Warrior: The Early Life of John J. Pershing* (New York: Charles Scribner's Sons, 1973), and Frank E. Vandiver, *Black Jack: The Life and Times of John J. Pershing* (College Station: Texas A&M University Press, 1977). Another biography of a soldier with a diverse and interesting career is Heath Twichell, Jr., *Allen: Biography of an Army Officer, 1859–1930* (New Brunswick, N.J.: Rutgers University Press, 1974). Robert L. Bullard did not reach the position of esteem achieved by John J. Pershing, nor was he so well connected socially and politically as Henry T. Allen, but his biography by Allan R. Millett, *The General: Robert L. Bullard and Officership in the United States Army, 1881–1925* (Westport, Conn.: Greenwood Press, 1975), intelligently traces a career molded by the institutional changes occurring in the pre–World War I army. A young reformer's interesting insights into military education, the General Staff, and citizen-soldiers may be found in I. B. Holley, Jr., *General John M. Palmer, Citizen Soldiers, and the Army of a Democracy* (Westport, Conn.: Greenwood Press, 1982). The portion of Holley's book covering the pre–World War I period is in actuality Palmer's autobiography.

CHAPTER 12

Over Where? The AEF and the American Strategy for Victory, 1917–1918

ALLAN R. MILLETT

No longer required to be neutral in thought and deed by Woodrow Wilson, the planners of the War Department General Staff analyzed in detail the army's role in World War I only after the American declaration of war on 6 April 1917. Although the General Staff lacked a full appreciation of the challenges of the Western Front and the future problems of industrial mobilization, its own hurried studies and the reports of American observers in France convinced the army that it faced its greatest test since the Civil War. Notorious for its appetite for lives and equipment, the Western Front, nevertheless, seemed to be the only place where America could play a decisive role in defeating Germany. So the General Staff reasoned. It soon convinced Secretary of War Newton D. Baker of the soundness of its strategic analysis. Allied leaders, with the exception of British Prime Minister David Lloyd George, supported its judgment.

Although he spent much of 1917 agonizing about sending American youths into the shell-drenched mud of France, President Wilson reached the same conclusions as the General Staff, though from different assumptions. The war would be won or lost in France. From Wilson's perspective, none of the war's other theaters, particularly the Balkans, provided an equal opportunity for military victory and diplomatic leverage on the peace to follow. Only in France would the United States escape the taint of imperialism that already marked Allied strategy and postwar planning. Although he vacillated until November 1917, the president eventually shared his advisers' opinion that the United States should throw its military weight into the strategic balance on the Western Front. Wilson and his advisers did not misunderstand the implications of this commitment: the United States would have to form a mass army virtually from scratch and send it into a type of warfare breathtaking in its complexity and scope.

Although constrained by its own limited size and skill and by Wilson's moral distaste for detailed contingency planning, the General Staff had some idea about the time it would take to form a wartime force large enough to play an important role in France. Educated by the threat of war with Mexico since 1914 and the public debates of the preparedness movement, the General Staff had few illusions about the nation springing to arms. In 1915 Assistant Chief of Staff Tasker H. Bliss calculated that equipment and munitions shortages alone would require nearly two years to correct in order to place an expeditionary force of just 500,000 men in the field—unless American industry could rapidly increase its production of military supplies. With the Allies already drawing heavily upon American manufacturers, the degree of industrial expansion became a critical unknown. Additional studies in 1916 and early 1917 reached much the same conclusion. Although the General Staff believed the nation could raise adequate numbers of men through conscription, it estimated that it would take between one to two years to field an army of 1 to 4 million men that would be adequately officered, trained, and equipped for combat against a first-class enemy. Certainly the German army fell into the first-class category. When the United States actually entered the war, therefore, the General Staff believed correctly (and unpopularly) that the United States could not play a significant part in the fighting until 1918 and that its army would not be ready for decisive operations until 1919.[1]

Almost immediately after America's entry, the General Staff learned of further complications in organizing an expeditionary force. Although it did not fully appreciate the additional problems, largely because of Allied lack of candor, a series of meetings with the Allied Balfour and Viviani missions in Washington and additional reports from Europe did nothing to revise the General Staff's conservative estimates. While no one disputed the Allied argument that American manpower would become the critical element in the strategic balance, the General Staff did not like the Allied plans for using American manpower. Stung by the collapse of the Nivelle offensive in 1917 and the subsequent mutinies in its army, France wanted American soldiers integrated into the French command and logistical system in order to prepare the Americans as quickly as possible for combat. Stunned by the appalling casualties suffered by the British Expeditionary Force (BEF) in 1916 and 1917, the British also favored some form of amalgamation. Neither the French nor the British believed that the United States Army could provide adequate commanders and staff officers for an independent army, and they privately wondered how they and the United States could find the shipping to transport all the necessary support troops and material to France. Since the German submarine campaign of 1917 had not yet peaked and Great Britain already was perilously close to economic disaster from the effect of the sinkings, the shipping question was critical.

With the amalgamation issue unsettled, the Wilson administration decided in May 1917 to send at least a token expeditionary force to France to bolster Allied morale, discourage the Germans, and solidify American public opinion behind the war. At Baker's urging Wilson selected Major General John J. Pershing to command the American Expeditionary Forces (AEF), primarily because Pershing was the most physically vigorous and tested field commander among the army's major generals. In addition, he had the advantage of being less partisan than his only real competitor, Major General Leonard Wood, the former chief of staff. Having commanded the Punitive Expedition into Mexico in 1916, Pershing had already demonstrated his ability to handle complex diplomatic and operational problems, and his contacts with the Republican party, primarily through his father-in-law, Senator Francis E. Warren, gave his appointment a healthy bipartisanship. Within the army Pershing commanded the respect of his peers (if not their affection) for his energy, intelligence, loyalty to the honor of the officer corps, political sophistication, and breadth of field and staff experience. Moreover, Pershing, never a military romantic, shared the General Staff's assessment that American troops should not be committed to the war in France before they had been trained and disciplined to exacting standards and not before Pershing had established the command and logistical system adequate to support an American army.

Secretary Baker and Acting Chief of Staff Bliss gave Pershing instructions that allowed him wide latitude in determining the scope and timing of the AEF's eventual use on the Western Front. Although one division would soon sail for France, perhaps to be joined in 1917 by a handful of additional regular and National Guard divisions, Pershing agreed that the AEF could not be ready for limited combat until 1918 and not for a major offensive until 1919. As commander in chief of all American land forces that eventually served in Europe, Pershing would make the critical recommendations on the AEF's use since Baker believed that the responsible field commander's judgment should carry the heaviest weight. (This assumption rerpresented a major victory for military professionalism in the United States.) Approved by Wilson, Pershing's instructions established the fundamental character of the American commitment without dictating either the degree of cooperation with the Allies or the exact place or timing of the AEF's major effort:

In military operations against the Imperial German Government, you are directed to cooperate with the forces of the other countries employed against the enemy; but in so doing the underlying idea must be kept in view that the forces of the United States are a separate and distinct component of the combined forces, the identity of which must be preserved. This fundamental rule is subject to such minor exceptions in particular circumstances as your judgment may approve. The decision as to when your command, or any of its parts, is ready for action is confided in you, and you will exercise full powers in determining the manner of cooperation. But, until the forces of the United States are in your judgment sufficiently strong to warrant operations as an independent command, it is understood that you will cooperate as a component of whatever army you may be assigned to by the French Government.[2]

When Pershing and his small staff finally arrived in France in June 1917, they found a staggering number of organizational problems for the AEF, complicated by a bewildering range of advice from the Allies and the American military missions already dispatched to France by the War Department. From the welter of words, some basic conclusions emerged. First, the French wanted the AEF to establish its training camps behind the portion of the Western Front that ran from Toul in Lorraine to the border of Switzerland. Relatively inactive since

1914, this portion of the front would give the Americans a chance to train with uncommitted French troops in a *bon secteur* and would eventually release French divisions for the more active front that ran from Verdun on the Meuse River all the way to the English Channel. In addition, the decision to place the AEF in Lorraine would lessen the problem of logistics since American supply lines could be established along the railroads that ran south of Paris to the ports along France's southwestern coast. The American logistical system would have to be superimposed upon the French army's in the southwest, but it would not tax the already strained depots and railroads supporting the BEF and French armies. After a quick, independent analysis of the logistical factors, Pershing agreed with the French that Lorraine would indeed be the best place to station the AEF while it went through the throes of organization and training.

Committed by personal, national, and professional pride to the creation of a field army that he would command—as well as by his guidance from the War Department—Pershing searched for a strategic plan that would justify an independent American army and fulfill his instructions to make an important (even decisive) contribution to the ultimate Allied victory. Dominated by graduates of the army's School of the Line and General Staff College at Fort Leavenworth and former members of the General Staff, Pershing's staff applied all its hard-learned Germanic operational theory to the problem. Fortuitously, many members of Pershing's General Headquarters (GHQ) staff knew the Lorraine area well since they had examined in detail the operations of the Franco-Prussian War. Now, in a twist of history, American officers found themselves fighting a war on the very terrain they had studied at Fort Leavenworth. They also shared "the Chief's" faith that national war aims and honor, as well as their own professional esteem, required a unique American solution to the stalemate on the Western Front. Without a definite strategic goal, the planners feared that the AEF might be amalgamated into the Allied armies. They also knew the highly centralized AEF organization that they preferred could not otherwise be justified. The GHQ staff, which included many personalities as strong as Pershing's, planned the AEF's employment with the full knowledge that its planning would ultimately shape every phase of the AEF's organization from troop strength and shipping schedules to training and tactics.[3]

After days of reading maps, assessing intelligence reports, touring the front, and debating the alternatives, the GHQ Operations Section produced a comprehensive strategic plan for the employment of the AEF. Although the plan appreciated the logistical need to establish the AEF in Lorraine, it drew its fundamental inspiration from geopolitical analysis and operational theory as well as from the assumption that the AEF could not function as a group of field armies until 1919. The plan advocated that the AEF mount a major offensive on the city of Metz in 1919 with the major weight of the attack east of the Moselle River. This offensive would break the German railroads that ran laterally south of the Ardennes Forest and north of the Vosges Mountains and, thus, force the German army to withdraw to the Rhine. In addition, the American offensive would seize the coal and iron mines of the Saar and, so the planners reasoned, cripple German war industry. By seizing Metz and the Briey-Longwy-Thionville triangle northwest of Metz, the AEF could force a peace settlement. Since this offensive could not begin before 1919, the planners advocated a limited American offensive to eliminate the St. Mihiel salient in 1918. Assuming that the Allies could contain any German offensive in 1918 without disrupting American plans, the AEF would use the St. Mihiel operation to seize critical terrain for the 1919 offensive, free the railroad along the Moselle in that sector, test American military effectiveness, and hearten civilian morale in the United States. Overly optimistic about the troop requirements for such an operation, the planners thought an AEF of 1.2 million would suffice.[4]

The Metz offensive drew much of its inspiration from Pershing's plan to command an independent army, the realities of logistics, and the existing position of the Allied armies in 1917. Nevertheless, this particular GHQ strategic concept shaped much of the AEF's future planning. From the autumn of 1917 until the Armistice a year later, the vision of a great AEF offensive toward Metz explains Pershing's adamant refusal to surrender permanently his forces to Allied commanders and his stubborn insistence that the AEF prepare for offensive action in the open terrain on either side of the Moselle Valley.

The selection of Metz as a strategic objective was not a particularly inspired decision. For one thing, the Germans had had ample time (nearly thirty-five years) to turn the Metz area into a formidable fortified area. Using the French fortifications they had conquered in 1870, the Germans had strengthened these defenses, anchored by the Ardennes Forest to the north and the Vosges Mountains to the south, as the French army had found to its sorrow in 1914. Moreover, the Germans had never intended that Lorraine would be a major theater of operations, and their railroad system had been developed accordingly. Capturing Metz would have given the AEF little, for the critical lateral railroad that Pershing stressed in his planning did not run through Metz at all. Instead, it turned west at Thionville (well north of Metz) and ran northwest through Longuyon and Montmedy until it reached the Meuse River at Sedan; the line then followed the Meuse to Mézières and turned north into German-occupied Belgium. To break this line would require an AEF offensive that advanced well past Metz.[5] In addition, the coal and iron resources of the Saar basin, another AEF objective, produced only about 10 percent of Germany's raw materials. The fall of the Saar might be a loss to the German war effort, but its capture did not appear decisive. The Allies, therefore, could honestly doubt whether Pershing's great 1919 plan offered any unique prospects for victory. The basic challenge remained the same: to destroy the moral and physical ability of the German army to hold the territory west of the Rhine. Pershing, on the other hand, held to the Metz plan with a determination that pleased his staff, but frustrated the Allies.

As Pershing's plans for the deployment of the AEF matured, the Allied cause suddenly worsened in the autumn of 1917. The Bolshevik Revolution in Russia ended the war on the Eastern Front, and an Austro-German army crushed the

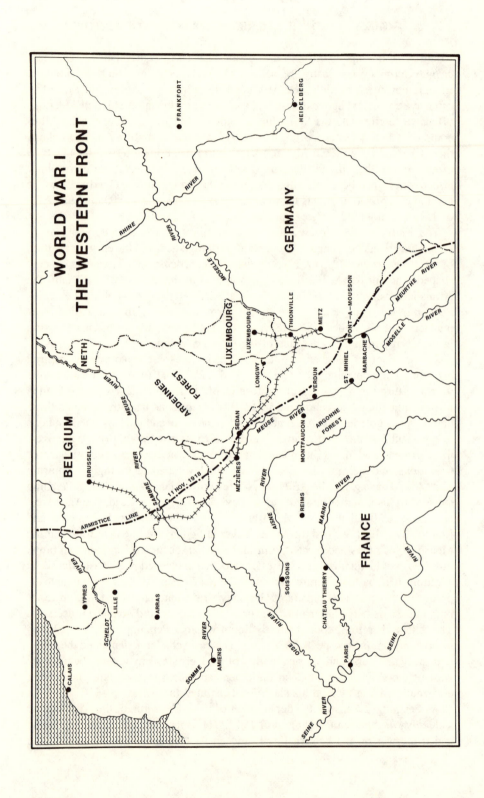

Italians at Caporetto. What had been a three-front war in April was by December a one-front struggle. Germany, on the other hand, could not afford to remain on the strategic defensive (or so the German high command reasoned) since the Allied blockade had stretched the German economy and eroded civilian morale. The German army commanders also recognized that their reservoir of military manpower was shrinking, but they believed that new tactics for massing artillery fire and infiltrating masses of infantry through the Allied Lines would bring victory. Counting on the assistance of divisions redeployed from Russia and Italy, the German high command began to plan a war-winning offensive on the Western Front for 1918.

Allied political and military leaders shared the German assessment, and they pressed the Wilson administration and Pershing to give up their plans for not committing the AEF on a large scale before 1919. Although he understood Allied pessimism and urged the War Department to speed the training of the American divisions in the United States, Pershing did not abandon his original concept: to form an independent American army of twenty-four to thirty divisions in 1918 and use it to reduce the St. Mihiel salient. He rejected an Allied proposal to deploy his 1918 divisions behind the juncture of the British and French armies in the valley of the Somme, a likely target for the German offensive. Pershing, however, did agree to commit the four divisions then in France to joint training with the French army—but only in the Lorraine sector he intended to occupy in force in 1918. His only other concession was to assign six divisions to the BEF for training—in return for the additional shipping that would bring those divisions to Europe.

When the GHQ staff reexamined its September 1917 plan and found it still valid, Pershing approved its conclusions and ordered his officers not to accept Allied pessimism about the seriousness of the German threat. Nevertheless, Pershing had many reasons to worry. He disliked the "trench warfare" tactics his troops were learning in France and America; he knew that the American industrial mobilization had not gone well; and he recognized that shipping short-ages would limit the growth of the AEF in 1918. Nevertheless, Pershing con-tinued to build his logistical system for the Lorraine campaign and rebuffed the Allied proposals to integrate the AEF into their armies. Neither Wilson nor Baker overruled him. As the spring of 1918 approached, GHQ held fast to its deliberate plans for organizing and training the AEF, which numbered only about 300,000 men in March 1918. Reflecting Pershing's emphasis on building the base for an independent American army, nearly 129,000 of these troops were committed to logistical and training assignments, not to combat units.[6]

If the AEF had turned instantly into a crack field army, Pershing's policies would not have distressed the Allies, but the American troops needed all the training that Pershing prescribed. The senior officers had little experience with European supporting arms, staff procedures, and the command of large units. The divisions which they commanded, for example, were larger than the entire United States Army into which they had been commissioned in the 1880s. The junior officers, the vast majority recent civilians, had little knowledge of the art of command and military techniques. The enlisted men impressed the Allies with their physical prowess and intelligence but appalled them by their lax discipline, carelessness with equipment and supplies, and cheerful overestimation of their own fighting skill. Although the AEF's school system attacked these shortcomings with some success, Pershing remained sensitive to Allied criticism. Equally worrisome, the AEF's logistical system—the Services of Supply—suffered from poor management, bureaucratic fragmentation, and organizational growing pains. The reality of such problems in France and the difficulty of coordinating policies with the War Department at home convinced Pershing and his staff that they had to pursue their slow, orderly buildup for the 1919 offensive. The Allies would have to survive the predicted 1918 German offensive without major AEF assistance.

The AEF's growing pains were only part of the larger problem of creating a mass army. The limited degree of American land force mobilization by the end of 1917 reflected the interplay of domestic politics, inefficient industrial mobilization, and conservative strategic planning. Of the some 1.2 million soldiers under arms by the end of 1917, more than 1 million remained in training in the United States. Built upon the 200,000 regulars and National Guardsmen in service in April 1917, this force had already grown by a factor of five and would expand by a factor of seventeen to 3.8 million at war's end. In early 1918, however, the wartime army had substantial weaknesses. First, in light of its eventual needs, it did not have enough officers. At the end of 1917 only one-quarter (about 53,000) of the eventual number of army officers who served in World War I (over 200,000) held commissions. Officers with regular army and National Guard experience numbered only 9,000. The enlisted force contained 678,000 volunteers and 517,000 draftees. Although Congress had passed a Selective Service Act in May 1917, the nation's political leaders hoped that conscription would bear lightly on the American people, serving principally as a spur to volunteering. In any event, the War Department could not house, clothe, or equip a larger force because the government's industrial mobilization policies had not yet produced the predicted cornucopia of arms. (Of the 2.8 million draftees who eventually served in the army, 2.3 million did not enter the service until 1918.) The ultimate result of the limited mobilization of 1917 was that the AEF fought in 1918 with officers and men who had insufficient training to compensate for their inexperience, immaturity, lack of leadership qualities, and modest physical ability.[7]

On 21 March 1918 the German army, enjoying numerical superiority on the Western Front for the first time since 1914, smashed the British Fifth Army in the Somme Valley and began a series of offensives that did not end until mid-July. The crisis almost destroyed Pershing's Lorraine campaign, but it also jarred the Wilson administration and the Allies into accelerating the movement of American troops to France. Although the Allies were most concerned about surviving the German 1918 offensive, Pershing used their desperate pleas for American infantry regiments and machine gun battalions to bargain for two important concessions to his strategic concepts: the acceptance in principle of an independent American army with a sector of its own and the use of Allied shipping to carry the combat support and service troops necessary to create a full American field army. During the first three months of the German offensive, the British also held some advantage in the complex inter-Allied negotiations on the use of the AEF, for the BEF had suffered the most serious losses and the British government controlled the ships that could be used to bring the Americans. Seizing the initiative in Washington and in the meetings of the Supreme War Council, the inter-Allied coordinating committee, the British managed to cajole and coerce Pershing into committing twelve American divisions to the BEF's front for training and emergency combat if necessary. The arrival of French reserve divisions and British replacements from England and the resiliency of the BEF, however, blunted the German offensive in the north. The new AEF divisions arrived too late to see extensive combat in the British sector.

At the end of May, however, the German high command delivered a crushing blow to the two French armies holding the Chemin des Dames ridges west of Reims and drove all the way to the Marne River, only forty miles from Paris. In the renewed crisis the Supreme War Council pressed Pershing to put more of his troops under Allied command and to postpone the creation of an American sector in Lorraine. In addition, Marshal Ferdinand Foch, the Allied supreme commander, urged the United States to plan for a 100-division AEF of between 3–5 million men, a proposal accepted by Pershing. Spurred by the crisis and the newly available British transports, the War Department sent more than 800,000 troops or the better part of 21 divisions to France in May–July 1918. Fortunately for Pershing, the Wilson administration (however timidly upon occasion) backed his assessment that the undertrained Americans should not see extended combat as long as British and French reserves were available. Fortunately, Marshal Foch and the French army commander, General Philippe Pétain, also agreed to husband the AEF for future operations. The result was that only three full American divisions saw heavy action during the German offensive, while most of the remaining divisions trained or occupied quiet sectors to release French troops for the active sectors. In both the British and French sectors, however, American infantry and machine gunners saw action, often with unhappy results, since the Americans had not mastered the tactic of withdrawal with the same skill as the Allies.

As the German offensive waned in July, the Allies examined the possibility of a limited counteroffensive to recapture the ground lost since March. They also looked forward to their 1919 operations. Anxious to commit both the French and Americans to his concept for the 1919 offensive, Field Marshal Sir Douglas Haig, commander of the BEF, proposed that the Allies conduct the offensive along a front running from Verdun on the Meuse River to the east all the way northwest to the English Channel. Such an offensive along a continuous front would stretch the German army thin and menace the German lateral railway system from south of the Ardennes Forest north to the key routes into Belgium.

The AEF should be used west of the Meuse for a drive north toward the twin critical railroad cities of Sedan and Mézières. In addition, the Americans should provide at least a full corps as part of the BEF.

General Pershing once again objected to Allied strategic concepts (or lack thereof in the case of the French) and argued that offensive operations in 1919 should be continuous in timing, but not in geography. He and his staff doubted that the Allies could remain on the offensive all along the front from the Meuse to the Channel. Instead, Pershing again advocated an American offensive in Lorraine, not only to Metz, but past it into the Saar and the German cities south of the Ardennes and west of the Rhine. Such an offensive would so menace Germany that at the very least it would draw off German divisions from the Allies' front, thus aiding the BEF's eastward thrust into Belgium. Pershing's 1917 reasoning still held: the Lorraine offensive on its own would force the Germans to sue for peace. The elimination of the St. Mihiel salient in 1918 remained a natural prelude to the Lorraine campaign.

AEF training still stressed tactics designed for the Lorraine offensive. Profiting from its study of the German offensive of 1918, Pershing's staff demanded that American division commanders stress widely dispersed infantry formations, the skilled use of machine guns and portable 37-mm cannon to reduce German strong points, and short, intense artillery barrages. Drawing upon British experience, the AEF staff also emphasized the use of tanks in the offensive. Unfortunately, the hard-pressed French could not provide tanks in quality and quantity, and the 1918 emergency retarded American training in other ways. Active operations with the French, the defensive occupation of sectors of the Western Front, and the scarcity of supporting artillery, tanks, and aviation prevented the extensive training in offensive operations the AEF staff prescribed. Nevertheless, Pershing and his planners insisted that the Lorraine campaign in 1919 should still shape AEF planning, and they did not retreat from this concept even under intense Allied pressure.[8]

The experience of the AEF Air Service dramatizes the difficulties in organizing technically specialized units for the Western Front. Few army planners doubted that the AEF would need a formidable air arm to perform three basic missions: provide air superiority above the American ground divisions, attack German troops and installations, and collect and distribute information on both enemy and friendly positions. Influenced by Allied recommendations and Pershing's own estimates, the War Department proposed an air force in France that would range between 202 and 206 squadrons (4,500–5,000 aircraft) by 1919. Every phase of the organization of this force fell behind schedule because the army could not train pilots and technical personnel rapidly enough and the War Department could not provide combat aircraft in quantity. The Allies could and did transfer their planes (more than 2,000) to American squadrons, but their own personnel shortages prevented them from lending men to the Americans. In January 1918 the AEF Air Service had only 723 officers and 14,559 men in France, and six months later it had only 14 operational squadrons in action. A massive deployment in 1918—which ruined any chance of an orderly buildup—brought the Air Service's strength to an awesome 7,692 officers and 74,272 men by the end of the war, but this flood of personnel did not bring an equally phenomenal growth in air capability. When the armistice was signed, the Air Service had only 45 squadrons in action (767 pilots, 740 aircraft) while the British and French provided 97 and 260 squadrons, respectively, to the air war above the Western Front. Like the AEF's ground divisions, the Air Service could claim enormous effort, modest accomplishments, and a deep sense of unfulfilled potential.[9]

As the strength of the AEF grew, so too did Pershing's power to dictate where and when the AEF would fight. He used his influence in July and August to force Foch to approve an American attack on the St. Mihiel salient. Pershing still saw this offensive as the prelude of the drive on Metz. In the meantime, beginning in mid-July American divisions under French corps command joined the Aisne-Marne counteroffensive, an operation designed to retake the ground lost in June. This successful offensive then shifted to a more ambitious French effort to drive the Germans northward from the ground between the Aisne and the Oise rivers, an attack for which General Pétain requested more American troops. Pershing, however, would not accept an army sector west of the Meuse. Instead, he persuaded Pétain to put the American divisions in their own corps sectors under American corps commanders; the result was that some AEF divisions fought under American generals, and others did not. The AEF's experiences of July and August under French generals further convinced Pershing that the Allies had nothing to teach the Americans about offensive warfare. Rather, he and his staff became convinced that French generals unnecessarily sacrificed American lives. As the program of corps consolidation continued, Pershing activated the headquarters of the United States First Army. On 24 July 1918 he personally took command of this army while retaining overall command of the AEF.

Inter-Allied strategic politics and the shifting fortunes of war on the Western Front once again affected the AEF's deployment. On 24 July, the day that Foch approved the St. Mihiel operation and Pershing activated the United States First Army, the Allied high commanders still saw no possibility of decisive victory in 1918. Pershing and General Bliss, now the American representatives to the Supreme War Council, agreed that prudence required a continued buildup of the AEF (now over a million men) to a force of from 80 to 100 divisions by 1919. As Pershing started shifting troops to the southern face of the St. Mihiel salient, however, the BEF won several spectacular victories in the north. Almost immediately, Field Marshal Haig pressured Foch to put into motion Haig's 1919 plan for a vast, compressing, double envelopment of the German army between the Channel and the Meuse with the Ardennes and the lateral railroad system forming the strategic rock upon which the Allies would grind the German armies into defeat. Pétain favored Haig's plan, and they both pressured Foch to force Pershing to abandon the St. Mihiel operation. Despite the AEF's growing strength, the pattern of the American war effort and the shipping priorities of 1918 placed Pershing at a disadvantage if he wanted to command a full American field army. Although he was growing manpower-rich, Pershing depended upon the French for artillery, tanks, aircraft, and vehicles. In a series of intense negotiations (30 August–2 September 1918), Pershing agreed to limit the St. Mihiel offensive and join the great offensive west of the Meuse in exchange for increased French arms (eventually including French divisions) and a sector of his own for the United States First Army.[10]

For the rest of the war, the American Expeditionary Forces' operations reflected Pershing's conviction that a Lorraine campaign might still be necessary, even in 1919. At the same time, Pershing refused to surrender the AEF to foreign command, even if his army's independence meant participation in the offensive west of the Meuse. In fact, he linked the two concerns by having Foch agree that the AEF might eventually mount operations in a sector that could run all the way from the Argonne Forest on the west to the Swiss border. What had become nonnegotiable for General Pershing was the creation of an independent American group of field armies, commanded by him and answerable only to the Wilson administration and the Supreme War Council and its agent, Marshal Foch. To assure that the AEF would fight as a unified command (although the United States II Corps fought out the war with the BEF and several American divisions saw combat west of the Argonne under French command), Pershing agreed to drive north toward Sedan-Mézières as Field Marshal Haig urged. Even while the St. Mihiel attack (12–16 September) went as scheduled, GHQ marshalled its scattered divisions for what became the Meuse-Argonne campaign on 26 September.

From 26 September until 11 November 1918, the American Expeditionary Forces battered through five German defensive zones until reaching the heights above Sedan. In forty-seven days of continuous battle, twenty-two of the AEF's twenty-nine combat divisions engaged one-quarter of the entire German divisional strength on the Western Front, drawing off critical German reserves from the BEF and French sectors to the west and north. In the course of the Meuse-Argonne campaign, 1.2 million American soldiers, a force larger than the whole Confederate army in the Civil War, engaged the Germans. During the campaign the AEF artillery fired more tons of shells than the entire Union army in the same war. To advance thirty-four miles in a sector of 1,500 square kilometers, the American First Army lost 120,000 men, of whom about 25,000 died in action. Typical of World War I battles, little of the First Army's original plan of attack survived the first few hours of the campaign. Some objectives to be seized in the first day's advance did not fall for two weeks, and the German defenders, though bludgeoned by 2,417 American cannon, did not break but fell back in decent order through their series of fortified positions. (In the Meuse-Argonne campaign the AEF took only 16,000 prisoners, about the same number it seized in four days at St. Mihiel.)

Despite Pershing's effort to keep fresh divisions at the front—the First Army's three corps never had more than nine divisions engaged at any one time—the AEF could not mount a continuous advance, and the First Army had to accept two major reorganization periods in the course of the campaign, allowing the Germans precious time to reestablish their defenses. Among the inexperienced divisions, unit disorganization and disorientation became common in the broken terrain and thick forests, and the famous "lost battalion" of the Seventy-seventh Division had many not-so-famous brethren. One division commander requested relief from battle because he believed the strength of his four infantry regiments had fallen to around 1,600 soldiers or about one-eighth of the troops with which he had begun the drive; when the division reassembled in a rest area, he found that it had 8,400 infantrymen left. High casualties among infantry officers and artillery liaison officers ensured that on-call fire missions on German machine gun nests did not occur often enough, and the First Army's small tank brigade did not stay in action with sufficient vehicles to give much aid to the embattled doughboys. Infantry replacements, hurriedly sent forward from incoming troopships, often went into battle with virtually no training; one division estimated that half its replacements had not fired their rifles. Even the most experienced divisions had difficulty maintaining unit cohesion, and no division received sufficient time to remedy its problems with additional training. Plagued by its casualties and its relative amateurism, the First Army's attacks bore considerable resemblance to the operations of the Army of the Potomac in 1864 or the Soviet armies of 1944.[11]

Logistical problems, especially moving cannon and artillery ammunition forward and removing casualties to the rear, contributed to the First Army's misery. Theater problems of storage, transportation, and distribution absorbed much of the energy of the Services of Supply (SOS) and did not improve until the AEF reduced its theater level-of-supply from ninety to forty-five days. Major General James G. Harbord, who left command of the Second Division against his will to reorganize the SOS, also decided to cut his planners' estimates of pounds per soldier from fifty to thirty pounds, another calculated risk that reduced the logistical burden. At the front the fundamental problem was transportation and engineering capability. During the campaign First Army estimated that it had only half the trucks it needed. Dependent upon horse-drawn wagons, the First Army estimated that it lost 44,000 horses in the St. Mihiel and Meuse-Argonne offensives. Four-legged replacements proved more difficult to find than men. Even with sufficient trucks and wagons, the First Army could not maintain the roads in its sector without using reserves as labor troops, a practice that ensured that combat units often returned to the front lines in less than rested condition. Infantry battalions locked in battle with the Germans depended upon carrying parties to get food, water, and ammunition forward, a practice that reduced foxhole strength in the heat of battle. Sporadic autumn rains thickened the mud of the shell holes and deepened the traffic jams that spread like tentacles behind the fighting divisions.[12]

Pressed by Haig and Foch to commit the bulk of his First Army west of the

Meuse in the hard fighting of October and early November, Pershing, nevertheless, pursued the Lorraine campaign concept until the last day of the war, 11 November. Irritated by continued pressure from London and Paris to place his divisions under French command and acutely aware that his troops faced a difficult combination of staunch German defenses and unfavorable terrain, Pershing widened his sector by committing American and French divisions east of the Meuse in October. As the fighting still raged around the third and central line of the German defense belt, the *Kriemhilde Stellung*, Pershing created another field army, the United States Second Army, for immediate operations toward Metz. Unconvinced that the Allied offensive then underway would defeat the Germans despite signs of German political and military collapse, Pershing intended to send the First Army no farther north than Sedan. Instead, he planned to shift the balance of his offensive against the German defenses protecting Metz west of the Moselle. This plan bore great similarity to the strategic concept he had approved more than a year before.

Acting on reports that the German army had begun to disintegrate (the evidence for the doughboys at the front was decidedly mixed), Pershing ordered the Second Army into action on 10 November. In fact, Pershing urged the Supreme War Council not to accept any peace terms other than unconditional surrender, an eleventh-hour opinion that threw the Allied political and military leadership into a crisis until President Wilson overruled his military commander. Nevertheless, Pershing believed that his Lorraine campaign would have been the *coup de grâce* to the German cause and the pride of the German military if he had been allowed to continue it. If the Germans had lost the Saar, he reasoned, they would have surrendered without terms and, thus, would have provided the Allies with a greater chance for reforming German politics and guaranteeing a lasting peace.[13]

Whether Pershing's aborted Lorraine campaign would have won the war in 1919 or forced an unconditional surrender in 1918 remains unanswerable in historical terms, but certainly the concept itself had as much to do with the deployment of the American Expeditionary Forces as the policy of fielding an independent army. The question of "where" (Lorraine or Alsace) cannot, therefore, be separated from the question of "what" (an independent army or amalgamation). While matters of logistics undoubtedly reinforced Pershing's commitment to a Lorraine campaign, that system followed and did not dictate the decision to go for Metz, a decision made in 1917 and projected for 1919 when the United States would reach full mobilization. And the AEF's logistical system just as easily could have supported operations west of the Meuse—as it did during the Meuse-Argonne campaign. On the other hand, capturing Metz would not have badly disrupted the German railway system. Instead, the AEF would have had to advance as far as Longuyon or Thionville to cut the lateral railway, a distance as far and as well defended as the muddy roads and ridges that led to Sedan. Yet, the AEF's Meuse-Argonne offensive—conceived by Field Marshal Haig—did indeed draw scarce reserves from the German armies facing the BEF and the French, an effect that probably contributed to the BEF's dramatic advances late in the war. The result was a less spectacular American military contribution to the Allied victory than Wilson and Pershing had sought. Just what influence this muted American effort had on the Versailles Treaty is worth debating.

Whether the AEF had the tactical skill to reach Metz, Thionville, and the Saar basin is as problematic as the strategy itself. Again, it is worth remembering that Pershing and his staff did not envision a grand offensive until 1919. By then, perhaps, the state of training and arming of the AEF and the very size of the American army in France would have made the campaign feasible. The commitment of the best-trained American divisions to the defensive and counteroffensive operations of May–August 1918 blunted the AEF's combat efficiency as did the hurried deployment of undertrained divisions fresh from the United States in the same period. Learning effective infantry-artillery coordination against the Germans on the battlefield proved as deadly for the Americans as it had for the British and the French.

Unlike its German opponents, the AEF had not yet concluded that it needed to reduce the thickness of its infantry attacks and to rely on smaller, more highly skilled assault units and shorter, more accurate artillery preparations. Even as astute a soldier as the First Army's operations officer, Colonel (later General of the Army) George C. Marshall, rejected the French tendency to husband infantry for dispersed, carefully prepared assaults. Assessing American operations shortly after the war, Marshall concluded that national characteristics and limited training gave the AEF no alternative to mounting thick frontal assaults:

Our men gave better results when employed in a "steamroller" operation, that is, when launched in an attack with distant objectives and held continuously to their task without rest or reorganization until unfit for further fighting. Their morale suffered from delays under fire, their spirits were best maintained by continued aggressive action, even though the men themselves were approaching the point of complete exhaustion. They bitterly resented casualties suffered while being held in position, without doing any damage to the enemy.[14]

Given the iron tactical constraints imposed by the immobility of 1918 infantry, the Americans faced tactical difficulties common to their allies and enemies. By 1918 those difficulties were well known, but unsolved. Essentially, infantry offensives could overwhelm enemy defenses as long as they were supported by artillery firing from fixed positions at preregistered targets. Some consideration for surprise and sophisticated infantry tactics—as the Germans proved in 1918—could reduce losses and increase the miles gained, but these changes could not overcome the casualties and physical exhaustion that the infantry faced when it moved beyond the range of its artillery. As the Americans learned in the Meuse-Argonne, moving guns and supplies over shell-plowed ground required more time than a sustained offensive allowed. Nevertheless, the best American divisions, even those ravaged by early casualties, demonstrated considerable tactical

General of the Armies John J. ("Black Jack") Pershing and his staff (Captain George C. Marshall, rear row, second from right), 23 September 1919
Library of Congress (USZ62-44595)

skill in the attacks of October and November 1918. Again, the problem was that the war ended before the AEF reached a uniformly high level of battlefield efficiency—whether that efficiency applied to army staffs, aviation squadrons, artillery batteries, or infantry platoons. Yet the American Expeditionary Forces in operational skill—as in so many ways—had come close to the best European standards by November 1918.

Although there was little doubt in the minds of the soldiers of the AEF—from General Pershing to the lowliest doughboy—that the Americans had won the war on the Western Front, a more accurate assessment is that the Allies might have lost the war without the American Expeditionary Forces. In almost every way World War I had become fixed by the time the United States entered the conflict. As both the Allies and Germans recognized, the theater of decision was France, and the Americans (for somewhat different reasons) agreed. Except for General Pershing's Metz concept, none of the Allied commanders in 1917 had a fresh plan for winning the war in France, and their earlier plans had proved bankrupt. In a strategic sense, the victory of 1918 was an extemporized counteroffensive shaped by the German offensives of the spring and the Allied counterattacks of the summer.

The only aspect of the American commitment that stood in sharp contrast to Allied preferences (and thus enhanced American national pride) was the question of amalgamation. Pershing's plan to create an independent American army remained central to AEF planning throughout the war. Yet the importance of the amalgamation question to American-Allied command relations should not obscure the fact that Pershing had a clear idea about how, where, and when his independent army should fight. As early as September 1917 Pershing decided that an offensive into Alsace-Lorraine in 1919 would so disrupt the German position west of the Rhine that the Allies would win the war without major offensives along the northern half of the Western Front. If the war had continued beyond 11 November 1918, the AEF would have marched toward Metz. Whether this offensive would have brought an unambiguous victory over Germany and simplified the peace that followed is another of the unanswered questions of World War I.

NOTES

The author appreciates the suggestions for revision and clarification he received from Professors Williamson Murray and Harry L. Coles (The Ohio State University), Edward M. Coffman (University of Wisconsin-Madison), Donald W. Smythe (John Carroll University), Peter Maslowski (University of Nebraska-Lincoln), Daniel Beaver (University of Cincinnati), Timothy Nenninger (National Archives), and Russell F. Weigley (Temple University). The author profited especially from Dr. Nenninger's study, "American Military Effectiveness in World War I," a draft essay done for the Mershon Center's "Military Effectiveness Project" for the Office of Net Assessment, Office of the Secretary of Defense.

1. Brig. Gen. T. H. Bliss, memo for the Secretary of War, "A Study of Deficiencies to be Supplied in Case the United States Should Ever Have to Organize a Military Force of 500,000 Men for Service at Home or Abroad," 19 May 1915, Tasker H. Bliss Papers, Library of Congress, Washington, D.C.; Brig. Gen. M. M. Macomb, memo for the Chief of Staff, "Organization and Cost of a National Volunteer Force," 21 June 1915, File 9053, Army War College Correspondence Files, Records of the War Department General Staff, Record Group 165, National Archives, Washington, D.C.; WDGS Report 12460, 28 February 1916, Correspondence of the Office of the Chief of Staff, Record Group 165, National Archives, Washington, D.C.; U.S., Congress, Senate, "Government Manufacture of Arms, Munitions, and Equipment," 64th Cong., 2d sess., 1917, S. Doc. 664 (Kernan Board Report with appendices); Adj. Gen. W. M. Wright to Maj. Gen. H. L. Scott, 24 March 1917, Hugh L. Scott Papers, Library of Congress; Brig. Gen. J. McA. Palmer to Maj. Gen. R. C. Davis, 7 August 1925, John L. Hines Papers, Library of Congress.

2. Secretary of War N. D. Baker to Maj. Gen. J. J. Pershing, 26 May 1917, quoted in full in Gen. John J. Pershing, *My Experiences in the World War*, 2 vols. (New York: Frederick J. Stokes, 1931), I, 38–39.

3. Brig. Gen. F. R. McCoy to Sen. J. W. Wadsworth, Jr., 22 April 1919, Frank R. McCoy Papers, Library of Congress; Brig. Gen. G. Van H. Moseley to Maj. Gen. C. C. Williams, 10 May 1928, George Van Horn Moseley Papers, Library of Congress; Maj. Gen. James G. Harbord (ret.), "Personalities and Personal Relationships in the American Expeditionary Forces," lecture to the Army War College, 29 April 1933, copy in the Hugh A. Drum Papers, in the possession of Mr. H. D. Johnson, Closter, N.J.; Edward M. Coffman, "The American Military Generation Gap in World War I," in Lt. Col. William Geffen, ed., *Command and Commanders in Modern Military History, Proceedings of the Second Military History Symposium, U.S. Air Force Academy* (Washington: Government Printing Office, 1969), pp. 35–43; Timothy K. Nenninger, *The Leavenworth Schools and the Old Army* (Westport, Conn.: Greenwood Press, 1978), pp. 134–54.

4. Office of the Chief of Staff, GHQ AEF, "A Strategical Study on the Employment of the A.E.F. against the Imperial German Government," 25 September 1917, GHQ AEF Secret General Correspondence, File 681, Records of the American Expeditionary Forces, Record Group 120, National Archives.

5. The rail system in Metz is shown accurately in Brig. Gen. Victor Esposito, *The West Point Atlas of American Wars*, 2 vols. (New York: Praeger, 1959), II, Map 68; U.S., Department of Defense, Department of the Army, Historical Division, *United States Army in the World War, 1917–1919*, 17 vols. (Washington: Government Printing Office, 1948), I, 26; Reichsarchiv, *Der Weltkreig, 1914–1918, Das Deutsche Feldeisenbahnwesen*, vol. I, *Die Eisenbahnen zu Kriegsbeginn* (Berlin: Reichsarchiv, 1928), pp. 110ff. and maps I, II, IV, and V.

On the other hand, the maps in Pershing's memoirs and the report of the American Battlefield Monuments Commission, which Pershing headed, erroneously show the major lateral route running directly from Metz to Sedan.

6. SecWar N. D. Baker to Gen. J. J. Pershing, 24 December 1917, quoted in Pershing, *My Experiences in the World War*, I, 271–72; Operations Section, GHQ AEF, memorandum for the C/S AEF, 24 November 1917 (approved by C-in-C, 15 December

1917), in *United States Army in the World War*, II, 80; résumé of conference between General Pershing and Gen. Pétain, 23 December 1917, *United States Army in the World War*, II, 105–7; HQ AEF confidential memo, "Pessimism," 13 December 1917, copy in Charles P. Summerall Papers, Library of Congress; C-in-C AEF to C/S USA, 13 December 1917; "AEF Confidential Cables Sent," James G. Harbord Papers, Library of Congress; U.S. Department of War, Army War College, Historical Section, *The Genesis of the American First Army* (Washington: Government Printing Office, 1938), pp. 9–20.

7. This analysis is based on Col. Leonard P. Ayers, *The War with Germany: A Statistical Summary* (Washington: Government Printing Office, 1919), pp. 13–22; Lt. Col. Marvin A. Kreidberg and 1st Lt. Merton G. Henry, *History of Military Mobilization in the United States Army, 1775–1945* (Washington: Department of the Army, 1955), pp. 241–243; Fred D. Baldwin, "The American Enlisted Man in World War I" (Ph.D. diss., Princeton University, 1964).

8. See the following documents in *United States Army in the World War*, II: memo of conference held between General Pershing and General Foch, 10 July 1918, 517–21; G–3 GHQ AEF, memo on conference with General Foch, 14 July 1918, 527–31; C-in-C AEF to C/S USA and SecWar, 19 June 1918, 476–79; GHQ AEF, memo on combat instructions, 29 June and 5 September 1918, 490–95; GHQ AEF, memo on tactical dispositions, 11 July 1918, 521–22. See also Gen. J. J. Pershing to Gen. H. L. Scott, 28 June 1918, Scott Papers; and C-in-C AEF to C/S USA, "AEF Confidential Cables Sent," 27 August 1918, Harbord Papers.

9. "Final Report of the Chief of the Air Service, American Expeditionary Forces," in Maurer Maurer, ed., *The U.S. Air Service in World War I*, 4 vols. (Washington: Office of Air Force History, 1978), I, 15–163.

10. Notes on conference between General Pershing, Marshal Foch, and General Pétain, 2 September 1918, *United States Army in the World War*, II, 589–92.

11. *Final Report of Gen. John J. Pershing, Commander-in-Chief, American Expeditionary Forces* (Washington: Government Printing Office, 1920), pp. 45–53; Ayres, *The War with Germany*, pp. 101–118; G–3, General Staff, First Army, AEF, "Special Operations Report: Part C: Meuse-Argonne Operations," 5 January 1919, AEF "Historical File," Record Group 120, National Archives; G–5, GHQ and 1st Army, AEF, "Notes on Recent Operations" Nos. 3 (12 October 1918) and 4 (22 November 1918), in G–5, GHQ AEF "Historical File," Record Group 120, National Archives; Paul F. Braim, "The Test of Battle: The American Expeditionary Forces in the Meuse-Argonne Campaign, 26 September–11 November 1918" (Ph.D. dissertation, University of Delaware, 1983).

12. James A. Huston, *The Sinews of War: Army Logistics, 1775–1953* (Washington: Office of the Chief of Military History, 1966), pp. 356–87; U.S., Department of War, General Staff, War Plans Division, Historical Branch, *Organization of the Services of Supply, American Expeditionary Forces* (Washington: Government Printing Office, 1921).

13. C-in-C AEF to CG 2d U.S. Army, "Instructions for Future Operations," 5 and 9 November 1918, appended to report of the CG, 2d U.S. Army, AEF Organization Records, Record Group 120, National Archives; Gen. J. J. Pershing to Lt. Gen. R. L. Bullard, 8 November 1918, John J. Pershing Papers, Library of Congress; Pershing, *My Experiences in the World War*, II, 359–69.

14. Gen. George C. Marshall, *Memoirs of My Service in the World War, 1917–1918*, ed. Brig. Gen. James L. Collins, Jr. (Boston: Houghton Mifflin Co., 1976), p. 179.

FURTHER READING

Although contemporary American scholarship on World War I and the American Expeditionary Forces is not voluminous, it includes some of the finest work in American military history. For short interpretations, see Edward M. Coffman, "The American Military and Strategic Policy in World War I," in Barry Hunt and Adrian Preston, eds., *War Aims and Strategic Policy in the Great War, 1914–1918* (Totowa, N.J.: Rowman and Littlefield, 1977); and Donald Smythe, "General of the Armies John J. Pershing," in Field Marshal Sir Michael Carver, ed., *The War Lords* (Boston: Little, Brown & Co., 1976). Edward M. Coffman, *The War to End All Wars: The American Military Experience in World War I* (New York: Oxford University Press, 1968), is an admirable popular history with a firm grasp of the military problems and personal experiences. For policy-making on the home front, see Daniel R. Beaver, *Newton D. Baker and the American War Effort, 1917–1919* (Lincoln: University of Nebraska Press, 1966); Robert D. Cuff, *The War Industries Board* (Baltimore: Johns Hopkins University Press, 1973); Edward M. Coffman, *The Hilt of the Sword: The Career of Peyton C. March* (Lexington: University of Kentucky Press, 1966); Bernard Baruch and the War Industries Board, *American Industry in the War* (New York: Prentice-Hall, 1941); and Marvin A. Kreidberg and Merton G. Henry, *History of Military Mobilization in the United States Army, 1775–1945* (Washington: Department of the Army, 1955), pp. 214–376. For a comprehensive account of the war's effect on American society, see David M. Kennedy, *Over Here: The First World War and American Society* (New York: Oxford University Press, 1980). To glimpse the AEF in the panorama of the entire American military experience, see Allan R. Millett and Peter Maslowski, *For the Common Defense: A Military History of the United States of America* (New York: Free Press, 1984).

A collective portrait of the American soldier and the Selective Service System that brought him into the army may be found in Fred D. Baldwin, "The American Enlisted Man in World War I" (Ph.D. dissertation, Princeton University, 1964), and John W. Chambers II, "Conscripting for Colossus: The Adoption of the Draft in the United States in World War I" (Ph.D. dissertation, Columbia University, 1973), summarized in "Conscripting for Colossus: The Progressive Era and the Origins of the Modern Military Draft in the United States in World War I," in Peter Karsten, ed., *The Military in America* (New York: Free Press, 1980), 275–96. The special experience of black troops is described in Arthur E. Barbeau and Florette Henri, *The Unknown Soldier: Black American Troops in World War I* (Philadelphia: Temple University Press, 1974).

For the organization and deployment of the American Expeditionary Forces in France, much of the most revealing literature remains the official and semiofficial writing and the document collections produced by the army itself. See especially *Final Report of Gen. John J. Pershing, Commander-in-Chief, American Expeditionary Forces* (Washington: Government Printing Office, 1920); U.S., Department of War, Army War College, Historical Section *The Genesis of the American First Army* (Washington: Government Printing Office, 1938); Leonard P. Ayres, *The War With Germany: A Statistical Summary* (Washington: Government Printing Office, 1919); U.S. Department of War, General Staff, War Plans Division, Historical Branch, *Organization of the Services of Supply,*

American Expeditionary Forces (Washington: Government Printing Office, 1921); U.S., American Battle Monuments Commission, *American Armies and Battlefields in Europe* (Washington: Government Printing Office, 1938); and U.S., Department of Defense, Department of the Army, Historical Division, *The United States Army in the World War, 1917–1919*, 17 vols. (Washington: Government Printing Office, 1948), an indispensable source of American, British, French, and German documents. Although commercially published, John J. Pershing, *My Experiences in the World War*, 2 vols. (New York: Frederick A. Stokes, 1931), is at least semiofficial since Pershing had access to classified documents, his own then-closed diaries and personal correspondence, and the staff studies of his own subordinates, who helped him with his research. The politics of command in the AEF are discussed in Edward M. Coffman, "The American Military Generation Gap in World War I: The Leavenworth Clique in the AEF," in Lt. Col. William Geffen, ed., *Command and Commanders in Modern Military History, Proceedings of the Second Military History Symposium, U.S. Air Force Academy* (Washington: Government Printing Office, 1969).

For general histories of the Allied campaign on the Western Front in 1918, see Barrie Pitt, *1918: The Last Act* (New York: Norton, 1962); John Toland, *No Man's Land* (Garden City, N.Y.: Doubleday, 1981).

Among other memoirs of AEF veterans, the most extensive and revealing accounts of the American strategic, organizational, and tactical problems are Hunter Liggett, *A.E.F. Ten Years Ago in France* (New York: Dodd, Mead, 1928); Robert L. Bullard, *Personalities and Reminiscences of the War* (Garden City, N.Y.: Doubleday, Page, 1925); James G. Harbord, *The American Army in France, 1917–1918* (Boston: Little, Brown & Co., 1936); and George C. Marshall, *Memoirs of My Services in the World War, 1917–1918* (Boston: Houghton Mifflin Co., 1976).

Among recent scholarly examinations of the AEF, see particularly David F. Trask, *The United States in the Supreme War Council* (Middletown, Conn.: Wesleyan University Press, 1961); volume II of Frank E. Vandiver, *Black Jack: The Life and Times of John J. Pershing*, 2 vols. (College Station: Texas A&M University Press, 1977); and Allan R. Millett, *The General: Robert L. Bullard and Officership in the United States Army, 1881–1925* (Westport, Conn.: Greenwood Press, 1975). For a professional, critical examination of American tactics, U.S., Department of War, Army Infantry School, *Infantry in Battle* (Washington: Infantry Journal Press, 1934), remains definitive. For a more personalized view of the war in France, see the contemporary writings and reminiscences of American soldiers in Frank Freidel, *Over There* (Boston: Little, Brown & Co., 1964), and Henry Berry, *Make the Kaiser Dance* (Garden City, N.Y.: Doubleday, 1978).

On the army's logistical problems, see especially Daniel R. Beaver, "The Problem of American Military Supply, 1890–1920," in Benjamin Franklin Cooling, ed., *War, Business, and American Society* (Port Washington, N.Y.: Kennikat Press, 1977), pp. 73–92; and Daniel R. Beaver, "George W. Goethals and the Problem of Military Supply," in Daniel R. Beaver, ed., *Some Pathways in Twentieth Century History* (Detroit, Mich.: Wayne State University Press, 1969), pp. 95–109.

The organization and operations of the AEF's Air Service may be found in three major works: I. B. Holley, Jr., *Ideas and Weapons: Exploitation of the Aerial Weapon by the United States During World War I* (Washington: Office of Air Force History, 1983); Maurer Maurer, ed., *The U.S. Air Service in World War I*, 4 vols. (Washington: Office of Air Force History, 1978); and James J. Hudson, *Hostile Skies: A Combat History of the American Air Service in World War I* (Syracuse, N.Y.: Syracuse University Press,

1968). See also William Mitchell, *Memoirs of World War I* (1960; reprint, Westport, Conn.: Greenwood Press, 1975).

For tactical analysis, see James W. Rainey, "Ambivalent Warfare: The Tactical Doctrine of the AEF in World War I," *Parameters* 13 (September 1983): 34–46, and Richard L. Pierce, "A Maximum of Support: The Development of U.S. Army Field Artillery Doctrine in World War I" (M.A. thesis, Ohio State University, 1983).

For further sources, consult Ronald Schaffer, comp., *The United States in World War I: A Selected Bibliography* (Santa Barbara, Calif.: ABC-Clio, 1978).

CHAPTER 13

The Interwar Army, 1919–1941

RUSSELL F. WEIGLEY

A column of horse cavalry clattering into an autumn dusk forms my earliest recollection of a mass of soldiers. The time was during the first beginnings of American mobilization in 1940. The mounts and the yellow piping of the uniforms bespoke a still older army than the riders' kettle-shaped helmets out of World War I. Together, the horses and helmets symbolized the central question of the army's history in the years between the world wars: which part of the army's past ought to shape it for the future—the long years of patrolling vast American distances against Indians and Mexican irregulars, or the brief moment of European intervention in 1917–1918?

Until 1940 the answer by no means seemed so obvious as hindsight now makes it. When General John J. Pershing came home from France, he warned against fixing his American Expeditionary Forces (AEF) tables of organization, or anything directly derived from them, upon the postwar army. "Our army is most likely to operate on the American Continent," he explained, "and mobility is especially necessary under all probable conditions of warfare in this theater." The bulky divisions of the AEF would surely have to go: "Our A.E.F. division (over 28,000 officers and men) was fairly suited to conditions in Europe but is entirely too unwieldy for war on this continent. . . . As a matter of fact, our division was so large that even during war of the character of that on the Western Front the division lacked mobility." For war in America, the most likely war of the future as Pershing saw it—some such small war as the Punitive Expedition that Pershing himself had led in 1916—the essential military requirement was not the massive power of the AEF but the mobility of the old Indian-fighting cavalry. "Maneuver," said Pershing, "is essential and vital for *all* units under all conditions, but more especially so on the American Continent. . . ."[1]

Yet the report of the AEF Superior Board on Organization and Tactics, which prompted Pershing's comments, assumed on the contrary that it was World War I that set the pattern for the most important future operations of the United States Army. The Superior Board consequently advocated retaining the four-regiment division and urged that it be reinforced with a large assortment of heavy supporting units in artillery and the division train. The relative immobility of the big square division, the board reasoned, accorded with certain intractable facts of modern war: that the division always attacks frontally, that it attacks in a severely constricted zone of action, and that accordingly it has little occasion for maneuver. The Superior Board insisted that with the First World War setting the pattern for the army's major future combats, the essential principle shaping the army ought to be power, not mobility.[2]

The implied strategic views of the Superior Board closely resembled those of General Tasker H. Bliss, former chief of staff and perhaps the best strategic thinker in the army at the time of the First World War. Despite that distinction, Bliss acquiesced in the reduction of strategy in modern war to the mechanical application of power:

War is, in a sense, a mechanical art. It is subject to the laws of mechanics which govern the application of power so as to perform the maximum of effective work in overcoming resistance at a given point in the shortest time with the minimum wear and tear on the machine. . . . In war the man who can accurately determine the point of hard resistance . . . and who can accurately function all parts of the machine to bring its maximum power to bear at this point, is the successful strategist. And strategy is the art of doing just that one thing.[3]

Pershing himself had favored a strategy of the frontal application of massed power in both his unrealized designs for an AEF drive against Metz and his actual offensive between the Meuse River and the Argonne Forest. The one other American war of mass armies, the Civil War, had similarly reached its military climax in the United States Army's destruction of the principal adversary army by means of a straightforward application of overwhelming power: U. S. Grant's campaign of 1864–1865 in which the Army of the Potomac and the Army of the James pounded to death the Army of Northern Virginia. Yet national policy after 1919—the rejection of the Treaty of Versailles and of American membership in the League of Nations and the revulsion against the American crusade on the Western Front—seemed to preclude repetition of military adventures on so vast a scale and, thus, to direct the American army back toward a career of small wars of maneuver, not large wars of massive application of power.

The legislative foundation of the post–World War I army paid some heed to its possible future involvement in either small wars or large wars but sought to ready the army mainly and immediately for the former, more traditional and more mobile style of combat. Shaped largely by Colonel John McAuley Palmer, a long-standing opponent of Emory Upton's plan for a skeletonized, expansible peacetime army, the National Defense Act of 4 June 1920 rejected the skeletonization of regular army divisions. It ensured that those divisions would instead be as ready as possible for prompt dispatch to scenes of trouble in the imperial possessions or in restless areas of the Western Hemisphere. Because the nine regular army infantry divisions were each to be stationed in a geographic corps area along with two National Guard and three Organized Reserve divisions and were to assist in the training of the citizen-soldier formations, the regular army divisions also vaguely served Palmer's ideas of a large, non-Uptonian citizen-army ready to spring forward in any new war of armed masses. But Palmer, strongly influenced by the Swiss model, expected the guard and reserve forces to be trained increasingly and as much as possible by their own citizen-soldier officers, not by regulars. The primary mission, and the only clearly foreseeable mission, of the regular army was readiness for small wars.[4]

Parsimonious Congresses and chief executives in the 1920s and 1930s prevented the design of the National Defense Act from attaining fruition. The statute authorized a regular army of 280,000 officers and men. Congressional appropriations failed to maintain any such level. The actual strength of the army was by 1922, 147,335; by 1932, 134,024. By 1939 there had been a gradual increase to 188,565. As a result of fiscal trimming, regular army formations became largely skeletonized after all. Yet the few formations that were kept at an approximation of full strength and readiness remained those most likely to be involved in small wars reminiscent of the old Indian campaigns—particularly the troops along the Mexican border. At the end of the 1930s, the First Cavalry and Second Infantry Divisions in the VIII Corps Area headquartered at Fort Sam Houston, Texas, remained the only nonskeletonized divisions, their horsemen and doughboys patrolling along the Rio Grande.[5]

The most vigorous army chief of staff in the years following World War I, the youthful and charismatic General Douglas MacArthur, reinforced this emphasis on a mobile army preparing for small colonial and border wars. When he began his tour as chief of staff in 1930, MacArthur found that despite the absence of prospects for another war of mass armies, his planners were busily at work on mobilization schedules for the mustering in of citizen-soldiers to wage a hypothetical grand-scale war. He turned the mobilization planners instead to designing an Immediate Readiness Force, to be drawn from the regular army for dispatch to colonial or Western Hemisphere trouble zones. "The War Plans Division," said the chief of the division on cue from MacArthur, "believes the immediate readiness force and the reinforcement of overseas possessions will be normal and the possibility of an orderly mobilization of Regular and National Guard units . . . exceptional."[6]

The concept of a light, fast-moving army tailored to wage war not against European mass armies but against elusive, highly mobile opponents emerged also, with a particularly conspicuous effect upon the subsequent combat capacities of the army in World War II, in the restriction of the weight of American tanks to 15 tons. Any heavier tank would have exceeded the limit of 15 tons placed by the War Department on the standard medium pontoon bridge, as well as the weight limits of most American highway bridges of the 1920s; a weight of anything over 25 tons would have exceeded the capacity even of Corps of Engineers emergency bridges. Thus, when World War II came, the United States had to develop in haste the 37.1-ton Sherman tank to compete with the 25-ton German Mark IV, but never to match the 45.5-ton Mark V Panther.

But more pertinent and fundamental than bridge capacity in shaping American tanks and their limitations were the basic principles set forth by the General Staff in 1922 in response to a request from the Ordnance Department for a policy statement on tanks. "In the development of the medium tank," said the General Staff, "consideration should be given to the essentials necessary to make it a fighting machine. Its speed should be the greatest possible consistent with the limitation in weight, economy in fuel, and radius of action." The concept of speed as the first requisite of a useful tank goes far to explain the army's lengthy preoccupation with the tank design of Walter Christie, featuring speeds as high as 42.55 miles an hour on tracks in the Model 1940 of 1929 and, with the tracks removed, capable of attaining speeds of almost 70 miles an hour on solid-rubber-tired bogie wheels. Armament and armor received considerably less attention and emphasis.[7]

MacArthur as chief of staff continued to seek an army that would be light and fast moving. For the sake of speed, MacArthur argued, even tanks designed for use with slow-moving infantry ought to have armor sufficient only to protect against small arms. More armor than that "would completely immobilize any machine of usable size. For protection of this kind [against field guns] the tank must rely upon rapid movement, surprise, proper use of ground, and the supporting guns of its own army." If speed was to be the hallmark of the infantry tank, still more was it appropriate that "cavalry interest in mechanization has therefore been centered principally in armored cars and cross-country vehicles possessing a high degree of strategic mobility, with fighting power and tactical mobility an important though secondary consideration."[8]

MacArthur's thinking not only limited the size of tanks, but also did much to kill one of the army's few promising ventures toward preparing for a possible return from small-scale colonial wars to European war. The choice of the small-wars army, akin to the American army of the Indian-fighting past, as the basis upon which to build the post–1919 force was a choice for mobility rather than power as the central principle of the army. Late in the First World War, however, there had emerged a new potential for combining mobility and power, for designing military formations that would emphasize neither principle to the debilitation of the other, but would harmonize both. As Colonel Samuel D. Rockenbach, formerly commander of the AEF Tank Corps, wrote in the *Infantry Journal* in 1921: "The tank was built to restore the balance between power and mobility that is essential to victory in war."[9]

The United States, the birthplace of the automobile revolution—and of track-laying vehicles, whose basic design feature was borrowed by Europeans from American farm equipment to create the tank—enjoyed advantages that might have been expected to place its army in the forefront of mechanized, armored warfare. The same Rockenbach had boasted, not without reason, to the General Staff College in 1919:

All that is claimed for the Tank Corps is that it is not fettered by English ideas in operation which are applicable only by the English or by their clumsiness in design; nor by French low mechanized knowledge which makes the self-starter too complicated and unreliable to be employed; nor by our own abnormal use of Tanks [in excessively restricted roles] with the First American Army. It has resisted entangling alliances and to date is not Infantry, Artillery, Motor Transport, Engineers or even Aviation, notwithstanding its great value to each of these services, causing deep thought as to which of them it should be.[10]

But American thought about employing tanks in an armored force separate from all the older, conventional branches of the service proved not at all so deep as Rockenbach apparently anticipated. The army's focus on wars of small expeditionary forces and the absence of any American memories of casualties on the Western Front comparable to the losses of the French, Germans, and British combined to deny the American army the Europeans' strong motivation to contemplate armored and mechanized forces as a means to escape repetition of the bloody deadlock in the trenches. Leadership in developing a theory of armored war passed to the British during the 1920s, especially to J.F.C. Fuller and B. H. Liddell Hart, and later to the Germans, with Heinz Guderian, and to a lesser extent to the French, with Charles de Gaulle.

As American theory stagnated, so did American development of the actual machines for armored war. Though it built experimental prototypes of designs drawn by Christie and others, until the close of the 1930s the army confined the tanks it placed in service with the troops to adaptations of the French and British designs of the First World War. The army had 23,405 tanks on order when the war ended in 1918. It carried 1,115 into the postwar years. These included 15 three-ton Ford "baby" tanks, 1,000 six-ton light tanks modeled on the French Renault FT, and 100 heavy tanks modeled on the British Mark VIII. At maneuvers at Pine Camp, New York, in August 1935, the army employed about one-third of its entire force of serviceable modern tanks; that is, two tanks were present, one of which broke down behind "enemy" lines, while the other immobilized itself on a stump. The scale of replacement after the mid–1930s is indicated by the production of 19 light tanks in 1936, 154 in 1937, and 74 in 1938; by March 1940, 18 M–1s of the new medium type had been manufactured and put into service, whereupon this model was declared obsolete.[11]

For a brief moment in the 1920s, American armored development had seemed about to be rescued from such stagnation. In 1927 Secretary of War Dwight F. Davis witnessed a demonstration at Aldershot of the British Experimental Mechanised Force, based partially on Fuller's ideas. American tank development lagged not least because design standardization awaited a doctrine for the employment of tanks; yet without tactical exercises to determine what it was that tanks could accomplish, there could be no agreement on doctrine. The army chief of staff under Davis, Major General Charles P. Summerall, already impatient because accomplishments were so slight, readily complied with Davis's request for emulation of the British mechanized experiment. "Organize a Mechanized Force," Summerall tersely directed his chief of operations, the War Department G–3.[12]

It was relatively rare for an artillerist with a gunner's appreciation of firepower to reach the summit of the American army. Summerall was such a rarity. He first made his mark in World War I during the summer of 1917 as a member of Colonel Chauncey B. Baker's board to study AEF organization and requirements, where he insisted that to break the deadlock of the Western Front guns would be needed in much greater quantities than Pershing's staff anticipated. Summerall did not get the quantities he wanted, but as commander of the First Field Artillery Brigade in the First Division, he orchestrated his weapons with such superb effect that in July 1918 he was elevated to command the division. Soon he headed a corps. Consistently an advocate of overwhelming power, particularly firepower, as the key to winning battles, Summerall also respected the American army's historic emphasis on mobility. His steady appreciation for both was another rarity. "The basic theme of the study," he said of the Experimental Mechanized Force, "is the question of how mobility with high striking power can be realized on the battlefield. . . . Movement is necessary to bring closer and more effective fire against the enemy; fire superiority minimizes hostile movement and neutralizes hostile fire."[13]

Summerall's Mechanized Force remained an experiment; throughout his term of office, he remained unsure how the problems of balancing mobility and firepower would eventually be resolved. "We are perhaps in a transitional period," he said, "the precise outcome of which no one can foresee." Yet of one point Summerall was sure: "Any great nation which fails to provide for the utilization of mechanization to the utmost practicable degree must suffer the consequences of neglect in future war."[14]

Then came MacArthur. Summerall's order to the War Department G–3 had brought together at Camp Meade, Maryland, in the summer of 1928 the Sixteenth and Seventeenth Tank Battalions; the Second Platoon, Fourth Tank Company; the army's only armored cavalry troop; a battalion of infantry; an artillery battalion; a company of engineers; a signal company; a medical detachment; an ammunition train; and a squadron of observation planes. The G–3 of this Experimental Mechanized Force, Major Adna Romanza Chaffee, Jr., reported on the force as a prototype of a new arm that was neither infantry nor cavalry but a blending of the power of infantry with the mobility of cavalry. A second Experimental Mechanized Force exercised at Fort Eustis, Virginia, in 1930. But MacArthur, succeeding Summerall as chief of staff late that year, broke up the experiment and rejected Summerall's and Chaffee's underlying ideas. Power and mobility became separated again.

The new chief of staff rejected the theory "that a separate mechanized force should be so organized as to contain within itself the power of carrying on a complete action, from first contact to final victory," because such an organization duplicated "the missions and to some extent the equipment of all other arms."

Therefore, MacArthur favored the alternative theory "that each of the older arms should utilize any types of these vehicles as will enable it better and more surely to carry out the particular combat tasks it has been traditionally assigned. . . . " Having dispersed the units at Fort Eustis, he ordered the cavalry to develop "combat vehicles that will enhance its roles of reconnaissance, counter-reconnaissance, flank action, pursuit and similar operations. One of its regiments will be equipped exclusively with such vehicles." He similarly ordered the infantry to "give attention to machines intended to increase the striking power of the infantry against strongly held positions.[15]

MacArthur's disposition of the Experimental Mechanized Force had at least the legalistic virtue of according with provisions of the National Defense Act of 1920 that had awarded the infantry exclusive control of tanks. The light tanks now restored to the cavalry for cavalry functions had to be disguised as "combat cars." The terminological restrictions mirrored the powerful influence that the National Defense Act granted the four traditional combat arms: infantry, cavalry, coast artillery, and field artillery. Each of these arms now had its own administrative headquarters in the War Department on a level with such historically potent and often almost autonomous staff bureaus as the Corps of Engineers and the Quartermaster Corps. Each of the combat arms' headquarters was to develop its own tactical doctrine. The National Defense Act nevertheless had heeded the experience of the First World War enough to create administrative headquarters in the War Department for three additional arms and services: the Air Service, the Chemical Warfare Service, and the Finance Department. Surely this divorcement of the Air Service from the traditional arms goes far to explain why the airplane advanced much further toward army recognition of its special potentialities and requirements than did the tank.[16]

Brigadier General William Mitchell and his most vociferous champions might have scoffed at this last assertion about the progress of army aviation. Indeed, it was Billy Mitchell's stated opinion that the army neglected air power to the point of revealing "the incompetency, criminal negligence, and almost treasonable administration of the National Defense by the Navy and War Departments."[17] But Mitchell was a prophetic zealot for whom anything less than perfect acceptance of his evangelical message was equivalent to complete rejection. Mitchell was personally frustrated, too, by his slide downward from wartime command of the American First Army Air Service to air officer at Fort Sam Houston by the mid–1920s. Mitchell's disgruntlement notwithstanding, the fact of the matter was that the romantic appeal of flight for its own sake, in combination with the appeal of military flight as a possible alternative to grubby infantry battles, sufficed to win military aviation a remarkably ample share of the meager army budgets of the 1920s and 1930s as well as to carry the organization of military aviation far along the road toward the independent air arm, emulating the Royal Air Force, for which Mitchell and his colleagues strove.

Mitchell's own court-martial in 1925 contributed to these results. He successfully turned the trial into a forum in behalf of air power as the primary instrument for winning wars. Mitchell was less successful in rescuing his own career, however. His zeal apparently blinded him to the near inevitability of a court-martial conviction for "disorders and neglects to the prejudice of good order and military discipline." Appalled by the sentence suspending him from rank, command, and duty, he resigned from the service. Nevertheless, amid the furor stirred up by the Mitchell trial, President Calvin Coolidge appointed Dwight W. Morrow to chair a board to investigate the issues of air power, while later in 1926 Congress transformed the Air Service into the somewhat more autonomous Army Air Corps and created the post of assistant secretary of war for air. Though the latter position fell before an economy axe in 1933, in that year another board investigating air power, chaired by Major General Hugh A. Drum, recommended that air units in the field be detached from the command of the regional corps areas and united under a General Headquarters (GHQ), Air Force, responsible directly to the General Staff. Endorsed by still another board under former Secretary of War Newton D. Baker, GHQ Air Force was created in 1935.

This headquarters concentrated its efforts on fostering the case for an altogether independent air force by advancing the idea that air power could be an independent weapon able to win wars on its own. To that end, the Air Corps also fostered the development of a four-engined bomber for "strategic" attacks on the "vital centers" of the enemy's economy well behind his military front lines, as advocated both by Billy Mitchell and by the Italian prophet who became the aviation strategy equivalent of Alfred Thayer Mahan, Giulio Douhet. At the same time Air Corps planners improved on Mitchell and Douhet by undertaking careful studies of the kinds of targets that, if destroyed by bombing, might paralyze an enemy's whole economy. As the four-engined bomber program produced the prototype Boeing B–17 in 1934 and the Air Corps planners moved toward their basic war plan, AWPD–1, of 1941, the Army Air Corps, though lacking the organizational independence of the Royal Air Force or even of the German Luftwaffe, nevertheless became in practice the best prepared of all the world's air forces for the independent application of air power through strategic bombing.[18]

It was the freeing of the Air Service from the doctrinal control of the traditional arms as early as the National Defense Act of 1920 and the growing autonomy of the air arm as the 1920s and 1930s rolled on that permitted aviation to concentrate not only on an independent role in war but also on a major war as the war for which to plan. If aviation had remained tied more closely in organization to the traditional arms, it likely would have been tied also to their persistent, lingering focus on small wars as the most likely wars of the future.

After all, through most of the 1920s and even more in the 1930s, the only war against a major power that the United States seemed likely to wage in the foreseeable future was a war that held out few charms for the army and little inducement for the ground arms to depart from their pre–1917 habits of thought or even to develop seriously the Experimental Mechanized Force. The only war they might have to fight against a major power, military leaders generally agreed, was a war against Japan. But a Japanese war would be preeminently the navy's war.

Referring to the color-coded war plans for a contest with Japan, a naval officer remarked to an Army War College audience in 1924: "An Orange War is considered the most probable. It is by far the most difficult for the Navy. It will require the greatest maritime war effort yet made by any nation."[19] The assessment was accurate. For this war the army members of the Joint Army and Navy Board cooperated in drawing up the various versions of Joint War Plan ORANGE, and the army planners in Washington and in the Pacific Ocean outposts contributed to the detailed army elaborations of the basic plan. Yet the more the planners labored, the more inglorious for the army the coming Great Pacific Ocean War had to appear. The war would begin for the army with one of the service's most costly and humiliating defeats, the sacrifice of the Philippine Islands and their garrison, with almost every officer experiencing the loss of friends and comrades to death or Japanese prison camps, and possibly becoming one of the victims himself. The more glorious side of the ORANGE war, the fight back westward across the Pacific through the mandated islands to the home islands of Japan, would be mainly the job of the navy and the marines, not the army.

In the early planning there was a minor share of glory for the army. As late as the 1924 ORANGE plan, the Philippine garrison was envisaged as defending Manila Bay until the navy could fight its way there with reinforcements and then base itself upon the Philippines for the final campaigns of the war. Already in 1924, however, there was more self-delusion than realism about the idea of clinging to Manila Bay until the battle fleet arrived in strength from Pearl Harbor. The army defenders of the Philippines would number only 15,000. The conception of the regular army as in large part a ready expeditionary force permitted the planners to contemplate an early reinforcement of 50,000—but how the 50,000 were to arrive through the Japanese navy and how the limited base facilities of the Philippines, restricted by the 1922 Washington Naval Treaty, were to sustain an eventual major naval offensive against Japan were matters left disturbingly unclear. The 1928 version of the ORANGE plan had the Japanese dispatching 100,000 men to the Philippines within fifteen days of the beginning of the war, 300,000 men within thirty days. In 1933 Brigadier General Stanley D. Embick, commander on Corregidor Island at the mouth of Manila Bay, estimated that his fortress garrison might conceivably hold out for a year against the Japanese, but he said that this would not be long enough and drew the only realistic conclusion: "To carry out the present Orange plan—with its provisions for the early dispatch of our fleet to Philippine waters—would be literally an act of madness."[20]

Then and two years later, when he had become chief of the War Plans Division of the General Staff, Embick drew the corollary conclusion that the United States should roll back its strategic frontier in the Pacific to places it could defend: Alaska, Hawaii, and Panama. Yet policy considerations prevented the army's applying to the Philippines the sort of realism that removed the army garrison from around the American settlement at Tientsin and elsewhere in China in 1938. The navy rejected Embick's strategic argument, and later versions of the OR-ANGE plan continued at the least to fudge the issue of the impossibility of an effective army defense of Manila Bay until reinforcements arrived. The diffi-culties of applying realism to the Philippines multiplied after 1935, when General MacArthur, upon stepping down as chief of staff and retiring from the United States Army, became a field marshal of the Philippine Commonwealth and returned to build a Commonwealth defense force in the archipelago so closely associated with his own and his father's careers.

MacArthur attempted to create a people's army on the Swiss model in a setting where the cultural and political prerequisites of the Swiss citizen-soldiery were scarcely to be found. The Philippine language problem alone dwarfed Switz-erland's and put thousands of recruits into companies whose officers' dialects were unintelligible to many of the men. In 1941 the army commander of the Philippine Department, Major General George Grunert, was warning as he had done consistently that, MacArthur's claims to the contrary notwithstanding, the field marshal's Philippine defense force was not a weapon on which to rely; but political considerations in the same year again overrode sound strategy to send Grunert home and restore MacArthur to active duty as commanding general, United States Army Forces in the Far East. MacArthur's illusions returned to active duty with him.[21]

By that time the illusions were all the more troublesome, in part because the long-expected war against Japan at last appeared imminent, but even more be-cause events not clearly foreseeable during most of the 1920s and 1930s had brought to the near horizon the storm clouds of another war with Germany. Through most of the years since the armistice, American foreign policy had seemed to rule out a second American campaign in Europe in the manner of 1918. But at the end of the 1930s, the eruption of a new German menace to American security, driven by leaders vastly more sinister than the darkest figures of the kaiser's regime, with relative abruptness recalled the army from planning for small wars and an unappealing naval war in the Pacific to the likelihood of another great campaign in Europe.

The prospect of another European war not only offered the army immensely more scope for proving its worth than did a Pacific Ocean war; it also posed a geographically nearer and militarily far more potent danger to the United States. To most army leaders the Philippines now seemed more than ever an irritating distraction. Though by long-standing tradition even the chief of staff of the army spoke with most muted tongue to civil leaders on issues touching civil policy, most such army leaders as had access to national policymaking at the beginning of the 1940s, and particularly the new chief of staff, General George C. Marshall, Jr., urged restrained and nonprovocative conduct toward the Japanese in order to free the nation's military resources for the greater challenge of Adolf Hitler's Germany.[22]

The potential menace of a militarized Hitlerian Germany had not been appreciated even for a number of years after Hitler grasped power in Berlin in 1933, and it was not until the fall of France in 1940 that American civil policymakers granted the army a renewed and unmistakable warrant to plan and prepare for another mass war in Europe. Yet since the homecoming of 1919 and the first debates inside the army over postarmistice military policy, the possibility of another European war could never entirely be discarded in the return to the lineaments of the traditional small-wars American army. While the army's campaigns had been, except for the Civil War, overwhelmingly a history of small wars, still the education of the officer corps, from Sylvanus Thayer's rehabilitation of West Point in the early nineteenth century onward, had helped direct attention toward European armies and sought to create a military professionalism derived from Europe. Intellectually, the American army's professional school system had always nourished a European orientation in somewhat uneasy tandem with the army's Indian-fighting experience. The post–1918 years had never completely extinguished the sense, awakened in 1917, that the prolonged education of the officer corps in European-style war somehow implied a military destiny awaiting the American army in Europe.

In particular during the 1920s and 1930s, industrial mobilization planning had anticipated an eventual return to mass war in Europe. The legislative foundation of the postarmistice army, the National Defense Act of 1920, had provided for this kind of hedge against a second European campaign amidst its redirection of the army toward colonial and American continental problems. In recollection of the disappointing contribution American industry had made toward supplying munitions of war in 1917–1918, the National Defense Act included the first permanent assignment of responsibility for planning for future industrial mobilization—an idea that made sense principally in the perspective of a possible renewal of large-scale war in a European setting. The act created the post of assistant secretary of war, charging the incumbent to make "adequate preparation for the mobilization of material and industrial organizations essential to wartime needs."[23]

In 1921 a board headed by Major General James G. Harbord, former chief of the AEF Services of Supply (SOS), sought to define a system of cooperation that would govern relations between the office of the assistant secretary of war and the General Staff, whose own planning functions had been reinforced when the National Defense Act granted it a reasonable complement of ninety-three officers not below the rank of captain. The Harbord report recommended that the General Staff prepare estimates of materiel requirements and the assistant secretary of war plan and accomplish their procurement. More broadly, the General Staff was to plan for the military aspects of mobilization, while the assistant secretary would plan for the business and industrial aspects of war. In 1922, furthermore, the War and Navy Departments together created the Army and Navy Munition Board for joint industrial mobilization planning.[24]

The army took much more interest in this kind of activity than the navy. The navy had to rely substantially on a fleet in being for peace or war; it did not anticipate nearly so large a wartime expansion of its materiel as the army. The navy could focus on strategic planning for an identifiable major enemy, Japan; the army, lacking so identifiable a potential major adversary, could not so satisfactorily join in strategic planning. To the extent that the army prepared for a major war, it could better do so through planning for mobilization, without identifying the enemy. The General Staff prepared a series of mobilization plans, chiefly those of 1923, 1924, 1928, 1930, 1933, and 1936. The Selective Service Act of 1917 had pointed the way toward solving wartime manpower problems; though the planners of the interwar period dealt at length with mobilizing men, the most difficult mobilization issues facing them were economic and industrial.

The assistant secretary of war meanwhile established his own office's Planning Branch to cooperate with the special staff supply departments in more detailed industrial mobilization planning. The Planning Branch's immediate practice of requiring all officers assigned to it to read the records of the mobilization agencies of the First World War helped lead to a formalization of education for industrial mobilization. On the recommendation of Assistant Secretary Dwight F. Davis, Secretary of War John W. Weeks established in 1923 the Army Industrial College, forerunner of the present Industrial College of the Armed Forces.[25]

By the early 1930s, the growing popular legend that malevolent "merchants of death" had led the country by the nose into World War I worked an unanticipated benefit for mobilization planning. During the Herbert Hoover administration, Congress created a War Policies Commission to study whether the Constitution should be amended to permit drastic controls over private profit making in wartime. The commission studied the current War Department Industrial Mobilization Plan and asked for recommendations on the subject from the Wall Street financier Bernard Baruch, thus giving the War Department the assistance of a high-level civilian review. The Senate's Nye committee similarly reviewed the 1933 revision of the Industrial Mobilization Plan, and the plan fairly well satisfied that extremely critical group. As the European war clouds gathered later in the decade, President Franklin D. Roosevelt proved a more severe critic, because he perceived in the Industrial Mobilization Plan grants of excessive economic power to both soldiers and private businessmen, a shift in economic gravity that might unbalance the New Deal. Roosevelt's initial inclination, therefore, was to use the War Department plans as little as possible. But in time several false starts toward economic mobilization for World War II were to compel the administration to return to many of the details of the prewar plans for acquisition of raw materials, allocation of productive capacity, and administration of a wartime economy, thus vindicating much of the War Department and army planning effort.

The central theme of the Industrial Mobilization Plans was a mass application of the American economy to war, avoiding the mistakes, and thus the disappointments, of 1917–1918 munitions production and permitting American productivity to overwhelm the enemy in a new mass war. This theme had little to do with the existing realities of the army of the 1920s and 1930s, but it fitted well into still larger themes of American military history.[26]

A mass war on the scale of 1917–1918, for example, is fought most appropriately, and military victory is won most swiftly and expeditiously, by overwhelming the adversary under a superior weight of men and resources. The American army's experience with large-scale war had been brief in proportion to its long years as an Indian-fighting constabulary, but from the American Civil War the army had drawn this conclusion, and the First World War had seemed to confirm it.

World War I gave no promise that victory in modern war could grow from anything but the application of superior resources, not in dazzling maneuver or in indirect approaches, but in hard fighting. In the army's professional school system—where European wars and armies had always taken precedence over immediate chores and foes—the war was fought and refought again and again after 1918 in lectures and student papers, and the emphasis always was on the intractability of modern strategic problems to any solution save that of overwhelming power. The four-year deadlock on the Western Front, which some critics interpreted as testimony to strategic bankruptcy, was most often seen in the American army not as a product of faulty generalship but as virtually implicit in the size and resiliency of modern armies and the economic resources behind them. With armies so huge and battle lines so long that flanks disappear, wars cannot be won by turning flanks and by maneuver. Victory depends on superior resources.

"If both [rival] initial plans fail in their object" of attaining prompt victory at the outset of war, said General Bliss, then "these huge masses [of modern armies] cannot be readily manoeuvered into new strategic combinations. The tendency then is for the two sides to take offensive-defensive positions which from the magnitude of the forces engaged, may extend across the entire theatre of war." The virtually inevitable outcome, as had proved to be the case in 1914, was that "thus the remaining struggle for four years became rather a test of the courage and endurance of the soldier and of the suffering civil population behind the lines than of the strategical skill of the general."[27]

Reasoning as General Bliss did, Colonel W. K. Naylor drew further conclusions for the students of the Army War College in 1922: "I wish to stress this point: that warfare means fighting and that war is never won by maneuvering; not unless the maneuvering is carried out with the idea of culminating in battle."[28] The purpose of battle is to pursue the true objective of war, which had been demonstrated by Grant in the Civil War to be the destruction of the enemy armed forces; as an Army War College committee studying the Civil War put it in 1927: "Prior to 1864, however, the end sought was the securing of vital areas rather than the defeat of the Southern armies and it was only after Grant was placed in high command that the *true strategic objective* was sought, that is, the 'enemies [sic] armies wherever found.' "[29]

In a modern battle where armies without exposed flanks fought to destroy each other, sound generalship sought not subtle maneuver but Grant's prescription: "We had to have hard fighting to achieve this."[30] Hard fighting was the means to the assertion of superior power. Colonel Oliver Prescott Robinson summed up much of the current thinking in a publication of the Infantry Association in 1928:

The objective for military forces is the defeat or destruction of the hostile main forces, and all the operations of war are indirectly, or directly, directed to that end.

. . . .

So let it be understood that, when war comes, there should be only one question that will ever be asked of a commander as to a battle, and that one is, not what flank did he attack, not how did he use his reserves, not how did he protect his flanks, but did he fight?[31]

The basic field manual, FM 100–5, gave the army's authoritative endorsement to this line of military thought, emphasizing the application of superior power in battle as the means to win wars. "The *ultimate objective* of all military operations is the destruction of the enemy's armed forces in battle. Decisive defeat breaks the enemy's will to war and forces him to sue for peace which is the national aim," stated Paragraph 91 of FM 100–5, *Field Service Regulations (Tentative), Operations* (Washington: War Department, 1939), just as the enemy's identity and the general shape of a new mass war were emerging at last. Commenting on this passage in *Military Review*, Captain Reuben E. Jenkins (destined to become chief operations officer of the Sixth Army Group in World War II) interpreted it in light of the army's usual conclusions about the significance of both the American Civil War and the First World War for strategy and tactics: "It should be remembered that the price of victory is hard fighting," said Jenkins in a direct echo of U. S. Grant, "and that no matter what maneuver is employed, ultimately the fighting is frontal. . . . And finally, although 'An objective may sometimes be attained through maneuver alone; ordinarily, it must be attained through battle' (Par 413 [of FM 100–5]). Blood is the price of victory. We must accept that formula or not wage war."[32]

Thus, a paradox underlay the history of the United States Army during the two decades when it recalled one world war and approached another. The debate about the shape of the army of the future immediately following the First World War pointed to a tension that was to strain the army throughout the interwar years, though never so much as at the close of the 1930s and the beginning of the 1940s, as the service began to prepare for the Second World War. The American army of the 1920s and 1930s was an army designed and deployed primarily to fight small wars. Psychologically as well as organizationally, it was an extension of the Indian-fighting constabulary that the army had been through the great bulk of its history, with the momentous but brief exceptions of 1861–1865 and 1917–1918. In its strategic conceptions, on the other hand, the army believed that victory in a major war must be achieved through the application of superior, overwhelming power against the enemy in battle. The strategic conceptions of the army were nurtured in particular by its professional school system, which had always looked to European military experience for guidance, even while the Indian wars lasted. These strategic conceptions demanded an army whose essence was power. But the Indian-fighting inheritance and an organization and deployment for small wars had created an army whose essence was not power but mobility.

When civil policy changed and another mass ground war against Germany began to appear imminent, the paradox and the tension persisted. The United States Army continued to shape itself for mobility. Its infantry divisions became the most mobile of their kind in the world. All their elements except their rifle companies were mechanized; the later addition of a few quartermaster truck companies would mechanize the riflemen as well. After the dissolution of the Experimental Mechanized Force, the most fertile doctrinal development for an American armored force came out of the cavalry tradition, especially out of the continued work of Adna R. Chaffee, Jr., the executive officer and then commanding officer of the Seventh Cavalry Brigade (Mechanized), the nearest approximation of a prototypical armored division in the army through most of the 1930s. As a result, the cavalry tradition and its emphasis on speed as well as endurance in movement shaped the American armored force that began to form after the German blitzkriegs in Poland and France. The preference for mobility rather than power appeared most dramatically in American tanks—the prominence of the M–3 General Stuart light tank as the only satisfactory American tank early in World War II, the inferiority of the M–4 Sherman medium tank to its principal German rivals in armament and armor throughout the war, the persistent unwillingness to build an American heavy tank. This same preference, moreover, went on to permeate every aspect of American armored organization and equipment. Nevertheless, American strategy for World War II, drawing on the different tradition of U. S. Grant and the army's professional schools, sought the defeat of Germany through the application of overwhelming American power in a massive offensive across the English Channel.

It was fortunate both for the American armed forces and for America's allies that the industrial mobilization planning of the War Department and the army had laid part of the foundation for a marshaling of unprecedented quantities of munitions of war. More than anything else, the success of the American power-drive strategy would hinge on sheer quantity. Vast numbers of American tanks would in the end compensate for deficiencies in armament and armor. An overwhelming abundance of military equipment of all kinds ultimately would enable an American army designed for rapid and sustained mobility to exert instead the sustained combat power that would be demanded by such logical outcomes of American strategy as the battles in the Normandy bocage and along Germany's West Wall.

These battles of World War II were to be not so much unlike the battles of the Western Front of the earlier European struggle after all, and they involved again the issues debated by the AEF Superior Board and General Pershing, with which this chapter opened. Pershing's recommendations of 1920 notwithstanding, it was not until late 1939 that the army actually got around to reorganizing its divisional structure from the four-regiment "square" division to the lighter three-regiment "triangular" division. In the interval, too few divisions had actually existed to give divisional tables of organization much meaning in reality. The purpose of the shift was to bring the infantry division into line with the army's general emphasis on mobility over power.

On the eve of the proposed shift in divisional structure from square to triangular, the First Army, under General Hugh A. Drum, conducted the most ambitious effort toward large-scale maneuvers seen in the army since the First World War. The effort culminated in an engagement between an army and a small corps on 23–25 August 1939. The BLACK army, a hypothetical invading force, had as much combat power as the troops could actually bring to bear within the assumptions of the exercise. The defending BLUE corps was much smaller than the army but featured mobility, including a mechanized cavalry brigade in addition to an infantry division and a separate infantry brigade. General Drum, admittedly a military conservative and very much a man of the old AEF— he had been chief of staff of the First Army in France—concluded from the maneuvers that the value of mobility could readily be overrated, and that while highly mobile mechanized forces ought to be created, the bulk of the army should be designed to exert sustained combat power.[33]

Drum's recommendation that the triangular division be rejected and the square division retained no doubt failed to take into account adequately the revolution in mobility that the German panzer divisions were preparing to unloose upon Poland and France. His criticism of the army for insufficiently appreciating the merits of sustained combat power nevertheless pointed toward flaws that in prolonged battle would become apparent in triangular infantry divisions and in American armored divisions as well. Drum's dissent from reorganization plans indicated that on the eve of World War II the tensions between mobility and power—in a historic sense, between the army's Indian-fighting past and its world-power future—had not been resolved. It was fortunate that behind the United States Army, already partially prepared for wartime mobilization by the army's planning during the interwar years, lay so vast a national reservoir of sheer material strength.

NOTES

1. Gen. John J. Pershing, Forwarding Report of AEF Superior Board on Organization and Tactics to the Secretary of War, 16 June 1920, pp. 1 (first two quotations), 7 (final quotation), Records of the American Expeditionary Forces, 1917–23, Record Group 120, National Archives, Washington, D.C.

2. Report of the Superior Board on Organization and Tactics (Maj. Gen. Joseph T. Dickman, Maj. Gen. John L. Hines, Maj. Gen. William Lassiter, Maj. Gen. Hugh A.

Drum, Maj. Gen. W. B. Burtt, Col. George R. Spaulding, Col. Parker Hitt), especially pp. 1–3, 18, 21, Pershing Papers, Record Group 200, National Archives, Washington, D.C.

3. Tasker H. Bliss, draft of article, January 1923 (?), p. 1, Box 274, Tasker H. Bliss Papers, Library of Congress, Washington, D.C.

4. *Statutes at Large*, XLI, 759–812; U.S., Congress, Senate, Committee on Military Affairs, *Reorganization of the Army: Hearings on S.2715*, 65th Cong., 1st sess., 1917; U.S., Congress, House, Committee on Military Affairs, *The National Defense: Historical Documents Relating to the Reorganization Plans of the War Department and to the Present National Defense Act*, 69th Cong., 2d sess., 1927; John McAuley Palmer, *America in Arms: The Experience of the United States with Military Organization* (New Haven: Yale University Press, 1941), pp. 101–103, 136–47, 168–70; James W. Wadsworth, introduction to John McAuley Palmer, *Statesmanship or War* (Garden City, N.Y.: Doubleday, 1927), pp. ix–xv.

5. Marvin A. Kreidberg and Merton G. Henry, *History of Military Mobilization in the United States Army* (Washington: Department of the Army, 1955), p. 379. On army deployment in the late 1930s, see Jim Dan Hill, *The Minute Man in Peace and War: A History of the National Guard* (Harrisburg, Pa.: Stackpole, 1964), pp. 358–59.

6. Kreidberg and Henry, *History of Military Mobilization*, p. 434, quoting Memo, WPD [War Plans Division] for DCofS [Deputy Chief of Staff Maj. Gen. Hugh A. Drum], 11 May 1933, subject: Fourth Army Organization, WPD 3561–16, DRB [Departmental Records Branch], TAG [The Adjutant General's Office]. For a general discussion of MacArthur's views on readiness, see ibid., pp. 424–34. On MacArthur as chief of staff, see D. Clayton James, *The Years of MacArthur*, 3 vols. (Boston: Houghton Mifflin Co., 1970–1985), vol. I, *1880–1941*, pp. 351–470.

7. Constance McLaughlin Green, Harry C. Thomson, and Peter C. Roots, *The Ordnance Department: Planning Munitions for War*, United States Army in World War II: The Technical Services (Washington: Office of the Chief of Military History, Department of the Army, 1955), pp. 190 (for quotation citing OCM [Ordnance Committee Minutes] 7814, 22 August 1929, pp. 9093–9096), 195–203.

8. Report of the Chief of Staff, in U.S., Department of War, *Report of the Secretary of War to the President, 1932* (Washington: Government Printing Office, 1932), pp. 82, 83; Green et al., *Planning Munitions for War*, pp. 192–93.

9. Samuel D. Rockenback [sic; actually Rockenbach], "A Visit to the Infantry Tank Center, Franklin Cantonment, Camp Meade, Md.," *Infantry Journal* 18 (April 1921): 367.

10. Army War College course, 1919–20, Vol. II, Intelligence, Part I, Lectures Miscellaneous, p. 181, Army War College Collection, U.S. Army Military History Institute, Carlisle Barracks, Pennsylvania.

11. Mildred Harmon Gillie, *Forging the Thunderbolt: A History of the Development of the Armored Force* (Harrisburg, Pa.: Military Service Publishing Co., 1947), pp. 9–34. On the Pine Camp maneuvers, see Hanson W. Baldwin, *Tiger Jack* (Ft. Collins, Colo.: Old Army Press, 1979), pp. 103–104. On tank production, see Green et al., *Planning Munitions for War*, p. 202.

12. Green et al., *Planning Munitions for War*, p. 192, quoting Maj. Gen. Charles L. Scott, Comments for History of Development of Combat Vehicles, 2 March 1950, OHF [Ordnance Historical File]. On the Experimental Mechanized Force and its successors, see Gillie, *Forging the Thunderbolt*, pp. 25–38.

13. Report of the Chief of Staff in U.S., Department of War, *Report of the Secretary of War to the President, 1928* (Washington: Government Printing Office, 1928), p. 81.

14. Ibid., *1930*, p. 122; *1929*, p. 108.

15. Ibid., *1931*, p. 43.

16. *Statutes at Large*, XLI, 759–61, 766, 768–75.

17. Alfred F. Hurley, *Billy Mitchell: Crusader for Air Power*, new ed. (Bloomington: Indiana University Press, 1975), p. 101, quoting "Statement of William Mitchell Concerning the Recent Air Accidents," mimeograph, William Mitchell Papers, Library of Congress, Washington, D.C.

18. For the Mitchell trial, see Burke Davis, *The Billy Mitchell Affair* (New York: Random House, 1967). For the Army Air Corps between the wars, see Wesley Frank Craven and James Lea Cate, eds., *The Army Air Forces in World War II*, 7 vols. (Chicago: University of Chicago Press, 1948–1958), vol. I, *Plans and Early Operations*; Alfred Goldberg et al., eds., *A History of the United States Air Force* (New York: Arno Press, 1974), chap. 3. For AWPD–1 see Haywood S. Hansell, Jr., *The Air Plan That Defeated Hitler* (Atlanta: Haywood S. Hansell, Jr., 1972).

19. Commander Richard B. Coffey, USN, "The Navy War Plans Division: Naval Plans and Planning," Army War College, War Plans Division Course No. 10, 11 March 1924, p. 6, copy in Bliss Papers, Box 280.

20. Mark Skinner Watson, *Chief of Staff: Prewar Plans and Preparations*, United States Army in World War II: The War Department (Washington: Historical Division, United States Army, 1950), p. 415, quoting Memo, ACofS, WPD [Assistant Chief of Staff, War Plans Division] for CofS, prepared by CofS, 5 April 1934, WPD 3251. For the ORANGE plans, see ibid., especially pp. 411–25; Louis Morton, *Strategy and Command: The First Two Years*, United States Army in World War II: The War in the Pacific (Washington: Office of the Chief of Military History, Department of the Army, 1962), pp. 24–44; and Morton's "War Plan ORANGE: Evolution of a Strategy," *World Politics* 11 (January 1959): 221–50. American and Japanese strategic planning is considered in a political context in Dorothy Borg and Shumpei Okamoto, eds., *Pearl Harbor as History: Japanese-American Relations, 1931–1941* (New York: Columbia University Press, 1973), pp. 165–259.

21. For MacArthur's plans for Philippine defense, see James, *Years of MacArthur*, I, 470–552; Louis Morton, *The Fall of the Philippines*, United States Army in World War II: The War in the Pacific (Washington: Office of the Chief of Military History, Department of the Army, 1953), pp. 15–73; Watson, *Chief of Staff*, pp. 425–52.

22. William L. Langer and S. Everett Gleason, *The World Crisis and American Foreign Policy: The Undeclared War, 1940–1941* (New York: Published for the Council on Foreign Relations by Harper and Brothers, 1953), especially pp. 843–48; Forrest C. Pogue, *George C. Marshall: Ordeal and Hope, 1939–1942* (New York: Viking, 1966), pp. 194–96; Watson, *Chief of Staff*, especially pp. 411, 446–52, 503–504.

23. *Statutes at Large*, XLI, 704; Kreidberg and Henry, *History of Military Mobilization*, pp. 502–40.

24. Kreidberg and Henry, *History of Military Mobilization*, pp. 380–81, 494–96, 499–502.

25. Ibid., pp. 496–98, 502–508, 511–12, 518–23, 527–32.

26. The larger themes are kept in mind throughout Paul A. C. Koistinen, "The 'Industrial-Military Complex' in Historical Perspective: The Interwar Years," *Journal of American History* 56 (March 1970): 819–39, reprinted in Carroll W. Pursell, Jr., ed.,

The Military-Industrial Complex (New York: Harper and Row, 1972), pp. 31–50, and in Paul A. C. Koistinen, *The Military-Industrial Complex: A Historical Perspective* (New York: Praeger, 1980), chap. 3.

27. Tasker H. Bliss, draft of article, January 1923 (?), p. 5, Bliss Papers, Box 274.

28. Col. William K. Naylor, "The Principles of War," Command Course No. 12, Army War College, 1922, Part I, 5 January 1922, p. 6, copy in Bliss Papers, Box 277.

29. Course at the Army War College, 1926–27, Command, Report of Committee No. 5, Report of Civil and Franco-Prussian Wars, Date of Conference, 25 February 1927, p. 7, Army War College Collection, U.S. Army Military History Institute, Carlisle Barracks, Pa.

30. Ulysses S. Grant, *Personal Memoirs of U. S. Grant*, 2 vols. (New York: C. L. Webster, 1885), II, 178.

31. Lt. Col. Oliver Prescott Robinson, *The Fundamentals of Military Strategy* (Washington: United States Infantry Association, 1928), pp. 75, 93.

32. Quoted in Capt. Reuben E. Jenkins, "Offensive Doctrine: Opening Phases of Battle," *Military Review* 20 (June 1940): 16. No page number cited for quotation from FM 100–5.

33. Jean R. Moenck, *A History of Large-Scale Army Maneuvers in the United States, 1935–1964* (Fort Monroe: Headquarters United States Continental Army Command, 1969), pp. 23–26.

FURTHER READING

The army between the world wars has been neglected by historians to an even greater extent than the army in most other peacetime eras, and the few historians writing about the army of the 1920s and 1930s usually treat the period largely as the prelude to the Second World War—which of course it was, but to view it only in that perspective is to miss its own atmosphere and values. A brief, judicious corrective may be found in Allan R. Millett and Peter Maslowski, *For the Common Defense: A Military History of the United States of America* (New York: The Free Press, 1984), chap. 12. The only comprehensive, book-length survey of the interwar army is Robert K. Griffith, Jr., *Men Wanted for the U.S. Army: America's Experience with an All-Volunteer Army Between the World Wars* (Westport, Conn.: Greenwood Press, 1982). Fortunately, the book is more comprehensive than its title suggests; while it emphasizes manpower policy, it deals with other issues as well.

Manpower policy—how best to prepare a small peacetime army for another possible mass mobilization on the 1917–1918 scale—was, as Griffith's title implies, always a central concern of the interwar army. Much of the evolution of the policy can be followed through an exceptionally able biography of a major military intellectual of the period who was particularly concerned with devising a manpower policy that would be appropriate to the army of a democracy: Irving B. Holley, Jr., *General John M. Palmer, Citizen Soldiers, and the Army of a Democracy* (Westport, Conn.: Greenwood Press, 1982). Holley follows General Palmer's contributions from the National Defense Act of 1920 to the Selective Service Act of 1940. Palmer offered his own detailed description of his contributions to the former measure, a somewhat less ample coverage of other aspects of his career, and a lucid summary of his views on military policy in *America in Arms: The Experience of the United States with Military Organization* (New Haven:

Yale University Press, 1941). The issues of manpower and conscription throughout American history, including the interwar period and the 1940 draft law, can also be followed through a useful collection of excerpts from documents, John O'Sullivan and Alan M. Meckler, eds., *The Draft and Its Enemies: A Documentary History* (Urbana: University of Illinois Press, 1974).

The experience of the First World War bequeathed to the interwar army a new set of planning problems equal in importance to the long-standing historic concern about manpower: the problems of economic and industrial mobilization for modern war. There is particularly strong coverage of the beginnings of the army's economic mobilization planning in Marvin A. Kreidberg and Merton G. Henry, *History of Military Mobilization in the United States Army, 1775–1945*, Department of the Army Pamphlet No. 20–212 (Washington: Department of the Army, 1955). The leading historian of the military-industrial complex relates industrial mobilization policy to larger economic and political issues in Paul A. C. Koistinen, *The Military-Industrial Complex: A Historical Perspective* (New York: Praeger, 1980), especially chap. 3, "The Interwar Years," pp. 47–67. Koistinen's detailed and informative doctoral dissertation (University of California, Berkeley, 1964), has been published in Richard H. Kohn, advisory ed., *The American Military Experience*, 43 books in 56 vols. (New York: Arno Press, 1979), as a photocopy of the original: *The Hammer and the Sword: Labor, the Military, and Industrial Mobilization, 1920–1945*.

There are satisfactory biographies covering the tenures of three chiefs of staff of the army for this period: Frank E. Vandiver, *Black Jack: The Life and Times of John J. Pershing*, 2 vols. (College Station: Texas A&M University Press, 1977); D. Clayton James, *The Years of MacArthur*, 3 vols. (Boston: Houghton Mifflin Company, 1970–1985); and Forrest C. Pogue, *George C. Marshall*, 3 vols. to date (New York: The Viking Press, 1963–). Of these biographies, James's vol. I, *1880–1941* (1970), and Pogue's vol. I, *Education of a General, 1880–1939* (1963), and vol. II, *Ordeal and Hope, 1939–1942* (1966), offer unusually distinguished examples of the endangered biographical species of the "life and times," informing us almost as much about the history of the army at large as about their individual subjects. In contrast, Douglas MacArthur, *Reminiscences* (New York: McGraw-Hill, 1964), is altogether unsatisfactory. Somewhat more useful is a sampling of MacArthur's speeches and writings compiled in the first flush of his post–1941 fame: Frank C. Waldrop, ed., *MacArthur on War* (New York: Duell, Sloan and Pearce, 1942). Just as Pogue's biography of Marshall illustrates the larger history of the army, so does the only volume thus far published of *The Papers of George Catlett Marshall*, ed. Larry I. Bland and Sharon R. Ritenour: *"The Soldierly Spirit": December 1880–June 1939* (Baltimore: Johns Hopkins University Press, 1981).

One of the most important themes of army history in the interwar years, the evolution of army aviation toward the status of a separate armed force and the controversies attending it, can also be best approached through two biographical studies, both focusing on the leading American prophet of air power, Brigadier General William Mitchell. By far the best comprehensive Mitchell biography is Alfred F. Hurley, *Billy Mitchell: Crusader for Air Power* (Bloomington: Indiana University Press, 1975). There is valuable supplementary material on Mitchell's sensational court-martial trial in Burke Davis, *The Billy Mitchell Affair* (New York: Random House, 1967). Indispensable in detail is the first volume of the official history of the Army Air Forces in World War II: *Plans and Early Operations, January 1939 to August 1942*, prepared under the editorship of Wesley Frank Craven and James Lea Cate by the Office of Air Force History, United States Air Force,

Wilfred J. Paul, Director, Albert F. Simpson, Air Force Historian (Chicago: The University of Chicago Press, 1948). There is much pre–1939 background material in this useful volume.

For the interwar evolution of the ground combat arms—viewed again from the perspective of the 1941–1945 war—a similarly indispensable official history is Kent Roberts Greenfield, Robert R. Palmer, and Bell I. Wiley, *The Organization of Ground Combat Troops*, United States Army in World War II: The Army Ground Forces (Washington: Historical Division, United States Army, 1947). The same topic can be approached through a study of the development of the ground forces' equipment in Constance McLaughlin Green, Harry C. Thomson, and Peter C. Roots, *The Ordnance Department: Planning Munitions for War*, United States Army in World War II: The Technical Services (Washington: Office of the Chief of Military History, Department of the Army, 1955). Both of the latter books are especially good on the development—or sometimes the lack of it—in tanks and armored forces. Setting American tank design and armored organization in a world perspective is the accomplishment of Richard M. Ogorkiewicz, *Armoured Forces: A History of Armoured Forces and Their Vehicles* (New York: Arco Publishing Company, Inc., 1970).

By the middle to late 1930s, the army could turn toward larger, strategic planning with the prospect of another war against Germany in mind. The reader should consult Mark Skinner Watson, *Chief of Staff: Prewar Plans and Preparations*, United States Army in World War II: The War Department (Washington: Historical Division, United States Army, 1950). The army was much less preoccupied than the navy with the danger of war against Japan. For the contrast between the services, the reader should compare Louis Morton, *Strategy and Command: The First Two Years*, United States Army in World War II: The War Department (Washington: Office of the Chief of Military History, Department of the Army, 1962), with John Major, "The Navy Plans for War, 1937–1941," and with Robert William Love, Jr., "Fighting a Global War, 1941–1945," both in Kenneth J. Hagan, ed., *In Peace and War: Interpretations of American Naval History, 1775–1984*, 2d ed. rev. (Westport, Conn.: Greenwood Press, 1984).

forces, but overseas to the combatant Allies; the British, and then the Russians, would take all they could get and ask for more. If Britons might occasionally grumble that the United States was prepared to fight to the last Englishman, they were still desperate for American goods, and such a policy, after all, was not entirely unacceptable to Americans. It did, however, leave American draftees and the activated National Guard divisions woefully short of their designated equipment allowances.

Such problems of shortage in one area, and waste in others, were inevitable concomitants of growth. Fortunately for the army and for the country, the higher command structure of the service, which had taken shape in the immediate prewar period, was not heavily dependent upon public and political perception. George C. Marshall became chief of staff in September 1939, and he guided the army through the entire crisis of the war years. A towering intellect, he was probably the greatest American military statesman since George Washington, and he remains one of the very few wartime leaders whom historians have treated with unreserved respect.

The peacetime army had been a close-knit organization in which almost everyone knew almost everyone else. There were only about 14,000 officers, and Marshall was therefore able to handpick the men who rose to high operational command. As the United States Army had seen relatively little large-scale combat in World War I, and no combat at all since then, most of these men had spent much of their career at school, as teachers or students, and on garrison duty. Dwight D. Eisenhower made his mark as a staff officer on maneuvers in 1941. He went from there to the War Plans Division in Washington, from which Marshall plucked him to command American forces in Europe. Omar Bradley had passed more than half his career as an instructor at various army schools; he remarked in his autobiography that when correspondents said he looked like a teacher that was because he *was* a teacher.[2] Jacob Devers and Mark Clark had similar backgrounds. One major commander who was not in this frame was Douglas MacArthur, who had been chief of staff nearly a decade before Marshall himself, from 1930 to 1935. He had actually resigned from the United States Army in 1937 to remain in the Philippines, where he was commanding the nascent Philippine army, and was recalled to command the American forces there as war clouds gathered. As a man who had been around forever, he proved a very difficult subordinate; so did George S. Patton, Jr., who was also senior in experience to most of the men who commanded him in the course of the war. Such were the men, hitherto largely ignored or unknown, who had to prepare a reluctant nation for war, turn a small army into a large one, and then lead that army in combat against experienced and formidable foes.

Russell Weigley has brilliantly reviewed the army's difficulties in arriving at a coherent tactical doctrine and its failure to decide firmly in favor of either the mass warfare tradition of the American Civil War or the mobile tradition of the old Indian-fighting army, a failure that plagued it throughout the entire war. An equally fundamental difficulty was the manpower problem, and General Lesley

J. McNair, who as Marshall's chief of staff commanded General Headquarters of the Army, later Army Ground Forces, spent his entire war trying to reconcile the demands of lower commands for troops with the restrictions placed upon the army's size by higher authorities.[3] Forced to compete with the other services and with civilian industry for bodies, the army never had as many men as it wanted, and it seldom had them in the right place. At the time of Pearl Harbor, there was only one division on a full wartime footing; General Headquarters had projected that it would need an army of two-hundred combat divisions to take the offensive against the Axis powers, but at the same time it was making that projection, President Roosevelt and his cabinet were actually moving toward decreasing rather than increasing the army's size.[4] The two-hundred-division target was never entirely realistic, and it was gradually watered down to one hundred; the army did not achieve that size, and at the end of the war in Europe it possessed eighty-nine divisions. Even this number was attained by a progressive weeding out of the strength of individual formations, doubling up of functions, and an attempt, not entirely successful, to reduce the number of specialized troops attached to units. The 15,000-man division called for by the 1941 Tables of Organization became a 14,000-man division by mid–1943, and it was these divisions that fought the war.[5] Theater commanders constantly demanded more troops and were equally constantly told to clean out their own rear areas to get them. But by May 1945, with 8,291,336 officers and men in uniform, the army still had only about 2,000,000 combat soldiers. The fact that in 1918 almost half the army was in combat units, while in 1945 only slightly over a third was in the same category, reflects not only the more complex military technology of the second war, not only that it was waged in more distant theaters, but also that it was a "fatter" army, a fact that was not always apparent to the men up in the rifle companies.[6] One is reminded of Winston Churchill's bitter remark about Anzio, on being told there were 18,000 vehicles and 70,000 men ashore: "How many of our men are driving or looking after eighteen thousand vehicles in this narrow space? We must have a great superiority of chauffeurs. I am shocked that the enemy have more infantry than we."[7]

The manpower problem was but illustrative of several others as well. If there was no basic agreement on tactical doctrine, on larger as opposed to smaller divisions, on specialized as against all-around formations, there was also disagreement on what kind of war should actually be fought. During the war, the Army Air Forces were not yet an independent service, though they were rapidly evolving in that direction. In early 1942 the Army Air Forces (AAF) achieved equal status with the other two basic commands, Army Ground Forces and Army Service Forces; the AAF commander, General H. H. ("Hap") Arnold, was naturally a firm believer in the efficacy of air warfare, and throughout the entire conflict the air force vigorously asserted its claim to fight its own kind of war, often at variance with, and even at the expense of, the war being fought by the army on the ground.

During the war, therefore, roughly one-quarter of the army's strength was not used by the army itself, but by the air force. Much of this energy, of course, went for air support, both logistical and tactical, but even more went for the strategic bombing campaign, the panacea of prewar air power theorists. From 1940 to 1945 the AAF took delivery of 12,677 B–17 Flying Fortresses and 18,188 B–24 Liberators, compared to 49,000 M–4 Sherman tanks for the ground forces. Only 945,000 machine guns were made for troops on the ground, while 1,575,000 were made for aircraft. Though the air force commanders were forced on occasion to conform to the needs of the larger war as perceived by higher leadership, such as in 1942 when their efforts were diverted to North Africa or to the antisubmarine campaign, or in 1944 when they made a major effort in the pre-invasion interdiction campaign in northern France, by and large they went their own way, followed their own sense of priorities, and fought their own war. In conjunction with the Royal Air Force Bomber Command's strategic campaign against Germany, they sought to cripple the German economy and its ability to wage war. They had major successes in this, and forced the Germans to divert substantial resources to countering their efforts. They also paid a very heavy price for their success, to the point where at several stages of the war the bombing campaign was nearly abandoned as being too costly and achieving too little. In the end the infantrymen and tankers found much of Germany in ruins, but they still had to fight their way through them to the final victory.

The strategic bombing campaign had demonstrably better results against Japan. By the time the Americans were able to mount a full-scale campaign against the home islands, they had better equipment, specifically designed for the distances of the war in the Pacific; they also had an enemy whose industrial plant and residential areas were more concentrated than Germany's and more vulnerable to attack from the air. Carrying war to the enemy in this way was a vast technological and administrative achievement and a saga of courage and endurance for the air crews involved. It also created a moral dilemma that has bothered historians increasingly as the war recedes into the past.

Tokyo in flames, Berlin in ruins, and American and Allied forces triumphant in 1945 were a long way off in the immediate aftermath of Pearl Harbor, and though Americans had unquestioning faith in the final victory, that faith was to be severely challenged in the desperate months of early 1942. The problems of manpower, logistics, administration, and doctrine, which had hitherto preoccupied military men and their civilian superiors, were now reduced to their true proportions as adjuncts to the fundamental matter of fighting. One of the great decisions of the war had already been made. American and British army officers had begun sounding each other out on strategic questions as early as the summer of 1940.[8] Through the end of that year and into 1942, American officers, though they were incurably—and correctly—wary of the British desire to fight the war in a way most beneficial to Britain, nevertheless reached substantially the same conclusion the British had reached: Germany presented the greater threat to both world and American security, and in the event of American involvement in the war against the Axis powers primary effort must be devoted to the defeat of

Germany, after which it would be possible to deal with Japan. The logic of this assessment simply could not be overcome, though proponents of a Pacific strategy and those who resented a reality that they saw as British domination of the war fought hard and repeatedly against it. It was a logic that was also fortunate for the army, because a war against Japan was going to be a naval war, with army help, while a war against Germany was going to be the army's war, with logistical support from the navy.

The first pressing problem of belligerency, though, was not what to do about Germany, but what to do about the Philippines. The weak American garrison there, plus the larger but barely formed Philippine Commonwealth forces, both commanded by General Douglas MacArthur, were immediately placed on the defensive and, in effect, under siege by the initial Japanese attacks. Prewar planning had called for a holding operation in the Pacific while the battle fleet steamed to the rescue; but the fleet was sitting on the mud of Pearl Harbor, MacArthur lost his air force in a surprise attack eight hours after news of Pearl reached him, and reinforcements already en route to the islands were quickly diverted to Australia. Though Washington sent reassuring messages, that was all it did, or could do, about a rescue operation. The simple fact was that overseas territories were hostages to sea power, and all the sea power in the western Pacific was Japanese. MacArthur conducted a highly creditable defense, though he delayed his retreat to the last bastion of Bataan until it was too late to organize his supplies properly.[9] He was then flown out to develop the defense of Australia, and the Philippine commander, General Jonathan M. Wainwright, surrendered unconditionally on 6 May 1942. Two days later MacArthur, now commander of the Southwest Pacific Area, recommended an offensive against the Japanese after appropriate strengthening of his forces. Obviously the "Germany first" strategy was going to be subject to some strains, especially as the United States Navy felt as did MacArthur.

Meanwhile, the United States had already extended its sphere of operations in the Atlantic. During 1941 there had been consideration of sending expeditionary forces to occupy various eastern Atlantic island groups, such as the Azores and the Cape Verdes, consideration that had played havoc with the army's training schedules and mobilization procedures. United States Marines landed in Iceland on 7 July and were later reinforced by army troops, though the full relief of the marines was not concluded until early 1942, so difficult was it to organize a mobile force of any numbers.[10]

Aside from the obstacles to getting American power deployed into the European theater, there arose yet another problem. In earlier conversations, the British had demonstrated a distressing tendency to want the Americans to move in such a way as to serve British imperial interests first and foremost. When Roosevelt and Churchill met for the first time in August 1941 in Placentia Bay, Newfoundland, the Americans found that the British idea of how to defeat Germany was far less straightforward than their own nascent thoughts on the matter. The entire Western European war had been warped by the fall of France and the entry of Italy as an active belligerent in the summer of 1940. Mussolini actually wanted the French North African empire. Balked of it by the early surrender of France, he turned instead upon British-held Egypt and had been soundly beaten for his efforts. But the British in turn had been sidetracked into adventures in the Balkans, where they lost much of their Middle East striking power, and the Axis had riposted by sending German units under the formidable Erwin Rommel to North Africa. The British thus had a lingering, seesaw battle on their hands. Desperately wary of the perils of a straightforward, cross-Channel attack—they had after all been pushed into the sea in 1940, and they had vivid memories of the bloodbath of 1914–1918—they found the Mediterranean an attractive alternative. Could not American forces be brought to bear in that area against Italy, even against France, and might this not have the effect of dispersing, distracting, and thereby weakening the German forces? Would not that, together with bombing and the possibility of large-scale risings in the German-occupied territories, be a cheaper and ultimately more effective way of defeating the enemy? The American response was lukewarm; American military strength was still minimal, but, more to the point, the Americans did not really see how an Allied conquest of North Africa was going to have a decisive effect on the Hitlerian empire.[11] Thus once more, even before hostilities began for the United States, a question of fundamental strategy arose whose resolution was to dog the entire history of the war and which has exercised historians ever since. For in the end the British got their way, and the first time American and German soldiers met was not on the beaches of France and the direct road to Germany, but rather in the hills and wadis of Tunisia, the first step on a long way around.

During the fifteen months between the meeting at Placentia Bay and the landing of Allied troops on the shores of Morocco and Algeria in November 1942, the American buildup continued. Japan launched the United States, united at last by the Pearl Harbor attack, wholeheartedly into the war; the Philippines went under, and the Japanese tide crested at the Coral Sea in May and at Midway in June 1942. Imperial Japanese forces and American sailors and marines reached a delicate, desperate equilibrium in the straits and jungles of the Solomon Islands, and a substantial American base was created in northern Australia, the prelude to MacArthur's eventual campaign in New Guinea and northwest toward the Philippines.

At the ARCADIA Conference in Washington immediately after Pearl Harbor, the British went all out for an attack in North Africa, to be followed in due course not by full-scale invasion of the Continent but possibly by a number of incursions of fast, mobile formations to set off general risings in the occupied territories. This was the Placentia Bay theme replayed, Churchill's commando raids writ large or, to revert to an earlier age, William Pitt's "breaking windows with guineas" in the Seven Years' War. General Marshall carefully refrained from negative comment, though his senior strategic adviser characterized the British view as " 'persuasive rather than rational' and as 'motivated more largely by political than by sound strategic purposes.' "[12] Such a comment hit not only the Churchillian but also the Rooseveltian nail on the head. Whatever the American military leaders, preeminently Marshall, saw as desirable, Roosevelt believed that for domestic political reasons there must be combat in the European theater at the soonest feasible time. A cross-Channel invasion in 1942 was not a realistic possibility, and Roosevelt thought it far too long to wait for one in 1943. Though a diversion to North Africa could have only the effect of pushing the invasion of France farther into the future, and thus of seriously compromising the American view of how the war ought to be fought, the British, aided by Roosevelt's political perceptions, got their way. The discussion was lengthy, but the decision was crucial.

Crucial, but not yet final. For even after ARCADIA, the Americans were not quite ready to give up. The Combined Chiefs of Staff, as the British and American high command was called, began planning for a North African invasion. But the American Joint Chiefs of Staff still did not like the idea. In April General Marshall was in London to discuss the invasion of France, the true second front as he saw it. Marshall and other American military leaders worried that Russia might be finally knocked out of the war; they also thought that shipping limitations would upset a North African operation. Their views had been summed up on 6 March by a statement of the Joint U.S. Strategic Committee which saw the defeat of Germany coming only from a direct assault across the Channel. Unfortunately, the Americans estimated that this would require at least 600,000 men and 6,500 aircraft, and after meeting their other commitments, they would have available in the British Isles by the start of 1943 only 252,000 of the former and 2,300 of the latter.[13] Their answer to this: the remainder should be supplied by the British.

The British reluctantly agreed, and planning for an attack in North Africa was shelved while the United Kingdom planning for an early invasion of France, code-named ROUNDUP, was pushed ahead for 1943. Then fate intervened again. The Germans cut loose both in Russia and in North Africa. Just after Marshall left London, Rommel jumped off on his second offensive, broke the British at Gazala, took Tobruk on the run, and advanced by the end of June as far as El Alamein, the last defensive position before Alexandria. Just as he closed up to El Alamein, the Germans opened their main summer offensive in Russia, and it looked like 1941 all over again. Russia appeared in serious danger of collapse, Churchill was heavily attacked in Britain for his handling of the war, and the Allies could not wait for ROUNDUP; North Africa, code-named TORCH, was on again.

An ironic contradiction of the American army's role in World War II was that history and geography made its leaders strategically bold, but their force limitations and general inexperience made them tactically cautious. Time and again against the Germans, the Allies achieved strategic surprise, in North Africa, in Sicily, at Salerno and Anzio in Italy, and in France. Almost invariably, the speed of the German reaction was such as to obviate the initial surprise, and in this as in much else, the North African invasion set the pattern.

The Allies landed at three widely spaced places; an American task force direct from the East Coast came ashore at Casablanca, another American force at Oran, and an essentially British force at Algiers. Here again was compromise. The Allied goal was Tunisia, and specifically Tunis. The British wanted to land at Bône, which is 125 miles west of Tunis. The Americans, fearing the power of the Luftwaffe and worried over the possibility of Spanish intervention—which shows the poor quality of their available military intelligence on Spain—wanted to land outside the Straits of Gibraltar altogether, as the western Task Force did at Casablanca. Yet Casablanca is just over a thousand miles from Tunis, that is, two and a half times the distance to Tunis from Rome. The British had agreed to an American commander for the operation, General Eisenhower, until August the commander of American forces in the United Kingdom, but they would not agree to a degree of caution that would foredoom the entire exercise. Thus the compromise landings. Even then the Allies were too fainthearted. Tunis is equidistant from Algiers and Rome; as soon as the landings took place, the Germans began shunting forces south across the Mediterranean, and while the British and Americans were untangling themselves from their landings and their convoluted relations with the Vichy French, the Germans won the race. They built up a line in the hills of eastern Tunisia and eventually linked up with a retreating Rommel, who had kept ahead of Montgomery's pursuit all the way from Egypt.

The Axis pocket in Tunisia was not crushed until May 1943. By then all hope of an invasion of France in the immediate future was gone. Tunisia cost Hitler at least a quarter of a million men but gained him at least a year. It also showed the Americans that they had a long way to go yet, for their first real combat against the Germans was a vastly sobering lesson. When the Germans launched a limited attack against the American II Corps in February around Kasserine Pass, almost everything in the defense went wrong. The American forces were dispersed, their chain of command was confused, their equipment was inadequate, and their general leadership inept. The British, who were like the old Aulic War Council of Austria in that having been beaten so often they thought they knew all about war, were thoroughly disappointed in their new allies, and their low opinion of American fighting prowess was to color strategy for the next year or better. Eisenhower replaced the II Corps commander and made various shifts of personnel. Assorted home truths were spelled out for officers and enlisted men alike. The American forces emerged from the Tunisian campaign sadder, wiser, and, most important of all, better than they had gone in.

The strategic arguments continued, but when Roosevelt and Churchill met in mid-January 1943 at Casablanca, the mood was lighter. At their last meeting only darkness had lain ahead. Now one German army was trapped in Tunisia, and another lay surrounded and dying at Stalingrad. France was back in the war, Italy desirous of getting out of it. The Japanese were losing the battle for Guadalcanal, and MacArthur's forces had started the long fight up the coast of New Guinea. China was still barely hanging on, but the war in Burma seemed at last to have stabilized, if not entirely to the advantage of the British. Clearly, the

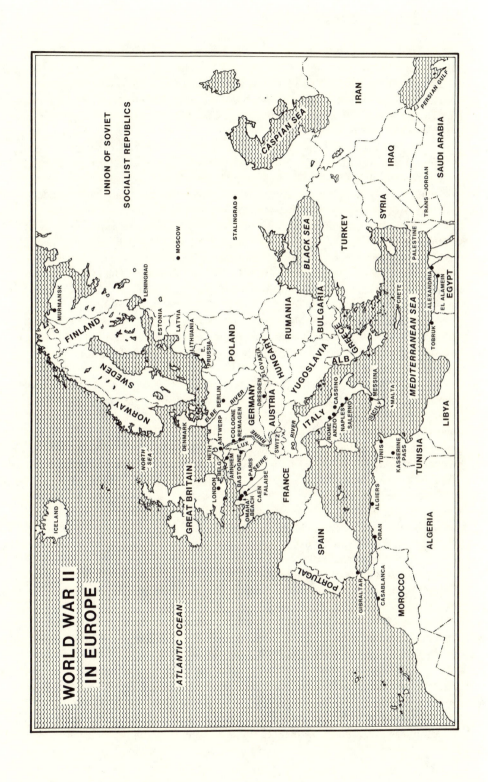

WORLD WAR II IN EUROPE

general initiative lay with the Allies. It was time for some clear-sighted decisions as to where to go next.

The American proponents of a direct invasion of Germany were now thoroughly disillusioned. Throughout 1942 they had been pulled three ways, between their own desire for a buildup in Britain, the British insistence on pursuing operations in the Mediterranean, and the pressing demands of the Pacific theater for additional army and air force commitments. By the end of the year, of seventeen divisions overseas, nine were in the Pacific, three had gone to North Africa, one to Iceland, and only four to the United Kingdom.[14] Once again, this was a measure of the extent to which the American strategic vision had exceeded the reality of the forces actually available. The three divisions for North Africa sailed in the last quarter of the year, so that may be taken as some indication of the way in which TORCH warped the intended buildup in Britain. But even had they not gone there, there still would have been as many units sent to the Pacific as to Europe itself. BOLERO, the buildup in Britain, had been downgraded; SLEDGEHAMMER, the ill-named plan for a limited cross-Channel assault in 1942, was gone; and now ROUNDUP, the plan—and hope—for a major invasion in 1943, was also pretty well moribund. As they met their British opposite numbers at Casablanca, American planners might well have asked themselves what they could hope to salvage of their concept of the way the war should be fought.

The answer was, not much. General Marshall really did not want any further commitment in the Mediterranean, yet by now saw little way to avoid it. The logic of what followed from TORCH was inescapable. Churchill for his part was rocketing about the map; he suggested looking at Sardinia, Sicily, Greece, other areas of the Balkans, and even the possibility of luring the Turks off the fence so that an Allied attack could be launched from the Black Sea against the Axis in Rumania and Bulgaria. Most of these prospects were wildly unrealistic and took little account of one of the Allies' most pressing problems, the availability of the shipping needed to support such long-range operations. Most of them, it may safely be concluded, were no more than trial balloons. In effect, the prime minister simply liked to play with maps and threw ideas as fires do sparks. The Americans probably took him more seriously than they should have done, but that is part of the price of dealing with prime ministers; and where he was all boyish enthusiasm, they tended to see deep imperialistic plots to carve out postwar spheres of British influence.

The professional British military men, in contrast to their political master, came to Casablanca fully armed with a complete set of plans: they now wanted to attack Sicily, in the hope of knocking Italy out of the war. Italy, which seemed to the Americans a minor matter, had always held for Englishmen such as Sir Alan Brooke, the chief of the Imperial General Staff, an importance far beyond its deserts. Taking Sicily, he argued, would probably make Italy collapse, would ease the strain on Allied shipping, and would do assorted other useful things in the central Mediterranean. General Eisenhower added his support to British ideas.

The Tunisian campaign was not yet going well; the Germans had proved far more formidable than anticipated, and American field commanders, from being vastly overconfident, had now become almost excessively respectful of their foes. With Marshall already half-convinced, the ill-prepared Americans were not going to argue against both the British and their own man. Eisenhower, while finishing off the Tunisian battle, was also ordered to plan for operation HUSKY, the invasion of Sicily in midsummer.

Now, with the planners agreed upon, or resigned to, a continuation of the Mediterranean thrust, rifts opened up at the operational level between the British and the Americans. Eisenhower found it very difficult to plan one campaign and fight another, and much of the work for HUSKY was left to his immediate, British, subordinates. The chief among them was Sir Harold Alexander, who was a first-rate field commander, a man of vast experience and ineffable charm. His one real failing was a disinclination to ride his underlings too hard, a trait that was taken full advantage of by the British Eighth Army commander, General Bernard Montgomery. The victor of El Alamein was to become virtually the Americans' *bête noir*, and many American military memoirs convey the impression that the Germans were in the war only incidentally; the real enemy was Montgomery. Omar Bradley, essentially a mild-spoken man, referred to him as an "arrogant egomaniac," while George Patton considered him a "tired little fart."[15]

The British, in their turn, were very disappointed with American performance in Tunisia, so when Sicily's turn came, they assigned the Americans basically a covering role on the left flank of the operation and assumed for themselves the task of driving directly for the main objective, the port of Messina in the northeast corner of the island. The planners were ultracautious, and at one point Eisenhower registered their unwillingness to proceed if there were even two German divisions on the island, a prudence that drew a viciously—and deservedly—scornful reply from Churchill.[16]

The Sicilian landing began on 10 July 1943, the day that General Patton activated the United States Seventh Army and took command of the American segment of the invasion. Patton soon proved himself one of the great masters of mobile, exploitative warfare. While Montgomery made his way slowly north against fairly heavy opposition, Patton's troops took off into the wilds of central and western Sicily. Furious at Montgomery's attitude of conscious superiority, enraged at British trespassing across operational boundaries, Patton goaded his people on. He had Bradley as one corps commander and General Lucian Truscott as a task force commander, and the Americans, whose Tunisian problems had been of innocence and inexperience, in Sicily both found their feet and hit their stride. By 17 August Sicily was secured, the Americans having gone the long way around and beaten the British into Messina. Once again the question arose, what next?

While the Americans and British squabbled about their differing ideas of how to wage a European war, the conflict with Japan ground steadily ahead. The eccentric or centrifugal tendencies of Japanese strategy and empire building had been such as to present the Allies with a wide variety of options. There were fronts in the Aleutian Islands, the central Pacific, the South Pacific, Burma, and China; and in different ways and different degrees, the Americans were involved in all of them.

The Aleutian area had opened up when the Japanese, as part of their plan to attack Midway, had landed troops on Attu and Kiska and struck at American installations along the island chain to Alaska. This was never more than a peripheral area for either Japan or the United States, though the American reaction to a violation of actual American territory was strong, and it was at one time thought that operations here might connect with the Russians if they could be brought into the war against Japan. They could not, but the Americans recaptured the islands, and for most of the war kept a quarter of a million men tied up there in not very profitable garrison duties.

The biggest problem with China was how to keep her alive and in the war. By 1943–1944 millions of Chinese were simply starving to death, as the Japanese launched "rice offensives" designed with just that end in mind. The Chinese had manpower, but not much else; the Americans were sensibly reluctant to commit many troops to the Asian mainland, but they consistently overestimated the capability of the Chinese. And here, as elsewhere, there was disagreement between proponents of different theories of war. General Joseph W. Stilwell, the American commander under a variety of titles in the theater until late 1944, wanted to train and equip a modern Chinese army, in spite of his outspoken reservations about the Chinese Nationalist leader, Generalissimo Chiang Kai-shek—"a vacillating tricky undependable old scoundrel who never keeps his word."[17] American air power was represented by General Claire Chennault, founder of the famous American Volunteer Group, or "Flying Tigers." Chennault believed that air power could win in China, and he and Stilwell were constantly at loggerheads, one insisting that the tenuous supply route from Burma to China be used for ground equipment, the other that it be used instead to ferry in material to sustain the air war. Eventually the Americans established the Fourteenth Air Force in China, and later in the war they attacked Japan with B–29s based there. But in the middle years of the war, it was Stilwell who was correct, as the Japanese graphically demonstrated when their offensives overran several of Chennault's bases without his being able to do much to stop them.

Burma and Malaya were designated a British sphere of command responsibility, with some American logistics presence there to support the effort in China. Isolated from India, and almost every place else, by climate, terrain, and geography, these two countries nonetheless proved essential as the only available Allied gateway to China. The British and Japanese fought a long, wasting campaign for control of this area, with occasional intervention by the Chinese, as well as by some American specialist forces.

This left the major American effort for the Pacific divided essentially between the Pacific Ocean Areas, under Admiral Chester W. Nimitz and controlled by

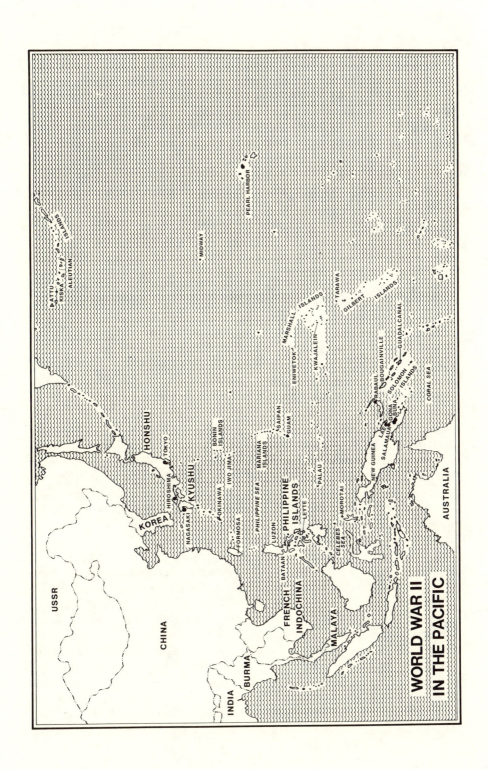

WORLD WAR II
IN THE PACIFIC

the navy, and the Southwest Pacific Area, commanded by MacArthur and run by the army. Here again General Marshall was forced to play the military statesman. In Europe he had to battle between the American desire to operate across the Channel and the British desire to continue in the Mediterranean; in the Pacific he had to balance MacArthur's determination to fulfill his promise to return to the Philippines against the navy's equally burning ambition to avenge Pearl Harbor. These views naturally found reflection in opposing plans. The navy wanted to operate in the Solomons and through the central Pacific island groups, using the army to garrison the islands that the naval forces and marines had already secured. The army wanted to advance up the coast of New Guinea and branch north through the Indies to the Philippines; MacArthur saw these as essentially land operations, with the navy serving in an ancillary role to provide transport and supply. If strategy was warped by personal predilection, it is also a fact that self-effacing men simply do not tend to rise to high military command. Admiral Nimitz and his superior, Admiral Ernest J. King, the chief of naval operations, combined with MacArthur to water down the Germany-first concept, but they then fought bitterly among themselves for priority in the Pacific. Their success in the former was indicated by the allocation of army divisions, as well as the amount of shipping that went to the Pacific in 1942.

Compromise had been achieved in July 1942; a month after Midway, Marshall and King had agreed upon a three-stage drive. The southeastern pivot of the Japanese defense perimeter was the great base at Rabaul, on the northern tip of New Britain. This was the American target. To get there, military and naval leaders planned to move both up the Solomons and along the coast of New Guinea. The first task was to secure the southeastern Solomons, and that was the navy's responsibility; the next stage was the taking of the rest of the Solomons, as well as the clearing of the northern coast of eastern New Guinea, and these undertakings would proceed essentially under MacArthur's direction. The third phase, which in the event was bypassed, was the taking of Rabaul itself.

During the latter part of 1942, the American and Australian troops led by MacArthur held on in eastern New Guinea and fought the Japanese to a standstill around Gona and Buna, Lae and Salamaua, all minor points on the northern New Guinea coast, while the Guadalcanal and eastern Solomons campaign was also being fought out. These were all desperate battles among men who were poorly equipped and insufficiently trained for the climate and conditions they encountered. As was happening across the world in Tunisia, several American commanders were relieved, and only slowly and painfully did the Allied forces first achieve equilibrium, then superiority over an enemy whom they had—as in Europe—initially underrated and then come to regard with almost self-defeating respect.

By early 1943 the first phase of the King-Marshall agreement was completed. The second phase took up most of the rest of the year and was accomplished at the cost of considerable army-navy friction. At Casablanca in January 1943, the Allied leadership had agreed to the advance on Rabaul, but it soon became apparent that MacArthur could not take Rabaul in 1943 without substantial reinforcements, something to which the Casablanca Conference had emphatically *not* agreed. The less ambitious Operation CARTWHEEL was developed instead, with MacArthur advancing along the northern New Guinea coast and the navy moving up the Solomons to Bougainville. The Japanese responded strongly, and through the middle months of the year there was bitter fighting along the Solomons and Bismarcks until the Americans achieved first air and then sea control. As the Japanese ability to move weakened, the possibility of bypassing Rabaul became more feasible, and that was basically what was done.

At the TRIDENT Conference held in Washington in May 1943, the Combined Chiefs of Staff accepted the Joint Chiefs' view of operations for 1944. These were to develop a two-pronged drive to the northwest, with a basically naval force going through the central Pacific island groups and the army up the coast of New Guinea through the Celebes Sea to the Philippines. The two drives would converge on the China coast somewhere around Hong Kong. All Japanese holdings to the south would be cut off, China would be revitalized, and the Allies would have a practicable base from which to move on the home islands of Japan themselves. The navy and MacArthur each tended to think that their drive was the only essential one and that the other might well be dispensed with, but by 1944 American strength was growing to the point where both drives could be afforded. After the Battle of the Philippine Sea in June 1944, the Imperial Navy was no longer a real threat to American operations. To the south, meanwhile, MacArthur fought a series of brilliant leapfrogging operations that carried American forces fifteen hundred miles in nine months. By the middle of September, the navy had reached the Palaus, and the army Morotai. The Philippines lay ahead.

During much of this time divisions among the Allies as to how to proceed in Europe remained as bitter as ever. The reduction of Sicily, Operation HUSKY, had been accepted as an admitted stopgap, and the Americans had explicitly demanded that it be an end in itself. But when Roosevelt and Churchill met at the May 1943 TRIDENT Conference, the prime minister started by blithely throwing all that out the window. He said that "the British came to the present meeting adhering to the Casablanca decisions," but immediately added, "There might have to be adjustments made necessary by our success." Since this was before Sicily was even invaded, let alone conquered, it might have been adjudged premature. But Churchill then went on to list his priorities, in the light of the future successes he so easily anticipated: "The first objective was in the Mediterranean. . . . The collapse of Italy would cause a chill of loneliness over the German people. . . . "[18] The chill was more likely to fall over the American Joint Chiefs, for they now discovered that the British were determined to go on into Italy, again at the expense of scaling down the BOLERO buildup and accepting the inevitable delay in the cross-Channel invasion. Churchill, as was inherent in his personality, expatiated at length on the benefits that would accrue from Italy's collapse, without giving much consideration to the difficulties that might be encountered in bringing on that collapse. His siren song about Italy was indeed remarkably similar to his World War I lyrics about all the delights that would flow from a successful forcing of the Dardanelles.

Like Ulysses tied to his mast, the Americans were able to resist Churchill's siren song, and his account of the remainder of TRIDENT laments the "hopeless breach" and "serious crisis of opinions."[19] In the end all he could get was a carefully worded and deliberately vague statement about concentrating maximum resources, so rather than settle for that, he carried General Marshall off to Algiers with him to discuss the matter with the Mediterranean commanders. Here Marshall played a somewhat weak hand very carefully while a whole entourage of British commanders bombarded him with arguments for invading Italy, the most impressive of which was that, after all, roughly three-quarters of the troops in the theater were British. The most he would give was that a final decision might be made when the Allies saw how things went in Sicily.

Things there went very well, of course, and as an added inducement, Mussolini's government collapsed during the Sicilian campaign. So when the next Allied conference, QUADRANT, was held at Quebec in August 1943, the Americans finally succumbed to an invasion of Italy. The utter irony of that seemed lost on everyone at the time. The British had pressed for further action in the central Mediterranean on the thesis that Italy must be "knocked out of the war." Mussolini was now safely in prison, his successors were surreptitiously negotiating to surrender, and on the basis of that, the British pressed for an invasion of the Italian mainland. They had, in other words, completely reversed their argument; from wanting to invade so that Italy would collapse, they now wanted to invade Italy because it had collapsed. Churchill envisaged the Allies securing much of the peninsula, at least the Naples-Foggia area, possibly Rome, and at his wildest the Ancona-Leghorn line. He was sure the Germans would not fight to hold Italy.

So when Eisenhower and his people in the Mediterranean, already charged with preparing plans to follow up success in Sicily, suggested a descent first on the toe of Italy and then an assault, AVALANCHE, up the coast at Salerno, the Combined Chiefs gave their approval—the Americans insisting only on a firm commitment that the cross-Channel invasion take place in May 1944 and that it have priority of resources. But Italy was on, and once again the British view of the war, and the logic of the Mediterranean theater, had carried the day.

Italy was invaded across the Straits of Messina on 3 September 1943, the anniversary of Britain's declaration of war on Germany. On the ninth, the U.S. Fifth Army, under command of General Mark W. Clark, and consisting of one British and one American corps, landed at Salerno.

Churchill's idea that the Germans would not hold Italy initially proved correct; their staff assessments concluded that the area was too vulnerable to an enemy possessing sea and air superiority to be defensible, and they saw little advantage to a major commitment there. Unhappily, this was changed by the hesitancy of the Allies themselves, and the German commander in Italy, Field Marshal Albert

Kesselring, threatened to push the Fifth Army back into the sea with what he regarded merely as a holding operation. He therefore convinced Hitler, always prone to issue stand-and-die orders, that there was no sense giving the Allies what they were not trying very hard to take. Instead of abandoning the peninsula, the Germans defended a series of river lines on both coasts; and the western Allies found themselves involved thereafter in some of the most bitter fighting of the entire war. Naples did not fall until 1 October; Eisenhower ordered the army group commander, Harold Alexander, to continue on to Rome, but November saw the Allies up against the German Winter Line, which extended from the Sangro River in the east to Cassino in the west. There they stayed.

Far from achieving what its advocates had so optimistically predicted, the Italian campaign became a long, wasting diversion, which both sides attempted to justify by claiming that it tied down enemy forces which were badly needed elsewhere. Before Cassino, "up among the mountains, in the mud and rain," as the bitter parody of "Lili Marlene" had it, the Allies and the Germans savaged each other in one brutal frontal battle after another, reminiscent of the trench fighting of World War I.

An Allied attempt to utilize the mobility of sea power by a landing up the coast at Anzio was poorly conceived and ill handled and resulted in yet another stalemate, with the Germans, as usual reacting rapidly, able to contain two fronts too far apart for mutual support. It was not until May 1944 that the Allies, reluctantly accepting that something must be done and that it might as well be done in support of the cross-Channel invasion, launched a major assault after a substantial force buildup. On 11 May a massive offensive cracked the German position and carried the Allies triumphantly to Rome by 4 June. But it took twenty-six Allied divisions to do it, as against approximately seventeen German, and one might well argue who was containing whom. Even after the Anzio breakout, probably misdirected by Clark to beat the British to Rome rather than to trap the Germans retreating from Cassino, the bulk of German forces got away to the north. Late in the summer the front stabilized in the northern Appenines, where Churchill had hoped to be without fighting a year earlier. Another bitter winter lay ahead before the American Fifth and British Eighth Armies broke through to the Po Valley; and even then, for all the valor of hard-used troops, their success remained a local one, achieved with great suffering and perhaps at the expense of greater accomplishments elsewhere.

At Normandy, on the coast of France, the great climax came at last. On 6 June 1944 forces of the United States, Great Britain, Canada, and France fought their way ashore, after years of agonized argument, intense planning, and a military buildup that threatened to tip southern England into the sea. It was in many ways the high point of the war. Both General Marshall and General Alan Brooke had hoped to command it, but the British had seen the political necessity of deferring to the Americans, and Marshall, to his intense disappointment, had succumbed to President Roosevelt's dependence upon him at home; the greatest command plum of the war thus went to General Eisenhower, the team man acceptable to both sides. The Allied force numbered close to 3 million men, with forty-five divisions on the ground, but the initial assault put five divisions over the beaches and dropped three airborne divisions on their flanks. As usual, the Allies achieved tactical and strategic surprise; the weather was bad, and the choice of objective had successfully fooled the enemy. And as usual, the German reaction was swift and violent. The hardest of the landings was at Omaha Beach, where the American First and Twenty-ninth Divisions had a desperate fight to get off the beach. General Montgomery, who had spoken blithely before the invasion of "rattling down to Falaise" and "knocking about with his tanks" on the afternoon of D day, did not take Caen, just behind his beach, until the third week of July.[20]

Nonetheless, the Allies were firmly ashore, assisted by confusion in the German higher command. The campaign refused to go as scheduled, however; Hitler insisted on his generals fighting forward, with the result that the battle of Normandy itself was brutal and prolonged. Thus, when the Allies did finally break out, in General Bradley's great COBRA operation on 25 July, when they did at last crack that hard German crust, they took off in a way that showed German generals what it was like at last to be on the receiving end of a blitzkrieg. The Germans barely escaped total annihilation in a pocket west of Falaise. Allied tactical air performed extraordinary feats of isolating the battle area. It took the Allies a month and a half to get the territory they had originally hoped to control in six days. But at the end of three months, when they had hoped to be closing up to the Seine, they were actually on the German border.

This was one of the most impressive campaigns of the war. Almost caught at Falaise, the Germans were then harried unremittingly back to the Seine, escaping over that river with the Americans and British hot on their heels and most of their armor and heavy weapons lost. Americans of what was now Bradley's Twelfth Army Group reached the river at Mantes below Paris on 19 August; Paris was liberated officially on the twenty-fifth and that day Patton's tanks rolled into Troyes, having advanced 175 miles, against admittedly light opposition, in eleven days.

In the next month, inevitably, an equilibrium was restored. As the Allies pressed on toward the frontier, the Germans coalesced, and the supply problem reared its ugly but inescapable head. So did inter-Allied ambitions and cross-purposes. The Americans had insisted on a supplementary landing in southern France, but it had been beset by logistical and scheduling problems. This landing, ANVIL, was made on 5 August by General Jacob Devers's Sixth Army Group; it made rapid progress northwards, but it did not do much to realize its initial intent of easing the strain on Allied supply lines.

Meanwhile, General Montgomery developed his own idea for winning the war quickly, an overly ambitious thrust across the lower Rhine with airborne troops and an armored drive. For the rest of the war, there was argument over the British preference for a "single thrust" to the heart of Germany versus the American idea of a "two thrust" or "broad front" advance. The Americans remained suspicious, correctly, that the British idea was self-serving, or in this case Montgomery-serving, and preferred a more even distribution of tasks, responsibilities, and resources. They did give in to the airborne-armored combination, Operation MARKET-GARDEN, only to see their fears realized. The advent of winter found them slowing at the German border; the end might be almost in sight, but it was still out of reach.

In the Pacific, meanwhile, American planners had changed their minds as the midocean war progressed. They decided Formosa was a better target than the China coast, and then, changing their minds yet again, they agreed to strike instead at the central Philippines. On 20 October 1944, American troops landed on Leyte, thus fulfilling General MacArthur's promise to return. The Imperial Navy made its last desperate bid to stop its great rival and went down in crushing defeat. American power could henceforth range at will, and the entirety of Japan's southern empire was cut off.

There had already been considerable argument among American planners about where to go after the central Philippines; Admiral King wanted Formosa, but MacArthur was emphatically in favor of Luzon, and in the end he won. There were about 250,000 Japanese soldiers on Luzon, poorly equipped and now isolated, but they fought hard, and at the end of the war there were still 50,000 of them left. Meanwhile, Formosa was bypassed, and the Americans began working their way up the island chain of the Ryukyus, landing on the largest of them, Okinawa, on 1 April 1945. It took almost three months to secure the island at a cost of 50,000 American casualties. But between Okinawa and the smaller but equally bitter battle for Iwo Jima in the Bonin Islands, the Americans were within 350 miles of the home islands of Japan, and their planners were actively working on the coming invasion.

While the fighting in the Pacific moved toward its awful climax, the Allied campaign in Europe gave signs of slowing down. The winter of 1944–1945 was hard on the American forces along the German frontier and on the northern slopes of the Appenines in Italy. Semistatic fighting and bad weather revealed the weaknesses of an army that had basically put a low priority on the man with the rifle and the bayonet. Fighting around Aachen and in the Huertgen Forest had worn infantry divisions down to a catatonic state; replacements were not easily found, and both the general manpower pool and the number of available new divisions were shrinking, not, indeed, by the standard of other belligerents, but rather by the standard of American ideas on how to wage the war. The combat forces were facing similar restrictions on their usually generous allotments of artillery and ammunition. Meanwhile, the air force's strategic bombing campaign had significantly failed to bring Germany down—how close it had come through a campaign against oil production facilities during the summer was not known—and it looked, therefore, as if the myth of the inexhaustible cornucopia of American manpower and productive capacity was about to be exposed as just that.[21] After a brilliant invasion, the Allies had now shown that they were not quite capable of winning the war in 1944, and unless the Germans began to crumble soon, some very hard choices were going to be necessary in the spring.

The Germans, however, were also at the bottom of their several respective barrels, in spite of the economic wizardry of their minister of production, Albert Speer. Hitler increasingly hoped for a miracle, especially the arrival of new weapons systems. To get time for it, he gambled on a sudden winter offensive in the west. Hitting the weak American line around Luxembourg, he expected to get all the way to Antwerp; instead he got the Battle of the Bulge. In ten days of confused, brutal winter fighting, the Germans drove a sixty-mile salient deep into the American lines. But the salient was only forty miles wide at its base, and the Germans never even got to the Meuse, let alone distant Antwerp. The Americans held hard at both shoulders and at crucial road crossings such as Bastogne; to the south General Patton expertly turned his army ninety degrees and drove into the Germans, while General Bradley sucessfully orchestrated the whole operation. By mid-January 1945 the bulge was gone, and so, though no one yet knew it, was Hitler's last strategic reserve in the west.

Argument continued as to whether Montgomery or the Americans should direct the main axis of advance, but in the end, circumstances gave that job to the latter. As the Allies pushed into the Rhineland, the Ninth Armored Division of Hodges's First Army got an intact bridge across the Rhine at Remagen on 7 March. Patton was across, south of that, on the twenty-second, and Montgomery crossed to the north on the twenty-third. The last German defense was definitively breached. There was still hard fighting, but it increasingly bore the character of a death gasp by the Germans with the Allies flowing in ever faster torrents over western Germany.

The final shape of the campaign was somewhat warped by two problems. One was the excessive American fear that the Germans would attempt some sort of Götterdämmerung in the highly propagandized "National Redoubt" in Bavaria; the effect of this was to send all of Devers's Sixth Army Group, as well as Patton's Third Army, off on an eccentric course to the southeast. The other was Eisenhower's interpretation of his general directive; he decided to stop his forces on the Elbe and link there with the Russians advancing from the east. This left Berlin to be conquered by the Russians; Berlin was already promised for their postwar zone of occupation, so Eisenhower concluded there was little sense, and much loss of life and possible danger of collision with his allies, if he went on. Logical at the time, the decision has since been widely criticized in the light of postwar relations with the Russians.[22]

By the time the Americans and British closed up to the Elbe, Germany was in complete collapse. In northern Italy the Fifteenth Army Group had at last broken into the Po Valley, and the enemy there surrendered on 2 May. In Germany itself there were several lesser surrenders, and the war in Europe officially ended on 7 May, with 8 May being proclaimed as V-E Day.

As American and Russian soldiers embraced along the Elbe, other Americans were still fighting against a desperate Japanese resistance in the Philippines and

GIs marching double file through barbed wire and tank traps of the Siegfried Line in World War II
National Archives (208-YE-193)

GIs passing through a German village in World War II
National Archives (208-YE-137)

American commanders in the European Theater of Operations. *Seated from left to right*: Lieutenant General William H. Simpson, Ninth Army; General George S. Patton, Jr., Third Army; General Carl A. ("Tooey") Spaatz, U.S. Strategic Air Forces in Europe; General of the Army Dwight D. ("Ike") Eisenhower; General Omar N. Bradley, Twelfth Army Group; Lieutenant General Courtney H. Hodges, First Army; Lieutenant General Leonard T. ("Gee") Gerow, Fifteenth Army. *Standing from left to right*: Brigadier General Ralph P. Sterling, Ninth Tactical Air Command; Lieutenant General Hoyt S. Vandenberg, Ninth Air Force; Lieutenant General Walter Bedell Smith, Ike's chief of staff; Major General O. P. Weyland, Nineteenth Tactical Air Command; and Brigadier General Richard E. Nugent, Twenty-ninth Tactical Air Command
National Archives (208-YE-182)

Heavy bombers high over Europe in World War II
National Archives (208-YE-70)

on Okinawa. The idea of an intermediate landing on the China coast had now been dropped, and instead plans were being worked up for Operation OLYMPIC, the invasion of Kyushu, in November, to be followed in March 1946 by CO-RONET, the invasion of Honshu itself. On the basis of past experience, the Americans expected bitter opposition, and figures of a million prospective casualties did not appear out of line. However, both the navy and the air force were developing a different view of events. The Japanese fleet was gone, and Japan's merchant marine had virtually disappeared in the face of the American submarine campaign. Japanese internal life was therefore collapsing. General Curtis LeMay's big B–29 Superfortress bombers, specifically designed for the Pacific distances, were laying waste the cities of Japan with intensive, low-level incendiary raids.

The significance of these developments for the final strategy and operations of the Pacific war was suddenly and irrevocably altered on 6 August when the first atomic bomb was dropped on the city of Hiroshima. On the eighth the Soviet Union declared war against Japan, and on the ninth Nagasaki was levelled by a second American atomic bomb. Destructive as they were, the bombs did not in themselves end the war; what they did do was convince the already faltering Japanese leadership that further resistance was hopeless. On the tenth the Japanese offered to surrender, fighting ceased on the fifteenth, and the actual surrender was signed aboard the USS *Missouri* in Tokyo Bay on 2 September 1945. World War II was over.

There are almost as many sets of figures available for World War II as there are compilers of them. Perhaps only one set really counts. During World War II, 10,420,000 men and women served in the United States Army and the Army Air Forces; 936,259 of them were battle casualities of one kind or another.[23] With all the waste of war, with all the disproportionate weight that war laid on one man as opposed to another, a casualty rate of 9 percent was still the lowest of any of the major belligerents, a tribute to the manner in which a small professional and large civilian body raised and trained its forces and fought its war. There will long be argument about who did what, and why, and if it all somehow might not have been done better, but to a generation which did not actively participate in it, World War II now seems like America's heroic age, "an appropriate climax to much of the history of the American Army and nation."[24]

NOTES

1. Admiral Sir Cyprian Bridge, *Sea Power and Other Studies* (London: John Murray, 1910), p. 104.

2. Omar N. Bradley and Clay Blair, *A General's Life* (New York: Simon and Schuster, 1983), p. 79.

3. Kent R. Greenfield, Robert B. Palmer, and Bell I. Wiley, *The Organization of Ground Combat Troops*, United States Army in World War II: The Army Ground Forces (Washington: Army Historical Division, 1947), passim.

4. Russell F. Weigley, *History of the United States Army*, enlarged ed. (Bloomington: Indiana University Press, 1984), pp. 435–36.

5. Greenfield et al., *Ground Combat Troops*, pp. 274–75.

6. Ibid., p. 192.

7. Winston S. Churchill, *The Second World War* (Boston: Houghton Mifflin Co., 1948–1953), vol. V, *Closing the Ring*, (1951), p. 488.

8. Maurice Matloff and E. M. Snell, *Strategic Planning for Coalition Warfare, 1941–1942*, United States Army in World War II: The War Department (Washington: Office of the Chief of Military History, 1953), p. 22.

9. H. P. Willmott, *Empires in the Balance: Japanese and Allied Pacific Strategies to April 1942* (Annapolis, Md.: Naval Institute Press, 1982), pp. 216–17.

10. Matloff and Snell, *Strategic Planning*, pp. 48–51.

11. Ibid., pp. 53–56.

12. Ibid., pp. 104–5.

13. Ibid., pp. 177–78.

14. Ibid., app. F, pp. 392–95.

15. Bradley, *Life*, p. 394; Martin Blumenson, *The Patton Papers*, 2 vols. (Boston: Houghton Mifflin Co., 1972–1974), II, 608.

16. Bradley, *Life*, pp. 163–64.

17. Barbara W. Tuchman, *Stilwell and the American Experience in China, 1911–45* (New York: Macmillan Co., 1971), p. 371.

18. Churchill, *The Second World War*, vol. IV, *The Hinge of Fate* (1950), pp. 790–91.

19. Ibid., p. 800.

20. Bradley, *Life*, p. 234.

21. These problems are more fully discussed in Russell F. Weigley, *Eisenhower's Lieutenants: The Campaign of France and Germany, 1944–1945* (Bloomington: Indiana University Press, 1981), pp. 370–82.

22. Stephen E. Ambrose, *Eisenhower and Berlin, 1945: The Decision to Halt at the Elbe* (New York: Norton, 1967).

23. M. H. Williams, *Chronology, 1941–1945*, United States Army in World War II: Special Studies (Washington: Office of the Chief of Military History, 1960), p. 551.

24. Weigley, *United States Army*, p. 480.

FURTHER READING

The number of works on World War II is legion; this short note is therefore divided into three specific categories: official studies and general studies; autobiographical or biographical works on the major commanders; recent studies of interest on particular topics. Unpublished collections of papers or documents are not included.

The most useful, as well as the most thorough, study of the United States Army is the U.S. Army in World War II series of the Office of the Chief of Military History, Washington, D.C., which has been published in several distinct subseries and now runs to over one-hundred volumes. A similar, smaller study is W. F. Craven and J. L. Cate, eds., *The Army Air Forces in World War II*, 7 vols. (Chicago: University of Chicago Press, 1948–1958). As this was coalition warfare at its best, even if it did not always look like it, the British official histories are equally useful, especially J. R. M. Butler et al., eds., *Grand Strategy*, 6 vols. (London: H.M. Stationery Office, 1956–1972). A good atlas is indispensable; the best is vol. II of V. J. Esposito, ed., *The West Point Atlas of American Wars* (New York: Praeger, 1960). For the best overviews of the American army, there are Russell F. Weigley's two volumes originally published in the Macmillan Wars of the United States series, *History of the United States Army*, enlarged ed. (Bloomington: Indiana University Press, 1984), and *The American Way of War* (New York: Macmillan Co., 1973). For an introduction to the war in the air, see R. J. Overy, *The Air War, 1939–1945* (New York: Stein and Day, 1980).

Almost all of the major participants wrote memoirs of their service or have had biographical studies or assessments written about them, or both. Needless to say, these vary considerably in quality. The reader should begin with the great study by Forrest C. Pogue, *George C. Marshall*, 3 vols. to date (New York: Viking, 1963-   ). Stephen E. Ambrose wrote *The Supreme Commander: The War Years of General Dwight D. Eisenhower* (Garden City, N.Y.: Doubleday, 1970); he also edited *The Papers of Dwight David Eisenhower: The War Years*, 5 vols. (Baltimore: Johns Hopkins University Press, 1970). Martin Blumenson wrote *Patton: The Man Behind the Legend, 1885–1945* (New York: William Morrow, 1985), and he edited *The Patton Papers*, 2 vols. (Boston: Houghton Mifflin Co., 1972–1974). Omar N. Bradley and Clay Blair collaborated on *A General's Life* (New York: Simon and Schuster, 1983), which is far better than Bradley's earlier *A Soldier's Story* (New York: Holt, 1951), and Martin Blumenson has written *Mark Clark* (New York: Congdon & Weed, Inc., 1984). Barbara Tuchman's *Stilwell and the American Experience in China, 1911–45* (New York: Macmillan Co., 1970) offers a good look at that controversial general. Clayton James has written a scholarly standard, *The Years of MacArthur*, 3 vols. (Boston: Houghton Mifflin Co., 1970–1985). For insight into some of the leading British figures, see Sir Arthur Bryant's *The Turn of the Tide and Triumph in the West* (London: Collins, 1957–1959), the published versions of Alan Brooke's diaries. None of the several biographies of Montgomery are as revealing as his own *Memoirs* (London: Collins, 1958).

Monographs on specific episodes continue to appear regularly. Among the more recent treatments of the Pacific theater are Gordon W. Prange, *At Dawn We Slept: The Untold Story of Pearl Harbor* (New York: McGraw Hill, 1981), and on the Philippines H. P. Willmott, *Empires in the Balance: Japanese and Allied Pacific Strategies to April 1942* (Annapolis, Md.: Naval Institute Press, 1982). The grand sweep of the entire Pacific war is masterfully portrayed by Ronald H. Spector, *Eagle Against the Sun: The American War with Japan*, The Macmillan Wars of the United States (New York: Macmillan Co., 1985). For Europe there are Max Hastings, *Overlord: D-Day, June 6, 1944* (New York: Simon & Schuster, 1984), and Russell F. Weigley, *Eisenhower's Lieutenants: The Campaigns of France and Germany, 1944–1945* (Bloomington: Indiana University Press, 1981). A new, rather episodic assessment is John Keegan, *Six Armies in Normandy* (New York: Viking, 1982). As it was at the time, the Mediterranean remains a poor relation; R. Trevelyan's *Rome '44: The Battle for the Eternal City* (New York: Viking, 1981) is something of a memoir; straightforward military critiques include W. G. F. Jackson, *The Battle for Rome* (London: Botsford, 1969), and John Ellis, *Cassino: The Hollow Victory— The Battle for Rome, January-June 1944* (New York: McGraw-Hill, 1984).

CHAPTER 15

The Armed Services and American Strategy, 1945–1953

STEPHEN E. AMBROSE

The years 1945 to 1953, from the end of the Second World War to the end of the Korean War, brought rapid and unexpected change to the armed forces of the United States. At the beginning of the period, the army was downcast, not only because of the trauma of the most rapid demobilization in history, but also because the atomic bomb seemed to make mass armies obsolete. The navy, too, was worried about its future in a nuclear world. The air force, meanwhile, claiming to represent the future, eagerly embraced the new technology and the wholly new defense organization (the Department of Defense) as it asserted simultaneously its independence from the army and its prominence over the older services.

But when the Korean War ended in 1953, the army was once again the service doing most of the fighting with the most men under its command, while the navy's crucial role in supplying the troops and protecting their flanks had grown rather than diminished. In Korea the air force had not been able to deliver the knockout punch it claimed it could. Therefore the idea, so popular from 1946 to 1950, that all the nation needed for its defense was an adequate force of heavy bombers had to be abandoned.

So, too, did the idea that America could go it alone. One of the most important military developments of the period was the creation of the North Atlantic Treaty Organization (NATO), America's first-time-ever commitment to a peacetime alliance with European powers. It came about primarily because of the revolution in weapons technology (radar, jet airplanes, guided missiles, super aircraft carriers, atomic bombs, etc.), a revolution that suddenly made the United States itself vulnerable to attack. To oversimplify, America came out of World War II convinced that it could order the affairs of the world through the possession of the world's largest air force, armed with atomic weapons (of which the Americans had a monopoly), and backed by a relatively modest army and navy. Eight years later American strategy relied on the NATO alliance, relatively heavy troop commitments to Europe, a strong and vigorous navy, and an air force that, although still wedded in theory to strategic bombing, spent most of its operational time supporting ground forces in Korea and Europe.

Shifts in strategic thinking which both reflected current political conditions and helped guide the creation of the postwar armed services occurred with alarming frequency throughout the period. In retrospect, it was inevitable that there would be much groping for a suitable strategy, because there were so many new facts to be dealt with, not only in weaponry, but also in the international scene. In the late thirties and early forties, the American armed forces had geared up to meet the German and Japanese threats. By 1945 those threats had disappeared, to be replaced by one from the Soviet Union that posed numerous new and unexpected military problems.

The towering figure in the American military establishment was General George C. Marshall, army chief of staff (1939–1945), secretary of state (1947–1949), and finally secretary of defense (1950–1951). His answer to the new problems was universal military training (UMT). Marshall was a great believer in the citizen-soldier; in addition, as the man who directed the huge buildup of the army in the early forties, he was keenly aware of the problems of trying to create a modern mass army from scratch. Like most men, Marshall believed that the future would resemble the past; when the next war came, he expected it to be like World War II, except that the country would not have as much time to prepare itself. Therefore, the United States needed a program of UMT in peacetime that would provide a mass army the moment the attack came.

Marshall convinced President Harry S. Truman. The army chief of staff, Dwight D. Eisenhower, was also enthusiastic. From early 1946 until the presidential election of 1948, Marshall, Truman, and Ike spent much of their time and effort advocating a program of UMT. All young men (and women, in some versions) would spend a year in the service after graduating from high school. Congress, however, never came close to passing such an expensive bill, not only because of the cost, but also because most congressmen, like most Americans, assumed that the days of mass armies were over.[1]

Meanwhile the army shrank and shrank. From a wartime high of over 8 million it fell to 4.2 million by 1 January 1946; by 30 June it was down to 1.89 million; a year later the army numbered 1 million (all figures include the Army Air Forces, which numbered about 40 percent of the whole). The navy fell back, too, from a wartime high of 3.4 million (including the Marine Corps) to less than 1 million. But the navy in the late war years had begun a building program that was less intended to fight Japan than to preserve the navy through the predictable budget cuts in the postwar world. The program emphasized aircraft carriers—the *Midway* and the *Franklin D. Roosevelt* were started in late 1943 and launched in March and April of 1945; the *Coral Sea* was finished in 1946. These giant vessels, combined with new heavy bombers that could operate from carriers, gave the navy a nuclear role, something the army tried desperately to achieve but was unable to find for itself.

Thrown on the defensive, the army argued that the air force would need forward bases to deliver the atomic weapons as well as troops to mop up the nuclear battlefield after the mushroom cloud had dissipated. The navy argued that the air force would need surface vessels to support overseas airfields. But in 1948, when the newly independent air force began accepting regular delivery of the B–36 bomber, those arguments were undercut because of successful experiments in midair refueling. The air force could and did argue that by itself it could deter war around the globe, punish aggression, and provide the muscle to ensure American foreign policy objectives.

Faith in the air force, a belief that it really could do it alone, was a factor in the passage of the National Security Act of 26 July 1947, which gave the air force its independence while putting all three services under one head. The army and air force had both favored a relatively strong unification plan (indeed, General Eisenhower, on the basis of his experience with triphibious warfare in Europe, advocated a single service with a single uniform and a single service academy). The army supported unification because it thought it could better protect its interests against the more glamorous rival services within a centralized defense department rather than in competitive appeal to Congress. The air force support came because it was confident of its future and was sure it could dictate in any unified command. The navy, however, feared subordination to commanders who did not understand sea power and feared in addition that it would lose its air arm to the air force. As a result of navy pressure, the defense structure created by the congressional legislation produced a "coordinated," not unified, National Military Establishment under a single civilian secretary of defense.[2]

The first secretary of defense was James Forrestal, formerly secretary of the navy and one of the chief opponents of unification. He found himself frustrated in his new job by the statute he had largely designed—he was unable to coordinate service policies or strategies. In March 1948 he held a famous meeting at Key West, Florida, with the Joint Chiefs of Staff (JCS). Forrestal ordered the chiefs to reach agreement on "who will do what with what." This attempt to set goals and missions (and thus lay the basis for appropriations) failed because the air force insisted on sole possession of a strategic role.[3]

Forrestal complained that he had responsibility but not power. Truman moved to correct that situation in March 1949 (the same month that Forrestal resigned) when he asked Congress for an amendment to the National Security Act that would create an executive department of defense (done on 10 August 1949). The new secretary of defense, Louis A. Johnson, got off to a terrible start, at least with the navy. Politically ambitious and mindful of public opinion polls that showed support for limits on defense spending and for a larger air force, Johnson's first act was to cancel the navy's first supercarrier, the 65,000-ton *United States*, just five days after the keel was laid.

Johnson's action provoked the "revolt of the admirals." Navy leaders "leaked" to sympathetic congressmen material critical of the air force in general, and of the B–36 in particular. The admirals thought that the navy was being stripped of offensive power, leaving the nation in a defenseless state. In hearings before the House Armed Services Committee, Admiral Arthur Radford called the B–36 a billion-dollar blunder and attacked the whole air force strategic concentration on atomic annihilation. "In planning to wage a war," Radford said, "we must look to the peace to follow.... A war of annihilation might possibly bring a Pyrrhic military victory, but it would be politically and economically senseless." His observation became all the more cogent when, during the hearings in September 1949, the Russians set off their first atomic bomb. The American nuclear monopoly was gone, and with it went the unexamined faith that the United States, through its nuclear-carrying bombers, could order the affairs of the world.[4]

From the first flash over White Sands, New Mexico, in July 1945, the bomb had dominated American strategic thinking. The basic strategy it underwrote was one of deterrence. America would have its way in the world not by fighting and winning wars, but by not fighting them, because the threat would suffice. As early as the summer of 1945, Truman had told Charles de Gaulle, who feared Russian moves in central Europe, that if Stalin did not behave the United States would use one or two bombs and force him to do so. The problem with a strategy of deterrence, however, was that it never met the real situation. Russian expansion, the major political problem of the postwar world, could not be halted with one or two of the relatively small bombs of the period—and one or two was all the bombs there were in the American arsenal until 1950. Further, it was always difficult to match provocation with response. The United States could hardly drop a bomb on Moscow because Stalin refused to live up to his promise to hold free elections in Poland. Only a massive Russian invasion of Western Europe could justify the use of the bomb, but if one waited until the invasion came, it would be too late—Europe would be overrun. Nuclear strategy, then and now, is an all-or-nothing strategy, and in the real world of international relations, all-or-nothing situations are seldom encountered short of all-out war.

Senator Robert Taft and other Republican conservatives had thought to balance the federal budget and cut taxes by continuing to reduce the army and navy while depending on a seventy-group air force for national defense. (The figure seventy, first used by the air force at the end of the war on the basis that seventy groups was the number Congress would pay for, took on a life of its own and was constantly cited during this period as the magic number that would ensure America's defense.) Whether the air force generals admitted it or not, their strategy, as Taft knew, was essentially isolationist, a Fortress America concept. The seventy groups might deter any Russian adventures in North America but not in Europe or Asia. But it would definitely be cheaper than playing a world role with active-duty soldiers and sailors, and much more popular, as Secretary of Defense Louis Johnson knew. After canceling the navy's supercarrier, he continued to "cut the fat" from the Defense Department's budget, which he promised to reduce to $13 billion for the fiscal year 1951.

The Truman administration's military and foreign policies were now rushing forward but in exactly the opposite directions, so that the gap between them increased daily. In foreign affairs Truman insisted on "getting tough with the

Russians," in Greece, in Western Europe, in Asia—everywhere. But there was little military muscle to back it up. Secretary of State Marshall later recalled, "I remember being pressed constantly to . . . give the Russians hell. . . . I was getting the same appeal in relation to the Far East and China. At that time, my facilities for giving them hell—and I am a soldier and know something about the ability to give hell—was 1 1/3 divisions over the entire United States. That is quite a proposition when you deal with somebody with over 260 and you have 1 1/3."[5]

Truman had to reduce America's world role or rearm. On 30 January 1950, to help him decide, he authorized the State and Defense Departments "to make an over-all review and re-assessment of American foreign and defense policy in the light of the loss of China, the Soviet mastery of atomic energy and the prospect of the fusion bomb." Through February, March, and early April, a State-Defense committee met. By 12 April it had a report ready, which Truman sent to the National Security Council (NSC). It came back as a policy paper, NSC 68. Senator Henry Jackson called NSC 68 "the first comprehensive statement of a national strategy."[6]

As one of the principal authors stated, NSC 68 advocated "an immediate and large-scale build-up in our military and general strength and that of our allies with the intention of righting the power balance and in the hope that through means other than all-out war we could induce a change in the nature of the Soviet system." How the change was to be brought about was unclear, except that it would not be through war. NSC 68 postulated that while the West waited for the Soviets to mellow, the United States should rearm and thereby prevent any Russian expansion. The program did not look to the liberation of China or of Eastern Europe, but it did call on the United States to assume unilaterally the defense of the non-Communist world.[7]

NSC 68 represented the practical extension of the Truman Doctrine of 1947, which had been worldwide in its implications but limited to Greece and Turkey in its application. The JCS representative on the State-Defense committee that drew up the plan had come to the meetings believing that the most money that could be gotten from Congress was around $17 billion a year. He quickly learned that the State Department representatives were thinking in much bigger terms, and he adjusted. In the end, although NSC 68 did not include any specific figures, the State Department estimated that defense expenditures of $35 billion a year would be required to implement the program of rearming America and her allies. Eventually, more could be spent, for NSC 68 declared that the United States was so rich it could use 20 percent of its gross national product for arms without suffering national bankruptcy. In 1950 this would have been $50 billion.

That was a great deal of money, even for Americans. It was necessary, however, because the danger was so great. The document foresaw "an indefinite period of tension and danger" and warned that by 1954 the Soviet Union would have the nuclear capability to destroy the United States. America had to undertake "a bold and massive program" of rebuilding the West until it surpassed the

Soviet bloc; only thus could it stand at the "political and material center with other free nations in variable orbits around it." The United States could no longer ask, "How much security can we afford?" nor should it attempt to "distinguish between national and global security."[8]

Truman recognized, as he later wrote, that NSC 68 "meant a great military effort in time of peace. It meant doubling or tripling the budget, increasing taxes heavily, and imposing various kinds of economic controls. It meant a great change in our normal peacetime way of doing things." He refused to allow publication of NSC 68 and indicated that he would do nothing about revising the budget until after the congressional elections. He realized that without a major crisis there was little chance of selling the program to the Congress or the public. He himself had only two and a half years to serve, while NSC 68 contemplated a long-term program. If the Republicans entered the White House, the chances were that their main concern would be to lower taxes, in which case the nation would have to wait for the return of the Democrats to get NSC 68 really rolling. Thus, when Truman received NSC 68 in its final form in early June 1950, he made no commitment. What he would have done with it had not other events intruded is problematical.[9]

In June 1950 North Korea invaded South Korea. Truman, called upon to back up his containment policy, did so at once, sending in first the air force and then the navy and the army to halt the aggressor. The United States was back at war. In the process, most of the expert's predictions about the nature of the "next war" proved to be dead wrong. General Omar Bradley, for example, chairman of the Joint Chiefs of Staff, had said that he doubted there would ever again be an amphibious operation, because of the nature of modern war; yet the decisive event of the first phase of the Korean War was Douglas MacArthur's amphibious invasion at Inchon in September 1950. Air force claims that the big bombers could interdict any supply line and thus bring victory from the air without the heavy casualties involved in ground warfare proved to be false claims. The common supposition that the "next war" would be a "push-button war," with the new weapons and machines taking over from men, could not have been more wrong. Korea was a classic infantryman's and artilleryman's war. The air support the soldiers needed and finally got was not big bombers on strategic missions (which were forbidden for political as well as economic reasons—there were no true strategic targets in North Korea or China), but close-in fighter and helicopter support. The navy, far from having lost its role in war, found that it was crucial not only in getting the fighting men over there and supplying them in battle but also because of its magnificent carrier fleet, which provided the troops with constant fighter cover.

But Korea was basically the army's war, and the heroes came from the army— Douglas MacArthur first of all, followed by Matthew B. Ridgway, William F. Dean, and J. Lawton Collins. It was a veteran army—most officers and many of the enlisted men had fought in World War II—and a good one. It used World War II organization charts, World War II weapons, and World War II techniques.

At Inchon MacArthur drew upon the vast experience of the navy and Marine Corps with amphibious assaults to score the greatest triumph of his long career. Unfortunately, this victory was followed in November and December 1950 by one of the worst defeats ever suffered by American armed forces, as Chinese troops surprised and overran MacArthur's men in North Korea. Eventually General Matthew Ridgway managed to force the Chinese back to the original demarcation line where the war settled down into trenches. Over the next two years, there was relatively little movement of the lines as the Chinese and Americans fought each other with weapons and methods quite similar to those used by the Germans and French in 1916. "Modern war" did not look very modern in Korea.[10]

Except in race relations. Perhaps the biggest difference between the army of 1941–1945 and the army of 1950–1953 was that in Korea the army was integrated. Indeed, in view of its social impact and in view of who was to do much of the fighting in the next war in Vietnam, it might be argued that integration of the armed forces was one of the most important political events of the period 1945–1953.

The United States Army in World War II was a Jim Crow outfit (the navy avoided Jim Crow by the simple method of having almost no black sailors). Only during the crisis of the Battle of the Bulge did the top brass consent to allowing a few black platoons (fifty in all) to fight as integral parts of white companies. They compiled an outstanding record. The report of the personnel officer of the 104th Division on his black platoon was typical: "Morale: Excellent. Manner of performance: Superior. Men are very eager to close with the enemy and to destroy him. . . . The colored platoon has a calibre of men equal to any veteran platoon." A few white officers declared that the black troops were too aggressive and occasionally overextended themselves, but when the black units suffered losses and could no longer function as platoons, the remaining men were formed into squads and served in white platoons, without complaints from either side. Although the black man's chance to prove himself came only at the war's end, the black platoons did so well that perceptive, younger army officers began to wonder if segregation really was the most efficient method of organization.

Not, however, the senior officers. After the German surrender the black platoons were gradually reassigned to all-black, usually noncombat, units, and kept in the occupation army in Germany while the division with which they fought went home for demobilization. The policy caused resentment. As one white commander explained to his superior, "These colored men cannot understand why they are not being allowed to share the honor of returning to their homeland with the Division with which they fought, proving to the world that Negro soldiers can do something besides drive a truck or work in a laundry. I am unqualified to give them a satisfactory answer."

The answer was that, with the exception of a relatively few officers, the army had no intention of making Jim Crow a casualty of the war. But in 1948 President

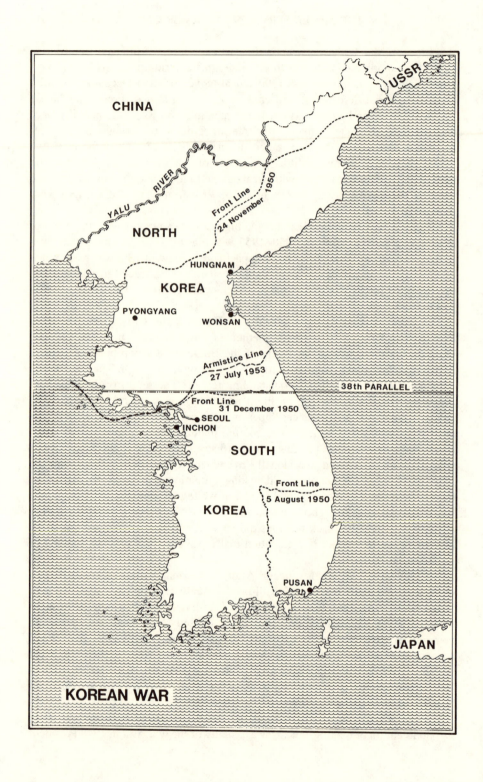

Truman, up for re-election and under tremendous pressure from black leaders, especially A. Phillip Randolph and the National Association for the Advancement of Colored People (NAACP), issued an executive order that barred discrimination in the armed forces.

Truman may have hoped to avoid an open, legal assault on Jim Crow (he promised only to end discrimination not segregation), but when General Bradley said that the army "is not out to make any social reform" and indicated that he would continue to segregate blacks in the army, the president had to rebuke him publicly. Truman said he wanted segregation ended and in September of 1948 appointed a committee of liberals and blacks to advise the military of its revision of race policies.

Over the next two years, the committee investigated the military and sought its cooperation in eliminating segregation. The navy promised to enlist more blacks. The air force, while holding to a quota system in some units, ended most segregation. The army, with a far larger percentage of blacks, lagged behind. Well into the Korean War the army retained some all-black units; integration among the forces in Europe did not even begin until the spring of 1952. The performance of individual black soldiers serving in integrated units in Korea was so far superior to anything white leaders had expected, however, and not incidentally better than black performance in segregated units, that the army brass gradually abandoned its opposition to integration. Some even became enthusiastic proponents when it became clear that white GIs accepted the new system. In time the army became the most thoroughly integrated service. After almost 200 years of continuous service in the army, black soldiers had finally achieved formal equality.[11]

In Korea, meanwhile, General MacArthur challenged President Truman at the end of 1950 on the conduct of the war, thereby setting off the Truman-MacArthur controversy—one of the great emotional events of American history, but one which need not detain us here, as it was a political, not a military dispute. What they were arguing about, rather than the way in which they argued, is important.

MacArthur's strategy put Asia first. Truman's strategy put Europe first. Thus, when Truman began the rearmament campaign sketched out in NSC 68, he sent most of the newly raised units or newly built weapons to Europe. MacArthur wanted them in Korea, or for use by the Nationalist Chinese against Red China. Truman insisted that the real threat was potential Russian aggression in Europe; MacArthur insisted that it was actual Chinese aggression in Asia. There could be no compromise between these views, and Truman was president. MacArthur got fired.

Truman had strong support from his cabinet, most of all from Secretary of Defense George C. Marshall. Indeed, it is possible to interpret the Truman-MacArthur feud as being in fact a dispute between Marshall and MacArthur over a proper American strategy. To oversimplify, MacArthur and other senior officers who fought in the Pacific in World War II, including many from the navy, believed that "Asia-first" was the proper American strategy, because Asia was the continent of the future, while Europe was old and worn out. Marshall, backed by Eisenhower, Bradley, and most of the senior officers who fought in Europe, were "Europe-firsters," convinced that America's historical, cultural, political, and economic ties with Europe were far more important than America's contacts with Asia. They thought military strategy and military dispositions ought to reflect that importance. Thus, even when the Korean War was going badly for the United States, Truman, Marshall, Eisenhower, and many others insisted on building up NATO at Korea's expense.

Their decision to strengthen Europe was carried out within the context of the North Atlantic Treaty, which the Senate had approved in July 1949 after a long debate on the strategy involved. Thoughtful Republicans, led by Senator Robert A. Taft of Ohio, questioned the wisdom of provoking the Soviets thousands of miles from America's shores. They raised other questions. Should the United States be a world policeman? How much should it pay to play such a role? And, at bottom, what was the nature and extent of the Soviet threat and how should it be met?

The United States already had the atomic bomb. NATO as it stood added nothing to this power. The ground figures remained the same, with the Red Army enjoying a ten to one advantage over the American army. Senators asked if the State Department or the Defense Department planned to send "substantial" numbers of American troops to Europe. Secretary of State Dean Acheson responded, "The answer to that question, Senator, is a clear and absolute 'No'." Did the United States plan to put Germans back in uniform? "We are very clear," Acheson replied, "that the disarmament and demilitarization of Germany must be complete and absolute."

This deepened rather than clarified the mystery. What would NATO do? The problem, as French Premier Henri Queuille put it in a much-quoted statement, was easily described: "We know that once Western Europe was occupied, America would again come to our aid and eventually we would again be liberated. But the process would be terrible. The next time you probably would be liberating a corpse."[12] The solution was not so easily seen. In the absence of an imminent attack, neither the Europeans nor the Americans were remotely prepared to undertake the rearmament effort on the scale required to match the Red Army. The Europeans were unwilling to jeopardize their economic revival by building standing armies, and the Americans relied on citizen-soldiers.

Each side was trying to carry water on both shoulders. In order to persuade their peoples of the necessity of accepting a provocative alliance, the European governments had to insist that the alliance could defend them from invasion. But the governments also simultaneously had to insist that no intolerable sacrifices would be required. As Robert Osgood has noted, "these two assurances could only be fulfilled, if at all, by the participation of West Germany in the alliance, but for political reasons this measure was no more acceptable to the European countries than a massive rearmament effort."[13]

German rearmament was also politically unacceptable in the United States

General of the Army Douglas MacArthur near Suwon, Korea; Lieutenant General Matthew
Ridgway, Eighth Army, third from right
National Archives (111-SC-356736)

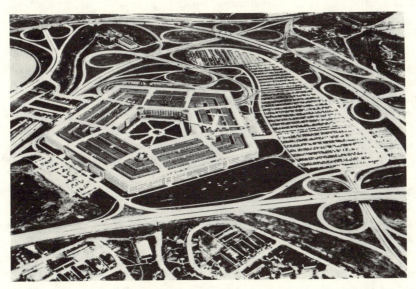

The Pentagon
National Archives (208-LU-61D-2)

and the Truman administration continued to insist that it had no intention of encouraging the resurgence of a militarily strong Germany. Nor, the senators were assured, would NATO lead to an arms race or require the Americans to provide military material to the Europeans. Taft was still opposed to the treaty, but was persuaded to vote for it after the Senate specifically repudiated any obligation either to build up the armed forces of the eleven allies or to extend them continued economic aid. On 21 July 1949 Taft and eighty-one other senators voted their approval of the NATO pact.

President Truman immediately ratified the treaty and sent to Congress a mutual defense assistance bill allocating $1.5 billion for European military aid. All the assurances that the treaty would not inaugurate an arms race or cost the United States were brushed aside. The president described the object of this legislation in disarmingly modest terms: ''The military assistance which we propose for these countries will be limited to that which is necessary to help them create mobile defensive forces.'' In other words, the administration had resolved to equip and bring up to strength Europe's twelve or so divisions.[14]

Taft was furious. He charged that the administration was committing the United States to a futile, obsolete, and bankrupt strategy of defending Europe by large-scale land warfare. He much preferred a unilateral American defense of Europe through enlarging the American air force and stepping up the production of atomic bombs.

In point of fact, however, the meaning of NATO was that the United States promised to use the bomb to deter a Russian attack. The alternative of building up Western ground strength to match the Red Army, an eventuality implied by the treaty and much feared by Taft, was politically impossible. Neither the United States Congress nor the Western European legislatures would fund large standing armies.

The United States promise to use the bomb to deter Russian aggression made sense only if the Americans retained their monopoly, but on 22 September 1949 Truman announced that the Soviets had exploded an atomic bomb. ''This is now a different world,'' Senator Arthur Vandenberg painfully recorded. It was indeed. The urge to do something, anything, was irrepressible. Congress swiftly appropriated the funds for NATO which Truman had requested in July, and the president ordered accelerated development of the hydrogen bomb. Nothing, however, could change the fact that America's promise to defend Europe with the bomb had been dissipated almost before it had been given. If the Russians could make the bomb, they surely could develop the means to deliver it. The Soviets now had two trumps, the bomb and the Red Army, to NATO's one.

German remilitarization and Western European rearmament were the obvious ways to counter the Red Army threat. The Americans could pay the bill with an updated version of lend-lease. But the Europeans were suspicious, the French especially so; they could see little point to accepting American arms if they also had to accept American orders, the central problem in NATO both then and later. A strategy that uses American equipment and European lives to counter the Red Army has little appeal to Europeans, especially since only the Americans can decide when or where to use the troops, only the Americans can pull the nuclear trigger, and the battlefield where Russia and America fight it out is Europe.

If the Europeans would not rearm, the Americans would have to do so themselves. Samuel Huntington stated the American dilemma: "Could a democracy arm to deter or could it only arm to respond?"[15] NSC 68 assumed it could arm to deter, and Korea gave the necessary impetus to make NSC 68 into policy. In December 1950, as MacArthur's troops fell back in Korea, Truman appointed the tremendously popular General Dwight D. Eisenhower as supreme commander of the allied powers in Europe. German rearmament then got underway, less than six years after the United States had helped to force Germany to disarm.

In 1951 Truman put the nation on a Cold War footing. He got emergency powers from Congress to expedite war mobilization, made selective service a permanent feature of American life, submitted a $50 billion defense budget that followed the guidelines of NSC 68, sent two more divisions (a total of six) to Europe, doubled the number of air groups to ninety-five, obtained new bases in Morocco, Libya, and Saudi Arabia, increased the army to 3.5 million men, pushed forward the Japanese peace treaty, stepped up aid to the French in Indochina, initiated the process of adding Greece and Turkey to NATO, and began discussions with General Francisco Franco which led to American aid to Spain in return for military bases there. Truman's accomplishments were breathtaking. He had given the United States a thermonuclear bomb by 1952 and rearmed Germany. He had established American military bases in Western Europe, Britain, and Japan.

There had to be a price. It was best summed up by Walter Millis, himself a Cold Warrior and great admirer of James Forrestal, the first secretary of defense. The Truman administration, Millis wrote, left behind it

an enormously expanded military establishment, beyond anything we had ever contemplated in time of peace. It . . . evoked a huge and apparently permanent armament industry, now wholly dependent . . . on government contracts. . . . The Department of Defense had become without question the biggest industrial management operation in the world; the great private operations, like General Motors, duPont, [and] the leading airplane manufacturers . . . had assumed positions of monopoly power which, however unavoidable, at least seemed to raise new questions as to the legal and constitutional organization of the state.[16]

The administration produced supergiant thermonuclear weapons, families of lesser atomic bombs, guided missiles, the B–52 jet bomber, new supercarriers, tanks, and other heavy weapons. It had increased the risk of war while making war immeasurably more dangerous.

One other thing bothered Millis. For all that the Truman administration accomplished, "what it failed to do was to combine these men and weapons into a practicable structure of military policy competent to meet the new political and military problems that now stood grimly before us. We were to face them in a large measure of bewilderment as to where the true paths of military policy might lead.''[17]

These misgivings were well founded. In 1945, at the end of World War II, many Americans had thought it would be possible to return to the good old days, when the United States got along fine with a miniscule army and navy. By the end of the Korean War in 1953, they had begun to learn that such a dream was just a dream, and in the years that followed they would come to accept as normal a degree of militarization of American life that an earlier generation would have called Prussian. Meanwhile, as the stockpile of atomic warheads grew—from 100 to 1,000 to 2,000 to 5,000 to 10,000 and ultimately to 50,000 and more—the chances of an atomic bomb actually being used in combat decreased, and men continued to fight their wars in old-fashioned, or "conventional," ways. And that was the ultimate lesson of the period 1945–1953: the atomic bomb had revolutionized international diplomacy, but not warfare.

NOTES

1. For an extended discussion of efforts to deal with these and other postwar problems while Eisenhower was chief of staff (December 1945–February 1948), see Stephen E. Ambrose, *Eisenhower*, vol. I, *Soldier, General of the Army, President-Elect, 1890–1952* (New York: Simon and Schuster, 1983), pp. 433–73. For Eisenhower's support of UMT, see especially pp. 472, 487, and 511.

2. On unification of the armed forces, see in particular Demetrios Caraley, *The Politics of Military Unification* (New York: Columbia University Press, 1966) and Paul Y. Hammond, *Organizing for Defense: The American Military Establishment in the Twentieth Century* (1961; reprint, Westport, Conn.: Greenwood Press, 1977), chap. 8. For the navy's response to the National Security Act of 1947, see Dean C. Allard, "An Era of Transition, 1945–1953," in Kenneth J. Hagan, ed., *In Peace and War: Interpretations of American Naval History, 1775–1984*, 2d rev. ed. (Westport, Conn.: Greenwood Press, 1984), p. 293, and the extended treatment in Paolo E. Coletta, *The United States Navy and Defense Unification, 1947–1953* (Newark: University of Delaware Press, 1981).

3. James Forrestal, *The Forrestal Diaries*, ed. Walter Millis (New York: Viking, 1951), pp. 389–91; Walter Millis, *Arms and Men: A Study in American Military History* (New York: G. P. Putnam's Sons, 1956), pp. 319–20.

4. The dispute over cancellation of the USS *United States* and the development of a new air force bomber is discussed in Allard, "Era of Transition," pp. 293–95 and at greater length in Paul Y. Hammond, "Supercarriers and B–36 Bombers: Appropriations, Strategy and Politics," in Harold Stein, ed., *American Civil-Military Decisions: A Book of Case Studies* (University: University of Alabama Press, 1963), pp. 465–564. Radford's comments may be found in U.S., Congress, House, Committee on Armed Services, *The National Defense Program: Unification and Strategy*, 81st Cong., 1st sess., 1949, p. 51.

5. Quoted in Samuel P. Huntington, *The Common Defense: Strategic Programs in National Politics* (New York: Columbia University Press, 1961), p. 40.

6. Quoted in Huntington, *Common Defense*, pp. 49–51.

7. Quoted in Huntington, *Common Defense*, p. 51. The origins of NSC 68 are discussed in Paul Y. Hammond, "NSC–68: Prologue to Rearmament," in Warner R. Schilling, Paul Y. Hammond, and Glenn H. Snyder, eds., *Strategy, Politics, and Defense Budgets* (New York: Columbia University Press, 1962), pp. 267–378; Sam Postbrief, "Departure from Incrementalism in U.S. Strategic Planning: The Origins of NSC–68," *Naval War College Review* 32 (March-April 1980): 34–57; and in Stephen E. Ambrose, *Rise to Globalism: American Foreign Policy Since 1938*, 3d rev. ed. (New York: Penguin Books, 1983), p. 164. The document itself was declassified in 1975 and first published in the *Naval War College Review* 27 (May-June 1975): 51–108.

8. For a thoughtful, albeit somewhat different analysis of NSC 68 than that presented here, see John Lewis Gaddis, *Strategies of Containment: A Critical Appraisal of Postwar American National Security Policy* (New York: Oxford University Press, 1982), pp. 89–117.

9. Quoted in Huntington, *Common Defense*, p. 53.

10. On the Korean War, see David Rees, *Korea: The Limited War* (New York: St. Martin's Press, 1964), and D. Clayton James, *The Years of MacArthur*, vol. III, *Triumph and Disaster, 1945–1964* (Boston: Houghton Mifflin Co., 1985), Pt. III.

11. The struggle to improve racial relations in the military during and after the Second World War is described at length by Richard M. Dalfiume, *Desegregation of the U.S. Armed Forces: Fighting on Two Fronts, 1939–1953* (Columbia, Mo.: University of Missouri Press, 1969). See also Stephen E. Ambrose, "Blacks in the Army in Two World Wars," in Stephen E. Ambrose and James A. Barber, Jr., eds., *The Military and American Society: Essays and Readings* (New York: Free Press, 1972), pp. 177–91.

12. Quoted in Robert Endicott Osgood, *NATO: The Entangling Alliance* (Chicago: University of Chicago Press, 1962), p. 37.

13. Osgood, *NATO*, p. 38.

14. Quoted in Osgood, *NATO*, p. 41.

15. Huntington, *Common Defense*, p. 52.

16. Millis, *Arms and Men*, p. 337.

17. Ibid.

FURTHER READING

The best general overview of the American armed forces—not only for the period 1945–1953, but for the whole of American history—is the magnificent book by Russell F. Weigley, *The American Way of War: A History of United States Military Strategy and Policy*, The Wars of the United States (New York: Macmillan Co., 1973). For more details on the army, see Weigley's *History of the United States Army*, enlarged ed. (Bloomington: Indiana University Press, 1984), which has become the classic work on the subject.

Works on the reorganization of the armed forces are numerous and generally quite good. Paul Y. Hammond, *Organizing for Defense: The American Military Establishment in the Twentieth Century* (1961; reprint, Westport, Conn.: Greenwood Press, 1977), is a basic book for all students on the subject. Samuel P. Huntington, *The Common Defense: Strategic Programs in National Politics* (New York: Columbia University Press, 1961), is another standard volume that must be read by anyone with a serious interest in national security. In "The Crisis of American Civil-Military Relations, 1940–1955," pt. III of his *The Soldier and the State* (Cambridge: Harvard University Press, 1957), Huntington deals with postwar organization and the political roles of the Joint Chiefs of Staff. The same topic is cast into broader context in John C. Ries, *The Management of Defense: Organization and Control of the U.S. Armed Services* (Baltimore: Johns Hopkins Press, 1964). Warner R. Schilling, Paul Y. Hammond, and Glenn H. Snyder, *Strategy, Politics, and Defense Budgets* (New York: Columbia University Press, 1962), is a model study; Hammond's section, "NSC-68: Prologue to Rearmament," is especially noteworthy. The significance of NSC 68 to the evolution of containment is assessed in John Lewis Gaddis, *Strategies of Containment: A Critical Appraisal of Postwar American National Security Policy* (New York: Oxford University Press, 1982). Gaddis's conclusions should be contrasted with those in Stephen E. Ambrose, *Rise to Globalism: American Foreign Policy Since 1938*, 3d rev. ed. (New York: Penguin Books, 1983). Forrest Pogue's volume on George C. Marshall's years as secretary of defense and secretary of state has yet to appear; when it does, it will be authoritative. For a stimulating interpretation of the first secretary of defense, see Arnold A. Rogow, *James Forrestal: A Study of Personality, Politics, and Policy* (New York: Macmillan Co., 1963).

On Korea, start with David Rees, *Korea: The Limited War* (New York: St. Martin's Press, 1964), still the best one-volume history. It should be supplemented with I. F. Stone, *The Hidden History of the Korean War* (New York: Monthly Review Press, 1969). Harry S. Truman, *Memoirs*, vol. II, *Years of Trial and Hope* (Garden City, N.Y.: Doubleday, 1956) gives the president's side of the story in Korea and also takes up NATO and NSC 68. MacArthur's memoirs are dull and of little help to students, but William Manchester, *American Caesar: Douglas MacArthur, 1880–1964* (Boston: Little, Brown & Co., 1978) can be used with profit. However, the authoritative work and incomparable biography is D. Clayton James, *The Years of MacArthur*, vol. III, *Triumph and Disaster, 1945–1964* (Boston: Houghton Mifflin Co., 1985), which is certain to remain the standard work on MacArthur for several generations.

Two of the generals who fought in Korea have published their accounts of the action: Matthew B. Ridgway, *The Korean War . . .* (Garden City, N.Y.: Doubleday, 1967), and J. Lawton Collins, *War in Peacetime: The History and Lessons of Korea* (Boston: Houghton Mifflin Co., 1969). The official history is by Roy E. Appleman, *South to Naktong, North to the Yalu (June–November 1950)*, United States Army in the Korean War (Washington: Office of the Chief of Military History, Department of the Army, 1960).

The Truman-MacArthur controversy can best be studied in U.S. Congress, Senate, Committee on Armed Services, *Military Situation in the Far East*, Hearings Before the Committee on Armed Services and the Committee on Foreign Relations, 82d Cong., 1st sess., 1951.

To understand the military's postwar role in Europe before the formation of NATO, read Lucius D. Clay, *Decision in Germany* (Garden City, N.Y.: Doubleday, 1950) and John Gimbel, *The American Occupation of Germany: Politics and the Military, 1945– 1949* (Stanford, Calif.: Stanford University Press, 1968). For the development of nuclear strategy, a good overview is David W. Tarr, *American Strategy in the Nuclear Age* (New York: Macmillan Co., 1966). On NATO, see Robert Endicott Osgood, *NATO: The Entangling Alliance* (Chicago: University of Chicago Press, 1962), an outstanding study in every way.

CHAPTER 16

From the New Look to Flexible Response, 1953–1964

DAUN VAN EE

On first inspection the inauguration of Dwight David Eisenhower on 20 January 1953 must have been seen by the United States Army as an indication that better times would come. Ike was the first professional soldier to have captured the presidency in almost a century. Army men could find additional comfort in recalling the nature of Eisenhower's forty-year career. Neither rebel nor critic, Eisenhower had epitomized the solidly professional staff officer. He had been thoroughly grounded in army doctrine at West Point, the Command and General Staff School, the Army War College, and the Army Industrial College. He was known as a skillful harmonizer of conflicting interests, and his great popularity within the army was due in large part to his congenial personality and sincere concern for the welfare of the troops. He had conferred great distinction upon both the army and himself by virtue of his splendid record as a theater commander in World War II. Most of the army's leaders—men like Omar N. Bradley, J. Lawton Collins, Matthew Ridgway, Maxwell D. Taylor, Mark W. Clark, James Gavin, Alfred M. Gruenther, and James A. Van Fleet—had served under Eisenhower in Europe, and many were his close personal friends. After the war he had fought skillfully for the army as its chief of staff. Of special interest to an army frustrated by the stalemated and limited war in Korea was Eisenhower's promise to take decisive action to end the struggle in one fashion or another. Surely he would be a president who would understand the army's problems and do much for his old service.

If the army had these high hopes, they were to be disappointed. Relations between Eisenhower and his wartime associates soon became strained as army leaders began to condemn what they believed were ill-advised presidential policies and inept Defense Department leadership exercised by Eisenhower's appointees. Army morale and effectiveness were thought to be at a low ebb as a result. Midway through Eisenhower's presidency, according to one official account, the army "had reached a post–World War II nadir . . . in terms of prestige and future outlook."[1] It was supposed that the other services—air force, navy, and Marine Corps—had captured the imagination of the public and would henceforth receive an ever larger share of defense funds. The future prospects for the army were grim: fewer roles and missions would be entrusted to it, and its strength would be reduced to the point of impotence. The chief villain, according to the army point of view, was Eisenhower's New Look and its corollary doctrine of massive retaliation. This strategy emphasized American technological superiority over the Soviet Union and stressed the atomic striking power of the air force's Strategic Air Command at the expense of army ground strength.

Although the New Look was by no means a complete policy revolution, it represented a dramatic and deliberate departure from the defense policies of the Truman administration as set forth in the National Security Council paper, NSC 68. The decision to break with those policies owed much to the experiences of Eisenhower himself as an executor and, to a lesser extent, a formulator of Truman's strategy of containment. As commander of the European occupation forces in the fall of 1945, he had assured General George C. Marshall, whom he was to succeed as chief of staff of the army, that there was no need for a large regular army: its size, he thought, "should be limited to that necessary for commanding, servicing, organizing and instructing a civilian army, and for providing the bulk of foreign garrisons." As chief of staff he again argued that reliance should be placed upon the mobilization potential created by a program of universal military training and the existence of reserve and National Guard forces, although he moderated his views to advocate a large (seventy-group, 400,000-man) air force. Not counting troops needed for occupation, only seven active divisions and two separate regiments were required by the regular army for national security.[2]

These requirements, however, were never fully met to Eisenhower's satisfaction, and he was responsible for distributing the shortages. On 7 February 1948, as he was leaving the Pentagon to assume the presidency of Columbia University, he warned Secretary of Defense James Forrestal about shortsighted economy measures in a fashion that would become familiar during his presidency:

The effect of budgets for '46, '47, and '48 have been to render the Army increasingly unable to mobilize effective land power to support air and sea power in any emergency requiring a major mobilization. With certain negligible exceptions we have purchased no new equipment since the war. . . . We should be much further along the road toward a fully air-transportable ground force. Lack of modern communications, radar and detection equipment, modern tanks, personnel carriers and other devices are fast reducing our regular land forces to obsolescence. Destruction of our reserve stocks are rapidly making our civilian component mobilization plan a paper fiction. And the curve of our materiel readiness is rapidly dropping.

By then the army was 100,000 men short of even the bare minimum that had been authorized and planned for (670,000). Having cut back wherever he could, Eisenhower said that if the downward trend continued, the army would no longer be able to perform its essential occupation tasks, and "the areas involved would have to be abandoned to chaos and communism."[3]

Leaving the post of chief of staff did not mean an end to the unhappy job of allocating increasingly scarce resources. Early in 1949 Forrestal called Eisenhower back to Washington to serve as his consultant and to preside over the Joint Chiefs of Staff (JCS). There he helped apportion the frugal defense budget planned for the 1950–1951 fiscal year (FY 51). It was a task he performed skillfully by giving priority to the air force's primary mission of strategic bombing, while at the same time recognizing the important (albeit somewhat symbolic) role played by the navy's fleet carriers. The army, even though its funds and forces were severely cut back in the course of the budget process presided over by Eisenhower, kept a fairly low profile and made no serious protest. Eisenhower himself repeated his earlier view that an overall budget figure of around $15 billion—$4.5 billion for the army, which meant at 1949 prices an army strength of only some ten divisions and nine separate, regiment-sized units—would be adequate if it were provided regularly. The feast-and-famine cycle that had prevailed in the past was wasteful because it interfered with systematic planning and procurement.[4]

Eisenhower gained a different perspective on the Truman defense system when he accepted the post of supreme commander of the North Atlantic Treaty Organization (NATO) forces in December 1950. By then the sense of crisis had deepened as a result of the Communist Chinese entry into the Korean War, and Eisenhower's ideas about the number of ground troops necessary for national security may have undergone some revision. Calling for "a good, solid combat force with immediate expansion possibilities," he estimated that it might be necessary to send from ten to twenty American divisions to Europe. He worked vigorously to establish a system of collective defense, with substantial American participation, until he returned to the United States in the spring of 1952 to run for the presidency against Democrat Adlai Stevenson. President Truman was accurate when he later described Eisenhower as "fully in accord" with his policies.[5]

While Truman's program of sending ground forces to bolster the NATO command was not criticized by Eisenhower during the 1952 presidential campaign, other defense policies did not escape his attention. Seeking to capitalize on the growing dissatisfaction with the Korean stalemate, the Republicans blamed the war on Truman's withdrawal of occupation troops from South Korea in 1949. Repeating and expanding upon this charge, Eisenhower said that America was at war because the Truman administration "allowed America, in a time when strength was needed, to become weak."[6] Eisenhower implied that the high number of American casualties had been unnecessary when he said that a greater part of the fighting should be turned over to the South Koreans. He finally promised that he would succeed where the Democrats had failed; he would end the war honorably.

Eisenhower won in a landslide, despite Truman's last-minute revelation that the general had participated in the 1947 decision to withdraw the troops from Korea. He made his promised preinaugural trip to Korea, and there he was greatly impressed by the rugged, mountainous terrain which he thought unsuitable for the mobile, American way of land warfare. Eisenhower also made it clear that he would have no part of the plan of the theater commander (his old comrade, General Mark Clark) for a moderate expansion of the war to achieve military victory. Returning home on the USS *Helena*, he took the first steps toward securing both a new set of defense leaders and a new strategic policy. Included among the passengers on board were John Foster Dulles (secretary of state designate), Charles E. Wilson (secretary of defense designate), and George M. Humphrey (secretary of the treasury designate). Also present were Joseph M. Dodge, soon to be director of the Bureau of the Budget, and Arthur W. Radford, the commander in chief of the Pacific Fleet, who was Eisenhower's selection as chairman of the JCS.

In their informal discussions concerning America's defense posture, Eisenhower and his advisers arrived at several areas of agreement. Perhaps the most important consensus reached was that the continued expenditures for the Korean War and the program of expansion called for by NSC 68 would not be tolerated. The Truman administration, it was thought, was spending its way into inflation and bankruptcy. From this premise two conclusions were drawn: the Korean War had to be ended, and unnecessary defense expenditures had to be cut.

Soon after the inauguration the new administration initiated its economy program. The army fared better than the other services at first, largely because it had to bear most of the Korean War's costs and would have been catastrophically affected by across-the-board cuts. Allowed to retain—at least temporarily—its twenty-division force, the army nevertheless felt compelled to present the JCS with a statement of risks involved in the revised budget and departure from the NSC 68 program. Chief of Staff J. Lawton Collins admitted that the biggest problem in providing ground strength for a general war was not the size of the twenty-division force but the result of the "maldeployment" of troops in Korea. If the war ended, and in June 1953 when Collins made his statement this was imminent, then a reserve striking force would be established and the army would be ready to wage a general war on the plains of Europe.[7]

Collins's characterization of the Korean War troops as maldeployed reflected the increasing frustration felt by the army. Truce talks had been going on for two years while offensives and counteroffensives had moved the fighting up and down the peninsula. As the talks moved toward their seemingly inevitable conclusion—partition of Korea roughly along the line of the thirty-eighth parallel—the United Nations went on the defensive and attempted to hold on to the main line of resistance. Eisenhower soon selected a new commander for the Eighth Army: General Maxwell D. Taylor, the World War II leader of the 101st Airborne Division. While he was not enthusiastic about the new policy, Taylor was prepared to make the best of it; he quickly instituted programs designed to encourage more aggressive patrolling and to retrain the entrenched units to take the offensive again if such a situation arose. At the same time Taylor was forced to fight a series of small but bloody battles in order to repel Communist thrusts at some of his outposts. One such position—Pork Chop Hill—was the scene of one of the war's most savage fights, and Taylor finally had to abandon it on the eve of the armistice.

Such incidents continued to reinforce the new president's determination that the stalemate should be ended. Having rejected Clark's earlier plans as too costly for the limited gains envisaged, Eisenhower began to let it be known that if the Communists continued to protract the negotiations, a major offensive using nuclear weapons was contemplated. As Eisenhower probably expected, the peace talks began making progress. After many tribulations caused by ally and foe alike, both sides signed the armistice on 27 July 1953.

Bolstered by this triumph of atomic diplomacy, Eisenhower set out to codify his ideas and experiences into a systematic restatement of American defense policy. He set up a number of high-level policy review committees composed of civilian and military defense experts to examine alternative national strategies. The results of this painstaking effort, named "Project Solarium" after the White House room where discussions first began, were sent to the National Security Council (NSC) in July 1953, and the resulting paper was designated NSC 162.[8]

NSC 162 contained most of the elements of the Eisenhower defense policies that collectively became known as the New Look; it also represented a return to the doctrine practiced by the Truman administration between World War II and Korea, as detailed in NSC 20/4, which Truman had approved on 24 November 1948.[9] There were two basic problems of national security, according to the NSC in 1953: meeting the Russian threat; and maintaining American values and institutions, including—especially—the United States economy. Excessive government spending resulted in either repressive taxation or (if the budgets were unbalanced) ruinous inflation followed by restrictive controls. Therefore, concluded the drafters of NSC 162:

The requirements for funds to maintain our national security must thus be considered in the light of these dangers to our economic system, including the danger to industrial productivity necessary to support military programs, arising from excessive levels of total Government spending, taxing, and borrowing.[10]

This rather pessimistic economic premise, so different from that upon which NSC 68 was based, led to an economy-minded defense posture that focused on the power of nuclear weapons even more than Truman had before 1950. The principal deterrent to war, and the main striking force in case the deterrent failed, was to be "the capability of inflicting massive retaliatory damage," i.e., an air-delivered atomic attack. To counter the increasing threat of a Russian atomic strike, "an integrated and effective continental defense system" was called for. In case of war nuclear weapons would be considered "as available for use as other weapons." The United States had to have allies, both to supply overseas bases for American retaliatory forces and to furnish the manpower to fight smaller, local wars.[11]

Two other features of NSC 162 made that paper markedly different from NSC 68. There was no mention of building up military forces in anticipation of a year of maximum danger; instead, the United States should be prepared to "continue, for as long as necessary, a state of limited defense mobilization." The absence of a crash program would, by implication, be beneficial to "a sound, strong, and growing U.S. economy" which would in turn "support over the long pull a satisfactory posture of defense." In addition, NSC 162 was critical of the way in which the previous administration had "over-extended" American armed forces, "thereby depriving us of mobility and initiative for future military action in defense of the free world." The solution would be to create a central strategic reserve that would permit "initiative, flexibility and support."[12]

This new Basic National Security Policy (BNSP) had obvious implications for the army: if strategic bombing and continental air defense were to be emphasized, then the relative importance of ground forces would decrease. General Ridgway, whom Eisenhower had chosen to succeed Collins as the army chief of staff, joined with the other members of the JCS to complain about the language used in a key passage. The BNSP called for "a strong military posture, with emphasis on" the forces of massive retaliation; the JCS twice tried to change the sentence so it would advocate a strong military posture "to include" those forces. The NSC refused to make the change, but NSC members were receptive to a proposal, suggested by Ridgway, to delete a section that would have precluded the United States from sending ground troops to help America's allies in limited wars. The earlier language had stipulated that allied forces must act "to counter local aggressions" because ground forces "cannot be furnished by the United States."[13]

Even before Eisenhower approved the final version of the new BNSP (NSC 162/2) on 30 October 1953, the new secretary of defense directed the JCS to translate the broad policy into an outline of military strategy, complete with a description of the forces necessary for the next three and a half years. The directive sparked bitter debate as the services squabbled over both their respective force allocation and the shares of the reduced defense budget they knew would be available. A compromise was finally engineered by Admiral Radford after he obtained Wilson's approval to raise the total projected manpower limitation so as to allow the army fourteen divisions (up from twelve) by the end of FY 57. The resulting document, JCS 2101/113, was sent to Wilson on 10 December and approved by Eisenhower five days later.[14]

Although in many respects JCS 2101/113 merely repeated the military provisions of NSC 162/2, there were a number of refinements and interpretations that affected the army. One of the most important of these was in effect an escape clause:

The strategy and other estimates in these papers reflect our agreed recommendations under the assumption that present international tensions and threats remain approximately the same. Any material increase in danger or reduction in threat would require complete new studies and estimates.

A second assumption was that both Germany and Japan would rearm and allow the United States to bring home enough troops to establish an effective strategic reserve. No more than six divisions were to be deployed overseas. JCS 2101/113 also called for "provision of tactical atomic support for US or allied military forces in general war or in a local aggression whenever the employment of atomic weapons would be militarily advantageous." Tactical nuclear weapons could substitute for the troops withdrawn from forward areas in Korea and Europe.[15]

The first dispute over army forces and budgets broke out soon after the new defense policy had been adopted. While Ridgway, the new army chief of staff, had agreed to cut back his strength to a maximum of fourteen divisions by the end of FY 57, he had never committed himself to any particular timetable. The budget cuts directed by Secretary of Defense Wilson forced the army to plan on a 1954–1955 force of no more than seventeen divisions, a level the army chief thought too low.

For the remainder of his term, Ridgway fought for a large army in confrontations with Wilson, in JCS meetings, and, in a more restrained manner, before congressional committees.[16] Most of the arguments Ridgway used in his attempts to evade the budget and forces limitations to which he had agreed in JCS 2101/113 would characterize the army's position for the rest of Eisenhower's presidency. Ridgway described himself as a professional military man and as such claimed no competence in economic matters. Eisenhower had asked the JCS to see national security problems in broad perspective; Ridgway thought such a request, since it required him to weigh economic factors when pondering questions of military policy, was improper. If the cost of the programs he proposed was "obviously fantastic," he should make that clear; if not, then questions of cost or of what the economy could bear were for others to dwell upon.

Furthermore, the members of the JCS had agreed on war plans, based upon guidance from their civilian superiors, and these plans obliged the military to provide certain forces. If these commitments were not changed—as in the case of NATO—then the army could not recommend in good conscience any military program that would render it unable to keep those commitments. Ridgway was not impressed with the New Look doctrine that reorganization and technological innovation would reduce the need for ground force manpower. Schemes to improve dramatically the ratio of combat troops to support personnel were dangerous, warned Ridgway. Cutting back on support troops weakened combat efficiency because it reduced the capacity for sustained combat. To counter the idea that the advent of tactical nuclear weapons would allow a sizable personnel reduction, Ridgway responded that foot soldiers would still be necessary in any war and it had not been shown that a nuclear battlefield required fewer men.

Furthermore, few of these weapons would be available by 1957, and the Russians would probably get them soon anyway.

The chief weakness in Ridgway's defense of a larger army was the fact that he had already agreed to a smaller one. Ridgway used the escape clauses in JCS 2101/113; his approval, he noted, was valid only so long as the situation and developments remained as described in that document. Since the forces that had been expected from Japan and Germany had not been provided, his agreement to maintain a smaller army was no longer binding. At first, the other services refused to go along with Ridgway; if army force limits were increased, then they also should get more. By July 1954, however, developments abroad had persuaded the JCS to ask for exactly that—increases all around.[17]

The events which had so emboldened the service chiefs took place in Indochina, an area specified in JCS 2101/113 as one that the United States would fight to protect. Obsessed by fears of losing their Southeast Asian empire, the French had been engaged in a bitter struggle against the Communist-nationalist Vietminh since the end of World War II. Late in 1953 the French decided to entice the Vietminh out of their jungle and swamp hideaways and established an outpost deep in enemy-held northwestern Vietnam where, they hoped, the enemy could be destroyed by superior firepower. The French garrison at Dien Bien Phu was soon besieged. Resupply and reinforcement by air became more and more difficult; it seemed likely that Dien Bien Phu would quickly fall without a massive effort to relieve it. The French appealed to the United States, which had been giving logistical support to the French effort since 1950. Eisenhower, after a series of consultations with his military and diplomatic advisers, congressional leaders, and allies, refused to intervene. Dien Bien Phu fell on 7 May 1954.

One of the advisers Eisenhower had consulted was General Ridgway, who was influential in killing the idea of intervention. Ridgway did not argue that stopping the Vietminh was an unworthy or impossible goal in itself; he was of the opinion that the real enemy was Communist China and that to correct the situation in Indochina would require a decisive thrust at this source of Communist power in Asia. To reinforce his argument, he sent an army survey team into Vietnam to determine the costs of intervention in terms of manpower and materiel. The costs, it turned out, were enormous: five to ten divisions, $3.5 billion per year, and an incredible engineering effort to fashion lines of communication in a roadless wilderness.[18]

In short, intervention was beyond American capabilities as they existed in the spring of 1954. In June the army asked for a combat-ready force of four divisions to be deployed in the Far East. Even though Wilson and Eisenhower were receptive for a time to the army's pleas and delayed the scheduled cutbacks and redeployments, they were nonetheless determined to reduce the size of the army. After the Indochinese crisis had abated, they continued to do so. The strength of the army dropped from 1,405,000 men (nineteen divisions and eighteen regimental combat teams) in the middle of 1954 to 1,026,000 men (eighteen divisions and ten regimental combat teams) two years later.

Since these cutbacks had fostered public and congressional criticism, Wilson tried to minimize their impact by keeping the number of divisions as high as possible. He grouped scattered and separate units, including training organizations, into divisions. Some existing divisions were skeletonized by maintaining them at less than authorized strength. All these divisions were then added to the total number with the implication that Wilson had conjured up more fighting strength out of a smaller force.

Such deviousness did not offend army leaders as much as the manner in which the budget and personnel cuts were implemented. Wilson never told the army forthrightly that certain ceilings would have to be kept. Instead, the Defense Department, after receiving and almost invariably rejecting the army's own recommendations and plans, asked the chief of staff to provide tentative deployments and programs based on maximum money and troop levels. When the army complied, the recommendations were approved, and the army was made to appear as if it had suggested the lower troop strengths.

Actions such as these were viewed with great uneasiness by army leaders, who feared that the facts about the reduction of American military strength were not reaching the public. General Ridgway, feeling that he had been tricked into advocating a program which would leave the United States dangerously weak, retired in June 1955. He soon gave vent to his unhappiness in an autobiography that was highly critical of Eisenhower's defense policies and the tactics used to produce a consensus among the JCS in favor of the New Look programs. In his book Ridgway revealed himself, perhaps unwittingly, as a somewhat naive and uncomplicated combat leader who was ill suited for a job requiring essentially political skills. His successor, Maxwell D. Taylor, was not thus handicapped. Handsome, urbane, intellectual, and ambitious, Taylor had combat credentials as a dashing airborne leader, like Ridgway. His strategy as chief of staff, however, differed from his predecessor's: whereas Ridgway had fought essentially a holding action, Taylor aggressively attacked the philosophical assumptions upon which the New Look was based. He advocated a program designed, as he later put it, "to improve the combat readiness of the Army . . . and to improve its morale depressed as it was by the precedence given to the needs of the Navy and Air Force by the ex-Army man in the White House."[19]

The obstacles facing him were formidable. The New Look was firmly entrenched as national policy. Deficit spending had been reduced, and Eisenhower's fiscal conservatism was reinforced by the prospect of an actual surplus in FY 56. The air force, navy, and marines were all reasonably content with the current program, and the influential chairman of the joint chiefs, Admiral Radford, was a strong proponent of the New Look.

Taylor's ability to change things was further diminished by Eisenhower's structural innovations and reorganizations. The effect of these changes was to increase the power of the chairman of the JCS and the secretary of defense at the expense of the civilian secretaries and the service chiefs; the top civilian and military officials of the Department of the Army were removed from the chain of command and served as mere staff advisers to, and executive agents for, the secretary of defense. The chief of staff was directed to relinquish most of his strictly army duties to his vice-chief so that he could devote more time to his advisory role as a member of the JCS. Eisenhower also increased the number and the powers of the unified commands (i.e., combat organizations made up of elements from all services). Henceforth unified commands, and not the army or any other service, would conduct operations under the direction of the secretary of defense. The army had, in effect, become merely an agency to organize, train, and equip its own forces.

Taylor could, however, use the prestige of his office to mobilize support for a new defense concept that would restore the army to its rightful place among the services. Before becoming chief of staff, he had worked out "A National Military Program" in which a strategy of Flexible Response (Taylor always capitalized the words) was outlined.[20] Taylor did not argue that a capacity for massive retaliation was unneeded. His point was, rather, that in an "era of atomic plenty, with mutual deterrence," the possession of a nuclear strike force was not enough. The United States could not always choose the kind of war it would become involved in, and the balance of terror made it more likely that the Soviet bloc would test America's determination by starting or sponsoring local aggression. Without a true capacity to fight a limited, nonnuclear war, America would be forced either to initiate a nuclear exchange or to do nothing. Since the American reluctance to strike first with nuclear weapons made the first alternative unlikely, the United States might well find itself sitting on the sidelines, clutching its thermonuclear horrors, and watching the strength of the free world erode as one by one its allies were nibbled away.

Taylor's proposal was simple: increase the priority given to limited-war forces to equal the priority given to the atomic deterrent forces. The catchword here was "deterrent"; Taylor proposed limiting the massive retaliatory forces to only those required to deter a Soviet attack. Only after forces designed to deter and defeat local aggression had been provided should the United States seek "to satisfy the full requirement for survival or victory in general war."

The logical group to which this proposal should be presented was the JCS. In March 1956 Taylor offered his program to them at a special meeting in Puerto Rico. It was ignored. The JCS decided instead to continue the New Look programs with only a small increase in manpower. Four months later Radford brought into the JCS his own proposal, one that would have carried the Eisenhower defense policy to its logical conclusion. He called for a radical reduction in army strength and a greater commitment to the idea that any Russian or Chinese provocation would meet a nuclear response. The army, which would be reduced by 450,000 men to a total of slightly over 575,000, would be able to supply only small nuclear task forces for deployment in Europe and Asia; the ground fighting, if any, would be done by allies or marines. When Taylor protested that Radford's ideas meant a return to Fortress America, he received no support from the other service chiefs, and it appeared as though the Radford plan would be accepted. Only a well-timed leak to the press stirred up enough embarrassing publicity to force Radford to postpone consideration of his proposals.

Such leaks were part of a deliberate army campaign to win public and congressional sympathy for its plight. Earlier in May, during the so-called Revolt of the Colonels, army staff officers had given the *New York Times* documents revealing Taylor's Flexible Response theories and providing details about interservice disputes. Taylor himself expounded upon his ideas in an article that was to appear in the prestigious periodical *Foreign Affairs*; Wilson and Radford, together with a nervous State Department, forbade its publication. Taylor's public relations campaign was taken up by his loyal ally, Secretary of the Army Wilber M. Brucker, who supported army programs and also sought to bolster army morale. Stressing the need for an American limited-war capability, Brucker embarked upon an ambitious speechmaking campaign, cultivated good relations with congressmen, and reinvigorated the Association of the United States Army as a promotional and lobbying organization. He also worked tirelessly to publicize and promote the army through a weekly television show, "The Big Picture," and he changed the mission of the official *Army Information Digest* from explanation to advocacy. From 1955 until the end of the Eisenhower administration its pages were filled with stories and pictures about the new doctrines and weapons which would enable the army to win limited wars. Typical of these articles was one celebrating the often neglected infantryman, who, like the army as a whole, could be counted upon "to be a decisive factor in keeping the Hammer and Sickle off our front lawn in the atomic age."[21]

The army also instituted two reorganization programs to enhance this image and, at the same time, to make the best use of its dwindling manpower. Drawing in part upon his experiments in postarmistice Korea, Taylor scrapped the triangular (three-regiment) divisions. In their place he organized more glamorous "pentomic" divisions, which could operate with fewer men (the new infantry divisions called for 13,748 men as opposed to 17,455; the new airborne divisions had 11,476 men as opposed to 17,085). The pentomic division had as its main striking force five battle groups, each capable of sustained, independent action. These battle groups, it was thought, could easily disperse and reunite on the nuclear battlefield, thus allowing American troops to avoid presenting a tempting target for atomic bombs and to concentrate quickly in order to set up and then exploit an American atomic strike. Taylor believed that improved communications now permitted a commander to control more than three major maneuver elements. The effect, as Anthony B. Herbert has noted, was somewhat the reverse; by eliminating the regiment the army had enlarged the difference in rank between the commanders and subordinate commanders and, hence, communication became less free than before. Furthermore, with the abolition of the regiment, many of the basic traditions of the army dating back to the earliest days of the Republic were lost. The army made a feeble attempt to endow each battalion with a ready-made regimental heritage, but the individual soldier found it difficult to identify with a "unit" whose components might be scattered across the globe in a number of different divisions.[22]

A second reorganization resulted in the creation of a Strategic Army Corps, whose acronym STRAC had long been used as an adjective to describe sharp, well-disciplined troops. Accordingly, the heart of STRAC was the XIII Airborne Corps, comprising the 82d and 101st Airborne Divisions. STRAC was to constitute the United States-based mobile reserve called for by NSC 162/2 and JCS 2101/113. Its commanders tried to keep it in a high state of readiness by constant training; continuing manpower reductions and the resulting high personnel turnover, however, made it very difficult to maintain STRAC readiness during the later 1950s.

The tight budgets of the Eisenhower years also made it difficult for the army to modernize its weapons and equipment. Development, procurement, and distribution of the infantry's new basic weapon, the 7.62-mm M–14 rifle, was painfully slow; when Eisenhower left office most units were still carrying the World War II Garand M–1. Infantrymen also had to make do with the old .30 caliber machine guns and the obsolete M–48 tanks. Their improved replacements had been developed and approved, but production was deferred in order to channel funds to more glamorous weapons systems.

The army was particularly energetic in the development of tactical nuclear weapons and doctrine, in part because such devices would be more likely to ensure a future role for ground troops than conventional weapons. Technological breakthroughs had resulted in a great reduction in the size and weight of nuclear warheads. The army developed a new generation of weapons and delivery systems to take advantage of the smaller size and to divest the Strategic Air Command of its near monopoly over atomic weapons. Among these new weapons were the Davy Crockett, a lightweight, 2- or 3-man rocket launcher; the Honest John and Little John short-range artillery rockets; and a variety of nuclear shells for heavy and medium weight artillery pieces.

The army's weapons innovation programs, together with its fears of future loss of mission, led it into a series of jurisdictional struggles with the air force. The fiercest contest was over guided missiles, in which field the army had retained an interest even after the air force had established itself as a separate service in 1947. The engineering team of Wernher von Braun at the Redstone Arsenal gave the army a superior capability for missile and space research, and the army began to attach more and more importance to missile development as the implementation of the New Look continued. Feeling that the new weapons would capture the imagination of the public and reaffirm the importance of the army, the army's leaders began to sacrifice other programs to fund von Braun's research. The air force, which to a certain extent had neglected missiles in favor of manned aircraft, soon became jealous of its prerogatives and tried to achieve complete control of missiles and space. The army won permission to develop the Jupiter, a mobile, intermediate-range ballistic missile whose range exceeded 1,000 miles. Late in 1956, however, Secretary of Defense Wilson gave operational employment of Jupiter to the air force and restricted the army's missiles to ranges of 200 miles or less. At the same time Wilson ruled against the army in the almost equally important field of air defense missiles by curtailing the range of the army's Nike series and by assigning overseas responsibility for air defense to the air force component commanders.

The army received a second blow at the same time when Wilson drew the reins in on the army's expanding aviation program. This effort was almost as important to the army as its missiles: the idea of "sky cavalry" attracted attention and funds, and air mobility helped compensate for America's relative disadvantage in manpower. The Defense Department placed strict limits on the weight and functions of the army's airplanes and helicopters, and their use was restricted to minor operations within the combat zone. Army aviation was not to provide its own aircraft for tactical airlift, reconnaissance, close air support, or battlefield interdiction. The air force threatened to take away the army's right to train its own pilots and the army was directed to use the research facilities of the other services whenever possible. Lieutenant General James M. Gavin, deputy chief of staff for plans and the best-known proponent of air mobility, was outraged; the effect of Wilson's decision, he said, was "to close the vast area between the Army's light vehicles and the large vehicles of the Air Force to further exploration and research." Gavin saw the decision as part of a "tendency to further restrict the Army's efforts to ready itself for limited war."[23]

The difficulties encountered by the army when it had to deploy troops quickly from Europe to Lebanon in 1958 served to illustrate a point that Ridgway, Taylor, and Brucker had all tried to make: the air force was concentrating too heavily on its strategic bombing role and neglecting its responsibility to provide air support for the army. The army had come to place great emphasis on its airborne troops; they were considered the elite of the army, and the mobility inherent in airborne operations made them important in both the New Look and the army's doctrine of limited war. Air force leaders, however, had been building up their strategic, tactical, and air defense wings at the expense of their troop-carrier wings. The army maintained that it had a need for approximately forty-five troop-carrier wings, enough to carry the assault echelons of three airborne divisions simultaneously; such a program would represent about one-third of the strength in wings in the air force. The army later scaled these demands down, and the other services agreed to a compromise proposal. Radford, however, recommended against any increase and told the army to count on using the older aircraft that it had previously deemed unsuitable. Wilson upheld the JCS chairman.

This pattern continued throughout the last years of the Eisenhower presidency, which were characterized by generally successful efforts to keep Congress and the military from scrapping the New Look. Wilson, Radford, and their successors (Neil H. McElroy, Thomas S. Gates, Jr., Nathan F. Twining, and Lyman L. Lemnitzer) continued to reduce the size of the army in accordance with Eisenhower's policies. On 30 June 1957 there were 998,000 men, eighteen divisions, and nine regiment-sized units; three years later the size of the army had diminished to fourteen divisions and 870,000 men, with a scattering of smaller nondivisional units. The army's budget rose slowly, but inflation and ill-considered space and missile programs devoured much of the increase. Although Taylor and other army leaders continued to press for the army's space and limited-war programs, they were unwilling to oppose the president and the Defense Department openly and publicly.

The Russian launching of its Sputnik satellite in the fall of 1957 and the reexamination of American preparedness and resources that it helped spark changed the situation drastically. The army's leaders discovered that Congress, hitherto as economy-minded as Eisenhower, was willing to spend more for defense. They also discovered to their chagrin that Eisenhower was going to maintain his fiscal restraint and would push on with the implementation of the New Look. The prospect of increased privation in the midst of potential plenty proved too much to bear. Dissent became open. The professional tradition of an apolitical officer corps, which had been weakened by the 1952 Eisenhower candidacy, was forgotten. Several prominent generals made their dissatisfaction known to the public in a variety of ways, including testimony before congressional committees, speeches to groups interested in defense problems, and leaks to sympathetic journalists and politicians. In 1958–1959 two of the most vocal army critics, Taylor and Gavin, retired and expressed their frustration in two widely heralded books. Taylor's *The Uncertain Trumpet* described the battles with the JCS and Defense Department over his Flexible Response policies. Gavin's *War and Peace in the Space Age* called for more army participation in programs involving missiles, space, air mobility, and tactical nuclear weapons. Both called for increased expenditures for defense, and both thought that an improved limited-war capability would enable the United States to frustrate the Communist drive for world conquest. Taylor and Gavin agreed that the French defeat in Vietnam had been a major setback for the free world; if America had possessed the military forces which they now advocated, the outcome would have been reversed. The implication, of course, was obvious: quick victories in limited wars would be very much to America's advantage, and if the Communists persisted in their tactics, avoiding such conflicts would hurt the interests of the United States. Taylor and Gavin were arguing in essence for a capability to fight limited wars, with every expectation that the capability would be used.

The Gavin and Taylor books made a substantial contribution to an intensifying debate over national strategy that culminated in the presidential election of 1960. Virtually all of the candidates were critical of Eisenhower's defense policies; even Vice President Richard M. Nixon, the eventual Republican nominee, implied that he would modify the New Look if elected. Of the Democratic candidates, Senate Majority Leader Lyndon B. Johnson and Senator Stuart Symington, a former secretary of the air force, had long been vociferously critical of what they felt was a lack of preparedness, particularly in the field of strategic weapons.

Senator John F. Kennedy, while also blaming Eisenhower for the "missile gap" that supposedly left America vulnerable to a Russian attack, had another defense cause to advocate: limited war. The United States, argued Kennedy, needed forces that could fight and win in situations short of general war; with such forces America could seize the initiative in the global struggle with the Soviet Union. In effect, Kennedy grounded this aspect of his campaign in the army's demands for a major new role in the nation's strategy.

The inauguration of President John F. Kennedy in January 1961 thus heralded a reaffirmation of the strategic assumptions of NSC 68 and the adoption of Maxwell Taylor's program of Flexible Response. Kennedy's secretary of defense, Robert S. McNamara, seemed to share with the president a conviction that the New Look had been a bad policy: limited wars could be fought successfully and should be prepared for. Although the first supplemental budget requests in 1961 continued the Eisenhower administration's priority on nuclear retaliatory forces, Kennedy and McNamara were determined to secure greater usable strength in the form of conventional forces. Symbolic of this determination was the recall to active duty of Maxwell Taylor, who had been serving on a committee to investigate the Bay of Pigs fiasco. As the special military representative to the president, and later as chairman of the Joint Chiefs of Staff, he successfully advocated the programs that Eisenhower had rejected. The principal beneficiary of the change in policy was, of course, the army.

In actual numbers of men on active duty, the change from the Eisenhower army to the Kennedy army was not nearly so great as the change from the Korean War army to the army of 1961. McNamara, after some initial reluctance, added 100,000 men to the total strength of the army in three years; he also increased the number of "combat-ready" divisions from eleven to sixteen (three of the fourteen Eisenhower divisions had been training units). Eisenhower, in contrast, had decreased army strength by about 650,000, with a roughly proportional drop in the number of combat divisions and smaller units. The importance of the Kennedy buildup lay in the increase of the army's strategic reserve: Eisenhower had only three divisions to work with, but his successor could call upon eight combat-ready divisions for deployment anywhere in the world.

Two foreign policy crises spurred the expansion. Early in the Kennedy administration the situation in Laos deteriorated to such an extent that many presidential advisers wished to intervene. General Lyman Lemnitzer (who had succeeded air force General Nathan Twining as chairman of the JCS) and General George H. Decker (who had taken Lemnitzer's place as army chief of staff) hesitated to commit the army. Since the military posture of the United States still reflected the New Look, they argued that a shortage of available troops made use of nuclear weapons necessary. Kennedy decided not to use force and to seek a political solution.

During the Berlin crisis of 1961–1962, the shortages again brought home to Kennedy the fact that an interventionist or activist foreign policy could not be pursued safely without a larger reserve of conventionally armed soldiers. To replenish the strategic reservoir depleted by troop deployment to Europe, Kennedy had to take the politically risky step of calling up reserve and National Guard units, which upon activation left much to be desired in the areas of combat readiness and overall efficiency.

The benefits of having a usable conventional ground force were most apparent in a third crisis. Kennedy not only established a naval quarantine to force the Russian missiles out of Cuba in October 1962; he also mobilized and deployed army divisions in preparation for an invasion of Cuba. Kennedy now had the ready forces he had not possessed in previous crises: fully 100,000 army troops were prepared to go into Cuba in what would have been the largest invasion since World War II. Army leaders naturally claimed that the invasion force played a large, if not decisive role in the Russian decision to back down and withdraw the missiles.

The force augmentation was accompanied by a thorough program of reorganization and modernization. Reflecting the Kennedy-McNamara distrust of over-reliance on tactical nuclear weapons and their determination that the United States should be capable of waging conventional war, the army even changed the structure of its basic fighting unit. The pentomic division was scrapped, and in its place was created the Reorganization Objectives Army Division (ROAD) which had a variable number of battalions and could be easily adapted to any kind of mission. The battalion replaced the division as the basic combat organization; brigades and divisions became flexible commands for either nuclear or nonnuclear war.

McNamara also pushed the army's modernization program to achieve more firepower and mobility. He accelerated production and delivery of the new rifles, machine guns, tanks, armored personnel carriers, and self-propelled artillery pieces. McNamara was especially energetic in his development of army aviation; under his prodding the army formulated air mobility tactics and formed the First Cavalry Division (Airmobile), whose organic transportation vehicle was the helicopter.

Recognizing that the army's new strength, firepower, and tactical mobility would be useless if it could not be brought to bear quickly, McNamara dramatically increased the strategic airlift capabilities of the air force. To this end he initiated the development of the C–141 long-range jet transport and accelerated deliveries of the C–130E turboprop carrier. By the middle of 1964 American airlift capabilities had increased 75 percent over what had been available in 1961.

The most radical change in the army was a result of direct action by Kennedy himself. Impressed by a Russian declaration in 1961 that seemed to signal an increased Communist emphasis on guerrilla wars, the president set up a special committee to develop and implement counterinsurgency programs. The ubiquitous Taylor became chairman, and he made certain that counterinsurgency training became increasingly important in the army's educational system. Kennedy also took special interest in the army's Special Warfare School at Fort Bragg, North Carolina. He greatly increased the size of the army's Special Forces units and attempted to create an elite organization that would be able to mix with the populations of underdeveloped countries and thus meet the guerrilla on his own ground. Special Forces teams were trained in various civic action techniques; their mission was as much nation-building as counterguerrilla warfare. The regular army, however, never readily subscribed to the idea that special warfare techniques were the most effective weapons to meet the Communists. After Kennedy's assassination in November 1963, much of the impetus behind the program was lost.

The Special Forces seemed tailor-made for the developing situation in South Vietnam where the army had been supplying advisory groups for over a decade. When Lyndon B. Johnson succeeded to the presidency in 1963, there were 10,000 army personnel in South Vietnam. The largest contingent was a support command that helped the Vietnamese army with its intelligence, communications, and logistical problems. The Special Forces concentrated on arming and leading the ethnic Montagnard tribesmen against the Viet Cong guerrillas in the highlands. The large army aviation contingent, equipped with the newest and most modern armed helicopters, was flying combat missions for the Vietnamese. In 1964 the total number of American combat deaths exceeded 100 for the first time, and the situation had become perilous despite the army's efforts.

By 1964 the army had regained the capability to fight major nonnuclear wars that it had lost during the Eisenhower era. It now had the size, weapons, and mobility to support an active, interventionist military policy. It was no accident that the United States decided to escalate the level of violence in Vietnam the following year; the restraint imposed by Eisenhower's policy of deliberate inability was no longer present. In retrospect, the army had forfeited its right to complain about what Vietnam would do to it. Displeased with the New Look cutbacks and fearful of a future that seemed to hold no place for them, the army's leaders had concentrated their efforts on finding reasons why ground strength should have been maintained after Korea. The proponents of limited-war capability had never stopped to think about the social, political, and economic ramifications of such conflicts. Perhaps a more graceful and thoughtful adaptation to the New Look might have enabled the army to ask the hard questions that could have prevented the tragedy that lay ahead.

NOTES

1. Office of the Chief of Military History, *The Office of the Secretary of the Army, 1955–60, Programs and Accomplishments* (Washington, n.d.), p. 45.

2. Dwight D. Eisenhower, *The Papers of Dwight David Eisenhower*, ed. Alfred D. Chandler et al., 9 vols. to date (Baltimore: Johns Hopkins University Press, 1970-), vol. VI, *Occupation, 1945* (1978), pp. 368–71 (quote from p. 369); vol. VII, *The Chief of Staff*, ed. Louis Galambos et al. (1978), pp. 679–81, 742–45.

3. Eisenhower, *Papers*, vol. IX, *The Chief of Staff*, ed. Louis Galambos et al. (1978), pp. 2253–55.

4. Eisenhower to Louis Johnson, 14 July 1949, CCS 370 (8–19–45), Sec. 18, Records of the Joint Chiefs of Staff, Record Group 218, National Archives, Washington, D.C.; Eisenhower Diary, 19 February 1949, Eisenhower Papers, Eisenhower Library, Abilene, Kansas; Kenneth W. Condit, *The History of the Joint Chiefs of Staff: The Joint Chiefs of Staff and National Policy*, vol. II, *1947–49* (Washington: Joint Chiefs of Staff, 1976), pp. 257–81.

5. U.S., Department of State, *Foreign Relations of the United States: 1950*, vol. III, *Western Europe* (Washington: Government Printing Office, 1977), pp. 378–80; Harry S. Truman, *Years of Trial and Hope* (Garden City, N.Y.: Doubleday & Co., 1955), p. 258.

6. Quoted in Ronald J. Caridi, *The Korean War and American Politics: The Republican Party as a Case Study* (Philadelphia: University of Pennsylvania Press, 1968), p. 226.

7. JCS 1800/205, 3 June 1953, CCS 370 (8–19–45), Sec. 41, Record Group 218.

8. For the final text of NSC 162 (162/2), see *The Senator Gravel Edition, The Pentagon Papers: The Defense Department History of United States Decisionmaking on Vietnam*, 5 vols. (Boston: Beacon Press, 1971), I, 412–29.

9. NSC 20/4 may be found in U.S., Department of State, *Foreign Relations of the United States: 1948* (Washington: Government Printing Office, 1976-), vol. I: *General: The United Nations* (1976), pp. 667–68.

10. *Pentagon Papers*, I, 422.

11. *Pentagon Papers*, I, 416, 424, 426.

12. *Pentagon Papers*, I, 417, 423, 425, 426.

13. *Pentagon Papers*, I, 424; Matthew B. Ridgway, memorandum, 26 October 1953, CCS 381 US (1–31–50), Sec. 30, Record Group 218.

14. JCS 2101/113, 10 December 1953, CCS 381 US (1–31–50), Sec. 32, Record Group 218.

15. Ibid.

16. See JCS 1800/215, 11 March 1954, Record Group 218; CCS 370 (8–19–45), Sec. 45; JCS 1800/221, 25 April 1954, Record Group 218; CCS 370 (8–19–45), Bulky Package, Pt. 5, Record Group 218; and Ridgway, *Soldier: The Memoirs of Matthew B. Ridgway* (New York: Harper and Brothers, 1956), p. 272.

17. JCS 1800/221, 29 April 1954, Record Group 218; CCS 370 (8–19–45), Bulky Package, Pt. 5, Record Group 218; JCS 1800/222, 1 July 1954, Record Group 218; CCS 370 (8–19–45), Sec. 46, Record Group 218.

18. Ridgway to the Secretary of the Army, 24 April 1954, Records of the Chief of Staff of the Army, 1954, 091 Indochina TS, Record Group 319, National Archives, Washington, D.C. See also *Pentagon Papers*, I, 471–72, 508–9.

19. Maxwell D. Taylor, *Swords and Plowshares* (New York: Norton, 1972), p. 166.

20. Maxwell D. Taylor, *The Uncertain Trumpet* (New York: Harper and Brothers, 1960), pp. 30–34.

21. Herbert B. Powell, ''The Infantryman in the Atomic Age,'' *Army Information Digest* 13 (April 1958): 39.

22. Anthony B. Herbert, *Soldier* (New York: Dell Publishing, 1973), pp. 88–89.

23. James M. Gavin, *War and Peace in the Space Age* (New York: Harper and Brothers, 1958), pp. 160–61.

FURTHER READING

As of this writing a truly accurate picture of the New Look, and the Taylor-McNamara-Kennedy reaction to it, cannot be written by unofficial researchers because most of the relevant documents remain classified. Researchers determined to use primary sources can, however, use the files of the Joint Chiefs of Staff (the ''CCS files''), in the National Archives, Washington, D.C. Two segments of these records, which run continuously from World War II through the 1950s, have recently been opened: the 1951–1953 files, which cover the origins and initial implementation of the New Look; and the 1954–1956 files, which document the army's increasing dissatisfaction and the many army-air force disputes engendered by that dissatisfaction as well as the army's search for a mission. Of the CCS subjective decimal files, the most rewarding is the 370 (8–19–45) series; the most valuable of the geographic files are those bearing the decimal number 381 US (1–31–50).

Because the period 1953–1964 falls between wars, good, solid secondary sources are scarce; few historians seem interested in examining the effects of Korea on the army or in seeking the origins of the Vietnam tragedy in the institutional history of the army. The best overall treatments may be found in two general surveys by one of the most imaginative military historians: Russell F. Weigley's *History of the United States Army*, enlarged ed. (Bloomington: Indiana University Press, 1984), and his more interpretive *The American Way of War: A History of United States Military Strategy and Policy*, The Wars of the United States (New York: Macmillan Co., 1973). Weigley's notes and bibliographies should be consulted with great care by scholar and general reader alike.

The official positions of the army and Defense Department may be gleaned from an examination of the annual and semiannual reports of the Department of Defense, to which the reports of the three military services are appended. Much of value can be found in the hearings and documents of the congressional armed services and appropriations committees. The army's publicity campaign can be sampled by scanning the pages of the official *Army Information Digest* and the semiofficial organ of the Association of the United States Army, *Army* magazine.

The best sources for the origins of NSC 68 and 162/2 are still two long essays in Warner R. Schilling, Paul Y. Hammond, and Glenn H. Snyder, *Strategy, Politics, and Defense Budgets* (New York: Columbia University Press, 1962): Hammond's ''NSC–68: Prologue to Rearmament'' and Snyder's ''The 'New Look' of 1952.''

Several memoirs written by major actors of the period also contain valuable insights: Dwight D. Eisenhower, *Mandate for Change, 1953–56: The White House Years* (Garden City, N.Y.: Doubleday, 1963), and *Waging Peace, 1956–61: The White House Years* (Garden City, N.Y.: Doubleday, 1965); Matthew B. Ridgway, *Soldier: The Memoirs of Matthew B. Ridgway* (New York: Harper and Brothers, 1956); Anthony B. Herbert, *Soldier* (New York: Dell Publishing, 1973); Maxwell D. Taylor, *The Uncertain Trumpet* (New York: Harper and Brothers, 1959), and *Swords and Plowshares* (New York: Norton, 1972); James M. Gavin, *War and Peace in the Space Age* (New York: Harper and Brothers, 1958); and John B. Medaris, *Countdown for Decision* (New York: Putnam, 1960). See also Robert H. Ferrell, ed., *The Eisenhower Diaries* (New York: Norton, 1981), and Omar N. Bradley and Clay Blair, *A General's Life: An Autobiography* (New York: Simon and Schuster, 1983).

The latest, most balanced biography of the author of the New Look is Stephen E. Ambrose, *Eisenhower*, vol. II, *The President and Elder Statesman, 1952–1969* (New York: Simon and Schuster, 1984).

Secondary sources for this essay—most written by political scientists or in the political science mode—include Richard K. Betts, *Soldiers, Statesmen and Cold War Crises* (Cambridge: Harvard University Press, 1977); Richard A. Aliano, *American Defense Policy from Eisenhower to Kennedy: The Politics of Changing Military Requirements, 1957–61* (Athens: Ohio University Press, 1975); Douglas Kinnard, *President Eisenhower and Strategy Management: A Study in Defense Politics* (Lexington: University Press of Kentucky, 1977); Lawrence J. Korb, *The Joint Chiefs of Staff: The First Twenty-five Years* (Bloomington: Indiana University Press, 1976); Samuel P. Huntington, *The Common Defense: Strategic Programs in National Politics* (New York: Columbia University Press, 1961); and Michael H. Armacost, *The Politics of Weapons Innovation: The Thor-Jupiter Controversy* (New York: Columbia University Press, 1969). See also William W. Kaufmann, *The McNamara Strategy* (New York: Harper and Row, 1964), and Frederick A. Bergerson, *The Army Gets an Air Force: Tactics of Insurgent Bureaucratic Politics* (Baltimore: Johns Hopkins University Press, 1980).

The U.S. Army's historical program has a large and growing number of official histories. Most of these, unfortunately, cover various aspects of World War II, Korea, and Vietnam; the interwar years are usually treated only insofar as they are important to wartime activities. Four Vietnam studies which should be consulted are George S. Eckhardt, *Command and Control: 1950–1969*, Vietnam Studies (Washington: Department of the Army, 1974); John J. Tolson, *Airmobility: 1961–1971*, Vietnam Studies (Washington: Department of the Army, 1973); James Lawton Collins, Jr., *The Development and Training of the South Vietnamese Army, 1950–1972*, Vietnam Studies (Washington: Department of the Army, 1975); and Francis J. Kelly, *US Army Special Forces: 1961–1971*, Vietnam Studies (Washington: Department of the Army, 1973). Relying on these and a wealth of other sources, Ronald H. Spector has produced the definitive work on American involvement in Vietnam during the 1940s and 1950s, *Advice and Support: The Early Years, 1941–1960*, United States Army in Vietnam (Washington: U.S. Army Center of Military History, 1983). Of the many unpublished manuscripts in the Center for Military History, the most valuable are Robert W. Coakley, et al., "Summary of U.S. Army Expansion and Readiness 1961–1962"; Office of the Chief of Military History, "The Office of the Secretary of the Army, 1955–60: Problems and Accomplishments"; and Ernest F. Fisher, "Relationship of the Road Concept to Moral Considerations in Strategic Planning." For the last months of the Korean War, see Walter G. Hermes, *Truce Tent and Fighting Front*, United States Army in the Korean War (Washington: U.S. Army Center of Military History, 1966).

CHAPTER 17

The Vietnam War, 1962–1973

B. FRANKLIN COOLING

United States Army participation in the war in Vietnam commenced officially during the administration of President John F. Kennedy. Battle streamers atop army flagstaffs and the campaign ribbons worn by the men who fought in Southeast Asia commemorate seventeen distinct periods of campaigning beginning soon after the creation of the Military Assistance Command Vietnam (MACV) in early 1962 and ending on 28 January 1973. Nevertheless, American military leaders first showed an interest in this part of the world as early as the Second World War. As the Vietnamese nationalist leader Ho Chi Minh and the Viet Minh tried to end French rule over Indochina in the early 1950s, army chiefs of staff such as Generals J. Lawton Collins and Matthew B. Ridgway counted on Brigadier Generals Francis G. Brink, Thomas J. H. Trapnell, and the other chiefs of the army's Military Assistance Advisory Group (MAAG) in Vietnam to keep a close eye on French political and military control of the area. But as the Korean War dragged on (1950–1953), top army officials worried about proliferating American commitments on the mainland of Asia, and everyone seemed quite content to allow a French surrogate to contain communism in Southeast Asia. Consultation and a massive infusion of military aid which it was hoped would build both French resolve and eventually a national Vietnamese military also formed part of this guarded American commitment. The bitter aftertaste of the Korean War precluded sending more American men to fight elsewhere in Asia. The acceptable pattern for American military policy in Southeast Asia therefore remained simply to tinker with ideas about strategy, training, manpower, and logistical aid while supporting the embattled French and their plans for that region.[1]

The French defeat at Dien Bien Phu in 1954 thus marked a crossroads for the United States in Southeast Asia. It led to the Geneva settlement and the withdrawal of France from the region by 1956. The American military would be drawn—slowly, subtly, but inevitably—into the vacuum left by the French. Yet no one foresaw this outcome at the time, in part because the United States Army had resisted the temptation to intervene in Southeast Asia during the siege of

Dien Bien Phu. Badgered by the French to relieve the garrison but worried that intervention might presage a longer and costlier commitment of men and resources to Indochina, military planners in the Pentagon wavered between the possible use of tactical nuclear devices to help the besieged French and plans to send seven army divisions and one marine division to replace the French should they withdraw precipitously from Southeast Asia. Navy and air force officials likewise prepared contingency plans, but in the end senior army leaders such as Ridgway and his assistant chief of staff for operations, Lieutenant General James H. Gavin, succeeded in averting any massive rescue of the French by the American army.[2]

Nonetheless, as the French departed from the area, the United States Army found itself in the position of helping to forge native military instruments to defend Indochina and avoid full-scale war. From 1955 through 1961 the army operated as part of "country teams" employing military, diplomatic, and economic aid in an effort to create strong, democratic states in the non-Communist part of what had been French Indochina. To succor the new state of South Vietnam, which had been formed at the Geneva Conference of 1954, the army advised the land forces of the Republic of Vietnam (RVN), as South Vietnam was officially named, through a Military Assistance Advisory Group located in Saigon. Similar groups operated in Cambodia and Laos.[3]

American military officers in this period emphasized building a conventional South Vietnamese army designed to counter the obvious martial threat posed by Communist North Vietnam, which had also been created at Geneva in 1954 and which lay beyond the seventeenth parallel of north latitude. Under the supervision of dedicated, if somewhat prosaic MAAG chieftains such as Lieutenant Generals John W. ("Iron Mike") O'Daniel, Samuel T. Williams, and Lionel C. McGarr, some 750 American advisers of all ranks and services (although roughly 50 percent came from the army) attempted to build a Vietnamese military machine capable of defending the South against an attack from the North as well as from internal subversion. But despite an awareness of the latter possibility, attention focused on a Korean-style invasion from North Vietnam, and American contingency plans of the late 1950s envisioned a conflict involving insertion of American air, ground, and naval combat forces in support of the South.

Much time was spent training, organizing, and equipping South Vietnamese forces for the anticipated invasion. It never came, yet the story of American military "advice and support" during the late 1950s is a revealing account of the American army's sometimes prickly relations with State Department officials as well as the many bureaucrats who helped administer the South Vietnamese regime of President Ngo Dinh Diem. Limited budgets, even more limited language capabilities, and a backward Vietnamese society evidencing little enthusiasm for the presence of yet another "colonial" power added to the frustrations MAAG personnel often felt during these years. As Vietnamese army divisions evolved from units and traditions formed during the earlier French period, American advisers were disturbed by the politicization, corruption, and mediocrity they saw permeating the Vietnamese officer corps. Yet the United States Army did successfully reorganize the Army of the Republic of Vietnam (ARVN), establishing a comprehensive school and training system, rationalizing (on paper, at least) the chain of command, and providing the basis of a logistics system. The South Vietnamese army by 1960 was no longer thought to be the weak, demoralized, and disorganized force of five years before.[4]

The test of this revitalized army came between 1959 and 1961 when the North Vietnamese government escalated its infiltration of subversives into South Vietnam in an effort to topple the Diem regime. Suddenly Diem and his generals found themselves faced with the threat of guerrilla war. In repeated firefights and smaller brushes with the National Liberation Front or Viet Cong (VC), as the guerrillas were styled, Republic of Vietnam forces proved unready for battle. Road-bound like the French had been, ARVN and paramilitary forces of the South displayed little stomach for fighting, even after the MAAG chief, General Samuel T. Williams, broke a long-established policy on 25 May 1959 and allowed American advisers to accompany Vietnamese units on operational missions.

While ARVN forces proved poorly prepared for an insurgency, few Americans had much experience with this type of warfare either. United States Army training and doctrine envisioned guerrilla war in the Korean sense—fighting behind established battle fronts to disrupt lines of communication to the rear. There would be no traditional battle line in Vietnam, however, as the whole country quickly became a battlefield. By July 1959 the first American advisers had been killed in a VC attack, and the situation was disintegrating badly.[5]

What was now called a "counterinsurgency" quickly came to dominate the attention of both American and Vietnamese officials. Contingency plans shifted to face this threat, while ARVN forces continued to lose in the field and the countryside became the domain of the Viet Cong. The American-Vietnamese answer always called for additional military aid and organizational reform. More men (better trained and armed than their predecessors), improved intelligence work, and a revamped chain of command—such was the collective wisdom of 1960 and 1961. It was perhaps natural that soldiers would offer military solutions; however, if ARVN defeats did not provide conclusive evidence of miscalculation, they did suggest a serious underestimation of the importance of the political side of the conflict.

Just how much influence any American soldier really had in South Vietnam at this stage remains unclear. Most American army advisers were little more than onlookers and instructors. They cannot be blamed for the failure of the South Vietnamese to develop the nonmilitary and paramilitary resources necessary to defeat the insurgents. Nevertheless, the public statements of MAAG headquarters in Saigon revealed the "can do" attitude of most military men at the time and their dogged determination to pursue a purely military solution to the problems facing the United States and its Vietnamese ally.

Men like General Matthew B. Ridgway, Secretary of State John Foster Dulles, Ambassador Elbridge Durbrow, and even some MAAG officials of the mid–

1950s sensed that the problems of Southeast Asia involved government and society as much as armies, but the advent of the more expansive and more confident administration of President John F. Kennedy in 1961 overcame the objections of naysayers everywhere. No frontier was too distant, no problem too large, no solution too elusive to the American way of thinking at this stage. As one senior army general commented later, "It was a period of national fumbling" during which the nation "was sucked into the maw of Vietnam." As always, the United States Army mirrored the society it defended. Nobody thought of quitting in 1961, and victory seemed to offer the only way out. Winning the war, however, would require additional American involvement.[6]

Given these developments, the American commitment and extent of advisory efforts in Southeast Asia changed dramatically from 1962 to 1965. The United States Army, for example, assumed a large-scale operational support role in addition to its training and logistical activities. Implementing the counterinsurgency plan developed in 1960–1961, the Kennedy administration replaced the Military Assistance Advisory Group in Saigon with the larger Military Assistance Command (MACV) under the command of General Paul D. Harkins and tried to bolster ARVN capabilities in irregular warfare. For the first time American army units directly supported each of the four South Vietnamese corps commands—particularly aviation companies with helicopters which could move ARVN infantry in and out of combat. By the end of 1962, some 11,000 American advisory and support personnel were in South Vietnam, twenty-nine Special Forces detachments were operating in the field, and American battlefield casualties were mounting. With over 500,000 South Vietnamese now in uniform, General Harkins and his staff pointed to the improved efficiency of their pupils.

Had it not been for the civil unrest and political instability that gripped South Vietnam from 1963 to 1965, the new American advisory and support role might have succeeded. Instead, the continuing politicization of the ARVN diluted its training and combat efficiency as well as its morale while the relentless pressure of a determined enemy strained the limited resources of the government of South Vietnam. As a result, necessary activities like the rotation of units from the field for training, the Strategic Hamlet Program, the Civilian Irregular Defense Group Program, and improvement of the territorial forces (Civil Guard and Self-Defense Corps) suffered. While the South Vietnamese army and government fell into even deeper disarray, the United States sought to compensate for the weakness of its ally by increasing its own commitment to the war effort. General William C. Westmoreland replaced General Harkins as commander, MACV, in June 1964, whle passage of the Gulf of Tonkin Resolution in August 1964 enabled President Lyndon B. Johnson to use American air, sea, and ground combat units as he deemed necessary in response to the increasingly frequent attacks of VC and North Vietnamese regulars. By the end of 1964, American military strength in the Republic of Vietnam had doubled and promised to go higher.

Despite these potentially significant changes, the army's mission in Southeast Asia still seemed clear to everybody at this stage. Worldwide communism had to be stopped in Vietnam as it had been in Korea. General Harold K. Johnson, the army chief of staff, told an Association of the United States Army audience on 17 November 1964:

Today we are confronted with a paradox. If our Free World deterrent posture against the Soviet Union and Red China remains effective, the Army is less likely to enter into direct combat with either or both of these major Communist powers. So long as our deterrent posture remains strong and versatile, the efforts of the Communists and their henchmen to gain their goals will be carried out by guerrilla warfare, revolutionary operations, insurgency, terrorism, and the entire catalogue of violence now described by the Communists as Wars of National Liberation.

The United States Army and the country had a role to play in countering such wars.[7]

To a reluctant president like Lyndon B. Johnson (who wished to avoid a heightened level of American involvement in Vietnam almost, but not quite, as much as he wished to avoid defeat) as well as to millions of his countrymen, the time seemed propitious to "Americanize" the war and get the job done. If South Vietnam could not solve its own problems, the United States would. Perhaps the trend could not have been otherwise—given the frustrations of Korea, the Eisenhower-Kennedy rhetoric of commitment and support for friends overseas, the ever-present dread of Red China, and the Communist presence in Southeast Asia. Perhaps the slowly growing level of American military activity and investment in South Vietnam had reached the point of no return by 1964–1965. Certainly, few military men objected openly to the decision to Americanize the conflict. For many military and political leaders alike, Vietnam seemed the ideal place to retrieve the elusive victory missed in Korea, to recoup the lost years of the Eisenhower administration, and to recover from the embarrassment of John Kennedy's Bay of Pigs fiasco in Cuba.[8]

Neither North nor South Vietnam wanted "Americanization" and Americans themselves did not want to be tied indefinitely to an interminable war in Asia. Yet it all seemed so necessary, so proper in the mid–1960s. Bands and banners greeted the first marine and army combat units when they arrived in South Vietnam in May 1965. The first army combat unit, the 173d Airborne Brigade, reached Vietnam on 5 May, and by early June the number of American military personnel there surpassed the 50,000 mark. Under General William C. Westmoreland, the MACV commander, they originally were ordered to defend specific areas; to conduct clearing operations designed to "search out and destroy" enemy forces, strong points, and supply caches; and to assist South Vietnamese units in defensive operations. The 173d Airborne Brigade and two South Vietnamese battalions initiated the first major American-Vietnamese combined offensive in late June just north of Saigon. Meanwhile, the United States Army buildup continued relentlessly with elements of the First Infantry, 101st Airborne, and First Cavalry (Airmobile) divisions all entering the war zone that summer.

As these and other units arrived in South Vietnam during 1965, military leaders divided the country into the major areas of responsibility that would govern operations for the next eight years. An interservice agreement assigned the marines to the I Corps Tactical Zone, as the military designated the five northernmost provinces of South Vietnam, while the United States Army was to operate mainly in the II and III Corps zones of the central highlands, adjacent coastal regions, and the area around Saigon. South Vietnamese troops retained the primary responsibility for conducting operations to the south in the Mekong Delta region of IV Corps. Admittedly, the boundaries separating these regions were not hard and fast, and it was not unusual for a unit from III Corps, for example, to join temporarily with forces from IV Corps for the purposes of a particular operation. The United States Air Force provided tactical air support (as did marine and naval air units) for these ground forces and, together with the navy, strategic bombardment of targets in North Vietnam. (In February 1965, under the code name ROLLING THUNDER, the air force had begun a particularly punishing series of raids against the North using B–52 heavy bombers.)

A late summer Communist offensive in the central highlands which tried to push through to the sea and cut South Vietnam in half, followed that autumn by battles in the Ia Drang Valley, introduced many of the American soldiers who arrived in Southeast Asia in 1965 to the type of fighting they could expect to encounter thereafter. A violent stand by the enemy to protect densely wooded, mountainous base areas close to the Cambodian border, ambushes and night infiltration, "hugging" of American units to forestall air and artillery strikes, and human-wave assaults always ended in retreat across the border into areas which were off-limits to American and South Vietnamese forces. There was no battlefield in the traditional sense and operations were fatiguing, frustrating, and mostly inconclusive. Despite the unfamiliar nature of such warfare, the United States Army succeeded in verifying its concept of airmobile operations and the ability of its fighting men to defeat enemy forces even in heavy jungle terrain. American leaders made the most of their ability to transfer entire brigades rapidly by air into a battle area to fight the more experienced North Vietnamese and Viet Cong who might require weeks to put their plans into action. Still, the European-oriented United States Army had to make a number of adjustments in its organization and equipment in order to function in a basically new environment.[9]

General Westmoreland intended to use 1965 and 1966 to keep the enemy off balance while constructing base camps and other logistical facilities for the larger campaigns of the future. To this end, MACV supported the South Vietnamese government's Revolutionary Development Program, a rural pacification endeavor which sought to overcome VC influence in the countryside, and undertook a series of ever larger search and destroy missions in which American, South Vietnamese, South Korean, and Australian combat units joined efforts to spoil Communist attack plans and smash Communist bases in South Vietnam. These actions marked the first part of a successful three-year counteroffensive against the Viet Cong and North Vietnamese Army units operating south of the De-

An army medic tending an injured lieutenant felled by a VC white phosphorus grenade booby trap
National Archives (306-MVP-16-1)

Helicopters of the First Air Cavalry Division returning to a landing field near An Khe after seeing action early in the Vietnam War
National Archives (306-MVP-16-5)

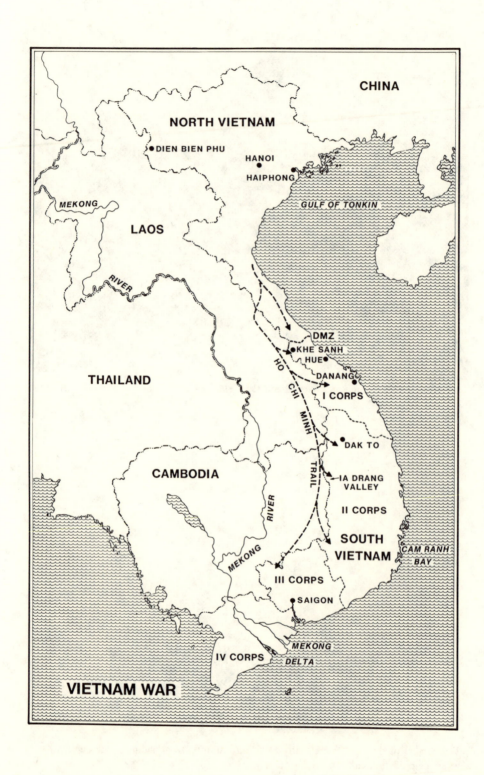

militarized Zone (DMZ) which separated the two Vietnams at the seventeenth parallel. The second phase of the counteroffensive (July 1966–May 1967) saw American forces occupy enemy-dominated areas in the Mekong Delta to the south and near the DMZ to the north. During this period newly arriving American units such as the Fourth Infantry Division and the 196th Light Infantry Brigade carried out a number of well-publicized operations—two of which (ATTLE-BORO near the Cambodian border and CEDAR FALLS in the "Iron Triangle" twenty-five miles northwest of Saigon) particularly encouraged American army officials with huge enemy casualty counts; tons of supplies, equipment, and documents captured or destroyed; and further proof that American soldiers could defeat an aggressive and shrewd opponent.

Operations by elements of the Ninth Infantry Division in the Mekong Delta in 1967 added another unique aspect to this war. Here in an area crisscrossed by canals and rivers and requiring close army-navy cooperation, United States Army units employed fire support boats, naval armored troop carriers, and artillery mounted on firing barges in riverine operations directed against the Communist Can Son Secret Zone. Repeatedly victorious by its own standards, the American military increasingly concentrated on discovering and annihilating enemy main force units and destroying long-established Communist base areas. South Vietnamese units—less aggressive and decidedly more defense-oriented—turned more and more to rural pacification.[10]

Events during the remainder of 1967 gave little indication of the dramatic turn the Southeast Asian conflict would take in the following year. By mid-June 1967 the United States armed forces had lost 11,099 men killed in battle and their total strength in South Vietnam reached 463,000. The South Vietnamese army contained over 600,000 men and had suffered 47,695 deaths. Communist forces in South Vietnam were estimated at 294,000, including 50,000 North Vietnamese, although these figures as well as the number of enemy casualties were rapidly becoming a controversial issue in Saigon and Washington. Bolstered by the arrival of fresh forces (including units of the Thai army), General Westmoreland and MACV continued to rely on search and destroy missions to inflict heavy casualties on the enemy and to keep the Viet Cong and North Vietnamese off balance. In September the South Vietnamese elected General Nguyen Van Thieu and Air Marshall Nguyen Cao Ky as their president and vice president respectively; and American leaders hoped the Thieu government would end the political instability which had plagued South Vietnam ever since the assassination of President Diem in November 1963. Two months later a major attempt by the Communists to take Dak To, which lay astride a series of infiltration routes known as the Ho Chi Minh Trail extending from North Vietnam into the central highlands in II Corps Tactical Zone, was soundly rebuffed.

Although American military leaders were cautiously optimistic, ominous signs also existed during the waning months of 1967. Westmoreland and other American officials thought that 67 percent of the South Vietnamese population lived in government-controlled safe areas. Nevertheless, the Communists still controlled much of South Vietnam and when danger threatened could always fall back on their bases in the neighboring sanctuaries of Laos and Cambodia. In addition, mounting Communist pressure on American units stationed along the DMZ and South Vietnam's western border with Laos and Cambodia took a heavy toll of killed and wounded—forcing General Westmoreland to reduce the army's strength in South Vietnam's populated areas in order to reinforce those units under attack along the country's outer perimeter. What Westmoreland did not realize was that this was what his North Vietnamese counterpart General Vo Nguyen Giap, architect of the earlier victory over the French at Dien Bien Phu, appears to have been counting on when the North Vietnamese army brought increasing pressure to bear on such outlying posts as Dak To and the marine base at Khe Sanh along the DMZ.[11]

Fearful that the North Vietnamese meant to do to the marines at Khe Sanh what they had done to the French at Dien Bien Phu and determined to prevent such a debacle, American leaders were caught off guard when the Communists suddenly launched a major offensive in the interior of South Vietnam in late January 1968 during Tet, the Vietnamese holiday celebrating the arrival of the Chinese lunar new year. Traditionally, Tet was a time of peace and good cheer. But it also offered an ideal cover for the Viet Cong to try to provoke a general uprising in the cities of the South. Orchestrated by General Giap, the simultaneous attack of Viet Cong units in major South Vietnamese cities like Saigon as well as in various provincial capitals was intended to fragment the South Vietnamese government and military and to drive the Americans from Southeast Asia. While the South Vietnamese forces did not break apart under stress and no general uprising spread to the countryside, such bloody encounters as the struggle for control of the provincial capital of Hue and the assault on the American embassy compound in Saigon were embarrassingly close calls. Except for some last-minute repositioning of United States Army maneuver battalions closer to the capital, thanks to Lieutenant General Frederick Weyand's suspicions of a surprise attack, that city might well have fallen to the enemy. As it was, by the end of February, a shaken American-Vietnamese command had mustered 495,000 American, 600,000 South Vietnamese, and 61,000 other allied combatants against an estimated 223,000–248,000 Communists. More than 50,000 total combat deaths on both sides attested to the intensity of the offensive. The ultimate result of Tet was a bloody battlefield repulse for Giap and the North Vietnamese premier, Ho Chi Minh. The South Vietnamese military had not collapsed, the foreigners had not been driven into the sea, and South Vietnam had not suc-cumbed to the North. Yet as one veteran soldier-historian of the Vietnam period, General Dave R. Palmer, has noted: "The *Tet* offensive was the most disastrous defeat North Vietnam suffered in the long war. Paradoxically, it was the North's most resounding victory during the years of American military presence."[12]

There were several reasons for this paradox. Weakened by heavy losses during the Tet offensive and disillusioned by the failure of that offensive to spark a general uprising in the South, the Viet Cong never fully recovered from the crippling blow dealt them during the first few months of 1968. In addition, the brutal methods the Viet Cong used during the offensive to intimidate civilians backfired and alienated many South Vietnamese, thus aiding the Thieu government in its increasingly successful efforts to suppress the guerrillas.

Although the military could say for these reasons that Tet had been an American victory, such a claim made little sense to the tired and increasingly skeptical American public. More important was the political and psychological fallout Tet produced throughout the United States. Military and political leaders from Lyndon Johnson on down had been proclaiming for three years or more before Tet that they could see "light at the end of the tunnel" and that "victory lay just around the corner." Westmoreland had but recently toured the United States, drumming up support for the war effort by assuring those with whom he spoke that "we are making real progress" over there. Suddenly, American taxpayers and the relatives of American servicemen in Vietnam saw a very different picture of the war on their television sets at home: shattered American embassy walls, body bags lying side by side on the ground, and the vacant stare of defeat in the eyes of soldiers who had given their all and had nothing left to give. All the while there were continual calls from Westmoreland for additional troops. As the sagacious dean of American newsmen, Walter Cronkite, so graphically put it: "What the hell is going on? I thought we were winning this war!" The Communists might well have lost the battle, but press reports filtering back from Vietnam conveyed the message to Main Street that America was losing the war. Tet had an even more startling impact on the political homefront, for 1968 was a presidential year, and political primaries to select the parties' candidates coincided with the Communist offensive. Tet shattered the grit, credibility, and stability of the Johnson administration. It also was one of the main reasons for the beleaguered president's announcement on 31 March 1968 that he would not seek reelection in the fall.[13]

Of course, much of this was not readily apparent until months after the Viet Cong and North Vietnamese had broken off the offensive and filtered back to their sanctuaries. By then the war had resumed its normal pattern. Westmoreland requested 206,000 more men (a 40 percent increase in a conflict where statistics seemed to be the sole measure of success or failure); and by the end of March 1968, Johnson announced a 13,500-man increase over the 525,000-man ceiling which had been set in mid–1967 for American troop strength in the Republic of Vietnam. This increase was designed to help restore the Thieu government's control over the country after Tet as well as to support the ongoing search-and-destroy operations of MACV. While Operation PEGASUS relieved the besieged Khe Sanh base in early April, the enemy proved stubbornly resilient. Ground fighting continued even around Saigon until May, with night rocket attacks against the capital persisting until late the next month. By the time Westmoreland left for Washington in June 1968 to become army chief of staff, almost as many Americans had died in Vietnam since the beginning of the year (10,503) as had been killed in all of 1967. Although no one knew for certain, the Communists were thought to have fared even worse, losing over 170,000 men and 39,800 weapons during their winter–spring offensive.[14]

In many ways then, 1968 was the pivotal year of the war. The Tet disaster led both sides to agree to sit down at the peace table in Paris on 13 May in order to negotiate an end to the fighting. The Viet Cong showed that it was not a viable instrument of revolution and the terrorist tactics used by Communist guerrillas in Hue and elsewhere during the Tet offensive actually united more than they intimidated the people against whom their fury had been directed. The army of South Vietnam proved its mettle during the spring offensive of the Communists, while American combat strength neared its apex under West-moreland's successor as the MACV commander, cigar-chomping General Creighton W. Abrams. Abrams had been Westmoreland's deputy commander in Vietnam and had supported "Westy's" earlier requests for more troops. As MACV commander, however, Abrams tried to get away from Westmoreland's strategy of attrition by introducing a "one-war" concept wherein all the armed services and allied forces, together with the various paramilitary units of the South Vietnamese government intensified and coordinated their operations. The Communists attempted to resume the level of their earlier offensives, but Abrams's "one-war" approach to operations consistently disrupted their troop movements, destroyed their staging areas and supply dumps, and thwarted their plans. As a result, in late August 1968 MACV was able to report that almost as much of the South Vietnamese population (66.8 percent) lived in government-controlled safe areas as had lived in secure areas during the pre-Tet period.

When Richard M. Nixon replaced Lyndon Johnson as president in January 1969, the new chief executive announced that, instead of Americanizing the war as Johnson had done, he would pursue the opposite policy of "Vietnamization." Nixon and his national security adviser, Henry Kissinger, decided that while the United States would continue to extend appropriate military and economic assistance to the Thieu regime, the nation of South Vietnam would increasingly have to provide the manpower for its own defense. Americans were simply tired of sending their boys to die in a war without apparent end or purpose, and the Nixon administration responded to this collective psychological exhaustion. There would be no precipitous withdrawal of American forces, but neither would the full military commitment of the United States continue indefinitely. It was a middle-of-the-road attempt to blunt opposition at home and buy time in Southeast Asia to strengthen the South Vietnamese military and to bolster nation-building efforts in the countryside.

Meanwhile, events in Southeast Asia continued to provide conflicting signals about who was winning the war. Soon after Nixon's inaugural, the Communists mounted a major offensive against 100 cities and bases throughout South Vietnam. The 1969 Tet offensive was a far cry from its namesake of the previous year, but before it ended American combat deaths in Vietnam had eclipsed the total number of Americans killed in the Korean War. By the end of April, United States military strength in Vietnam peaked at 543,000. Shortly afterward President Nixon announced that he planned to begin withdrawing American forces from South Vietnam in July. In late August the Ninth Infantry Division brigade and two navy river-assault squadrons which formed the Mekong Delta Mobile Riverine Force were replaced by South Vietnamese units. A similar transfer of responsibility for the Capital Military District around Saigon took place in October.

To make it more difficult for the North Vietnamese to come south and take advantage of the American troop reduction, Nixon also authorized a partial renewal of the air war which President Johnson had halted in 1968 as an inducement to get the Paris peace talks moving as well as to assuage domestic critics of the war. As early as March 1969, Nixon began a fourteen-month clandestine bombing campaign over Cambodia in retribution for the use of Cambodian bases by large numbers of North Vietnamese regulars during the Tet offensive. In July American pilots began bombing the Ho Chi Minh Trail in Laos. By then Nixon had also approved the limited use of "protective reaction" strikes against aircraft and antiaircraft sites in the southern part of North Vietnam whenever aggressive action against allied planes could be traced to one of these sites. The reasons for launching "protective reaction" strikes against the North in time became much more flexible, as did the choice of targets for those strikes.

The Nixon administration sharply accelerated the withdrawal of American forces from South Vietnam beginning in 1970. General Abrams protested, saying that the South Vietnamese were not ready to fight the war alone and that too rapid a withdrawal would ultimately endanger the goal of Vietnamization. The South Vietnamese army of over 1 million men had more than quadrupled since the early 1960s and as a result was hampered by a severe shortage of trained officers who were qualified to lead their men into combat. United States Army officers returning to Vietnam for a second or third tour of duty in the early 1970s were sometimes shocked to discover how "woefully weak [the South Vietnamese army was] because of lack of leadership at the regimental and battalion level." As if this were not enough, Geneal Matthew Ridgway had warned in 1968 that it would take at least two years for the South Vietnamese army to learn how to use American equipment and doctrine properly, and his prediction proved all too true. While American military strength in South Vietnam declined to 335,794 by the end of 1970, to 158,119 by the end of 1971, and to 24,200 by the end of 1972, the United States still had to provide extensive air, artillery, logistical, and advisory support for the South Vietnamese throughout this period.[15]

Although Nixon did not feel that public opinion would allow him to withdraw American forces as slowly as General Abrams had requested, the president sought to buy time for Vietnamization by bringing as much pressure to bear on North Vietnam as he could during the final years of American involvement in the war. To this end, American helicopters supported a South Vietnamese attack against a Communist sanctuary in Cambodia in March 1970. At the end of the following month, more than 40,000 troops from the United States First Cavalry Division and the South Vietnamese Airborne Division took part in Operation ROCK-CRUSHER, the controversial invasion of Cambodia which led to angry, often violent demonstrations at Kent State University and other college campuses throughout the United States. By the time the last American troops withdrew from Cambodia in June, the combined operation had resulted in an estimated 2,000 enemy troops killed along with the capture of 9,300 tons of enemy munitions, weapons, rice, and other supplies. No longer could the Communists depend on their Cambodian sanctuaries. The performance of South Vietnamese troops during this operation, moreover, convinced officials in both Washington and Saigon that Vietnamization was working and that the South Vietnamese army was rapidly approaching the point where it could begin operating on its own.[16]

President Nixon sought to put additional pressure on the Communists by intensifying the bombing campaign north of the DMZ soon after the 1970 Cambodian incursion began and by authorizing massive B–52 raids over the Vietnamese-Laotian border later in the same year. In February 1971 MACV announced that it was giving support to the South Vietnamese army in operations then underway in both Cambodia and Laos. Although American soldiers did not accompany the ground forces in either of these two operations, MACV provided the South Vietnamese with badly needed aerial and artillery support. American airpower may well have saved the ARVN infantry division and armored brigade which entered Laos as part of Operation LAM SON 719 in February–April 1971 in order to disrupt the movement of supplies from North to South Vietnam along the Ho Chi Minh Trail. The South Vietnamese were almost routed when they unexpectedly encountered a larger force of approximately 36,000 North Vietnamese regulars equipped with modern Russian weapons and tanks. Nearly one-half of the South Vietnamese troops participating in this operation were killed or wounded, while the Americans suffered over 1,200 casualties and lost more than 100 helicopters. Officials in both Washington and Saigon should have paid more attention to this campaign for it revealed at virtually every level of the military hierarchy serious weaknesses in the South Vietnamese system of command and control. It also underscored the very dangerous possibility that the South Vietnamese army had grown too dependent over the years on American advice and combat support for it to stand and fight on its own with any assurance of success. The seeds of later disaster could have been seen in this operation had anyone cared to notice them, but by the spring of 1971 officials in the Nixon administration were looking for ways to hasten the withdrawal of American forces from Vietnam, not reasons to slow that process down.[17]

Growing disillusionment at home with Nixon's expansion of the war into Cambodia and Laos as well as the apparent inability of American and South Vietnamese forces to make any significant headway against the Communists led the Nixon administration to step up the rate of troop reductions in 1971 and to try for a major breakthrough in the ongoing Paris peace talks by promising to remove all American soldiers from South Vietnam without insisting that North Vietnam also agree to withdraw from the South. Adding to the incentives the administration already had to bring the troops home and to try to reach a negotiated settlement was the much publicized court-martial conviction in March 1971 of Lieutenant William Calley for murdering at least 22 unarmed South Vietnamese civilians during a search-and-destroy operation three years earlier. In that infamous episode American soldiers from the Twenty-third American Infantry Division had massacred some 450 inhabitants of the village of My Lai. The brutal, sometimes senseless nature of a struggle in which Americans had grown so frustrated that they deliberately killed the very people they were supposed to aid reinforced a growing belief that American involvement in this war was a mistake. By the summer of 1971 more than 70 pecent of the American people thought it wrong to have sent American troops to Vietnam and only 31 percent approved of Nixon's handling of the war. Most Americans felt the president was moving too slowly, and publication by the *New York Times* in June of a series of classified Defense Department documents which became known as the *Pentagon Papers* and which shed light on the origins of American involvement in the war reinforced a growing public conviction that the sooner the last American left Vietnam, the better.

Perhaps the most important reason so many Americans were disillusioned with this war, however, was that it seemed no nearer a solution in late 1971 and early 1972 than it had a decade before. Henry Kissinger's secret talks with the North Vietnamese representative Le Duc Tho in Paris broke down in late November. Worried by signs of an enemy buildup north of the DMZ, American pilots flew massive, prolonged "protective reaction" strikes against fuel and supply depots, airfields, and antiaircraft installations in North Vietnam. They also participated in a series of secret bombings of the North for which the commanding officer of the Seventh Air Force was later cashiered. These precautions notwithstanding, the wiley General Giap began a massive invasion of the South in late March 1972 that has since become known as the Easter invasion. Eschewing the unconventional tactics for which he had become best known in the past, Giap launched a conventional attack in which twelve North Vietnamese divisions with full armor and artillery support drove into South Vietnam on four separate fronts. This was the biggest offensive of the war since Tet 1968, and General Giap and Ho Chi Minh's successors in Hanoi ("Uncle Ho" had died in 1969) hoped that it would not only end the stalemate that had stymied military operations ever since the 1968 Tet offensive but also force the Americans in a presidential election year to make further concessions at the Paris peace talks.[18]

Before it was over, the 1972 Easter invasion almost cut South Vietnam in half and gave the Nixon and Thieu administrations much food for thought. The South Vietnamese army still lacked enough qualified officers. It was also ill equipped and unprepared to carry out the type of large-scale operations that were needed to stop the advancing North Vietnamese divisions. As part of the process of Vietnamization, MACV had helped to transform the South Vietnamese military into a force that excelled in the type of small-unit actions characteristic of counterinsurgency and pacification operations. The best ARVN units were engaged in pacifying the countryside when the invasion began and subsequently had to rush to reinforce those points along the border in greatest danger of being overrun by the enemy. This enabled the Viet Cong to mount an offensive of their own in the Mekong Delta and near Saigon.

Aided by their American advisors, as well as by a heavy dose of American air and naval gunfire support, the South Vietnamese eventually stopped the invasion and initiated a counterattack that saw them regain by the end of September most of the territory they had lost in April and May. In the meanwhile President Nixon had ordered several North Vietnamese ports mined, including Haiphong Harbor, and had imposed a naval blockade on North Vietnam. Nixon also resumed the full-scale bombing of North Vietnam with B–52 airplanes from the Strategic Air Command (SAC). Known as LINEBACKER I, this aerial bombing spree lasted from May to October and proved much more damaging to the North Vietnamese economy than Operation ROLLING THUNDER had been—in large part because of the greater accuracy of the new "smart bombs" which, guided by television cameras and laser beams, were used for the first time in 1972. By 23 October when Nixon ordered a temporary halt to all bombing north of the twentieth parallel, no one could deny that North Vietnam had suffered another costly defeat. Approximately 100,000 North Vietnamese and 25,000 South Vietnamese were thought to have died during the Easter offensive. Yet South Vietnam had had to have massive amounts of combat support to repulse the invasion and such help could not continue indefinitely.[19]

Even before LINEBACKER I ended, Henry Kissinger and Le Duc Tho had resumed serious negotiations in Paris. When the talks stalled just short of an agreement in mid-December, Nixon ordered a resumption of the bombing north of the twentieth parallel. From 18–29 December air force and navy planes flew almost 1,800 sorties and dropped thousands of tons of bombs (most of them over the heavily populated corridor connecting Haiphong Harbor and Hanoi) in the heaviest bombing campaign of the war, dubbed LINEBACKER II. The Paris discussions resumed on 8 January and a cease-fire agreement initialled by Kissinger and Le Duc Tho on 23 January and formally signed on 27 January 1973 took effect the next day. The last American troops left South Vietnam on 29 March, and on 14 August the Nixon administration discontinued the bombing of Cambodia in compliance with a congressional prohibition banning all further military involvement of the United States in Indochina.[20]

The war had ended for the United States Army. A temporary Defense Attaché Office in Saigon and the United States Activities Group in Thailand together took the place of MACV in order to supervise the transfer of the vast amount of hardware, munitions, and supplies that had been promised to the Thieu regime. In 1973 South Vietnam received more than $2.3 billion in military aid. It received less than half that amount in the following year and only $700 million in 1975. Many Americans later felt that greater congressional largess might have prevented the final collapse of the South Vietnamese army and government when General Van Tieng Dung and a heavily armored North Vietnamese force swept south in March–April 1975. With more military aid from the United States, the South

Vietnamese army could have relied on greater air and artillery support to blunt the Communist thrust southward. That antidote had saved the South Vietnamese army before—in Laos during Operation LAM SON 719 in 1971 and again during the 1972 Easter invasion. But the South Vietnamese had barely escaped defeat on each of those occasions and there was no guarantee that heavy firepower could again compensate for the poor leadership, inadequate training, low morale, and rampant corruption that existed in many ARVN units. Besides, a South Vietnamese victory in 1975 would merely have postponed that country's inevitable defeat; for the cornucopia of American support—even if extended through 1975—could not have continued indefinitely, and without that support the South Vietnamese army eventually had to fall before the onslaught of its powerful and relentless adversary to the north.

Nevertheless, the final victory of Hanoi came as a rude jolt to many Americans. No one was prepared for the sudden collapse of the South Vietnamese army or the final throes of that country's panic-stricken people as they desperately fought with each other for space on board one of the seventy helicopters used to evacuate some 7,000 Americans and Vietnamese from Saigon in the last hours before enemy troops entered the city. Military men in the United States were no less deeply moved by these events and often would appear to have found them a good deal more disturbing than did other Americans.

That this was so is hardly surprising. More than 2.5 million American military men and women had served in South Vietnam since the late 1940s. Of these, some 62,000 had died or been captured or reported missing in action. Another 154,000 had been wounded in a futile attempt to contain communism and preserve the freedom and independence of the South Vietnamese. The fate of South Vietnam in 1975 caused many Americans to question the very policy of containment that had led to their country's original involvement in Southeast Asia. But the Vietnam War had been primarily a land war, and the army more than any other service had been responsible for implementing that policy. Soon after France had signed the 1954 Geneva accords, the United States Army had begun training the South Vietnamese army in order to strengthen the new government of Prime Minister Ngo Dinh Diem. When political instability in the early 1960s had threatened to reverse earlier gains, army officers had been in the forefront of those urging Presidents Kennedy and Johnson to Americanize the war. When President Nixon later embarked on his Vietnamization program, it had been the United States Army's job to prepare ARVN units to take over their country's defense. The failure of those units to stop the onrushing North Vietnamese army in 1975 was thus particularly disturbing to many American army officers.

Like so many of their countrymen, America's military leaders at first tried to forget the war and its unhappy ending. But denial has gradually given way to a desire to learn more about the past in order to avoid making the same mistakes again. Officers and civilian historians employed by the army have embarked on what promises to be a long-term, critical investigation of almost every aspect of the service's involvement in the Vietnam War. Teachers at the Command and

General Staff College at Fort Leavenworth, Kansas, and the Army War College at Carlisle Barracks, Pennsylvania, have incorporated analysis of Vietnam into their classes more and more in order to encourage their students to think about some of the civil-military and professional issues raised by the war. It is impossible to predict the results of this searching self-analysis, but it does seem likely that the effort will have a significant impact on military thinking and doctrine for some time to come.

NOTES

1. Ronald H. Spector, *Advice and Support: The Early Years, 1941–1960*, United States Army in Vietnam (Washington: U.S. Army Center of Military History, 1983), especially chaps. 2–9.

2. Ibid., chaps. 10–11; George C. Herring and Richard H. Immerman, "Eisenhower, Dulles, and Dien Bien Phu: 'The Day We Didn't Go to War' Revisited," *Journal of American History* 71 (September 1984): 343–63.

3. In addition to Spector, *Advice and Support*, see George S. Eckhardt, *Command and Control, 1950–1969*, Vietnam Studies (Washington: Department of the Army, 1974), chap. 1.

4. James Lawton Collins, *Development and Training of the South Vietnamese Army*, Vietnam Studies (Washington: Department of the Army, 1975), pp. 2–21; David Ewing Ott, *Field Artillery, 1954–1973*, Vietnam Studies (Washington: Department of the Army, 1975), pp. 18–31.

5. Spector, *Advice and Support*, chaps. 17–18.

6. Ibid., pp. 375, 378–79; Murray Fromm, "The American Military in Vietnam: 1950s," in Harrison E. Salisbury, ed., *Vietnam Reconsidered: Lessons From a War* (New York: Harper and Row, 1984), pp. 38–40; Stanley Karnow, *Vietnam: A History* (New York: Viking, 1983), chaps. 6–7. See also William E. Depuy, Oral History Interview, 26 March 1979, sec. 5, p. 2, Senior Officer Oral History Program, Manuscript Archives, U.S. Army Military History Institute (USAMHI), Carlisle Barracks, Pennsylvania.

7. On the critical years 1962–1965, see Collins, *Development and Training*, pp. 25–43; Ott, *Field Artillery*, chap. 2; Eckhardt, *Command and Control*, chap. 2; Harold K. Johnson, Speech, 17 November 1964, Box 1946–1970, A. S. Collins Papers, Manuscript Archives, USAMHI.

8. Robert Manning, "Development of a Vietnam Policy," in Salisbury, ed., *Vietnam Reconsidered*, pp. 41–44; Karnow, *Vietnam*, chaps. 10–11; A. S. Collins to Creighton Abrams, 7 March 1966, and copy of speech, Harold K. Johnson to Civilian Aides Conference, Fort Bliss, 22 March 1965, both in Box 1946–1970, Collins Papers, USAMHI.

9. Eckhardt, *Command and Control*, chap. 3; Collins, *Development and Training*, chap. 3; Ott, *Field Artillery*, chap. 4. See also Office of the Chief of Military History, "Miscellaneous Named Campaign List, U.S. Army: Revolution to Vietnam" (Washington: Department of the Army, 1968 and 1973), an unpublished study, for Vietnam campaigns; and John J. Tolson, *Airmobility, 1961–1971*, Vietnam Studies (Washington: Department of the Army, 1973), especially chaps. 1–7.

10. See especially Willard Pearson, *The War in the Northern Provinces, 1966–1968*, Vietnam Studies (Washington: Department of the Army, 1975), chaps. 1–3; Bernard

William Rogers, *Cedar Falls-Junction City: A Turning Point*, Vietnam Studies (Washington: Department of the Army, 1975); Robert R. Ploger, *U.S. Army Engineers, 1965–1970*, Vietnam Studies (Washington: Department of the Army, 1974), chaps. 1, 4, 9; and William B. Fulton, *Riverine Operations, 1966–1969*, Vietnam Studies (Washington: Department of the Army, 1973).

11. Office of the Chief of Military History, "Campaign List"; Karnow, *Vietnam*, chaps. 12–13.

12. On the military aspects of Tet, see Dave Richard Palmer, *Summons of the Trumpet: U.S.-Vietnam in Perspective* (San Rafael, Calif.: Presidio Press, 1978), chaps. 21–22; Pearson, *War in the Northern Provinces*, chaps. 3–4; Tolson, *Airmobility*, chap. 8; Ott, *Field Artillery*, pp. 137–48; and Fulton, *Riverine Operations*, chap. 8.

13. For the larger implications of Tet, see Palmer, *Summons of the Trumpet*, chap. 23; and Karnow, *Vietnam*, chap. 14.

14. Post-Tet counteroffensive operations can be followed in Pearson, *War in the Northern Provinces*, chaps. 5–7; Tolson, *Airmobility*, chap. 8; Office of the Chief of Military History, "Campaign List."

15. Arthur S. Collins, "Debriefing Report, 5 January 1971," Box 1946–1970, Collins Papers, USAMHI.

16. Palmer, *Summons of the Trumpet*, chap. 26.

17. Palmer, *Summons of the Trumpet*, chap. 27; and Karnow, *Vietnam*, pp. 629–31.

18. Guenther Lewy, *America in Vietnam* (New York: Oxford University Press, 1978), pp. 407–10; Palmer, *Summons of the Trumpet*, chap. 28; and Karnow, *Vietnam*, pp. 639–43.

19. Palmer, *Summons of the Trumpet*, chap. 28; Karnow, *Vietnam*, pp. 643–46; and Lewy, *America in Vietnam*, pp. 410–12. For an American adviser's first-hand account of the 1972 offensive, see Gerald H. Turley, *The Easter Offensive: The Last American Advisers, Vietnam, 1972* (Novato, Calif.: Presidio Press, 1985).

20. Palmer, *Summons of the Trumpet*, chap. 29; Lewy, *America in Vietnam*, pp. 412–17; and Karnow, *Vietnam*, pp. 647–54.

FURTHER READING

We stand only at the threshold of understanding the army and the part it played in the Vietnam War. Considering how recently the war ended, we already possess a formidable number of studies which detail its long and tragic history. Four books in particular provide essential reading for anyone interested in learning more about the war in general. George C. Herring, a diplomatic historian, offers a succinct and balanced introduction to the war in *America's Longest War: The United States and Vietnam, 1950–1975* (New York: John Wiley & Sons, 1979). The journalist Stanley Karnow provides a more detailed account of the war in *Vietnam: A History* (New York: Viking, 1983). Two books—the first by an army officer who served in Vietnam, the second by a political scientist—provide a good overview of American military operations during the war: Dave Richard Palmer, *Summons of the Trumpet: U.S.-Vietnam in Perspective* (San Rafael, Calif.: Presidio Press, 1978); and Guenther Lewy, *America in Vietnam* (New York: Oxford University Press, 1978). A slightly older, more impassioned study that still merits careful attention is Frances Fitzgerald, *Fire in the Lake: The Vietnamese and the Americans in Vietnam* (Boston: Little, Brown & Co., 1972).

Two brief but excellent accounts of the United States Army's role in the war and the impact of the war on the army can be found in Allan R. Millett and Peter Maslowski, *For the Common Defense: A Military History of the United States of America* (New York: Free Press, 1984), chap. 17; and Russell F. Weigley, *History of the United States Army*, enlarged ed. (Bloomington: Indiana University Press, 1984), pp. 542–73. More detailed treatment of the army's involvement in the war can be found in the Department of the Army's Vietnam Studies, as well as in the various studies that have been published by the U.S. Army Center of Military History as part of its United States Army in Vietnam series—many of which have been cited in the footnotes to this chapter. An invaluable reference for anyone interested in the Vietnam War is Shelby L. Stanton, *Vietnam Order of Battle* (Washington: U.S. News Books, 1981).

Critical studies of the army during this period include William L. Hauser, *America's Army in Crisis* (Baltimore: Johns Hopkins University Press, 1973); William R. Corson, *The Betrayal* (New York: Ace, 1968); Edward L. King, *The Death of the Army*, (New York: Saturday Review Press, 1972); and Ward Just, *Military Men* (New York: Alfred A. Knopf, 1970). Paul L. Savage and Richard A. Gabriel, "Cohesion and Disintegration in the American Army in Vietnam," *Armed Forces and Society* 2 (May 1976): 340–76, presents a provocative view of the impact the war had on the army, while Herbert C. Kelman and Lee H. Lawrence, "American Response to the Trial of Lt. William Calley," *Psychology Today* 6 (June 1972): 41–45, 78–81, addresses the My Lai issue. Some earlier books that are still useful include Don Oberdorfer, *Tet!* (Garden City, N.Y.: Doubleday, 1971), and Peter Braestrup, *Big Story: How the American Press and Television Reported and Interpreted the Crisis of Tet 1968 in Vietnam and Washington* (Boulder, Colo.: Westview Press, 1976).

A former small-unit commander in Vietnam, Shelby L. Stanton, provides a history of army and Marine Corps operations in his detailed account, *The Rise and Fall of an American Army: U.S. Ground Forces in Vietnam, 1965–1973* (Novato, Calif.: Presidio Press, 1985). For good eyewitness accounts of what it was like to participate in army operations, see Frederick Downs, *The Killing Zone: My Life in the Vietnam War* (New York: Norton, 1978), and James R. McDonough, *Platoon Leader* (Novato, Calif.: Presidio Press, 1985). In order to understand how senior army leaders viewed the war, see in particular Maxwell D. Taylor, *Swords and Plowshares* (New York: Norton, 1972); William C. Westmoreland, *A Soldier Reports* (Garden City, N.Y.: Doubleday, 1976); and Bruce Palmer, *The 25-Year War: America's Military Role in Vietnam* (Lexington: The University Press of Kentucky, 1984). But see also Douglas Kinnard, *The War Managers* (Hanover, N.H.: University Press of New England, 1977).

The stirrings of revisionism can be profitably explored in Timothy J. Lomperis, *The War Everyone Lost—And Won: America's Intervention in Viet Nam's Twin Struggles* (Baton Rouge: Louisiana State University Press, 1984). See also *The Senator Gravel Edition, The Pentagon Papers: The Defense Department History of United States Decisionmaking on Vietnam*, 5 vols. (Boston: Beacon Press, 1971–1972).

The definitive story of the background to intervention has now been told in Ronald H. Spector, *Advice and Support: The Early Years of the U.S. Army in Vietnam, 1941–1960* (New York: Free Press, 1985).

CHAPTER 18

The Army after Vietnam _____

COLONEL HARRY G. SUMMERS, JR.

The United States Army's recovery from Vietnam began while the war was still in progress. General William C. Westmoreland, recalled from Vietnam in June 1968 to become the army chief of staff on 3 July, was especially concerned with the army's discipline, integrity, ethics, and professionalism. In April 1970 he directed the Army War College to analyze the moral and professional climate in the army. The result was a hard-hitting study published in June 1970 which set the tone for further self-analysis and introspection.[1] In 1971 General Westmoreland appointed Lieutenant General George I. Forsythe as his special assistant for the modern volunteer army and charged him with reassessing the army's internal rules and regulations as well as devising innovative ways to improve the attractiveness of service life.

In October 1972 General Westmoreland was succeeded as chief of staff by the man who had been his successor in Vietnam, General Creighton W. Abrams. This change in leadership brought with it changes both in style and in emphasis. General Westmoreland was meticulous in his appearance and was seen as an aloof and somewhat aristocratic figure who was quite formal in his dealings with his staff and other subordinates. Yet, as chief of staff he devoted less personal attention to operational matters (which in large measure were left to his vice chief of staff, General Bruce Palmer, Jr., and his deputy chief of staff for operations and plans [DCSOPS], Lieutenant General Richard Stilwell) than to the morale and welfare of his soldiers. General Abrams, on the other hand, was to all appearances a rough and unpolished field soldier who had won his reputation in World War II as one of General George Patton's outstanding tank battalion commanders. Careless in his appearance (he was once described as "looking like an unmade bed"), his leadership style was informal and direct. If in his appearance, his demeanor, his aristocratic southern heritage (and, some might say, in his tactical but not strategic battlefield successes), General Westmoreland was the personification of Robert E. Lee, Abrams was Ulysses S. Grant. Like Grant, he was one of the finest strategic thinkers the army has ever produced, and he possessed the uncanny ability to see directly to the heart of a problem.

Deeply concerned with the army's personnel problems (one of his admonitions was that "soldiers aren't in the army, soldiers *are* the army"), General Abrams saw that the army's deteriorating morale, discipline, and professionalism were symptoms of a much more serious malaise—the army's loss of confidence in itself and in its missions. General Abrams's first priority, therefore, was the restoration of his soldiers' feelings of self-worth which had been weakened by the nuclear age and had been almost destroyed by public reaction to the Vietnam War. To that end, he directed his DCSOPS, Lieutenant General Donald H. Cowles, to create an ad hoc Strategic Assessment Group to determine the legitimate role for conventional strategy and for the army in the post-Vietnam world. Better known as the "Astarita Group" (after its chairman, Colonel Edward F. Astarita), the panel's findings on the need for an army as an essential element in the American national security apparatus were widely discussed throughout the defense establishment.[2] In March 1981 General John W. Vessey, Jr., then army vice chief of staff and later chairman of the Joint Chiefs of Staff (JCS), commented that the Astarita Report and the decisions it fostered marked a turning point in the post-Vietnam army.[3]

In and of themselves the findings of the Astarita Group were unremarkable. After conducting an intensive examination of political, economic, sociological, and military trends and making a detailed analysis of American foreign policy, the members of the group concluded that the nations of the world were clustered in rough equilibrium, and that the United States occupied a relatively advantageous position. It was allied with Western Europe and Japan, next to the United States the world's dominant economic power centers. Its potential adversaries—China and the Soviet Union—were also adversaries of one another. The United States, therefore, was still the world's greatest power. The task, as the Astarita Group saw it, was to retain that position of relative advantage.

While some critics complained that the army strategists had merely legitimized the status quo, such comments missed the essential point. Answering the detractors in a 1976 article, General Fred C. Weyand, General Abrams's successor as army chief of staff, quoted T. S. Eliot to emphasize the importance of the Astarita Group's findings: "At the end of all our exploring," Eliot wrote in *The Wasteland*, "will be to arrive where we started and know the place for the first time." Knowing the place for the first time had great therapeutic value. It shifted the army's focus from the frustrations of Southeast Asia to the successful role played by the army's forward-deployed units in undergirding and supporting American foreign policy objectives in the critical areas of Western Europe and northeastern Asia.[4]

These forward-deployed units—the army divisions stationed in West Germany and in Korea—and the divisions in the United States designed to reinforce them in the event of war had been severely depleted to support combat operations in Vietnam. General Abrams ordered these units restored to strength. He reversed a planned reduction in the number of active divisions and instead added three divisions to the thirteen already authorized for the active army. In what came to be called the "round-out" program, several of these divisions were created by combining two active army brigades with one brigade drawn from the Army Reserve. In addition, Abrams wanted eight reserve divisions brought up to full strength in personnel and equipment in order to provide an immediate reinforcement capability for the active army. Many of the units in the National Guard and the Army Reserve were affiliated with active units in order to improve their training and readiness. This revitalization of the Army Reserve was designed to return it to the position of importance it had enjoyed in World War I, World War II and the Korean War.

By returning to the traditional relationship between active and reserve forces—the so-called total army concept—General Abrams had two objectives in mind. First was the reestablishment of the army's capability to deter war, especially in areas critical to United States national security. Equally important to Abrams, however, was the restoration of the traditional linkage between the army and the American people. With the revitalization of the Army Reserve, the citizen-soldier—the centerpiece of American military history—could once again act as a bridge between the active army and the American people.

The post-Vietnam army General Abrams sought to create was designed deliberately, therefore, to form an interrelated structure that could not be committed to sustained combat without mobilizing the reserves. This structure became a reality by 1983, when roughly 50 percent of the army's combat elements and 70 percent of its combat service support units—engineers, maintenance, transportation, communications, and supply—were in the National Guard and Army Reserve. General Abrams hoped this return of the army to the structure it had known throughout much of the twentieth century would correct one of the major deficiencies of the American involvement in the Vietnam War—the commitment of the army to sustained combat without the explicit support of the American people as expressed by their representatives in Congress.

By focusing on the past, General Abrams prepared the army for a future in which conventional, nonnuclear war appeared to be the most likely form of combat. This conviction was reinforced by the 1973 Arab-Israeli war—particularly the large-scale battles in the Sinai which army leaders in the United States saw as reaffirmation of the decisive role conventional forces and land combat still played in modern warfare. One of the specific lessons drawn from the 1973 war was the need to develop better doctrine for the close coordination of combined arms. To fill that and other needs, the Training and Doctrine Command (TRADOC) was formed under the direction of General William E. DePuy.

TRADOC was designed to supervise and control the entire army training and educational system, including the basic training centers as well as combined arms schools such as the Infantry School at Fort Benning, Georgia, the Artillery School at Fort Sill, Oklahoma, the Armor School at Fort Knox, Kentucky, and the Command and General Staff College at Fort Leavenworth, Kansas. TRADOC also supervised education at the different combat support and combat service support schools such as the Engineer, Intelligence, Ordnance, Quartermaster,

Signal, and Transportation schools which were located at army posts scattered across the entire United States. In addition, TRADOC was responsible for developing and publishing all army instructional and doctrinal manuals.

In the area of training, much emphasis was given to hands-on, practical work. Instead of attending classroom sessions on how to assemble and disassemble weapons or how to conduct squad battle drills, soldiers were now required to perform these tasks in a field setting. Through a series of Soldier Qualification Tests involving actual job performance, an effort was made to find an accurate method of measuring and quantifying each soldier's proficiency. A series of how-to-fight manuals was produced with explicit instructions intended to facilitate such common battlefield tasks as siting weapons, organizing terrain, and engaging enemy forces.

In this new setting, ''counterinsurgency doctrine'' disappeared as rapidly and abruptly as it had begun a decade earlier, and the army began revising its doctrinal capstone on operations, Field Manual 100–5. The new version consciously drew lessons from the 1973 war and sought to focus the attention of its readers not on the Third World, as counterinsurgency training had done, but on the European battlefield. Published in 1976, the new FM 100–5 addressed what the army then saw as its most immediate problem—the defense of central Europe against large, modern, Soviet armored forces. Because the army was still recovering from Vietnam, the manual concentrated heavily on defensive operations; but it simultaneously emphasized fire power and attrition, the so-called American way of war that had been the army's mainstay in World War II and Korea.[5]

Concurrent with his efforts to restore the self-confidence of the army, General Abrams faced the problem of convincing the Congress that not only was there no ''peace dividend'' as a result of the American withdrawal from Vietnam, but far-reaching and expensive steps would have to be taken if the army was to meet its postwar commitments. One of the first necessary steps was to stabilize army personnel strength and stop the turbulence caused by President Richard M. Nixon's decision in 1972 to end conscription and rely on an ''all-volunteer army.'' General Abrams took his case to the House and Senate Appropriations and Armed Forces committees, where he tactfully reminded the legislators that it was their constitutional responsibility to raise and support armies. In return for an army of three-quarters of a million soldiers, Abrams promised the legislators that his service would provide enough combat divisions to accomplish the missions assigned to it by the National Security Act of 1947: safeguarding internal security, protecting the American homeland, and upholding and advancing the national policies and interests of the United States, including securing areas vital to those interests.

Another pressing requirement brought home by the 1973 Arab-Israeli war was the need to strengthen (or ''heavy-up'') the light forces with which the United States Army had fought the Vietnam War. Electronic warfare and precision-guided missiles had taken on a new importance, and their deadly use in the 1973 war spurred Congress and the army to agree on the need to develop the long-delayed main battle tank, to provide an infantry fighting vehicle, and to upgrade army helicopter capabilities for the modern battlefield. These decisions gave rise to the army's new, appropriately named M–1 Abrams tank, the Bradley infantry fighting vehicle, the Apache helicopter, and other new battlefield weapons systems. It is thus evident that General Abrams's success in winning the confidence of the Congress and gaining its support for rebuilding combat capabilities was a major factor in the army's post–Vietnam War recovery.

In September 1974, two years after he had begun to lead the army out of its post-Vietnam depression, Creighton Abrams died. He was succeeded by his vice chief of staff, General Fred C. Weyand, who in 1972 had followed Abrams as field commander in Vietnam. A 1939 graduate of the University of California at Berkeley, General Weyand was an intellectual as well as a warrior. He saw his role as chief of staff partially as that of a caretaker nurturing to fruition the programs General Abrams had initiated. But Weyand also left his intellectual imprint on the army through a series of articles in military journals, and during his tenure the Army War College was directed to undertake an extended and searching reassessment of the army's role in Vietnam and in American society generally.[6] The War College study took five years to complete and when published as *On Strategy* in 1981 became a pivotal piece in the administrative, philosophical, and historical reevaluation of the American army.

The ongoing reassessment and revitalization of the army in the meantime continued under the direction of Abrams's successors. In October 1976 General Weyand was followed in office by General Bernard W. Rogers, a former Rhodes scholar who had been General Abrams's deputy chief of staff for personnel. Intimately acquainted with Abrams's plans for the army and desirous of contributing to their implementation, Rogers faced a unique challenge. A month after he became chief of staff, the American people elected Jimmy Carter president of the United States. Eight years of Republican rule ended as the new Democratic administration set fresh priorities for social and defense spending, and General Rogers began the thankless task of gaining the new administration's endorsement to continue rearming and reequipping the army along the lines sketched by General Abrams.

While army chiefs of staff thus focused on immediate political and material issues, they also encouraged internal criticism by less senior officers and thereby helped to lay the foundation for more far-reaching changes in an attempt to recapture the professional excellence that marked the army of the late 1930s and early 1940s. This movement to strengthen a sense of professional dedication in the service culminated in 1979 when the former Army War College deputy commandant and former army chief of operations and plans, General Edward C. Meyer, became chief of staff. General Meyer's appointment marked a watershed in several respects. Unlike his four immediate predecessors, who had served as general officers in Vietnam, Meyer had fought in that war at the tactical level. As a lieutenant colonel and colonel commanding a battalion and later a brigade in the army's new and innovative air assault formation, the First Cavalry

Division, Meyer had not personally been involved in the strategic decisionmaking of the Vietnam War. Commissioned in 1951 during the Korean War, he broke the hold of the world war veterans who had led the army for two generations and whose battlefield experience, to a greater or lesser degree, had predisposed them to see total war and absolute victory as norms rather than historical aberrations.

Unwedded to any historical imperative, General Meyer prodded the army to intensify, broaden, and publicize its continuing reassessment of itself and its place in American society. As chief of staff, he restored military history to its former place of prominence in the army's educational system and in 1981 sponsored formal publication of *On Strategy*, the Army War College's long-term study of American military strategy in Vietnam.

On Strategy advanced the thesis that a lack of appreciation of military theory and strategy—especially the relationship between military strategy and national policy—had led to a faulty American appraisal of the nature of the Vietnam War. As a result, the army exhausted itself fighting a secondary guerrilla force, and military strategy ultimately failed to support the national policy of containment of Communist expansion. Since adopted as a textbook at the Army War College, the National War College, the Naval War College, the Air War College, and the Army and Marine Corps Command and General Staff Colleges, this work has been credited with making a major contribution to a better understanding of the Vietnam War and to a deeper appreciation of strategy and the art of war. It helped to raise the level of the critical analysis of the Vietnam War and, by extension, the quality of debate over how to correct the deficiencies uncovered by the war.[7]

Previously published critiques of the army's performance in Vietnam had concentrated on symptoms rather than causes.[8] They had drawn two primary lessons: first, that the army's leadership collapsed or, more precisely, was overwhelmed by an emphasis on business-type management, which had led to the disintegration of American fighting forces; and second, that because the army overemphasized conventional large-unit operations and failed to implement counterinsurgency doctrine properly, it was defeated by the more mobile and elusive Viet Cong guerrillas.

In decrying an inordinate emphasis on managerial techniques, however, these early critics based their arguments on a false distinction between "leadership" and "management." These are interrelated, not exclusive concepts, for both "management" (the material aspects of combat) and "leadership" (the skillful use of materiel on the battlefield to defeat the enemy) are essential for the successful conduct of war. In *On War*, the classic nineteenth-century work on the theory and nature of warfare, Carl von Clausewitz illustrated this interdependence by drawing an analogy between the "art of the swordsmith" and the "art of fencing."[9] More to the point, "management" did not cause the failure of American arms in Vietnam. On the contrary, "management" enabled the United States to move a million soldiers a year half-way around the world, and then to feed, clothe, shelter, arm, and equip them at a historically unprecedented level of abundance. Neither was "leadership" at the tactical (battlefield) level the cause of the army's failure. Indeed, by promoting the idea that the army "disintegrated" in Vietnam, critics did a major disservice to American soldiers who, despite the exceptions highlighted in exhaustive detail, performed bravely and admirably under difficult circumstances and defeated the Viet Cong and North Vietnamese in every major engagement.

The second criticism commonly made of the army's performance in Vietnam— that it tried to apply the rules of conventional warfare to a counterinsurgency— obscured the fact that Vietnam represented a strategic defeat rather than a tactical failure for the army. The defeat of the United States and its South Vietnamese allies had less to do with how well American soldiers followed the principles of counterinsurgency doctrine than it did with the doctrine itself. If the United States did not win, neither did the insurgents, for as the results of the war demonstrated, the Viet Cong were defeated at every turn by the United States, by the South Vietnamese, and, most conclusively of all, by the North Vietnamese.[10] No one perceived at the time that the Viet Cong were being used in a kind of economy-of-force operation which caused the United States to exhaust itself against a secondary enemy while the North Vietnamese regular forces remained relatively safe in their homeland sanctuaries awaiting the moment when their enemy had been weakened sufficiently for the killing blow. As Colonel Stuart Herrington put it in his recent book on counterinsurgency operations, "Like us, Hanoi had failed to win the 'hearts and minds' of the South Vietnamese peasantry. Unlike us, Hanoi's leaders were able to compensate for this failure by playing their trump card—they overwhelmed South Vietnam with a twenty-two division force. . . . "[11]

Herrington's book, coming on the heels of On Strategy and the renewed respect accorded the study of military history throughout the army, suggests that the army of the late 1980s finally will place the Vietnam War in broad historical perspective and shed its collective institutional embarrassment over the American defeat in Southeast Asia. Nevertheless, the contemporary army remains to some extent hobbled by structural legacies of the 1960s, and one of the major liabilities the army inherited from the Vietnam era was the inefficient mechanism used by the Washington defense establishment for command and control of combat forces in the field. This operational aspect of warfare, what Clausewitz called the "conduct of war proper," has been almost totally overshadowed by the administrative matters which Clausewitz said were a necessary part of the "preparation for war."

This imbalance derives in large measure from the Planning-Programming-Budgeting System (PPBS) which Secretary of Defense Robert S. McNamara instituted in 1962 to maintain better control of military forces. Using the tools of the economist, this system relies heavily on quantified computer data and highly sophisticated programs which lead in turn to decisions based on a so-called cost-benefit analysis. The fallacy of this approach to waging war lies in the fact that while military "costs" are tangible, their "benefits" are often difficult to quantify. McNamara's system also unrealistically ignores the human element of warfare. Wars are fought not by things but by men. Such intangibles as morale (the fighting spirit of the soldier) and esprit de corps (the feeling of confidence and sense of identification with one's battlefield unit which holds soldiers together under the terrible strains of combat) play an essential role in determining the outcome of a military struggle. Intangible factors of this sort are virtually impossible to quantify or computerize and are thus often disregarded by contemporary planners in the Pentagon.

Oversight of the army by both the Office of Management and Budget (OMB) and the Congress further militates against effective command and control. The OMB and Congress assess the army's performance primarily in terms of programs and budgets. As a result, the army staff has structured itself to respond to budgetary questions. It therefore has become concerned more with "preparation for war" than with the "conduct of war proper." This structural deficiency is beyond the army's ability to correct, but it is of particular concern to a diverse and increasingly active group of congressmen, military officers, and academics known as the military reform movement. Unlike other knowledgeable observers of the military who are primarily interested in questions of hardware, the members of this movement pay more attention to the larger issues of military doctrine, strategy, and tactics.[12]

One of the early members of the military reform movement, Georgetown University Professor Edward Luttwak, has drawn an important distinction between civil efficiency and military effectiveness.[13] This distinction is best illustrated by the debate over which is more desirable: centralized or decentralized control of the army. The advent of modern communications and data processing technology, along with the efforts of civilian authorities to oversee army finances in as much detail as possible, led to the imposition of a series of vertical, centralized controls on army field operations. For example, at one time commanders paid, fed, clothed, housed, promoted, reduced, and controlled the duty hours of the soldiers under their command, but now they can do almost none of these things. Soldiers are paid by computers located in the Army Finance Center at Fort Benjamin Harrison, Indiana. They are fed en masse in consolidated "dining facilities," and many live away from their posts in civilian housing. Promotions and reductions are strictly controlled by the army's Military Personnel Center in Alexandria, Virginia, and the pass system which was used to reward exemplary performance of duty has long since become a thing of the past. Considered in isolation, each of these administrative controls can be proven to be "cost effective" and efficient. Taken together, they have had an unintended but highly deleterious impact on operational effectiveness, for they have severely weakened the bond linking the leader and the led—a bond that military history tells us is absolutely essential for success on the battlefield. In effect, "authority" has been centralized while "responsibility" remains in the hands of field commanders. This dilution of the field commander's authority through excessive administrative centralization is the most critical problem facing the army of the mid–1980s.

Another serious problem facing the army following the Vietnam War was whether it would continue to adhere to the battlefield doctrine of attrition or whether it would adopt the doctrine of maneuver, as many members of the military reform movement urged. In simple terms, attrition relies on a massive use of firepower to defeat the enemy by gradually wearing him down. Maneuver, on the other hand, calls for the skillful application of military power at a point where the enemy is vulnerable, so that a relatively small attacking force can disrupt and destroy a much larger enemy formation.

Disagreement over which of these doctrines to use is not new. As Russell F. Weigley pointed out in his analysis of the army's campaigns in France and Germany in World War II:

The American army's two principal inheritances from its past were also conflicting legacies. . . . The memory of the Western border wars [against the Indians] suggested that the primary military virtue is mobility. . . . The memory of the Civil War [by contrast] suggested that the primary military value is sheer power. . . . To reconcile mobility and power, to arrive at the appropriate military compound of the two, proved the central problem of the transformation of the old American army of the frontier to the new army of European war.[14]

Mobility and power can be reconciled, and the doctrines of attrition and maneuver can actually complement each other; but this possibility of reconciliation is overlooked by many recent critics of American military doctrine. They condemn General Ulysses S. Grant for his "bloody" campaign of attrition against General Robert E. Lee during the closing stages of the Civil War, and they praise General William Tecumseh Sherman's brilliant campaign of maneuver in his "March to the Sea" which cut the Confederacy in half. They perversely fail to see, however, that it was precisely because Grant fixed Lee with his campaign of attrition that Sherman was able to mount his campaign of maneuver.

Using more recent historical examples, some of these same critics have praised the "maneuver doctrines" of the North Vietnamese and Viet Cong and condemned the "attrition strategies" of General Westmoreland. Yet the casualty figures for the Vietnam War are most revealing. Some 57,000 soldiers were killed in action or died of other causes during that war, but the North Vietnamese military commander, General Vo Nguyen Giap, admitted that he lost 600,000 soldiers killed between 1965 and 1968.[15] If this is the price of maneuver (the equivalent, adjusted for population, of over 6 *million* American lives), then such a doctrine makes no military or political sense—especially since it was not Viet Cong or North Vietnamese "maneuver doctrines" that decided the Vietnam War but instead the 1975 blitzkrieg in which more than twenty North Vietnamese divisions overwhelmed the South Vietnamese defenders by sheer power alone.

Misinterpretations of history notwithstanding, some of the criticism of army doctrine following the Vietnam War did have a valid point. As noted earlier, the 1976 edition of the army's basic operational manual, FM 100–5, was a stopgap that concentrated on defensive operations and the massive use of firepower. Criticism within and without the army soon caused this manual to be rethought and rewritten. The revised 1982 edition emphasized the importance of maneuver in the dynamics of battle, while continuing to acknowledge that "firepower provides the enabling, violent, destructive force essential to successful maneuver."[16] Although still a matter of concern, the debate over whether to adhere to a doctrine of attrition or one of maneuver has gradually become less of an issue than the related question of whether the army should key its thinking, training, and structure to a particular theater of operations or instead should maintain the flexibility needed for world-wide operations.

It was this issue that became the prime concern of General John A. Wickham, Jr., who replaced General Meyer as chief of staff in June 1983. Like his predecessor, General Wickham also represents a new generation of top-level army leadership. Although he was commissioned in 1950, he served in Europe during the Korean War. During the Vietnam War he was wounded in action and decorated for bravery while serving as a lieutenant colonel in command of an infantry battalion. General Wickham later served as commmander in chief, United Nations Command in Korea and as army vice chief of staff immediately prior to his assumption of the office of chief of staff.

As noted above, the army saw a need to "heavy-up" immediately after the Vietnam War in order to meet the requirements of the European battlefield. But this change came at the price of strategic mobility, for heavy forces proved difficult to deploy rapidly to areas of crisis. Thus, under General Wickham the army began to consider restructuring its forces to include more light divisions capable of rapid movement by air and sea.

These ongoing changes in the army's organization for combat, as well as the army's continual modifications of operational doctrines, reveal an army leadership flexible in both thought and action. Yet it may be that the most important military response to Vietnam is the response that never happened. Unlike the French army after its defeat in Indochina and the Portuguese army shortly before its withdrawal from Angola, the United States Army did not vent its frustrations against either the American people or their elected representatives. In 1975, addressing this very point, army chief of staff General Fred C. Weyand credited the army's restraint to its officers' oath to support and defend the Constitution of the United States. He went on to say:

The United States Army withdrawal from Vietnam after a nine-year involvement was taken by most Americans, in and out of the Army, as a matter of course. There were no screams of betrayal, no bitter remorse, just a simple carrying out of orders. This is as it should be. . . . When you consider that this withdrawal took place during the most serious governmental crisis in the history of our Republic, culminating in the resignation of the

President—the Commander-in-Chief—then the loyalty, steadfastness, and stability of the Army is particularly remarkable . . . so remarkable that it is unremarked.[17]

Reflecting these sentiments, the mood today among serving army officers who fought in Vietnam is best illustrated by the attitude of General Joseph W. ("Vinegar Joe") Stilwell when he walked out of Burma in 1942. "I claim we got a hell of a beating," Stilwell said. "We got run out of Burma and it is humiliating as hell. I think we ought to find out what caused it, go back and retake it."[18] Today's army officers have no wish to go back and take Vietnam, but they are determined to find out what caused the army's failures in Southeast Asia so that their service will be able to fight and win the next time the American people commit it to a contest of arms.

NOTES

1. *Study on Military Professionalism* (Carlisle Barracks, Pa.: US Army War College, 1970).

2. The Strategic Assessment Group was under the direction of Maj. Gen. Rolland V. Heiser, the ODCSOPS director of plans, and was headed by Col. Edward F. Astarita. It included Lt. Cols. Warren Anderson, Harold Brandt, Robert Carpenter, Neal Kempf, Thomas Noel, Harry Summers, and John Todd; Maj. Theodore Frederick; and Sgt. 1st Class Ignatius Dolata from ODCSOPS; Lt. Col. Joseph Stallings and Maj. Tyrus Cobb from the Office of the Assistant Chief of Staff for Intelligence; and Col. W. G. Allen from the Office of the Deputy Chief of Staff for Logistics.

3. The complete findings of the Strategic Assessment Group were never published. For an unclassified version of its recommendations written in 1974, see Col. Harry G. Summers, Jr., "The Astarita Report: A Military Strategy for the Multipolar World," *Occasional Paper* (Carlisle Barracks, Pa.: Strategic Studies Institute, U.S. Army War College, 1981), p. v.

4. Gen. Fred C. Weyand and Lt. Col. Harry G. Summers, Jr., "Serving the People—The Need for Military Power," *Military Review* 56 (December 1976): 8–18.

5. General William E. DePuy, "FM 100–5 Revisited," *Army* 30 (November 1980): 12–17.

6. For Weyand's imprint, see "Serving the People: The Basic Case for the United States Army," *Commander's Call* (May-June 1976); "Serving the People: The Need for Military Power," *Military Review* 56 (December 1976): 8–18; and "Vietnam Myths and American Realities," *Commander's Call* (July-August 1976)—all of which were widely disseminated throughout the army.

7. Col. Harry G. Summers, Jr., *On Strategy: The Vietnam War in Context* (Washington: Government Printing Office, 1981) was originally published in paperback but is now available in hard cover as *On Strategy: A Critical Analysis of the Vietnam War* (Novato, Calif.: Presidio Press, 1982).

8. Two of the more widely acclaimed public accounts were Richard Gabriel and Paul Savage, *Crisis in Command: Mismanagement in the Army* (New York: Hill & Wang, 1978), and Cincinnatus [pseudonym], *Self-Destruction: The Disintegration and Decay of the United States Army During the Vietnam Era* (New York: Norton, 1980). None of

these authors served in Vietnam, and without the leavening of first-hand experience, they evidently failed to understand that their source material was distorted by its very nature. In the main, they drew from internal army critiques that emphasized the negative in order to facilitate change—critiques that took the positive aspects of American military involvement as a given.

9. Carl von Clausewitz, *On War*, ed. and trans. Michael Howard and Peter Paret (Princeton, N.J.: Princeton University Press, 1976), bk. II, chap. 2, p. 133.

10. See Senior General Van Tien Dung, "Great Spring Victory," *Foreign Broadcast Information Service*, vol. II, FBIS–APA–76–131, 7 July 1976, which is remarkable for the absence of mention of the Viet Cong's contribution to final victory. See also Al Santoli, "Why Viet Cong Flee," *Parade*, (11 July 1982), pp. 4–6, for comments of former Viet Cong leaders, as well as Stanley Karnow, *Vietnam: A History* (New York: Viking Press, 1983), pp. 27–43.

11. Lt. Col. Stuart A. Herrington, *Silence Was A Weapon: The Vietnam War in the Villages* (Novato, Calif.: Presidio Press, 1982), p. 203.

12. For an overview of the military reform movement, see Jeffrey G. Barlow, ed., *Reforming the Military* (Washington: The Heritage Foundation, 1981).

13. Edward N. Luttwak, "On the Meaning of Strategy . . . for the United States in the 1980's," in W. Scott Thompson, ed., *National Security in the 1980's: From Weakness to Strength* (San Francisco: Institute for Contemporary Studies, 1980), p. 268.

14. Russell F. Weigley, *Eisenhower's Lieutenants: The Campaigns of France and Germany, 1944–1945* (Bloomington: Indiana University Press, 1981), p. 2.

15. Chalmers Johnson, *Autopsy on People's War* (Berkeley: University of California Press, 1973), pp. 46–48. See also John E. Mueller, "The Search for the 'Breaking Point' in Vietnam," *International Studies Quarterly* 24 (December 1980): 503–7.

16. U.S., Department of Defense, Department of the Army, *Operations*, Field Manual 100–5 (Washington: Government Printing Office, 1982), pp. 2–4. See also Lt. Cols. Huba Wass de Czege and L. D. Holder, "The New FM 100–5," *Military Review* 62 (July 1982): 53–70.

17. General Fred C. Weyand, speech to the Minuteman Chapter, Association of the United States Army, reprinted in U.S., Congress, House, *Congressional Record*, 94th Cong., 1st sess., 1975, 121, pt. 30: 39506–7.

18. Quoted in Barbara W. Tuchman, *Stilwell and the American Experience in China, 1911–45* (New York: Macmillan Co., 1971), p. 385.

FURTHER READING

Historians have yet to show as much enthusiasm for military developments since the Vietnam War as have soldiers, political scientists, sociologists, and economists. An important exception is Russell F. Weigley who provides an overview of the changes the army underwent during the 1970s and 1980s in his *History of the United States Army*, enlarged ed. (Bloomington: Indiana University Press, 1984), chap. 23. More extended assessments of the post-Vietnam army include Zeb B. Bradford, Jr., and Frederic J. Brown, *The United States Army in Transition* (Beverly Hills, Calif.: Sage, 1973), and Thomas H. Etzold, *Defense or Delusion? America's Military in the 1980s* (New York: Harper and Row, 1982). For a brief examination of the nation's armed forces and defense policies during this period, see Allan R. Millett and Peter Maslowski, *For the Common*